D1426750

# CRUCIBLE

# CRUCIBLE

*Thirteen Months That
Forged Our World*

JONATHAN FENBY

**SIMON &
SCHUSTER**

London · New York · Sydney · Toronto · New Delhi

A CBS COMPANY

First published in Great Britain by Simon & Schuster UK Ltd, 2018
A CBS COMPANY

Copyright © Jonathan Fenby, 2018

The right of Jonathan Fenby to be identified as the author
of this work has been asserted in accordance with
the Copyright, Designs and Patents Act, 1988.

1 3 5 7 9 10 8 6 4 2

Simon & Schuster UK Ltd
1st Floor
222 Gray's Inn Road
London WC1X 8HB

www.simonandschuster.co.uk
www.simonandschuster.com.au
www.simonandschuster.co.in

Simon & Schuster Australia, Sydney
Simon & Schuster India, New Delhi

The author and publishers have made all reasonable efforts
to contact copyright-holders for permission, and apologise
for any omissions or errors in the form of credits given.
Corrections may be made to future printings.

A CIP catalogue record for this book
is available from the British Library

Hardback ISBN: 978-1-4711-5501-7
Trade Paperback ISBN: 978-1-4711-5502-4
eBook ISBN: 978-1-4711-5504-8

Typeset in Sabon by M Rules
Printed and bound by CPI Group (UK) Ltd, Croydon, CR0 4YY

Simon & Schuster UK Ltd are committed to sourcing paper
that is made from wood grown in sustainable forests and support the Forest
Stewardship Council, the leading international forest certification organisation.
Our books displaying the FSC logo are printed on FSC certified paper.

To my family

# CONTENTS

# ACKNOWLEDGEMENTS

My first debt is to Iain MacGregor at Simon & Schuster for proposing the idea from which this book grew, encouraging its development and then shepherding it through to publication with his able staff. As always, Renée was the invaluable companion in research, as first reader and in offering support. Andre Villeneuve was a stalwart source of information, discussion, suggestions and assiduous reading of the first draft.

This book, as Tony Judt put it in the preface to *Postwar*, 'rests, in the first instance, on the shoulders of other books'. I am indebted to the many authors listed in the bibliography, both historians and writers of contemporary diaries, memoirs and letters that bring the period alive. I benefited greatly from conversations with a range of experts on the various themes, from Europe to China via the Middle East, South Asia, the Soviet Union and the United States. Arne Westad was as illuminating as ever. Gordon Barrass provided valuable reflection on the Cold War. Mick Cox and Sverozan Rajak were generous with time, knowledge and opinions. Among others who helped me along the way, I would like to mention in particular Alice Arguden, Andrew Burns, Frank Dikötter, Tim Garton-Ash, Rana Mitter, John Nilsson-Wright, Sidney Rittenberg, Timothy Snyder and Steve Tsang. Christopher Sinclair-Stevenson not only looked after my interests, but also provided enthusiasm to help drive work forward. The staff and resources of the London Library were, once again, a godsend.

# PREFACE

The past is not another country. Even a relatively short period can have deep effects that persist decades later. So it is with the thirteen months covered in this book that saw an extraordinary coalescence of events across the globe. The twenty-first century has brought challenges unimagined then, ranging from climate change to terrorism, sectarianism and the impact of technology. The global balance has shifted with the rise of Asia and relative decline of the West. Still, the time from June 1947 to June 1948 really did change the world, shaping much of it in a form that gives the period a lasting relevance for our day.

Two years after the end of by far the most devastating conflict the planet had experienced, with 55 million or more dead, the Cold War became entrenched between two great powers, which, drawing on the ideological divide between capitalism and socialism that had marked the twentieth century, each believed the inexorable tide of history was on its side as its political, economic and social model would sweep away the old world epitomised by Europe and the traditional societies of China and Japan.[1] By far the world's leading economic power after building on its enormous growth in the later nineteenth century and first half of the twentieth, the United States took on the global political involvement it had refused in 1919.[2] As a logical development of its wartime role, the Truman administration rejected George Washington's admonition to avoid foreign entanglements, especially with Europe. Instead, it drew closer to the west of that divided continent, as well as to East Asia and Latin America through formal agreements, trade, military strength and soft power while laying a network of strong and stable diplomatic, economic and military engagements. With a defence budget of $9 billion in 1948, the US occupied more than two hundred military bases around the world, was the predominant naval power and had a huge strategic air force. The only nation with the atom bomb, it now felt responsibility for what happened elsewhere, its confidence boosted by victory on a two-front global conflict and the economic uplift as wartime activity put a final end to the downturn that had begun in 1929.

America's emergence was balanced by the presence of a very different power in the vast Soviet land empire stretching from Asia to the heart of Europe, motivated by the belief that the iron laws of history would ensure eventual victory. Though America dominated most meaningful measures of power and ruled the oceans, the Union of Soviet Socialist Republics (USSR), inheriting the land empire of the Tsars, appeared to embody the vision of the geo-politician Halford Mackinder, of a superpower embracing the Eurasian Heartland. Its armed forces had played the major part in the defeat of Hitler's Germany with a victory that handed it a deep security zone for the hard state system directed by its Vozhd (Boss) from his red-walled corner office in the Kremlin. While far behind the United States in its development, the Soviet economy grew strongly after 1945, averaging 8 per cent annual expansion, as it brought under-used potential into play and mobilised resources under strong political control. Big projects organised on military lines, re-armament and production of capital goods acted as a spearhead for expansion. But the scale of destruction was such that output did not regain its pre-war level until the end of the 1940s and, in sharp contrast to the US, consumption was a low priority.[3]

The struggle between the two great powers would last more than four decades and shape global events, with effects still felt as Russia seeks to restore its influence and the international community comes to terms with the prospect that the United States may no longer be ready to exercise the function it took on in the later 1940s. Still, for all its dangers, particularly after the USSR developed atomic weapons in 1949, the conflict in Europe was always circumscribed by the way in which neither of the superpowers challenged the other in their respective security zones. Despite the declaration at the Yalta summit promising the peoples of Europe the right to choose their form of government and create democratic institutions of their own choice through free elections, the US did not intervene to defend non-Communists in East and Central Europe, whose division Churchill had set out in his 'percentages' proposal to Stalin in 1944.[4] The Cold War would have moments of great danger, but the way its early years were managed shows how big-power governments can pursue national interests while balancing strategic advantages and acknowledging that some issues are best left to work themselves out in their own fashion.

Though most international histories of the period focus largely on the emergence of the struggle between the US and USSR played out primarily over a Europe unable to fend for itself, the direct influence of the two powers in the rest of the world was often absent or marginal. Seeing this period through the prism of the Cold War is to distort events that determined the fates of hundreds of millions of people in Asia and Africa in ways that persist to our day. Reducing it to a trial of strength between the countries led by Harry Truman and Josef Stalin is to ignore the extraordinary multiplicity of major developments across the globe and the way in which, at this stage at least, nationalism played a more important role in liberation struggles than allegiance to an ideological master in a far-away capital.

The Soviet–American contest had no impact on the independence of India and Pakistan. Despite intelligence service warnings that Jewish refugees included Communists and fears that Arab nations might lean towards Moscow if a Zionist state was created, the Cold War was not a significant factor in the ending of the British Mandate in Palestine, the creation of Israel and the Arab invasion that followed. In South Africa, proponents of apartheid made much of the 'Red threat' but Communist influence was slight while independence movements elsewhere on the continent were driven by nationalism, not allegiance to the Kremlin. There was much US but little Communist presence in Latin America, where the challenge to right-wing governments came from populist movements calling for economic and social reform. Even in China, Cold War parameters were subject to local distortion. Soviet help had been vital for the

survival of the Communist forces in 1945–6, but they then evolved
in their own way, with Mao Zedong frequently ignoring advice from
Stalin. Preferring to keep the huge neighbour divided and believing
the Chinese revolutionaries were not yet ready to take power, the
Kremlin signed a treaty of friendship and alliance with Chiang Kai-
shek's Nationalist regime and advised the Great Helsman to check
the advance of the People's Liberation Army (PLA) at the Yangtze to
divide the country on the lines of Germany and Korea. For its part,
Washington grew increasingly unready to bail out its wartime ally
and came to regard China as peripheral to its core Asian strategy.

Though Stalin said he wanted to 'unleash a movement of liberation' and talked of using anti-imperialist sentiment to bring down
capitalism, the Cold War at this stage did not play much of a role in
the struggle in Vietnam, Indonesia, Malaya and parts of Africa. The
Kremlin was suspicious of the nationalism that powered the fight
against colonialism. The Cominform, the international Communist
organisation created in 1947, was exclusively European in membership. Stalin thought Asian revolutionaries were dangerously petit
bourgeois. 'Oh, you Orientals. You have such rich imaginations,' he
remarked when Ho Chi Minh asked for aid.

Indonesian Republicans worked for a time with the Communist
Party but then turned against its ally in a brutal settling of scores.
In the Philippines, which gained independence from the US in 1946
and gained a $620 million aid package, despite sharp economic and
social disparities, it was not until 1950 that the Communist Party
decided a 'revolutionary situation' existed. Communists in Malaya
took action earlier, but did not operate under Soviet guidance and
drew more support from the Chinese community's resentments than
from ideology. The British high commissioner, Malcolm MacDonald,
concluded in 1948 that there was 'little sign' of Soviet activity in the
region, noting that 'if you suppress a nationalist severely enough, you
will find him tending towards Communism'.[5]

This was a period of great violence as confrontations persisted that
had outlived the world war, or had been fanned by it. The processes
of nation building or regime change were often extremely lethal
with a combined death toll of millions. Mass population movements

brought enormous suffering, altered nations and deprived cosmopolitan cities of their historic flavour amid ethnic cleansing.

The power of governments was greatly extended. State authority buttressed by violence was at the core of the Soviet system and Stalin made public in 1946 his belief that any partial liberalisation allowed during the war should end. In the US, the state played a bigger role in helping business than free-market zealots would care to admit, while the heritage of government research during the war acted as a catalyst for peacetime technological development. The dominant Indian Congress Party aimed to create a strong central government, absorbing hundreds of princely states and creating what became known as the 'licence Raj'. Mao's vision of a new China was based on renewed national unity in the image of the old empire with a new ideological overlay. In South America, Peronism made corporatism as directed by the charismatic general its guiding light.

In Europe, nationalisation of key industries and the central banks was widely adopted. After the disasters of the 1930s, Keynesian economics ruled with the acceptance of the state's role in manipulating aggregate demand to stimulate economic activity for the good of the citizenry at large. Welfare provisions were embraced together with redistributive tax systems. Social mobility increased. Inequalities lessened in many countries as the rich became less rich and the poor less poor.

Obstacles to democracy were reduced as women got the vote and property and wealth restrictions on electoral eligibility were removed. New global institutions came into being in an attempt to spread international collaboration and foster peace. Technology advanced in many fields, often building on wartime innovations. Mechanisation boosted farm productivity, particularly in the United States. The global energy balance shifted, with important geopolitical implications.

However, whatever the aspirations for social justice at home, European powers held on to their colonies across large swathes of the globe, and their influence marked many leaders of nationalist movements, notably in the Raj. Though granting independence to India, Pakistan, Sri Lanka and Burma, Britain resisted further decolonisation. Herbert Morrison, the deputy prime minister, said giving independence to Africans would be 'like giving a child a latch-key, a bank account and a shot-gun'. Hugh Dalton, the chancellor of the Exchequer, wrote in his diary of 'a horrid vision of pullulating, poverty-stricken, diseased nigger communities, for whom one can do nothing in the short run, and now, the more one tries to help them, are querulous and ungrateful'.[6]

The French Union ensured Paris retained control of a complex structure exploited by the powerful imperial lobby; Socialists joined the centre-right in backing the use of military force in Vietnam and suppression of rebels in Madagascar in the name of defending civilisation. The Dutch army fought Nationalist Republicans in the East Indies. Portugal applied the full toughness of the Salazar dictatorship to its colonies while Belgium, in the words of the historian Martin Meredith, saw the Congo as 'a valuable piece of real estate that just required good management' by Brussels.[7]

What made these thirteen months unique as a crucible of global change was how so much of importance happened at the same time. If we think our present day is crowded with changes and uncertainties, the period covered here was even more challenging both in terms of immediate events and long-term trends, sometimes linked, sometimes self-contained but all with consequences that continue seven decades later.

On 1 June 1947, India and Pakistan were under British imperial rule and the state of Israel did not exist. The United States had become weary of attempts to perpetuate the wartime alliance with the Soviet Union but had not yet committed itself to the vast programme of aid that would revive Western Europe. The Chinese Nationalist government still held most of the country. Germany and Japan were being constrained to ensure they did not threaten world peace once again. Harry Truman was thought to be consigned to inevitable defeat in the 1948 presidential election and the veteran statesman-soldier-philosopher Jan Smuts seemed a solid bulwark against the advance of Afrikanerdom and apartheid in South Africa.

Thirteen months later, the subcontinent was divided into two new nations with a combined population of 380 million and hostilities raged between them in the Himalayas. Jews and Arabs were at war in the Middle East. The Marshall Plan had gone into action, bringing not only material aid but a major psychological boost vitally under-pinned by the continuing presence of American troops in Western Europe. The continent was divided into hostile blocs as never before. Czechoslovakia, the one semi-independent country east of the Iron Curtain, had been brought to heel by a Communist putsch. Stalin had created the Cominform to keep the Soviet satellites in line – though Yugoslavia soon declared its independence of Moscow. The US, UK and ten of their allies had launched their eleven-month air-lift to beat the Soviet blockade of Berlin as the division of Germany became cemented in ways that suited both sides in the Cold War and the West of the country embarked on economic and political revival. Chinese Communist armies had inflicted a series of major defeats on government forces and were on their way to final victory. Occupation policy had been reversed to allow Japan to grow into a major economic power and the principal American ally in Asia. The white population of South Africa had voted for apartheid, and Harry Truman had found the electoral recipe that would earn him a second term in the White House.

Running through this global saga was an unparalleled cast of adversaries and allies whose characters did much to determine the course of history. It is fashionable to decry the personal factor in the shaping of events, but the nature of those at the top of their coun-tries' political systems made a huge difference, from the accidental occupant of the White House and the Vozhd in the Kremlin to China's enemies of two decades and the mutually antagonistic rulers of India and Pakistan and of Israel and the Arab Nations. In their hands, the period yields multiple examples of crisis manipulation and management and the foundation of the international system that is now under strain. Amid all the violence and suffering across much of the globe, these thirteen months provide a relevant and valuable framework and instructive prelude for our times; a period when, for all the deep divisions, the future was often a matter for aspiration and construction.

Spheres of influence on the eve of WWII

- British Empire
- French Empire
- Axis Alliance
- Soviet Union
- Belgian/Dutch
- Portuguese Empire
- USA
- Major conflicts post-WWII
- Frontiers, 1955

*Independence war, from 1952* (MOROCCO)

*Independence war, from 1954* (ALGERIA)

*Greece, civil war 1946–49*

LIBYA *Independence 1951*

UNION OF SOVIET
SOCIAL REPUBLICS

MONGOLIA

MANCHURIA

Chinese Civil War, 1946–49

Korean War, from 1950

JAPAN

CHINA

Independence,
1948

IRAN

Independence,
1947

INDIA

Indo-China, 1946–54

*Pacific*

*Ocean*

PHILIPPINES

GYPT

SUDAN

ADEN PROTECTORATE

ETHIOPIA

The Emergency, from 1946

*Indian*

*Ocean*

DUTCH EAST INDIES

Indonesia, 1945–49

MADAGASCAR
Anti-French rising,
1947–48

AUSTRALIA

NEW ZEALAND

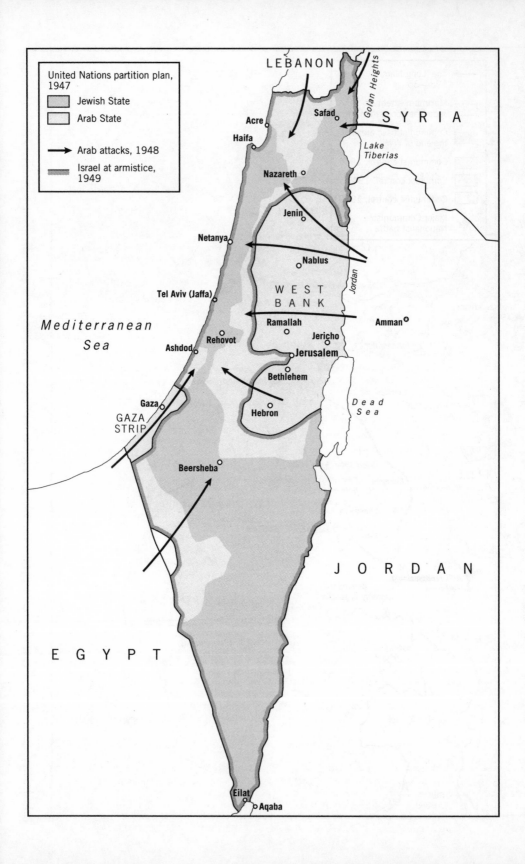

LEBANON

SYRIA

Golan Heights

Acre
Safad
Haifa

Lake
Tiberias

Nazareth

Jenin

Netanya

Nablus

Jordan

WEST
BANK

Tel Aviv (Jaffa)

Ramallah
Amman

Jericho

Mediterranean
Sea

Rehovot
Ashdod
Jerusalem

Bethlehem

Gaza
Dead
Sea

GAZA
STRIP
Hebron

Beersheba

JORDAN

EGYPT

Eilat
Aqaba

United Nations partition plan,
1947

Jewish State

Arab State

Arab attacks, 1948

Israel at armistice,
1949

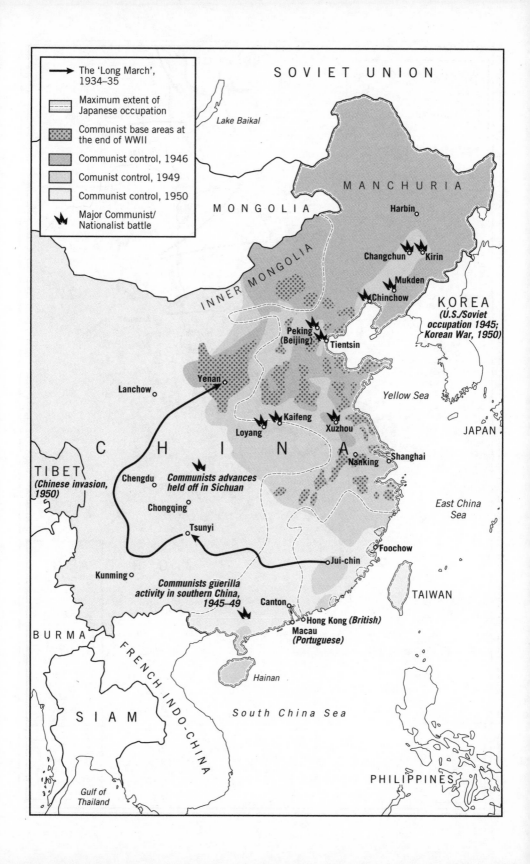

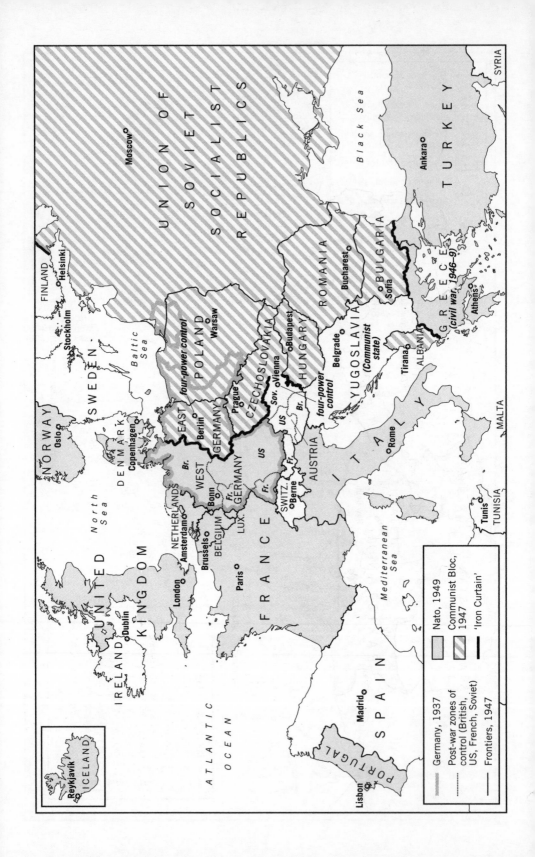

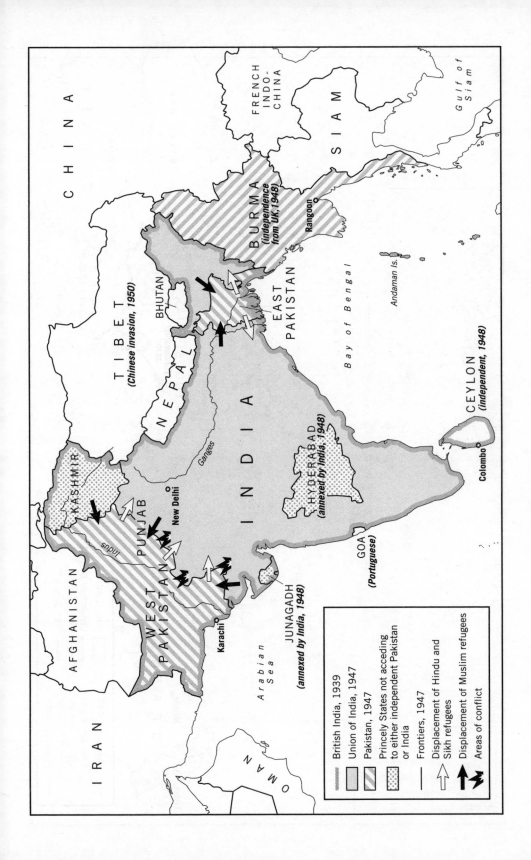

British India, 1939

Union of India, 1947

Pakistan, 1947

Princely States not acceding
to either independent Pakistan
or India

Frontiers, 1947

Displacement of Hindu and
Sikh refugees

Displacement of Muslim refugees

Areas of conflict

CHINA

FRENCH INDO-CHINA

SIAM

Gulf of Siam

BURMA
(independence
from UK, 1948)

Rangoon

TIBET
(Chinese invasion, 1950)

BHUTAN

NEPAL

EAST PAKISTAN

Bay of Bengal

Andaman Is.

Ganges

INDIA

HYDERABAD
(annexed by India, 1948)

CEYLON
(independent, 1948)

Colombo

KASHMIR

PUNJAB

New Delhi

AFGHANISTAN

WESTERN PAKISTAN

Indus

JUNAGADH
(annexed by India, 1948)

GOA
(Portuguese)

Karachi

Arabian Sea

IRAN

OMAN

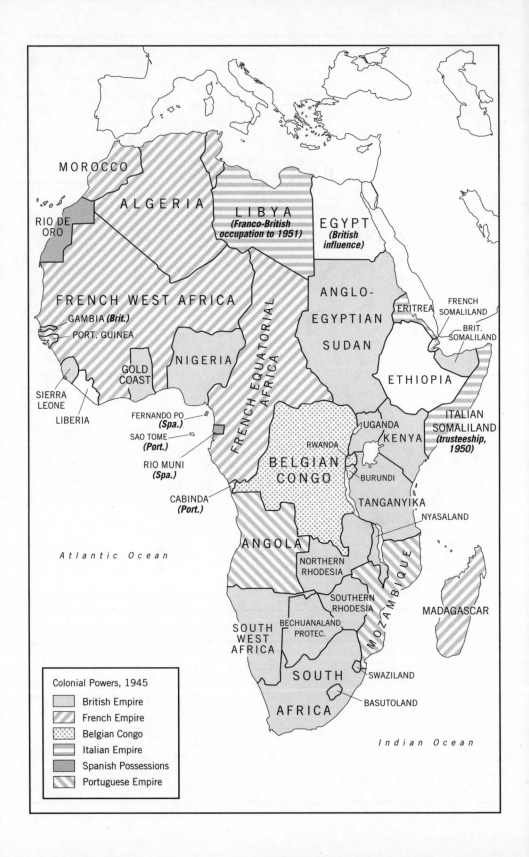

MOROCCO

RIO DE ORO

ALGERIA

LIBYA
*(Franco-British occupation to 1951)*

EGYPT
*(British influence)*

FRENCH WEST AFRICA

GAMBIA *(Brit.)*

PORT. GUINEA

SIERRA LEONE

LIBERIA

GOLD COAST

NIGERIA

FRENCH EQUATORIAL AFRICA

ANGLO-EGYPTIAN SUDAN

ERITREA

FRENCH SOMALILAND

BRIT. SOMALILAND

ETHIOPIA

ITALIAN SOMALILAND
*(trusteeship, 1950)*

FERNANDO PO *(Spa.)*

SAO TOME *(Port.)*

RIO MUNI *(Spa.)*

CABINDA *(Port.)*

RWANDA

BELGIAN CONGO

BURUNDI

UGANDA

KENYA

TANGANYIKA

NYASALAND

*Atlantic Ocean*

ANGOLA

NORTHERN RHODESIA

SOUTHERN RHODESIA

BECHUANALAND PROTEC.

SOUTH WEST AFRICA

MOZAMBIQUE

MADAGASCAR

SWAZILAND

BASUTOLAND

SOUTH AFRICA

*Indian Ocean*

Colonial Powers, 1945

British Empire

French Empire

Belgian Congo

Italian Empire

Spanish Possessions

Portuguese Empire

# PART ONE

# A NEW WORLD ORDER

# CHAPTER ONE

# LEGACY OF WAR

## I: THE COST OF VICTORY

'WAR IN EUROPE OVER. There is absolutely no reason to get up in the mornings any more,' wrote the photographer Robert Capa in his diary when the news of Germany's capitulation was announced. Few other people could take such an insouciant attitude as the cataclysm, which had killed an estimated 15 million military personnel and 40 million civilians, gave way to continuing high anxieties and turbulence that escalated beyond any expectations, gathering pace between the summers of 1947 and 1948.[1]

The conflict had seen a high build-up in industrial output to fuel the war machine on all sides, but, across much of the globe, recovery from the devastation it caused was slow; in some places things actually got worse. In 1947, the United Nations concluded that the previous two years had been 'characterized by retardation of economic progress'. While the US grew greatly, the potential of many other important countries diminished even more. Inflationary pressures increased. The dollar, the main vehicle for international exchanges, was in critically short supply. 'The far-reaching post-war dislocations of international trade have remained acute,' the UN noted in its global report for 1948. 'Productive facilities were still not generally significantly larger than before the war while progress in agricultural output still lagged seriously in many areas.'[2]

Wartime destruction stretched from Western Europe to China, where, after occupying Manchuria for six years, Japan launched a full-scale invasion in 1937. Killing and devastation had been indiscriminate. Civilians died in much greater numbers than fighting troops, including 6 million Jews slain in the Holocaust, Slavs and other groups targeted by the Nazis and Asian civilians massacred by the Japanese. The number of Soviet dead has been put officially at 26.6 million though another estimate raised this to 40 million. Anywhere from 15 to 22 million Chinese perished. Ten per cent of the population of Yugoslavia was killed. Of the two defeated Axis powers, Japan lost 2.6–3 million troops and civilians while German deaths amounted to between 5 and 8 million, with several million held as prisoners of war. (In contrast, the US death toll ran to 419,000, and that of the UK and its dominions and colonies to 450,000.)

In some Russian villages, a hundred or more men went off to fight and only five returned. Belarus lost up to 30 per cent of its population. The new weapons of strategic bombing and fire raids on cities took more than 1.5 million lives, followed by the atomic explosions at Hiroshima and Nagasaki, which killed up to 250,000. In Germany, which suffered 600,000 civilians killed by bombing, there were 1.6 million disabled veterans and 1.2 million war widows. In Manila, hundreds of thousands of civilians died in the fiercest urban fighting of the Pacific War as Japanese troops killed and raped indiscriminately – a doctor recalled being among only fifty survivors from a group of more than 3,000 men herded together to be killed. A quarter of the inhabitants of Okinawa perished in fighting there after US troops landed in 1945.[3]

One-third of the wealth of the USSR was destroyed. The damage to the Netherlands was put at one-third of pre-war gross domestic product. In European Russia, the Ukraine and Belarus, which were occupied by the Germans and then pummelled by the Soviet westward offensive, 5 million homes were destroyed, leaving 25 million people without shelter, some living in holes in the ground. Eighty per cent of Warsaw was blown away. 'Here is a burial ground. Here is death,' a Polish writer lamented on return to the city. Ten million Germans and 9 million Japanese were homeless. A German Communist arriving in Berlin after the defeat of the Reich described the city as 'a picture of hell. Fires and ruins, aimless people dressed in rags.' In France, a million houses were laid waste from the air, most after D-Day; in the Norman town of Saint-Lô, only two hundred of the 2,600 buildings escaped, while 100,000 mines were buried or floated off the beaches of the fashionable resort of Le Touquet. In Finland, the Germans laid waste 35,000 square miles of territory as they retreated, sending 170,000 people fleeing from their homes.[4]

In France and Italy, the economy ran at 40 per cent of the 1938–9 level. Though Britain had emerged among the victors, the war had cost a quarter of its wealth and put it deeply in debt; exports in 1945 were down by a third and almost half its old markets had been lost, mainly to the US. Coal and steel production in Germany was less than 50 per cent the pre-war level. Half of Hungary's industrial capacity was devastated in fighting in 1945. In the Philippines, towns, farms and factories had been razed, 80 per cent of schools were in ruins and the sugar industry was devastated. Japan lost a quarter of its national wealth in its quest for regional supremacy. The industrial belt between Tokyo and Yokohama was a mass of rubble.

Famines had killed millions in the later stages of the war in Bengal, China and Vietnam. In Manchuria, 400,000 people were short of food and sometimes starving. In Budapest, 30,000 inhabitants died of hunger at the end of the conflict; 'the bodies choked the gutters,' the mayor remembered. In the USSR, an estimated 2 million citizens starved to death during the two years after the end of the war. People 'survived on grass' and there were cases of mothers eating their babies in the Ukraine, which had already been the target of the Holodomor famine engineered by Moscow in the 1930s that took some 4 million lives.[5]

More than half the locomotives and rolling stock were out of service in major European nations; bridge and viaducts were down; canals were blocked; of the big ports, only Bordeaux and Antwerp were still functioning. Ninety per cent of lorries in France were out of service. Fuel was scarce and coal supplies ran short. Becoming prime minister at the Liberation in 1944, Charles de Gaulle described his country as 'ruined, decimated, torn apart'. In China, only 10 per cent of the rail network was operational, rivers were mined and most shipping had been destroyed.[6]

The plight of European countries was aggravated by their trade deficits with the US, which meant they had to export everything they could to earn dollars to buy vital imports, reducing the availability of consumer goods and increasing pressure on supplies. Annual price rises hit 60 per cent in France and inflation rose so fast in Hungary that the government stopped collecting taxes because the money in which it was paid was useless by the time it was banked by the treasury; bank notes issued in 1946 had twenty zeros. Queues, hoarding, barter and black markets were the order of the day. Harry Lime, the *Third Man* black marketer of Vienna, became emblematic of the times, as did the British spiv with his striped drape jacket, garish tie, rakish trilby hat and pencil moustache offering goods that had fallen of the back of a lorry, epitomised by the popular comedian Sid Field's character of Slasher Green, the cockney wide boy. Spanish landowners circumvented controls to sell grain in a parallel system. Japan had 17,000 'blue sky markets' dealing in black market goods.[7]

Health care was lacking in many nations. A fifth of the inhabitants of Warsaw were reported to be suffering from tuberculosis. Infant mortality in Vienna was nearly four times the rate in 1938. In Czechoslovakia, premature civilian mortality rose by 100,000 a year, the birth rate declined and there was a high level of disease among babies.[8]

The UN calculated that average per capita consumption across the globe in 1945–6 was 10 per cent below the pre-war level overall. Harvests were poor; Soviet grain output in 1946 was less than half that of 1940. Arable land had been depleted by fighting. Large numbers of farm animals had been killed – in Western Russia and adjoining territories, 20 million pigs and 11 million horses had died. In Western Europe, more than 100 million people lived on one-third of the average calorie consumption of the United States. In China, a United Nations mission reported that 40 million people were at or barely above starvation level. Japanese plundering and then the collapse of supply chains with its defeat added to the destruction caused by war and the removal of equipment, reducing much of East Asia to, at best, mere self-sufficiency and what one historian described as 'dilipadation and decrepitude as was not seen in Western Europe'.[9]

A severe winter in Europe in 1946–7 followed by heavy rains in the west and drought in the east made things even more dire. As Britain suffered the worst blizzards for seventy years, electricity supply was cut to a few hours a day, factories closed and unemployment rose. There was concern about whether the railways could keep operating and the BBC suspended its fledgling television service for a month to save energy. Orme Sargent, the permanent under secretary at the Foreign Office, told a colleague that he expected 'a very severe slump indeed'.[10]

The wheat crop in Belgium dropped by 70 per cent. Spanish government policy was summed up as being 'to avoid starvation'. In Germany, Italy, Greece, Poland, Hungary and Yugoslavia, the level of calories per day was below the 'temporary maintenance' level, the UN reported. Similar shortages hit Brazil, Colombia, Chile, Mexico and Peru. Fishery production fell sharply in Asia because of war damage to boats and the sea. Rice, the staple food for almost half the world's population, was 'in critically short supply' according to the international body.[11]

Truman made the world food crisis the subject of the first televised presidential address from the White House;[12] he cancelled state banquets and urged Americans not to eat meat on Tuesdays or poultry or eggs on Thursdays as part of a 'Save Food for Europe' campaign. US distilleries were shut down for sixty days to conserve grain to be sent across the Atlantic. Louis Meyer, head of the MGM film studio, decreed that Tuesday would be a meatless day at the commissary when its big star, the collie Lassie, was served a diet of apple pancakes. The Heinz company distributed posters to be put up in shops reading '500,000,000 People Are Hungry. DON'T WASTE FOOD.'[13]

The former American president, Herbert Hoover, whom the president sent to study the food situation in Europe, warned that starvation would open the gates to Communism. After a trip across the ocean in early 1947, Will Clayton, the US Under Secretary of State, reported that 'Europe is steadily deteriorating ... One political crisis after another merely denotes the existence of grave economic distress.' Depending on loans from the United States to keep going, Britain and France would run out of foreign exchange reserves by the end of the year, he warned; Italy even sooner.[14]

## II: Brutal new world

Whatever the high ideals of the newly created United Nations and declarations of 'Never Again', the world conflict left deeply dehumanising effects. Though proclaimed as 'the good war', it had seen the shelving of the mutually accepted rules of engagement generally respected in 1914–18. The killing of civilians laid a legacy that infected the psyches of many parts of the world for years after the fighting ended. Morality was often inverted in an age which lived in the shadow of the Holocaust, mass killing of civilians as well as troops and Japan's brutal attempt to dominate Asia. Inhabitants of countries occupied by the Nazis or the Japanese had come to believe that 'their patriotic duty was to cheat, to lie, to run a black market, to discredit and to defraud; these habits became ingrained after five years,' as Belgian Foreign Minister Paul-Henri Spaak put it.[15]

Once-dominant elites had lost their pre-eminence and the ability to control societies. In Central and Eastern Europe, institutions already sapped by pre-war authoritarian rulers were further weakened. The rights of citizens, the protection of property and the sanctity of life itself had been shown to be fragile. Millions of German and Japanese were held as prisoners of war. Families were split by the fighting, deportation and displacement. Children separated from their parents or living in camps became feral survivors; there were estimated to be 280,000 orphans as a result of the fighting in Yugoslavia alone while, in Germany, 1.5 million children were without parents.[16]

In the Philippines, criminal gangs armed with wartime weapons robbed banks and staged kidnapping in big cities while guerrillas turned to banditry. In Japan, crime and use of alcohol and drugs increased in what was called the 'kyodatsu condition', or 'state of lethargy'. China's society was hollowed out; summing up a trip to regions of China held by the Nationalists, the American diplomat, John Melby, wrote of the prevailing 'despair and decadence and corruption'. The Communist siege of the city of Changchun in Manchuria resulted in more than 100,000 civilian deaths from starvation. A similar death toll was reported at the time as the French put down a rising in Madagascar, while fighting on the Korean island of Jeju involved mass killings.[17]

Independence for India and Pakistan was accompanied by spreading communal violence on a huge scale between Hindus, Muslims and Sikhs. The Viet Minh, the Indonesian Republicans and Nationalists in Madagascar battled colonial authorities, which hit back with counter-attacks. In Palestine, the Zionist army launched a campaign of violence while extremist groups staged terrorist attacks against the Mandate authorities, the Arabs vowed to drive 'the British to the sea and the Jews to the grave' and police and troops resorted to increasingly heavy-handed methods.

The Chinese Communists and the Nationalist government both repressed any form of opposition. A generally sympathetic American journalist who visited areas in the north occupied by the People's Liberation Army described the 'extermination of large sections of the population'. A Norwegian missionary told of landlords being hung up by their toes or thumbs, whipped with thorns, their arms and legs broken, starved to death or sent out as beggars with the death sentence for anybody found giving them alms.[18]

In parts of Eastern and Northern Europe, where the Nazis had found willing local collaborators, partisans fought bitter wars against the Soviets; 70,000 Red Army soldiers, militias and death squads were needed to suppress the 'Forest Brothers' of the Baltic states. The Greek government clamped down ruthlessly on Communists, whose army raided villages, press-ganged peasants into service and sent children to be brought up in Communist neighbouring states. French resistance fighters set up summary tribunals to execute collaborators and women accused of having slept with Germans had their heads shaved before being paraded through the streets.

Tito made the royalist Chetnik resistance army his first target once the Germans were gone as well as wreaking revenge on Croatian fascists who had slaughtered Serbs in death camps. In neighbouring Albania, Enver Hoxha liquidated non-Communist partisans in a settling of scores that would lead to the killing and imprisonment of hundreds of thousands of people.

Women were often particular targets. The convulsions at the end of the Raj were accompanied by mass rapes and abductions of victims to be sold to brothels or to private clients; those who escaped were often rejected by their families as shameful. Soviet troops raped an estimated 1.4 million women in East Prussia, Pomerania and Silesia; a woman in a camp in East Prussia said she had suffered 128 times. The historian Antony Beevor put the number of rapes by the Red Army in Germany at 2 million. An estimated half a million Hungarian women suffered, as did 100,000 Romanians. In the northern half of Korea, Soviet troops duplicated the rapes and pillage of their comrades in Europe.[19]

When the Yugoslav Communist Milovan Djilas raised the subject with Stalin, the Vozhd replied that it was understandable if 'a soldier who has crossed thousands of kilometres through blood and fire and death has fun with a woman or takes some trifle'. Though recent studies have highlighted brutality by some American troops, and French soldiers attacked women in the Black Forest region, there was nothing comparable on the Western Front, while the Japanese were amazed at the generally good behaviour of the occupation forces. The US occupation chief in Germany, General Lucius Clay, remarked, 'We began to look like angels, not because we're angels, but we looked that in comparison to what was going on in Eastern Europe.'[20]

In a re-ordering of the global map, territories from the middle of Europe to Korea were divided, the apparatus of governments split and populations subjected to mass movements, either enforced or motivated by fear – and without the right to return to their old homes. Germany and Austria were cut into separate occupation zones for each of the wartime Allies. Palestine was partitioned. Asia was fragmented with China in the grip of civil war, Japan on its knees, Korea split and significant parts of Vietnam, Indonesia, Malaya and the Philippines were outside the control of the central authorities. Anticipating defeat in the civil war on the mainland, Chiang Kai-shek's Nationalists prepared to split the island of Formosa (now Taiwan) from the mainland following its return to China's sovereignty after half a century of Japanese occupation, looting and repressing the indigenous population as they prepared their safe haven.

The USSR was the major beneficiary of the re-drawing of frontiers, which introduced changes of sovereignty that endure to this day. It took 70,000 square miles of territory from Poland, which was partially compensated with 40,000 square miles of what had been East Prussia and German Silesia, and a new frontier on the line of the Oder and Neisse rivers decided at the last Allied summit at Potsdam. Pursuing a Tsarist-era expansion course designed to ensure the security of the Russian heartland, Moscow held on to Red Army conquests in the three Baltic states, from which half a million people were deported between 1944 and 1949 in an attempt to make the region more subservient. It acquired western Ukraine (from Poland), the port city of Königsberg/Kaliningrad (from Germany) and part of the Carpathian region (from Czechoslovakia) as well as one-tenth of Finland's territory, a fifth of its industrial capacity and important ports. To the south and east, it asserted control of the Black Sea littoral with acquisition of Bessarabia and Bukovina (from Romania) as well as the Sakhalin and the Kuril Islands off its north Pacific coast, which it had taken from Japan.

In China, an official with the United Nations Relief and Rehabilitation Agency wrote of 50 million 'homeless, wandering people [in] the greatest trek in history' after eight years of war. More than 12 million people fled their homes or were driven out in a ceaseless movement between Hindu, Muslim and Sikh regions as the Raj was divided. Fighting in Java and Sumatra between the Dutch and Indonesian Republicans is estimated to have uprooted 7 million people. The number of people who fled from the north of Korea to the south was put by American estimates at 400,000. Japan absorbed a flood of settlers and military personnel who returned to their home country after being expelled from lands which had fallen under Tokyo's imperial expansion, nearly 3 million of them from China.[21]

The partition of Palestine and creation of Israel led to the displacement of some 700,000 Palestinians and the sacking of 400–600 villages in what Arabs called the 'al-Nakba', 'the catastrophe'. Half a million Jews travelled from East Europe and Arab countries to Israel. The Zionist authorities paid Romania and Bulgaria $5 million to allow 160,000 migrants to depart. Nearly 40 per cent of Jews living in Egypt left after a wave of killings, detentions and confiscations while a pogrom and destruction of the synagogue in Aleppo precipitated flight from Syria.

Nations and cities changed their nature as living cheek-by-jowl with those of different ethnic groups or religions was no longer the norm. Instead, people defined themselves by what they thought they were or how they were told to think of themselves. Integrated, if imperfect, communities were destroyed in the interest of settling old scores or in pursuit of Stalin's idea that rule by a single ethnic group was the best guarantee of stability since the culture and roots of minorities might threaten imposed uniformity. As Władysław Gomułka, the general secretary of the Polish Communist Party, put it, 'countries are built on national lines and not on multinational lines', though the only permissible national identity in the Soviet sphere of influence was the one approved in Moscow. Hindu zealots saw no place for Muslims in India unless they conformed religiously, and Muslims responded with massacres of Hindus and Sikhs. David Ben-Gurion thought that the fewer Arabs in the new Jewish state the better. Chaim Weizmann, the Zionist patriarch, believed Palestine should be 'as Jewish as England is English', while Arab leaders spoke of driving out both the Jews and the British.[22]

The Holocaust had wiped out the Jewish professional class of doctors, businessmen, lawyers, scientists and teachers in countries occupied by the Nazis and the mixture of peoples, cultures and traditions that had characterised the heyday of the Hapsburg Empire was as unacceptable to Stalin as it had been to Hitler. Class warriors equated the bourgeoisie with Fascism. Some 20 million people were moved from their homes in Central and Eastern Europe in what the British prime minister, Clement Attlee, called 'one of the most horrible events in human history'. A million and a half were lodged in camps for displaced persons. The *New York Times* correspondent Anne O'Hare McCormick wrote that 'the scale of this resettlement, and the conditions in which it takes place, are without precedent in history. No one seeing its horrors first hand can doubt that it is a crime against humanity.'[23]

Those expelled included 12–13 million Germans, some of whom could trace family trees there dating back seven centuries. Most came from Czechoslovakia, whose president Edvard Beneš warned them, 'Woe woe, woe thrice woe to the Germans, we will liquidate you,' and from land taken by Poland where the wartime leader Stanisław Mikołajczyk held that it was 'impossible for people of Polish and

German extraction to co-exist in one state'. The low-lying eastern farmlands which had been Germany's granary and home of the Junkers were reduced to empty space and deserted villages; 'the fields were fallow, the weeds thigh-high,' a British journalist wrote after driving between Berlin and Warsaw. 'Shutters flapped and doors creaked, dirty curtains flew out of empty windows. Inside, furniture and beds, even sideboards and cupboards stood complete with their contents, rain-soaked, filthy, abandoned.'[24]

Half a million Germans died in the population movement and as many were unaccounted for. Some were massacred as they made their way west packed into railway wagons or pillaged by bandits. Women were taken off to be raped and never returned. An observer recorded that one group arriving in Berlin, some freezing to death, were 'more cattle than human beings, more dead than alive'. A militia made up mainly of young men, many of whom had been pressed into labour service by the Nazis and were out for revenge, terrorised those leaving Poland. In a Silesian camp commanded by a sadistic eighteen-year-old, nearly 6,500 people died, 828 of them children.[25]

Lucius Clay reckoned that the flow of refugees who did get through increased the population of the US and British occupation zones of Germany by 20 per cent. Apart from the drain on scarce supplies, the newcomers were different from the locals in culture, language and background. Four hundred thousand would still be in camps in 1950 without jobs. The scale of the movement of people also weighed heavily on Austria – divided, like Germany, among the four powers – which became the destination for a million refugees but had trouble feeding its own inhabitants.[26]

Despite the horrors of Nazi rule, anti-Semitism remained visceral in parts of Europe. There was resentment at the relatively high proportion of Jews among the new rulers who arrived from Moscow with the Red Army. Nor could concentration camp survivors count on a good welcome home in countries such as France, where they were seen as embarrassing evidence of collaboration.

Poland witnessed more than three hundred attacks on Jews between 1944 and 1946; forty-two were massacred and fifty seriously injured in the town of Kielce, where Jews returning from concentration camps had claimed back their homes and mobs ran

riot after rumours were spread of gentile children being ritually murdered for their blood to be used to make matzos. Police and armed
workers joined in. In the next four months, an estimated 100,000
Jews left Poland, many joining others who fled to Palestine.

Stalin had always been suspicious of Jews and his anti-Semitism
grew as he aged: 'every Jew is a nationalist and an agent of American
intelligence,' he would say. In Soviet thinking, the class struggle took
precedence over genocide and the Jewish sense of community and
identity ran counter to the required homogenisation of society. As
Hersh Smolar, a resistance leader in Minsk and a prominent cultural
figure in post-war Poland, put it, 'If there turn out to be some people
who are going to buzz on like flies about some sort of supposedly
higher and more essential Jewish national goals, then we will eliminate those people from our society.'[27]

CHAPTER TWO

# NEW DEPARTURES

## I: The state expands

For all the turbulence that followed the end of the world war, this was a time of major social, economic and political change which would become embedded as a new world took root. The escalation of government involvement on behalf of citizens at large appeared the best way to repay the sacrifices made during the conflict. Redistributive tax and wage policies, the destruction of assets of the rich and the enhanced power of organised labour were deemed necessary to diminish inequality. Governments and political parties of the left promised justice and reform to alter society radically. In the US, the slice of income taken by the wealthiest 10 per cent of the population declined.

In the UK, the Labour Party sent Churchill into opposition with its victory in the 1945 election on a platform that promised sweeping economic and social change. Post-war governments in Western Europe contained Socialists and Communists alongside Christian Democrats but few from the right. New regimes revolutionised East and Central Europe in coalitions that morphed to the Soviet model. In Asia, with 47 per cent of the world's population, state power seemed to many the only path to progress. India's Congress Party brought in the 'licence Raj' while the looming Communist victory in China heralded the establishment of the strong centralised authority the country had lacked. In Australia, the Labour government of the fiscally prudent Joseph Chifley introduced a raft of social reform while transforming the wartime economy into a peacetime regime that boosted prosperity. In South Africa, the implementation of apartheid brought a big expansion of the state in pursuit of social engineering on a national scale.

The reaction to the destruction of the war and the failure of laissez-faire economics in the 1920s and 1930s was the adoption of central planning and nationalisation and the pursuit of increased output. Soviet Five-Year Plans set elevated targets and France embarked on an ambitious programme of state planning under the future 'Father of Europe', Jean Monnet.[1] 'Produce, produce and produce more [as] the highest form of your duty as Frenchmen,' the Communist leader, Maurice Thorez, exhorted miners.[2]

Public spending surged to 20–30 per cent of national wealth in Western Europe. As welfare provisions expanded, people came to regard health care, education, housing, employment and pensions as rights owed to them by the state. Sweden's path-setting Social Democrats developed a comprehensive system of health insurance, pensions, child and rent allowances and the expansion of education in a system that combined private enterprise production and socialised consumption under agreement between employers and unions to enshrine industrial peace as a national interest. Post-war reconstruction of cities produced housing estates and town planning. Le Corbusier began work on his giant steel and concrete Cité Radieuse apartment buildings in Marseilles as a model project. State-sponsored culture blossomed – popular theatres in France, the BBC's Third Programme, city arts programmes in Germany.

Trade unions gained increased power. In Britain, they constituted virtually an arm of government, while in France and Italy they became the blunt instrument for Communist parties. Across the Atlantic, where Truman wanted to continue Roosevelt's policy of using the federal state to bolster the capitalist system, labour power was on display in strikes on the railways, coal mines, steel mills, automobile manufacturers, meat packing, film studios and mortuaries. While the Republican majority returned to Congress in 1946 ensured the United States remained firmly on the capitalist path, the Full Employment Act proclaimed that it was the duty of government to 'foster the general welfare' and promote 'conditions under which there will be afforded useful employment for those able, willing, and

seeking to work; and to promote maximum employment, production, and purchasing power'. Truman's State of the Union message
in 1948 called for a national health insurance scheme, increased
support for farmers and education along with a big increase in the
minimum wage and a cost-of-living credit to all taxpayers to be paid
for by raising corporate taxes.[3]

Still, while parties of the left could benefit from the discredit
accruing to the right for its pre-war performance and, in some places,
collaboration with Fascism, the centre revived in the form of new
Christian Democratic parties – the CDU in Germany, Democrazia
Cristiana in Italy, the MRP in France, and the Volksbeweging in
the Netherlands. In the United States, the Republicans, preaching
reduced government spending and limits on labour rights, were
confident of capturing the White House in 1948 after an absence of
sixteen years. International capital was strengthened.

Internationally, the US-led international financial system gained
its third leg when the General Agreement on Trade and Tariffs
(GATT) went into operation at the start of 1948 following the
International Monetary Fund (IMF) and World Bank. Bringing
together twenty-three nations, it introduced 45,000 tariff concessions affecting $10 billion in trade.

In other areas of co-operation between nations, the World
Health Organization (WHO) was brought into being and twenty-
one countries became inaugural members of the Organization of
American States (OAS). A conference in Geneva agreed to set up an
International Civil Aviation Organization. As well as the Security
Council and General Assembly, the United Nations operated councils
and sub-units covering each continent, social, economic and fiscal
matters, statistics, population, children, labour, food and agriculture.
As the post-war order evolved, there was also a constant stream of
bilateral economic agreements – seventy were concluded in the first
three months of 1948 alone.[4]

## II: SOCIETIES SHIFT, TECHNOLOGY ADVANCES

Even if the world was male-dominated, women built on their wartime service to establish their role in society – though, in the Soviet

Union, the nearly one million female gunners, snipers and pilots were told that their primary duty was now motherhood. Female participation in the workforce rose. In Japan, where the Americans insisted that women get the vote, they not only went to the polls in greater numbers than men at the 1945 elections, but seventy-nine ran for seats in the House of Representatives, thirty-nine successfully.

After decades of opposition from the right and from republican politicians afraid of the influence of the Catholic Church on them, women won the vote at last in France, where Marthe Richard, a former prostitute and spy turned Christian Democratic politician, got state brothels closed in 1946. Education became more widespread for both sexes. In Britain, the government aimed to create a million more school places and Cambridge University accepted full degrees for women. Across the Atlantic, the GI Bill led to a stream of veterans attending universities and vocational colleges.

The assumption of the supremacy of white colonialism had crumbled with the surrender of 85,000 British and Dominion troops to 36,000 Japanese at Singapore, the fall of Hong Kong, the capitulation of 93,000 Dutch troops in Indonesia and the readiness of Vichy French to work under the victorious Asian in Indochina. The power and privileges of feudal rulers who had worked with the Europeans was also seriously hit, most dramatically in the absorption of the more than 555 princely states by the new nations of India and Pakistan.

Though European monarchs who had spent the war years in London returned home, their powers were reduced in the new political and social environment. A referendum in Italy dethroned the House of Savoy in favour of a republic. The new governments in the east of the Continent forced their monarchs, many of them descendants of Queen Victoria, to abdicate; in Romania, the Communist Party leader pointed a revolver at King Michael to get him to agree to step down. More broadly, the traditional European ruling classes were edged out or more forcibly dispossessed. 'Everything is going nowadays,' King George VI said to the writer Vita Sackville-West, whose family home was being taken over by the National Trust. 'I shall also have to go.' In fact, the resistance of royal houses to eviction was considerable; the British monarch held on, as did his peers in Scandinavia, the Netherlands, Greece, Egypt, Transjordan, Saudi Arabia, Iran and South East Asia.[5]

Emperor Hirohito of Japan, who was fortunate not to be tried as a war criminal, was described by an American correspondent in 1945 as 'a tired, pathetic little man about five foot two inches in height, in a badly cut striped grey suit, with trousers a couple of inches too short. He has a pronounced facial tic and his right shoulder twitches constantly. When he walks, he throws his right leg a little sideways as if he had no control over it.' But by 1947, Hirohito was more at home in public and attracted huge crowds on tours of the country, some waving the banned flag of the rising sun. Conservative politicians, who were re-emerging and winning American backing, jostled to join the imperial train and motorcades that took on the appearance of victory parades as Hirohito started to assert his political role once again.[6]

This was a time of great technological advances, some based on military innovations from the war turned to civilian use, backed financially by governments and companies convinced of the value of investing in research and development for power or profit. 'Science has been in the wings,' a leading engineer, Vannevar Bush,[7] wrote to Truman. 'It should be brought to the centre of the stage – for in it lies much of our hope for the future.' In keeping with that spirit, the US government became a major patron of scientific inquiry, sponsoring the National Science Foundation and extensive university research as munitions factories were transformed for civilian purposes. The concentration of the latest technology in the West deepened the divide with under-developed nations as most of the 2.5 billion people on earth had little or no access to it. As a result, while many developed nations became more equal societies, the inequality between richer and poorer countries widened – life expectancy in the former was twice that in the latter.[8]

The transistor was demonstrated at Bell Labs in California at the end of 1947. Under the professor and academic administrator Frederick Terman, Stanford University was built up as a great centre for technical excellence. At Harvard, Howard Aitken and colleagues worked on the electro-mechanical Mark computer for the American navy. The American mathematician Claude Shannon formulated information theory. The Hungarian-British physicist Dennis Gabor developed the hologram. The first modern use of the 'computer' was recorded. The AT&T company offered the first mobile telephone service. A 200-inch telescope was unveiled in California. Bing Crosby made the first pre-recorded radio broadcast. French engineer Constant Martin invented the clavioline electronic keyboard, precursor of the synthesiser.

The development of the antibiotic Streptomycin made effective treatment possible for tuberculosis. The Zika virus was isolated in the Ugandan forest of that name. Defibrillation was used for the first time and the anti-thyroid drug was introduced in the USA. In Italy, insecticides, which formed part of American aid, brought under control the deadly malaria that had been a scourge, particularly in the Po Valley and the marshlands around Rome. DDT was sprayed from aircraft and 3 million Italians had their bodies daubed with the chemical.[9]

The global energy balance was shifting as increasing Middle Eastern oil output heightened the region's strategic importance. The Anglo-Iranian Oil Company was a UK crucial asset, making more money out of oil than the government in Teheran. In Saudi Arabia, where the biggest oil field to date was discovered at Ghawar in 1948,[10] an alliance of Bedouin rulers and Texas oilmen produced a state within a state in the shape of the Aramco company with its own ports, roads, towns and schools. A US consortium put up the unheard-of sum of $7.5 million cash, a minimum annual royalty of $625,000 and 15 per cent of the profits for Kuwait's Neutral Zone concession, throwing in a million-dollar yacht for the Amir as part of the deal. The independent operator, J. Paul Getty, paid even more for the Saudi concession in the zone.

Everyday life was radically changed by the widespread application of pre-war inventions such as plastics, polystyrene, polyethylene and synthetic rubber. The 5,000 television sets in the US at the end of the war rose to 350,000 in 1948 before increasing sixfold the following year. The Republican and Democratic conventions of 1948 were held in the same city, Philadelphia, partly to enable the first television coverage of both.

Refrigeration, vacuum cleaners and other appliances spread

through households in the US and then in other developed nations where plastic became ubiquitous. The first long-playing records became available. The Michelin company commercialised the radial tyre. The American Harold Land, with 535 patents to his name, produced the Polaroid camera. A six-foot-tall microwave oven was available for $5,000.[11] Earl Tupper launched the food containers that bore his name. Teflon began to coat pots and pans. The Frisbee was launched. A resident of Newtown, Connecticut, set about commercialising a word game he called Scrabble.

Experts who had worked for the Nazis turned their skills to the American space programme; a rhesus monkey given the name of Albert was fired to an altitude of 39 miles on a rocket – he died of suffocation during the flight. Visitors from other planets were said to have been spotted in Washington State, to have landed in New Mexico and to have made off with an airliner that disappeared in the Andes.

The Air Travel Plan pioneered by American Airlines and the Air Transport Association became the first internationally valid charge card. A Frenchman promoted bikini swimsuits which, he said, had to be small enough to be pulled through a wedding ring, but met with little initial success. The Land Rover was exhibited for the first time at the Amsterdam Motor Show. A Scottish woman used her sewing machine to run off four hundred Paddi disposable nappies with a cellulose pad inside a plastic baby garment made of old parachutes – they went into full production in the early 1950s. Christian Dior launched his New Look fashion line of wasp-waisted, full-pleated 'Satan red' gowns as a flamboyant response to post-war austerity; when the new mode was staged for a photo shoot in the streets of Montmartre, angry women attacked the models to protest at such profligacy.[12]

The era saw the publication of *Under the Volcano*, *Exercises in Style* and *The Heart of the Matter*. *The Caucasian Chalk Circle* and *The Maids* were put on stage while *Bicycle Thieves*, *Red River*, *Monsieur Verdoux*, *Springtime in a Small Town*, *The Lady from Shanghai* and *The Treasure of the Sierra Madre* hit the screen. Primo Levi's account of Auschwitz, *If This is a Man*, was published in an edition of 2,500 copies and George Orwell worked on *Nineteen Eighty-Four* while suffering from tuberculosis on the island of Jura. Robert Capa, Henri Cartier-Bresson and other leading photographers created the Magnum agency to exploit the possibilities of 'mini-cameras and maxi-minds', as one of the founders put it.[13]

Anne Frank's diaries were published, as were the war memoirs of Churchill and Eisenhower. Toscanini conducted the NBC Symphony Orchestra to take classical music to a mass audience. The revolutionary Kinsey Report on sexual behaviour was published in the United States, where Freud's teachings were setting the conventional wisdom for explaining why people acted as they did. Across the Atlantic, the initial Edinburgh International Festival was held and Princess Elizabeth and Philip Mountbatten were married in Westminster Abbey. The first organised group of 492 Caribbean emigrants arrived in Britain from Kingston, Jamaica, on the *Empire Windrush* liner. Most of the men had served in the British forces during the war; the Nationality Act of 1948 entitled any Commonwealth subject to settle in the UK.[14]

The Olympics resumed with the 1948 summer games in London (the US topped the medals table with eighty-four followed by Sweden with forty-four and France with twenty-nine; the host nation netted twenty-three). Pope Pius XII ensured the Catholic Church remained conservative. Amid a religious boom in America, Billy Graham began his career as an evangelist and Martin Luther King Jnr entered a theological seminary. The influential Egyptian Islamist theorist, Sayyid Qutb, went to the United States, where he disapproved of the sexuality of women, found artistic tastes primitive and dismissed jazz as invented to satisfy the 'primitive inclinations' of black people, 'as well as their desire to be noisy on the one hand and to excite bestial tendencies on the other'.[15]

The US brought the first jet bomber, the B-45 Tornado, into service. The USSR showed off a range of new military jets and a Tupolev heavy bomber modelled on the US Boeing Superfortress. Commercial planes became bigger and faster, changing the nature of air transport. American and British jets broke the sound barrier, and a British pilot set an altitude record. Round-the-world airline flights were inaugurated. The UK's Bristol Aeroplane Company worked on plans for a huge transatlantic airliner, the Brabazon, with eighty sleeping berths, a dining room, cinema, promenade and bar.[16] Howard Hughes piloted his five-store-high flying boat, nicknamed the 'Spruce Goose' and designed to carry 750 troops, 150,000 lbs of cargo or two Sherman tanks on its first and only flight over one mile in California. Recurrent air accidents killed hundreds of passengers and crew in a dozen countries. On the high seas, the Cunard line anticipated a revival of up-scale cruising by launching the luxurious 34,000-tonne *Caronia* 'Green Goddess',[17] which set a new transatlantic speed record, while the Kon-Tiki raft skippered by the Norwegian ethnologist and explorer Thor Heyerdahl crossed the Pacific to show the historic possibility of migration across the ocean.

On the ground, California built the 800-mile highway between its borders with Mexico and Oregon as part of a $2.4 billion plan for a 14,000-mile state highway system. The southern part of the state, centred on Los Angeles, became the hub of an automobile culture with its multi-lane roads, drive-ins, motels, coffee shops, filing stations and 'exaggerated modern' architecture of cantilevered plate-glass and parabolic roofs. In Siberia, work began on the 2,700-mile Baikal-Amur mainline railway which would take a quarter of a century to complete.[18]

France's Citroën company launched the cheap, innovative Deux Chevaux motor car with its front-wheel drive, unique suspension and detachable doors and roof. The bombed Volkswagen plant in Wolfsburg, Germany was partially restored under a British engineer who went to work in uniform to make sure his instructions were followed; by 1946 it was turning out a thousand vehicles a month, though the lack of roofing and windows meant work had to stop when it rained. Ferrari began to produce commercial cars, and Porsche and Saab went into business. A British Vincent Black Shadow motorcycle set a world record of 150 miles an hour at Bonneville Salt Flats in Utah, the driver perched horizontally wearing only bathing trunks, a rubber cap and sneakers.

# CHAPTER THREE

# THE SUPERPOWERS

## I: SHINING HOUR

Though the conditions were different from those he had envisaged and it was the Americans rather than the British who took the lead, the 1835 prophecy of French writer and sometime politician Alexis de Tocqueville appeared to be being borne out. 'There are now two great nations in the world which, starting from different points, seem to be advancing towards the same goal; the Russians and the Anglo-Americans,' he had written. 'Each seems called by some secret design of Providence one day to hold in its hands the destinies of half the world.' Or, as Hitler had proclaimed in his testament in April 1945, 'With the defeat of the Reich ... there will remain in the world only two Great Powers capable of confronting each other – the United States and Soviet Russia ... The laws of both history and geography will compel these two Powers to a trial of strength, either military or in the fields of economics and ideology.' For Dean Acheson, the Under Secretary of State, 'Not since Rome and Carthage, has there been such a polarisation of power on earth.'[1]

The population of the two nations was broadly comparable – 170 million in the USSR to 145 million in the USA. Each had a political, economic and social model that claimed to offer a new way ahead in an age when progress was seen as entirely attainable.

The confrontation that followed the defeat of the Axis powers may have surprised some, but it merely heightened a hostility stretching back at least to the Bolshevik Revolution. The 1930s had been notable for the lack of understanding between Moscow and Western capitals, including the absent Washington. Hitler had brought together the two sides of this ideological divide; now that the common threat was removed and the territorial make-up of Europe had altered, it was hardly surprising that the conflict should resume, the Soviet zone's advance to the Oder–Neisse line and the weakness of Germany bringing Communism and democracy into direct contact with the vital difference from the inter-war period that the United States was now not only in the game but the prime player on one front.

In stark contrast to the dire state of much of the world, the United States emerged from the great conflict in strong and confident mode. Though it had fought on two fronts and spent more than $4 trillion on the war effort, its territory had remained unscathed since Pearl Harbor. With its vastly superior resources in everything from industry and armaments to food and soft power, and protected by two vast oceans, it was in an unchallengeable position, the world's major source of both supply and demand, supremely sure of the superiority of its way of life, its political and economic systems, and its consumer society.

If the war had been won by machine tools as much as by machine guns, no power had pursued the industrialisation of conflict more than the United States. The resulting economic activity finally brought recovery from the Great Depression, with rising consumer demand and a doubling of industrial output in the war years. With economic primacy came the predominant role for the dollar with what would later be termed[2] its 'exorbitant privilege' of being the world's dominant reserve currency. America was home to the biggest multi-national manufacturing and technological corporations, and its financial institutions moved into the international gap left by the impact of the conflict and post-war politics on European banking houses. It controlled two-thirds of the world's financial reserves, its strength and wealth enabling it to offer other countries security and a rules-based international trading system, which was certainly in its interests but also seen by democratic governments abroad as being in theirs.

Industrial production in late 1947 was 63 per cent above a decade earlier and exports were up by more than four times. Such was the American predominance that the UN report on the world economy for 1947 noted that the big fear was that 'any serious decline of production, employment and incomes in the United States may have devastating deflationary effect on the economies of other parts of the world'.[3]

Leadership of the International Monetary Fund, the World Bank and the GATT trading arrangement meant that it was not only the prime player but also managed the system in the developed non-Soviet nations while using them for what has been called 'vectors for plugging countries into the liberal order created by the United States'. Realising how the absence from global affairs before the war had harmed not only the world but also their own country, its leaders accepted an international role commensurate with its strength, hoping, in the words of future president Bill Clinton, that foreigners would be 'more impressed by the power of our example than the example of our power'. American thinkers who provided the intellectual framework for the new role pointed to the way their country, as a freeloader in the inter-war period, had failed to take Britain's place as the prime contributor to global security, leaving the Axis powers free to act as the world descended into economic depression and political anarchy. That now had to change, in the interests of the United States and the broader international community of like-minded nations.[4]

This role was given a solid domestic political base by the bilateral approach engineered by Truman and Senator Arthur Vandenberg, who overrode the more isolationist sentiments of fellow members of the Republican majority in Congress. Vandenberg had once been opposed to international entanglement, but said Pearl Harbor had 'ended isolationism for any realist'; now, he declared that 'the greatest nation on earth either justifies or surrenders its leadership. We must choose ... I can only say I prefer my choice of responsibilities.' Though his party belittled the president at every turn, the senator from Michigan insisted on the importance of a bipartisan foreign policy that meant 'a mutual effort ... to unite our official voice at the water's edge so that America speaks with maximum authority against those who would divide us and conquer us and the free world'. 'We could not have gotten much closer unless I sat in Vandenberg's lap or he sat in mine,' Secretary of State George Marshall remarked. The domestic cohesion gave America's global policy enormous strength.[5]

While Europe struggled to survive, for America, the post-war world was the age of the middle class and those who aspired to join it. Jobs were generally secure. The birth rate hit a record 4.7 million in 1947 following an unprecedented 2.2 million couples getting married the previous year.[6] Though Socialism was a dirty word, increased government spending provided a safety net. Subsidised mortgages for returning GIs meant millions could afford to buy homes; residential construction increased fifteen times between 1944 and 1950. William Levitt launched the biggest private housing project in the country's history in 1947 on 4,000 acres of potato farms on Long Island, its units made in assembly-line fashion, each with a tree in the front yard. Residents were required to cut the grass round their houses at least once a week and were forbidden to hang laundry outside on weekends and holidays.[7]

Defence Secretary James Forestall worried that demobilisation would make it impossible to deploy troops on the scale which might be required to back up the new global role. But the country's military might now lay primarily in more modern projections of force epitomised by the atomic weapon – the arsenal consisted of only a dozen bombs in 1946 but was to be increased to fifty by the end of 1948. After a huge build-up of its aviation industry that had seen 2 million workers producing nearly 300,000 planes during the war,[8] the US had the biggest strategic air force and a fleet of some 6,000 vessels, 1,200 of them major fighting ships – 70 per cent of the world's total. It, or its allies, controlled the choke points on shipping routes: Panama, Suez, the Malacca Strait.

Truman wanted to continue the legacy of the Roosevelt era in its extraordinary construction programme that included building 650,000 miles of roads, 78,000 bridges and 40,000 schools. Abroad, as befitted its wealth, the US was the world's big donor – in the eight years after the end of the war its aid would total $44 billion, $13 billion of it in the Marshall Plan for Europe ($140 billion in 2017 value). It underwrote the recovery of its two principal wartime foes; as

Truman put it in his memoirs, 'Never before in history has one nation faced so vast an undertaking as that confronting the United States of repairing and salvaging the victors as well as the vanquished.'[9]

There was, however, a big scar running through this positive story of the exceptional nation, though it was not one that was specific to the United States – racism. As Roosevelt took care to keep Southern Democrats on side for the New Deal, his administration's liberalism had not extended to black citizens – even public housing projects were strictly segregated. After the war, the South saw lynchings and attacks on returning Afro-American military veterans. Jim Crow electoral laws remained in force along with 'whites only' public facilities and transport. In the northern suburbs of cities like Chicago, black workers migrating from the southern states were often crowded into what became ghettos. It was not until 1947 that Jackie Robinson broke the baseball colour line by appearing for the Brooklyn Dodgers. Levittown touted itself as offering 'A New Way of Life', but homes there were for Caucasians only. 'As a Jew, I have no room in my mind or heart for racial prejudice,' its developer said. 'But, I have come to know that if we sell one house to a Negro family, then 90 or 95 per cent of our white customers will not buy into the community.'[10]

World-weary Europeans could easily see Americans as naïve and insensitive to the Old World. The Spanish writer, Salvador de Madariaga called the US 'a land of boys who refuse to grow up', while the British intellectual Harold Nicolson wrote that though its people were 'decent folk in every way, they tread on traditions in a way that hurts'. A transatlantic exodus took a stream of American writers to Paris in search of inspiration they could not find at home or, in the case of James Baldwin, Richard Wright and jazz musicians, to escape from racism at home.[11]

But the new global presence of the United States boosted English as the main global language while blue jeans and dark glasses were symbols of modernity and swing music echoed around the globe. America became the centre for modern art and architecture, cinema, fiction and music. Its advertising and marketing helped to standardise language and exported new terms to foreign lands. People in Western Europe and parts of Asia might resent GIs for their easy money and sometimes gauche manners but, as the French writer

Simone de Beauvoir put it, they also appeared to many as 'the incarnation of freedom'.[12]

Norman Mailer published *The Naked and the Dead*, Robert Lowell won a Pulitzer Prize for his first collection of poetry, *A Streetcar Named Desire* and *Kiss Me Kate* hit Broadway while Elia Kazan and Lee Strasberg opened the Actor's Studio to teach the Method way of acting in keeping with what the artist Mark Rothko described as 'the secret of direct access to the wild terror and suffering which lay at the bottom of human existence'. With London, Paris and Berlin impoverished by war, New York could well feel entitled to proclaim itself 'the capital of the world'.[13] The foundations of rock and roll were being laid by songs like Roy Brown's 'Good Rocking Tonight' and Louis Jordan with five consecutive number-one hits. As bebop took jazz into its third age, Manhattan was, even more than before, the heart of the country's original music, from 52nd Street to Minton's, the Apollo Theatre and the 10,000-square-foot Savoy Ballroom, reaching to Carnegie Hall, where Charlie Parker and Dizzy Gillespie fronted their big band at a historic concert.[14]

In the US, there was a general belief that, in the words of the wartime song, this was the American nation's shining hour. What had worked for the New Deal would work for the rest of the world, be it in free markets or great public utility projects on the model of the Tennessee Valley Authority. Victory over Germany and Japan boosted the self-confidence ingrained into the national narrative of the exodus from the Old World covered by divine providence, which offered the prospect of affluence to everybody who signed up along with a culture filled with faith in itself.

Not that the new international role weighed heavily on most Americans at a time when, as one senior figure put it, 'most people wanted simply to go to the movies and drink Coke' while their country exulted in its model of modernity distinct from the old and troubled world of Europe. Clement Attlee thought that it was not until the Berlin crisis of 1948 that 'the American public really wakened up to the fact of life'. The growth of escapist entertainment reflected the desire of Americans to put the war and Great Depression behind them, with the sudden stardom of Jerry Lewis showing a desire to indulge in what his *New York Times* obituary described as 'a long-suppressed taste for silliness' in a 'dialectic between adult and infant, assurance and anxiety, bitter experience and wide-eyed innocence, that generated a powerful image of post-war America, a gangly young country suddenly dominant on the world stage'.[15]

The writer Martha Gellhorn entitled a series of articles written after a motor trip through small-town America 'Journey through a peaceful land'. She contrasted the sense of permanence and peace she found there with

> the reality of most of the world now [which] is hunger and des-
> olation, gutted houses and factories, the car that lies by pocked
> with bullet holes at the side of the road, the burned-out tank, the
> ration tickets, the black market, the hopelessly repaired cloths, the
> cracked shoes and the wretched allotment of coal. I do not see how
> anyone can make that reality clear to Americans because they have
> not felt it and experience is not communicated through the mind.[16]

Harry Hopkins, Roosevelt's normally phlegmatic lieutenant, was moved to declare that 'We believe our dynamic democracy is the best in the world.' The magazine publisher Henry Luce advised that 'Americans must be the elder brother of nations in the brotherhood of man', though he also recognised the global responsibility that came with this, warning that 'It is no longer the case that we can lie in the sun without having to worry about the Koreans and the Azerbaijanis.'[17]

As the novelist Philip Roth would recall, looking back to his New Jersey boyhood after the war,

> America from 1941 to 1945 had been unified in purpose as never
> before. Later, a collective sense of America as the center of the
> most spectacular of the post-war world's unfolding dramas was
> born not just out of chauvinistic triumphalism but out of a real-
> istic appraisal of the undertaking behind the victory of 1945, a
> feat of human sacrifice, physical effort, industrial planning and
> military mobilization – a marshalling of communal morale that
> would have seemed unattainable during the Great Depression of
> the previous decade.[18]

## II: SECURITY FIRST

The Soviet Union's size of 8.5 million square miles, covering one-sixth of the world's surface in more than a dozen constituent republics spanning Europe and Asia, meant that the USSR could only be budged from its position as a great power by its internal weaknesses. Severely damaged by the war, it could in no way rival the United States in economic and military power, innovation or attraction. It was widely seen as more threatening than it really was outside its geographical security zone, but, having achieved its aims in the construction of a deep security belt reaching to the middle of Germany, it was never likely to expand further by force if it encountered firm opposition.

Stalin would consolidate Soviet rule through his sphere of influence, but 1948 marked the frontier of his expansion as he blinked in the face of Western resistance in Berlin. He still believed in Lenin's 'who, whom?' formulation positing only one winner from the struggle between Communism and capitalism, rather than co-existence. But he saw limits for the time being with the divisions that brought. As he told Milovan Djilas in the later stages of the war, 'The West will make Western Germany their own, and we shall turn Eastern Germany into our own state.'[19]

Still, psychologically, he was unable to relinquish his certainty of eventual domination as guaranteed by Marxist theory. If core beliefs are essential to strong leaders, nobody needed that conviction more than Stalin. Once his country had got over its huge wartime losses, he said, 'We shall recover in fifteen to twenty years, and then we'll have another go at it.' For the time being, however, his priority was rebuilding and strengthening the system atop which he sat, rejecting Western bourgeois principles of representation and rights, indifferent to the happiness of the people, the proud heir of the autocratic tradition of the Tsars, a devotee of Russian–Slavonic values who ruled as if he was a despot from the Asian lands that made up most of the USSR.[20]

Force was his essential weapon. As he had noted in the later stages of the war, 'Whoever occupies a territory also imposes on it his own social system. Everyone imposes his own social system as far as his army can reach. It cannot be otherwise.' He would take opportunist advantage of any chance to weaken the principal opponent across the Atlantic and its allies closer at hand – but with a keen sense of knowing when to stop before he endangered the regime he had constructed since establishing himself as Lenin's heir and the master of the USSR.[21]

Yet the Father of the People who had rallied his country to play the major role in defeating Nazi Germany ended up by driving West Europe closer to the US rather than exploiting the potential for transatlantic discord. This made the Soviet Union less of a threat than it could have been as the period spanning 1947–8 brought a shift of influence towards the USA, which became unavoidable as the devastated old continent was confronted by recession, hunger and global challenges. The inevitable development of the atom bomb by the Soviet Union changed the nature of warfare and froze the confrontation between the two superpowers; but still, as George Orwell had written presciently in 1945, it was likely to have the effect of 'prolonging indefinitely a *"peace that is no peace"*'.[22]

Still, the Red Army's record in the war and the resistance role of west European parties once Hitler had undone the pact with the USSR in 1941 helped to give Communism an appeal from afar, boosted by the image of 'Uncle Joe' puffing on his pipe and giving a reassuring smile to the world. Soviet Communism presented itself as a haven for workers and the oppressed around the world, an inter-Nationalist creed that surmounted the petty, oppressive frontiers of nationalism. The certainty of its ideologues was bolstered by the way Marxism–Leninism could be seen as having been proved correct by the economic woes of the 1930s. To criticise Stalin's regime was to open oneself up to accusations of neo-Fascism. Communist parties were allowed to preach in Western Europe, operating freely in sharp contrast to the elimination of opposition east of the Iron Curtain. In West Europe, Moscow enjoyed the support of leading intellectuals. Though he did join the party, Jean-Paul Sartre, the polymath philosopher who was a landmark of the intellectual world on the Parisian Left Bank, argued that Communism should be judged by its intentions and not by its actions. His fellow philosopher, Maurice Merleau-Ponty, celebrated 'proletarian humanism' and explained away the purge trials of the 1930s as being in the tradition of revolutionary violence. Some of those closer to reality saw things very differently, as the Polish poet Czesław Miłosz wrote of the rules of history:

> Learn to predict a fire with unerring precision.
> Then burn the house down to fulfil the prediction.[23]

Fear of a revival of German power further heightened the appeal of the USSR's protective shield in Eastern and Central Europe while, despite the soft power of Hollywood movies and American music, many people in the west of the Continent resented the material advantages of the United States and joined in the jibe that its troops, with their abundant supplies of everything from cigarettes to nylon stockings from military stores, were 'over-paid, over-sexed and over here'. Communism offered a new faith, what one Polish intellectual called 'a refined catechism', and the certainty of being on the winning side of history which made it easy to dismiss reports of what was happening on the other side of the Iron Curtain as fake news spread by reactionaries.

Seeking to find a 'third way' between what British Foreign Secretary Ernest Bevin described as 'the red tooth and claw of American capitalism and the Communist dictatorship of Soviet Russia', some west European Socialists and influential newspapers like *Le Monde* dallied with a notion of neutralism which would bring the two halves of the Continent together. In France, Léon Blum floated the idea of an 'international third force'. But economic reality tied the west of the Continent to the United States just as Stalin's obsession with security for the USSR left the east no choice. By the end of the summer of 1947, the Manichaean die was cast on both sides of the Iron Curtain.[24]

National security took on a broader meaning as it melded politics, military and economic interests in the toolboxes of the two superpowers, particularly since the vetoes of the five permanent members of the Security Council limited the effectiveness of the United Nations. The Truman administration established the CIA and instituted loyalty checks on government employees; the head of the board in charge of the checks said the government was entitled to sack people 'for any reason that seems reasonable with no hearing. Any suspicion may suffice.' The spy became the emblematic figure of the east–west confrontation.[25]

For Stalin, the Cold War provided the ideal excuse to roll back the partial liberalisation of the war years and resume the attack on society that had always been integral to Bolshevism. In a hard-line speech at the Bolshoi Theatre in Moscow in early 1946, he declared the need for heightened political control which would exert extreme pressure on the population and mean forced labour, few consumer goods and a focus on building up the military. In the following two years, taxes of collective farms rose by a third. The Vozhd of the USSR instructed his subordinates to 'deliver a strong blow' to any talk of competitive democracy.

The NKVD political police was reorganised and reinforced. Legislation banned marriages between Soviet citizens and foreigners. Anybody and everybody was liable to fall under suspicion, and subversive youth groups were suddenly 'discovered' in many cities and put down. The number of people held in Gulags rose steadily from the 1.46 million total at the end of the war; those in 'special settlements' was put at 2.46 million in 1946.[26] Returning prisoners of war were sent to remote penal colonies in remote regions for fear that they had been contaminated by contact with other systems; when liberated at Dachau concentration camp, some begged to stay rather than being put on trains to the East. In the mass population movements in Eastern Europe, Soviet citizens sometimes posed as Poles or Ukrainians to avoid being consigned to the USSR.

'Strict regime' labour camps were set up in which inmates were kept in chains and had no blankets. Victorious commanders were sidelined in case their popularity made them a threat to the ruler, including the architect of the push to Berlin in 1945, Marshal Zhukov. Poets were reproved for writing love odes. Shostakovich was cast into disgrace and Pasternak concentrated on translating Shakespeare. The second part of Eisenstein's *Ivan the Terrible* was banned because of its unflattering portrait of one of Stalin's great heroes. The economist Eugen Varga, who had argued that capitalism might be inherently stable and that workers could gain power in a parliamentary democracy, had his institute closed down, though he was still called on to give advice when Stalin was confronted with the challenge of the Marshall Plan.[27]

While the United States promoted a model of economic liberalism that sought to balance the market and the state's protective role, the Soviet Union retreated into autarky and rigidity that reflected the mindset of its ruler, cutting itself off not only politically but also economically, in ways that would, eventually, help to weaken the regime to the point of collapse. By its nature, the USSR stood in opposition to the United States, the great external adversary Stalin needed to buttress his authority on top of the internal enemies he was so adept at finding. But, as the British ambassador Frank Roberts wrote to London in 1946, 'World revolution is no longer part of its programme, and there is nothing in the internal conditions within the Union which might encourage a return to the old revolutionary tradition.'[28]

## III: JOE AND HARRY

The difference between the superpowers was epitomised by their leaders. Stalin took an essentially pessimistic view of humanity; Truman was by nature an optimist. One operated in a rigorous ideological framework; the other was, for the most part, an unideological pragmatist. The dictator distrusted those he ruled and believed that people had to be kept in order by whatever means was required; the president thought nations did best when their citizens were allowed to follow their own inclinations. Truman gained succour from meeting ordinary people, and asked what was wrong with being average. Stalin remained immured in the Kremlin, his isolation an apt reflection of his view of himself as a historic figure and his obsession with security.

With purges, repression and all-embracing policing, the dictator had made sure he faced no opposition, continuing and developing the ruthlessness practised by Lenin. As the illusions of the Old Bolsheviks about the melding of scientific rationalism, social engineering and revolutionary mysticism were replaced by the politics of force and expediency, the Communist Party's quasi-religious nature was subsumed into one-man echo-chamber rule. Any problems the regime encountered must be the result of sabotage. Enemies were everywhere and, if there were innocent victims along the way, they were isolated cases which could not impede the necessary rooting out of agents of imperialism. Truman, in contrast, had to put up with and, in foreign policy at least, seek accommodation with a Republican majority in Congress. He also faced a wide degree of dissent within his own party from those who sought another stand-ard bearer for the 1948 presidential election.[29]

At the end of 1947, Stalin was sixty-nine, Truman sixty-three. The two most powerful people in the world had been born and brought up far from the centres of power. Ioseb Besarionis dze Jughashvili, who took the name of Stalin (Man of Steel) as a young revolutionary, was from Georgia, the son of a drunken cobbler and a housemaid. Harry S.[30] Truman came from a farming family in Missouri.

Both were largely self-educated and were hard workers – Stalin's bureaucratic mastery and attention to detail had paved the path to power while Truman pored over documents late into the night, wear-ing a green eyeshade. They read widely – Truman liked to parade his historical and geographical knowledge while Stalin kept a library of 20,000 books, many of which he annotated; he also collected watches and liked gardening. They were each of stocky build; Stalin was sensitive about his lack of height, standing at five foot five, three inches less than the president; when he accompanied Tito to a dinner with the Soviet leadership, Djilas noted that most of his subordinates were no taller than the dictator.

Both suffered from physical defects from early in their lives. A protracted bout of diphtheria seriously weakened Truman's eye-sight and obliged him to wear thick spectacles – he memorised the vision charts in advance to get into the National Guard. Stalin had two adjoined toes on his left foot,[31] which, along with an accident in his youth, made him walk pigeon-fashion. Childhood smallpox had scarred his face – though this was airbrushed out on photo-graphs – and his left arm was shorter and stiffer than the other from a boyhood encounter with a horse-drawn carriage. A defect on his vocal chord meant he spoke softly. He had a strong memory but his intellectual horizons were limited, his personal paranoia melding with the structural paranoia of Leninism.[32]

The dictator had a stroke in 1946 and put on weight. He could eat to the point of gluttony, but his bad teeth meant he had to be served the most tender meat and ripest fruit. His hair turned grey and the bags grew under his amber eyes. His teeth and moustache were stained yellow by his smoking of choice Herzegovina Flor cigarette tobacco shredded into his pipe to provide 'the man of the people' touch. As he aged, he exploded without notice, the hardening of his arteries aggravating his mood swings. Under pressure, he suffered from tonsillitis with high temperatures. At a dinner for a visiting Yugoslav delegation at the end of 1947, Stalin tried to dance to a gramophone record, his arms flailing in rhythm, but soon had to give up, sighing, 'Age had crept up on me and I am already an old man.' But, when he raised this with those around him, they all replied that he looked fine.[33]

Though he was in generally good health and kept up his routine of early morning walks at the pace of 120 steps to the minute, which he had adopted during service in the National Guard before the First World War, Truman let work get on top of him early in his presidency; at one point he did not manage to find time for a swim in the White House pool for five months. He worried about his mother who was approaching her hundredth birthday. Feeling lonely in the White House with his wife back at their Midwestern home, he told his daughter that 'No man in his right mind would want to come here of his own accord.'[34]

Neither man had much time for nuances or hindsight or agonised over possible mistakes. Truman, who said he fell asleep as soon as his head hit the pillow, never regretted dropping the atom bombs. Stalin was convinced that the iron laws of history were working for him. Each recognised that, in the words of the sign on the White House desk, 'the Buck Stops Here'. Stalin might equally have adopted the phrase the president picked up from a local Mid-Western politician, 'If you don't like the heat, get out of the kitchen.'

Neither had much direct experience of the world outside their home countries. Stalin's travels abroad were largely limited to his early revolutionary career. Truman served in the army in France in 1917–18 but did not go abroad again until the Potsdam summit in 1945, after which he did not venture outside the western hemisphere or leave the USA after a visit to Brazil in 1947.

In many other ways, however, the two could hardly have been more different in character, outlook and personal history, their differences framing the way they evolved the policies of their nations through their perception of the world.

Despite his avuncular wartime nickname and the amiable pipe-smoking image that went with it, the pope of international Communism lacked emotional attachments and grew ever more suspicious in his seclusion in the Kremlin and heavily guarded dachas; he rarely appeared in public and was presented in the media as a figure who might, at most, be glimpsed from afar. Truman greeted fellow pedestrians he passed on his early morning walks. He was the first head of state for twenty years to go into the White House kitchen to thank the head cook for baking him a birthday cake. He liked to wear two-tone shoes as well as double-breasted suits and, when he visited the presidential retreat at Key West, donned gaudy sports shirts. Stalin kept to uniforms and colourless tunics.[35]

Truman knew how to dissemble and wield the power of his office to great effect, but he was not, as he said, one 'to man a chopping block', unlike the leader who had presided over the deaths and persecution of tens of millions in the purges and Gulags. Whereas Stalin made the rules, the president believed in keeping to those laid down by the constitution and the courts, even if political expediency might induce elasticity. His great historical hero was Andrew Jackson, 'the man of the people' (though his foreign policy would run counter to Jacksonian unilateralism). Stalin's model was Ivan the Terrible; he extolled the tsar to the film director Sergei Eisenstein as a 'great and wise ruler' who had known the need to be ruthless, had excluded foreign influences from Russia and whose secret police he hailed as a 'progressive army'.[36]

Though he had a circle of cronies with whom he played poker, went on cruises on the Potomac and exchanged barnyard jokes, Truman kept relations with his advisers on a professional level with none of the often sinister and drunken socialising that formed part of Stalin's power games. He was punctilious in dealing with those around him and famed for his punctuality. As befitted a poker-playing 'good ole boy', he was partial to bourbon, including a nip in the morning, but a long-time friend recalled that he could make a single highball last for hours, and he was never seen under the influence.

Where the dictator thrived on collecting material to use against others, Truman dismantled the bugging system Roosevelt had installed in the presidential office. When J. Edgar Hoover, the FBI chief, sent an emissary to say the agency would do anything the president wanted, Truman waved him away. 'We want no Gestapo or Secret Police,' he wrote in his diary after a month in the White House. 'FBI is tending in that direction. They are dabbling in sex life scandals and plain blackmail ... This must stop.'[37]

Stalin said the suicide of his mentally unstable second wife[38] in 1932 after a row between them at a dinner party 'crippled' him; there 'died my last warm feelings for humanity,' he added. Truman was devoted to his wife, Bess, whom he met in Sunday School and whom he called 'the only person in the world whose approval and good opinion I value'.[39] On their twenty-ninth wedding anniversary, he wrote to her, 'It seems like twenty-nine days ... You are still on the pedestal where I placed you that day in Sunday school. What an old fool I am.' At Potsdam, he gave a lift to a young officer who told him he had only to ask if there was anything he wanted, 'like women'. 'Listen, son, I married my sweetheart,' the president replied. 'She doesn't run around on me, and I don't run around on her. I want that understood. Don't ever mention that kind of stuff to me again.'[40]

Truman was also close to his daughter, Margaret, taking pride in her career as a soprano singer. Stalin's family was less happy. One son died after being captured by the Germans in the war. The second was an alcoholic who had a distant relationship with his father while the dictator sought to run the private life of his daughter, Svetlana.

Though he could change tack under pressure, as with the nationalist appeal above ideology during what became known as the Great Patriotic War with Germany, the Soviet leader operated along fundamental, long-term lines as a strategic juggler set in his ways by decades of power struggles. The president, who had lacked the grooming for high office, was driven far more by instinct and tactical considerations, a leader who could get himself caught in corners but who embodied the new internationalised spirit of his nation. If Stalin epitomised the totalitarian system he had built on the foundations laid by Lenin and the repressive, autocratic tradition inherited from the Tsars, with no place for an independent civil society, Truman was a pure product of American politics, a symbol of the pluralistic notion of democracy and individualism, however imperfect it might be in application.

In the early 1920s, a document attributed to Lenin noted that Stalin had accumulated 'unlimited authority' and wondered whether he would be capable of using it with sufficient caution. (Some historians have branded the 'Letter to the Congress' a forgery but, if so, it was a prescient fiction.) For the dictator, what counted was strength, adopting Lenin's dictum 'Probe with a bayonet. If you meet steel, stop; if you meet mush, push.' Individuals were an impediment to be eliminated or brought into line; as the prosecutor at his show trials had told a British minister, it was historically impossible for Soviet policy to accord with Western values of democracy and human rights. For Truman and the American vision he incarnated, people were the essence of the system. Whatever the influence of big corporations, political parties, the evolving national security network and the racism that held back Afro-Americans, individuals at different levels were the final shapers of American society and its state; in the USSR it was the other way around.[41]

The Soviet leader was the longest-serving world leader. He had been named general secretary of the Communist Party in 1922 at a time when the future president was running a haberdashery business which would fail. While the Man of Steel was eliminating his rival, Trotsky, and consolidating his power through purges, centralisation and industrialisation, the Midwesterner became a county court judge before being elected to the Senate as the candidate of the notoriously corrupt boss of wide-open Kansas City, Tom Pendergast. When the Father of the People was directing the gargantuan Soviet war effort after Hitler had reneged on their pact and invaded the Soviet Union in 1941, the 'Senator from Pendergast' was heading a legislative commission inquiring into misuse of war funds.

As the Red Army was advancing in late 1944 to clinch the Allied victory, Harry Truman was propelled to the vice-presidency by the managers of the Democratic Party ahead of the incumbent, Henry Wallace, whom they regarded as too left-wing. The other main candidate to be Roosevelt's running mate, the congressional manipulator James Byrnes, was ruled out because his southern roots made him a negative for the black vote and his lapsed Catholicism was likely to alienate another significant section of the electorate. So Truman was a safe choice. Confident of a fourth term, Roosevelt paid little attention to his running mate. After the ticket won, he had only a couple of tête-a-tête meetings with him, froze him out of foreign affairs and did not inform him about the summit with Stalin at Yalta or the atom bomb programme.

At the death of Roosevelt in April 1945, his successor was a very unknown quantity. He told reporters in his first full day as president – a Friday the thirteenth as it happened – 'Boys, I don't know whether you fellows ever had a load of hay fall on you, but when they told me yesterday what had happened, I felt like the moon, the stars, and all the planets had fallen on me.'[42]

He was generally dismissed, not only by Republican opponents but also by the media and New Dealers. 'It's as if the correspondents had made up their minds when Mr Truman became President that he was a country bumpkin, and I'm afraid a great many of them never changed their mind,' Dean Acheson said later. 'He is a small opportunistic man, a man of good instincts but, therefore, probably all the more dangerous,' Wallace, who had no cause to speak well of his successor as vice president, wrote in his diary. But the editor of his local newspaper, Roy Roberts of the *Kansas City Star*, commented, 'What a test of democracy if it works!'[43]

## IV: The education of a president

'In those days nobody seemed to think I was *aware* of anything,' as Truman put it later. His main drawback for most people was simply that he was not FDR, to whom the country had grown used over the previous dozen years. How he would deal with the Soviet Union was a mystery. Four years earlier, he had rated Nazi Germany and the Soviet Union as morally equivalent and thought they should be left to fight one another to the death; now he said that nothing was more important than the continued co-operation of the anti-Axis powers. But his idea of co-operation with Moscow came with a proviso based on his perception that 'the Russians are like bulls in a china shop – they are only 25 years old'.[44]

Eleven days after being sworn in as president, Truman was visited at the White House by the Soviet foreign minister, who was in the US for the inaugural conference of the United Nations in San Francisco. The president's lecture on how Moscow had to live up to its obligations was so forthright that Molotov objected that he had 'never been talked to like that in my life'. To which Truman responded, 'Carry out your agreements and you won't get talked to like that.' He characterised his approach as a 'straight one-two to the jaw'.[45]

But then he grew worried that too much toughness would tip the Kremlin over the edge. A Cabinet meeting discussed whether to share US knowledge of atomic weapons with the USSR; the idea was rejected by nine votes to five. Truman sent Roosevelt's close lieutenant, Harry Hopkins, who had recommended aid to the USSR in 1941, on a mission to Moscow to try to build bridges. His briefing included the instruction to say 'that Poland, Rumania, Bulgaria, Czeckoslovakia [sic], Austria, Yugoslavia, Latvia, Lithuania, Estonia et al., made no difference to U.S. interests only so far as World Peace is concerned'. Polish elections were to be 'as free as US big city bosses would allow and Uncle Joe should make some sort of gesture – whether he means it or not'.[46]

The Hopkins mission, his last before he died of long-standing ailments, was counted a success, even if it had little lasting impact. But the president was at sixes and sevens as he tried to find his bearings in international affairs. 'I want you to understand that I am trying my best to save peace and follow out Roosevelt's plan,' he told the former ambassador to Moscow, Joseph Davies, who favoured friendship with the USSR. But, at the Potsdam summit of the wartime allies in August 1945, a change of tone from FDR's emollient approach was evident. Truman was 'a man of immense determination', Churchill told his doctor, Charles Moran. 'When Stalin gets tough, Truman at once makes plain that he, too, can hand out the right stuff . . . if only this had happened at Yalta.'[47]

Still, Stalin got much of what he wanted, notably on Poland's frontiers. At the US embassy in Moscow, George Kennan regarded the outcome as 'unreal and unworkable', showing 'casualness and frivolity [and] apparent indifference on the American side'. Truman's main initiative was to propose an agreement on freedom of canals and waterways. In a later letter, he painted himself as 'a naïve, innocent idealist (good definition for a diplomatic darnfool)'.[48]

After getting back to Washington, Truman drafted a letter to a friend saying he was 'tired of babying the Soviets', but decided not to send it. Two months later, he scribbled a note to himself that 'unless Russia is faced with an iron fist and strong language another war is in the making'. His attitude could only be influenced by growing realism about Moscow's stance; when an American diplomat asked the former Soviet foreign minister, Maxim Litvinov, what Washington could do to satisfy Stalin, the answer was simple – 'nothing'.[49]

There were, however, signs that the Vozhd could moderate his ambitions if faced with a firm line. The USSR pulled back from a bizarre claim to set up a military base in Libya. There was also a compromise on Soviet influence over Finland and the USSR accepted its exclusion from any role in post-war Italy. Confronted by Western resistance over the status of the disputed city of Trieste, Stalin ordered the Yugoslavs to abandon their claims in favour of an international settlement. In Greece, he refused to funnel help to Communist rebels. In France and Italy, Moscow instructed the powerful Communist parties to join coalition governments with class enemies rather than using the muscle of their resistance movements to bid for power. At a four-nations foreign ministers' conference in Paris, Molotov dropped Soviet objections to ratifying peace treaties with Germany's allies, Italy, Bulgaria, Finland, Hungary and Romania. The Kremlin pushed Soviet interests in Turkey but pulled back after a war scare swept the US with plans for mass strategic bombing raids of the USSR, the dispatch of an aircraft carrier to the Eastern Mediterranean and economic and military aid to Ankara.

In Iran, Moscow backed a rebellion by Azerbaijanis, seeking to exploit regional differences and divisions between reformers, the messianic Nationalist politician Mohammad Mossadeq, Islamic fundamentalists and the young shah, who had been put on the throne after wartime intervention by the British and Soviets. The British were highly unpopular because of the huge profits being made by the Anglo-Iranian oil company. But Moscow retreated when the national army blocked a march on Teheran by the shah's opponents. Pressure from tribal leaders forced the ejection of pro-Communist ministers and the US and UK came to the aid of the ruler following strikes by oilfield workers. As Stalin reflected, 'We must leave before it is too late.'[50]

Despite such evidence of underlying caution, the steady evolution of the Cold War made up Truman's mind for him as Stalin delivered his hard-line speech at the Bolshoi Theatre in February 1946, and refused to join the new International Monetary Fund (IMF). Asked for an explanation of that decision by Washington, the diplomat George Kennan filed a 5,500-word despatch from the embassy in Moscow on 22 February 1946 that laid the basis for the administration's policy containment. Kennan had been warning about Moscow's intentions for eighteen months but felt it was 'like talking to a stone'. Now, ill with influenza, fever, sinus trouble and tooth pains, he decided that 'they had asked for it. By God, they would get it!'[51]

The Soviet leaders had a fanatical commitment to the belief that there could be no long-term peaceful coexistence with the United States, he wrote. They thought it was 'desirable and necessary that the internal harmony of our society be disrupted, our traditional way of life destroyed, the international authority of our state broken'. But the threat was not rooted in Communist ideology, he argued. Rather, 'at the bottom of the Kremlin's neurotic view of world affairs is [the] traditional and instinctive Russia sense of insecurity'. The 'fig leaf' of Marxism provided 'justification for their instinctive fear of the outside world, for the dictatorship without which they do not know how to rule'. Soviet power was 'impervious to the logic of reason, but it is highly sensitive to the logic of force'.[52]

The telegram fell on fertile ground in Washington, appearing to make sense of Soviet intentions at a very confused time. 'If none of my previous literary efforts had seemed to evoke even the faintest tinkle from the bell at which they were aimed,' Kennan wrote later, 'this one, to my astonishment, struck it squarely and set it vibrating.' It was, as he noted, one of those moments when official Washington 'was ready to receive a given message'.[53]

He advocated a low-risk response to Soviet power which melded politics, economics and national security while encouraging the revival of Germany and Japan as democratic 'workshops'. Freedom would be the banner for the struggle. The United Nations would become a vehicle for collective security. Republicans and Democrats would unite in what Truman termed 'the will to co-operate' and those who preached a more understanding approach to the USSR like Henry Wallace would be marginalised in a seemingly perfect meld of domestic and international politics.

Kennan's Long Telegram was followed in March 1946 by Churchill's address in Fulton, Missouri warning of an Iron Curtain descending across Europe.[54] Truman had read and approved the speech in advance, but backed off when it came in for wide criticism in US media – the leading commentator, Walter Lippmann, described it as 'an almost catastrophic blunder'. After Stalin denounced 'a call to war', the president offered to send a battleship to bring him to Fulton to make a reply.[55]

Fearing that the Kremlin was 'going to run hog wild', he commissioned a report to 'be ready to reveal to the whole world the full truth about the Russian failure to honor agreements'. This was entrusted to his fellow Missourian, Clark Clifford, an increasingly important aide at the White House with movie-star good looks, and George Elsey, a young naval officer.[56]

Delivered in September 1946, it argued at great length that the USSR was a determined, sure-footed adversary set on world domination. The US had to aim at 'restraining and confining' the Kremlin while informing the American public so that it would 'support the stern policies which Soviet activities make imperative'. The president judged the report so explosive that he kept all copies to himself; 'if it leaked, it would blow the roof off the White House,' he noted. But, in similar vein, his adviser Averell Harriman told a British diplomat that 'the Russians had clearly declared ideological war on the democracies', while Byrnes, who had become secretary of state, made plain in a speech in Stuttgart that the US was ready to keep troops in Europe indefinitely and intended to build up the Western occupation zones of Germany.[57]

The Soviet ambassador Nikolai Novikov warned Moscow that the US was aiming for world domination and was preparing for 'the prospect of war against the Soviet Union'. He described the president as 'politically unstable ... with certain conservative tendencies'. Byrnes, he added, was 'strengthening the reactionary circles of the Democratic Party'.[58]

Truman was under considerable strain at home. Coal miners and rail and automobile workers went on strike. There was a shortage of meat and a debate about maintaining wartime price controls. His opinion poll support, which had hit 87 per cent in 1945, dropped to 32. Even the ending of the big railway strike after a threat to draft workers into the armed forces did not lift his reputation. Wallace, the last New Dealer in the Cabinet as secretary of commerce, caused a storm with a speech saying the danger of war stemmed 'much less from Communism than ... from imperialism'; after some hesitation, Truman sacked him, glad to be rid of a man he described as 'a real Commie and a dangerous man'. For him, as he remarked, 'No professional liberal is intellectually honest.'[59]

'The world picture is none too bright,' the president wrote to his wife in the autumn of 1946. He had sent the wartime chief of staff George Marshall on a mission to try to bring the Nationalists and Communists together in China, but after some initial success, this floundered on the intransigence of both sides. Truman was not sure that Byrnes would 'bring home the bacon' from negotiations with the Soviets. A new wave of strikes was welling up at home. 'The army and navy are at each other's throats again and my Cabinet family keeps bickering all the time,' he noted. 'So it goes and I have to keep a straight face and grin about it.' Congressional elections in November were forecast to give the Republicans control of both legislative houses. 'To err is only Truman' people quipped.

To guide him in the unfamiliar thickets of foreign affairs, the president had the benefit of a circle of half a dozen experienced, savvy operators who were comfortable with the exercise of national power and had no other political master. Dubbed 'the Wise Men' by their collective biographers, they consisted of two diplomats, two lawyers and two bankers who came together to mould American foreign and strategic policy.

They all served under the man Truman called 'the greatest American alive', Marshall, whom he appointed to succeed Byrnes after becoming increasingly unhappy with the latter's performance and what he saw as his lack of respect for the presidency. The two men developed a mutually reinforcing relationship, the general's gravity compensating for accusations that the president was a lightweight.

A man of few words, Marshall said at a birthday dinner for the president in 1948, 'The full stature of this man will only be proven by history; but I want to say here and now that there has never been a decision made under this man's administration, affecting policies beyond our shores, that has not been in the best interests of this country. It is not the courage of those decisions that will live, but the integrity of the man.' When the general sat down, Truman rose to his feet with his arms half-outstretched, only able to say in response, 'He won the war.'[60]

A country boy from Pennsylvania, the secretary had a bad memory for names, kept mislaying his spectacles and stayed away from the Washington social whirl. He called everybody by their surname and was addressed as 'General Marshall' – 'a title fitting him as though he had been baptized with it', as his deputy, Acheson, remarked. He insisted that he would exercise office in a non-political manner. His subdued speaking style and demeanour marked him as a dispassionate public official who stood above partisan divisions in keeping with his belief that his country had to accept 'a sense of responsibility for world order and security' given its 'special position ... geographically, financially, militarily and scientifically'.[61]

Reserved in character, with grey hair, lips tightly drawn and piercing blue eyes, he believed in clear lines of command and was intensely loyal though nobody's servant – he had declined to laugh at Roosevelt's jokes. He told Acheson that he had 'no feelings except a few which I reserve for Mrs Marshall'. *Time* magazine, which twice named him as its Man of the Year, described the general as 'the tall man, with a weathered homely face, in which there was a visible touch of greatness'. For Churchill, he was 'the noblest Roman of them all'. One of many admirers from outside politics, Orson Welles, called Marshall 'the greatest human being who was also a great man ... He was a tremendous gentleman, an old fashioned institution.'[62]

At meetings, Marshall would listen patiently to lengthy discussions and then intervene in his low but incisive staccato voice to say,

'Gentlemen, don't fight the problem; decide it.' He advised subordinates to 'avoid trivia'. Walter Bedell Smith, the US ambassador to Moscow from the spring of 1946, recalled how, whatever the strain and stress, Marshall never failed to dominate any gathering 'by the sheer force of his integrity, honesty and dignified simplicity'. In an all-embracing appreciation of his boss, George Kennan recalled 'his unshakable integrity; his consistent courtesy and gentlemanliness of conduct; his ironclad sense of duty; his imperturbability ... his deliberateness and conscientiousness of decision; his serene readiness – once a decision had been made – to abide by its consequences, whatever they might be; his lack of petty vanity or ambition; his indifference to the whims and moods of public opinion ... and his impeccable fairness and avoidance of favouritism in the treatment of subordinates'.[63]

'I am not a diplomat,' the secretary said at his first meeting with French leaders in the early spring of 1947. 'I mean exactly what I say and there is no use in trying to read between the lines because there is nothing to read there.'[64]

In contrast to his boss, the tall, broad-shouldered, debonair under secretary of state Dean Acheson was described by one of his former law partners as 'the shiniest fish that ever came out of the sea' and by the Treasury Department's number two, Harry Dexter White, as 'a throat-slitter of a very vicious kind'. His plummy voice, hawk nose, socks held up by garters and waxed red-grey moustache[65] meant he was easily derided by critics as a 'smarty pants' diplomat but with a 'low boring point' and 'ruthlessly logical mind'.[66]

For all his fastidious superiority, 'the Dean' was adept at playing the Washington political game and gaining tactical advantage. As 'the Number One Number Two man', he preferred concrete action to abstract thought, and adopted a steadily harder line towards the USSR while exploiting openings for the United States to spread its influence over nations worried by the Soviet stance. In the frequent absences of Byrnes, he had overseen the running of the department as it revived from its neglect under Roosevelt, who had handled top-level foreign policy as a personal matter.

This brought him close to the president, seeing him four or five times a week and speaking to him more often by telephone. When

Truman returned from Missouri to Washington after the disastrous 1946 mid-term elections, Acheson was the only official waiting to greet him at the station. A great one for loyalty, the president prized such fidelity and said later that he 'sensed immediately that he was a man I could count on in every way, I knew that he would do what had to be done, and I knew that I could count on him to tell me the truth at all times'. The result, as biographer Robert Beisner put it, was that 'his fingerprints – and whole hands and footprints – are all over the president's diplomacy and national security policies'.[67]

The under secretary seized his moment on Friday 21 February 1947, when the British embassy in Washington delivered a message saying the UK could no longer afford to shoulder the job of protecting Greece and Turkey from Soviet expansion. In the absence of Marshall at a university function, Acheson took charge. The decision by the Attlee government was part of a broader retreat which included withdrawal from the Raj and Palestine, and he saw it as the moment for the US to step up to a global commitment – the War Department had already warned that, if Greece gravitated into the Soviet orbit, there would be 'most unfavourable repercussions in all those areas where political sympathies are balanced precariously in favour of the West and against Soviet Communism'.[68]

Acheson's staff worked through the weekend on its recommendation, toasting the outcome with martinis. Marshall was back in town for the White House meeting with Truman and congressmen on the Monday but the under secretary judged that, much as he esteemed his boss, the general did not make the case for action forcefully enough. So he stepped in to say that, 'like apples in a barrel infected by one rotten one, the corruption of Greece would infect Iran and all to the east'. This could spread to Africa and the Near East and then contaminate Europe through the strong Communist parties in Italy and France. The Kremlin was playing one of the great gambles in history at minimal cost, and only the US was 'in a position to break up the play'. After Acheson had spoken, the president, who had long been fascinated by the region, took a large map from a drawer of his desk and gave a short lecture on its history and strategic importance. Since there was no dissent from what the under secretary had said, the administration began work on a proposal to channel aid to the two East Mediterranean countries, reassured that Senator Vandenberg would ensure bipartisan backing as the domino theory came to life and the new world power moved into the vacuum left by the decline of Europe.[69]

Three former members of the embassy in Moscow joined Marshall and Acheson in crafting the administration's approach to the developing Cold War. The wartime ambassador, Averell Harriman, whose lugubrious demeanour belied his $100 million fortune[70] built up from banking and the inheritance from his railway baron father, tended to mumble. But he was known as 'the crocodile' for the way in which, after appearing inert, he would suddenly snap into action. The journalist Theodore White wrote that 'once he was wound up and pointed in the direction the government had told him he must go, he was like a tank crushing all opposition'.[71]

Harriman had grown increasingly concerned about Soviet intentions as he moved away from the hopeful Rooseveltian view of post-war relations. In a message from the Moscow embassy to Washington in 1944, he depicted Soviet leaders as 'bloated with power ... they expect they can force acceptance of their decisions without question upon us and all countries'. The US 'might well have to face an ideological crusade just as vigorous and dangerous as Fascism or Nazism,' he added, warning that there was 'every indication the Soviet Union will become a world bully'.[72]

Kennan, who could show signs of personal insecurity, and the debonair Charles 'Chip' Bohlen, a genial, subtle master of the Washington bureaucratic machinery who was fluent in Russian, were other major players in forming policy. Together with John McCloy and Robert Lovett, who held senior posts at the War and State Departments, they constituted the elite who moulded America's emergence as a global power, especially in its relations with the USSR.

When Acheson stepped down in June to return to private life and make some money at law in June 1947,[73] his job was taken by Lovett, described by Kennan as 'one of the most charming of men, a seasoned financier and a very smooth, capable operator'. Their focus on the burgeoning Cold War, virtually to the exclusion of the rest of the world, gave policy an introverted, self-perpetuating character. If it was understandable that what happened between Washington and

Moscow was their priority, this tended to exclude the wider ambit of a world which included China, India, Pakistan, South East Asia, the Middle East, Latin America and Africa – and where their Cold War considerations could deform policy in the face of what were fundamentally nationalistic rather than ideological movements.[74]

## V: THE BRILLIANT GENIUS

Western envoys had been mightily impressed by their wartime contacts with Stalin as he sat at the conference table at the Teheran and Yalta summits doodling wolves heads with a thick pencil. Detecting 'a composed, collected strength', Harry Hopkins called him 'a perfectly co-ordinated machine'. Averell Harriman judged the Vozhd 'better informed than Roosevelt, more realistic than Churchill ... the most effective of the war leaders'. Britain's wartime foreign secretary, Anthony Eden, ranked Stalin as the toughest negotiator he encountered.[75]

Still, at the embassy in Moscow, Kennan detected 'depths of calculation, ambition, love of power, jealousy, cruelty and sly vindictiveness' behind the unpretentious, even-tempered façade assumed with high-ranking Westerners. Eden was struck by 'the intense cruelty of his face ... like an Oriental potentate'. Meeting him at Potsdam, the British prime minister, Clement Attlee, found 'a pretty ruthless tyrant ... like a despot from the Renaissance era – no principle, any methods, but no flowery language – always Yes or No, though you could only count on him if it was No'.[76]

The dictator was the subject of an enormous personality cult, hailed as 'The Brilliant Genius of Humanity' and 'The Gardener of Human Happiness'. If he mispronounced a word in a speech, his subordinates followed suit. When he insisted that Benelux consisted of only Belgium and Luxembourg, a Kremlin meeting went along with his omission of the Netherlands. 'When I say "no", it means NO,' he growled.[77]

After victory over Germany, the 'old tiger', as Kennan called him, had turned in on himself. He believed that conflict between the capitalist powers was inevitable, that Britain, France as well as a revived Germany and Japan were bound to break away from the US. He had been struck by a throwaway remark from Roosevelt at a wartime summit about the probability of US troops being withdrawn from Europe within a few years of the end of the war. Until James Byrnes signalled a change of course with his Stuttgart speech in September 1946, he took this to mean that the USSR had only to wait for ultimate victory to come its way following the acceptance of the extension of its control in East and Central Europe.

His court was marked by its heavy drinking, though the leader usually restricted himself to white wine. There were alcohol-fuelled games and crude practical jokes, such as placing a tomato on the seat of an unwary guest. Stalin liked to play a record of a woman opera singer accompanied by the howling of dogs. 'It's clever, devilishly clever,' he told one guest.[78]

The dictator sang in his good tenor voice while the ideological enforcer, Andrei Zhdanov, who was widely seen as a likely successor, played the piano and Molotov the violin and mandolin. This was followed by all-male dancing to the gramophone, at which the foreign minister showed off his talents as a ballroom performer. Nicknamed 'Iron Arse' for his ability to sit through unending meetings, Molotov had been demoted from his position as Stalin's deputy after the end of the war. Given his unbending attitude at conferences, it was ironic that he was accused of excessive friendliness towards foreign powers; more probably, his boss simply wanted to prevent any of his subalterns becoming too entrenched.

This did not affect the loyalty of the 'professional revolutionary' who had known his future leader since 1911 and had helped consign victims of the Great Purges of the 1930s to their deaths. When the Jewish Anti-Fascist Committee with which Molotov's wife was associated came in for official attack in 1948, Stalin told him he would have to divorce her. They duly split and Molotov abstained in the vote on whether to expel her from the party before she was sentenced to forced labour for 'treasonable activities'.[79]

As Molotov's star waned, others consolidated their positions in the leading groups around Stalin. Georgy Malenkov, chubby-faced but with prominent Mongol cheekbones, had marked himself out as a consummate bureaucrat during the purges – Zhdanov gave him the peasant woman nickname of 'Malanya' (Melanie). Stalin's fellow Georgian, Lavrentiy Beria, the highly capable and deeply sinister police chief, had been put in charge of the atom bomb programme helped by information from Soviet spies in the West; Djilas described him as exuding 'a certain self-satisfaction and irony mingled with a clerk's obsequiousness'.[80]

Anastas Mikoyan, the trade commissar and a great survivor, had belonged to the Communist Party Central Committee since the 1920s. He spent three months in the US in the mid-1930s meeting Henry Ford, visiting Macy's department store and studying the food industry – on his return he arranged for the introduction into the USSR of corn flakes, popcorn, hamburgers and ice cream. An early Bolshevik figure, Lazar Kaganovich, the only Jew at court, was prized for his ruthless execution of Stalin's orders. The future leader, Nikita Khrushchev, a Kaganovich protégé who succeeded him in charge of the Ukraine, joined the charmed circle along with the stout, goatee-bearded armed forces minister Nikolai Bulganin. Marshal Georgy Zhukov, the military architect of the defeat of Germany on the Eastern Front, was, however, exiled from the centre of power to command the Odessa region, victim of his own independence of mind and Stalin's lurking fear that his popularity might make him an alternative national leader – the cheers he received when riding a white horse at the victory parade could have but set off alarm bells in the leader's mind.

The paranoia of the 'Great Stalin', as he was greeted by crowds, grew with age – several body doubles were employed to impersonate him in public. He was subject to fits of personal uncertainty. 'I'm finished, I trust no one, not even myself,' he remarked to some of his lieutenants. Growing ever more secretive and self-protective, he was increasingly lonely. He made sure that those around him all had blood on their hands. Though their rivalries could make them deadly 'scorpions in a jar', his comrades harboured genuine respect for his leadership and his historic status. Having survived his monumental misjudgement of Hitler in 1941, he was never in danger of being overthrown. Not that this made him any less wary or any less dedicated to bolstering the security rampart he had erected on the ashes of Germany's defeat in the face of a president across the ocean who was so far outside the realm of his experience.[81]

# CHAPTER FOUR

# ALLIES AND ADVERSARIES

## I: THE HUMAN FACTOR

The personal element counted for much in the unfolding of events in these thirteen months as antipathies and ambitions influenced policies among the exceptional cast of leaders. They included autocrats and democrats, Nationalist guerrillas and smart statesmen, power holders and independence fighters, exiles and long-entrenched rulers, military men who had been fighting all their adult lives, veterans of the First World War marked by its death toll of more than 15 million – and newcomers catapulted to power by the second great global conflict.

Some were divided by hostilities stretching back for decades while others sought new forms of co-operation between their nations. Some were guided by rejection and personal animosity. Some were on their way to founding dynasties or were the objects of huge personality cults. For some, power and ideology were inextricably entwined in a struggle for supremacy. Others were more modest and accepted the possibility of electoral defeat.

Despite the deepening Cold War, Stalin and the president were relatively mild about one another. After their only encounter at the Potsdam summit in the summer of 1945, Stalin merely dismissed the new American leader as a 'noisy shopkeeper' who was 'neither educated nor clever'. 'I like Stalin,' Truman wrote to his wife from the conference. 'He is straightforward. Knows what he wants and will compromise when he can't get it.' On his return to Washington, he told his staff the Soviet leader was 'an SOB, but of course he thinks I'm one too'. Looking back in 1960, he recalled of Stalin, 'I liked him a lot. But he was always talking through his hat ... He didn't mean what he said.'[1]

In the South Asian subcontinent, the antagonism across the new frontier between India and Pakistan was personal as well as political between Muhammad Ali Jinnah, the Quaid-e-Azam (Great Leader) of the Muslim nation, and Nehru and Gandhi. In the Middle East, Arab leaders were deeply divided by their own rivalries, which helped to facilitate the establishment of Israel and its victory in the subsequent war, while Zionists had been split between the Jewish establishment and rival terrorist groups and the prime minister was waging a power struggle with the military command. In China, Chiang Kai-shek and Mao Zedong had been at war since the Kuomintang turned on their erstwhile Communist allies in the 'White Terror' of 1927.

Truman and the domineering pro-consul in Japan, Douglas MacArthur, were chalk and cheese as the president insisted on the primacy of civilian control of the military and the general pursued his own course as much as he could. MacArthur and Lucius Clay, the US occupation commander in Germany, enjoyed enormous authority, with blurred lines of communication to Washington that enhanced the scope for independent action. Like Clay and MacArthur, the last viceroy of India, Lord Louis 'Dickie' Mountbatten, a cousin of King George VI, enjoyed considerable autonomy as the Raj moved to independence and statehood for India and Pakistan.

In Europe, Tito's identification with the new Yugoslavia after his wartime leadership of the partisan fight against German occupation made inevitable a clash with Stalin given his insistence of the primacy of the USSR. French Communists made vituperation of their post-war coalition partners their leitmotif after the Kremlin instructed them in 1947 to step up their militancy. In Western Germany, the Christian Democrat Konrad Adenauer and the Social Democrat Kurt Schumacher were poles apart temperamentally as well as politically.

Health was a problem for quite a few of those involved. So was age for some and the pressure of business for all. Stalin was in marked medical decline and work could get on top of Truman, as we have seen. King Abdullah of Transjordan was diabetic. His Egyptian counterpart, Farouk, with his gluttony and taste for teenage girls, grew unhealthily fat; he was described as 'a stomach with a head'.[2] The Zionist patriarch, Chaim Weizmann, a distinguished biochemist born in Belarus who had worked for the Balfour Declaration on a homeland for the Jews in 1917, was in his seventies, his health poor, his face deeply lined, his sight nearly gone. The other leading Zionist figure, David Ben-Gurion, had bad backache, which he treated by weekend bathing in the Dead Sea.

The patron saint of French Socialism, Léon Blum, was increasingly frail in his later seventies, and found it hard to get through parliamentary speeches as he sought to form a 'Third Force' government between the Communists and Gaullists. The governments in Athens to which the US channelled aid were headed by a series of veterans – one of them eighty-seven – while Turkey, the other East Mediterranean country Washington pledged to defend from Soviet pressure, was led by the ageing, deaf President İsmet İnönü who had first been prime minister in 1923.

Kurt Schumacher bore the burden of severe injuries in the First World War when he had lost an arm followed by years in a Nazi concentration camp; aides bought milk for him on the black market to soothe his stomach – he preferred black coffee and cigarettes.[3] Churchill, out of office but Britain's best-known international figure at the age of seventy-three, had a mild heart attack in 1941 and went through periods of his 'Black Dog' of depression. At one point in 1947, as Britain faced a currency crisis, Attlee's four principal colleagues in the Cabinet were simultaneously in poor medical state, with the chancellor of the Exchequer depending on Benzedrine to keep himself going.[4]

Ernest Bevin, the British foreign secretary, weighed in at eighteen stone – Acheson described him as 'short and too fat'. He lumbered rather than walked and had trouble negotiating a single flight of stairs. A shrewd, earthy and sometimes emotional man, he suffered from angina, arteriosclerosis, liver and kidney damage and cardiac trouble, took no exercise and slept badly. A doctor who examined him in 1943 said his feet were the only sound part of his body.[5]

Tumours were growing on Marshall's kidneys. Kennan suffered

from ulcers as did the US ambassador in Moscow, Bedell Smith. The under secretary, Robert Lovett, was physically frail, with 'glass insides' and recurrent gall bladder trouble. Ho Chi Minh had tuberculosis and diabetes. Tito developed gallstones during his confrontation with Stalin in 1948. At sixty-three, the teetotal, non-smoker President Edvard Beneš of Czechoslovakia was impeded by two strokes and arteriosclerosis; at times he could not speak. Jan Masaryk, his country's 61-year-old foreign minister who tried to maintain its independence from the USSR, was subject to strong mood swings – a British friend noted the 'mad streak' in his family.[6]

Jinnah, seventy-one when Pakistan came into being, had tuber-culosis and lung cancer. Sadar Patel, the 72-year-old power broker of India's Congress Party, suffered a severe heart attack after independence. Nearing eighty, Gandhi was in seriously declining health, his kidneys failing, his weight dropping before his assas-sination at the beginning of 1948. Nehru, who kept in trim with a morning yoga session that included headstands, was in his late fifties but the press of events sometimes led him to take to his bed. Though his Pakistani counterpart, Liaquat Ali Khan, was only fifty-one, he was hit by a major thrombosis and had painful ulcers. One reason the partition of India and Pakistan was adopted, Nehru reflected later, was that 'we were tired men and we were getting on in years' and wanted a way out. 'I am run down,' Jinnah lamented. 'I have too much to do.'[7]

For some, age seemed no problem; indeed, advancing years increased their self-belief and accentuated their behaviour. Syngman Rhee, seventy-three when he became president of South Korea, did not let his years impede his pursuit of autocracy after decades in exile. MacArthur, nearing seventy, dominated the scene in Tokyo. The leading Japanese politician, Shigeru Yoshida, who wanted his country to reclaim its identity after the eclipse of defeat, headed governments while in his seventies. The president of Finland, Juho Kusti Paasikivi, conducted a sensitive balancing act with the USSR. Adenauer and Jan Smuts in South Africa were also septuagenarians. The latter had fought the British in the Boer War at the turn of the century, while the former had been mayor of Cologne before Hitler assumed power, but the British poet Stephen Spender found that he had 'the quietly confident manner of a successful and attentive young man'.[8]

In some cases, alcohol took its toll. The prime minister of Czechoslovakia, Klement Gottwald, was sometimes too inebriated to function; Molotov remembered him as 'a good fellow, very good, but he drank'. Bevin also consumed too much alcohol for his own good; the Soviet minister recalled him throwing up over his wife's skirt as they left an embassy reception; 'what kind of man was he, what kind of diplomat if he couldn't take care of himself?' he asked. France's foreign minister, Georges Bidault, had a low tolerance for drink, compounded by his eating habits – a slice of bread with mustard for breakfast, nuts, radishes and gherkins for lunch.[9]

## II: AUTOCRATS AND DEMOCRATS

Nationalism was important for many of those who appear in this book, often expressed through ethnicity and religion and spilling over into personal cults and demagogic showmanship, even if this sometimes hid uncertainty. In Europe, despite the forced removal of Germans and others, the sentiment was generally sublimated to the dictates of Communist unity and the desire of French and German leaders to avoid a fresh outbreak of the hostility that had led to three wars in three-quarters of a century. But, elsewhere, the independence struggle against colonialism and internal conflicts drew heavily on ethnic and religious elements and the charisma of leadership.

Chiang and Mao were both deeply Nationalist, as were Syngman Rhee and Kim Il-sung. Sukarno and Ho drew on the desire to create, or recreate, a nation and used their charisma to the full. The apartheid leaders of South Africa harked back to the era of the Boer Great Trek and elided the promotion of the interests of the white population with a belief that apartheid fulfilled a divine purpose. Striding forth as a figure from history who spoke of himself in the third person, de Gaulle pursued the greatness of the country of which, he said, he had 'a certain idea'.

Tito was a national hero; heavy-set and handsome with bright blue eyes, he cut a dashing figure in uniform or white suits with his flashing diamond ring. The leader of the Communist army in

Greece, Markos Vafiadis, a former trade union official in the tobacco industry who had led resistance to the Italians and Germans in Macedonia, was described by a BBC correspondent as having the 'halo of a guerrilla chieftain ... shrewd, temperate, his moustache drooping at the ends ... he wore the outfit of a mountain brigand, carried a walking stick rather than a gun and had the romantic image for his followers of King of the Mountains'. In Argentina, Juan Perón set the model for a populist military strongman swaying the crowds at vast rallies outside the presidential palace, offering workers economic and social inducements and using the instruments of state and violence to quell opposition while employing his wife's charisma to buttress support and welcoming fugitive Nazis.[10]

Jinnah's chilling aloofness did not stop him being mesmerising. The great leader was, as the wife of Pakistan's first prime minister put it, 'a dictator to the fingertips ... who could talk for hours at public meetings to crowds of people who didn't know any English in pin-drop silence'. After accompanying him on a visit to the North-West Frontier during which he received the homage of tribal barons, Louis Heren of the London *Times* decided that he saw himself as the heir of the Mughal emperors – 'the epitome of arrogance'.[11]

Nehru swayed crowds with his rhetoric; his opiate, a diplomat remarked, was the adoration of the people. Energetic, well read and well connected, and with a fierce temper, he charmed Westerners with his easy conversation and internationalism, as well as showing his ability to walk fast backwards up hills, turn somersaults and stand on his head. Vallabhbhai Patel, who became India's first home affairs minister, could be benevolent and smiling in private, but was remorseless in politics and government – 'leather tough' as the *New York Times* correspondent wrote. Three decades on from the start of his campaign of disobedience against the Raj, Gandhi still had enormous charismatic appeal, even if his non-violent teachings were submerged by the turmoil of partition and his advocacy of turning India back into a village society bereft of modern inventions made little sense.[12]

Most heads of European governments were more conventional, many of them grey figures in dark three-piece suits and Homburg hats, frequently smoking a cigarette or pipe. With his cricketing metaphors and modest personal life, Attlee was the epitome of a member of the bourgeoisie who compared socialism to gardening. The French prime minister Robert Schuman was so lacking in charisma that a leading journalist compared his speeches to a pharmacist counting out pills – 'his audience did not grow impatient; it fell asleep'. The Dutch prime minister, Willem Drees, went to work on foot or by bicycle – when an American diplomat visited him at home, he was struck by the way in which the politician's wife served him a single biscuit with his cup of tea. In two former enemy countries, Adenauer was a highly reassuring presence for the Allies, while his Christian Democrat counterpart in Italy, the pale, frail Alcide De Gasperi, cut an unassuming but determined path as he led his party into battle with the Communists. Progress towards democracy could be trusted to such reliable men, the Americans and their allies felt.[13]

Eastern Europe leaders were easily seen as faceless apparatchiks whose only concern was to curry favour with the Kremlin, notable for their taciturnity rather than their popular appeal. Most had fled from authoritarian regimes at home to seek shelter in Moscow during the 1930s and spent the war years there. Life might have been made comfortable for them in the Lux Hotel and other well-upholstered establishments, with access to special rations and sanatorium treatment, but the purge police came round to pick up foreign Communists who had fallen under a cloud – nearly all the senior Poles in the Soviet capital were liquidated as suspected Trotskyites.

Some had a degree of historical legitimacy, such as the Bulgarian Georgi Dimitrov, who had won fame for his successful defence after being accused by the Nazis of being responsible for the burning of the Reichstag in Berlin in 1933 and had then headed the international Comintern organisation after reaching Moscow. The Hungarian party chief, Mátyás Rákosi, known as 'potato head' on account of his shaven skull, had been a junior minister in the country's short-lived Soviet Republic after the First World War and was then imprisoned by the right-wing regime in Budapest for thirteen years before being exchanged for a set of national flags the government wanted to reclaim to enable him to go to Moscow in 1940. Tito stood out as the leader of resistance to the German occupation of

Yugoslavia who had triumphed without Soviet intervention and now commanded the third largest land forces in Europe.

Most of those who arrived with the Red Army in 1945 were strangers in their own lands with little popular support and dependent on Soviet backing, their task further complicated by traditional antipathy towards the Soviet Union in countries like Hungary and Poland – and suspicion of some of them as Jews. They entered coalition governments, ensuring that they had control of the Interior Ministries and the police; after the Gestapo and its local emulators came the NKVD and its pupils. Opponents were marginalised and elections rigged. Otherwise, as the Polish Communist Jakub Berman acknowledged later, his party would have lost at the polls, and 'what's the point of such an election? You can't be honest if you want to stay in power.' Or, as Walter Ulbricht of East Germany explained, though the acquisition of power had to have a democratic façade, 'we must have everything under control'.[14]

Thoroughly schooled in the Stalinist system, they owed their prime loyalty to unity of the Communist movement under Moscow's leadership. This had no room for independent routes to the socialist goal. Disputing the wisdom emanating from the Kremlin was the ultimate treason. The systems they headed parroted the Soviet model with the government subservient to the Communist Party and its political bureau (Politburo) headed by a general secretary. The 'Little Stalins' were flanked by other once-exiled Moscow Communists who could be counted on to keep a watch on them and report any failings to the Kremlin. Figures like Gomułka who had spent the war in their native country were suspect. Fealty to Moscow was all. In Hungary, Rákosi boasted that he was 'Stalin's best pupil'. A joke in Romania had it that the foreign minister, Ana Pauker, who had remained loyal to the Soviet cause despite the shooting of her husband in Russia as a Trotskyite, was asked why she was carrying an umbrella when she left home on a sunny day, to which she replied, 'Ha! Have you not seen the meteorological report? In Moscow, it is raining.'[15]

In the west of the Continent, the principal Communist Party leaders, Maurice Thorez of France and Palmiro Togliatti of Italy, had both spent the war in Moscow. As a former miner, Thorez projected himself as a true son of the proletariat with his burly presence – after a lunch they both attended at the Paris City Hall in 1946, Senator Vandenberg kept repeating to himself, 'How can such a healthy-looking man be a Communist?' Stalin said, however, that the Frenchman 'lacked bite' and called Togliatti 'a professor who could write a good theoretical article but couldn't lead people towards a well-defined goal'. The Italian party allowed a degree of internal debate but the French were rigorous in their loyalty to the Kremlin. Both exerted great influence through the major trade union federations, the CGT in France and the CGIL in Italy.[16]

Despite their rejection of socialism as an ideology, many in Washington, rightly, saw the Social Democrats of Western Europe as a strong bulwark against Communism. As a result, the Cold War cannot be seen simply as a conflict between Communism and capitalism and has to be shaded with West European Social Democratic characteristics as politicians like Clement Attlee and Ernest Bevin, Léon Blum, Paul Ramadier and Jules Moch or Kurt Schumacher and the West Berlin mayor Ernst Reuter proved stalwart allies for the struggle against the USSR, whatever their criticisms of the American model. Right-wing parties were tarnished by the failure of pre-war policies and, in some places, their collaboration with Fascism. In contrast, men like Blum and Schumacher had spent their lives fighting Moscow-aligned Communism as well as the Nazis, while the long antipathy of Attlee and Bevin to Communism made them reliable Cold War allies for Washington.

Rebutting the warnings of Austrian economist and philosopher Friedrich von Hayek about the dangers of socialism to freedom and the need for a fightback by liberals against collectivism, such politicians set out to show that democracy and the interventionist state were not only compatible, but could save Europe from a return to the disasters of the 1930s. 'A weak and perverted bourgeois democracy has collapsed and must be replaced by a true democracy, an energetic and competent democracy, popular instead of capitalist, strong instead of weak,' as Blum put it. 'This popular democracy will be, indeed can only be, Social Democracy.'[17]

# PART TWO

# JUNE 1947

## ACTS

*George Marshall sets out his plan; India and Pakistan move towards independence amid communal violence; the United Nations takes on Palestine; Chinese Communist armies advance.*

## SCENES

*Harvard, Washington, London, Paris; Delhi, Karachi, Calcutta, Bengal and Punjab; Palestine; the Central Plains of China, Shandong and Manchuria.*

## CAST

*Marshall, Truman, Kennan, Bevin, Bidault; Nehru, Jinnah, Mountbatten; Arab and Zionist leaders; Mao, Chiang, 'One-Eyed Dragon', Liu Bocheng, Deng Xiaoping, Lin Biao.*

# CHAPTER FIVE

# POWER POLARISATION

## I: The Secretary has a plan

George Marshall was no orator. Rather than soaring rhetoric, his deliberate, quiet manner implied that great thought had been given to his words, and that he meant what he said – never more so than in his address to the Alumni Association at Harvard University on a sunny afternoon on 5 June 1947. George Kennan now at the State Department's planning section had developed the basis for what the secretary of state would say on the evolution of American thinking he had set in motion with his 'Long Telegram' from the embassy in Moscow sixteen months earlier. Reports from State Department envoy Will Clayton on the parlous state of Western Europe added to Washington's concern about a collapse there which would benefit only the Soviet Union.[1]

A note from Kennan had laid out the main objective of US strategy as being 'to render principal European countries able to exist without outside charity'.

'Necessity of this,' it went on:

(a) so that they can buy from us;
(b) So that they will have enough self-confidence to withstand outside pressure.[2]

The injection of aid on a massive scale would enable recipients to surmount their dollar shortage and open the way to currency convertibility and multi-national trading arrangements which would promote co-operation between participating states. Despite Kennan's (a) point, the programme as it developed was not essentially an effort to find markets for surplus American production. Rather, it aimed to boost trade in both directions and recognised the need to encourage imports to revive transatlantic economies, particularly in the western half of Germany. Simply using the aid to soak up unwanted US domestic production would not have served the broader aim of rebuilding the European economy to make the west of the Continent a bastion in the competition with the USSR, underpinned by alliances with independent, self-sufficient, like-minded nations. The US wanted allies, but it did not wish them to be weak, dependent states, preferring to help build up their strength so that they would be effective partners in a world where economic co-operation ranked alongside political alignment in a broad global strategy.[3]

Marshall had been awarded an honorary degree from Harvard earlier in the day together with the poet T. S. Eliot, the D-Day general Omar Bradley and Robert Oppenheimer, director of the atom bomb project. Taking the podium in the afternoon, the general looked down at his text, fiddling with his spectacles. As always when reading from a script, he spoke in a flat, businesslike tone, but what he had to say was momentous. In a concluding passage he had composed on his way from Washington, he said, 'The whole world's future hangs on ... the realization by the American people of what can best be done and what must be done.'

Pointing to 'the dislocation of the entire fabric of European economy', he noted that the Continent's requirements for the coming three or four years were so much greater than its ability to pay that it 'must have substantial additional help, or face economic, social and political deterioration of a very grave character'. The remedy lay in 'breaking the vicious circle and restoring the confidence of the European people in the economic future of their own countries and of Europe as a whole'. He continued, rarely looking up from his notes:

> It is logical that the United States should do whatever it is able to do to assist in the return of normal economic health in the world,

without which there can be no political stability and no assured peace. Our policy is directed not against any country or doctrine but against hunger, poverty, desperation and chaos. Its purpose should be the revival of a working economy in the world so as to permit the emergence of political and social conditions in which free institutions can exist.

Setting out what had become the core of the Truman administration's thinking, he argued that aid should provide 'a cure rather than a mere palliative'. How the money would be used was the business of the Europeans and 'the program should be a joint one, agreed to by a number, if not all European nations'.[4]

Marshall's speech was couched in very general terms. There was no worked-out project. The State Department had not alerted the future partners. 'The initiative, I think, must come from the Europeans,' the secretary said. That was asking a lot given the state of the Continent and the lack of collaborative institutions – and, as Kennan would say later in the year, it would be up to Washington to tell the recipient nations what they would get.

Still, the initial reaction was enthusiastic. Ernest Bevin called the proposal 'a lifeline to sinking men bringing hope where there was none', while Georges Bidault hailed a 'noble initiative of the Government of the United States ... which we cannot ignore'. They welcomed the chance to boost productivity and resource utilisation, leading to rising prosperity which would foster stability and enable participating countries to join a revived international trading network.

The mixture of altruism and self-interest made the plan a landmark in political and economic strategy. Unlike policies adopted by the victors after the First World War, it aimed to rebuild the economies of both the winners and the losers of the Second, and thereby strengthen them politically along lines of which Washington approved, melding the promotion of an open, competitive international system with mechanisms of economic planning, co-operative arrangements and private–public partnerships. The historian Michael Hogan has characterised this as 'the New Deal synthesis', applying federalism on US lines to achieve 'the fusion of separate economic sovereignties into an integrated market capped by supra-national institutions of economic planning and administration'.[5]

The secretary of state blushed when Truman told him the scheme would be known as the Marshall Plan, but the president knew what he was doing. As always, foreign policy initiatives have to be set in the context of domestic politics, in this case the control of Congress by the hostile Republican Party.

'I can't allow a thing like that to happen, Mr President,' Marshall replied.

'You won't have anything to do with it, but that's what will happen and that's what I want to happen,' Truman replied, well aware that the general's name would command far more respect than his own as his opinion poll standing sank and given the need to get the programme through the congressional majority. As he commented later, 'Can you imagine its chances of passages in an election year in a Republican Congress if it is named for Truman and not Marshall?'[6]

## II: The patient is sinking

The Harvard speech was the result of a lengthy process which dated back to 1945 but had been given a sharp edge by an inconclusive conference meeting of the foreign ministers of the US, USSR, UK and France in Moscow in March and April 1947 that began soon after Truman had agreed America should commit itself to defending Greece and Turkey. Molotov, Marshall, Bevin and Bidault gathered in a large ornate chamber of the Aviation Industries House to which they were ferried through driving snow, stared at by tobogganing children. They met for four hours each afternoon around a table with a yellow cloth in a grey painted room. They had made little progress at sessions over the previous two years in London, New York, Paris and Moscow, and stayed far apart on the key issue of Germany, with the USSR insisting on reparations of $10 billion from the defeated enemy. That would have to be funded by America, meaning, as Marshall put it, that 'we put in and the Russians take out'.[7]

In a cable to Truman, the secretary of state summed up US objectives as being to obtain (A) a politically and economically unified Germany under a democratic government with effective safeguards of human rights and fundamental freedoms; (B) a sufficient increase in Germany's level of industry to assist in the economic recovery of Europe; (C) guarantee of security from German aggression by a treaty among the four occupying powers; (D) an adjustment in connection with the provisional eastern boundaries to provide additional food for Germany and to reduce her present population density.

Despite the first aim, the Western side was highly suspicious of pressure by Moscow to form a single centralised German government in place of the separate occupation zones. The general saw this as aiming to achieve 'the seizure of absolute control of a country which would be doomed economically . . . and would be mortgaged to turn over a large part of its production as reparations, principally to the Soviet Union'.[8]

The prospect of reaching understanding receded further only two days after the ministers met when Truman sent a message to Congress asking for approval of a $400 million aid programme to Greece and Turkey and accompanied this by laying out the doctrine which would bear his name. 'I believe that it must be the policy of the United States to support free peoples who are resisting attempted subjugation by armed minorities or by outside pressures,' he said. The world faced a choice between different ways of life, one 'based upon the will of the majority' and governments providing 'guarantees of individual liberty', the other on 'the will of a minority forcibly imposed upon the majority' and relying on 'terror and oppression'. The foreign policy and the national security of the United States were, the president argued, involved in the fates of the two East Mediterranean nations, though, naturally, he did not mention that one was run by a small circle of sometimes corrupt right-wing politicians and the other by an aged military autocrat.[9]

Still, the foreign ministers went through the routine as if there was still a hope of agreement – though their main motivation may have been simply to avoid the responsibility for breaking off the top-level contact between the wartime allies. Molotov lived up to his nickname of 'Iron Arse' – an American aide wrote to his wife that the Soviet minister adopted 'his usual pose. Hand covering chin, elbow on table, slowly nodding his head' while Bidault tried 'to give the impression that he is bored and thinking above the lot' and Bevin glanced with raised brows through papers and books, a cigarette hanging from his lips.[10]

The foreign secretary, who had caught a bad cold on the four-day train journey to Moscow, wrote to Attlee that the four powers were 'perilously near a position in which a line-up is taking place' after five weeks of 'very cold, frank but firm' talking. 'There is courtesy, there are no high words being used, no tempers,' his letter added. 'But all of it is cool, calculated and the two big boys look to be pretty determined.' The virtual breakdown 'would have been farcical were it not so tragic'. At least the three Western ministers agreed, in meetings of their own, on the foreign secretary's suggestion that their countries should develop their German occupation zones separately from the Soviets. The US and Britain went further to merge their zones into a 'Bizone' or 'Bizonia'.[11]

The conference was a particularly bitter experience for the always-sensitive Bidault. Disquieted by the American desire to revive Germany and aiming to build up its economy, France pressed for annexation of the mineral-rich Saarland, just across the frontier from Lorraine. It wanted guarantees of coal supplies, continuing reparations and international ownership of the industries in the Ruhr. Marshall expressed sympathy but without committing himself. The Soviets backed Bidault on reparations and the Ruhr, but, on the Saarland, Molotov offered no support, while Stalin, who was still contemptuous of the surrender to Germany in 1940, omitted the Frenchman from the first round of toasts at a banquet for the ministers.[12]

'You look just the same as when I last saw you,' the Soviet leader told Marshall when they met in Kremlin at 10 p.m. on 15 April. 'But I am just an old man.'[13]

The secretary of state, who had met the Soviet leader at Allied wartime summits in his capacity as chairman of the chiefs of staff, found that the dictator looked unwell and shrunken. Sitting down in the wood-panelled conference room, the American explained he had become 'very concerned and somewhat depressed at the extent and depth of misunderstandings and differences'. He noted 'a serious and steady deterioration' in public regard for the Soviet Union, but assured his host that there was 'no desire on the part of the United States to attempt to convert the Soviet people to our form of government'. As for Germany, he supported economic union of the occupation zones, but feared a centralised government controlling industry, education, finance and other matters would 'constitute a real danger for the peace of the world'. The US was, he added, 'determined to do what we can to assist those countries which are suffering from economic deterioration which, if unchecked, might lead to economic collapse and the consequent elimination of any chance of democratic survival'.

Stalin, who doodled with a thick pencil, insisted that the USSR must get $10 billion in reparations and said the economic unity of Germany could not be achieved without political unity between the occupation zones. As for the foreign ministers, their differences were 'only the first skirmishes and brushes of reconnaissance forces on this question'. As a rule, he added, people recognised the need for compromise once they had exhausted themselves in disputes. If no great success would be achieved at the current session, nobody should grow desperate. It was necessary to have patience and not become depressed. Marshall left after ninety minutes and remarked subsequently that he found the Soviet leader 'completely evasive' about substantive issues behind his calm and gracious exterior.[14]

He took Stalin's comment about the need for patience as an indication that the Soviet leader was playing for time and counting on deteriorating conditions to deliver Germany, and perhaps the rest of Western Europe, into the Kremlin's hands. 'He came to the conclusion that Stalin saw the best way to advance Soviet interests was to let matters drift,' his aide, Charles Bohlen, wrote in his memoirs. On the journey home, Marshall referred repeatedly to his staff on the plight of Europe and the need to bolster non-Communist forces to prevent 'a complete breakdown'. The Continent's economic woes were 'the kind of crisis that Communism thrived on'. Looking back, Marshall recalled that 'we thought they could be negotiated with . . . I decided finally at Moscow that they could not be.'[15]

Bevin and Bidault were of the same mind. When he reached Paris, the French minister told the prime minister, Paul Ramadier, that he was convinced it was impossible to do business with the Soviets, who were out 'to eradicate Western civilisation'. Bevin was so relieved to be leaving Moscow he burst into song at the station, and was in no doubt of the need for a tougher line towards the Soviets.

Back in Washington, Marshall told Congress what was required was not 'general talk or vague formulae' but 'concrete solutions for definite and extremely complicated questions' of politics and economics. In Europe, he went on, 'disintegrating forces are becoming evident. The patient is sinking while the doctors deliberate. So I believe that action cannot await compromise through exhaustion. New issues arise daily. Whatever action is possible to meet these pressing problems must be taken without delay.'[16]

He was in tune with a growing belief in Washington that, rather than Soviet military expansion, the real and immediate danger to the West lay in what George Kennan described as 'the disruptive effect of the war in the economic, political and social structure of Europe and from a profound exhaustion of physical plant and of spiritual vigour'. Military factors were not discounted – the Truman administration ordered a hundred six-engined B-36 bombers, the biggest warplanes on earth.[17] But Will Clayton warned that 'We have grossly underestimated the destruction of the European economy by the war,' and he estimated that three years of aid running at $6–7 billion annually would be needed.

'We have concluded that we must use to an increasing extent our ... economic power in order to call an effective halt to the Soviet Union's expansionism and political infiltration, and to create the basis for political stability and economic well-being,' Acheson noted. In a speech in Mississippi in May, the under secretary outlined the need for a programme of grants to revive Europe's agriculture, industry and trade. The fundamental aim of a coordinated economy for the Continent should be pursued without Four Power agreement, if necessary, he added, stressing the importance of German reconstruction.[18]

Since the end of the war, Washington had sent 82 million tons of products valued at $9 billion to Europe. It was shipping 450,000 tons of grain to Germany each month. In July 1946, it had granted Britain a $3.75 billion loan at 2 per cent interest, to which Canada had added $1.19 billion. The Truman administration had also wiped out the UK's Lend Lease programme that had made US output available to its wartime ally, selling assets held by Britain at 10 cents on the dollar after the wartime aid programme was curtailed in September 1945. It agreed to write off $2.8 billion of debts owed by France as well as granting a $650 million low-interest credit. The help came with conditions. Britain had to agree to make sterling convertible within a year while France was obliged to open its markets to American products, especially films.[19]

This help was not enough. The transatlantic trade deficit was forecast to more than double from 1946 to 1947 to $4.7 billion. The severe weather in 1946–7, oscillating between extreme winter cold and an overheated summer, exacerbated the damage done. The east of the Continent was worst hit and least able to deal with the resulting shortages, particularly of food. 'Things are in very bad shape in Europe as a whole,' Stalin told a visitor.[20]

In Germany, a Catholic archbishop gave his blessing to those who stole to feed their families. In Denmark, a mob attacked a train carrying coal. In France, where annual inflation ran at 60 per cent and the wheat harvest was the worst for 130 years, rationing was tightened on bread, milk, fats and textiles. In Britain, where cyclists rode on the frozen Thames, Bevin noted 'almost unrelieved gloom'. Ten per cent of annual industrial production was lost. Unemployment rose to 15 per cent. Output of cereals fell by 10–20 per cent, and a quarter of the sheep died. 'The margin of safety in Europe, both from an economic and political viewpoint, is extremely thin,' the State Department's planning department warned. The annual dollar gap in West Europe shot up from $7.8 billion to $11.6 billion in 1946. Bevin noted 'the need to co-ordinate our foreign policy with that of the only country which is able effectively to wield extensive economic influence – namely the United States'. Without its help, he added, 'our financial nakedness [would] be fully apparent to the world'.[21]

In June, the Attlee government announced drastic cuts in imports of petrol and tobacco to try to stem the deterioration of the trade position and the drain on its reserves. Reductions in the meat and tea rations followed. London suffered a severe potato shortage. The

Treasury warned that the credit line with the US was being drawn down 'much more rapidly than we expected'.

French railwaymen, miners and bakers went on strike – coal output was cut by 700,000 tons in June. The previous month, Paul Ramadier had dropped the Communists from his government after a series of clashes over wages restrictions and colonial affairs. That facilitated policy-making but left Maurice Thorez and his colleagues free to go on the offensive both in Parliament and through the CGT labour federation. The government also came under pressure from a new movement set up by Charles de Gaulle, who pledged to sweep away the Fourth Republic, declaring the country to be on the edge of an abyss.

Food supplies were reported to be nearly exhausted in Italy, Austria, Greece, Hungary and Poland. In the Cologne region of Germany, 30,000 workers stayed away from their factories, saying food shortages meant they had insufficient energy to do their jobs. In Italy, encouraged by Washington, de Gasperi also ejected Communist ministers and formed a minority Christian Democratic government that depended on support from parties to its right. The Mafia chief, Salvatore Giuliano, declared war on the left in Sicily, where a tommy gun attack on Communist headquarters killed four people and provoked a general strike.

In the east of the Continent, Communist pressure rose steadily while, in Greece, Communist-led forces staged repeated attacks in the north of the country, including a ten-hour battle in Salonica. The Soviet occupation authorities in Berlin ruled that the election of the Social Democrat Ernst Reuter as mayor was unacceptable because of his 'anti-Soviet attitude'. Poland remained a tricky matter given the strength of anti-Russian sentiment and the way the Red Army had stood by as the Nazis suppressed the rising in Warsaw. Stalin had told Harry Hopkins in 1945 that implementing Communism in Poland would be like putting 'a saddle on a cow' but he now showed no compunction about doing whatever was necessary as prominent Socialists were detained, accused of 'terrorist subversive activity'.

In Bulgaria, which had been allied with Germany until the Red Army entered its territory in 1944, the Communists engineered a split in the main political group, the Peasants' Party. Its leader, Nikola Petkov, was arrested for espionage; colleagues who tried to protect him were beaten up. Another member of the party recounted being detained for ninety days on charges of burning Russian cotton stock and plotting a coup, interrogated round the clock, beaten with a rubber whip and deprived of food and water before suddenly being released. The Communist-led coalition in Romania, another German ally till near the end of the fighting, used fraud and pressure to win the post-war election. Political prisoners at the country's main prison smuggled out a statement charging that they were being starved to death, with six being held in cells designed for a single occupant and water available for only two hours a day.

Despite doing badly in elections and having only 3,000 members at the end of the war, Hungary's Communists were able to follow Stalin's instructions to secure the interior ministry and a deputy premiership, benefitting from the country's economic dependence on the USSR and the fear of alienating Moscow among other parties. To increase the pressure, Stalin then told the Communist leader, Mátyás Rákosi, to get rid of the prime minister, Ferenc Nagy of the Smallholders Party, 'or it will be very hard for you'. Nagy was induced to resign while on holiday in Switzerland after getting a pledge of safe conduct out of the country for his four-year-old son to join him. He was replaced by a left-wing member of the Smallholders at the head of a coalition in which the Communists played an ever-growing role; the new premier called for 'a purge of anti-democratic elements'. Ahead of fresh national elections, 180,000 people were removed from the voting roll.[22]

Despite its ruined state, fear of Germany remained widespread. However, a report by former president Herbert Hoover after a trip to Europe at Truman's behest recommended lifting post-war restraints on the defeated nation's economy. The revival of the western sectors of Germany became increasingly fused with the promotion of the Continent's economic unity envisaged by at least some politicians on either side of the Rhine.[23]

As Truman would put it, the European Recovery Program (ERP), as the Marshall Plan was officially known, aimed to induce recipient nations to 'develop their own solution of Europe's economic problems, viewed as a whole and tackled co-operatively rather than as separate national problems'. Kennan's planning staff recommended promoting 'the supra-national idea of European unity' with financial leverage deployed to bring about currency convertibility and lower tariff barriers, and to promote joint economic programmes. Under Secretary Clayton looked to 'a European economic federation' to replace economies which had become 'divided into many small watertight compartments'. An appeal for a United Europe was signed by eighty-one prominent American figures. A congressional resolution called for economic and political federation across the ocean and columnist Walter Lippmann urged Washington to draw up a comprehensive recovery plan aiming at the 'unification of Europe'.[24]

Hammering home the transatlantic link, Truman argued that a healthy Europe was 'essential to the maintenance of the civilization' in which the American way of life was rooted. 'The recovery of production abroad is essential both to a vigorous democracy and to a peace founded on democracy and freedom,' he said. 'It is essential also to a world trade in which our businessmen, farmers and workers may benefit from substantial exports and in which their customers may be able to pay for these goods.'[25]

When Sam Rayburn, the Democratic leader in the Senate, told him the ERP would 'bust this country', the president replied 'If we don't do it, Europe will have the worst depression in its history, and I don't know how many hundreds of thousands of people will starve to death, and we don't want to have a thing like that on our consciences, not if it's something we can prevent, we don't. If we let Europe go down the drain, then we're going to have a bad depression in this country.' But, if the money was spent, 'we can save the world with it'.[26]

By tying the ERP so closely to national security and strategic and economic interests, the administration ensured bipartisan support while making it a cornerstone in the evolution of the Cold War as $13 billion[27] was disbursed over four years. The plan marked a decisive step on the road to a new American international role which had been evolving since 1945 as Truman's realism replaced Rooseveltian schemes and dreams and presidential advisers elaborated a global policy for the times. Robert Lovett, who succeeded Acheson as under secretary of state that summer, would sum up: 'Our choice was ...

between becoming a little island of prosperity and democracy, or fulfilling the second corollary of our foreign policy and supporting an atmosphere in which our international exchanges of goods and services is possible and in which our future would be most secure.' Yet, while Washington's eyes were fixed on Europe, other parts of the world were burning or in ethnic conflict and hot wars that the administration found it possible to overlook, but which also demonstrated just how complex the globe was.[28]

# CHAPTER SIX

# VOLCANO OF HIDDEN FIRES

## I: BIG CALENDARS AND MASS KILLINGS

As the administration embarked on the Marshall Plan, the British government commissioned a 48-year-old English lawyer to try to get to grips with the intricacies of dividing up the Raj. Cyril Radcliffe, an outstanding member of the Bar in London who had never been to India, went to work in the intense summer heat in a village in the grounds of the Viceroy's palace in Delhi, guarded by a very tall Indian soldier with pistols and a bandolier. Four months after the Attlee government announced its intention of leaving the Raj, Mountbatten had abruptly announced on 4 June that independence for India and Pakistan would come into effect on 15 August. It was now up to the scholarly Radcliffe, who had been Britain's director of information during the world war, to rule on borders between the two nations running for 3,800 miles through densely inter-mixed communities, especially in Punjab and Bengal. He had forty days to complete his findings on the partition between Hindus, Muslims and Sikhs; they were deemed so sensitive that the viceroy decided to keep them secret until after independence had been declared.

The two men did not hit it off. The viceroy found the visitor 'upright, proud, frigid, haughty' and one of Radcliffe's staff recalled how Edwina Mountbatten 'had to use all her adroitness to keep conversation between them on an even keel'. The short time allowed to Radcliffe made a proper study of the mass of conflicting claims impossible and reflected Britain's attitude that the interests of the people of the Raj should not be allowed to interfere with its haste to leave. The intransigence of local officials from the different communities ruled out sensible compromises: 'It is not that I do not wish to make modifications, but I dare not,' Radcliffe quoted a Muslim representative as telling him. 'If I did, my life would be in instant danger.'[1]

British rule was tightly stretched and the government was unable to afford to spend any more on security. Ministers in London could be under no illusion about the danger of conflagration. Attlee saw the subcontinent as 'a volcano of hidden fires'. Archibald Wavell, the viceroy since 1943, had warned Nehru and Gandhi that 'India is on the verge of civil war'. Considerable authority had been devolved to an Executive Council, with Nehru as prime minister, Patel running home affairs, Jinnah's deputy, Liaquat Ali Khan, in charge of finance and the Sikh leader, Baldev Singh, holding the defence portfolio. But relations were testy; Congress leaders resented the finance minister's questioning of their proposals while his budget put financial pressure on their business backers.

Regarding him as insufficiently supportive and prone to take too much notice of Muslim concerns, Congress intrigued in 1946–7 for the replacement of Wavell, a former Allied commander in North Africa whose military service dated back to the Boer War. A stenographer in his secretariat was passing his correspondence to the party. The viceroy grew increasingly exasperated; when Gandhi and Nehru accused him of giving way to Muslim blackmail, he shot back, 'For God's sake, who are you to talk of blackmail?' He drew up a secret proposal entitled 'Breakdown Plan' for withdrawal; privately, he entitled it 'Operation Madhouse'. Attlee responded that it was 'unreasonable' to 'expect us to envisage failure' and decided to name a new viceroy, Lord Louis Francis Albert Victor Nicholas 'Dickie' Mountbatten.[2]

The 47-year-old cousin of King George wanted no delay. His energy amazed observers – he would watch a film till midnight and then work through the early hours, ringing aides at 2.30 a.m. to call for reports by breakfast time. Giant calendars were distributed to his staff to remind them of the countdown to 15 August, a page for each day stating how long there was to go to the transfer of power.[3]

Communal violence had been on the rise since what became

known as the Great Killing of Calcutta the previous August. Two-thirds of the city's inhabitants were Hindus, but the surrounding province of Bengal was 56 per cent Muslim. The provincial government was headed by a deeply dubious politician, H. S. Suhrawardy, who had been the responsible minister during the Bengal famine of 1943, which killed an estimated 3 million people. Wavell regarded him 'as one of the most inefficient, conceited and crooked politicians in India, which is saying a good deal'. The British journalist and author Leonard Mosley described the Muslim political boss as somebody 'who believes that no politician need ever be out of office once his strong-arm squads have gained control of the polling booths ... He loved money, champagne, Polish blondes and dancing the tango in nightclubs and was reputed to have made a fortune during the War. He loved Calcutta, including its filthy, festering slums.'[4]

Suhrawardy sought initially to work with Congress, but by the summer of 1946 had moved away from communal conciliation to throw himself behind a Direct Action Day declared by the Muslim League on 16 August 1946. Though saying the occasion should be peaceful, Jinnah stoked passions by references to Congress as a 'Fascist Grand Council' and warned, 'We have forged a pistol and are in a position to use it.' Suhrawardy declared that 'bloodshed and disorder are not necessarily evil in themselves if resorted to for a noble cause.' Leaflets invoked a holy jihad. Preachers stirred up congregations at prayers. A Muslim civic leader warned infidels that their doom was approaching.[5]

Addressing a march through the city on Action Day, Suhrawardy appeared to tell the Muslim crowd that police would not intervene against it. Fighting between Hindus, Muslims and Sikhs broke out in poor districts and the docks. Thugs led mobs in gang warfare under cover of religious differences. Sikhs in armoured vehicles rode about slashing victims with swords. Hundreds of Hindus were slaughtered in a cotton mill. The streets were littered with mutilated corpses. In one place, four lorries stood piled with bodies oozing blood and brains. The Bengal governor, Sir Frederick Burrows, called the killings as bad as anything he had seen in the First World War.[6]

The violence lasted for ten days before 45,000 British, Indian and Sikh troops gained control. The official death toll was 4,000, though

Wavell put it at 5,000 with 16,000 hurt, and other estimates went up to 6,000. Three-quarters of the dead were Muslims. 'This is not a riot,' the main newspaper of Calcutta, *The Statesman*, wrote. 'It needs a word from mediaeval history, a fury. Yet fury sounds spontaneous and there must have been some deliberation and organization to set this fury on its way.'[7]

The idea that it was simply inconceivable for Hindus and Muslims to live together gained force, and was exploited by political leaders on both sides. Jinnah warned that the Great Killing showed what Muslims should expect from a Hindu-majority undivided India. In Hindu histories of the time, it went down as the moment when the League showed its true nature and Muslims revealed themselves as bent on killing those of different religions. At a meeting later in the month, Wavell found Nehru 'full of hate against the League' and Gandhi 'malevolent'. 'If India wants bloodbath she shall have it,' Gandhi was reported to have said.[8]

Two months after the Great Killing, reports spread of Muslims attacking Hindu landlords and raping and abducting women in the watery Bengal delta region of Noakhali. Organised by a local politician and former military men, the assaults sent thousands fleeing. Estimates of how many died range from a few hundred to thousands. Troops soon restored order. Gandhi went to the region for four months to spread a message of peace, though, dispirited by the contrast between his teachings and the violent reality around him, he was heard to mutter, 'What can I do?' Reporters flocked to capture the image of the lone prophet of peace with his shaven head, large pocket watch, dhoti and long bamboo staff rising at 4 a.m. and walking barefoot along the dykes around flooded paddy fields to visit villages, trying to stay in Muslim homes but being refused. The reporting did not mention the entourage that followed him, the police guards, the microphone system set up when he travelled by train so that he could address people at stations, or the helpers who carried a commode, a wash basin, his books and syringes for enemas.[9]

News of the killings in Noakhali provoked mass rallies and attacks on Muslims in neighbouring Bihar, a backward region of 36 million people. Visiting the state, Nehru was told the death toll was three hundred, but it was certainly very much greater; some estimates put it as high as 7,000 while the League claimed 30,000. The number of people who fled, many of them to Muslim areas of Punjab, may have reached almost half a million. The prime minister raced around trying to quieten the mobs; in one place, he wrestled a man to the ground and choked him to unconsciousness. Still, he blamed the trouble on the 'unpatriotic and highly objectionable attitude' of the League in pressing for a separate nation of Pakistan. Muslim leaders noted that the attackers seemed to benefit from immunity from the authorities. Jinnah became even more embittered and suspicious of Congress, authorising the expansion of the League's paramilitary National Guards to more than 60,000.[10]

As the violence moved westwards, 350 people were killed and there was extensive destruction of property in a district close to Delhi orchestrated by the extremist Hindus of the RSS organisation. But it was further west in Punjab, the 'land of the five rivers' covering 172,000 square miles on the border between India and Pakistan, that the greatest tragedy of partition gathered pace.

Just over half of the province's 28 million inhabitants were Muslims, 30 per cent Hindus and 15 per cent Sikhs with a small scattering of Christians and other religions. Its interlaced communities included the Sikh holy place of Amritsar with its Golden Temple and the great city of Lahore, once a major Mughal centre and a cultural hub for the north of the Raj. It was a major agricultural area with an intricate system of canals to irrigate the fields. Its Muslim, Hindu and Sikh population often lived close together in the 52,000 villages and forty-three princely states.

Since the 1930s, Punjab had been run by a coalition government under the Unionist Party, a cross-communal movement led by big Muslim landlords and rich Hindu farmers. The administration concentrated on dealing with local problems and avoiding communal clashes. But, for provincial elections in 1946, the League staged a big campaign calling on Muslims to support the struggle for Pakistan in the name of Islam. Religious festivals rallied support. Activists held meetings in mosques, telling Muslims they faced a simple choice – were they true believers or infidel traitors? Party membership rose as workers, professionals and businessmen heeded the call of 'Islam in danger' and feared the prospect of living under a Hindu Raj. The League won seventy-nine seats in the 175-member provincial assembly, a big increase in strength but not enough to form a government.[11]

Dreaming of absorbing the whole of the Punjab into Pakistan, Jinnah was on bad terms with the Unionist premier, Malik Khizar Hayat Tiwana, who supported the unity of the subcontinent. When the British governor asked Khizar to form a new administration after the election, the League leader was outraged at the idea of a largely non-Muslim government in a Muslim-majority province led by a Muslim who opposed the establishment of a Muslim state which would absorb Punjab. A campaign of mass opposition was launched. National Guards stocked arms and made ready for action. 'You are heading for disaster,' Jinnah barked at the end of an acrimonious telephone conversation with Khizar. 'I wish you Godspeed.'[12]

Khizar banned both the Guards and the RSS at the start of 1947. League officials were imprisoned, but continued to orchestrate their followers from behind bars while Hindu newspapers printed incitements to violence and encouraged Sikhs to prepare for action after the spring harvest. After a League member was killed by a flying brick during a demonstration, a big protest procession marched through Lahore. Muslim leaders ordered all businesses to close down in mourning. When the demonstrators found the High Court was still sitting, they stormed the building and replaced the Union Jack flying on the roof with their flag before attacking Hindu and Sikh policemen. In reprisal, the RSS launched a bombing campaign.

The prime minister resigned at the beginning of March, and the governor, Evan Jenkins, entrusted the formation of a new government to the provincial League chief, the Nawab of Mandot, a faithful follower of Jinnah. Non-Muslims grew increasingly alarmed. Waving his sword over his head, the Sikh leader, Master Tara Singh,[13] proclaimed 'Death to Pakistan' and quoted a traditional verse looking forward to the liquidation of his people's enemies.

'Position in Lahore has deteriorated with many dead and widespread incendiarism,' Jenkins reported. He declared emergency powers and worked on a provincial partition plan though he thought this would ruin the province. On 5 March, the Holi spring festival,

Muslims killed hundreds of people in Amritsar and mobs swept over Sikh and Hindu villages. In one, Thoha Khalsa near Rawalpindi, a Muslim resident who was sixteen at the time recalled:

> We were living peacefully. People were very friendly and co-operative. Sikhs were very rich people as they ran the shops and had thriving businesses. They often helped us on money matters.
>
> On the evening of March 6, Muslim mobs from the surrounding villages entered Thoha Khalsa and gave ultimatums to the Sikhs to convert ... the actual clashes started the next morning, when their numbers swelled to some thousands.
>
> After resisting for three days, the Sikhs hoisted white flags. They had only acted in self-defence. But when defeat and dishonour was imminent, Sikh men started killing their own women ... For six days, the whole village witnessed orchestrated looting and killing. While their men fought, the Sikh women started gathering near a well around the garden. It was almost after noon, and I watched from nearby with two of my friends. Some of the women held their children in their arms. They sobbed desperately as they jumped into the well. In about half an hour, the well was full of bodies. I went closer and realised that those who were on top were trying to submerge their heads. No space remained. A few came up and jumped again. It was a terrible scene. They were determined to die rather than sacrifice their honour. In one week, all the remaining Sikhs and Hindus were compelled to leave their native place.[14]

Tara Singh urged Sikhs to set up jathas, the fighting units that had conquered the Punjab in the eighteenth century. Armed with guns, grenades, spears, axes, staves and kirpan sabres, they organised attacks on military lines under commanders dressed in blue. The groups, sometimes several hundred strong, advanced on villages, the first wave firing at Muslims who usually climbed to the roofs of their homes, beating drums and gongs to summon help. The second wave threw grenades. The third went in for the kill with kirpans and spears. Finally, older men, many with long white beards, ran forward with torches. Mounted out-riders with sabres cut down anybody who got away. Sometimes women and children joined in.[15]

Justifying the attacks, Tara Singh said Sikhs had been the particular target of Muslim violence, some being 'burned alive as if mere faggots' together with 'crimes against their womenfolk which even the vilest wretch would feel ashamed to narrate'. Nehru suspected the Sikhs of wanting to provoke war between India and Pakistan in the hope of creating a state of their own. Jenkins put the death toll at more than 2,000 a considerable under-estimate.[16]

The administration of the province broke down. 'When it was made clear that we were to leave on 15 August, we became politically impotent,' the governor recalled. The Boundary Force set up by the British at the last moment to try to keep the peace was far too small and poorly equipped to carry out its task, which was complicated by not being able to conduct pursuit across the border of princely states where gangs of killers sought refuge. 'Why talk of compromise when there is no basis for compromise?' Jinnah asked an American diplomat.[17]

## II: LEADERS AT ODDS

By the summer of 1948, the leaders in the two future states had shown themselves incapable of controlling events, their impotence heightened by mutual disdain underscored by personal rivalry stretching back to the 1930s. For Jinnah, a separate entity was essential to secure the safety of Muslims; for Nehru, Pakistan was 'a mediaeval state with an impossible theocratic concept [which] should never have been created', 'mad and foolish and fantastic and criminal'. Jinnah dismissed Nehru as 'vain, loquacious, unbalanced, unpractical', a 'Peter Pan ... who never learns or unlearns anything ... a busybody ... who must poke his nose into everything except minding his own business'. For Nehru, Jinnah was 'an obvious example of the utter lack of a civilized mind' who showed 'opportunism raised to the nth degree, pomposity and filthy language', 'vulgarity ... total incomprehension of the events & forces that are shaping the world'. But his distaste for the other man was such that he thought it 'better to have Pakistan or almost anything if only to keep Jinnah away and not allow his muddled and arrogant head [to be] interfering continually in India's progress'. For his part, Gandhi characterised the founder of Pakistan as 'an evil genius [who] believes he is a prophet ... He has cast a spell over the Muslim who is a simple-minded man.'[18]

Both men had trained as lawyers in London, Jinnah being far the more successful. Born into a middle-class Muslim family in the port city of Karachi, the future Great Leader had gone to London at the age of sixteen as an apprentice with a shipping and trading company which he soon quit to study for the Bar. Returning home as the only Muslim barrister in Bombay, he won fame and earned a lot of money in high-profile cases, showing enormous self-confidence and remorseless logic. A political career followed as he became a leading advocate of a joint Muslim–Hindu campaign for independence, steering through the Lucknow Pact of 1916 laying out the path to co-operation between the two communities and dismissing Muslim fears of Hindu domination as 'a bogey' designed to prevent 'the co-operation and unity which are essential to self-government'. His opposition to British rule was unyielding. When the government in London sent out a commission in 1929 as part of a review of India policy, he refused to meet it because it had no native members.[19]

A constitutionalist and an elitist to the tips of his elegantly manicured fingertips, Jinnah opposed Gandhi's policy of mass non-co-operation with the British. He distrusted the way the mahatma was stirring up popular opinion by marches against the salt tax and other British exactions. But his opposition was swamped within Congress as the seer gained sway over the movement; at a session in Nagpur, he was shouted down when speaking against passive resistance to British rule. He nurtured something close to hatred towards Congress, his secretary recalled. As Gandhi himself noted, 'Jinnah and other Muslim leaders were once members of Congress. They left it because they felt the pinch of Hindu patronising.'[20]

Blocked in his political career, Jinnah went back to London, where he was again successful as a lawyer, living in a large house in Hampstead, a tall, elegant figure in perfectly cut suits, silk ties and two-tone shoes. His second wife, the daughter of a prominent Parsee who had left home against her family's wishes at the age of eighteen to be with him, grew increasingly erratic, and died in 1929, after which Jinnah was cared for by his forbidding sister. His political ambition was fuelled by anger when he heard that Nehru, twelve years his junior, had described him as 'finished', and he found his cause in a pamphlet published in 1933 that proposed the creation of 'a land of the pure' combining Punjab (P), the region bordering on Afghanistan (A), Kashmir (K), the coastal province of Sind (S) and the deserts and mountains of Baluchistan (TAN) to make Pakistan. Despite this, he revived the idea of a Hindu–Muslim alliance to press for independence when he returned to the subcontinent in 1934, taking up residence with his sister in a white mansion in Bombay. But Gandhi had promoted Nehru to lead Congress, and the younger man was adamant that the fight for freedom was to be conducted by his party alone. 'Congress is the country, and the country is Congress,' he said.[21]

Born in 1889 in India's second oldest city of Allahabad, Jawaharlal Nehru had grown up in luxury in a family of Kashmiri Brahmin origin. His father, an early member of Congress, was a highly successful lawyer with a casual attitude to religion. He was the first Indian to move into the previously all-European district of the city, equipping his mansion with electric light, a tennis court, a swimming pool and two kitchens, one for Indian food and one for European cuisine. There was wine and cigars, many servants and the city's first motor car. The patriarch believed in working with the British until he adopted Gandhian principles in the 1930s.

Nehru was educated at home by a British tutor and then sent to the English public school, Harrow, but he did not distinguish himself academically either there or at Trinity College at Cambridge, where he studied science and frequently asked his father for more money to pursue his social life. His academic star was equally dim when he turned to the law at the Inner Temple in London before returning home to an arranged marriage with another Kashmiri Brahmin in a lavish ceremony in 1916. Their daughter, Indira, was born the following year; a son born in 1924 lived for one week.

Nehru recorded that on his return from Britain, he had 'a sense of the utter insipidity of life'. That changed when he took up the cause of Indian independence after the British massacre of nearly four hundred unarmed demonstrators at Amritsar in 1919. He joined Gandhi's non-co-operation movement, going into the countryside for his first glimpse of rural India to witness the population 'naked, starving, crushed and utterly miserable' and was horrified by the lack of concern or knowledge among educated Indians about the 'the degradation and overwhelming poverty'.[22]

Rather than being deterred by the scale of poverty, he was, he wrote later, 'full of excitement and optimism' as he joined peaceful protests that landed him in jail several times. Independence and alleviation of the suffering of the masses became entwined. 'Politics irritates me,' Nehru said in 1945. What counted was 'the freedom of India and ... of ending poverty by rapid economic advancement. It is a politics of revolutionary changes.'[23]

A good speaker, he soon became Gandhi's principal apprentice, more malleable than the militant left-wing Bengali radical Subhas Bose and better able to incarnate spirituality than Vallabhbhai Patel, the principal organiser of the support base embracing family, caste and grassroots organisations, institutions that permeated Hindu society and businesses that provided funding.

Congress conservatives were confident they could control the young man's Social Democratic leanings. Indeed, his advocacy of economic policies to protect Indian industry and agriculture were welcome to big business and landlords. His charisma and love of playing to crowds provided a populist edge to lay on top of Patel's hard-nosed party management and he was useful in checking the rise of the forceful Bose, who regarded non-violence as weakness, espoused socialism and wanted to stir up workers and peasants, setting up a paramilitary force with himself as commanding officer in breeches and leather boots.[24]

Nehru's whole life was bound up with the movement. He was, judged the leading businessman G. D. Birla of the Marwari clan in Calcutta, 'a typical English democrat ... giving expression to his ideology, but he realizes that action is impossible and does not press for it'. At a Congress conference in 1936, the tycoon noted with satisfaction that 'Jawaharlalji's speech was thrown into the waste paper basket' while Gandhi ensured that no new left-wing commitments were made. 'He frets and fumes, he storms, he is often in a rage,' Patel commented. 'But after all he is a great sport and so quickly regains his balance and sees that there is no unpleasantness left behind.' His taste for modernisation clashed with Gandhi's reactionary vision of India, but he remained loyal to the mahatma who picked him to lead the party, describing him as 'truthful beyond suspicion ... a knight *sans peur et sans reproche*'.[25]

Nehru's status and his rejection of the Muslim League was enhanced by a successful campaign at elections in eleven provinces in 1937 for which only 10 per cent of the population was entitled to vote and the lists of candidates were divided between Hindus and Muslims as Britain practised divide and rule tactics. He carved out a reputation abroad as the polished, cultivated Congress ambassador to the world, a committed Nationalist with the veneer of an English gentleman. Travelling in Europe, he was elected to the executive council of the Brussels-based League against Imperialism. On these trips, he visited his wife who was being treated for tuberculosis from which she died in a Swiss sanatorium in 1936.

An anonymous article that year in Calcutta's *Modern Review* warned that Nehru

> has all the makings of a dictator in him – vast popularity, a strong will directed to a well-defined purpose, energy, pride, organizational capacity, ability, hardness, and, with all his love of the crowd, an intolerance of others and a certain contempt for the weak and the inefficient ... in this revolutionary epoch Caesarism is always at the door, and is it not possible that Jawaharlal might fancy himself as a Caesar? Therein lies danger for Jawaharlal and for India.

It emerged later that Nehru himself was the author.

Under a strategy engineered by Patel, Congress followed the election success by assuming responsibilities offered by the British at provincial level. Its expanding reach widened the division between Muslims and Hindus. Despite the claim to stand for all Indians and that 'the tremendous and fundamental fact of India is her essential unity', the party's membership was 97 per cent Hindu. At Muslim League congress in 1937, at which he appeared in the traditional sherwani coat of a Muslim nobleman, Jinnah promoted a resolution calling for an independent India to consist of a federation of democratic states to protect the rights and interests of the Muslims.

Insisting that an independent state must have a strong central government, Patel and the Congress high command would have nothing to do with such ideas. Jinnah, however, was equally insistent that the 60 million Muslims were bound to be second-class citizens in a nation dominated by more than 300 million Hindus and led by Congress.[26]

There will always be debate about whether Jinnah really wanted a separate nation or was simply pushing the idea as a negotiating tactic to achieve a loose federal system that would allow for Muslim self-rule in a single country. The probability is that he would have preferred the second but was pushed to the first by the wall of opposition and rejection from Congress and his unfulfilled personal political ambition. The result was that, from 1937, the secular, whisky-sipping believer in the law and due process adopted his other persona as leader of a separatist movement whose binding force was religion. 'Hindus and the Muslims belong to two different religions, philosophies, social customs and literature,' the one-time advocate of unity declared. 'It is quite clear that Hindus and Muslims derive their inspiration from different sources of history. They have different epics, different heroes and different episodes.' The League's aim, he said, could be summed up by the name Pakistan.[27]

Some leading Muslim politicians and big landowners in Bengal, Punjab and the North-West Frontier did not go along with this, fearing that the League would undermine their privileges and unsure of their position in a new nation. Jinnah's record as a secularist who drank alcohol and rarely visited a mosque led to him being distrusted by the main religious party, the Jamaat-e-Islami, which preferred the pursuit of a more perfect Muslim society in a united India and a supra-national Islamic brotherhood to the creation of a new nation. But the Second World War boosted his position when he offered co-operation to the British in contrast to a 'Quit India' campaign launched by Congress.[28]

The protests led to almost all the Congress leadership being arrested; Nehru kept the police waiting while he ate a breakfast of cornflakes, eggs and bacon, toast and coffee. He was sentenced to four years' imprisonment in an old fort with other party leaders; they were left free to confer on policy between reading, sleeping, gardening and playing cards. Gandhi was kept in the Aga Khan's palace in Poona where three goats were brought in to provide milk. In contrast, Jinnah urged League members to join the British forces – many came from Muslim areas of the Punjab and the north-west. The League took over posts in provincial government and the legislative council to fill the vacuum left by Congress. Jinnah later admitted that the war was a blessing in disguise while, for the colonial power, it presented a fresh chance to implement divide and rule.[29]

If Muslims thought they were a nation, they were a nation, Jinnah argued. Pakistan was life or death issue, he insisted. When the British government, under American pressure for decolonisation, sent a mission to India in 1942, it got nowhere with Congress, but the League was pleased when its leader, Stafford Cripps, spoke at a press conference of provinces forming 'a separate union' with exchanges of population.[30]

The war buttressed the cause of independence which returning troops saw as the natural reward for the service of 2 million men in Africa, the Middle East and Burma, where they suffered 36,000 deaths, as many wounded and twice as many taken prisoner. Resentment of imperial rule was heightened by the callous way the British had reacted to the famine that killed some 3 million people in Bengal in 1943, and by the racism Indian soldiers often suffered from their officers. The treatment of the 11,000 prisoners from an army raised by Subhas Bose to fight alongside the Japanese against the British in 1944 also aroused controversy, since many saw them as misguided patriots rather than traitors. Three members of the 35,000-strong force – a Hindu, a Muslim and a Sikh – were put on trial; Nehru took out his barrister's robes to plead for their defence. Convicted of treason, they were ordered to be deported. This set off riots in which twenty-two people died and three hundred were injured after police opened fire. The sentences were quashed and the three men became heroes at celebratory events.

Ratings at a naval signals school in Bombay mutinied, accusing their British commanding officer of habitually calling them 'coolie bastards', 'black buggers' and 'jungli Indians', as well as demanding higher pay and faster demobilization. They were joined by a corvette lying offshore which trained its guns on a yacht club for officers. Twenty thousand ratings across the country joined in the protest.

A strike brought the city's docks to a halt. The British ended the protest with a show of force, including a mortar bombardment, but imperial rule looked increasingly fragile amid soaring food prices and outbreaks of cholera.[31]

For elections in 1946, at which 28 per cent of the adult population was entitled to vote, the League enrolled the backing of preachers in mosques. Its activists made speeches after prayers and linked the creation of Pakistan to Islam and the Koran. Jinnah was shown in giant portraits held aloft by supporters wearing traditional robes riding a white horse and brandishing a scimitar. At meetings, he sat in solitary splendour like a prophet in traditional garb. The League's main newspaper, *Dawn*, printed quotations from the Koran on its front page. The flag adopted for the new nation had clear Islamic connotations.

The appeal to religion, as well as better management, swept the League to 89 per cent of the Muslim vote. It took nearly all the seats for Muslims in Bengal and seventy-five of the eighty-six in Punjab, also doing well in Bombay, Madras, Assam, United Provinces and Bihar. Jinnah got British agreement that his party alone would select Muslim members of the Executive Council. The time for action had come, *Dawn* proclaimed.

III: HEADING FOR THE EXIT

Mountbatten demonstrated where his sympathies lay by inviting Nehru to stay at the vice-regal lodge in the hill station of Simla in May 1947. He felt that he would get nowhere if he did not have a strong relationship with the Indian party in contrast to the frosty feelings between him and Jinnah, who, at one point, raged that the viceroy had 'virtually become a Hindu' and that, given his wife's closeness to Nehru, he 'fully expected to see her wearing a caste mark in the centre of her forehead'. On the contrary, his relations with Nehru were warm, the Indian politician delighting in showing his hosts his ability to walk fast backwards uphill.[32]

Since his arrival in India in March 1947, the viceroy had been casting around for a plan to cover Britain's withdrawal. His solution, 'Operation Balkan', proposed that the eleven provinces of the

Raj should decide their own fate, with Punjab and Bengal free to divide on Hindu–Muslim lines if they wanted to. After sending it to London, he handed a copy to Nehru over late-night drinks in his study at Simla. When he read it in his room, the visitor was highly alarmed, seeing the plan as a recipe for anarchy and war. In the morning, he wrote a 'Personal & Secret note' to the viceroy, dismissing it as 'a picture of fragmentation and conflict and disorder'.[33]

Desperate for a way out, the viceroy turned to a leading civil servant, Vapal Pangunni Menon, who was in Simla though not invited to stay at the lodge. A remarkable figure from a poor family who had worked as a clerk in a tobacco firm and in a goldmine, Menon rose to the top of the Reforms Office and became a leading constitutional expert. A conservative Hindu closely linked to Patel, he was hailed by Mountbatten as 'my brilliant Indian Staff Officer' whose ideas 'very greatly influenced ... my own negotiation development'.[34]

At high speed, Menon typed up a plan on which he had been working for months. This provided for two central governments, one for India and the other for Pakistan, both taking constitutional authority and assuming Dominion status within the Commonwealth to assuage British feelings. The provincial assemblies of Punjab and Bengal would vote on whether they wanted division. Mountbatten sent telegrams to Delhi and London cancelling Operation Balkan, and flew home to confirm the new plan with the government. Menon kept Patel informed throughout – the politician, he recorded, 'was delighted by the turn of events'.[35]

Running the Home Affairs Department in Delhi, the Congress strongman instructed that Muslim officials 'should be got rid of as soon as possible'. They were thrown out of their offices and forced to work on tables in tents or in the open air under the trees. Muslims were banned from working on the Indian railway as a security risk. The division of the army between the two countries was rushed through. Congress leaders agreed that India would be better off without Muslim-majority areas since Pakistan was bound to collapse and be obliged to beg to return to a united nation. Jinnah complained that the new state he would head was a 'moth-eaten' entity which its larger neighbour was intent on destroying.[36]

Communal violence spread across the Gurgaon plain outside

Delhi and Muslims huddled into camps which Mountbatten's chief of staff, Hastings Ismay, compared to 'Belsen – without the gas chambers'. Volunteer militias headed from Delhi to the Punjab; one had an elephant. Fires raged in Lahore. Amritsar was under a curfew, its markets closed by rioting, looting and arson. There was fresh unrest in Calcutta while, on the North-West Frontier, the Red Shirts movement called for an independent Pashtun state. 'There is a civil war on and you are doing nothing to stop it,' Patel told the viceroy.[37]

# CHAPTER SEVEN

# BATTLE FOR PALESTINE

## I: CALL IN THE UN

If Britain was managing to get out of India and Pakistan without itself becoming the target of violence, the same was far from the case in its other retreat, from Palestine with its population of 600,000 Jews and 1.2 million Arabs. The Attlee government had announced in February 1947 its decision to seek the advice of the United Nations on the future of the Mandate it had been handed by the League of Nations after the First World War. Partition would open the way for the creation of the state of which Jews had dreamed since the expulsion from the Temple almost 2,000 years earlier and, in more codified form, since Theodor Herzl's formulation of Zionism at the end of the nineteenth century embodying a spiritual desire to revive a very long heritage in what has been termed a 'regenerative transformation'. But Arab insistence on the territorial integrity of Palestine meant the two communities would inevitably come to blows, bringing the probable intervention of regional states and another mass population displacement.[1]

By the summer of 1947, any prospect of co-operation between Jews and Arabs was out of the question. Jews were not employed in Arab enterprises and very few Arabs worked for Jewish undertakings except for seasonal labourers in citrus groves. Government offices and the oil refinery in Haifa were virtually the only places where the two communities met as co-workers. The 'Iron Wall' theory of the Zionist Revisionist leader Vladimir Jabotinsky foreseeing inevitable conflict and calling for the creation of a sovereign state with sufficient military power to impose itself on the territory came to reflect reality on the ground. Agents of the fiercely anti-Jewish Grand Mufti of Jerusalem killed the rare Arabs who co-operated with Jews.

Demonstrations against Zionism had been organised at the end of 1945 in Egypt, Syria, Iraq and Lebanon. In Libya, a hundred Jews were killed. In Alexandria, synagogues and Jewish property were attacked. The leader of the dominant left-leaning Mapai party, David Ben-Gurion, had written in the 1920s of Jews and Arabs living in 'harmony and friendship', but now saw a zero-sum conflict in which his people faced extermination if they did not construct adequate defences. Though he led the Zionist left in fierce debates against the Revisionists and viewed the creation of a Jewish state as a step-by-step process, by 1937 Ben-Gurion envisaged expelling Palestinians to make room for Jews and 'a Galilee free from Arab population'.[2]

The UN formed a Special Committee (UNSCOP) with representatives of eleven nations chosen for their neutrality and excluding permanent members of the Security Council. A Swedish judge was appointed to chair the group, which arrived in Palestine on 15 June 1947 and visited Jerusalem, Haifa, Tel Aviv, Acre, Hebron and other centres as well as settlements in the Negev desert. At Jewish kibbutzes, its members were impressed by progress in agriculture and irrigation; at one farm on the shore of the Dead Sea, they saw how damming of winter rains and a water pipeline enabled the cultivation of tomatoes, dates, olives and pomegranates in salty soil that had never previously supported crops. The Jewish Agency made sure settlers were on hand who spoke the languages of committee members.

While the Jews co-operated with the UN group, the Arab Higher Committee boycotted the proceedings, claiming to represent all Palestinians. It called a one-day protest strike as the mission arrived and banned Arabs from attending the UN sessions or conferring with its members. Representatives of Arab states met the delegation in Beirut, but took a hard line on using force to prevent any form of Jewish state. Representatives of Arab states in Washington submitted a memorandum to UNSCOP with similar wording, and the Grand Mufti spoke fiercely against partition from exile in Cairo where he formed a militia for Palestine.[3]

King Abdullah of Transjordan, who ruled with British support, lamented the Committee's attitude. The Hashemite monarch, known in Britain's Foreign Office as 'Bevin's little king', met the delegation in Amman – one of the UN team described him as 'a small, poised handsome man who spoke in a most musical cadence'. While stating publicly that his kingdom 'will take, as it always has, the same stand taken by the other Arab countries on the Palestinian problem' and that the rights of the Arab population must be protected, he was ready to work secretly with the Zionists to expand his realm across the river.[4]

It was thirty years since the government in London had addressed the Balfour Declaration to Baron Walter Rothschild for transmission to the Zionist Federation of Great Britain and Ireland. It stated that 'His Majesty's Government view with favour the establishment in Palestine of a national home for the Jewish people, and will use their best endeavours to facilitate the achievement of this object, it being clearly understood that nothing shall be done which may prejudice the civil and religious rights of existing non-Jewish communities in Palestine, or the rights and political status enjoyed by Jews in any other country.' From the start, the Declaration had been regarded by the Arabs as contradicting undertakings they had received on nationhood to encourage them to side with the Allies in the First World War – the British said that these had not covered Palestine.

The carving up of the Ottoman Empire by Britain and France led to a wasps' nest of ambiguities in the region and especially over the 'twice promised Holy Land'. The 'non-Jewish communities' referred to in the 1917 Declaration made up 90 per cent of the inhabitants of Palestine at the time and owned even more of the land. But Britain thought support of Jewish ambitions for a national home was useful to help maintain its influence in the region while the Zionist leader, Chaim Weizmann, who had been instrumental in the 1917 statement, found it useful to 'hitch a lift with the British empire'.[5]

Given the preponderance of Arab inhabitants, Jewish immigration was essential to constitute the Zionist state. The movement of people from Europe boosted by the rise of the Nazis amounted to more than 300,000 between the start of the Mandate and the end of the

Second World War, taking the Jews to a third of the population as they bought and farmed land more productively than ever before. At the same time, Palestinian society became steadily more urbanised, weakening the traditional feudal structure and producing a more radicalised working class.[6]

The Mandate frustrated British administrators. Ronald Soars, who became governor of Jerusalem and Judaea in 1921, reflected that 'two hours of Arab grievances drive me into the synagogue while, after an intensive course of Zionist propaganda, I am prepared to embrace Islam'. Tension between the communities boiled over in 1929 when Palestinian attacks killed 133 Jews, followed in the next decade by an Arab revolt for independence, sharpened by rising Jewish immigration and economic influence, the impact of the Great Slump and conflicts over land and religion. Britain's repression was relentless, with torture, collective punishment, destruction of property and crops as well as aerial bombardments. Official figures set the death toll at more than 3,000 but the historian Rashid Khalidi puts it at 5,000 with 10,000 wounded, 5,000 detained and thousands more exiled or forced to flee – amounting in all to 10 per cent of the adult male Palestinian population. Estimates of Jewish deaths ranged from ninety-one to several hundred.[7]

Village-level Palestinian units did most of the fighting independently of any overall command, and local leaders would use that experience fighting against the creation of a Zionist state. The Jewish paramilitary organisation, the Haganah, with 10,000 men and 40,000 reservists, worked with the Mandate authorities to help quell the revolt. It found an unexpected ally in the charismatic and eccentric British soldier, Orde Wingate. A believer in ruthless unorthodox warfare and a passionate convert to Zionism, he organised counter-guerrilla Special Night Squads of Jewish fighters uniformed in blue police shirts, linen trousers and Australian bush hats. His attachment to the Jewish cause led to him being recalled home, leaving a legacy in those who fought under him including the future commander Moshe Dayan, who said Wingate had 'taught us everything we know'.[8]

British policy at the end of the 1930s veered between acceptance of partition between Jews and Palestinians and then the conclusion that 'the political, administrative and financial difficulties involved in the proposal to create independent Arab and Jewish States inside Palestine are so great that this solution of the problem is impracticable'. Immigration was restricted to 75,000 over five years. Placating Arab states that might side with the Nazis was seen a major objective – as one official put it, 'The Jews would be on our side in any case ... Would the independent Arab nations adopt the same attitude?'[9]

The Zionist position hardened in May 1942, at a conference of six hundred delegates from eighteen countries convened by Ben-Gurion at the Biltmore Hotel in New York City. The meeting adopted a resolution that Palestine 'shall be constituted as a Jewish Commonwealth as part of the structure of the new democratic world'. The Mandate could not ensure the establishment of a Jewish national home, it added. The desired immigration target was set at 2 million. Ben-Gurion declared the goal as 'not a Jewish state in Palestine but Palestine as a Jewish state'.[10]

The conference cemented Ben-Gurion's position, but his relations with Weizmann deteriorated steadily as they operated in different spheres: while the younger man worked on the spot from Zionist headquarters in Tel Aviv, the patriarch communed with statesmen and intellectuals in London and New York, dismissing the Biltmore Programme as 'just a resolution like the hundred and one resolutions usually passed at great meetings'. The clash reflected the very different characters of the old-school Zionist who believed that links with the British could bring about the promise of the Balfour Declaration and the hard-charging, power-hungry local leader with strong left-wing beliefs. Weizmann was seventy-three and in declining health; Ben-Gurion, twelve years his junior and leader of the majority Mapai party in Jewish Palestine, was a force of nature in full flow.[11]

After an explosive exchange of letters during which the younger man told Weizmann he was 'no longer linked to him', the leading New York rabbi, Stephen Wise, convened a peace meeting between the two. But Ben-Gurion used it to accuse the Zionist elder of running the movement as a personal court, and of being capable of doing 'incalculable harm, when he acts alone'; if he did not change, he should resign. Replying heatedly, Weizmann spoke of 'political assassination'.[12]. The half-dozen other participants in the meeting were stunned by the argument. One left with tears streaming down his cheeks.

Wise wrote to Weizmann asking him to withdraw his accusations of 'untruths' and 'delusions' against Ben-Gurion, which he refused to do, charging that the other man 'suffered from some mental aberrations' and was 'in a constant state of jitters [and] nervous tension' which turned meetings into 'the gyrations of an insane asylum'. In a letter to the Jewish Executive, he compared his critic to 'a petty dictator ... humourless, thin-lipped, morally stunted, fanatical and stubborn, apparently frustrated in some ambition ... a small man nursing his grievance introspectively'. Recalling the struggle against Jabotinsky and the Revisionist Zionists, he pointed to the danger of 'a new and more dangerous brand of Fascism under the leadership of Ben-Gurion'.[13]

Ben-Gurion flew home and, when he had given an account of the quarrel, the Jewish Agency invited Weizmann to visit Palestine. He declined, saying London was where the centre of Zionist activity lay. But a World Zionist Organization conference in late 1946 demonstrated to him the way the movement had changed as he recorded the 'dreadful experience' of seeing how, after the Holocaust, so many old, familiar faces from Europe were missing and how delegates from Palestine and the US now dominated. The meeting rejected his proposal for negotiations with the British and did not renew his mandate as the organisation's president. Ben-Gurion took over on an acting basis which lasted for ten years.

The hardening of the movement's stance reflected a more radical mood among Zionists in Palestine. As future prime minister Golda Meir (then known by her married name of Meyerson) recalled: 'We kept hearing the argument "The Arabs can create so much trouble, therefore you have to give in." So in the end we decided, very well *we'll* create trouble, therefore you have to give in.' The Jewish Agency's Haganah strike forces blew up railway lines and bridges and attacked the oil refinery in Haifa. In the autumn and winter of 1945–6, twenty-seven British soldiers, officials and police were killed and 164 wounded. Police headquarters in Jerusalem was bombed along with two coastguard stations, military installations and an airstrip where twelve planes were destroyed. A raid on a train netted £35,000 in cash on board.[14]

The British sealed off the Agency buildings, imposed curfews and arrested 3,000 Jews; Ben-Gurion escaped detention because he was in Paris, where he met Ho Chi Minh who offered him an alternative national home for the Jews in central Vietnam, an offer that was politely declined. The Lehi/Stern Gang group[15] shot dead Lord Moyne, British minister of state for the Middle East in Cairo, which set off a Haganah campaign to bring freelance Zionist extremists under control. Dubbed the 'Sezon' (Hunting Season), it was aimed more against the Irgun underground movement led by Menachem Begin than the smaller Lehi. The Jewish Agency gave the British the names of seven hundred Irgun members, most of whom were arrested, though its chief remained at large in hiding.

Begin, born in Belarus, had arrived in Palestine in 1942 after serving in the Polish army fighting alongside the Allies. Adopting the mantle left by Jabotinsky, he saw violence as the way to political power with direct action acting as a catalyst. But, treasuring Jewish unity, he refused to fight back against the Hunting Season and emerged with his status enhanced, even if he was denounced by the Zionist establishment as 'crazy and strange'.

The Irgun military commander Amichai Paglin masterminded the bombing in 1946 of the King David Hotel in Jerusalem, the city's most stylish spot and seat of the Mandatory government; ninety-one people were killed. The Lehi mounted attacks on British personnel and property and a letter bomb campaign against members of the Attlee government by a ring operating in Paris, which also hatched unfulfilled plans to poison London's water supply with cholera bacteria and to blow up a British destroyer. An ex-servicemen's club in London was bombed. An agent left devices in the women's lavatory of the Colonial Office after saying she had to enter it to fix her stockings; they did not go off, and she was later caught wearing a corset fitted with dynamite. Other members of the group set off two suitcases packed with high explosives outside the British embassy in Rome, blowing out the façade.[16]

British security forces in Palestine retreated into heavily guarded compounds known as 'Bevingrads'. The chief of the imperial general staff, Bernard Montgomery, called for harsher action, accusing the government of appeasement. The new high commissioner, Alan Cunningham, privately described the psychology of Jews as 'quite abnormal and unresponsive to rational treatment'. The anti-Semitic British commander, Evelyn 'Bubbles' Barker, banned British troops from frequenting Jewish restaurants as a way of 'punishing the Jews in a way the race dislikes as much as any, by striking at their pockets'. In letters to his Lebanese mistress he hoped that the Arabs would kill 'more bloody Jews ... loathsome people'.[17]

The War Office set up secret underground units to combat Jewish terrorism with a veteran of the Special Air Service (SAS), Roy Farran, sent in to lead operations. In one of his first sorties, he chased and caught a young man putting up Lehi posters. Farran, whose presence on the scene was established by his trilby hat, which fell from his head in the chase, confessed that he had killed the prisoner during interrogation. He then fled to Syria, returned to Palestine as the UNSCOP team arrived, was arrested, escaped and finally gave himself up and was put on trial. The case collapsed for lack of evidence.

In the last year of the world war, the British Labour national executive had proposed that the solution to the Palestine problem lay in encouraging the Arabs to move out with generous compensation as Jews moved in. 'The Arabs have many wide territories of their own; they must not claim to exclude the Jews from this small area of Palestine less than half the size of Wales,' it added. Strongly pro-Zionist voices in the Attlee government included the left-wing leader, Aneurin Bevan. But British policy from 1945 set London increasingly at odds with the Zionists.[18]

For the foreign secretary, Palestine was a growing irritant as he sought to buttress a position for his country in the Middle East. He thought the best outcome was a unitary bi-national state with autonomous areas. The creation of a Jewish nation, he warned, might prove a constant factor of unrest in the Middle East and jeopardise British interests. Bevin feared that leftist Zionists would side with the Soviet Union; at one point, he even believed that Moscow had mustered a Jewish army in Odessa ready to invade the Middle East. Jewish rights should be protected, he agreed, but with measures 'to prevent a real flooding of the country by immigrants'. 'The consequences of permanently alienating the Arabs would be so serious that partition on this ground alone must be regarded as a desperate remedy,' he told the Cabinet.[19]

The foreign secretary was egged on by the Arabist civil servant Harold Beeley, who believed that Britain must not support the creation of a Jewish state because of the damage this would do to regional relations and access to oil. The numbers seemed to back up Beeley. Arab states covered 1.18 million square miles with more than 14 million people compared to the 10,000 square miles and 1.65 million people in Palestine, only some 600,000 of whom were Jews. Britain had already concluded a partnership agreement with Transjordan. Negotiations were under way to retain control of the Suez Canal and maintain air bases and oil concessions in Iraq.

Bevin's biographer Alan Bullock denies he was anti-Semitic; but Christopher Mayhew, his parliamentary under secretary, recalled him as 'passionately unshakeably anti-Zionist', holding that the movement was 'basically racialist, that it was inevitably welded to violence and terror, that it demanded far more from the Arabs than they could or should be expected to accept peacefully'. The foreign secretary 'tended to attribute the character of his Zionist enemies to the Jewish people as a whole', added Mayhew, who, as the pressure rose, wrote in his diary of the 'anti-Semitism and detestation of Jews' of his boss. For the pro-Zionist Labour politician Richard Crossman, Jewish opposition to Bevin's plans 'tipped him into overt anti-Semitism' and 'the step from anti-Zionist to anti-Jew was instinctive'.[20]

## II: No place to go

By the start of 1947, the foreign secretary said he was 'at the end of his tether' over Palestine, which was tying down 100,000 troops amid the rising wave of terrorism. A paper he submitted to Cabinet in mid-January painted a bleak picture. The Jews would reject the unitary independent state sought by the Arabs while the Arabs would reject the partition on, which the Zionists insisted and which he thought would be unacceptable to the United Nations. Dalton, the pro-Zionist chancellor of the Exchequer, warned of the cost of hanging on which he judged to be 'of no real value from the strategic point of view – you cannot in any case have a secure base on top of a wasps' nest – and it is exposing our young men, for no good purpose, to abominable experiences and is breeding anti-Semitism at a most shocking speed'. Henry Gurney, the tough-minded chief secretary to the British administration in Palestine, was scathing about his country's record: 'In the last 30 years, we have seen nothing but fluctuations of policy, hesitations or no policy at all,' he wrote in his diary. 'It is this continual surrender to pressure of one sort or another – American Jewry or Arab rebellion – that has made British policy in Palestine ... unintelligible and mistrusted by both sides.'[21]

When Britain brought Jews and Arabs together for a conference in London early in the year, the two delegations sat in separate rooms. Bevin presented a proposal for a four-year British trusteeship with limited Jewish immigration followed by independence if both sides could agree. As he finished speaking to the Zionists, a power cut blacked out the lights. With a heavy-handed attempt at wit, the foreign secretary said there would be no need for candles because the Israe*lites* were present. That did not go down well. Neither side took up Bevin's proposal. Two days before announcing the decision to withdraw from India, Britain turned to the UN, asking for advice on how the Mandate could be administered or amended.[22]

Zionist extremists were spurred to renewed action in the spring, their suspicions of the authorities fuelled by the involvement of British army deserters in Arab attacks. The Irgun blew up the British Officers' Club in Jerusalem, killing a dozen people. The British oil refinery at Haifa was attacked; the blaze took three weeks to put out. The head of the police Special Branch in the city was shot dead as he parked his car. A mine derailed a train, killing eight aboard. An Irgun attack in May blew a hole in the wall of the crusader castle in Acre, which was now a jail; hundreds of prisoners escaped, mainly Arabs but also Jews accused of terrorist offences.

Ben-Gurion called a meeting of Jewish commanders to assess their preparations for war with the Arabs. Could the new state for which they were working repel an invasion, he asked? The basis was there, the military chief Yigal Allon replied, but more people and equipment were needed: they had 10,000 rifles, 2,000 sub machine guns and nearly 800 mortars but no cannons, heavy machine guns, anti-tank weapons, naval ships or aircraft. Talk of withstanding regular Arab armies seemed 'lunacy', future army general and prime minister Yitzhak Rabin recalled.[23]

The Arabs were, however, seriously split both within Palestine and on the broader canvas of the Middle East. Locally, the Husseini Palestinian clan, led by the Grand Mufti of Jerusalem, Mohammed Amin al-Husseini, with his private militia, were the most militant against the British while the rival Nashashibi family was more ready to entertain compromises. Palestinian nationalism was, in any case, suspect to Arab rulers. Across the Jordan, King Abdullah negotiated secretly with the Zionists and accepted payment from them in pursuit of his scheme for a unified Jordan and Palestine under his rule with separate Arab and Jewish areas to complement his broader scheme to extend his influence over Iraq and Syria and restore the power of the Hashemite dynasty. He was at loggerheads with the Saudi rulers who had forced his father to flee from the land of Mecca in the mid-1920s. His visceral dislike of the Grand Mufti was reciprocated, not so much for his wartime collaboration with the Nazis as because of their contending aims in Palestine, while the rulers in Baghdad and Damascus were suspicious of the king's ambitions to create a Greater Syria under his leadership. In dealing with the Western powers, the Arabs were seriously off-message. As Christopher Mayhew recalled, they were

> separated by the totally different culture and procedures and politics of their countries and ours. If they did make some kind of submission in writing, it would be wrongly worded, the arguments would be all wrong and it would be sent to the wrong person. On the other hand, there were Zionists so close to the Cabinet that there had been instances where Cabinet members actually telephoned the result of a Cabinet meeting straight to the Zionist concerned.[24]

Like other Western foreign ministries, the State Department contained a powerful contingent of Arabists who warned against destabilising existing relations by supporting the Zionist cause.

Marshall listened to the experts on his staff and disapproved of what many saw as an electoral streak in support for Zionism from the White House ahead of the presidential election. As Truman put it later, the Department's thinking was that 'Great Britain has maintained her position in the area by cultivating the Arabs; now that she seems no longer able to hold this position, the United States must take over, and it must be done by exactly the same formula; if the Arabs are antagonized they will go over to the Soviet camp.'[25] Defence Secretary James Forrestal was concerned about oil supplies and thought sheer numbers meant the Arabs were bound to submerge the Jews.

The Zionists faced an additional hurdle in the form of an American arms embargo on the region. This hit them hardest since the Arab nations got most of their arms from the British who did not stop supplies. A complex covert Zionist weapons procurement network was set up in the US, but was expensive and hazardous to operate. A safer conduit was provided by European countries, notably Czechoslovakia, ready to supply weapons for hard cash.

Truman's close adviser Clark Clifford backed the creation of a Jewish state. White House aide David Niles, a strong Zionist, told American Jewish leaders – in Yiddish – that Truman accepted there would be a new state. The lobby in the US, led by Rabbi Wise and the accomplished Russian-born Nahum Goldmann, was highly organised. In contrast, the often-elderly Arab diplomats seemed detached and unbending, unable to recognise the impact of the Holocaust on opinion and showing aversion to Jews, whom the 73-year-old Syrian UN delegate insisted were of Mongolian origin and, as he declared in one speech, 'had always sought the extermination of men, women, children and animals'.[26]

The president's stance would be crucial and, as on some other sensitive issues, his attitude melded principle – support for the creation of state, which he felt was deserved, especially after the Holocaust – and political advantage – Jewish backing for his re-election. 'Everyone else who's been dragged from his country has someplace to go back to,' he said on one occasion. 'But the Jews have no place to go.' When Forrestal talked of the importance of energy supplies from Arab states, Truman replied that he would handle the issue in the light of justice, not oil. But when Arab diplomats pressed their case, his reported response was, 'I'm sorry, gentlemen, but I have to answer to hundreds of thousands who are anxious for the success of Zionism; I do not have hundreds of thousands of Arabs among my constituents.'[27]

His call for Britain to admit 100,000 immigrants following a report he had commissioned which highlighted the desire of European Jews to go to Palestine could be seen either as a humanitarian gesture or as sop to the Jewish electorate – or both. It did no good, however. The Attlee government, which had not been told of the statement in advance, was highly annoyed and the prime minister fired off an unusually blunt personal message to the White House before announcing that the restrictions of the 1939 White Paper would remain in force.

Transatlantic relations on the issue did not improve. In one outburst, Bevin said the Americans were calling for increased quotas only because 'they did not want too many Jews in New York'. Truman was outraged. When the foreign secretary next visited the US, dockers refused to handle his luggage and he was pelted with eggs and booed at a baseball match. Ben Hecht's stridently emotional Zionist play, *A Flag is Born*, was a sellout on Broadway; one character, a Holocaust survivor played by Marlon Brando, joins the struggle after being urged by three Zionist fighters to join the cause to 'battle the English, the sly and powerful English ... in a new Jewish language, the language of guns. We fling no more prayers or tears at the world. We fling bullets. We fling barrages ... We promise to wrest our homeland out of the British claws.'[28]

Bevin and his colleagues were also annoyed by French backing for the Zionists. The Socialist interior minister, Édouard Depreux, freed an arms consignment ordered by Jews for Palestine when it was intercepted by police in south-west France and ensured that visa checks on refugees were minimal. Blum called the King David Hotel bombing 'nothing but a desperate form of revolt'. Sartre joined the French branch of the League for a Free Palestine set up under a pseudonym by a senior Irgun member who used it to get to know Bidault and other politicians anxious to make amends for anti-Semitic persecution during the Occupation.[29]

CHAPTER EIGHT

# ANNIHILATE THE ENEMY

## I: Towards the turning point

As June drew to a close and the summer heat rose, the vanguard of a Communist army of 100,000 men crossed the Yellow River in Central China. Their commander was a 54-year-old veteran of more than three decades of war, the 'One-Eyed Dragon', Liu Bocheng. The political commissar was the diminutive Deng Xiaoping. The crossing of the silt-laden waterway known as 'China's Sorrow' for its destructive flooding took place in the cradle of the country's civilisation. The objective was to sweep across the vast Central Plains, breaking away from the guerrilla tactics employed by the Red Army since the Long March of 1934–5 in favour of frontal warfare, which Liu had learned at the Frunze military academy in Moscow.

Long an advocate of military force as the essential complement to mass political movement, Mao Zedong had laid out a strategy of annihilating the enemy as straightforward as it was uncompromising. A government offensive had forced the Communist leadership out of its long-time base at Yan'an in northern China in March. The Nationalists made much of the event – Chiang Kai-shek flew in and walked briskly through the town, visiting Mao's house, while photographers took pictures of the building that had housed the 'Local Products Company' – the cover name for the Communists' opium enterprise. But the capture of the town made little difference to the course of the war and diverted troops from more important operations. The leadership escaped after being tipped off by a spy in the government army, taking with it weapons, medicines, radio equipment and printing presses.

A series of offensives the previous autumn by superior Nationalist forces had reduced Communist-held territory by a quarter and its population from 150 to 100 million. Mao took this, and the loss of Yan'an, as calling for a bold new move by the PLA, a display of military strength to score a propaganda coup and restore confidence. Such a move, he felt, was needed 'under even the most problematic circumstances ... when we are facing difficult times'.[1]

So he turned to Liu Bocheng, whose career had taken him from being a brigand to fighting in the Kuomintang ranks[2] and then joining the PLA at its foundation in 1927 before going to Moscow to learn military tactics, siding with Mao during the Long March and commanding troops against the Japanese. The advance across the Yellow River was an enormous military gamble given the resources that the Nationalists could bring to bear, but Liu and Deng walked into a promising revolutionary situation in which peasants flocked to join them and their troops were able to live off the land. The region had been devastated by earlier wars and heavy flooding after Chiang had the course of the Yellow River diverted for a second time to try to block his adversaries, submerging five hundred villages and driving 100,000 people from their homes. Initial Communist victories led government regiments to retreat into the shelter of towns, leaving the way free for a 600-mile march southwards to a long-established base in the Dabie Mountains at the junction of Hubei, Henan and Anhui provinces.[3]

Government forces were in low spirits, their regional commanders unwilling to risk battle – Chiang would sack all of them by the end of the summer. Still the advance came at heavy cost. Half Liu's men were killed or otherwise put out of action. They lost much of their heavy artillery. But when they reached Dabie, they threatened the Nationalist heartland along the Yangtze River. Mao hailed the operation as the turning point in the war while his comrades held it up as fresh evidence of his military genius.[4]

Other PLA armies advanced in Manchuria in the north-east while, in the big province of Shandong, Communist forces under the short, stout Chen Yi, a beret-wearing twenty-year PLA veteran who wrote poetry, scored successes with a series of ambushes of government units. Chiang poured in reinforcements, which forced the enemy to fall back into the mountains with heavy losses. But the survivors marched westwards to link up with Liu's army and trap government troops in a series of pincer movements. They cut a key east–west railway line, and opened up a corridor from the east to Communist positions deep inland.

Despite such advances, Mao thought the civil war would last for another five years or more. Even pessimists in Washington did not seriously entertain the prospect of a Communist victory. Stalin, for his part, was happy to see China divided. But the nature of war was changing in China, opening the way to a swifter resolution of the power struggle that had been going on since the late 1920s. Both sides departed from the tradition of fighting battles in which the defeated adversary was allowed to leave the field with substantial forces intact so that the winner would be allowed to do the same if things turned out differently in future. Chiang sought to crush the Communists in big set pieces with superior manpower and weaponry. For Mao, the prime aim was to wipe out as many enemy troops as possible. His military creed declared:

First strike isolated and scattered groups of the enemy, and later strike concentrated, powerful groups.

First take small and middle-sized towns and cities and the countryside, and later take big cities.

The major objective is the annihilation of the enemy fighting strength, and not the holding or taking of cities and places. The holding or taking of cities and places is the result of the annihilation of the enemy's fighting strength, which often has to be repeated many times before they can finally be held or taken.

In every battle concentrate absolutely superior force – double treble, quadruple, and sometimes even five or six times those of the enemy – to encircle the enemy on all sides, and strive for his annihilation, with none escaping from the net ... we are inferior taken as a whole – numerically speaking – but our absolute superiority in every section and every specific campaign guarantees the victory of each campaign. As time goes by, we will become superior taken as a whole, until the enemy is totally destroyed.[5]

The Communists were aided by a series of weaknesses in their adversary. Chiang's efforts to control battlefield tactics from afar did not help. Nor did the way he prized loyalty over competence among subordinates. The factionalism of the Kuomintang was a constant problem. Government armies were notoriously corrupt and predatory, earning the hostility of the population. Their numerical superiority over the PLA was made less effective by the inclusion, alongside well-trained central army units, of a ragbag of soldiers of doubtful motivation or ability, some taken in from warlord troops, some forced into battle, roped together. The way commanders sought the safety of towns left the countryside to the Communists who could then isolate them by ripping up the tracks of the railways on which they depended for supplies and reinforcements.

The generalissimo's Kuomintang (KMT) regime had punched well below its weight throughout its twenty years. Based in the Middle and Lower Yangtze Region, it lacked roots elsewhere in China and had been unable to institute a system of effective governance since proclaiming itself the national government in Nanjing in 1927 after defeating some of the warlords who had ruled the country since the fall of the empire in 1912. It survived by forging alliances with the remaining militarists but was still faced with recurrent regional revolts. Its economic base was weak and was further weakened by its dependence on printing money. The high-minded precepts of the regime's father figure, Sun Yat-sen, were undermined by its authoritarian, factionalised, corrupt nature as Chiang Kai-shek developed what has been aptly termed 'Confucian Fascism'.[6]

Its first decade had been marked by repeated convulsions that added to its endemic weaknesses in aborting the promise of a national rebirth. In 1931, Japan took over Manchuria and expanded its influence in northern China. Despite repeated encirclement campaigns, the main group of Communists escaped from their base in the south-east on the Long March to reach Yan'an in the north in 1935. The following year, Chiang was kidnapped by a former warlord and forced into a united front with his domestic adversaries against the Japanese. The full-scale war that broke out in 1937 brought a string of disasters and forced the Nationalists to sit it out from 1938 in their capital of Chongqing behind the Yangtze Gorges until the United States won the struggle in Asia.

## II: Between the superpowers

To make matters worse, the Nationalists knew that, as during the world war, China ranked second to Europe among Washington's priorities; it had received some 2 per cent of the assistance granted by the US between 1941 and 1945 and now there was no Marshall Plan for Asia. As an extremely proud man, Chiang Kai-shek had no liking for allies from across the Pacific who sought to influence his policy and get him to implement reforms that would weaken his control. He had been on extremely bad terms with Joseph 'Vinegar Joe' Stilwell, whom Roosevelt sent in to be his chief of staff and reform the army, both of which the generalissimo was bound to oppose since the army was his power base and he was, in any case, not a man who took advice.

The Stilwell mission was a prime example of the wrong man being sent on the wrong mission at the wrong time; the acerbic American referred to the generalissimo in his diary as the 'peanut' and the 'rattlesnake'. After one meeting, he noted in his diary that the Chinese leader was a 'crazy little bastard with that hickory nut he uses for a head [harbouring] cockeyed reasons and idiotic tactical and strategic conceptions. He is impossible!' The Nationalist leader's distaste for Americans seems to have gone even further; after the Republican Wendell Willkie, who fell for his wife on a mission to Chongqing, left the room following a meeting, he told aides to open the windows to let out 'the smell of dead meat'.[7]

After the war, Chiang faced a more elevated form of pressure from George Marshall, whom Truman sent to China to try to bring the two sides together, warning that 'China disunited and torn by civil strife could not be considered realistically as a proper place for American assistance'. Though Washington's provision of weapons and transport planes to the Nationalists to ferry troops compromised its ability to act as an honest broker, the wartime chief of staff brokered a ceasefire and agreement on troop reductions. The KMT promised political reform. Russia started to withdraw from positions it had occupied in Manchuria after its last-minute entry into the war against Japan, but only after having grabbed substantial booty including modern Japanese plant and equipment – and after Communist troops had entered the region. The American envoy went to meet Mao; they watched a film together in the evening sitting on reclining chairs with rugs pulled up against the winter cold. But both sides in China were out to buy time to build up their forces. Pledges to reduce troop numbers meant nothing and political reform was not on their agendas while the Red Army handed the Communists in Manchuria many millions of rifles, plus machine guns, artillery and seven hundred vehicles, including tanks.[8]

By the spring of 1946, the civil war was spreading across Manchuria and the generalissimo had become bitter towards the American envoy, accusing him of acting aggressively, 'his face and voice ... harsh'. Marshall imposed another ceasefire by threatening to stop providing American planes for government use in Manchuria; Chiang acceded and halted the advance in Manchuria by government troops, which had reached the outskirts of the main Communist-held city of Harbin. He later regarded this as 'a most grievous mistake'.

Still, the Communists attacked Marshall as an imperialist allied with their adversary while Chiang said the American did not care whether 'China survives or perishes'. At a final meeting, the envoy warned the generalissimo that the Communists could not be defeated militarily; Chiang forecast victory in ten months. In January 1947, the visitor flew home to become secretary of state, attributing his failure to 'almost overwhelming suspicion' aggravated by KMT reactionaries and 'dyed in the wool Communists'. Meeting a group of editors, Truman described the situation in China as 'very, very bad'.[9]

A report by the US joint chiefs of staff at the beginning of June recommended an immediate increase in military aid to prevent the collapse of the government and ensure that China 'be free from Soviet domination'. But the State Department expressed doubts that the Nationalists could hold their own even if they got more help on top of the $700 million already extended. Preventing a Communist victory, it added, would mean direct American involvement, probably including control of the military and of administration of the country, something Truman and Marshall were not prepared to contemplate and Chiang would resist. It was a dilemma that would continue through the following two years.[10]

Mao was, meanwhile, having trouble with the other great power. He was keen on boosting his status in the international Communist movement and getting more Soviet aid. The way to meet those aims, he reasoned, was to visit Moscow. Stalin was not enthusiastic.

At the Yalta summit, the Soviet leader had accepted Chiang as China's national leader. Though helping Communist armies in Manchuria after Japan's defeat and providing military, technical and medical assistance to the PLA in the north-east, he cautioned Mao to limit his ambitions, which he regarded as too aggressive and headstrong. In keeping with his classification of China as a country in an early stage of revolution, he favoured a 'national revolutionary-democratic government, rather than a Communist one' after a defeat of the Kuomintang.

He had delayed the departure of the Red Army from Manchuria until government troops were ready to move in, and suggested that the Communists should adopt the 'French way' of disbanding or incorporating resistance forces into the national army. Though the USSR subsequently made major arms deliveries to the Chinese colleagues, Stalin's aim was to have a weak neighbour to the east in which he could play off the contending parties rather than facing a single determined movement such as that led by the chairman (or by a victorious Chiang who might put right the failings of his regime after gaining supremacy).[11]

That attitude went back a long way. Chinese Communists under Moscow's orders and egged on by a Comintern adviser had opposed Mao before the Long March. The Soviet leader had ordered the leaders of the Chinese party to abandon their plan to try Chiang before a people's court when he was kidnapped in 1936. After Germany withdrew its aid to the Nationalists the following year, the USSR became their biggest source of assistance. During the war with Japan, the Comintern envoy sat on the sidelines in Yan'an, reduced to lamenting the ideological errors of Chinese comrades while noting how they raised funds from opium and refrained from engaging the enemy to keep their powder dry for the civil war to come. In 1945, Moscow signed a Treaty of Friendship and Alliance with the Nanjing government; Molotov stated that moral and military support would be 'entirely given to the National Government as the central government of China'.[12]

While not disputing Moscow's leadership of international Communism, Mao took only as much notice of instructions from the Kremlin as he wanted to. After Stalin's death, he told the Soviet ambassador in Beijing that, in the later part of the civil war, the dictator 'made wrong estimates of the situation in China and of the possibilities of revolutionary development. He continued to believe more in the Kuomintang's strength than in the Communist Party ... When our troops were winning victories, Stalin insisted on striking a peace with Chiang, because he doubted the strength of the Chinese revolution.'[13]

In 1947, the chairman was developing his thesis of an 'Intermediate Zone' between the US and the USSR, which was home to the 'principal contradictions' in international affairs. For the moment, he entertained hopes of maintaining relations with Washington, but his main diplomatic objective that summer was to get invited to Moscow to take his place in the global Communist pantheon with the public approbation of the grand chief in the Kremlin. Stalin had to react carefully. He did not want to build up a leader who might upset his China strategy. But he could not simply reject the leader of the biggest military struggle against imperialism. So he responded that, in view of forthcoming military operations and the prospect that Mao's absence would have an adverse effect, 'we consider it appropriate to postpone [the] trip temporarily'.[14]

## III: MANCHURIAN COCKPIT

Important as the Central Plains and Shandong were, the main focus of the civil war in the summer of 1947 was on Manchuria. It was the most developed area of the country. Home of the last imperial dynasty, the Manchu Qing, the 600,000-square-mile region had a population of 40 million and major industrialised cities in Harbin, Changchun and the north-eastern capital of Mukden.[15] After Japan's crushing victory over China in the war of 1894–5, the rising Asian power had developed the north-east, notably with the South Manchurian Railway Company, with 700 miles of track and 13,000 staff, schools and hospitals, public offices, storage depots and coal mines.

As the Kuomintang regime formed a national government in 1927, the region was under warlord rule and outside its control.

The Japanese Kwantung Army based there became a law to itself, blowing up the warlord Zhang Zuolin after deciding he was insufficiently pliant, and then taking over the region when his morphine-addicted son proved no more biddable, proclaiming the puppet state of Manchukuo under the last Qing emperor, Puyi. Resistance by semi-bandit gangs was squashed. Roads were built and railway extended. Mining developed. Immigrants from Japan were given land seized from local owners. The army nurtured a 'national defence state', which ran the economy and industry using Chinese and Manchurians as slave labour. By the late 1930s, Manchukuo's steel output exceeded that of Japan.

When the Red Army crossed the border in August 1945, after the USSR joined the war in Asia, it met hardly any resistance. Puyi was captured and flown to Russia. The Soviet commanders handed some areas to the Chinese Communists, but kept them out of others. The main concern of the victors was loot – an estimated $2 billion worth of assets were shipped back to the USSR, including railway trains and whole factories. For Mao and his colleagues, the north-east's proximity to the major Communist power made it the obvious place in which to fight the Nationalists, whose home base was far away in central China.

But Chiang was fixated on taking over the region, to the extent that he allowed this to distort his overall war game and soak up many of his best troops as he refused to withdraw in the face of Communist advances. If the enemy took the north-east, he reflected, 'it would mean the beginning of another world catastrophe'. He built up troop levels using American air transport, but was doomed by his heavy-handed tactics and pervasive suspicion of others, in this case the Manchurians.

Chiang preferred to send commanders from elsewhere at the head of troops with no local links or knowledge. He failed to appeal to local sentiment. His armies were concentrated in the cities and the government's few local allies were the urban elite and big landowners who had taken over property after Japan's defeat. Government forces, many from the south, 'conduct themselves as conquerors not as fellow countrymen and have imposed a "carpet-bag" regime of unbridled exploitation', a US observer noted.[16]

In contrast, by persuasion and force, the Communists put down roots in the countryside, offering land reform and recruiting both Manchurians and members of the ethnic minorities that dotted the region. But they, too, faced a number of challenges. Their capital of Harbin was the first big city that they had administered and the initial period there was a time of repression as class enemies were executed and expropriated. In rural areas, they struggled against bandit groups which had emerged in the vacuum left by Japan's defeat, members of secret societies, and former members of militias set up by the occupation authorities.[17]

Imposing order in uncertain times became an important element in the Communist message. Policies were overseen by a five-man civilian leadership in which one of Mao's protégés, the forceful Gao Gang, played a major political role.[18] Communist areas became laboratories for the development of policies later implemented elsewhere. Land reform, regarded by the party as 'the mother of all other work', was engineered from above, rather than stemming from a spontaneous peasant movement. Its severity was modulated according to the circumstances and it was not allowed to get in the way of creating a supply base for the PLA.

In this as in other respects, organisational strength and discipline were vital to Communist success, along with the ability to mobilise armed forces at short notice through a network of militia, local defence units, women's brigades and peasant associations. Villagers were required to provide labour to erect defence works, help the wounded and act as the eyes and ears in watching for enemy activity. Cadres coordinated the overall effort and organised body searches of landlords suspected of hiding gold, jewels or other valuables about their person.[19]

Under the regional commander, Lin Biao, the PLA developed its expertise in applying in Manchuria methods learned largely from Russian advisers and the example of the Red Army as it moved from guerrilla warfare to conventional tactics. It had Japanese weapons passed on by the Russians and then American arms captured from the Nationalists, who rarely bothered to destroy them before defeat or flight. Though resented by some of his colleagues, Lin was a powerful figure, with a strong direct link to Mao and a political position as Communist first secretary for the Northeast Bureau.[20]

A Nationalist build-up forced the PLA to pull back in early 1947, but it launched a counter-offensive in May and, by mid-June, had surged forward, threatening major cities and sabotaging railway tracks. A state of siege was declared in the regional capital of Mukden after the railway line was cut. To the south, the province of Jilin was encircled and government troops were forced to abandon the strategic Liaodong Peninsula.[21]

However, Chiang sent in reinforcements that beat back the Communists from the big cities and restored some rail communications. In the industrial centre of Changchun, they withstood a Communist attack using tanks manned by captured Japanese. Still, with Mao's enthusiastic backing, Lin Biao organised an advance on the town of Siping, commanding the southern route into Manchuria. But, under orders from Chiang that the place must not be lost, aircraft and heavy artillery pounded the attackers in twenty-three days of house-to-house fighting that ended when the PLA withdrew at the end of the month after losing half its men.[22]

When torrential rains brought an end to fifty days of fighting in the north-east, the government had lost half the territory it had controlled at the start of the year, along with forty towns. Its casualties were around 100,000 men; some units were down to a fraction of their original strength. As the Communist hold on the countryside tightened, landlords and their associates crowded into government-held cities adding to the flood of refugees and creating a homeless, underfed mass in the absence of any welfare assistance.

Though they had also suffered big losses, the PLA had shown considerable mobility and demonstrated greater discipline. By using local recruits (or conscripts) it could bring numerically superior forces to bear and took large quantities of supplies abandoned by retreating government forces. For popular support, it traded on the unpopularity of the adversary. Strategically, it was now able to link their bases in the north and south of Manchuria as Lin Biao prepared a fresh offensive.

## IV: DESPAIR, DECADENCE AND RECTIFICATION

After the devastation of eight years of war, Nationalist China was in a desperate state, to which the government had no answer. Mao reckoned that it had lost three-quarters of a million men since 1945 while the Communist casualties totalled 300,000. However distorted those numbers might have been, there could be no doubt that the tide of war had shifted. It was not just a matter of battles won and lost.[23]

Though designated by Roosevelt as one of the 'four policemen' of the post-war world, the country was increasingly dysfunctional as the defeat of Japan was followed by civil war. The reasons for discontent were manifold. The bureaucratic capitalism practised under Chiang fostered corruption as it linked business and the authorities, excluding those who did not earn or buy favour. Instead of being returned to the original owners, property seized by the Japanese was grabbed after 1945 by officials and well-connected carpetbaggers. Closure of plants for wartime production hit employment in inland areas. Collaborators with the invaders not only often escaped punishment but also sometimes seemed to prosper in the post-war world. The long war, with its puppet government in the eastern provinces, had hollowed out society while hopes that Japan's defeat would bring a new national start for China were dashed before they could take shape.

Labour discontent and wage demands escalated; there were 1,716 work stoppages and disputes in Shanghai in 1946 and 2,538 the following year. The government's agreement to wage increases linked to inflation alienated business owners at a time when they had extra costs from rising energy and transport prices, high interest rates, and suffered from stagnant demand. Then policy was reversed with a pay freeze but this proved ineffective. The tax system penalised companies and largely exempted personal incomes, including those of speculators. In the countryside, levies bore down on the population and local officials were stigmatised as 'blood suckers' for the way they extorted money.

The annual shortfall in the output of rice was put at 5 million tons. Military requisitioning of food made things worse – after troops grabbed rice in Sichuan province, the price trebled. In Shanghai, the cost of living rose by 54 per cent in May 1947, and the price of rice went up by a fifth in four days. Food riots broke out in cities. An American visitor to the big Central Yangtze River city of Hankow found the local civil and military administrations 'stagnant, corrupt and inept'.[24]

Production of coal, tin, cotton and soya beans was below that of the late 1930s. Government revenue, mainly from land taxes, was lower than during the war with Japan when the invaders occupied much of the country. But military expenditure was now higher than in the first half of the 1940s. The inefficient, rigid fiscal system could not cope with inflation. The government was unable to tap domestic resources for funding, and was obliged to draw on expensive foreign sources.[25]

As industrial production stalled, unemployment rose, reaching 20 per cent in the big southern port city of Canton and 30 per cent in the Nationalist capital of Nanjing. The currency more than halved in value against the dollar at one point. Export-import regulations were exploited by the Shanghai financiers, including the generalissimo's relatives in the Soong family, experts at insider trading who added to their fortune by playing the gold market.[26]

The regime was increasingly militarised and closed in on itself as right-wing cliques predominated. The KMT, founded at the start of the century by 'the Father of the Republic' Sun Yat-sen, had traditionally drawn support from the urban population, government employees and business circles with some backing from intellectuals. But now, as a leading political commentator noted, 'no one among these people has any positive feeling' towards the government and the KMT's 'tyrannical style' as bounding inflation and low pay impoverished civil servants who should have been the regime's bedrock and alienated intellectuals.[27]

In the key area of Manchuria, the regional administration was collapsing. Nationalist morale was low; some senior officers used planes that brought in reinforcements and supplies to evacuate themselves, their families and their belongings. Press gangs seized men from their homes or on the streets and forced them into army service – those who had the cash paid poorer men to take their places as conscripts. In Mukden in May, only eighty-two out of 4,000 men called to the recruiting stations turned up and thirty-nine were fit for service. The American Consul General in the city noted the 'jumpy nerves of military garrisons ... apathy, resentment and defeatism ... growing indignation over [the] disparity between officers' enrichment and soldier's low pay'.

Reporting on the 'extremely serious situation' after a visit to Manchuria, the US ambassador, John Leighton Stuart, told Washington, 'military officers of the Central Govt of all ranks are exploiting the populace, enriching themselves and consequently there are stirrings of separatist feelings ... discontent is rapidly becoming intensified'.[28]

In contrast, the Communists displayed steely resolve both on the battlefield and with a vicious 'rectification campaign' which imposed ideological conformity to instil discipline, along with the development of the paramount Mao personality cult. More than 10,000 had been killed in 1942–4 as the party's political police tightened its hold under the murderous enforcer, Kang Sheng. Young, progressively minded, idealistic Chinese who had trekked to the base were suspect for their urban, bourgeois background. The tenets of the May the Fourth modernisation movement of the 1920s, to which Mao had subscribed at the time, were swept away and replaced by the dogma of his thoughts to mould minds in a straitjacket of obedience and conformity to whatever was decreed from above.

The concept of the 'mass line' promulgated in 1943 provided the template for the revolution and revealed the leader's dictatorial bent. The party was told to establish the closest possible relationship with the people and learn from them, but the aim was to take the 'scattered and unsystematic ideas of the masses' and turn them into 'concentrated and systemic ideas'. Then cadres would 'go to the masses and propagate and explain these ideas until the masses embrace them as their own'. The party and its chiefs would determine what the people really wanted. Those who did not adopt this would have no place in the new China.[29]

The government had no answer. In late 1946, the National Assembly adopted a constitution to provide for a strong elected executive regime. But, when the KMT made it clear it intended to dominate, other parties staged a boycott. The unpopularity of the authorities was heightened by their ban on public gatherings and arrests of dissidents. On 1 June, following student protests and calls for an end to the civil war, police raided universities, hitting half a dozen colleges in Shanghai, detaining two hundred people in the wartime capital of Chongqing and killing three students in Wuhan on the Yangtze with dumdum bullets.

The State Council declared that, since 'nothing has succeeded in dissuading the Communists from staging a rebellion', national mobilisation was needed to achieve 'the acceleration of economic reconstruction, reform of local governments, mobilisation of manpower and resources, improvement of food and conscription administrations, maintenance of social order, the mitigation of the people's sufferings, protection of their basic rights, the practice of thrift, the increases of agricultural and industrial production'. To anybody who had followed the regime for the past two decades, it was hollow noise.[30]

~

## MEANWHILE

- Railwaymen, coal miners and bakers go on strike in France.
- The French government reveals that it held talks with the Viet Minh in the spring, but France refuses to recognise the Democratic Republic of Vietnam headed by Ho Chi Minh as entitled to speak for the whole country and insists on moving its forces wherever it wished. This makes agreement impossible.
- A new French commander arrives in Madagascar with four battalions of troops trained in anti-guerrilla warfare. Four warships and the air force join the battle against the rebels.
- US courts sentence three men to fines and prison for contempt of Congress in refusing to say if they belonged to the Communist Party; one of them, Francis Xavier Waldron, going under the name of Eugene Dennis, is the party's general secretary. Henry Wallace tells a crowd of 10,000 in Washington that the Truman Doctrine may drive Europeans into the Communist camp. Coal miners go on strike, cutting output in half.
- After a dialogue of the deaf following a ceasefire agreement at the start of the year, Sukarno accepts Dutch proposal for an interim federal government to cover the whole of Indonesia. Republican and Dutch delegates meet.
- Jomo Kenyatta becomes President of the Kenyan African Union; other groups fear his Kikuyu tribe so much that they prefer to stay outside and some support the British.

- Eva Perón tours Europe; in Switzerland, a protestor throws a tomato at her open car – it hits the Swiss foreign minister sitting beside her. She is received by the pope but Britain says King George VI will not see her if she visits London, so she does not. In Buenos Aires, her husband sends troops to clear up rotting garbage after dustmen strike. The leading police chiefs resign.
- A constituent assembly meets in Rangoon to draw up the constitution for an independent Burma. Strikes by labourers, dock workers and civil servants in Ceylon, which is also due for independence, lead to clashes in which police fire into crowds; the colonial authorities blame Communists.
- Troops from Outer Mongolia cross into China – the Chinese allege they are supported by bomber planes with Soviet markings.
- Douglas MacArthur says Japan's military potential has been destroyed for 'at least a century'. He advocates building up the country's exports so that it will earn enough to be able to import 15 per cent of its food. In Singapore, two Japanese officers are hanged for their part in the massacre of 5,000 women after the capture of the city in 1942.
- Pan-American Airlines launches the first round-the-world passenger service, taking ninety-three hours flying time to span the globe. The *Queen Elizabeth* liner registers a record by crossing the Atlantic in four days, eight hours and six minutes. Air crashes in Maryland and at New York kill ninety-five people.
- Cricketers Denis Compton and Bill Edrich set a Test match third wicket partnership record of 370 runs at Lord's.

# PART THREE

# JULY 1947

**ACTS**

*The deepening of the Cold War, Stalin calls
Czechoslovakia to heel; France and the Netherlands
fight for their colonies; the UN considers the future
of Palestine amid rising violence, the Exodus drama
and the hanging of two British sergeants by Zionist
extremists.*

**SCENES**

*The US, USSR, Prague; Madagascar; Vietnam;
Indonesia; Palestine.*

**CAST**

*Stalin, Molotov, Truman and Marshall, Gottwald,
Masaryk; Ho, Thierry d'Argenlieu; Sukarno;
Weizmann, Ben-Gurion.*

# CHAPTER NINE

# A MATTER OF FRIENDSHIP

## I: Confrontation by the Seine

In the weeks after George Marshall floated his plan for European recovery, a crucial question predominated; would the USSR and countries in its sphere be invited to join and, if invited, would they accept? In his speech, the secretary of state had said that 'any government that is willing to assist in the task of recovery will find full co-operation, I am sure, on the part of the United States Government'. But he then added: 'Any government which manoeuvers to block the recovery of other countries cannot expect help from us. Furthermore, governments, political parties or groups which seek to perpetuate human misery in order to profit therefrom politically or otherwise will encounter the opposition of the United States.'

Planners around him thought Moscow would refuse, and were quite happy with that prospect – their fear, as one put it, was that 'the Soviet bear might hug the Marshall Plan to death'. If Moscow joined the ERP, the State Department expected the Republican Congress to reject the whole programme. Will Clayton went to London to discuss with Bevin how to prevent Soviet participation without publicly shutting out Moscow. The US ambassador in Paris, Jefferson Caffery, reported that the French and British had told him they hoped the Soviets would refuse to co-operate and that they were ready go 'full steam ahead' if this happened. For the foreign secretary, the main priority was to reinforce Western unity and do whatever was possible to weaken the Kremlin's grip over its satellite nations. Britain and

France had made a start on the first target with their mutual defence pact signed at Dunkirk in March and Bevin saw the European Recovery Plan as 'the quickest way to break down the Iron Curtain' since the Kremlin would be unable to 'hold its satellites against the attraction of fundamental help towards economic revival'.[1]

The USSR and Eastern Europe could certainly do with assistance given the wartime destruction they had suffered. There was a precedent; during the conflict with Germany, the USSR received Western goods and arms to the tune of $11.3 billion. But the world had changed. Stalin was loath to enter into any system depending on the US and knew the danger that countries like Czechoslovakia and Poland might well open up to the West economically, potentially leading to political liberalisation. A report drawn up for him, Molotov and Beria by Soviet economist Evgenii Varga, depicted the ERP as an imperialist attempt to create an anti-Soviet bloc, but did not recommend rejection. He forecast that the American economy would go into a slump, which would give Moscow negotiating room to avoid unacceptable conditions such as Washington's desire to make its aid Continent-wide with a monitoring mechanism that it would oversee. The Soviet embassy in Washington also warned of US intentions, but also recommended participation to achieve a 'decisive role' in heading off the US politically and breaking the programme down into a country-by-country scheme which Moscow could control in its sphere of influence. Rejection by governments in East and Central Europe 'would have given grounds to accuse them of a lack of political independence', the veteran Bulgarian apparatchik Georgi Dimitrov observed.[2]

Deciding to test the waters, Stalin sent Molotov to Paris at the head of a hundred-strong team to meet Bevin and Bidault. Soviet embassies in Prague, Warsaw and Belgrade were told to inform the governments there that Moscow 'thought it desirable that the friendly allied countries, from their side, take the initiative in arranging their participation in the drawing up of such an economic programme'.

As the tripartite conference opened in intense summer heat in the Salon des Perroquets in the Quai d'Orsay by the Seine, Molotov's tone was 'unusually mild', in the words of a French diplomat. Bidault told Ambassador Caffery that his Soviet counterpart 'clearly does not wish this business to succeed. But on the other hand his hungry satellites are smacking their lips in expectation of getting some of your money. He is obviously embarrassed.' But he stuck to the Soviet hard line on Germany, insisting on reparations and that aid should not increase its industrial capacity. The British and French did not agree; nor did they go along with his suggestions that the plan should be turned into a series of bilateral agreements which each recipient orchestrate.[3]

Taking time out from the conference, Molotov met Milovan Djilas, who was in Paris to attend the French Communist Party Congress. Over lunch, he told the Yugoslav that 'he had at first leaned towards participation but that the Politburo had disavowed the Marshall Plan and directed him to oppose it'. Giving him a lift afterwards, the foreign minister remarked that, once they got aid, the French would 'spend it on brothels and luxuries and be right back where they started'.[4]

After four days of wrangling, Bidault decided to extend the meeting by a day to give Molotov a chance to compromise. Instead, the atmosphere grew even frostier after the Soviet delegation received a cable from Moscow passing on information from its spies at the Foreign Office that Bevin and Clayton had agreed that committees would be set up to oversee steel, coal, transport, agriculture and food, and that Washington and London would oppose payment of German reparations from current output. It is safe to assume that the cable was accompanied by instructions from Stalin to take a tougher line.[5]

Molotov now 'answered invective for invective', as he put it later, denouncing 'behind-the-scenes collusion of the USA and Great Britain'. Washington was out to destroy the sovereignty of participating nations, he charged. The only acceptable approach was for it to guarantee funding on the basis of recovery plans put forward by individual states. Pointedly, he asked Bidault if France was ready to give up receiving reparations and see German industry reviving. In reply, the Frenchman accused the Soviets of seeking to undermine the meeting, of trying to incite opinion and of preventing 'hungry satellites' from receiving aid. Bevin pointed out that the Soviet piecemeal approach would simply mean no assistance. Faced with that united front, the Russian turned pale and the bump on his forehead, which betrayed pressure, swelled up.[6]

On 2 July, the Soviet delegation issued a statement accusing

Britain and France of trying to create 'a new organization standing over and above the countries of Europe and interfering in their internal affairs'. They were laying claim to 'a predominant position in this organization'. Participant countries 'would find themselves placed under control and would lose their former economic and national independence because it so pleases certain strong powers'. The United States would determine the Continent's economic rehabilitation in 'a denial of economic independence ... incompatible with national sovereignty'.[7]

At dawn the next day, Molotov flew home where he was notable by his absence at the 4 July American embassy reception. 'If Western writers believe that we were wrong to refuse the Marshall Plan, we must have done the right thing,' he reflected in old age. Marshall assured Bevin and Bidault of his 'complete understanding'. 'At least the Soviet attitude in these questions has been clarified at this stage and will not continue to represent an uncertainty in the working out of a recovery programme for other countries,' he added. Truman wrote to his wife that he would 'like to explode on the Bolshies', but added, 'Marshall hopes I won't. So, of course, I won't.'[8]

Six hours after the Soviet delegation flew out, Bevin and Bidault met at the Quai d'Orsay to draw up plans for a broader conference to open on 12 July. As well as being addressed to most west European governments, invitations were sent to Yugoslavia, Poland, Romania, Bulgaria, Hungary, Albania and Czechoslovakia. They did not go to the USSR, Germany (which had no government) or Spain, which was in political purdah because of the Franco regime.

As Bevin and Bidault pressed ahead, Stalin was still uncertain how to proceed. A cable from Moscow to Belgrade warned that the aid programme was a step towards 'enslavement' to US interests, but still advised participation to 'prevent the Americans from unanimously pushing through their plans'. After putting in an appearance, friendly governments should leave 'taking with you as many delegations of other countries as possible'. The Kremlin could count on most governments in its sphere to follow its lead, whatever that might be. But there was one country that retained a degree of independence on the cusp of the deepening division of Europe. What happened there would be key to the evolution of the Cold War.[9]

## II: THE COUNTRY IN BETWEEN

Wedged between Poland, Germany, Austria, Hungary and Ukraine, landlocked Czechoslovakia had been created out of the ruins of the Austro-Hungarian Empire. It was an ethnic mixture of Czechs, who made up 51 per cent of the population mainly in the west, and Slovaks, who constituted 16 per cent in the east. A fifth of the population was of German origin before their post-war expulsion. All citizens were proclaimed to be equal, but unity had not been easy.

Czechs ran advanced industries making cars, weapons, planes, shoes and machinery – the country ranked among Europe's leading half dozen industrial states. With 65,000 employees around the world, the Bata shoe firm diversified into energy, newspapers, construction, insurance, mining and aviation, operated a profit-sharing scheme for workers and set up 'Batavilles', which provided schools and welfare. Slovakia, formerly part of Hungary, was agrarian, backward, politically reactionary and deeply religious. The Nazis had set up a puppet regime there under a Catholic priest Jozef Tiso, who was hanged after the war, charged with a hundred crimes, including treason and the mass deportation of Jews to concentration camps. The Germans had been prominent in industry and modernised agriculture, and included leading writers and musicians, but had been enthusiastic about the Nazi takeover that began in the Sudetenland following the Munich Agreement in 1938.

Under its first president Tomas Masaryk and his successor Edvard Beneš, Czechoslovakia had been the only properly functioning democracy in the region between the world wars. The Communist Party had been free to operate, though its leader, Klement Gottwald, told ministers he had gone to Moscow 'to learn from the Russian Bolsheviks how to twist your neck'. The Munich Treaty betrayal by Britain and France followed by the German occupation of the whole country the following year led Beneš to view the USSR as the best guarantor of his country's future, particularly against a revival of Germany. In any case, Yalta put Czechoslovakia in the Soviet sphere. Prague was liberated in 1945 in the last major Soviet military action of the war after American troops were ordered to stop their advance 60 miles from the capital.[10]

Described by Attlee, who had seen much of him when he headed the government-in-exile in London during the war, as 'strong but narrow' and 'too clever by half', Beneš had no illusions about the Communists and their ambitions. A note he scribbled to himself during a visit to Moscow at the end of the war noted that national committees to be set up after the liberation of his country were 'in fact Soviets, in the Communist understanding'. 'The Communists' totalitarian tendencies remain,' he went on. 'Under the guise of the National Front, in fact one party should govern. The Communists' participation in the government has one aim; to get hold of positions and have direct influence in preparation for seizing all power in the state.'[11]

But he thought he could 'swallow and digest' the Communists at home while hoping the Soviet regime would evolve away from autocracy. During the Moscow visit, the government-in-exile reached an understanding with the Czechoslovak Communists, including Gottwald, who had spent the war there. Beneš promised Molotov that Prague would do nothing without Soviet approval. In return, Stalin assured him that 'this time we shall destroy the Germans so that they can never again attack Slavs' and pledged that 'the Soviet Union will not interfere with the internal affairs of its allies'. For Beneš, his country could be a bridge between east and west, though the foreign minister Jan Masaryk observed, 'Horses walk over bridges and often litter them with droppings.'[12]

Most of the Czechoslovak democratic political parties were ready to work with the Communists in a post-war National Front. The ambassador to the USSR, Zdeněk Fierlinger, nominally a Social Democrat but in reality a fellow traveller, became prime minister. A shifty figure with what were described as 'a rat's face and an oily grin', he was, as Beneš put it to the American ambassador, 'superficial, unreliable, tricky and ignorant'. While he had been in Moscow, George Kennan judged him to be 'to all intents and purposes a Soviet agent'.[13]

A hard-line Communist, Václav Nosek was installed at the Interior Ministry controlling the police. The defence minister General Svoboda asked to join the party but was told he would be more useful sitting as an apparent independent in the government and voting in the Communist interest. Prokop Drtina, who had been Beneš's private secretary, became justice minister. Masaryk, son of the country's first president and a member of no political party, took the Foreign Ministry and acted as the regime's international face. He referred privately to the prime minister as 'that bastard' and worse than the Communists: 'I'd rather deal with the devil face-to-face than with something crawling in the woodwork,' he told his American partner Marcia Davenport.[14]

Gottwald became deputy head of the government and chairman of the National Front, as well as running the Communist Party. He and his wife moved into a villa in a smart district of Prague, decorating it with socialist realist works of art from state galleries and shelves of gleaming crystal. A stocky, pipe-smoking former carpenter with a ruddy nose who drank heavily and moved slowly in a manner that reminded Djilas of a Slovenian inn keeper, Gottwald knew that 'for all Communists, Stalin's words are an immutable law' and thought he had the master's blessing for his belief that his party could win power legally through open elections. He refused to cut his links with the Catholic Church and liked to recall that Stalin had once told him the Soviet model and the dictatorship of the proletariat was not the only path ahead.[15]

'Socialism here is going to be different,' he declared. Democracy was secure 'so long as other parties remain progressive', he told the visiting British historian, A. J. P. Taylor. Communist Party membership rose from half a million in 1945 to nearly 1.5 million by late 1947 (out of a population of 12 million). Its leading role in redistributing confiscated German land and property buttressed support among Czechs in the Sudetenland.[16]

The party was far from homogenous, with adherents ranging from moderates to radical revolutionaries. The common strand was nationalism, the desire to win control of the country, Pan-Slavism, a belief in spreading egalitarianism – and the insistence that Czechoslovakia should do nothing to annoy Moscow. So long as the membership remained committed to that, and the president stuck to his Soviet-friendly foreign policy, Gottwald and his colleagues could let a hundred flowers bloom, and Stalin was prepared to give them leeway in the hope of finally seeing a Communist regime take power with popular consent in a nation with a developed economy, as prophesised by Marx.[17]

The other partners in the National Front were no match. The National Socialists, Beneš's party, which counted 600,000 members in 1947, based their appeal on Czech nationalism but were poorly organised outside Parliament. Though a third of its 364,000 members were industrial workers, the Social Democratic Party leadership was mainly drawn from the urban middle class; its ideology remained rooted in Marxism and many members felt an instinctive pull towards united action with the Communists. The People's Party (400,000 members) drew support from Catholic peasants and suffered from weak leadership. The Democratic Party of Slovakia, with a similarly sized membership, was a regional movement rooted in rural areas with a strong anti-Communist streak.[18]

One thing on which all parties agreed was that it was, as Beneš said, time to 'liquidate the German problem in our republic'. Retribution for the Nazi occupation, which had caused 150,000 deaths, was fierce. 'So bitter is the hatred of all things German after the country's sufferings during the six years of occupation that there is no talk of toleration or compromise,' the Reuters correspondent reported.[19]

Two million Germans were deprived of citizenship and expelled. Tens of thousands died in the process. German property was seized. Women were raped. Former Nazi camps[20] were used to house prisoners. Germans were made to wear white armbands and banned from walking on pavements or attending theatres, cinemas and inns; they were permitted to leave their homes only at certain times of the day and their rations did not include meat, milk, cheese, eggs or fruit.

In the Bohemian town of Postoloprty, eight hundred Germans were killed by an army unit sent to 'cleanse' the area, while soldiers took 265 Carpathian German men, women and children from a train, forced them to dig their own graves and shot them. In one incident, a woman was attacked by a mob and stripped naked; her limbs were attached to horses which were driven off in different directions. Anti-German hatred was fuelled anew by the trial and public execution of the Nazi viceroy of Prague, Hans Frank. The Gestapo torture chamber in the capital was preserved, the blade of the guillotine was left caked with blood as a memorial to the dead, a tattered Czechoslovak flag and a small wreath beside it. With its history of collaboration, Slovakia remained deeply suspect to progressives in the Czech lands.[21]

As politics swung to the left, a new economic and social order was enforced, based on socialism and nationalisations – among the companies taken over was Bata, whose management set up a new headquarters in Canada. As elsewhere in East and Central Europe, the means of production were to be in public ownership. Pre-war land reform was extended with distribution of 1.3 million hectares to half a million families and a limit of fifty hectares on the size of farms. The state absorbed industrial firms with more than fifty employees including most mining, iron and steel and chemicals enterprises.

While democratic institutions and freedom of speech and worship were maintained, the limits were evident in a ban on the emergence of new political groups and the stipulation that all parliamentary deputies had to vote as ministers from their parties did. Criticism of government policy in areas such as nationalisation was forbidden. So was any questioning of the USSR. A law provided for the exile to labour camps of workers who resisted the new economic policies.

The Soviets took over a big uranium mine at Jáchymov. A secret treaty formalised their access to its output to fuel their atom bomb programme. NKVD political police penetrated deep into the state machine; their cars flanked the presidential reviewing stand at the march past on Liberation Day in 1945. They trained the local force, the SDTB, whose agents aped the Gestapo's garb of long leather coats; an opinion survey reported widespread fear of the security apparatus among a public that 'still lived under the influence of the past'. At celebrations for the first anniversary of the end of the Nazi occupation, Moscow underlined its links with the country by sending a hundred officers including two marshals – the Western Allies had seven or eight representatives each.[22]

But there were still hopes that a new model of relative democracy and freedom could develop. In recognition of the country's good behaviour, Red Army occupation troops were withdrawn at the end of 1945 at the same time as American forces, which had moved into the west of Czechoslovakia in the final stages of the war. Imports from the US were as large as those from the USSR. Western films and

books were highly popular – a trade agreement with the USSR provided for an increase in Soviet films but they were poorly attended.
The American ambassador, Laurence Steinhardt, took a generally
benign view of the situation.[23]

In its review of the year of 1946, the London *Times* commented
that Czechoslovakia 'has distinguished herself by the speed, vigour
and relative moderation with which economic recovery and a political revolution have been carried through'. Output of coal, iron and
steel was back at pre-war levels and food production had increased,
though a high proportion of industrial and consumer goods were
exported to earn much-needed dollars. Negotiations for a US loan
stalled but, as secretary of state, Byrnes thought the government in
Prague could follow a 'more discriminating course' than other East
European states, remaining friendly with the US while not provoking
the ire of the USSR.[24]

Parliamentary elections in 1946 gave the Communists 38 per cent
of the nationwide vote and 114 of the 300 seats with 40 per cent of
the vote in the Czech lands and 30 per cent in Slovakia, well ahead
of the second-placed National Socialists who secured fifty-five representatives. Gottwald became prime minister while remaining party
chairman. Communist and non-Communist ministers were evenly
balanced in numbers in the new Cabinet, though the former held the
key ministries of the Interior, Finance, Defence and Information.

By July 1947, events were closing in on the non-Communists
in Czechoslovakia. The initial post-war economic revival stalled.
Production costs were high and exports faced growing competition.
There was heavy pressure from Moscow to export industrial goods
at low prices. The financial system, which had been broken by the
Germans, remained frozen. The supply of machinery and materials
under the United Nations Relief and Rehabilitation Administration
(UNRRA) ended. Drought hit agriculture. The loss of the skills of
German Czechs weighed heavily.

In its ceaseless hunt for enemies, the Interior Ministry announced
the discovery of a separatist conspiracy in Slovakia. State Security
headquarters set up a special unit staffed by Communists working
with Soviet intelligence agents. Gottwald declared that it was 'necessary to step on this hydra right on its throat'.[25]

Disputes erupted in the ruling coalition. 'Once, the National Front was like the start of a marriage, a time of kissing; we made love and could not keep ourselves apart from each other,' a Communist propagandist and ideologue, Václav Kopecký, recalled. 'Today it looks like a marriage does after one year. There is a lot of surliness. We are throwing pots and pans at each other.' Masaryk told Marcia Davenport of Cabinet fights about economic priorities. 'I'm damned if we make heavy goods for the Russians before our own people get [what] they need,' he added. The Social Democrats were increasingly split as the left wing, under former premier Fierlinger, did all it could to work with the Communists while the moderate party leader, Bohumil Laušman, made a speech saying that Czechoslovakia wanted to remain free and not be a Soviet satellite.[26]

After suffering two strokes, Beneš was increasingly weak both politically and physically. Though he still regarded the USSR as his country's best defence against aggression, he told his secretary, 'The Russians will do whatever they can so as to broaden and strengthen their domination over Germany and Central Europe.' The only ultimate salvation from a Soviet advance lay in a 'striking show of strength by the West', he advised a visitor. But, while ready to come to the aid of the governments of Greece and Turkey, the Truman administration was inhibited when it came to Czechoslovakia by the wartime agreement with Stalin, the country's geographical location and the strength of Gottwald's party in its government. Any suggestion of assistance to a government headed by a Communist could have destroyed the bipartisan front with the congressional Republicans in Washington. So the Truman administration took a negative attitude to aid, much to the dismay of non-Communists in Czechoslovakia.[27]

Still, the non-Communists could take comfort from a parade in the streets of Prague of 120,000 young Catholics chanting slogans in favour of private enterprise and denouncing 'Dictatorship whatever its colour'. An opinion poll reported that only 13 per cent of respondents regarded themselves as living behind the Iron Curtain. Beneš told a British visitor: 'The Communists had failed. The Czechoslovak people ... were not to be dragooned. There had been anxious moments. There were still difficulties, but the

Communists were now losing ground ... Czechoslovakia was out of the woods.'[28]

Yet, the growing pressure was clear. Masaryk, the leading independent figure in the government with an extensive network of friends and contacts on both sides of the Atlantic, wrote to an American acquaintance that he found the faith people had in him 'very touching'. But he added, 'How will I fail them the least – that's the question because ... I cannot deliver the goods they so vitally need and so deeply deserve. For the time being we can hold our own. How long I do not know.'[29]

Living in splendour in the Baroque Czernin Palace in Prague, the foreign minister was tall, bulky, jowly and balding, with small hands and a domed forehead above mobile eyes. A fine pianist with a taste for frogs' legs, he had a pronounced inability to say no to anybody, avoiding confrontations and making commitments that put him under heavy strain. He spoke perfect English – his mother was American and, as a young man, he had lived in the United States where he married an heiress; they were divorced after seven years. There was a history of mental instability in the family on his mother's side. Robert Bruce Lockhart, the British diplomat, writer and one-time secret agent in Russia who knew him well, recorded the 'melancholic tendency and the mad streak in the Masaryk family'. His fatalism could plunge him into depression; returning from tiring foreign trips he sometimes kept his doctor with him for twenty-four hours. Then he would swing to good humour and ribaldry.[30]

Marcia Davenport, the author of a bestselling family saga novel, described his face as showing his duality – 'the right side is the face of sadness and bears the intimation of tragedy ... the left half of the face is the other person – the wit, the warm and intuitive companion, the man of the boisterous laugh and appetites and rich expletives'. His judgement, she wrote, would 'sway and wheel from desperate hope to more desperate hopelessness' as he walked a constant tightrope between independence and the need to maintain a good relationship with the Soviets and their acolytes, convinced, as he put it, that 'One day, they'll kill me.'[31]

## III: Midnight in Moscow

The invitation to the Paris conference on the European Recovery Program faced the government in Prague with a crucial choice. At an all-night Cabinet session, Masaryk led the argument for acceptance. Since Moscow had not ruled that out, Gottwald and his colleagues went along, though Fierlinger denounced the programme as being directed against the Soviet Union and the United Nations.[32]

The American embassy reported that the government appeared 'extremely anxious to participate in the Marshall plan'. Masaryk said the country had 'a vital interest in economic co-operation with the West, as far as exports and raw materials are concerned'. He sent the British ambassador a note of assurance that 'according to the opinion of my government, there is no reason for Europe to be divided into East and West'. He told American correspondents the government was ready to 'take actions in line with the proposal of the US Secretary of State Marshall'.[33]

The delegation to the Paris meeting was to be headed by the Czechoslovak ambassador to France, Jiri Nosek, who would advise if higher-level representation was warranted. Nosek was suspected in Moscow as being anti-Soviet, but Czechoslovakia did not seem to be alone. Poland's foreign minister told the American envoy in Warsaw he felt certain his government would also be represented in Paris.

As news of the acceptance became known in Prague, there was an explosion of rejoicing – Davenport saw 'people literally dancing in the streets, embracing total strangers'. Still, the country was walking on eggshells, and Masaryk wanted to plumb the Kremlin's intentions. When a Soviet diplomat handed him a note giving Molotov's reasons for having walked out in Paris, he asked three times what this meant for Czechoslovakia's participation. 'On this matter, I do not have any instructions,' was the only reply. A cable from the Kremlin transmitted through a secret radio link to Gottwald was clearer as it instructed him that the delegation should go to Paris only to show that the American plan was 'unacceptable and prevent its unanimous acceptance'. It should then walk out.[34]

To be sure of their ground and avoid alienating the USSR, the Czechoslovaks decided to send a three-man team to Moscow first.

Gottwald and Masaryk were joined by Justice Minister Prokop Drtina. At a preliminary meeting before setting out, Masaryk told fellow ministers that 'our allied obligations towards the Soviet Union, Poland and Yugoslavia have the highest priority'. He was hoping for a loan from the USSR; 'Russia is like a big fat cow with its head grazing in Prague and its udders in Moscow,' he told a reporter. 'I'm hoping to turn it round.'[35]

The weekend before the delegation left was the occasion for the annual parade to commemorate the country's Legionnaires who had fought in the First World War for the Allies and in the Russian civil war against the Bolsheviks. Beneš and the foreign minister both spoke at the event in fierce summer heat. The president was taken ill, officially put down to the effect of the sun. That evening, Masaryk joined Davenport at a country house where she was staying. Wearing a short-sleeved summer shirt hanging out over his trousers, he looked worried and said little over dinner. Later, he confided that Beneš had suffered a stroke. When he and the American passed the presidential palace on their return to the capital the next day, he gave a hoarse sigh and let his head drop on his chest; Davenport described his mood as one of 'black pessimism'.[36]

Arriving in Moscow on 9 July, the delegation was kept waiting for hours at its hotel, during which Gottwald left his colleagues, saying he wanted a rest. After a while, Masaryk sent an aide to fetch the prime minister but he returned with word that the head of the government was sleeping. In fact, he was getting his orders at the Kremlin. Returning at night, still wearing his hat and coat, he told the others, 'Everything is all right. I've just come to an agreement with Stalin. We're to see him.'

When the delegation was ushered into the dictator's presence, he was, by Masaryk's account, 'very gracious – of course, he'd kill me if he could'. Stalin explained that, initially, Moscow had thought it would be 'more correct to go to the conference and then to leave it if that should turn out to be necessary'. But, gesturing to a map, he said it had now become clear that the Western powers were trying to form a bloc against the USSR. So the Czechoslovaks would be acting against the Soviet Union if they accepted American aid. Not going to Paris was simply 'a question of friendship', he added. Attendance would 'show that you want to co-operate in an action aimed at iso-lating the Soviet Union', breaking the united front of Slav states and handing a success to the West.[37]

Gottwald seemed overawed; Masaryk did not demur. They assured their host of unconditional friendship. The prime minister said his government had accepted the invitation to be present at the Paris meeting only 'with serious reservations which give us the possibility of a free decision'. In Czechoslovakia, the Communist deputy foreign minister, Vladimír Clementis, went to see Beneš at his country home with another emissary to tell him what Stalin had said. The president was too incapacitated to understand what they told him or to speak. But, on his return to Prague, Clementis told fellow ministers that he had authorised cancellation of participation in the Paris meeting. Some ministers resisted during a Cabinet ses-sion held without Gottwald or Masaryk, though the prime minister telephoned twice from Moscow for news of how the discussion was going. After seven hours, a statement was issued repeating the argu-ments advanced by Stalin.[38]

The Polish leadership swiftly fell into line as well, declining to go to Paris and getting a promise of $450 million worth of credits from the USSR plus a five-year trade agreement. The American ambassador in Warsaw told Washington he had the impression the government had been overruled by a higher authority; the foreign minister, he added, had been 'extremely apologetic and at least apparently regretful'. Acutely conscious of the need not to give Moscow an opportunity to intervene in its affairs, the Finnish gov-ernment decided not to accept US aid.

Returning to Prague, Gottwald said that the delegation had come back 'with great results'. Moscow offered a trade agreement to exchange Soviet grain, cotton, wool and raw materials for Czechoslovak machinery. Molotov reflected later that the USSR had acted as it did towards the Czechoslovaks because 'we could not count on them'. 'The vast majority of Czechoslovaks are extremely distressed that second thoughts have caused the government to with-draw its acceptance of the invitation,' the London *Times* reported. 'The last thing [they] want is to be forced to choose between two water-tight compartments.' As for Masaryk, he later told a British friend, 'I went to Moscow as the foreign minister of an independent sovereign state; I returned as a lackey of the Soviet government.'[39]

## IV: COUNTERFORCE

The division of Europe was set. Sixteen West European nations met in Paris on 12 July to start laborious negotiations on the details of the Marshall Plan, each government seeking to maximise its advantage but knowing that aid was dependent on Congress and its Republican majority, which wanted to see positive steps towards economic integration in the west of the continent.

At American urging, a Committee of European Economic Cooperation was set up under the senior British civil servant Oliver Franks. The ERP was, a State Department official wrote, like a flying saucer: 'Nobody knows what it looks like, how big it is, in what direction it is moving, or whether it really exists.' Washington would listen to what the Europeans had to say, George Kennan wrote, 'but in the end . . . we would just tell them what they would get'.[40]

The Soviet rejection and the importance of the Marshall Plan for Britain and France buttressed the broader dimension of Western policy. The US and UK agreed to boost their zone in Germany by increasing the annual steel output quota to 12 million tons. The mutual defence treaty between Britain and France went into effect. Kennan followed his earlier memorandums with an article in *Foreign Affairs* monthly which depicted the Soviet system as preventing 'any sincere assumption of a community of aims between the Soviet Union and powers which are regarded as capitalist' and forecasting that 'the Russians look forward to a duel of infinite duration'. The article was published under the pseudonym of 'X' but the identity of its author soon became known, and it was enthusiastically circulated by administration hawks. Though insisting that the US must act as the 'unalterable counterforce' to the USSR, it suggested war was unnecessary so long as Washington pursued 'the adroit and vigilant application of counterforce at a series of constantly shifting geographical and political points corresponding to the shifts and manoeuvers of Soviet Policy'.[41]

No change could be expected in Moscow's approach, 'which

cannot be charmed or talked out of existence', Kennan argued. The US must exercise 'long-term, patient but firm and vigilant containment of Russian expansive tendencies'. Soviet power 'bears within it the seeds of its own decay and the sprouting of those seeds is well addressed,' he added. As with the telegram from Moscow, the article was perfectly timed as providing intellectual backing for the policy the administration had adopted. Extracts were run in leading magazines. 'At no time in my recollection have I ever seen a world situation which was moving so rapidly toward real trouble,' Robert Lovett at the State Department noted at the end of July. 'I have the feeling that this is the last clear shot we will have at finding a solution.'[42]

# CHAPTER TEN

# HANGING ON

## I: FRANCE DIGS IN ACROSS AFRICA

While Britain bowed to the inevitable in India and relinquished its Mandate in Palestine as well as acknowledging its inability to continue its role in Greece and Turkey, governments in Paris and The Hague fought to maintain their imperial reach by military force. France had no intention of withdrawing from its global presence stretching over 5 million square kilometres from West Africa and the Caribbean to Indochina and the South Pacific. Equally, the Netherlands resisted Nationalist pressure for independence in the 735,000-square-mile colony of the East Indies, originally claimed by the Dutch East Indies Company but taken over by the state in 1800.

While polls showed public opinion as evenly divided, politicians in Paris worried about a domino effect if they gave way in one colony. The most they would offer was the prospect of joining a French Union in which the metropolitan government would have the upper hand. The only political party favouring granting independence was the Communists, who had been ejected from government in May.[1]

Closest to home, important economic links reached across the Mediterranean, notably to Algeria, which the royal forces of Charles X had invaded in 1830. The *pieds-noirs* European settlers regarded themselves as full citizens of the Republic stretching 'from Dunkirk to Tamanrasset' in the southern Sahara. Deputies from across the Mediterranean elected on a strictly restricted franchise sat in the National Assembly by the Seine. But tension had been rising since 1945 as nationalists called for an autonomy and economic conditions worsened after poor harvests. A series of major clashes broke out between nationalists and police and troops in which both sides used extreme violence, laying the seeds for the later war of liberation. The death toll ran into thousands. The government in Paris agreed to the creation of an Algerian Assembly, but half its members were to be chosen by a European electoral college of 460,000 French citizens plus 58,000 'assimilated' Muslims who had been granted French citizenship.[2]

The next challenge to the French Empire in Africa came at the beginning of 1947 on the other side of the continent in Madagascar, where the Democratic Movement for Malagasy Reform (MDRM) won local elections in January and got three deputies elected to the National Assembly in Paris. The party's left-wing nationalism clashed with the repressive attitude of the colonial 'native affairs service' backed by 35,000 settlers intent on preserving their privileges.

France had completed its conquest of the Indian Ocean island, the world's fourth largest, covering 226,000 square miles, at the end of the nineteenth century. Its predominantly rural economy depended on rice, coffee, vanilla and cloves. To establish themselves, the French had to supplant the Merina dynasty based in the central highland plateau, which ran a slave-labour society and had been converted to Christianity by British Protestant missionaries. The Europeans were met by a peasant revolt, known as the *menalamba* ('red shawls') from their garments smeared with the red highland soil.

It took a year for the French military to suppress the movement. Members of the Merina court were executed for complicity.[3] The last monarch, Queen Ranavalona III, was exiled. The celebrated colonial administrator, General Joseph Gallieni, an ardent proponent of spreading French republican values wherever the tricolour flew, was sent in as governor-general. Slavery was abolished. Education became mandatory up to the age of thirteen. The royal palace was transformed into a museum. But the colonial authorities were unable to check an outbreak of plague that persisted for decades after being brought on a ship from India.[4]

British forces took the island from the Vichy French after protracted fighting and restored sovereignty to the post-war French state. The colonial regime exploited the economy and played on ethnic differences in the population. Though slavery had been abolished, labour service was imposed to build railways and roads; when the government in Paris announced in 1946 that this would end, the settlers resisted. In the highlands, where France's writ did not run, secret societies flourished and fifty years after the Red Shawls revolt, members of two of them attacked a police camp in early 1947, and stormed a rail junction and a jail, freeing prisoners and making off with money and hostages.

Putting their faith in talismans, magic potions, ancestor worship and appeals to their gods, the rebels then raided settler plantations, sometimes torturing the European residents and hacking them to death with farm implements. Roads and railways became unsafe; open wagons mounted with machine guns and manned by French soldiers were attached to trains. Food was parachuted to isolated settler estates. Rice output plummeted. Coffee exports were disrupted.[5]

The leader of one group made his determination plain. 'My ancestors were killed during the French occupation, shot by Senegalese firing squads. I had to fight to avenge my father. I was angry. I told myself: we went to France, fought the Germans, defended France, country of the French. Why aren't we defending our own country? Let's stand up and be counted. Let's abolish forced labour.'[6]

A second revolt erupted in the north of the island and an 18,000-man expeditionary force was sent in; its size would increase to 30,000 with four warships providing support in fighting along the coast. The French drew a 'cage' area of nearly 40,000 square miles in rebel areas in which they fought a very dirty war of repression, killing and arresting at will in the first of a series of colonial conflicts that became cancerous for the army of the Fourth Republic. 'It was a real bludgeoning,' a French priest on the island recalled. 'They called it pacification once they'd flattened everything.'

Villages were burned down, sometimes with inhabitants still in their homes. Farmers suspected of supplying the rebels had their crops and livestock destroyed. People were thrown from helicopters, dropped into the sea from planes or massacred while being moved on trains. Thousands of natives were imprisoned in harsh penal colonies. Twenty alleged leaders of the revolt were executed. There was

widespread torture and raping. Starvation spread. Whole communities were devastated. Backing an indigenous group against the main
rebel movement, the colonial authorities set off a civil war within the
broader conflict. The Socialist-led government in Paris sought moral
justification by portraying the rising as a reactionary attempt by the
Merina-linked aristocracy to restore slavery and oppress the mass of
the population whose only defence lay in French rule.

Estimates of fatalities among the native population have varied
widely over the decades. The figure given by a Catholic priest at the
time, of 80–100,000 killed by the French, compared to several hundred Europeans and 1,900 Malagasies slain by the rebels, was long
accepted. More recent historical analysis has suggested the total was
far smaller. Still, taking into account those who died from malnutri-
tion or other causes associated with the fighting, the number, even
on this lower count, was in the tens of thousands.[7]

Though it disavowed the rising and denounced 'barbaric crimes'
by the rebels, the MDRM was outlawed. Its size – with an estimated
membership of 300,000 and its melding together of different anti-
colonial movements – made it a threat which the authorities felt they
had to quash. Its three parliamentary deputies were arrested and,
after a prosecution based on false or insecure evidence, sentenced to
death (though later reprieved). The French media paid little attention
to the events. Vincent Auriol, the Socialist President of the Republic,
merely noted in his diary 'There were excesses.' The writer, Albert
Camus, the conscience of his generation, was one of the few critics of
the repression, writing in his newspaper column that 'we are doing
what we blamed the Germans for'. But the French high commissioner
was predictably adamant in declaring, 'France is in Madagascar –
she will stay there.'[8]

## II: Impasse in Vietnam

The same state of mind applied to Indochina, where attempts to
find a common ground between Paris and the Democratic Republic
of Vietnam (DRV), which Nationalists had declared in 1945, got
nowhere. On 14 July 1947, Raoul Salan, commander of French forces
in the north of the country, organised a big Bastille Day ceremony

in Hanoi, the first for many years. The next day, he flew through clear skies to survey the region between the city and the frontier with China where the Viet Minh enemy was entrenched. Then he took a plane south to Saigon with a battle plan to submit to the overall commander, General Valluy.

Covering nearly 300,000 square miles, Indochina was a particularly prized possession for the French. Three-quarters of its population of 25 million were Vietnamese, 3 million Cambodians and a million Laotian. With the kings of Cambodia and Laos loyal to the French, opposition to colonial rule came from Vietnam, a 130,000-square-mile land of three different regions – Tonkin in the north, Annam in the centre and Cochin-China in the south – with substantial ethnic minorities and big religious sects.

The European conquest began in the 1860s when a naval expedition forced the ruling Nguyen dynasty to allow the French into the south of the country. Further military expansion led to the creation of the Union of French Indochina at the end of the 1880s as governments in Paris were spurred to join the imperial game alongside Britain and assert national glory after the humiliation of the defeat by Prussia in 1870. There was a powerful notion of spreading French civilisation and considerable Catholic missionary enthusiasm. Vietnam became a big producer of rubber, coffee, tobacco, indigo and tea with a well-entrenched population of plantation owners and traders in Cochin backed by a political lobby in Paris.

Infrastructure and schooling were developed while hospitals helped to combat disease. Classic colonial buildings went up in Saigon and Hanoi to house government offices, banks and companies. Though Chinese dominated local business, some Vietnamese entered business or joined the civil service, the law and the teaching profession, albeit paid less than Europeans. Rural landlord families moved into steadily expanding cities. An urban working class lived a harsh existence and was forbidden to form trade unions or strike.[9]

Material benefits were directed overwhelmingly at the colonial class and there was no real progress towards sharing political power. This bred recurrent rebellions, including a decade-long royalist rising, a 25-year insurrection in the northern mountains, a failed mutiny by Vietnamese soldiers, attacks on Catholics and a movement led by a mystic millenarian who claimed to be a Living Buddha. As was the case for other European powers in Asia, the aura of colonial rule was dealt its biggest blow when the Japanese invaded in September 1940, mainly to block the supply route from the northern port of Haiphong to south-west China, which the imperial army had not penetrated. The French authorities quickly gave in, four months after the fall of their home country to Tokyo's Nazi ally. Loyal to the Vichy collaborationist regime, they granted Japan the right to station troops in Indochina and operated under its supervision. In early 1945, concerned about a possible Allied invasion, the imperial army assumed full direct control, overwhelming the French, killing 4,000 of their soldiers and taking 15,000 military and civilian prisoners.[10]

Bao Dai, the last emperor of the Nguyen dynasty, was installed to head a puppet state, which began to dismantle the colonial bureaucracy and education service. There was some resistance – a French general who refused to sign a surrender document after the outpost he commanded had been overrun was beheaded on the spot. But the Japanese action further lowered the status of the Europeans while two resistance movements that had taken shape during the war continued to operate after it ended. One was made up of non-Communist Nationalists under the aegis of the Kuomintang government in China and with backing from liberal Nationalists in the south of Vietnam. The other was set up by the man originally called Nguyen Sinh Cung, who now adopted the nom de guerre of Ho Chi Minh (Bringer of Light).

Son of a Confucian scholar, teacher and magistrate, he had gone as a young man to Europe, where he nurtured an interest in politics and nationalism. After joining the French Communist Party in 1920, he spent two decades as a wandering, tubercular revolutionary,[11] attending the Whampao Military Academy in Canton headed by Chiang Kai-shek and forming the Indochinese Communist Party in Hong Kong where he was arrested. The French pressed the British to extradite him, which they did not wish to do for reasons that are not clear; instead, a report was issued that he was dead and he was covertly released in 1933, going to Moscow for medical treatment. Seven years later, he presided over the establishment of the resistance movement the Viet Minh (Vietnam Independence League) across the border in south China waiting for the defeat of Japan to return home.

A brilliant underground operator, Ho was a committed Marxist who believed that 'only Socialism and Communism can liberate the oppressed nations and the working people through the world from slavery'. He purged dissidents and rivals and set up 'traitor elimination committees', which killed not only political rivals but also Vietnamese women married to French men. But he knew how to broaden his appeal and compromise when necessary, proclaiming a post-war united front and formally disbanding the Communist Party (though, in fact, it simply went underground, adopting the name of the Association for Marxist Studies). He was adept at beguiling foreigners with airy turns of phrase, evocations of the *Rights of Man* and the American Revolution projecting his whispy-bearded image in simple peasant garb with rope sandals pecking at his Hermes Baby typewriter in jungle hideouts. When he went to Paris for talks with the French in 1946, the head of Foreign Ministry protocol expressed his admiration for 'this self-taught man, his language skills, his ability to make his views accessible, to make his intentions seem moderate, and his politeness'.[12]

His ambition to take the helm of the Nationalist movement had been facilitated when the principal non-Communist campaigner for independence died in a French prison in 1943 and the focus of the struggle swung to the north of the country, where the Viet Minh was based. It gained popular sympathy by managing the distribution of food during a huge famine in 1945 caused by Japanese food seizures and poor French administration. As the war drew to a close, advisers from the US Office of Strategic Services (OSS) trained its guerrilla fighters, received intelligence about the Japanese from them – and treated Ho for malaria and dysentery.

France was, however, intent on re-establishing colonial rule after the defeat of Japan. Paris did not respond when Bao Dai wrote to plead for the independence of Vietnam, leading the emperor to abdicate and associate himself with the Viet Minh for a while. But France had no troops with which to impose itself; the Potsdam conference, which it did not attend, decided British forces should move into the south while Chinese Nationalist forces occupied the north. In September 1945, Ho declared the Democratic Republic of Vietnam (DRV) with himself as chairman of its Provisional Government, warning that anybody who tried to block it would be 'smashed'. Though dominated by a Communist core, members of other groupings held 40 per cent of ministerial posts and formed a majority at its first legislative congress.

The new republic had only a primitive administrative structure and a regular army of 1,200 men. The famine and floods ravaging its heartland in the north of the country took anywhere from 400,000 to 2 million lives. There was extensive looting by the 20,000 Nationalist Chinese soldiers; given the antipathy felt by many Vietnamese for their larger neighbour and the Chinese links with the non-Communist resistance group, Ho could not wait to see them gone.[13]

In the south, violence broke out between Vietnamese and the French after DRV supporters in Saigon hung out banners reading 'Long Live Vietnamese Independence' and 'Vietnam Has Suffered and Bled under the French Yoke'. A dozen French people were killed. The British commander General Douglas 'Bruiser' Gracey declared martial law. The Viet Minh called for a general strike and attacked the airport, the main market and the docks. Gracey used Japanese and freed French prisoners of war to help his mainly Indian troops gain control. After a series of encounters outside the city, the British handed over to a newly arrived French Expeditionary Force. Around a hundred British, French, Indian and Japanese soldiers had died in the fighting while the Viet Minh toll was officially estimated at 2,700.[14]

Ho's movement shifted to guerrilla tactics in the south while assassinating non-Communist politicians and sending death threats to Vietnamese managers working with the French or running casinos and brothels in Saigon's Chinese quarter of Cholon. In the north, it liquidated political opponents, ensuring overwhelming victory at elections in early 1946. When the National Assembly met later, in the year, only thirty-seven of the 291 deputies were from opposition parties.[15]

French hopes were bolstered under the new commander, Philippe Leclerc, de Gaulle's favourite general who had led an armoured division into Paris at the Liberation. His expeditionary force advanced south into the Mekong Delta and north-west into the Highlands, while gunboats scoured the Mekong Delta and French forces landed along the coast. The messianic Cao Dai sect in the Delta sided with the

French. In February 1946, Leclerc felt able to declare that 'the pacification of Cochin-China is entirely achieved' in the first of many claims
of victory that would prove premature over the following decade.[16]

However, a split emerged between Leclerc and the high commissioner, Thierry d'Argenlieu. A Carmelite monk who had become a
Free French naval icon, the admiral had been told by de Gaulle to
constitute an Indochinese Federation in which France would have the
last word. An arrogant figure, he was strongly backed by the settlers,
business interests and long-time colonial civil servants who believed
that the south should break from the north and form a separate entity
under their control based on French military power. Leclerc, on the
other hand, came to believe that a political solution was necessary.

Acting in the high commissioner's place during an absence abroad,
he backed negotiations with Ho conducted by an envoy from the
government in Paris, Jean Sainteny, who reached a tentative agreement in March 1946 by which France recognised the DRV as a free
state with its own government, Parliament, army and treasury as a
member of the Indo-Chinese Federation and the French Union. At
the same time, the French negotiated the withdrawal of the Chinese
troops by agreeing to hand over its concessionary areas in China and
provide trading agreements in Vietnam.

The accord caused problems on both sides. Ho had to call a mass
meeting to explain it to northerners. Settlers and the colonial lobby
were up in arms. In private, d'Argenlieu spoke of 'an Indochinese
Munich' and said he was 'amazed that France's fine expeditionary
corps in Indochina is commanded by officers who would rather
negotiate than fight'. A meeting between the high commissioner and
Ho aboard a French naval vessel went badly, and was punctuated
by a rough exchange between d'Argenlieu and Leclerc. The admiral
was horrified when Ho embraced him as he left.[17]

Undeterred, the Viet Minh leader and Sainteny left for follow-
up talks with the government in France, accompanied by General
Salan. The admiral decided it was time to act, emboldened by the
lack of control from Paris and backing he enjoyed from settlers
and the colonial lobby. In June 1946, he declared an Autonomous
Republic of Cochin-China without referring to the government at
home. Learning of the creation of the southern republic on his way to

France, Ho said he wanted to return home. Salan dissuaded him. But the government in Paris did nothing to reverse the admiral's move, casting a heavy pall over the talks at the Château de Fontainebleau.[18]

Non-Communist politicians were recruited to join the Cochin administration, headed by a big landowner, Nguyen Van Thinh. Believing they would enjoy a large degree of independence, they saw d'Argenlieu's initiative as a means of bolstering their own positions and keeping the Viet Minh out of the south. But they soon came under pressure to follow local French wishes as the admiral called a conference in the hill resort of Dalat to assert the autonomy of Cochin and push for a federal assembly of states kept under colonial control. Thinh was pressed to drop nationalists from the government, and attacked by both settlers and nationalists. The high commissioner refused his requests for a meeting. On 9 November 1946, he threw a rope around the lock on a window in his office and hanged himself. His suicide note called for an end to the 'criminal wait-and see game', adding, 'I die to show the path of duty, liberty and honour.'[19]

Despite a subsequent ceasefire agreement, the Fontainebleau talks failed to produce overall agreement. The French would not relinquish the degree of control the Viet Minh saw as a minimum. 'Can the French Union base itself on force on one side and hatred on the other?' Ho asked in a letter to Salan. 'Can it put itself together with member countries which are amputated, ruined, in mourning and soaked in blood? Certainly not! If it wants to become a reality, the French Union must base itself on friendship and mutual confidence.'

He warned the French, 'You can kill 10 of my men for every one I kill of yours, yet even at those odds, you will lose and I will win.' 'It will be a war between an elephant and a tiger,' he told an American journalist in one of those analogies beloved of guerrilla leaders. 'If the tiger ever stands still, the elephant will crush him with his mighty tusks. But the tiger will not stand still ... He will leap upon the back of the elephant, tearing huge chunks from his side, and then he will leap back into the dark jungle. And slowly the elephant will bleed to death. That will be the war of Indochina.' But, as they shook hands at the end of the Fontainebleau talks, Salan had a warning of his own: 'We are going to fight and it will very tough.'[20]

The Viet Minh leader chose to return home by the long sea journey rather than by air. While he was on his way, positions hardened on both sides, with the French determination to hold on matched by the Viet Minh's faith in ultimate victory. After a clash in Haiphong harbour, the French shelled the city, killing thousands. The nationalists drew up a new constitution that made no mention of any link with France. In a series of planning and strategy notes entitled 'Urgent Work Now' after his return to Vietnam, Ho advocated 'protracted resistance'. The enemy, he wrote, 'will run out of steam, and we will win'.

Meeting at night on 18–19 December 1946, under Ho's chairmanship, the Communist Party Central Committee decided to launch a resistance struggle across the whole of Vietnam. But, playing his habitual double game, Ho also sent new proposals to Paris and dispatched an emissary to Sainteny to suggest local talks. The message to France was held up by d'Argenlieu's staff in Saigon. Sainteny refused the offer of talks. Learning of this, the Viet Minh leader frowned, thought for a few moments and exclaimed, 'Huh! Then we fight.'[21]

At 8.03 p.m. on 19 December 1946, explosive charges cut off electricity from Hanoi's main power plant. As the lights went out, the French opened fire with rifles and sent up parachute flares. The Vietnamese ran trams and a railway train across main streets to block them. Some twenty French residents were killed in their houses. Two hundred were taken prisoner. Sainteny was badly hurt when a mine exploded under his car.

A Vietnamese unit occupied a central French government building and held off Legionnaires backed by cannons, tanks and armoured cars for twelve hours. The city's water plant was damaged, but the defences at the airport and the oil tanks withstood attack. Planes dropped bombs as Viet Minh suicide squads wielding charges on wooden poles attacked armoured vehicles. French troops steadily outflanked the guerrillas, though fighting continued until mid-January when the last Viet Minh fighters escaped across the Red River in twenty boats.[22]

After that, the Viet Minh focused on building up its capability for irregular warfare with a string of bases and underground arms caches for a long-term struggle. They were strongest in the 'free zones' such as a big area south of the Red River in the north, with markets, schools and health clinics. There were military drills and propaganda meetings held at night to avoid air attacks. Weapons were manufactured. Taxes were levied and food stocks built up along with literacy campaigns and land reform. But the rebels had few trained officials or soldiers and their administrative apparatus was disjointed. Militias often operated autonomously, each following its own tactics and organisation. Messages between Hanoi and Saigon had to be carried by boat and on foot. They were also isolated internationally; the Soviet Union did not recognise the DRV and the French Communist Party provided no material aid while an approach to the US embassy in Bangkok got no response.[23]

The French command, meanwhile, radiated confidence. D'Argenlieu declared that colonial power extended to wherever the tricolour flew. 'I consider that there is no longer a military problem in Indochina,' the war minister, Paul Coste-Floret, said after a visit in the spring of 1947. 'The success of our arms is complete.' Such optimism ignored the bulk of the country with its deep jungles and inaccessible mountains which the French could not reach. While Coste-Floret was visiting, a Viet Minh ambush killed forty-four people, including two ministers from the Cochin-China government and a French colonel. After he returned home in 1947, Leclerc warned that ministers had been 'misinformed about the gravity of the situation'. France could not use force to block the desire for change of the Vietnamese population, which was coloured by xenophobia and nationalism, he argued, adding 'The solution can only be political. Anti-communism will be a lever without traction so long as the national problem is not resolved.'[24]

Another departing general reported that the situation in the south of the country was steadily deteriorating. 'One leaves Saigon only in convoys,' he noted. 'Eighty per cent of the population is on the side of the Viet Minh. The government's authority is non-existent . . . We are fighting not only against the Viet Minh, but against the great majority, if not the totality, of the population. Ho Chi Minh has retained all his prestige. However effective the French troops are, guerrilla warfare goes on . . . there is no purely military solution.'[25]

When d'Argenlieu made a vague offer to step down as high

commissioner in early 1947, the government in Paris grabbed the chance to get rid of the obstinate admiral, who retreated to a monastery. The job was offered to Leclerc, but he made acceptance dependent on raising troop levels to achieve a position of military strength from which negotiations could be conducted. Under severe budget pressure and fighting a simultaneous war against the rising in Madagascar, the government could not agree.

So the job went to solid civil servant Émile Bollaert, a leading figure in the Radical Party who had never been to Indochina. He sought to open negotiations by sending a liberal administrator, Paul Mus, to see Ho. But the encounter got nowhere as the French laid down preliminary conditions unacceptable to the Viet Minh, which said it was ready to talk only if Paris recognised the independence and unity of Vietnam. A plan by Bollaert to make a speech holding out the eventual prospect of independence led to him being called to a meeting at the Élysée Palace of seven senior ministers and President Auriol. This rejected any talk of independence. When the high commissioner made his speech, there was no mention of the 'i' word. France's course was set – refusing to relinquish control and seeking a military solution to eliminate the Viet Minh as Salan worked on his plan for a decisive offensive.[26]

## III: Return of the Dutch

To the south, the Dutch launched their biggest military initiative against the Nationalists who had declared an independent republic two years earlier. On 21 July, three divisions advanced in the main island of Java and three more in Sumatra. The government in The Hague alleged that the Republicans had breached an agreement reached four months earlier, and wanted to re-establish its position shattered by defeat at the hands of the Japanese in 1942.

The Dutch had been in the archipelago of 13,500 islands since 1602, completing their conquest at the end of the nineteenth century. In the 1930s, their colony produced a third of the world's rubber, as well as large amounts of sugar, copra and pepper – and provided from 14 to 17 per cent of the national income of the Netherlands. Colonial society was slow and conservative, dominated by families that had been there for decades and lived in old aristocratic houses built in the Dutch style with oak staircases and heavy furniture, though there was also a transient population of those who came, made money and left. Most of the settlers lived in urban areas while more than 90 per cent of the native population was in the countryside, where the literacy rate was 10 per cent and most people lived on a subsistence rice diet. The authorities co-opted local sultans and repressed nationalist movements; a Communist rising in Java was put down in 1926 and the only form of representation was a largely powerless People's Council.

In 1927, a group of nationalists set up the *Partai Nasional Indonesia* (PNI), calling for independence, secularism and unity for a new nation. One of its leading members, Sukarno,[27] was arrested and put on trial, which he used to deliver speeches attacking colonialism and imperialism. He was sentenced to four years in jail, and then exiled to the remote island of Flores.

The son of a village schoolteacher, he had graduated with a degree in engineering in 1926, one of a handful of natives who received a full education, and set up a firm providing architectural, planning and contractor services. Fluent in Javanese and several other languages of the Indies, he also spoke German, English, French, Arabic and Japanese, and had a photographic memory. His political approach sought to meld nationalism and indigenous customs with the majority religion of Islam and a dash of Marxism to unify people of greatly differing ethnic, cultural and religious backgrounds. A charismatic speaker, Bung Karno (Brother Karno) said he 'lived to intoxicate the masses'. 'He seemed to direct a current of electricity into the crowd,' a Western observer wrote. 'It was as if he were a heart pumping oxygen into the Indonesian body politic.'[28]

Still in detention when the Japanese invaded in 1942, he reacted by declaring, 'God be praised ... Independent Indonesia can only be achieved with Dai Nippon,' and co-operated with the occupiers, ignoring the way they set out to exploit Indonesian manpower and natural resources while toying with nationalism to their own advantage. The Japanese dragooned millions of people as forced labour to build railways, airfields and other facilities. Indonesians were ordered to bow deeply in the direction of Tokyo. A local army was created to help the imperial cause. Occupation forces seized rice and other food while forcing the peasantry to cultivate castor oil plants to be used as aviation fuel and lubricants. A famine in Java caused by requisitioning killed more than a million people in 1944–5.

But, in speeches on the Japanese-run radio and over loudspeaker networks across Java and Sumatra, Sukarno urged people to fight on the invaders' side, forming a committee to link the creation of 'an independent, united, sovereign, just and prosperous Indonesian state' with 'a single front with Dai Nippon in this life-and-death struggle'. For him, the defeat of the Japanese could only mean the return of the Dutch, which he regarded as the greater evil. He and a fellow leading Nationalist, Mohammad Hatta, were sent on a tour of Japan, where they were decorated by Emperor Hirohito and entertained in the prime minister's house.[29]

After US forces took the Philippines in the spring of 1945, the Japanese continued their policy of trying to solidify Nationalist support by allowing a quasi-legislature consisting of sixty-seven representatives from most ethnic groups. Sukarno was appointed to head it; in an attempt to forge unity, he put together his principles of Nationalism, Internationalism, Democracy, Social Justice, Belief in God and Religious Freedom. After Japan's defeat, he tried to play for time, but impatient Nationalists kidnapped him and got him to proclaim independence in August 1945, with a simple statement: 'We, the people of Indonesia, hereby declare the independence of Indonesia. Matters concerning the transfer of power etc. will be carried out in a conscientious manner and as speedily as possible.' The red-and-white flag of the Republic was raised and the anthem 'Indonesia Raya' sung. Sukarno became president and Hatta vice president. The spectators numbered five hundred.

The Republic established itself in Java and Sumatra as Japanese troops retreated to their barracks awaiting arrival of Allied forces. The situation was chaotic in many places, with local warlords taking charge and weapons easily available from the arsenals of the former occupiers. Armed gangs attacked Europeans, Chinese, Christians, native aristocracy and anyone perceived to oppose independence. Former Dutch prisoners of war went on shooting rampages against Indonesian civilians. Gunmen tried to assassinate the prime minister.

The economy was in a mess. As one historian put it, Indonesia had become 'a land of extreme hardship, inflation, shortages, profiteering, corruption, black markets and death'.[30]

The first Allied soldiers, a battalion of the British Seaforth Highlanders, reached Indonesia in September 1945. Most were Indian. Their mission was to keep the peace for the return of the Dutch. The Republicans tried to counter this by seeking international recognition and support. Though officially they were not at war, the British became embroiled in clashes with Indonesians. Artillery duels raged round the West Java city of Bandung. In the capital, as a young British soldier, the future actor Dirk Bogarde, recalled, 'Every building was covered with patriotic graffiti screaming for "Bloodshed or Freedom", and the blood flowed. Nightly, the explosion of bombs ... rocked the city. Machine-guns stuttered and chattered on the deserted suburban streets, fires drenched the starry nights with orange and crimson light, and the crump and crash of mortars and grenades was a familiar sound.'[31]

Thousands of Indonesians and three hundred British Army soldiers were killed in a full-scale three-week battle in November 1945, in the major port of Surabaya after Dutchmen who had raised their national flag were lynched on the lawn of the Colonial Club. The nationalists probably had more than 100,000 troops, while the Indians of the British forces numbered 4,000. Sukarno and Hatta broadcast unavailing appeals for peace. The British commander was shot dead in his car after trying to defuse one confrontation. A final assault by land, sea and air drove away the Republican forces as shelling set off firestorms in the densely crowded city.

At the beginning of 1947, the British withdrew from Indonesia and Dutch troops flooded in. The colonialists set up separate states in Bali and Eastern Indonesia to weaken the Republicans and unleashed a campaign of terror on the big island of Sulawesi. Sukarno and most of the Republican government sought shelter in the city of Yogyakarta, ruled by a friendly sultan.

The veteran colonial administrator, Hubertus van Mook, a large, reserved man, refused to deal with the Nationalists because of the collaboration of their leaders with the Japanese, but, above all, because he regarded the 'so-called republic of Indonesia' as an impossible dream. For him and his colleagues, the islands could exist only in a European-run commonwealth in which The Hague would have the last word.[32]

The Dutch government was, however, keen to reduce the cost of the 100,000 troops stationed in the Indies at a time of financial strain at home. A decline in earnings from Indonesia made it less important economically. When Marshall Plan aid arrived, it would best be used for reconstruction, not colonial defence.[33]

International opinion was moving in the direction of the Nationalists as pressure rose for an agreement. In March 1947, the Netherlands acknowledged de facto Republican sovereignty over Java, Sumatra and the island of Madura, but insisted on having the last word in any administration and said independence could be granted only under a commonwealth headed by Queen Wilhelmina. The decision to negotiate with the colonial power aroused strong opposition from militant Republicans and the Indonesian army, which briefly kidnapped the prime minister. Charismatic as he was, Sukarno could not be sure of being the master of the different forces in his movement bent on pursuing their own interests. Always a proponent of compromise, he put unity first and did not impose his will on the politicians and military commanders around him who wanted to expand Republic control. Nor did the Dutch let the agreement constrain them from preparing military action as van Mook concluded that 'a surgical operation was necessary to save the patient from the cancer of lawlessness and terrorism'.

Accordingly, they launched Operation Product on 20 July, their troops moving into towns in Java and Sumatra and forcing out Republican forces. They estimated it would take two weeks to conquer the main Republican cities and six months to subdue the whole country to recover sugar plantations and oil and rubber reserves. Air raids set ablaze ports, oil tanks and transport centres. The colonial army took all the deep-water ports in Java and plantations and oil and coal facilities in Sumatra. No attack was planned on the Republican capital of Yogjakarta because of the likely scale of fighting and the possibility of another battle of Surabaya. Retreating Nationalist forces destroyed property owned by Chinese and Indians, and killed Indonesian aristocrats; in West Java, there was a pogrom of Chinese.[34]

The Dutch offensive brought strong international condemnation. Bevin expressed 'keenest regret'. Washington was unhappy. At the UN, the chief Soviet delegate, Andrei Gromyko, denounced an 'unprovoked military attack'. Australia urged a settlement. Nehru said no European country had any business using its army against the people of Asia. For its part, the Dutch government worried that Marshall Plan aid might be jeopardised, and agreed to take the matter to the United Nations, where the Security Council called for immediate ceasefire. Operation Coupon was ended after a month, though the Dutch continued to mop up Republican units in areas they controlled. The colonial army put its losses at fifty-nine dead, 132 wounded and sixteen missing. There was no figure for Republicans and civilians, but casualties ran into thousands, with many more fleeing their homes.

UN negotiators moved in. The US tried to bring the two sides together. A Good Offices Committee was set up with American, Australian and Belgian members to work for a lasting ceasefire. But the Republicans were not ready to accept anything except full independence, while the Dutch believed that they could only negotiate from a position of strength after military victory. Nothing had been solved. However much talk might go on, neither side would yield.

# CHAPTER ELEVEN

# NEXT YEAR IN JERUSALEM

## I: THE UN, EXODUS AND THE SERGEANTS

The day after Molotov flew home from the Marshall Plan talks in Paris, the United Nations mission to Palestine began two weeks of public hearings at which representatives from twelve Jewish organisations testified and submitted a mound of written material. The Zionists were particularly well placed because they had bugged the meeting rooms. In his evidence, Chaim Weizmann said a Jewish state could absorb 1.5 million more people. He called the Jews 'a disembodied ghost'. Whatever was done, he added, should be done quickly. 'Do not let it drag on. Do not prolong our agony. It has lasted long enough.' Ben-Gurion said that for Jews, 'the countries of their birth are a graveyard of their people'. They simply wanted to regain 'their dignity, their homeland'. So he called on the international body to 'restore freedom to Palestine, give justice to the people and stability, progress and prosperity to the Middle East. These three objectives can be accomplished by ... the establishment of a Jewish State and the promotion of Jewish–Arab alliance.'[1]

Jorge García-Granados, the Guatemalan member of the team, recalled later that 'the legal case of the Jews, it seemed to me, was far stronger than that of the Arabs. But there were still the moral aspects on the problem to be considered. It was impossible, I told myself, to ignore the claim that Palestine was an Arab land, inhabited from remote times by an Arab majority, characterised by an Arab culture, a land in which, according to the Arabs, the Jews were interlopers and invaders.'[2]

While the UN Committee held its hearings, British armoured cars and army lorries were blown up by bombs laid by Zionist extremists in Jerusalem. Heavy gunfire erupted with tracers and parachute flares lighting the night sky. Barbed-wire fences lined the streets patrolled by soldiers. A British constable was shot dead in Haifa. 'Tel Aviv mortars' made from drainpipes were fired at an army camp.

The Irgun movement, which had declared all British in Palestine as legitimate targets, adopted a policy of kidnapping soldiers to hold as hostages against the lives of Jews sentenced to death for terrorist attacks and, on 12 July, grabbed two sergeants as they left a café in the town of Netanya. Drugged with chloroform, they were driven to a disused diamond-polishing plant south of the town where they were held in an underground chamber fashioned for the purpose with an airtight hatch hidden beneath sand. There was a week's supply of food, a canvas bucket and oxygen cylinders.

A Jewish colleague, who had also been taken and was released before they reached the diamond plant, told the police what had happened. But searches of the area by both the British and the Jewish Haganah army failed to find the men. The situation was all the more tense because three Irgun members were under sentence of death for the prison breakout in Acre the previous month. When the father of one sergeant wrote to appeal for his son's life to the Irgun chief, Menachem Begin responded, 'You must appeal to your government that thirsts for oil and blood.'

At the same time, the biggest crisis to date erupted over the attempts by Jewish refugees to reach Palestine. For the Zionists, immigration was essential not simply to enable Jews to join a state of their own but also because the demographics were pitted against them. A study for the UN Commission forecast that, without immigration, the total population of Palestine would rise from 1.845 to 2.394 million between 1947 and 1960 but that the Jewish share would drop from 31 to 28 per cent.[3]

Zionist groups in Europe had, by now, established a well-organised system for Jews wanting to go to Palestine and forged links with European police and border authorities to ensure their passage. Emigrants gathered at local centres and set off in groups of twenty to forty. The main routes from Poland ran through Silesia and Czechoslovakia to the American zone of Germany, or through Austria to Italy before reaching the Mediterranean, where French officials helped them board ships. The British navy turned back the larger vessels but smaller craft slipped through. Some 50,000 would-be immigrants were sent to internment camps in Cyprus, where they staged hunger strikes.[4]

The largest of the refugee ships left the French port of Sète in the early morning of 11 July, watched by British military ships and aircraft. On board were 4,500 people, most of them Holocaust survivors. Flying the Honduran flag, the ship's crew claimed to be headed for Turkey. The twenty-year-old American vessel had been bought in Baltimore the previous year by a Haganah agent. To repel British boarding parties, pipes were installed to spray out steam and boiling oil. The wheel house, radio room, machine room and steam room were all reinforced and covered in wire. The steel hull promised protection against being rammed while the ship was taller than the Royal Navy destroyers it would face. Its original name of *President Warfield*, after the head of a shipping firm, was changed to *Exodus*.[5]

The British boarded the boat on 18 July, 40 kilometres from the Palestinian shore. Those aboard tried to block them; two were killed by gunshots and one was clubbed to death. A blow-by-blow commentary on the struggle transmitted over the ship's radio was picked up by Zionist stations and relayed to the world.

*Exodus* was towed into Haifa port and those aboard transferred to land before being put on three other vessels. The British authorities decided to ship them back to Europe; the camps in Cyprus were overcrowded and Bevin wanted to send a message to other governments and those organising the journeys that refugees would be returned to their point of origin. 'It will be most discouraging to the organisers of this traffic if they end up by returning from whence they came,' the foreign secretary declared. But negative publicity rolled in. The future Israel foreign minister, Aubrey (Abba) Eban, got four members of the UN team to go to Haifa to watch what he called 'a gruesome operation' of sending away the refugees; when they returned to Jerusalem, he recalled, the diplomats 'were pale with shock ... preoccupied with one point alone; if this was the only way the British Mandate could continue, it would be better not to continue it at all.'⁶

When the ships carrying the refugees arrived in southern France, the authorities there insisted that the disembarkation had to be voluntary. Haganah agents pulled up beside the ship and urged those aboard not to leave. They started a hunger strike instead. Three weeks passed during which both sides refused to budge and criticism of the British rose, particularly in America, where the *Exodus* became a Zionist rallying cry. The French Communist newspaper *l'Humanité* described the ship as 'a floating Auschwitz'. Léon Blum, who had spent two years in Nazi concentration camps, joined the criticism, and his fellow Socialist Jules Moch accused the British of 'closing, one after another, all the avenues of hope to Jews of Palestine and Zionists across the world'.⁷

At dawn on 29 July, the three Irgun members sentenced to death after the Acre prison breakout were hanged. They sang the national anthem of the future state of Israel as they went to their deaths and shouted 'Avenge our blood!' The corpses were left dangling from the gallows for twenty minutes.

Four Irgun members drove to the polishing plant and took the two sergeants from the chamber, hooded and with their wrists and ankles bound. Nooses around their necks, they were mounted on chairs which were kicked away. Early the following morning, the bodies, stuffed into bags, were taken to a eucalyptus grove where they were hung five yards apart from two trees beside which a mine was buried. Their shirts were wrapped round their heads. The corpses were blackened and bloodied. Notes attached to their chests said they had been convicted of 'criminal anti-Hebrew activities', including illegal entry into the Hebrew homeland, membership of 'a British criminal terrorist organization known as the Army of Occupation', illegal possession of arms, anti-Jewish spying in civilian clothes. 'Found guilty of these charges they have been sentenced to hang and their appeal for clemency dismissed. This is not a reprisal for the execution of three Jews but a routine judicial fact,' the notes added.

When the first of the bodies fell to the ground after being cut down with a knife on the end of a pole, the mine went off, blowing the corpse into fragments. As the news spread, British soldiers and police assaulted Jews, broke shop windows and attacked buses in Tel Aviv; five people were killed and fifteen injured. Bevin told Marshall that anti-Jewish feeling in Britain was greater than it had been for a hundred years. Synagogues and other Jewish buildings were attacked in London, Glasgow, Blackpool, Plymouth and other cities. In five days of rioting in Liverpool, more than three hundred Jewish properties were damaged.[8]

The refugees from the *Exodus* continued to pose a problem for the British government. The Foreign Office decided that, if France would not agree to their forcible landing, they should be taken to the British zone of Germany despite the outcry officials knew this would provoke. The best the Attlee government could do was to state that they would not be put into former concentration camps or guarded by Germans.

When the Jews arrived in Hamburg, British soldiers and military police were given extra rations of beer and cigarettes and fresh uniforms to raise morale before boarding the ships to force the passengers ashore. An eyewitness from the World Jewish Congress, Noah Barou, recalled that the soldiers were 'very young and I am told some were stationed before in Palestine. They went into the operation like a football team and did not understand the languages of the refugees. They were met with volleys of everything that came to hand, from biscuits to bulks of timber and cries of "Hitler commandos" and "gentlemen fascists".' One young woman appeared at the top of a stairway and shouted, 'I am from Dachau.' 'The Jews were fighting madly all the way,' the British commander reported. 'In several cases the resistance, even by children, was fanatical.' One trooper 'was downed with half a dozen Jews on top kicking and tearing at him'.[9]

Once ashore, the refugees were taken to camps in northern Germany and Austria. British soldiers were photographed dragging them from trains to a camp near Lübeck. In Austria, they burned an effigy of Bevin. More than half eventually found their way to Palestine, often via the US occupation zone. Zionist militants blew up the police headquarters in Haifa in retaliation for their treatment, killing ten people and injuring fifty-four. By the late summer of 1947, the Attlee government could hardly wait for the UN Committee to deliver its verdict.

~

## MEANWHILE

- The Chinese government asks the US for a loan of $500 million to $1 billion. Truman charges General Albert Wedemeyer, who had been the US military envoy to China in the later stages of the war against Japan, to carry out 'an objective survey' of conditions in China and Korea.
- In Burma, which is set for independence at the beginning of 1948, seven members of the Executive Council including the prime minister, Aung San, are killed by men in uniform who machine-gun a Cabinet meeting.
- In Greece, Communist rebels launch their biggest offensive in the north of the country but are beaten back by government forces. Thousands of alleged members of 'Communist terrorist organisations' are arrested as US aid flows in.
- In Japan, Douglas MacArthur says demilitarisation has been completed and the country is embarked on course to 'a peaceful and constructive future'.
- In France, a week-long strike cuts coal output by 700,000 tons.
- The Swedish diplomat, Raoul Wallenberg, who saved thousands of Jews in Hungary and was then taken prisoner by the Russians, is said to have died of a heart attack in the Lubyanka jail in Moscow. This is later disputed with reports that he was shot – or is still alive.
- A world conference in Paris forecasts an annual global deficit of 18 million tons of cereals.
- The AK-47 Kalashnikov assault rifle enters production; some 75 million will be made in the following decades.
- The Tour de France resumes after wartime suspension and is won by a little-known French rider.
- The betrothal is announced of the heir to the British throne, Princess Elizabeth, and Philip Mountbatten. It is, the *Manchester Guardian* comments, 'clearly a marriage of choice, not of arrangement'.

# PART FOUR

# AUGUST 1947

ACTS

*The independence and partition of India and Pakistan; communal violence in the Punjab and elsewhere; Gandhi's attempts at pacification; the fate of the princely states.*

SCENES

*New Delhi, Karachi, Punjab, Bengal, Hyderabad and other princely states.*

CAST

*Nehru, Patel, Gandhi, Jinnah, Liaquat, Baldev Singh, Mountbatten, maharajahs and nawabs.*

# CHAPTER TWELVE

# THE BIRTH OF TWO NATIONS

## I: The midnight hour

'Long years ago, we made a tryst with destiny and now the time has come when we redeem our pledge, not wholly or in full measure but very substantially,' Jawaharlal Nehru declared to an audience of 2,000 politicians, princes and grandees gathered in the Constituent Assembly building in Delhi late on the night of 14 August to celebrate the independence of India, which came into force the following day, a date approved by soothsayer. 'At the stroke of the midnight hour, when the world sleeps,[1] India will awake to life and freedom,' the prime minister declared. 'A moment comes, which comes but rarely in history, when we step out from the old to the new, when an age ends and when the soul of a nation long suppressed finds utterance.'

As the clock struck the midnight hour that brought independence, the sound echoed through the chamber of a conch shell into which a Hindu was blowing to invoke the approval of the gods. Nehru covered his smile with his hand. Outside, an artillery salvo saluted the new nation, temple bells rang, fireworks exploded, the crowd exulted. To complete the handover of power, Nehru and Rajendra Prasad, the president of the Constituent Assembly, were driven from the Assembly to the palatial Viceroy's House.

Watched by journalists, Prasad started to invite Mountbatten to become independent India's first governor-general, but stumbled over his words. The prime minister prompted him. 'I am proud of the honour and will do my best to carry out your advice in a

constitutional manner,' the British monarch's cousin replied. Nehru
handed over a large envelope saying it contained the names of government ministers. Mountbatten, who had watched a Bob Hope
film before the visit, poured port and proposed 'To India.' 'To
King George VI,' Nehru replied, a significant accommodation for
a leader of the independence movement who had earlier refused to
join in such toasting of British royalty. After the visitors had left,
Mountbatten opened the envelope. It was empty.[2]

As Independence Day continued, more than a million people
massed round the Red Fort in Delhi to watch Nehru raise the flag
of the nation of 330 million inhabitants covering 1.5 million square
miles. The future Nobel Prize winner Amartya Sen recalled being
'glued to the radio in our little school a hundred miles from Calcutta'
as he listened to the prime minister's speech 'with rapt attention – we
felt powerful, inspired'. Three thousand guests mingled at an evening
reception among the jacaranda trees of the former Vice-Regal palace;
thousands of small lights twinkled in the branches. W. E. B. Du Bois,
the African-American sociologist and civil rights campaigner, hailed
'the greatest historical date' of modern times as marking the end of
the era in which 'the white man, by reason of the color of his skin,
can lord it over colored people'.[3]

The newly appointed governor-general had returned that day from
Karachi where he had attended Pakistan's independence ceremonies. Jinnah had been greeted by jubilant crowds when he arrived in
Karachi earlier in the week. But, though there was wild cheering in
some places, impartial observers were struck by the often-flat mood
and some half-empty streets on the historic day. The Great Leader
took the position of governor-general of Pakistan for himself. Setting
out his vision of the future, he told the people of the new country,
'You are free. You are free to go to your temples. You are free to go
to your mosques. Or to any other place of worship in this State of
Pakistan. You may belong to any religion or caste or creed ... We
are starting with this fundamental principle that we are all citizens
and equal citizens of the State.'

He looked to the day when 'Hindus would cease to be Hindus
and Muslims would cease to be Muslims, not in the religious sense,

because that is a personal faith of each individual, but in the political sense as citizens of the state'. In a gesture of togetherness and a rebuke to the caste system across the border, a Hindu Untouchable was elected as temporary chairman of the Constituent Assembly. English was laid down as the working language; a member who tried to speak in Urdu was told to switch tongues.[4]

There were some troubling portents. The ancient Rolls-Royce carrying Jinnah and Mountbatten to the independence ceremony caught fire. Inside the building, many seats for the public and distinguished guests were empty. Nineteen of the sixty-nine members of the assembly did not turn up. Only one Hindu and no Sikhs attended the swearing-in of the new governor in Lahore, Francis Mudie, a member of the Indian civil service known for his hostility to Congress. An electricity failure cut off power from fans and lights during the reception after his inauguration, which he described as 'the worst party ever given by anyone'. The only illumination was from the burning city. 'All around the garden, there was firing going on – not isolated shots, but volleys,' Mudie recalled.[5]

Hindu nationalists denounced the 'vivisection' of partition. Its leader, L. B. Bhopatkar, insisted that 'India is one and indivisible and ... there will never be peace unless separated areas are brought back into the Indian Union and made its integral parts'. The newspaper of the RSS paramilitary organisation declared 15 August as a day of mourning for the destruction of the 'sacred indivisibility of Mother India'.[6]

But Nehru's deputy, Patel, said that 'the poison has been removed from the body of India', while Jinnah held 'We have either a divided India or a destroyed India'; without it, his newspaper *Dawn* warned, Muslims in a Hindu-dominated subcontinent would have been in the same position as Jews in Nazi Germany. As the senior British civil servant Penderel Moon noted, Hindus 'may loudly lament their brethren in Bengal and Punjab being torn from the embrace of Mother India, but they are not likely to have the will or the power to undertake a Crusade on their behalf'. Agreeing to partition after insisting for decades on the unity of the subcontinent had not been the only concession Congress made to gain freedom for the nation; it also agreed to drop its long-standing opposition to becoming a Dominion of what would shortly be the British Commonwealth.[7]

Though a pall of smoke hung over Delhi from the burning of official documents, Britain constructed a narrative of dignified retreat. There was no mention of the long decades in which British business had exploited the Raj while political concessions were granted with extreme parsimony and a policy of divide and rule buttressed imperial rule. Nobody on the British side mentioned that only one-eighth of the population was literate, that only 1,500 out of 640,000 villages had electricity or that life expectancy was twenty-seven; nor how imperial dominance had impoverished the two new nations and left 90 per cent of the population below the poverty line in a land where the economy grew by an average of less than 1 per cent a year while the population rose at more than three times that rate.[8]

Rather than the reality of pell-mell withdrawal under economic stress at home with a minimum of planning and a maximum of improvisation or sheer failure to anticipate events, the image was propagated of a progressive, far-sighted decision to withdraw, leaving multiple benefits of a high-minded empire. The violence of nationhood was not directed against the British as the new rulers took on much of the heritage left by the imperialists. English was the lingua franca of the leaders of both new nations. The colonial administrative structure remained in place. Police who had repressed protests by Congress leaders served under those same men. Preventive detention was retained. The armies of the two new states were placed under a British field marshal, Claude Auchinleck. Assemblies elected in 1946 under a limited franchise dictated by the British continued as legislatures.

For the Congress chiefs, the best way of ensuring the strong state they sought was to perpetuate the existing organs of government, not to initiate revolutionary change. Nor, despite the progressive views proclaimed by Nehru, did they make any attempt to combat India's caste system, even though the brilliant leader of the Untouchables, Bhimrao Ramji Ambedkar, was put in charge of drawing up the constitution. Jinnah would have liked a similar strong state for Pakistan, but the chronic lack of resources, the influence of religion, geographical division and the hostility shown by the larger neighbour all made it hard to achieve the kind of authority enjoyed by Nehru, Patel and their colleagues.

## II: The poison cup

The best-known person in India was not present at the ceremonies in Delhi. Approaching his seventy-eighth birthday, Mahatma Gandhi had chosen to spend Independence Day in Calcutta.

Bengal's greatest city had been hit by a fresh outbreak of violence in the preceding days, a year after the Great Killing. In a gesture of conciliation and hope that his message of peace still had force, the mahatma passed the day in the company of former premier Shaheed Suhrawardy, who had asked him to use his influence to defend the Muslims of the Hindu-majority city. Gandhi agreed, provided the politician joined him in the Hydari Mansion, a deserted, dilapidated building surrounded by refuse and stagnant water in the middle of a turbulent Muslim–Hindu district, described by Patel as 'a veritable shambles and a notorious den of gangsters and hooligans'. 'And in what choice company too!' the politician added. 'It is a terrible risk.'

Cyril Radcliffe's partition ruling allocated the west of Bengal to India and the east to Pakistan. India got the great prize of Calcutta, with its 64 per cent Hindu majority. Violence ebbed and flowed in the weeks before independence. Bodies were found in the streets, in boxes and sacks, and in sewers. 'The city remains full of fear,' a correspondent reported.[9]

On the night of 14 August, Gandhi held a prayer meeting attended by more than 10,000 people outside the house, calling for communal unity to a mixed audience, and hoping that the 'poison cup of disturbances' would be replaced with the 'nectar of friendliness'. But Hindu youths stoned the house and demanded Suhrawardy's blood. The former premier lay on the floor until Gandhi returned from prayers and opened the window to appeal for calm, standing at the window with his arm around the other man's shoulder.[10]

'It is Bengal's good luck that the mahatma is in our midst at this hour,' Suhrawardy said. 'Will Bengal realise its high privilege and stop the fratricide?'

'Are you not responsible for the Great Calcutta Killing?' the crowd shouted back.

'We all are,' the politician replied and then, as the crowd kept after him, he admitted, 'Yes, it was my responsibility.'

That cooled things down and the two men were able to walk unmolested through the city for an hour at night while Hindus and Muslims chanted slogans in favour of unity and friendship. The next day, thousands went to the mansion to join Gandhi in prayer. He fasted and worked his spinning wheel while Suhrawardy did without food too. The mahatma was then driven around the city for two hours. Crowds pouring out their grievances blocked the passage, but it was his day of silence so he did not respond, making notes in a little book instead.[11]

## III: New lands, old quarrels

In 1946, Nehru had told a journalist, Jacques Marcuse, of his three convictions: 'One, India will never be a Dominion. Two, there will never be a Pakistan. Three, when the British go, there will be no more communal violence in India.' Meeting Marcuse just after independence, he could only murmur, 'Wasn't I wrong?'[12]

After Radcliffe's findings were published on 17 August, the flood of refugees and the killings intensified. All sides criticised his decisions. In private, Radcliffe was recorded as considering that partition was a great mistake and could only bring a rising tide of communal war. 'We could have held India quite easily but having let things go so far we had no alternative but to get out,' he told friends after returning to London.[13]

'Since I assumed charge of my office, I have done nothing but tried to keep people from killing each other or visited refugee camps and hospitals,' Nehru reflected. 'All the plans which I had drawn up for making India a prosperous and progressive country had to be relegated to the background.' Surveying the violence, he worried at 'an upheaval of the lower middle class – the classes who first supported Hitler' and detected 'madness in its worst form' in the violence. His faith in Indians was being shaken; 'I could not conceive of the gross brutality and sadistic cruelty that people have indulged in,' he wrote to a friend. It was 'more than I can bear'. One of Mountbatten's aides described him as looking 'inexpressibly sad' at 'the crucifixion of his life-work'.[14]

Jinnah was even gaunter than ever, his cheekbones standing out like horizontal ridges, his teeth in bad condition. A Western observer thought he resembled 'a walking, talking corpse'. His appetite was minimal and he could not sleep. He was more alone than ever, living in a largely empty wing of Government House in Karachi with his sister, described by Edwina Mountbatten as 'almost fanatical ... like Mr Jinnah she has a persecution mania'. He had not seen his only child, Dina, since she married a Christian from a prominent Parsee family; she stayed in England, never visiting Pakistan in his lifetime. His sister recalled that when they discussed the latest news at breakfast, 'his handkerchief furtively often went to his moist eyes'. Shooting his portrait, the American photographer Margaret Bourke-White noted that his hands were 'desperately clenched' and detected 'a spiritual numbness concealing something close to panic'.[15]

The country he had brought into being was in a sorry state. Its 361,000 square miles of territory and 70 million people were dwarfed by India's 1.27 million square miles and population of 390 million. It had low levels of literacy. Large provinces in the north were made up of barren mountains and stony plains while poverty-stricken Pakistani Bengal was subject to floods. Feudal landlords held sway over agricultural areas such as the south Punjab. The economy was backward, depending on agriculture, textiles and jute. The treasury in Karachi was short of money from the start. As Jinnah acknowledged in his inaugural address, the country suffered from the 'poison' of bribery and corruption, the 'monster' of black-markeerting and 'the great evil' of nepotism and jobbery. Big landlords held sway in farming regions.

Dreams for the 'land of the pure' had been clouded by the failure to gain the whole of the Muslim-majority provinces of Bengal and Punjab. Jinnah called the Radcliffe adjudication 'unjust, incomprehensible and even perverse'. One Pakistani minister condemned them as 'a parting kick of the British ... a sop to Sikhs and Goondaism (Hindu hooliganism)'. The two halves of the new state were separated by 900 miles of Indian territory and Delhi turned

down proposals for a land corridor between them. The sea journey
between the main ports of Karachi in the west and Chittagong in
the east took at least five days.[16]

India, as a saying went, was the elephant and Pakistan its two
ears. Pakistan was, in Jinnah's words, 'mutilated' and 'moth-eaten';
Reuters correspondent Doon Campbell described it in a letter home
as 'a lame, truncated, bisected country'. It lacked internal cohesion.
Bengalis were alienated by the refusal to give their tongue official
status. Nor did they relish being ruled by politicians from far off.
Thirty million Muslims stayed in India.[17]

Some of the richest parts of Punjab had gone to India. Sindh was
divided between its largely rural hinterland and the fast-developing
capital of Karachi. Balochistan, with 43 per cent of the country's territory but only 7 per cent of its population, had mineral and energy
reserves but was economically backward, its princely states retaining
local influence. The North-West Frontier, covering nearly 30,000
square miles, was an isolated area populated largely by independent-
minded tribes given to plundering raids in the name of religious jihads.

The flood of refugees exerted pressure the new state was not
equipped to absorb. The newcomers lacked cultural or linguistic
links with the existing population. Most were peasants who brought
few skills to the new nation, while Hindu professionals, merchants
and bankers fled eastwards, taking with them currency, bullion and
jewels. 'We are leaving the "Pakistan" an economic desert,' one
financier told the *Civil and Military Gazette* of Lahore. Imports
of cloth, coal and petrol from India petered out. Cotton for export
piled up because almost all the brokers had left. Only 10,000 of the
300,000 Hindus who had lived in Lahore remained. Three years after
independence, the city's economic output was still below the level of
1946 as property prices crashed and transport barely functioned.[18]

Politicians in Delhi were in no mood for co-operation. Most
Congress leaders thought their neighbour was bound to collapse. A
free trade agreement between the two countries soon broke down
and each slapped levies on goods from the other. 'Every effort is
being made to put difficulties in our way by our enemies in order
to paralyse or cripple our State and bring about its collapse,' Jinnah
wrote to Attlee.[19]

In theory, Raj government property and equipment was to be divided 80 per cent to India and 20 per cent to Pakistan, but Patel and his colleagues put obstacles in the way, forbidding officials moving to Pakistan to take files or furniture with them. In Karachi, they worked on packing cases as desks, sometimes using thorns as paper clips. 'The government ... is being created overnight,' Major General Shahid Hamid, Jinnah's military secretary, recorded. 'There are no Government officials, no secretaries, and no office furniture or stationary. Typewriters are a luxury. It is utter chaos.' Or, as somebody at the independence ceremonies put it, 'Pakistan was being improvised.'[20]

A bomb on the tracks blew up a train carrying government staff and equipment from Delhi.[21] When the finance minister went to his office to start work, he found it empty except for a single table. Such was the lack of readiness in the capital that the new administration suggested holding the first sessions of the Pakistani Constituent Assembly in Delhi, an idea rejected by the Indians.

Pakistan received only fourteen of the Raj's eighty-nine regiments, the rest going to India. Its army was dominated by men from western Punjab and the North-West Frontier, who became a key element in the new country. Its air force was made up of two squadrons to India's eight. Its navy consisted of two frigates, six minesweepers and eight other small craft, while its neighbour had twenty-four ships plus a cruiser bought from Britain and with three destroyers on order. Of 160,000 tons of ordinance allocated to Pakistan, no more than 23,000 arrived.[22]

A loan was obtained from the Muslim nizam of Hyderabad, but would cover only four months of the expenses of the army, which took three-quarters of the first budget. A request for a big credit from Washington brought just a few million dollars. Still, Jinnah had the Pakistani representative in the United States order a green Cadillac 'super limousine' at a cost of $6,000 to replace the antiquated Rolls.[23]

On the flight back to Delhi from Karachi, Mountbatten and his wife had looked down at the plumes of smoke rising from the Punjab. The spiral of attacks and reprisals seemed unending, mestastasizing as it spread across the province. Three days before the declaration of independence, Louis Heren of the London *Times* stared from a bridge at a train headed for Pakistan that had been diverted into a siding; all 4,000 Muslims on board had been killed, he reported. 'The Sikhs will tell you that this is retaliation for what Muslims did to the Sikhs in Rawalpindi in March which was retaliation for Hindu massacres of Muslims in Bihar which was retaliation for Noakhali which was retaliation for Calcutta,' he wrote.[24]

'*Murder and Arson Reach New Peak. Lahore Walled City a Veritable Sea of Flames*', read the main headline in the *Civil and Military Gazette* on Independence Day. Muslims and Sikhs fought in the streets. Large areas were in ashes after arson attacks; the city's two fire engines were unable to penetrate the narrow streets of the Old City where scores of thousands of people were trapped without water. The only impartial security force consisted of two hundred Gurkhas under a twenty-year-old British officer.[25]

Seventy thousand refugees arrived in Lahore in the week after independence. The crowded trains heading westwards, with people sitting on the roofs of carriages or on the buffers and bogeys, were repeatedly attacked by Sikh and Hindu gangs. The city's station, built in the style of a castle with thick walls and turrets, became a charnel house circled with barbed wire. Railway drivers refused to work without military guards. Miles of bodies stretched on each side of the Grand Trunk Road to the Indian border.[27]

Out in the countryside, the hugely undermanned Punjab Boundary Force, set up to try to maintain order, was unable to intervene to any effect. Visiting East Punjab, Penderel Moon wrote of villages 'just being allowed to run amuck as they pleased'. The Sikh leader Tara Singh said Punjab was to the Sikhs what Palestine was to the Jews. After a six-hour attack on one village, only forty of 350 Muslim inhabitants remained alive. In another, Sikhs hacked mothers and children into small pieces and cut off the hands of women kneeling in supplication for mercy. In reprisals, Muslims stormed trains to kill refugees fleeing the province.[26]

The industrial town of Sheikhupura near Lahore, whose population was divided between Muslims and Sikhs and which had been allocated to Pakistan, erupted after a false rumour spread that mosques were about to be assaulted. Muslim mobs rampaged through the town, joined by police and troops with machine guns.

'Street after street was surrounded by Muslim mobs, military and police,' a young Sikh survivor, who took refuge with his family in a Christian church, recalled. After Muslim thugs forced them into the street where his father was beaten to death, the boy ran away and hid in a poor district. On the fourth day, Christian peace volunteers rescued him, imploring him to cut his long hair. He refused. On his way to a refugee camp, he saw that most houses and shops of Hindus and Sikhs had been burned. People fleeing to the station were surrounded and shot with machine guns. The main street was covered with hundreds of bodies and the air was heavy with the stink of death.

Anywhere from 10,000 to 20,000 people were estimated to have been killed by shooting, stabbing, beating and burning alive in Sheikhupara. Hospitals were desperately short of medicines and staff to deal with men and women whose hands had been cut off, whose forearms were black putrescent fly-covered stumps, and children, even babies, who had been cut and slashed. Visiting at the end of the month, Nehru said he was 'sick with horror'. When a Muslim crowd stopped his car, he shouted at them, 'Are you not ashamed of yourselves? Have you no conscience left?[28]

There were instances of mercy and of members of one community protecting those of another. In Sheikhupura, the civil surgeon recorded how the lives of his children and some six hundred Hindus and Sikhs were saved 'by the efforts of some God-fearing Muslims who gave them shelter in their houses, even at the risk of their lives'. But, more often, the divisions between Hindus, Muslims and Sikhs, and some smaller groups, were sealed in blood and suffering and what Nehru called 'a competition in retaliation'. Paramilitary groups were ruthless, well organised, well armed and backed by local politicians and landowners, or, in some cases, by the rulers of princely states.[29]

The RSS movement was estimated to have half a million members by August 1947, including adherents in the police and magistrature. Its leader, Madhav Sadashiv Golwalkar, demanded that non-Hindus in what he called Hindustan must adopt 'the Hindu culture and language, must learn to respect and hold in reverence Hindu religion, must entertain no idea but those of glorification of the Hindu race and culture ... wholly subordinated to the Hindu nation, claiming nothing, deserving no privileges, far less any preferential treatment – not even citizens' rights'. While Gandhi still held out the hope that the people of India and Pakistan 'shall ever be friends and brothers helping and respecting one another', Penderel Moon wondered if the two new nations would 'sink into utter and irretrievable chaos'.[30]

Neither government could guarantee the basic duty of protecting its citizens in regions such as Punjab, where administration had largely broken down, food ran short in some areas and British officers told reporters that what they were witnessing was 'a thousand times more horrible than anything we saw in the war'. Refugees carried stories of atrocities and rumours flew, fuelling a cycle of reprisals.[31]

Nehru made two trips to Punjab in the last week of August. On the first, he was driven through deserted, wrecked villages littered with bodies to a dusty plain where a column of 100,000 refugees wended its way across the countryside. 'I cannot imagine another day when he could have felt more strongly that all his hopes, his dreams, his faith in human nature were crashing down in pieces,' his secretary wrote. On his second visit, he had what would turn out to be his last encounter with Jinnah at Government House in Lahore. They made a joint broadcast appeal for peace, but this did nothing to stop the violence. As the correspondent of the London *Times* put it, 'Speeches by prominent politicians and visits by them to the disturbed areas have had no visible effect, the reason being that the machine has broken down and the respective administrative Governments have no means of implementing their policies and desires ... only the physical disappearance of the minority concerned will end the trouble.'[32]

Under pressure from the Indian and Pakistani governments, which each wanted to take formal control, the Punjab Boundary Force was disbanded at the end of the month. In Lahore, the roads were empty except for military and police vehicles. No Hindus or Sikhs were visible outside refugee camps, which had no food, sanitation or care. The official death toll for the month in Amritsar alone was put at 3,000, but authoritative estimates were up to four times higher. An army officer reported seeing four babies roasted to death over a fire.[33]

The killing spread to Delhi and the surrounding region, leading

Mountbatten to note in his daily journal, 'I've never been through such a time in my life. The War, the Viceroyalty were jokes, for we have been dealing with life and death in our city.' Calcutta was hit by fresh violence. A crowd of angry Hindus massed around the shabby mansion where Gandhi was staying. He had gone to bed, but got up as a brick crashed through a window. The mob invaded the house, bringing with it a boy said to have been wounded by Muslims and demanding Gandhi issue a call for revenge. Doors and windows were broken. One man threw a stick, which narrowly missed the mahatma. There were shouts of 'Go back, Gandhi'. After five hours, police used tear gas to disperse the crowd. The next day, Hindu mobs attacked Muslims, killing at least fifty.[34]

Gandhi said he would fast to the death unless the violence ceased, lying in a cot and refusing anything but sips of water. He told Hindus and Muslims who came to apologise for the violence that he 'intended to stir the conscience and remove mental sluggish-ness'. After two days, city leaders signed a pledge there would be no more violence. Gandhi drank a glass of sweet lime juice. Calcutta remained quiet.

## IV: Maharajahs, nizams and nabobs

The end of the Raj posed an existential challenge for the rulers of the 550 princely states that occupied two-fifths of Indian territory. They had been an important prop for British rule, which allowed them authority over internal affairs, including their own legal systems, while the Raj took charge of defence, foreign affairs and communi-cations and approving, or proposing, their chief ministers. They had been offered blandishments in honours such as the Star of India, titles and invitations to grand receptions; a quarter of the princes headed 'salute states' meaning they were entitled gun salutes on ceremonial occasions. Conrad Corfield, head of the Indian Political Service that oversaw them, flew to London to intercede on their behalf and had more than four tons of confidential documents burned and shipped back to the UK to avoid any embarrassing disclosures. But Patel and his lieutenant, V. P. Menon, were intent on getting the princes to adhere to the new nation on their terms.[35]

The size and nature of the states varied hugely. Hyderabad and Jammu and Kashmir stretched over some 80,000 square miles each. Others were tiny, one covering only an acre. A few had industrialised and were relatively progressive with efficient civil services – Mysore and Baroda had good universities and Hyderabad spent a significant amount on education. Thirty-two states had railways operating on their own gauges. Others were extremely backward and reactionary, practising female infanticide and rural slavery.

Jai Singh of Alwar, ruler of Rajasthan, wore silk gloves for fear of his skin coming into contact with anything unclean. A heavy drinker, he employed a procurer to get him good-looking male youths. He was said to have once become so angry with a poorly performing polo horse that he set it alight with kerosene. But contemporaries judged him as well read and articulate, in the words of one British secretary of state, 'a man of imagination and of industry, of knowledge and of reasoning power'.

The nawab of Junagadh, on the west coast, a Muslim ruling a majority Hindu population, kept hundreds of dogs for whom he staged elaborate birthday parties and weddings. The ruler of Rampur, in the United Provinces, liked to show off his collection of two hundred radio sets, and kept a private jazz band. In mineral-rich Travancore, on the south-west coast, the maharajah, in his mid-thirties, was the puppet of his beautiful mother, the junior maharani, described by a British political agent as 'arrogant, uncharitable, egotistical, bad-tempered, insular and vindictive'. The ruler of one Punjab princedom who ran short of money arranged for the state treasury to be burgled and pocketed the cash before absconding. Another ruler from the Punjabi plain threatened to shoot Nehru if he visited his territory. At a meeting in Mountbatten's office, the maharajah of Jodhpur brandished a revolver at Menon.[36]

The biggest state, Hyderabad, with 16 million inhabitants, had its own currency, army, transport and postal system, as well as a big university. Its reserves of precious metals and his ownership of 10 per cent of the state's land led to its ruler being ranked as the richest man in the world.[37] Diminutive and shy, His Exalted Highness Nizam Sir Mir Osman Ali Khan Siddiqi Asaf Jah VII had seven wives and a large number of concubines; he was said to father a child every four months. He padded through his sprawling palace with its huge library in faded carpet slippers and a thin white dressing gown with a brown fez perched on the back of his head, and liked to take photographs of European visitors in the nude with hidden cameras; he also prowled graveyards at night and watched operations in hospitals.[38]

Despite his wealth, he was famed for his stinginess – at a dinner he gave for the ex-king of Spain and fifty guests, he provided a single bottle of champagne. His car was a rattling 1918 model and his office was described by a British visitor as 'an excessively mean and squalid little room with two decrepit swivel chairs, two or three kitchen chairs, an antique safe, a few boxes and a pile of dusty letters and documents' looking out onto 'a very small and smelly yard'. Cobwebs hung from its dirty ceiling and walls.[39]

The Muslim nizam ruled an 87 per cent Hindu state. His dynasty was the oldest Indian ruling house of its religion, giving it a special historical and cultural significance. Many Hindu businesses supported him, as did landowners and lower caste Dalits. He faced pressure from Congress in Delhi and Hyderabad for adhesion to India, but the Muslim Razakar movement, with a militia and a charismatic, rabble-rousing leader, held that sovereignty rested in the Islamic community rather than in the ruler and distributed leaflets declaring 'Free Hyderabad for the Hyderabadis'. Jinnah warned that if the state was forced to join India, 'every Muslim throughout the whole of India, yes, all the hundred million Muslims, would rise as one man to defend the oldest Muslim dynasty in India'. But Patel said its independence would create 'a cancer on the belly' of the nation.[40]

Refugees streamed over the border in both directions. Communists in the state's largely agricultural Telangana region led an uprising which redistributed big estates to peasants, abolished forced labour and ran a parallel government in more than a thousand villages. The complexity of the state's politics were heightened by support the nizam received from Churchill and British Tories who saw him as a weapon in their long-running war against Congress.[41]

For all his tightfistedness, the ruler extended a loan to Pakistan and paid a reputed 90,000 guineas a year for the services of his British legal adviser, the well-connected Conservative Walter Monckton, to keep India at bay. The lawyer claimed that treaties between Hyderabad and the British should preserve his state's autonomy after the Raj ended, and that Congress was exerting 'intolerable black-mail' in 'an exhibition of power politics ... an exact replica of those in which Hitler indulged'.[42]

The nizam was not alone in seeking to stay outside India or form an attachment to Pakistan. The chief minister of Travancore declared independence, with the support of the junior maharani; Jinnah promised 'a relationship which will be of mutual advantage'. The dog-loving Muslim nawab of Junagadh wanted to become part of Pakistan despite having no land border with it and in defiance of his state's mainly Hindu population. Though Hindu, the young maharajah of Jodhpur, whose state bordered Pakistan, toyed with the idea of joining it; Jinnah offered port facilities in Karachi, arms and grain supplies.[43]

London was not interested in such moves. It repudiated its treaties without hesitation and Mountbatten told a group of rulers who planned to form a union and then join Pakistan that there could be no question of their states not being incorporated into India. 'Most agreed, feeling that they could not go against the wishes of the king's cousin,' a political agent recorded. 'A few who were intransigent were taken to see Lady Mountbatten who told them peremptorily that they must do as they were told.'[44]

Patel made plain that India would use its authority over defence and communications to impose its rule if there was opposition. He and Menon allowed the rulers to keep their titles and palaces, and they were paid a 'privy purse' calculated according to the revenue of their states; by Menon's reckoning, the central government made ten times as much money from tax earning as it paid out in stipends. But the acquisition of territory was what counted most. As Patel told officials, 'We do not want their women and their jewellery – we want their land.'[45]

MEANWHILE

- Yugoslavia and Bulgaria sign a treaty of alliance without informing Moscow. Stalin tells Tito the agreement was mistaken and premature. Soviet officials call Yugoslav proposals for a Balkan federation far-fetched.
- Parliamentary elections are held in Hungary but, despite extensive rigging, the Communists get only 22 per cent of the vote.
- The British government announces new targets for output of coal, steel and agriculture and trade goals. Miners are told to work an additional half hour but strike at fourteen pits. Convertibility of sterling is restricted. The petrol ration is cut by a third and the meat ration reduced. The US and UK open negotiations on loan terms.
- The Americans and British agree to a further 30 per cent increase in industrial production in their zones of Germany; France objects that output is not being controlled.
- The USSR demands oil concessions in Iran, attacking 'the intrigues of the Anglo-Iranian company' and the 'strangling of the working class'.
- The trial starts in Germany of senior executives of the IG Farben chemical group accused of war crimes and crimes against humanity for collaboration with the Nazis, including work at gas chambers at Auschwitz.
- 10,000 Boy Scouts gather for the World Jamboree at Moisson outside Paris.
- The first Edinburgh Festival is held, opened by a concert by the Colonne Orchestra of Paris which the *Times* reviewer finds 'oppressively loud'.
- Pilot William Odom makes a 20,000-mile round-the-world flight in seventy-three hours and five minutes.
- The *Kon-Tiki* raft skippered by Norwegian ethnologist and explorer Thor Heyerdahl arrives in French Polynesia after 101 days crossing the Pacific, showing the possibility of historic migration across the ocean.

# PART FIVE

# SEPTEMBER 1947

**ACTS**

*The UN Committee backs partition in Palestine; the Soviet Union forms a new Communist organisation for European parties; the envoy sent to China by Truman delivers his report on the situation there, and is told to keep quiet; Post-independence violence continues in India and Pakistan before ebbing.*

**SCENES**

*Lake Success; Washington; Szklarska Poręba; Nanking; Delhi, Punjab.*

**CAST**

*Ben-Gurion, King Abdullah, Truman; Zhdanov, Duclos, Djilas, Gomułka; Albert Wedemeyer, Chiang; Nehru, Gandhi.*

# CHAPTER THIRTEEN

# LAND AND LIVES

## I: PARTITION ADVANCES

In its report issued on 3 September, the United Nations Special Committee on Palestine came out for independence and partition of Palestine at the earliest possible date. It proposed splitting the territory into separate Arab and Jewish states linked in an economic union with a special status for Jerusalem where both communities would have rights. There should be freedom of movement and unrestricted commercial relations. Each state would have 'a self-operating control of immigration' and the plight of displaced European Jews should be handled as a matter of extreme urgency. The Jewish state would contain 498,000 Jews and 407,000 Arabs, the Arab state 725,000 Arabs and 10,000 Jews. Jerusalem would house 105,000 Arabs and 100,000 Jews. The Negev desert was to be included in the Jewish state and Western Galilee in the Arab entity.

The UNSCOP report, which would go to a vote by the General Assembly two months later, noted that the Jewish entity would have 'a considerable minority of Arabs' but saw this as inevitable under any plan that did not place the whole of Palestine under Arab rule. The Jews, it went on,

> bring to the land the social dynamism and scientific method of the West; the Arabs confront them with individualism and intuitive understanding of life. Here then, in this close association, through the natural emulation of each other, can be evolved a

synthesis of the two civilizations, preserving, at the same time, their fundamental characteristics. In each State, the native genius will have a scope and opportunity to evolve into its highest cultural forms and to attain its greatest reaches of mind and spirit. In the case of the Jews, that is really the condition of survival. Palestine will remain one land in which Semitic ideals may pass into realization.[1]

While the Jewish Agency supported most of the findings, the Arabs rejected it, insisting Zionist claims had no legal or moral basis. At a secret meeting in London with the secretary of the Arab League, Azzam Pasha, Jewish representatives argued that their presence in Palestine was an established fact. Azzam replied that the Arabs were 'not in a compromising mood' and would try to crush any Jewish state. 'Nationalism, that's a greater force than any which drives us,' he added. 'We have only one test, the test of strength.' A Jewish delegate, economist David Horowitz, described the meeting as having destroyed any remaining hope of a peaceful settlement.[2]

The League decided in mid-September to establish an Arab Liberation Army (ALA). To an Egyptian newspaper, Azzam spoke of a 'war of elimination ... which history will record similarly to the Mongol massacre or the wars of the Crusades'. Egypt's King Farouk forecast an Arab victory that would drive the Jews from Palestine. 'We shall eradicate Zionism,' the Syrian president declared.[3]

Ben-Gurion instructed the Haganah to mobilise 'the full capacity' of the Jewish community to safeguard its position. It set up operational units for the north, south and centre of the future state and for Jerusalem. The Palmach strike force created in 1941 to fight alongside the British in Syria was expanded to 2,100 men and women with a reserve of a further thousand. Supply chains were established. Hideouts and arms caches were built. Conscription was stepped up for both men and women. Medical services were developed. Veterans of the Second World War with the British Jewish brigade were recruited. Military training was undertaken in the refugee camps in Cyprus, using wooden rifles. The future Israeli prime minister said the aim might be not only to defend existing lands but also 'to conquer the whole country or most of it, and to maintain its occupation until the attainment of an authoritative political settlement'. 'We shall not restrict ourselves territorially,' he added.'[4]

## II: OH HELL!

The probability of partition found King Abdullah of Transjordan at increasing loggerheads with other Arab rulers. The monarch saw the situation as propitious to his ambitions to restore the Hashemite fortunes, forging a union with Syria, and then adding Palestine as a gateway to the sea. He had concluded a friendship treaty with Turkey which he hoped would back him, and had a strong fighting arm in the shape of the Arab Legion, the best Arab military force.

His great fear was that Palestine would fall under the sway of the Grand Mufti, whom he described as 'the greatest obstacle to settling matters in Palestine, Transjordan and Syria ... he must be removed from the scene at any price and quickly'. That made him keen to reach agreement with the Zionists, offering them semi-autonomy in return for support, money and expertise. Meeting a Jewish envoy in 1946 in his palace in Amman, he had told the visitor: 'You do not have any realistic leaders like me in the entire Arab world. You have two alternatives; to join with me and work together or to give me up.'[5]

Iraq was ready to treat with Abdullah in the hope that it too could get access to the Mediterranean. But he faced substantial opposition from other regional states. His plan was an anathema to Ibn Saud, who had chased the Hashemites from the Arabian Peninsula and had no desire to see them restore their strength to the north. The rulers in Damascus had nothing to gain from a Greater Syria run by Abdullah. Lebanon was equally hostile. The Palestinian clans, Egypt and the Arab League were all dedicated to opposing partition.[6]

British frustration over Palestine mounted as public opinion tired of the lack of an agreed solution and deaths from terrorism increased. A Zionist group in Paris headed by an American rabbi born in Ukraine tried to get a former US pilot to fly over London and shower Whitehall with incendiaries; the pilot prevaricated and informed the authorities – the rabbi was arrested when he arrived at the airfield to see the plane off.[7]

Bevin thought the UNSCOP conclusion was unjust and would stir further trouble. Britain told the UN it did not feel able to implement any agreement not acceptable to both Arabs and Jews. The government's overriding desire was to get out as swiftly as possible. A cartoon in *Punch* magazine summed up the mood as it showed a list of proposals for Palestine chalked on a wall, each crossed out, and a soldier in tin hat and shorts writing underneath, 'Oh Hell!'[8]

In Washington, the State Department continued to insist on the need to maintain good relations with the Arabs, the importance of oil and, as future secretary of state Dean Rusk put it, the fact that 'war in that area was not very inviting because it might draw us in, and draw the Soviets in'. On top of which, as Rusk added, some of his colleagues 'were not willing to accept that the Books of Moses constituted a land title in the twentieth century'.[9]

Despite his instinctive sympathy with the Zionist cause, Truman was growing fed up with the intensive lobbying by its supporters. He worried that, if the creation of a Jewish state led to war, the US might find itself involved in its new international role and saw the Zionist lobby as one of the special interest groups he deplored. 'I wish you would caution all your friends who are interested in the welfare of the Jews in Palestine that now is the time for restraint and caution,' he wrote to the Jewish former treasury secretary Henry Morgenthau Jr. He was further alienated when Rabbi Abba Hillel Silver, co-chair of the American Zionist Emergency Council who had close links with the Republican, hammered on the president's desk and shouted at him. Truman mused of the Jews that 'Jesus Christ couldn't please them when he was on earth, so how could anyone expect that I would have any luck?'[10]

# CHAPTER FOURTEEN

# SEPARATE CAMPS

Having brought Czechoslovakia to heel and ensured the loyalty of other states of East and Central Europe, Stalin felt it time to formalise the unity of the Soviet domain with an organisation to succeed the international Comintern he had dissolved during the war as a sop to the Allies. He put his close lieutenant, Andrei Zhdanov, whose son would marry his daughter Svetlana, in charge of this disciplinary exercise. The timing was probably influenced by the rolling out of the Marshall Plan, but Stalin had mooted the idea of establishing an organisation to ensure obedience the previous year.[1]

In charge of Leningrad in the 1930s, Zhdanov had conducted purges on behalf of his master with the required ruthlessness before helping to organise the defence of the city against the Germans. Described by the Yugoslav Milovan Djilas as 'rather short, with a brownish clipped moustache, a high forehead, pointed nose', he suffered from asthma and heart and liver trouble which meant he sometimes had to replace alcohol with fruit juice. Well educated and regarded in the Politburo as an intellectual, he took charge of culture and ideology, insisting that only socialist realism was acceptable to advance the class struggle. He branded the leading poet Anna Akhmatova as 'half-nun, half whore' and compared the music of Dmitri Shostakovich to a road drill and a mobile gas chamber. His attacks on Sergei Prokofiev for 'formalism' and 'anti-democratic tendencies' reduced the composer to a shell of his former self, who wrote celebrations of Stalin as the 'sun of our lives'.[2]

In late September, Zhdanov and Malenkov travelled to the Silesian mountain resort of Szklarska Poręba in Poland to meet leaders of Communist parties in other European countries. They maintained constant radio contact with Moscow from the State Security rest home in the midst of meadows chosen as the venue for the meeting with delegates from the Bulgarian, Czechoslovak, French, Hungarian, Italian, Polish, Romanian and Yugoslav Communist parties. Albania was considered too inconsequential to merit an invitation and the Greeks too much of a provocation to the West.

The opening Soviet statement pointed to the conference of foreign ministers in Moscow earlier in the year as evidence of the West's aggressive policies, particularly in Germany. International politics was 'dominated by the ruling clique of the American imperialists', it stated, calling on European Communist parties to step up the struggle against 'reactionary imperialist elements' aiming at enslavement of the Continent and creating a launching pad for an attack on the USSR. 'Reactionary imperialist elements' wanted to revive Germany and Japan as weapons against the USSR. Communist parties had to struggle against this by any means necessary, including sabotage in countries accepting US aid.[3]

Djilas followed with a swingeing attack on 'imperialists in Washington' and 'the sharks of Wall Street', while asserting that 'Moscow radiates freedom and justice for all mankind'. Rudolf Slánský, the Czechoslovak party's secretary-general, spoke of his country being under harsh pressure from American imperialism and pointed to the continuing presence of 'many reactionary bureaucrats', especially in Masaryk's Foreign Ministry.[4]

Zhdanov then laid out the doctrine by which the meeting would become known, positing the division of the world into two camps. There was 'the imperialist and anti-democratic camp on the one hand, and the anti-imperialist and democratic camp on the other'. The choice stretched from politics and culture to plant biology. Though cloaked in ideological language, this was designed to embody Moscow's mastery and reject any idea of 'national communism'.[5]

The French and Italian parties came in for violent criticism, led by two of the Yugoslavs, Edvard Kardelj and Djilas, who had resented the superior airs of comrades he had met at their party's congress in Paris in the summer. The sin of the West Europeans was held to have been their participation in governments led by bourgeois politicians – the fact that they had done so on Moscow's instructions was forgotten. They were told that they were guilty of having underestimated the power of the working class and allowed themselves to become 'victims of imperialists' intimidation and blackmail'.

Zhdanov described the French party as 'helpless and unprincipled' and guilty of 'parliamentary cretinism'. The Italians were ridiculed as 'bigger parliamentarians' than the Christian Democrats. Zhdanov warned the two parties that, if they failed to consult Moscow on all matters, they would suffer 'extremely harmful consequences'. Their aim must be to 'destroy the capitalist economy' – the French asked if they should prepare for armed revolt, to which Zhdanov did not reply.[6]

The Italians accepted the criticism and personal relations remained good. But Jacques Duclos, the short, bald, spherical leader of the delegation from Paris, tried to navigate his way through the attacks, further annoying Djilas who found him 'supercilious and self-confident'. The Frenchman later lamented that 'certain comrades seemed to have decided to put us on trial'. Matters were not helped by the fact that his delegation was the only one unable to conduct the discussion in Russian; their translator was not familiar with the political terminology being used and a Pole had to step in.[7]

Faced with Zhdanov's unrelenting attacks, Duclos admitted to 'opportunism, legalitarianism and parliamentary illusions'. The task now, he agreed, was to 'motivate the people against American imperialism'. He was later seen sitting on a bench in the compound, disconsolately swinging his legs and apparently sobbing.[8]

The only dissident voice came from the host, the Polish party leader, Władysław Gomułka, who advocated working with other parties of the left to 'follow the Polish road to Socialism'. In his speech opening the meeting, he had advocated 'collaboration with the petty bourgeois', a suggestion directly counter to the line about to be laid down by Moscow.

Gomułka already had several things against him as far as Stalin was concerned. He had spent the war inside his homeland, rather than joining the 'Moscow Communists', and had then spoken out against one-party rule while trying, with scant success, to stop the

Red Army removing goods and assets from territories allocated to Poland from Germany. The dictator found him personally annoying, complaining that 'he sits there all the time looking into my eyes as though he was searching for something. And why does he bring a notepad and pencil with him? Why does he write down every word I say?'

When Zhdanov set out the 'two camps' policy, Gomułka reacted by saying he had been duped. One of his colleagues drove to Warsaw to warn the Politburo of the clash. The central party organisation swiftly despatched an order to its first secretary to toe the Soviet line. He did so with a sinuous speech and survived – for the time being.[9]

The impact of the new Soviet line was felt as soon as the delegates got home, anxious to show their fealty to the new orders. In Bulgaria, Nikola Petkov, the leader of the Agrarian Party, was tried and convicted on espionage charges: 'to a dog, a dog's death', the Central Committee declared as he was hanged at the end of the month. German Communists were told that there was no 'German way' to socialism. On his return to Prague, Slánský declared that other political parties in Czechoslovakia were 'no longer just reactionary but treasonable' and drew up a plan for a general strike to be followed by a new administration to end 'the shackles of formal parliamentary democracy'. The Communist-controlled Interior Ministry announced the discovery of a plot to assassinate President Beneš; eighty people were arrested.[10]

Churches in Eastern Europe came under attack. Five million Ukrainian Catholics found themselves forcibly merged into the Russian Orthodox Church. Polish priests were accused of spying for the US and the Vatican. Romania's Greek-Catholics were branded as 'anti-national and anti-historical' and their assets transferred to the Orthodox Church. Hungary's Cardinal Mindszenty, who had been preaching at huge Marian Year celebrations and defending Catholic education, became a major target of the authorities; an official slogan vowed to 'annihilate Mindszentyism'. Leaders of the country's big Smallholders' Party were arrested or forced to leave the country or co-opted into the regime. The rightist Independent Party and the clerical Democratic People's Party, which had won 30 per cent of the vote between them at the summer general election, disintegrated. In

Yugoslavia, Tito denounced the Truman Doctrine as 'an endeavour to provoke war in Europe and to enslave other people'. Though it had not been invited to the Cominform meeting, Albania joined in the repression, executing sixteen people convicted of working for the US and UK, followed by a rolling pattern of mass arrests and executions.

Communist militancy surged in Italy and France. Though he had initially not wanted an outright rejection of US aid, Togliatti now accused Washington of 'splitting Europe in two' and warned that the Marshall Plan 'presented a grave danger of foreign control of our development'. The policy of 'progressive democracy' followed by his party might no longer be appropriate, he added. Millions of workers in agriculture and metallurgy stopped work, calling for higher wages in what the Communist leader termed the start of 'a major battle'. Deputies came to blows in the Parliament in Rome.

French Communist chiefs unleashed violent rhetorical attacks on the government and the Marshall Plan. Party publications ran cartoons of bomb-carrying American military officers planting Stars and Stripes flags across Western Europe. Thorez told the party's Central Committee that US aid was aimed at the 'colonization of France' and would turn it into 'an anti-Soviet operational base'. Duclos called for a new 'democratic government'.

'Russia has at last shown her hand and it contains the cards Marshall and I thought it would,' Truman wrote to his wife after hearing of the creation of the Cominform. 'All we can do is go ahead working for peace – and keep our powder dry.' The world, he added, seemed to be 'topsy-turvy' and the situation 'fraught with terrible consequences'. In a radio broadcast from the White House, the president said the most immediate danger lay in France and Italy. 'If the economies of these countries collapse and people succumb to totalitarian pressures, there will be no opportunity for them or for us to look forward to their recovery so essential for world peace.'[11]

'Suppose for example, that Italy should fold up and Tito then would march into the Po Valley,' his letter to his wife went on. 'All the Mediterranean coast of France is then open to Russian occupation and the iron curtain comes to Bordeaux, Calais, Antwerp and the Hague. We withdraw from Greece and Turkey and prepare for war.' Receiving a congressional delegation, the president warned of the prospect that 'the governments of France and Italy will fall, Austria too, and, for all practical purposes, Europe will be Communist ... This is serious. I can't over-emphasise how serious.' In a letter to his daughter he speculated that if a British bankruptcy shattered global prosperity, 'Uncle Joe Stalin can have his way. Looks like he may get it anyway.'[12]

The administration finalised plans for the National Security Council to coordinate military, diplomacy and intelligence activities and for the creation of the Central Intelligence Agency (CIA), which funnelled help to the Christian Democrats in Italy ahead of elections the following spring, and encouraged US labour groups to work with non-Communists to form a new union movement in France. The army and navy were brought together under James Forrestal, a former bond salesman who had made a fortune on Wall Street, with a separate department for the Air Force.

But the most important European initiative, the Marshall Plan, was demonstrating its inherent complexities. The European participants were split despite Washington's insistence on a unified approach. Germany, which would be at the core of a European recovery, was not represented at the coordinating conference in Paris. Governments jockeyed for allocation of funds. The UK still hoped for a bilateral deal of its own. France was suspicious of British intentions, wanted access to the Ruhr, and was concerned that the revival of Germany would take precedence over its own recovery. George Kennan, for one, was concerned that time was running out fast. 'As a body politic, England is seriously sick,' he thought. Economic conditions there and in France were deteriorating with 'terrifying rapidity'. Unless something was done by the end of the year 'both faced hunger by winter, and other complications of unpredictable dimensions, with unforeseen effects in other areas of the world'.[13]

The evidence was plain to see. In France, the Ramadier government ordered the power supply to be cut to four days a week for industry and five for households. The country's wheat harvest fell well short of requirements and there were demonstrations against food shortages in major cities; police used tear gas and fire hoses to beat back attacks on prefectures in Caen and Alençon. The government won a parliamentary confidence vote but only thanks to abstentions.

Rations of bread, milk and cheese were reduced in the Netherlands, where the budget deficit reached a record level. Strikes against longer working hours spread through British coal fields against trade union advice. A congressional delegation which toured Western Europe warned of the peril of Communist expansion and of trade unions with Communist 'overlords' disrupting industry 'to produce chaos and put an end to freedom'. Referring to the aid programme, one of its members, Everett Dirksen of Illinois, urged simply, 'Do it – do it now – and do it right.'[14]

CHAPTER FIFTEEN

# THE GENERAL REPORTS

I: MILITARY FORCE IS NOT ENOUGH

As the United States committed itself to bailing out those European nations that would accept its assistance, the Truman administration's policy towards its wartime ally on the other side of the world remained confused. The report delivered to the White House on 19 September by General Wedemeyer after his mission to China at the president's request further clouded the outlook. He had been a surprising choice for the task, and his findings presented the president and secretary of state with a dilemma that underlined the contradictory nature of their policy.

The clean-cut general had prior experience of China, having been sent as adviser to Chiang Kai-shek in 1944 to replace the acerbic Joseph Stilwell. Relations between 'Vinegar Joe' and the generalissimo had become impossible as the American fumed about the incompetence of the Nationalists and their poor leadership. Wedemeyer was more accommodating, which enabled him to get more done and, after his return home and his appointment as army chief of plans and operations, he did not hide his belief that the administration should give the Nationalists increased backing.

As the pro-Kuomintang 'China Lobby' gained in strength, the president may have thought the choice of the general to conduct an inspection of the situation on the ground might deflect their attacks. But, before he left the US in July, Truman had warned that more aid would be forthcoming only 'if the Chinese government presents satisfactory evidence of effective measures looking towards Chinese recovery and provided further that any aid which may be made available shall be subject of the supervision of representatives of the United States government'.

Though welcoming Wedemeyer's appointment, Kuomintang leaders were increasingly disturbed by the realisation that their country took second place to Europe in Washington's concerns. They sensed that the administration had reached a watershed in its China policy and that the Truman Doctrine of aiding allies against aggression was not going to apply to them as they thought it should. This pushed them to ally themselves even more closely with the Republicans, Madame Chiang acting as a go-between as they hoped that a new occupant of the White House would help their cause. That, in turn, further alienated Truman in a sharp demonstration of the interweaving of global and domestic politics.

The general was certainly shocked by what he found in China after an absence of two years. 'The more places Wedemeyer visited, the more people he saw, the more despairing he became about this Government,' the diplomat John Melby noted in his diary. 'His last two or three conversations with the Generalissimo were angry ones in which neither man minced any word and in which no common understanding was reached.'

Meeting the government in Nanjing on 22 August, Wedemeyer criticised the military effort, corruption and inefficiency and then made a public statement before leaving that 'To regain and maintain the confidence of the people, the Central Government will have to effect immediately drastic, far-reaching political and economic reforms. Promises will no longer suffice. Performance is absolutely necessary. It should be accepted that military force in itself will not eliminate Communism.' Recovery for the government, he told reporters before flying out, 'awaits inspirational leadership, and moral and spiritual resurgence that can only come from within China'. From somebody regarded as a deeply anti-Communist friend of the Nanjing government, that was a devastating verdict for the Nationalists and for the generalissimo, in particular.

Wedemeyer's criticism had been echoed in a stream of reports from the American embassy while, at a meeting of the Kuomintang

Executive Committee on 9 September, Chiang scathingly denounced
his own party. The Communists had shown themselves to be abler
and more dedicated to the welfare of China, he said. The country
could not rely on the United States, he warned, implying that it
should seek closer relations with the USSR. Meeting a delegation
from the House of Representatives, the generalissimo said military
reverses in Manchuria were 'an American responsibility'. If the
Communists won the civil war, it would be because the US had failed
to honour its commitment.[1]

Despite his strictures to Chiang, the main thrust of Wedemeyer's
report was to denounce Communism as presenting 'even greater
dangers to world peace than did the Nazi militarists and the Japanese
jingoists'. China, he wrote, had been jeopardised by 'forces as sinister as those that operated in Europe and Asia leading to World
War II. The pattern is familiar – employment of subversive agents;
infiltration tactics; incitement of disorder and chaos [designed]
to undermine popular confidence in government and leaders.' He
denied that Communist policies were popular, and asserted that,
despite corruption, 'it is a certainty that the bulk of the people are
not disposed to a Communist structure'. It was wrong to deny fresh
aid at a time when help was going to Greece and Turkey, which were
less important. The report proposed putting Manchuria under a UN
Trusteeship including the USSR and Britain, and sending US military
advisers to the Nanjing government. Its basic argument was that, if
the regime made political and military changes, it should be given
more assistance, which would enable it to come out on top.

The administration's reaction was frosty. At a short meeting in
New York, Marshall told the general he must not discuss its contents
with anybody under any circumstances. The secretary particularly
disliked the idea of a trusteeship for Manchuria. He proposed delet-
ing some passages, which the author refused to do. In answer to
questions, the administration stuck to the line that the report contained 'confidential material the publication of which might cause
embarrassment to the nations concerned'. Wedemeyer thought of
resigning from the army but soldiered on, and published his version
of events only eleven years later.[2]

American policy thus remained stranded between a desire not to see a Communist victory but an even stronger will to avoid becoming more involved in preserving the Nationalist regime. Given the military situation, that could only lead to one outcome. George Marshall seemed resigned to this, influenced no doubt by sour memories of his abortive mission to try to bring together the two sides in the civil war. There were those who still saw Mao and his colleagues as 'agrarian socialists' as Roosevelt had put it, with whom the US might be able to work. Others, as George Kennan recalled, believed that the weaknesses of the Nationalist regime 'would be more apt to be indulged and encouraged than corrected by further infusions of American aid'. A Communist victory would not be fatal to American interests because China was not a strong industrial power and 'could not become in any short space of time a strong military power anywhere beyond the mainland of Asia', he added.[3]

## II: MANCHURIAN PIVOT

In early September, Lin Biao launched a fresh offensive across the broad Sungari River as freezing winds whipped the region, causing particular pain for government reinforcements newly arrived from southern provinces. In a battle starting at dawn on 14 September, two Nationalist divisions were pushed back with heavy losses and a third retreated. In a series of attacks along the main railway line, the PLA inflicted heavy casualties. By the end of the fighting, the Communists said they had taken nineteen towns.

The zones in the north-east still controlled by government forces were surrounded by a far larger Communist area, where cadres set up administrative machinery and implemented land reform while raiding parties gathered crops from farms within Nationalist territory. The PLA established trading links with the Soviet Union, exchanging minerals, furs, grain and meat for vehicles, boats and telephones. Helped by Soviet technicians, it set up arsenals to produce armaments and conscripted advisers and medical staff among captured Japanese troops. At the end of the month, it mounted a fresh offensive to capture several more towns, but, after Chiang despatched reinforcements, a lull in the fighting set in that lasted until December.[4]

Other Communist armies advanced elsewhere in northern China, isolating major urban centres including the Shanxi provincial capital of Taiyuan, where the long-time warlord Yan Xishan, the 'Model Governor', held out, protected by 5,000 stone pillboxes, 700 artillery pieces and an army into which he had incorporated Japanese troops at the end of the world war. He showed a Western reporter a stock of poison pills which he said he and his officers would take if the PLA got through the city walls.[5]

Having established its position in the Dabie Mountains of Central China after its summer offensive across the Yellow River, the army led by 'One-Eyed Dragon' Liu Bocheng advanced to cut road and rail communications, seizing 150,000 rifles from government stores. This threatened to open up a new front along the Yangtze River, Chiang's main power base, while PLA units also moved forwards across the strategic Longhai railway in the lower Yellow River. In Shandong province in the east, the Nationalists were estimated to have lost nearly 100,000 men, killed, injured or, for the greater part, captured in big battles as Communist forces moved on the provincial capital of Jinan, where the US consul-general reported that the population 'no longer considers [the] Government merits continued support'.[6]

Apart from such reverses on the battlefield, the government had lost the allegiance of the scholar class, which was always highly respected in China. Students were siding with the Communists. The elimination of liberal political groups by the Kuomintang left them with no alternative. Big anti-regime strikes broke out during the month in Shanghai, where inflation, corruption and lack of hope undermined the country's main commercial centre. The hard right-wing CC Clique tightened its grip on the party. Chiang's brother-in-law, former prime minister T. V. Soong, who favoured some liberalisation while keeping his huge fortune intact, was sent off as governor of Guangdong province in the south.

Attempts at economic reform came to naught. As inflation roared on, Nationalist China became a barter economy amid an air of unreality about what was happening on the battlefields. 'Last spring the Government announced the war would be over in three months,' John Melby noted. 'Yesterday the Chief of Staff said Chefoo in

Shantung would be taken today, which would mean the end of the war. It has not been taken. The Communists announce the capture of places which never existed and the destruction of divisions no one ever heard of . . . If you added up the total of announced casualties it would run into the millions since the end of the war.'[7]

# CHAPTER SIXTEEN

# MY HEAD HANGS IN SHAME

After the slaughter in the Punjab, the violence that had marked independence engulfed the Indian capital, killing hundreds. Huge crowds attacked Muslim shops in Connaught Circus, Delhi's neo-classical central plaza. Nehru plunged into the crowd waving a stick and chasing rioters from the Odeon cinema. Looters walked off with goods from the shops. There were widespread arson attacks. Hindu goonda hoodlums stormed into a school, separating out Muslim boys and killing them all. Six bombs were thrown at refugees at the main railway station. A twelve-hour clash between troops and rioters north of the city left roads littered with bodies and a town burnt to ashes. 'If we go down in Delhi, we are finished,' Mountbatten told a meeting attended by a furious Patel and a shaken Nehru.

Some reports estimated that more than half a million people took part in the rioting. Muslims put their death toll at 10,000. The post, telegraph and telephone systems broke down. Police and troops were told to shoot to kill. Twelve thousand Muslims sought shelter in the Transfer Office. Hindus left their shirts unbuttoned to exhibit white sacred thread across their chests. 'The atmosphere is such that a Muslim appears in public only at the risk of his life, and there is no assurance that either police or Indian army troops will interfere if he is attacked,' an American diplomat wrote.[1]

'We are dealing with a situation which is analogous to war and we are going to deal with it on a war basis on every sense of the word,' Nehru declared on the radio. He went to see Mountbatten to 'unburden his soul and to obtain ... comfort'. He and Patel clashed, the prime minister saying he felt humiliated by the slaughter but his deputy insisting that everything possible was being done to maintain security. Nehru set up a tent city for refugees in the garden of his home; among those in it were two Muslim children he rescued from a roof. Driving through the dangerous streets, he ordered a Hindu pulling a cart full of loot to take it back to its Muslim owner. When the man refused, the politician grabbed him by the throat to force compliance.[2]

In Punjab, evacuation between the two parts of the region was made the 'first priority'. That was no more than a recognition of reality but opened the door to organised ethnic cleansing as officials forced Muslims to leave India while Hindus and Sikhs were obliged to move eastwards on hugely overcrowded trains or, more often, on foot or in carts along roads lined with corpses. One caravan over which Nehru, Patel and Mountbatten flew on an inspection trip stretched for 50 miles. Muslim and Sikhs moved almost side by side in opposite directions. 'There was no sign of a clash,' Mountbatten's press secretary, Alan Campbell-Johnson, noted. 'As though impelled by some deeper instinct, they pushed forward obsessed only with the objective beyond the boundary.'[3]

A refugee train going east from Pakistan arrived in Amritsar carrying victims of Muslim attacks. Enraged Sikhs assaulted a train carrying Muslim peasants from the Delhi area bound for Pakistan; at least 1,500 people were killed, according to the British commander of the escort. 'The Punjab is convulsed with insanity,' wrote a British resident of Lahore after a journey out of the city during which he saw 'scenes from Dante's *Inferno*'. Women were often the greatest victims. Suicides, sometimes by throwing themselves into wells, were common. Mothers who offered themselves to save their daughters saw their children abused as well beside them. In Amritsar, Muslim women were stripped naked, paraded through the streets and raped – most were then burnt alive. After one massacre, an official wrote that 'the girls were distributed like sweets'. An eyewitness reported how 'the better "stuff" was taken by the police and the army while the "small coin" would be given to the rest'. The girls were passed from one man to another, sold four or five times before ending up in brothels or being kept in 'safe-custody' for the pleasure of police.[4]

In the rich market town of Harnoli in the Mianwali district of Pakistan, more than 3,000 non-Muslims were massacred. 'Children were snatched away from their mothers' arms and thrown into the boiling oil,' a district official recorded.

> Hundreds of women saved their honour by jumping into wells or throwing themselves into burning houses ... Girls of eight to ten years of age were raped in the presence of their parents and then put to death mercilessly. The breasts of women were cut and they were made to walk all naked in rows of five in the bazaars. About eight hundred girls and women were abducted and small kiddies were wandering in the jungles and were kidnapped by passers-by.[5]

Partition of farmland and the continuing violence aggravated an already dire food situation after poor rice and wheat harvests which threatened starvation in some areas. Planes dropped 12,000 lbs of cooked food. Cholera broke out in refugee camps.

'My head hangs in shame when I think of the inhuman acts committed by my own countrymen,' Nehru declared. The main correspondent for the London *Times*, Ian Morrison, compared the situation in Punjab to 'a sort of infectious hysteria or mental derangement carried by the refugees and accelerated by irresponsible politicians and journalists and those gangster elements who profit from anarchy'. He pointed to 'a psychosis of fear, a terror that it is about to be attacked [or] a psychosis of revenge, [in which] often both fear and revenge are mixed, and are soon absorbed in wild and indiscriminatory hostility'. Each side passionately believed the other to be solely responsible, but questions of responsibility and blame might be irrelevant. 'Either all parties concerned are responsible, officials who have sanctioned communal solutions, and politicians who have made inflammatory speeches equally with illiterate peasants who have speared women and children, or else there are certain cataclysms in human affairs in which men do not retain control over their destinies,' he concluded.[6]

Still, though the number of people of the road was put at 4 million, the intensity of attacks in Punjab decreased as September went on. One reason, a correspondent wrote, was that there were 'few villages left to burn and few minority communities left to kill'. Heavy rain washed away some refugee columns and train tracks, submerging roads, bringing down bridges and hampering the movement of attack gangs.[7]

But Jinnah noted how 'one disaster follows another' as the violence spread to the United Provinces, where Muslims made up 14 per cent of the population. After the arrival of Gurkhas and troops from south India to restore order in Delhi, some rioters there moved to the hill resort of Simla, where they killed a Muslim family in the Grand Hotel. Fighting was reported on the North-West Frontier as tribesmen moved down towards the plain.[8]

Gandhi travelled to Delhi in the middle of the month. He was suffering from influenza and a visitor found him 'physically weaker and mentally disturbed'. In contrast to his shabby lodgings in Calcutta, he stayed at the mansion of his rich businessman supporter G. D. Birla, occupying a ground-floor room with a bathroom attached – he slept on the terrace outside. But his fresh fast for peace alienated Hindu extremists; some threw a bomb during a prayer meeting.[9]

~

## MEANWHILE

- The Allies sign peace treaties with Italy, Austria, Romania, Hungary, Bulgaria and Finland.
- Trieste becomes an independent city-state under the United Nations divided into two zones, one run by the American and British, the other under the Yugoslavs.
- The USSR rejects an American proposal for four-power talks on Korea (with the UK and China) but then suggests the withdrawal of all foreign troops in three months.
- Douglas MacArthur marks the second anniversary of the end of the war in the Pacific with a speech saying the occupation has brought enlightenment, truth and reality 'to a race long stunted by ancient concepts of mythological teaching'.
- Truman is greeted by huge crowds on a state visit to Brazil. He and his doctor elude their secret service escort to climb a 1,000-foot-high mount to pick orchids.

- The Argentine Parliament passes legislation sponsored by Eva Perón enfranchising women.
- A food conference in Paris forecasts that consumption per head in 1951 will still be below 1934–8 levels.
- Muscovites dance through the night as the city celebrates its 800th anniversary. A hundred million light bulbs illuminate streets and buildings, 100,000 of them on the Kremlin. Stalin hails 'the capital of the great peace-loving Power'.
- A four-engine jet plane is tested in Columbus, Ohio.
- Charlie Parker and Dizzy Gillespie give a concert at Carnegie Hall with a bop big band.
- British racing driver John Cobb sets world land speed record of 394.2 mph at Bonneville Salt Flats in Utah in a 24-cylinder car.
- The black baseball player Jackie Robinson is named Rookie of the Year after finishing the season with a batting average of .297.
- A surgeon in Cape Town reports removing 2,422 nails from the stomach of a carpenter who says he swallowed them to combat depression.

# PART SIX

# OCTOBER 1947

**ACTS**

*French politics are in turmoil as the Cold War deepens the colonial army launches a major offensive against the Viet Minh; War erupts in the Himalayas.*

**SCENES**

*Paris, Strasbourg, Hanoi, Bac Kan, Saigon, Hong Kong, Jammu and Kashmir.*

**CAST**

*De Gaulle, Thorez, Salan, Bollaert, Bao Dai; Maharajah Hari Singh, Sheikh Mohammad Abdullah, Nehru, Jinnah.*

# CHAPTER SEVENTEEN

# A REPUBLIC UNDER SIEGE

## I: THE GENERAL'S GAUNTLET

On the afternoon of 5 October, Charles de Gaulle stepped onto a huge white rostrum at Vincennes racecourse on the edge of Paris. Above him flew a tricolour flag and a banner emblazoned with his wartime emblem of the Cross of Lorraine. The organisers of the occasion said the crowd numbered half a million. Even if that was an exaggeration, the number of people in serried ranks below him was enormous.

Before the general appeared, the rally had resembled a popular festival as people ate and drank at stands while the band played military airs, music hall acts performed and regional troupes went through their routines. Opponents had scattered nails on the road to the racecourse but this did not stop the enthusiasts who had to come to hear the Free French leader tell them what was wrong with their country and what he intended to do about it.

There was a deep rumble from the crowd as he strode into view, the effect of his height increased by his position above the throng. He denounced the 'abyss' into which the ruling political parties had led the nation. Each had devoted itself to 'cooking its little soup, on its little fire in its little corner,' he said. Now, he would show the way to national salvation. 'Fortune has never betrayed a France that stands together,' he cried, raising his arms in a great V-shaped salute.

'Do you agree with me?' he asked.

'Yes! Yes!' the crowd shouted back.

René Serre, a former boxer who was a member of the security service for the event, felt that the crowd displayed 'the ardour of a neophyte at his first religious experience, mixed with the modesty of a woman who is going to give herself for the first time and knows it. One felt that the General could have done as he wished with the crowd.'[1]

After stalking out of the premiership at the beginning of 1946 when members of the post-war coalition government blocked his attempt to exercise the authority he thought necessary to rule the nation, de Gaulle had taken up residence just outside Paris, expecting to be called back to office. When that did not happen, he moved to his country home at Colombey-les-Deux-Églises in the east of the country, which he described as a melancholy place of grey skies, frost, fog and rain. He worked on his war memoirs, scrawling the words in sloping script with his black fountain pen as he chain-smoked, endlessly refashioning his text before passing the pages to his daughter Élisabeth to be typed on her portable. At times he sank into self-pity; putting logs on the fire, he lamented, 'This is all there is left for me to do.'

Life was in keeping with de Gaulle's personal frugality and a lack of money. Since his promotion to the rank of general had not been confirmed by the time he flew to England and raised the standard of resistance in 1940, he and his wife Yvonne had to live on a colonel's retirement pay. The cuffs and collars of his shirts were turned so that he could continue to wear them for as long as possible. Meat came from chicken and rabbits kept in the garden. Wine was served sparingly in small glasses.

Seven years on from his eruption into history, he appeared to be at risk of becoming a man of the past, a highly assertive leader who could not co-exist with the constitution of the Fourth Republic adopted by a referendum at the end of 1946 which perpetuated the supremacy of the legislature, with the president reduced to a largely ceremonial figure. But, though the main political parties backed the new order, popular enthusiasm was lacking. The abstention rate at the referendum was 31 per cent, meaning that the text was approved by only 36 per cent of the electorate. As de Gaulle remarked, the text had been 'accepted by 9 million voters, refused by 8 and ignored by 8'.[2]

In Colombey, the general pondered a return to politics, imagining an initiative similar to his BBC broadcast speech on 18 June 1940, calling on France to resist the Germans. It was time, he thought, for a new liberation. 'My poor friend, nobody would follow you,' his wife told him. At which, the general threw out his arms and replied, 'Leave me alone, Yvonne! I am big enough to know what I have to do!' After conferring with wartime aides and visiting Paris for a month in early 1947, he told his former secretary, Claude Mauriac, that what was needed was not a new political party but a *rassemblement* (rally or union) to bring the French people together under a strong leader.[3]

To advance his project, the general went to Normandy to address a gathering of resistance fighters on the towering cliffs by the hamlet of Bruneval. Facing 50,000 people from a platform decorated with a tricolour and a giant Cross of Lorraine, he told them that the time was coming to set aside 'sterile games' and reform the political system, after which 'the immense mass of the French will rally to France'. Cries of '*de Gaulle au pouvoir*' rose from the crowd.

The prime minister Paul Ramadier made a secret night-time visit to Colombey to sound out the general's intentions. 'I will remain the guide for the nation,' de Gaulle told his visitor. 'I serve only France.' The following weekend, in a speech in Strasbourg, he told a large crowd that the Republic had to be 'brought out of its tomb' by a popular movement. As he finished, he flung up his long arms in a V-shape while the crowd sang the national anthem followed by the familiar shouts of '*De Gaulle au pouvoir!*' On 14 April, he announced the launch of the Rally of the French People (*Rassemblement du peuple français*) (RPF). The country had three choices, its posters declared: the Communists; the parties which were 'burning France's cards'; or the 'rally of the mass of French people'.[4]

Groups were set up to cater for families, students, ex-servicemen and civil servants. Left-wing Gaullists advanced ideas of capital and labour working together. The movement was strongly anti-Communist, warning that the distance separating the Red Army from the French border was equivalent to only two days' stages in the Tour de France. As for colonial affairs, the general remained firm in his insistence that France's overseas territories must remain under the control of Paris, even if a degree of self-government was allowed.

By 1 May, the movement claimed 810,000 membership applications. The general made whirlwind provincial tours, appearing in uniform before enthusiastic crowds of up to 100,000 people. 'The RPF is like the métro,' the Gaullist writer André Malraux remarked of the movement's diverse appeal. Its leader said privately that it consisted of 'one third good folk, one third idiots and one third collaborators', and remarked that 'if there's a cuckold, a pederast or a crook somewhere, I'll find him in the RPF'.[5]

For all the general's anti-party rhetoric, however, the Rally came increasingly to resemble a partisan political group appealing mainly to right-wing voters as it organised mass meetings for municipal elections in mid-October 1947. Forty-one National Assembly deputies formed a parliamentary group. There were fierce physical clashes with Communists, which raised morale but threatened to give the movement a violent reputation and played into the hands of those who accused the general of fascist leanings.

Operating on a shoestring from headquarters in the rue de Solférino on the Left Bank of the Seine in what one of the faithful described as 'Franciscan austerity', the RPF was run on military lines with orders transmitted from the top and the equivalent of a regimental commander in each region. Its governing council was made up primarily of Free French 'companions' de Gaulle felt he could trust. It remained within the democratic system but its aim was clear – to replace the Fourth Republic with a regime crafted for its leader.

## II: BREAD AND STRIKES

France was deeply in the grip of shortages – the government cut the bread ration and the price of baguettes doubled. Black markets flourished; potatoes sold for double the official rate. The cost of living had risen by 8 per cent in September; the government said it needed $120 million in aid each month to keep going until Marshall Plan help arrived.[6]

Settlements of strikes during the summer hoisted wages by 11 per cent, boosting already huge inflation; but fresh stoppages broke out on a local basis. Workers occupied Renault and Citroën factories in the Paris area. The northern coal fields were paralysed and workers at some pits held managers hostage in their offices. The Paris public transport system was hit. The left wing of the prime minister's Socialist Party hankered after a united front with the Communists and a reversal of their expulsion from government in May. Policy was confused: the Christian Democrat finance minister, Robert Schuman, advocated a lessening of state intervention but the Socialist economics minister, André Philip, pressed for government controls to be strengthened. President Auriol warned that public concern was approaching the panic level. All in all, de Gaulle had little difficulty in depicting a government that was failing to control events.

The outcome of the municipal elections in late October was all he could have hoped for. The RPF captured 38 per cent of the vote in major cities, winning control of thirteen of the twenty-five biggest urban centres and finishing top of the poll in Paris, where de Gaulle's brother, Pierre, became the president of the city council. Civil servants made up the single biggest group of its electorate, followed by industrial workers and shopkeepers and artisans. It attracted considerably more men than women, and enjoyed greater support in cities than in rural areas, which its rudimentary organisation had found it hard to penetrate.

Still, the Communists showed their strength by finishing second in the elections nationwide as they slammed American assistance as 'shameful speculation on the poverty of the French' and accused the government of being lackeys of Washington, as Pétain had been of Berlin. At a big meeting in the Vel d'Hiv cycle stadium in Paris, Thorez thundered that the 'very existence of France as a sovereign, independent nation' was at stake. What was needed, he went on, was the imposition of a 'democratic government in which the working class and its party finally take the leading role'. Referring to the execution the previous month of Nikola Petkov, the leading non-Communist politician in Bulgaria, Thorez said that 'we should imitate the Bulgarian democrats and strike the traitors'.[7]

It all served to reinforce de Gaulle's jeremiads about the threat orchestrated from Moscow, while street clashes at home kept the temperature high. A big confrontation erupted at the end of the month down from the Arc de Triomphe, after a meeting held to denounce Soviet crimes. Ten thousand Communists marched to the scene but were held back by police. In the ensuing clashes, one person was killed and three hundred injured. Elsewhere, Gaullists fought street battles with Communists and the republic faced a mounting challenge from the unions in the winter of 1947/8 as the general wrote to his son that 'the success of the Rassemblement is a triumph. The frogs are croaking in desperation.'[8]

There was no lack of shortage of evidence for the concerns expressed by the RPF about Communism in the autumn of 1947. The increased repression in countries in the Soviet orbit following the initial Cominform meeting continued. Dragoljub Jovanović, leader of the Yugoslav People's Agrarian Party, was sentenced to life imprisonment. In Romania, where the number of political prisoners was put at a quarter of a million, the leader of the Peasant Party, Iuliu Maniu, aged seventy-four, was sentenced to life imprisonment after being accused of planning to flee the country to set up an opposition government-in-exile and of plotting treason with the US and UK. Stalin urged the Communist general secretary, Gheorghe Gheorghiu-Dej, to 'keep the masses occupied. Give them a big project to do. Have them build a canal or something.' So the Danube–Black Sea canal project was launched, to be dug by tens of thousands of political prisoners to improve waterborne transport and serve Soviet naval purposes.[9]

In Greece, where a state of emergency was declared, the rebel army backed by Yugoslavia staged widespread attacks and was reported to be building an airfield on the Albanian border with conscripted labour. The Communists stepped up the pressure in Czechoslovakia, calling for stronger action against 'reactionary elements' as they tightened their grip on the Interior Ministry and the police and attacked their Social Democrat coalition partners for being in league with 'millionaires, big landowners, black markets' and working with 'foreign reactionaries'.[10]

The division of Germany deepened. The Anglo-American control group decided to return responsibility for the coal industry in the Ruhr to the Germans. The number of plants to be dismantled in the west was set at less than half the original target, the occupation commanders saying the aim was to 'ensure that a balanced industrial economy, capable of self-support and of making a large contribution to economic rehabilitation – not only of Germans but also of Europe – is left'. The Christian Democrat leader Konrad Adenauer described the programme as the 'plundering of German industry', but steel production in the western zones reached its highest level since the end of the war. At elections in the Saarland, the Christian Democrats got almost half the vote, with the Social Democrats finishing second and the Communists a distant third. A Writers' Congress in Berlin saw hard-line speeches from Soviet delegates and a walkout by the Russians when the principal American speaker praised authors who 'carried the seeds of rebellion and revolt into people's minds and hearts', though he received enthusiastic applause from the audience.[11]

On the other side of the divide, General Agreement on Tariffs and Trade (GATT) was concluded in Geneva to complete the Western-led post-war global economic system. Wanting to preserve as much of the imperial preference system as possible, Britain dragged its feet in the negotiations – the imperialist *Daily Express* newspaper called the outcome 'a big bad bargain', while *The Economist* groused that it was 'one of the longest and most complicated public documents ever issued'. But the hardball tactics of the chief British negotiator, Stafford Cripps, won the UK extensive concessions – the US Committee on Trade Agreements calculated them to be worth $584 million.[12] Though American congressmen went to bat for local interests, the agreement embodied Washington's belief in free trade as a positive global force, and the Truman administration's faith in the liberalisation of international commerce as an important weapon in its attempt to use economics to build up a global network of common interests, in particular in stimulating European reconstruction and aiding the recovery of Japan. It hailed the accord as 'the most extensive action ever taken with respect to trade barriers'. The president called it 'a landmark in the history of international economic relations'. In fresh evidence of the divisions of the Cold War, the USSR and its allies did not participate, and none of the twenty-three signatory nations appears to have made any attempt to get them to join.

## III: GLOVES OFF IN VIETNAM

As voters were going to the polls at municipal voting booths across metropolitan France, the country's paratroopers were dropping on the isolated mountain forests of Bac Kan 6,000 miles away in a major campaign designed to destroy the Viet Minh. The assault on the guerrilla headquarters in the north of the country was intended to capture Ho Chi Minh and his senior colleagues, to destroy their main force and to free hostages taken in fighting earlier in the year. Named Operation Léa after a 1,400-metre-high pass, it had been carefully prepared by General Salan, who had accompanied Ho to the Fontainebleau talks the previous year and was the commander in Tonkin.

French intelligence had identified Bac Kan, a sparsely populated region of mountainous forests, as the main Viet Minh base close to the frontier with China over which supplies could be ferried. Salan had decided that a mass drop provided the best chance of catching the elusive enemy unaware. The operation had to be delayed until the end of the rainy season when the 1,200 paratroopers were able to descend on their target while two columns set out to join them by road and river.

The operation began in the early morning of 7 October, two days after de Gaulle's speech at Vincennes. The troops had slept on the tarmac by their planes the previous night. Salan flew overhead in a Catalina seaplane and received radio messages from the ground reporting that the attack had caught the Viet Minh completely by surprise. Their main buildings had been taken with many losses, while the French had suffered only a few wounded. Ten minutes later, a second message said the Viet Minh government had been caught. Four further communications in the following half hour reported that Ho had asked for an end to the war. Salan felt jubilant, and headed back to Hanoi to pass the news to High Commissioner Bollaert in Saigon.[13]

The next morning, however, a message from Bac Kan asked for reinforcements, followed by further messages that Salan found alarming. He sent in a battalion of paratroopers. But then a cable signed in Ho's name arrived asking to be released to permit armistice talks. 'Thank you for the good conduct of your troops towards the population,' it added. Sensing something was amiss, the general ordered the reinforcements not to drop on Bac Kan. But his instruction arrived only after one stick had jumped. The ground commander was amazed to see them and sent an officer to Hanoi in a small plane to say that everything was going well.

No sooner had Salan received that news than Bollaert arrived from the south, full of smiles and congratulations, and ready to open talks with Ho. The general told him they had been victims of a hoax. The subsequent investigation pointed to the false messages having been concocted by a radio operator, who was sent back to France, though the case against him was not proved and his motives remained undetermined.[14]

Ho and his senior colleagues had, in fact, escaped, their departure so precipitate that the fires were still warm in their headquarters. The paratroopers freed the hostages, who prostrated themselves on the ground in front of Salan when he arrived for an inspection. The column moving on the ground ran into ambushes and had to deal with poor roads, arriving after the fighting was over. The river-borne troops had an even more difficult time, delayed by low water levels, sandbanks and obstacles floating in their path. As well as destroying the headquarters, the French took over tin and zinc mines in the area. Once the initial surprise had worn off, the Viet Minh fought back, mainly with ambushes and short, sharp attacks.

The French reported suffering forty killed, forty lost and 580 wounded, while counting 7,200 enemy corpses and taking a thousand prisoners. They seized hundreds of rifles, automatic weapons, artillery pieces and radio transmitters as well as destroying ten weapons factories and tons of munitions. Salan reckoned the scale of losses meant the main Viet Minh force would be unable to stage attacks for a long time and would have to fall back on local militias. However, the colonial army was unable to maintain its presence in the isolated hills and pulled back after a month, enabling the guerrillas to return. A second drive into the same area at the end of the year seized supplies but resulted in no big encounters, and the French withdrew to the lowlands just before Christmas.

Since the government in Paris was unable to finance reinforcements, the thrust of military policy became to secure the main highways and restrict Viet Minh movement, rather than mounting fresh forays into enemy territory. The guerrillas had little difficulty in slipping through the lines and went on receiving supplies from Communist forces in southern China. Still, for Salan and his colleagues, Operation Léa had been an example of what the army could do if given its head. General Valluy, the overall French commander, expressed his satisfaction that 'positive action' had replaced 'paper plans'. Army officers were 'straining at the leash with a full sense of superiority,' he added; one wrote to thank Salan that they had 'finally been able to assert ourselves'. It was the kind of sentiment that would run through the military up to the denouement of its uneasy relations with politicians in Paris in the coup in Algeria in 1958 and its aftermath that would see Salan becoming head of the terrorist OAS Secret Army.[15]

Operation Léa took place as France sought to promote the former emperor, Bao Dai, as the rallying point for non-Communists, an option favoured by the settlers and anti-Viet Minh politicians in Cochin. Known for his playboy ways, he was, however, indecisive. Though promoting the Bao Dai option, the senior civil servant in Saigon, Léon Pignon, described him as 'always very nervous and diffident'. The Americans were even more dismissive: Charles Reed, head of Southeast Asian Affairs at the State Department, called him 'a French-inspired and French-dominated political zero'. Now living in Hong Kong, the ex-emperor was described by the American writer S. J. Perelman, who saw him sitting with several hostesses in a nightclub there, as 'a short, slippery-looking customer rather on the pudgy side [who] wore a fixed, oily grin that was vaguely reptilian'. When Perelman tried to engage him in conversation in his rudimentary French, the former emperor 'shrugged evasively and buried his nose in his whisky-and-soda' after confiding that his favourite screen actress was Jeanette MacDonald.[16]

The French authorities hoped the Bac Kan operation would help to 'rally the popular masses who have been suffering for so long around a new national government headed by Bao Dai'. The Overseas Ministry said peace could 'only be restored by a truly national Vietnamese government, which, while aspiring to independence and unity, will respect undertakings and be capable of putting an end to a state of terror and assassinations'. The Viet Minh had just organised the killing of two anti-Communist politicians.[17]

Two dozen politicians, mainly from the south and centre of the country, flew to Hong Kong to appeal to the former emperor as 'the only qualified representative of the Vietnamese people to take power and open negotiations with France to restore peace and bring about unity and independence'. While Bao Dai hesitated on how to respond, Bollaert proposed the granting of internal autonomy while insisting that Vietnam must be a member of the French Union with Paris retaining control of defence and foreign affairs as well as having the last word on its relations with Laos and Cambodia. Nationalists in the south expressed their disappointment and the Viet Minh said control of the army and diplomacy were essential for true independence.[18]

Bao Dai was not keen on the limitations laid down by the French and faced the problem of leading non-Communist Nationalists while collaborating with the colonial power, which always saw him primarily as a figurehead to serve its interests. He issued a statement full of lamentations about the suffering that the conflict had brought to the people of Vietnam, but gave no details about how he intended to proceed. The Viet Minh immediately rejected the initiative, saying it was the sole representative of the Vietnamese people entitled to negotiate.

The situation was further complicated by the return from Paris of the only Vietnamese general in the French army, Nguyen Van Xuan. He had links with French politicians who disliked the idea of restoring the monarchy and favoured 'a social and lay Vietnamese Republic'. Xuan, who had been educated in France and was not fluent in Vietnamese, proposed a confederation of Tonkin under the Viet Minh, Annam under Bao Dai, and Cochin under himself. He would play the balancing role between Ho and Bao Dai with the backing of Socialists in the government in Paris. On 1 October, he organised a coup against the leader of the Cochin Republic and had himself elected as its president, interior minister and defence minister.[19]

But the Viet Minh refused to talk to him and the settler lobby distanced itself while Bao Dai called for the Cochin government to be replaced by an administrative council. The general retreated, expressing his readiness to drop his separatist ambitions. High Commissioner Bollaert opened negotiations with Bao Dai and got the agreement of the government in Paris that he could now use the word 'independence'; but he assured the overseas minister that this would not go beyond 'verbalism of an almost religious character'.[20]

# CHAPTER EIGHTEEN

# THE GREAT GAME

## I: INVASION IN THE HIMALAYAS

Two weeks after the paratroops dropped on Bac Kan, the vanguard of a jihad invasion in the Himalayas crossed the river marking the border between the North-West Frontier province of Pakistan and the princely state of Jammu and Kashmir, whose maharajah had not decided on the future of his domain. Thousands of Pashtun tribesmen in black turbans followed in trucks, jeeps, station wagons and buses flying Pakistani flags. Some of the attackers were reported to be regular Pakistani soldiers in local garb. Tribal rulers sent in fighters while other guerrillas moved east from the frontier area. In some places, Kashmiri Muslim troops refused to resist the invaders who killed wantonly as they rampaged forward, looting as they went. 'We shot whoever we saw,' one said later.[1]

Set in dramatically beautiful scenery of lakes, forests and mountains, its summer capital of Srinagar clustered around Lake Dal with its fleet of houseboats, the 85,000-square-mile region was strategically important given its borders with both India and Pakistan as well as Russia, China and Afghanistan. Its five disparate regions varied from well-populated valleys and stretches of arable land to sparsely peopled mountain areas, where the terrain compounded the backwardness and isolation. Trade and communications links were mainly with western Punjab, now part of Pakistan. Most inhabitants spoke their own language, Koshur.

Three-quarters of the population were Muslims, though the

lowland Jammu region to the south and the winter capital in the city of that name contained a large number of Hindus. The overall preponderance of Muslims pointed to union with Pakistan. But the maharajah, Hari Singh, was Hindu, the descendant of Dogra rulers who had acquired the state from the British after they had taken it from the Sikhs in the mid-nineteenth century. His dream was to achieve an independent and neutral 'Switzerland of the East'. But he was a weak ruler who had little contact with his subjects and, as his fourth and youngest queen put it, 'just sits surrounded by fawning courtiers and favourites, and never really gets to know what is going on outside'.[2]

A procrastinator, the maharajah avoided confrontations and decisions, taking to his bed and pleading an attack of colic when Mountbatten visited before independence to urge him to choose between India and Pakistan. A familiar figure at the racecourse in Bombay, he spent much time hunting in the jungles of his state. While a young man, he had been trapped in a sting operation by an English woman with whom he was caught in bed at a Paris hotel. He was only saved from paying the £150,000 blackmail when her gang was rounded up; a razor he took with him to shave her pubic hair was a prize exhibit at the trial.[3]

For Jinnah, it seemed only a matter of time before the predominantly Muslim state came into the fold – after all, Kashmir provided the third letter of the nation's acronym. A trip to the mountains after independence can only have bolstered the great leader's confidence. He had been feted at huge banquets; carpets were laid across the roads on which his car drove; his eyes glowed as he received pledges of fealty.[4]

Though the regular forces of Pakistan did not officially join the offensive, there was aid and logistical support from Karachi. Liaquat, the prime minister who was bedridden after suffering a coronary thrombosis, clearly knew what was going on. Jinnah cut off an official who tried to brief him by saying, 'Don't tell me anything about it. My conscience must be clear.'[5] As the debate on the future of the territory swirled, the US ambassador in Delhi, Henry Grady, warned that it was 'the one great problem that may cause the downfall of India and Pakistan'. The maharajah banned public meetings and all political activity. He replaced the pro-Pakistan chief minister with one who had close ties to Congress, and refused to let Jinnah visit his state, even for a holiday. He appointed a Hindu governor in largely Muslim Gilgit on the southern slopes of the Hindu Kush where the British had based a mercenary force known as the Gilgit Scouts. In another mainly Muslim area, Poonch, close to Pakistan, new taxes on everything from cows to wives and widows provoked protests in which some twenty people were killed and led to appeals to Karachi for support against 'atrocious military oppression'.[6]

Hindus massacred Muslims in the Jammu region. The state's first British-trained barrister, Sardar Muhammad Ibrahim Khan, called a Muslim assembly in his home region of Azad Kashmir bordering Pakistan, which voted unanimously for accession to its western neighbour. Gathering arms, ammunition and men, he declared a jihad against the maharajah and proclaimed the independence of Azad Kashmir, becoming its president.[7]

Pakistan halted truck traffic at the frontier and suspended rail services. In Delhi, Patel ordered improvements to be made to the rough road leading into Kashmir and weapons and wireless equipment to be flown in. Nehru was determined to get Jammu and Kashmir into India. His family's roots in the region gave him a strong emotional attachment to the land of his ancestors; he said that it gave him 'a mild intoxication – like music sometimes or the company of a beloved person'. He believed the maharajah should be got rid of as a feudal relic and the state should join India as proof of the new nation's multi-ethnic, multi-religious nature.[8]

The prime minister had struck up a close relationship with the territory's most popular figure, the extremely tall Sheikh Mohammad Abdullah, who headed a Conference of Muslims but felt no enthusiasm for Pakistan, regarding Jinnah as little more than an atheist and his country as an 'an unscrupulous and savage enemy'. Famed for his recitations from the Koran and his advocacy of progressive policies, the 'Lion of Kashmir' had been sent to jail after heading a movement to get the maharajah to quit. But now, in a placatory move, Hari Singh had him released from jail. Addressing a crowd at the main mosque in Srinagar, the sheikh called for a 'complete transfer of power to the people of Kashmir' who should decide between India and Pakistan while Muslims, Hindus and Sikhs formed a joint government.[9]

As the invaders advanced, refugees poured down the road to

Srinagar where the maharajah was holding his annual durbar banquet at which local nobles pledged allegiance to him. His palace had its own electricity generator but, outside, the city was plunged into darkness after invaders disabled the state power station. Though the road to the capital was open to them and they far outnumbered the defenders, the tribesmen lost the momentum that was their best chance of facing the government in Delhi with a fait accompli.

Pausing at the town of Baramulla, they burned Hindu and Sikh shops and went into an orgy of looting and rape. A Christian convent was smashed up; the mother superior was wounded, a retired British colonel and his wife who lived there were killed – her corpse was found in a well. European nuns were lined up to be shot but were saved at the last moment by a tribesman who had studied at a Catholic school. Twenty-three children also escaped. The nuns tended to the fighters' wounds as they turned the building and its grounds into a transport depot.[10]

The maharajah asked Delhi for military help. The government's troubleshooter with the princes, V. P. Menon, was dispatched to Srinagar where he found 'the stillness of the grave [and] an atmosphere of impending calamity'. Hari Singh 'had gone to pieces completely', he reported. 'Unnerved by the rush of events and the sense of his lone helplessness', he was unable to make a decision and left with his jewels in a convoy of cars heading for the safety of Jammu on the edge of the great north Indian plain.

The state's chief minister was more resolute. Agreeing with Menon that adhesion to India was the best course, he flew with the envoy to Delhi where they went into conference with Nehru, Patel, Mountbatten and Sheikh Abdullah, who had been brought in and was staying with Nehru. The meeting agreed troops should be dispatched, but the governor-general suggested that, before this, Hari Singh should sign a document formally asking for accession to India. This was drawn up for Menon to take to Jammu, but he missed his plane and got the ruler's signature only the next day, by which time Indian forces were already on the ground at Srinagar airfield. The document was duly backdated to maintain the cover of legality. India said the accession would be subject to a popular vote 'when law and order have been fully established'.[11]

The last summit: Joseph Stalin, Harry Truman and Clement Attlee at Potsdam, 1945. (Imperial War Museum)

Foreign ministers go on meeting: Ernest Bevin, George Marshall, Vyacheslav Molotov and Georges Bidault. (Alamy)

For the president, George Marshall was 'the greatest American alive'. (Getty)

Truman signs the European Recovery Act – the Marshall Plan. (Getty)

Comrades together: Stalin with Mao Zedong, Walter Ulbricht and
Nikita Khrushchev. (Getty)

The ideological enforcer: Andrei Zhdanov with Stalin. (Getty)

Alcide de Gasperi leads Christian Democrats to Italian election victory. (Alamy)

The Communist challenge led by Palmiro Togliatti fails. (Getty)

Black market in ruined Berlin. (Getty)

German rivals: Kurt Schumacher and Konrad Adenauer. (Associated Press)

Relief flies in: the Berlin airlift. (Getty)

## II: Stalemate

On the first day of India's troop movement, 27 October, a fleet of twenty-eight Dakotas landed, followed by more than a hundred planes by the end of the month. In all, 4,000 men arrived, many of them Sikhs. They set up a defensive perimeter, and used armoured cars and howitzers to repulse an attack. In one battle near the airfield, they reported killing half of a raiding group of seven hundred tribesmen. Then they advanced to recapture towns, enjoying the important tactical advantage of aerial backing. RSS militants helped to secure the airfield and defend the Vale of Kashmir.

The Indian soldiers took Baramulla with the support of Spitfire fighter planes. The power plant was captured before the tribal forces could blow it up. As they retreated, the invaders set fire to villages and looted at will, blocking roads with trees and rocks and destroying bridges. They grabbed women for brothels in Pakistan; reports spoke of 'a very large number of abducted women and children who were sold like cattle and chattle'. In one town, four hundred bodies were found in a well of women who had preferred to die than be taken off.[12]

Sheikh Abdullah became 'head of administration'. He was, Nehru said, 'the only person who can deliver the goods'. Srinagar was festooned with banners and bunting, as his supporters chanted, 'What is the order of the Lion of Kashmir? Hindus, Muslims and Sikhs be united.' Reporters visiting from India were amazed at the 'amity and indeed fraternity' between different communities in the capital. Nehru visited; grasping the sheikh's hand, he pledged to defend Hindu–Muslim unity. But the outlook for an agreement was bleak as the war of words between Delhi and Karachi escalated and fighting continued in the hills.[13]

Learning of the accession decision, Jinnah was said to have downed several glasses of brandy and instructed the Pakistani army to cross the border. But their British commander refused to heed the order to pit British Dominion forces against one another without the approval of his chief, Auchinleck, which was not forthcoming. News of the accession to India was particularly badly received in Gilgit, with its overwhelmingly Muslim population who called for immediate union with Pakistan. At evening prayer in the mosques, mullahs preached a jihad, urging the killing of the Hindu governor and non-Muslims. Three thousand Muslims armed with rifles and daggers gathered on the polo ground while another thousand roamed through the streets. The British commander of the Scouts, Major William Brown, took charge.

After a night-time gun battle at his residence lit by moonlight, the Hindu governor was replaced by a local council pending the arrival of an agent from Pakistan. The Pakistani flag was raised over the headquarters of the Gilgit Scouts' headquarters. Mountain tribesmen arrived amid festivities and prayers during which a mullah called for the liquidation of non-Muslims. But, on his arrival the following month, the agent sent by Pakistan dispersed the local council, telling its members, according to Brown, 'You are a crowd of fools ... I shall not tolerate this nonsense for one instance.' Though not formally absorbed, Gilgit remained under Karachi's control while a dozen other princely states in the border region, some of them tiny, joined Pakistan.[14]

Mountbatten flew to Lahore to see the Pakistani leaders; Nehru said he was feeling too ill to make the trip. Liaquat was suffering from a bleeding ulcer and looked cast down during the fruitless talk. At a subsequent 'arduous and concentrated conversation', Jinnah put forward a litany of complaints and self-justification. His bad mood was heightened by his seriously declining health as he coughed blood and whispered to a friend when he woke from a doze in the garden of his official residence, 'I am so tired, so tired.' Mountbatten's press aide, Alan Campbell-Johnson, described his mood as one of 'depression, almost fatalism'.[15]

The Great Leader tried to barter Kashmir for the much smaller and less strategically important state of Junagadh, whose dog-loving ruler was still aiming to join Pakistan. He said the decision to join India was based on 'fraud and violence' and attacked Britain for having failed to come to the rescue of his country in the face of Indian attempts to destroy it. He had 'lost interest in what the world thought of him', he added. But he undermined Pakistan's plea of non-involvement in the invasion by saying that, if India withdrew its troops, 'I will call the whole thing off.' The situation, he told Mountbatten at the end of the meeting, 'was so bad that there was little that could happen to make it worse'.[16]

Patel was particularly adamant in warning of a domino effect if

Delhi did not stand firm. India had begun to send troops into Junagadh to keep it from joining Pakistan. But the larger issue of Hyderabad still loomed and the home affairs minister drew a direct connection between it and Kashmir and Junagadh. If both did not join India, a significant bloc to the north and south of the region around Delhi would emerge, which would constitute a major threat. It was important to stand firm so that the nizam was not encouraged to seek his own path.

On the ground in the north-west, tribesmen harried towns and forced Indian troops back from a key road junction after a battle in heavy rain that inflicted substantial losses on both sides. RSS fundamentalists converged on Jammu where they alleged that Muslims had amassed arms for a coup. They got a group of more than a thousand Muslims to board buses, saying they would be driven to Pakistan, and then forced them to disembark in a forest clearing where they were slaughtered with daggers, staves and swords. The following day, a second convoy was also ambushed and the bodies thrown into a canal. A journalist travelling through the region reported being 'confronted everywhere with burning houses and despoiled crops and rotting carcasses befouled the road. Whole valleys were apparently deserted except for small groups of refugees wandering aimlessly in all directions.'[17]

~

## MEANWHILE

- As Communist forces advance in Manchuria, Mao Zedong issues a manifesto calling for the unity of workers, peasants, soldiers, intellectuals, businessmen and 'all the oppressed' in a national united front to overthrow the 'dictatorial Chiang Kai-shek'. The US grants only $27.7 million in economic aid to the Nationalist government.
- Arabs in Jerusalem stage a general strike. Two thousand refugees aboard a converted pleasure steamer renamed *Jewish State* are turned back by the British – one of those on the ship holds up a dead baby as the boat is directed to Cyprus.
- Iraqi tribal chiefs meet to plan 'active measures' against the partition of Palestine. Syrian troop movements are reported.

- Belgium, the Netherlands and Luxembourg ratify the Benelux customs union agreement originally drawn up in 1944 and due to go into effect in 1948.
- The use of the word 'computer' is recorded for the first time.
- Bing Crosby makes the first broadcast of a show recorded on magnetic tape, complete with canned laughter.
- American test pilot Chuck Yeager flies a rocket plane faster than the speed of the sound, the first time this has been achieved.

# PART SEVEN

# NOVEMBER 1947

**ACTS**

*New government takes office in France amid huge strike wave; UN General Assembly votes for the independence and partition of Palestine; Foreign ministers of big four powers meet for what turns out to be their last summit; Revival of West Germany begins while Communists dig in in the East.*

**SCENES**

*Paris, Marseilles; Lake Success, Palestine, Middle East; East and West Germany, Berlin, Bizone.*

**CAST**

*Blum, Schuman, Moch, Thorez, Duclos; Truman, Ben-Gurion, Weizmann, Eddie Jacobson, King Abdullah; Marshall, Molotov, Bevin, Bidault; Adenauer, Schumacher, Ulbricht, Clay.*

# CHAPTER NINETEEN

# THE REPUBLIC SHOWS ITS GUTS

## I: INDESCRIBABLE PANDEMONIUM

On 19 November, the frail figure of Léon Blum rose from his seat in the National Assembly in the Palais Bourbon by the River Seine. It was eleven years since he had led the Popular Front government which had introduced a tornado of social reforms and then crashed out of power on a combination of its unrealised ambitions and relentless hostility from the right, fuelled, in part, by anti-Semitic attacks on the 'Talmudic' prime minister. Now, at the age of seventy-five, he had been called on to try to form a government after the ministry of his fellow Socialist, Paul Ramadier, had been brought down by growing economic strains and a wave of civil and industrial unrest.

Workers across the country were suffering not only from shortages but also from the drop of purchasing power, which was one-third lower than in 1938. They were under constant pressure to increase output as laid down by the state planners. Strikes hit the building trade, steel mills and public services. In the north-eastern coal fields, union members fought with miners who continued to work. In the Paris region, occupations of car plants spread and teachers announced a two-week stoppage. The national train network was paralysed. Marseilles was torn between the forces of left and right – an increase in tram fares provoked a general strike and the invasion of the city hall by a Communist-led mob which beat up the newly elected Gaullist mayor and tried to throw him out of the window.[1]

It was a perfect context for the Communist Party to pursue the militant line laid down by Zhdanov and the Cominform, while Italy saw a similar wave of strikes, demonstrations and street violence as Togliatti called for 'a ruthless offensive' against the government and the lira had to be devalued by 15 per cent. Parliamentary debates in Paris became chaotic. In one session in mid-November, the normally placid Ramadier had to shout his speech to make himself heard, thumping his fist on the desk in front of him amid what one newspaper called 'indescribable pandemonium'. President Auriol did not want to call on either the Gaullists or Communists to form a government, though they had taken first and second place in the municipal elections the previous month. So he turned to the elder statesman of the left.[2]

Son of a prosperous businessman from Alsace, Blum had become involved in politics during the Dreyfus Affair. A disciple of the Socialist leader Jean Jaurès, he rejected Marxist ideas of class warfare and headed the SFIO Socialist Party after the break with the Communists in 1921 over whether to line up with Moscow. Following the collapse of France in 1940, he was arrested and put on trial by the Vichy collaborationist regime, for treason and having weakened national defences, but made such a spirited defence that the Germans ordered the hearings to be stopped. He was transported to a series of concentration camps in Germany where his wife voluntarily joined him. There, he wrote his main political work, *À l'échelle Humaine* (The Human Scale). In the final weeks of the war, the Nazis ordered his execution but the commandant of Dachau decided not to comply.

Blum became prime minister at the end of 1946 but lasted for only five weeks. However, he was a key figure in the attempt to find a 'third way' internationally between American capitalism and Soviet Communism and, at home, between the PCF and Gaullism. 'We want to be neither Americanised nor Sovietized,' he argued. His problem was that, for all his historic status, events were moving against the progressive non-Communist movement he sought to construct while calling for adhesion to the Marshall Plan by Europe's Socialists.

At seventy-five, the patriarch of the non-Communist left walked with difficulty to the podium of the National Assembly. He had trouble finding his spectacles and spoke in a weak, faltering voice. His cheeks were hollow and he appeared haggard, hardly fit to provide the firm leadership France needed. But his message was clear. The country must reject both Communism and Gaullism; the Republic faced a double danger – 'On the one hand, international Communism has openly declared war on French democracy. On the other, a party has been formed in France whose object, and perhaps its only objective, is to remove fundamental rights.'[3]

The Communist riposte was savage. Duclos painted Blum as a 'lackey' of Washington and Thorez said the Socialists were 'the most zealous agents of Yankee imperialism' as he warned that the Marshall Plan would reduce France to the status of a colony. Gaullists, Christian Democrats and Radicals were unwilling to give the old man a chance, greeting his speech with cries of 'Shame!' Blum got three hundred votes, fourteen short of the number needed to form a government. It was the end of his political career, and he retreated to his home at Jouy-en-Josas outside Paris, where he died in 1950.[4]

## II: THE PHARMACIST TAKES OVER

In Blum's place, the Christian Democrat Robert Schuman formed a ministry to confront the crisis facing the Fourth Republic. Born in Luxembourg to a German father, the 61-year-old prime minister grew up in German-occupied Lorraine and was called up for the Kaiser's army in the First World War though excused service on medical grounds; he became a French citizen in 1919. Entering politics and elected to Parliament, he joined the government in 1940 as an expert on eastern France, staying on to serve in the Vichy regime. Among the deputies who voted to give full powers to Philippe Pétain, he soon resigned his government post and was detained before escaping and joining the resistance. Like others who had voted for Pétain in 1940, he was condemned to 'national indignity' and lost his political rights after the Liberation, but he petitioned de Gaulle and was restored.

Elected to Parliament from the Moselle in 1946, Schuman played a leading role in the rise of the MRP, trying to restore order to France's economy as finance minister in Ramadier's government. De Gaulle dismissed him as 'a man as fitted to resist events of the gravity of those we must face today as I am to become pope'.[5]

However, after negotiations with other parties lasting until 5 a.m. on 24 November, he was able to rally a hundred more deputies than Blum to back the formation of a government including Socialist and Radical ministers and a 31-year old independent anti-Communist, François Mitterrand, who was made responsible for war veterans and victims. Bidault stayed at the Quai d'Orsay, and was immediately off to London for the opening of the latest meetings of the four power foreign ministers to discuss Germany. 'My government is determined above all to act and to talk as little as possible,' the new prime minister told reporters.[6]

Schuman made restoring the economy his priority, promising to campaign against inflation, strive for a balanced budget and use foreign aid wherever it came from. But, for most people, the more pressing issue was the spreading strike wave which made Jules Moch, who had moved to the Interior Ministry in charge of the police and national order, the key member of the government. With his professorial air, tortoiseshell spectacles and toothbrush moustache, he was a resolute, methodical character and had an impeccable record as a Socialist and Jewish member of the Resistance that made him difficult to attack. At his previous post as transport minister, he had turned the Esplanade des Invalides in the centre of Paris into a vast bus and lorry station to ferry people and goods around during the railway strikes and made contact with non-Communist railway workers who were thinking of breaking away from the party-led CGT.[7]

The Interior Ministry was at the centre of intense government activity. Moch said that, at one point, it received 2,300 official telegrams reporting of the state of the country in twenty-four hours – most were in code so the cypher clerks were overwhelmed. The minister stepped up the use of the CRS riot police set up at the Liberation, and worked closely with the army. Eighty thousand reservists were called to the colours. African colonial troops were mobilised. Pickets were dispersed. Government agents stepped up their encouragement of Christian trade unionists and non-Communist members of the CGT's *Force Ouvrière* (Workers' Force) branch to oppose strike action. Communists were weeded out of the police. The CIA undertook black propaganda against Thorez and his comrades and engaged Corsican gangsters in Marseilles.[8]

Still, the stoppages intensified, spreading in the coal mines to the prime minister's homeland of Lorraine. Industrial output slumped, rail lines to and from Paris were at standstill and tracks were sabotaged. Food began to run short in cities. A shortage of paper reduced newspapers to two pages. The Paris water, gas and electricity systems came under severe strain – a concert by Arthur Rubinstein had to be held by candlelight. A work stoppage by dustmen left the capital's streets lined with overflowing bins. The state executioner refused to guillotine eight men unless he got a pay rise and a bonus for each beheading.[9]

There were violent clashes between police and strikers in Nice, Beziers, Montpellier and other towns and cities. An express travelling through the Jura and a Paris metro train was derailed. Communists occupied the station at Limoges, one of their provincial bastions. Thirty thousand strikers, some carrying iron bars, marched through the industrial centre of Saint-Étienne; when soldiers refused to stop them, they took over three military vehicles equipped with machine guns, grabbed weapons and forced back police in clashes that injured a hundred people.

Violence continued in Marseilles where strikers set up barricades and attacked government food lorries. At the important railway junction of Valence, demonstrators led by the local Communist parliamentary deputy stormed the station, were driven out by police and returned in larger numbers to reassert control. Two people died. Electricity pylons were blown up outside Bordeaux, threatening the power supply to western France. In the north, North African troops sent to clear coal mines near Lens laid down their rifles and had to be replaced by riot police.

De Gaulle, who passed his fifty-seventh birthday on 22 November, forecast an imminent collapse of the franc and pressed the demand for a general election. He ordered the reorganisation and enlargement of the RPF to provide 'a framework in which, rising above its divisions, the Nation can attain its salvation'. Calling for a 30 per cent cut in government spending to balance the budget, he evoked a union of West European nations led by France against the USSR.[10]

But he remained sphinx-like as to his immediate plans; some supporters forecast that he would wait for the end of winter before making a move while others recalled his remark after the municipal elections about having reached a Rubicon and noted that he had been seen lunching with his wartime intelligence and covert operations chief, Colonel Passy. While content with his political success, the general suffered a blow when Philippe Leclerc, the army commander he had seen as his putative heir, was killed on 28 November in a plane crash in Algeria. Rumours flew that he had been urging the RPF leader to stage a coup and that sugar had been put into the aircraft's fuel supply to remove him. De Gaulle did not reply to an invitation from Schuman to attend the state funeral.[11]

As the Schuman government withdrew subsidies for coal, gas and rail fares, the CGT called for 25 per cent pay increases and set up a committee to prepare for a general national stoppage. 'We must arm against all of those who seek to bring about the disintegration of the forces of state and to sap the authority of the government,' the Prime Minister told Parliament. He warned that the country was approaching 'the point of insurrection' and denounced 'factious undertakings synchronised through Europe'. He won a confidence vote, but with the support of ninety fewer deputies than at his investiture.[12]

In Paris, where fog engulfed the city and snow fell for the first time that winter, National Assembly proceedings were constantly disrupted by Communists who took no notice of the speaker, 75-year old Radical Édouard Herriot. They staged filibusters to block government business, joined in renditions of the Marseillaise and Russian revolutionary songs during debates, and bellowed insults at ministers. Moch, who was Jewish, was greeted with cries of 'Heil Hitler'. Thorez told Mitterrand, 'You speak like Goering.' When the prime minister appeared, Duclos shouted, 'There's the Boche.' 'Where were you as a soldier in 1914?' another cried. In response, right-wingers recalled the Soviet–Nazi Pact, setting off further pandemonium.[13]

After a Communist deputy, Raoul Calas, made an incendiary speech urging police not to take action against strikers, a motion was adopted for his exclusion, but he refused to leave. The session was suspended and other deputies filed out except for Communists clustered round him. As Herriot left the chamber, one shouted, 'Where are your Republican guts now?' The comrade deputies stayed on until dawn, sleeping on the benches. When Republican Guards arrived with a warrant to clear the place, they sang the national anthem, forcing the soldiers to stop and stand to attention. Eventually, their colonel reached Calas, who said 'I give in to force' and let himself be led away.[14]

CHAPTER TWENTY

# MISSION ACCOMPLISHED

## I: DECISION AT LAKE SUCCESS

The General Assembly of the United Nations met on 26 November at its temporary headquarters in the former offices of the Sperry Gyroscope company at Lake Success outside New York City to vote on the recommendation of its commission on Palestine. Though the US and Soviet delegations had come out the previous month in support of the partition it proposed, there was no certainty of the necessary two-thirds majority when the vote came. While the debate evolved through the day, that majority became ever more elusive as speakers stressed the negative aspects of splitting the territory.

The Jewish Agency delegation realised it had to play for time. The cigar-chomping American Nahum Goldman huddled with the Assembly's pro-Zionist president, Osvaldo Aranha of Brazil, and then spoke to two other Latin American delegates who backed partition. He told them they had to mount a filibuster. One objected that he had already spoken three times but Goldman told them, 'Read from the Bible. Read the Psalms, the promises of the prophet Isaiah.'

In the evening, the two men swept into action despite shouts of 'To vote!' from Arab delegates. Aranha came up with a list of other speakers, which filled in an hour until he rose in front of the vast map of the world on the wall behind the platform and said such an important matter required further consideration – and adjourned the meeting for two days.[1]

The Jewish Agency and American Zionists went to work. 'We

took the list of undecided countries and began to seek ways of influencing them,' the diplomat Abba Eban recalled. 'How shall we influence Liberia? They say that the American Firestone Rubber Company carries weight there. How do we reach Firestone? How shall we approach the President of the Philippines? Is there any Jew who knows him? How can we influence Haiti, which is still straddling the fence?'[2]

Zionists had listening devices planted in the chief Syrian delegate's hotel room and in a rental car used by the British. Twenty-six senators were enlisted to sign a letter backing partition which was sent to undecided countries – Congress was considering the American aid programme at the time. Liberia fell into line after a threat of the withdrawal of aid and pressure from Firestone, which underwrote its economy. Haiti was offered assistance of $5 million for a positive vote. The Philippines switched sides to back partition after speaking initially of a decision 'clearly repugnant to the valid nationalist aspirations of the people of Palestine'.[3]

Nehru said an unsuccessful attempt had been made to bribe India to abandon its negative stance. When France hesitated over the possible negative reaction among Arabs in its African territories, Bernard Baruch, the prominent financier, Democratic Party elder and ardent Zionist, warned its chief delegate that failure to support partition might lead to a reconsideration of Marshall Plan aid. 'Jewish and non-Jewish opinion, leaders and masses alike, converged on the Government and induced the President to assert the authority of his Administration to overcome the negative attitude of the State Department,' Truman's least favourite rabbi, Abba Hillel Silver, recalled. 'The result was that our Government made its intense desire for the adoption of the partition plan known to the wavering governments.'[4]

A Saudi delegate called the Zionist campaign a demonstration in actual political science in action ... the pressure politics that was applied, the economic promises and persuasion. The propaganda, the breathing down the throats of the delegates, the long-distance telephone calls to various heads of state to get their UN delegates to shift the votes. To the Arabs, the sessions were left to luck and

they relied mostly on the good faith of the delegates. To the Jewish
people, politics was not a gamble, it was a science so they used
every technique possible to win the vote.[5]

Still, the State Department did not give up. 'I've given my word to
the Arabs,' Loy Henderson, chief of the Near Eastern and African
Affairs section, told his country's UN team. The Department criticised the proposal to give the Jews Jaffa, Palestine's cultural capital,
and was strongly opposed to the inclusion of the Negev desert in a
Jewish state. Marshall circulated a warning from Bevin that Jewish
groups moving illegally from the Balkans to Palestine included many
Communists. Defence Secretary James Forrestal kept up a drum-
beat of concern about oil supplies and his warning that 'there are
45,000,000 Arabs and 350,000 Jews and the 450,000,000 Arabs
are going to push the 350,000 Jews into oceans. So that's all there is
to it.' A memorandum by the joint chiefs of staff argued that partition would enable the Soviet Union to replace the US and UK in the
Middle East and would threaten access to oil, a point also made by
Arab representatives in Washington.[6]

The case for backing the creation of a Jewish state was pressed
by two presidential aides, the increasingly influential White House
Counsel, Clark Clifford, and David Niles, the special assistant for
minority affairs. Apart from his Zionist sympathies, Niles was
keenly aware of the importance of the Jewish vote in the following
year's election – at one meeting he turned to the State Department
representative and said, 'Look here, the most important thing for the
United States is for the President to be re-elected.'[7]

They had to deal with Truman's mounting irritation with Zionist
lobbying – he said that he wished they would care more about their
country and less about their own particular interests. 'I do not think
I ever had as much pressure and propaganda aimed at the White
House as I had in this instance,' he wrote in his memoirs. 'The per-
sistence of a few of the extreme Zionist leaders – actuated by political
motives and engaging in political threats – disturbed and annoyed
me.' To Eleanor Roosevelt, a UN delegate, he wrote that 'the action
of some of our United States Zionists will eventually prejudice everyone against what they are trying to get done. I fear very much that

the Jews are like all underdogs. When they get on top they are just as intolerant and as cruel as people were to them when they were underneath. I regret this situation very much because my sympathy has always been with them.'[8]

One person the president did listen to was his old friend and one-time Kansas City haberdashery partner, Eddie Jacobson, a devout Jew concerned about the admission of refugees into Palestine who now broke with his normally apolitical relationship with the president. 'When the day came when Eddie Jacobson was persuaded to forgo his natural reluctance to petition me and he came to talk to me about the plight of the Jews ... I paid careful attention,' Truman remembered. Acheson would recall that his boss's 'deep conviction' on the creation of a Jewish state was 'in large part implanted' by Jacobson.[9]

At Jacobson's urging, Chaim Weizmann had been received at the White House a week before the UN session. The meeting was kept secret. The Zionist patriarch spread a map of the Negev on the presidential desk. In Arab hands, he said, the desert would continue to be as it was, but the Jews would 'make it into a flourishing garden'. The Gulf of Aqaba would be dredged to enable the port of Eilat to become an international maritime centre, perhaps with a canal from the Mediterranean to rival the one at Suez. Truman was impressed. 'You can bank on us,' he said. When his guest left, he put in a call to the ambassador at the UN with instructions to change the delegation's position on the Negev.[10]

## II: Secret meeting by the Jordan

Unknown to all but the royal entourage in Amman and a few insiders at the Jewish Agency, a sub-plot for Palestine was evolving in the run-up to the UN vote. King Abdullah of Transjordan was as intent as ever on making the most of the changing situation to advance his ambitions for a Greater Syria under his rule. His main weapon would be his Arab Legion. Subsidised by the British who supplied its top officers, including the commander John Glubb Pasha, a First World War veteran whose jaw had been shattered in fighting on the Western Front, who spoke fluent Arabic. It was highly mechanised, well disciplined and had an efficient artillery arm. The king was confident it would assert his control over areas allocated to the Arabs by the UN. He wanted to avoid coming to blows with the Jews, with whom he planned to co-operate while receiving subsidies and technical expertise.[11]

On 17 November, the Hashemite monarch went to lunch at the home of his private secretary by the Jordan River. The meal was also attended by the Jewish manager of a nearby electricity generating plant who worked for the Hanagah intelligence service and who laid on power to his palace and the home of his concubine. After the meal, the manager invited the monarch to accompany him to his white-painted house for a siesta. Waiting there was Golda Meir, with two of the Jewish Agency's Arab experts.

Born Golda Mabovitch in Kiev, her earliest memory was of her carpenter father boarding up the front door against a pogrom. She followed him to the US in the early twentieth century, becoming a committed Zionist and marrying a sign painter, Morris Meyerson. They moved in 1921 to Palestine where their kibbutz elected her as its representative to the Histadrut Labour Federation and she rose to become number two in the Jewish Agency's political department. In the absence of its chief, Moshe Sharett in New York, she was the natural choice to meet Abdullah, though he was taken aback to be confronted by a woman.

After introductory cups of coffee, they discussed the outlines of a possible deal if the UN voted for partition. The king spoke of sending in the Legion with the aim of bringing Arab Palestine under his rule with the Jews forming a republic of their own. He said he would stop other countries intervening against a Zionist state as well as blocking any moves by the Grand Mufti.

The monarch's freedom of action was circumscribed by the need to keep his contacts with the Zionists secret, especially since other Arab rulers were hostile to his grand designs. He also needed to balance between British financial and military support and appearing to be a puppet of London, ready to work with enemies of the Arabs. Still, the conversation seemed promising enough for them to agree to meet again after the vote at Lake Success.[12]

## III: JOY AND LAMENTATION

On 29 November, the General Assembly gave more than the required two-thirds majority for the creation of separate Arab and Jewish states with a Special International Regime for Jerusalem. Eddie Jacobson's condensed record of events laid out the sequence:

> Nov. 6th – Wash – Pres. Still going all out for Palestine.
> Nov. 17th – Again at the White House.
> Wed 26 – Received call from White House – everything O.K.
> Nov 27. Thanksgiving. Sent two page wire to Truman.
> Friday, received call from his secretary not to worry
> Nov. 29th – Mission accomplished.[15]

Thirty-three countries, or 72 per cent of those voting, came out in favour. Thirteen were against. There were ten abstentions. The USSR joined the US in voting positively, Stalin having decided that the left-wing character of the Zionist movement meant the new state would be a thorn in British and American sides in the Middle East. Supporting the resolution, Andrei Gromyko, the chief Soviet delegate, said that 'as a result of the war, the Jews as a people have suffered more than any other people' and that it would be unjust to deny them a state of their own.[13]

Other countries backing the resolution included thirteen from Latin America and the Caribbean, led by Brazil, and eight from Western Europe, among them France, which ignored the potential reaction in North Africa, plus Canada, Australia, New Zealand and the Philippines. From Eastern Europe, partition was backed by Poland, Ukraine, Byelorussia and Czechoslovakia. India, Cuba and Greece joined Arab and Muslim countries in voting against. Britain abstained, citing its position as the mandatory power, as did China, Yugoslavia, Ethiopia and six Latin American and Caribbean nations. Thailand was absent.

When the result of the vote was announced, Arab delegates walked out, accompanied by the Indians and Pakistanis. A member of the Indian delegation told an Israeli diplomat that his government knew the Jews had a case but had to take account of the Muslim population of his country.[14]

Under partition, only 1 per cent of the Arab state's 725,000 inhabitants would be Jewish while Arabs would make up 45 per cent of the 407,000 people in the other entity. Jerusalem, with 105,000 inhabitants, would be evenly split. Despite the population figures and the fact that Arabs owned most of the land, the Jews got 60 per cent of the territory, including three fertile lowland plains, sole access to the Red Sea and most of the 4,700-square-mile Negev. Arabs were given the highlands, source of most of the territory's water and the city of Jaffa. The expectation was that immigration would swell the number of Jews as soon as the British left. Haifa was to be a free entry port.

The mainstream Zionist leadership under Ben-Gurion was overjoyed at this huge step towards achieving the millennial goal of celebrating the next year in Jerusalem. Hard-liners denounced the territorial division as insufficient, Begin insisting that partition would never be recognised since 'the land of Israel will be restored to the people of Israel. All of it. And for ever.' But most Jews celebrated through the night. Huge bonfires were built at kibbutzes. 'We were happy that night, and we danced and our hearts went out to every nation whose UN representatives had voted in favour of the resolution,' wrote the future general Moshe Dayan.[16]

'After the darkness of 2,000 years, the dawn of redemption has broken,' the chief rabbi of Jerusalem declared, hailing 'an epoch not only in Jewish history, but in world history'. Cafés in Tel Aviv served free champagne. A brewery threw open its doors to the crowd. 'For two thousand years, we longed for deliverance,' Golda Meir told the crowd in front of the Jewish Agency headquarters. 'We awaited this great day with awe. Now that it is here, it is so great and wondrous that it surpasses human expression.'

In New York, a beaming Weizmann was carried aloft by a celebratory crowd at the St Nicholas Skating Rink. The following day, Ben-Gurion reflected simply, 'I know of no greater achievement by the Jewish people.' But the reality of the conflict ahead soon made itself felt. Arab snipers fired at ambulances going to the main Jewish hospital in Jerusalem, six Jews were killed in machine-gun and grenade attacks on two buses and a 25-year-old Jew was shot dead between Tel Aviv and Jaffa.[17]

In contrast to the Jewish rejoicing, 'Arabs were found going about their business silently, resentful at having been flouted by the west,' the London *Times* reported. The Arab Higher Committee declared a three-day general strike in Palestine. There were clashes in Jerusalem, Lydda and Jaffa. The Grand Mufti's men were training for a guerrilla campaign in towns and villages allocated to the Jews.[18]

For the Arab states, which still did not recognise the extent to which many countries felt the need to atone for the destruction of European Jewry, the UN vote was a spectacular failure built on the intransigence that had marked their non-diplomacy with UNSCOP. They insisted that partition violated the principle of national self-determination. 'The [UN] Charter is dead,' the Syrian delegate declared. The Palestinians and their allies warned of a holy war. The Iraqi prime minister, Nuri al-Said, vowed that the Jewish state would be smashed along with every other place where Jews sought shelter.[19]

Britain set 14 May 1948 as the final day for the Mandate with complete withdrawal by the beginning of August. The Cabinet decided not to join in enforcement of partition and told the UN it would be 'intolerable' if it sought to exercise authority in the territory before the Mandate ended. This made it impossible for the international organisation to orchestrate the process and, on top of the deeply entrenched hostility between the communities, could only deepen the risk of war when the Zionist state was proclaimed.

As news of the UN vote came over the radio, Abdullah was meeting representatives of the Arab Higher Committee in Amman. He had begun to infiltrate troops from his Legion into Palestine, but the Committee turned down his proposal to act as protector for Arabs there. 'You have rejected my offer,' the king told his visitors. 'You deserve what happens to you now.'[20]

# THE GREAT DIVIDE

## I: ONE MORE ATTEMPT

As the United Nations delegates were voting on Palestine and Robert Schuman's government was squaring off against the Communists in France, George Marshall flew to London on his first visit since just before D-Day three years earlier. He was there for the latest meeting of the foreign ministers of the big four powers, as agreed at their session in Moscow earlier in the year. The focus was once more Germany, though Austria was also on the agenda. But the context had changed with the European Recovery Program and the Soviet attempt to derail it. A committee headed by Averell Harriman had just put the plan's cost at $12–17 billion and the administration proposed an initial package of $597 million for France, Italy and Austria to show what Truman called it 'sincere determination to support the freedom-loving countries of Western Europe'.

The secretary of state had told a meeting in Chicago before leaving that there could be no revival of Europe without the return of German production. The two issues were intimately linked; the recovery of the western half of the country was essential for the success of the ERP. Soviet insistence on the need to press ahead with German unity could only impede that since it would involve further laborious negotiations and the deadlocked issue of reparations. Marshall expected the Soviets to come up with 'various ruses to try to get us out of Western Germany'. Robert Murphy, political adviser to the US commander, Lucius Clay, noted that if the conference failed to produce an agreement, 'shortly thereafter we would be obliged to develop a political organization' in the Western sectors.[1]

West German politicians were unhappy at how the fate of their half of the country was being decided without them having a say, but other West European countries were growing fed up with the lack of progress; the three Benelux governments sent a message to London calling for the political and economic structure of Germany to be fixed 'to bring an end to the uncertainty in Europe'. Bevin rumbled that 'we cannot go on for ever with chaos in Europe', though the American ambassador to the USSR, Bedell Smith, noted that 'it will require careful maneuvering to avoid the appearance of inconsistency if not hypocrisy'.[2]

The Soviet media rampaged against the 'imperialism' of the West. In a speech on 6 November, Molotov accused the US of wanting to impose 'capitalist slavery'. At the annual dinner of the Foreign Press Association in New York, his deputy, Andrey Vyshinsky, denounced 'Anglo-American reactionaries and war mongers' who were attacking the USSR 'with hatred and a vicious animus'. In Berlin, the propaganda director of the Soviet zone, General Tulpanov, told a public meeting the US was seeking war, the first time an official of one Allied power had attacked another before a German audience.[3]

## II: SICK AND TIRED

'The forthcoming meeting will be one of transcendental significance,' Edwin Pauley, the US special adviser on reparations, wrote as the conference opened. 'It will constitute one of the Great Divides of American policy in the era.' However, the atmosphere as the delegations settled around the big circular table in the conference chamber in the early nineteenth-century grandeur of Lancaster House, close to Buckingham Palace, was described as being of 'utter gloom'.[4]

There was an immediate procedural wrangle over the order of topics on the agenda, which produced the usual three-to-one division. The Western powers wanted Austria to be dealt with from the start but the Soviets insisted it be put off till the end. Bevin, Marshall and Bidault thought the question of a peace treaty with what the secretary of state described as the first victim of Nazi aggression could be cleared up quickly. Post-war elections had brought convincing victories for Austrian conservatives and Social Democrats and there was no prospect of the Communists gaining the kind of support at the polls they enjoyed in Czechoslovakia, while the division of the country into four occupation zones meant that Moscow could not impose its will. So Moscow was aiming to perpetuate for as long as possible occupation by the Red Army of a state bordering on the Soviet domain.[5]

This disagreement led the foreign secretary to ask if the Kremlin's only method of procedure was that the others must always agree to what it proposed. Molotov responded by charging that the Soviet side had been threatened by the United States. To which the foreign secretary replied that he had seen no threats; indeed, he had gained exactly the opposite impression. Molotov then contrasted the 'imperialist peace' sought by the West with the 'democratic peace' offered by Moscow. Bevin tried to make light of this by remarking, 'If we treat the charges with the humour they deserve, we may get more peace. We are so used to it by now, being called warmongers. The only good country in the world is the Soviet Union. And the rest of us, we come from somewhere down below, I suppose.' That earned him a tight smile from the Russian, but did not stop Molotov pursuing his familiar tack that the other powers wanted to use Germany as a military base. When he complained that the USSR had been threatened by the Americans and attacked by the Western press, Bevin replied that the British people were sick and tired of delays and obstructions from Moscow, and wanted a prompt settlement 'with mutual concessions not from one side only'.[6]

At a bilateral meeting, Bevin confronted Molotov over Soviet insistence on German unification under a single government. 'Why do you want that?' he asked. 'Do you really believe that a unified Germany would go communist? They might pretend to. They would say all the right things ... but in their hearts they would be longing for the day when they could revenge their defeat at Stalingrad. You know that as well as I do.'

'Yes,' Molotov replied. 'I know that. But I want a unified Germany.'[7]

The foreign secretary's question reflected the growing reality – the

US, UK and France wanted their occupation zones in the richest half of the former enemy to develop on their own as a single unit. Stalin might worry that this could become a base for a Western offensive at some point in the future. But, for the moment and whatever rote response Molotov trotted out about wanting unity, Moscow was being forced to admit that, if it wanted to keep the east of the country as the forward element in its security zone, it would have to accept the Iron Curtain division in the centre of Europe.

'The Soviet Government would, under present conditions, treat any scheme for German economic unity solely as a means for trying to influence events in the Western zones', Bevin noted. In the plenary session of the conference, he laid out his position: 'When I say I want a democratic Germany, I do not want a dangerous Germany, and I refuse to agree to a type of centralised Germany that can become a danger to us again. On the other hand, I want Germany to have sufficient central powers for her economic and political development.' By now, the former foe had become a key element in the deepening split in Europe that would include its own inevitable division for four and a half decades.[8]

CHAPTER TWENTY-TWO

# REVIVING GERMANY

## I: DEVASTATED LAND

The development Bevin spoke of seemed very far away in the Germany that emerged from the war. The country that had aspired to rule Europe was in ruins. Between 10 and 15 per cent of the male population was killed or missing; in Berlin, men and boys made up only 37 per cent of the population. After a visit to Germany in 1945, John McCloy, the under secretary for war, said the situation there was 'probably worse than ever happened in the world'.[1]

Industrial output ran at a third of pre-war levels with coal production down 75 per cent. Bombing had destroyed up to 40 per cent of factories and half the locomotives as well as more than 2,300 railway bridges and the power and water supplies. Food was scarce: the daily ration in the American occupation zone in 1945 was a quarter of the average consumed in 1940. In many places, even the low rations could not be met. The financial and currency systems were in chaos.

More than a million German women had been raped by Red Army troops. Millions of women were without husbands, and 10–15 per cent of children grew up without their biological father. The Russian occupation authorities shipped at least 1,300 factories to the USSR along with 4,500 miles of railway track. Their total takings have been estimated at about $4 billion between 1945 and 1948. 'Take everything,' a Russian officer told his troops before other Allied armies arrived. 'What you can't take, destroy. Only leave nothing for the allies: no machines, not even a single bed, not even a chamber pot.'[2]

Air attacks and ground fighting had flattened cities across the country. Intensive bombing had devastated Hamburg and destroyed 1,600 acres of the Saxon city of Dresden. The old middle of Frankfurt am Main was gone. In Cologne, 262 air attacks, including the first 'thousand bomber' offensive, left only three hundred houses standing in the centre. Mainz, another Rhineland city, looked as if it had been hit by an earthquake: 'All one could see were ruins, faceless people, twisted beams, empty façades,' the writer Alfred Döblin recorded.[3]

Berlin, where the Nazis had staged their last stand, was, in Truman's words to his wife from the Potsdam summit meeting, 'a hell of a place – ruined, dirty, smelly, forlorn people, bedraggled hangdog look about them. You never saw as completely ruined a city.' For the film director Billy Wilder, returning for the first time for a dozen years, the city was 'a desert of rubble. It looks like the end of the world.' The economist John Kenneth Galbraith, with the State Department, wrote home from the city that the inhabitants were 'sallow, distressed and demoralised'. A German Communist arriving from Moscow recalled, 'People looked absent-minded as if they couldn't see or understand anything any more.'[4]

Able-bodied women were enlisted to clear the mountains of rubble; there were estimated to be 75 million tons of rubble in Berlin. The *trümmerfrau* were rewarded with food rations well above the normal and some made 40 marks a week, the equivalent of the price of four cigarettes on the black market. Thousands of bodies lay buried under the ruins in the capital of the Reich, polluting the air in the intense summer heat. Many more floated on the waterways or lay in abandoned allotments. Old people, pale and haggard, trudged through the streets carrying everything they owned in wheel-barrows, hand carts and rucksacks.

Hitler's vast Chancellery was a gaunt ruin. The great dome of the cathedral in the centre of the city had collapsed after a bombing raid. The entrance to the once fashionable Adlon Hotel was through a mound of rubble, and its restaurant served the most basic of fare to those with the appropriate coupons. Only the thirteenth-century St Marienkirche stood as before among the ruins of the centre of the devastated Reich.

One big black market stretched out in front of the blackened

Reichstag building while another, at the Brandenburg Gate, offered
everything from watches, clocks, items of clothing, rings, jewels,
boots, binoculars, cameras, razors and fur coats to stockings and
women's silk underwear, a resident recalled. Medicines provided
a lucrative commerce and, at the top of the traffic, flawless diamonds were sometimes on sale together with narcotics – 10.8 kilos
of opium were confiscated from a woman. In early 1948, it was
officially estimated that a third of all goods traded in the city went
through its seventy-five markets; police raids which detained up
to a hundred people a day did nothing to stop the trading, joined
by Allied soldiers selling goods from their own stores and buying
watches, cameras, antiques and jewels. American cigarettes were the
preferred medium of exchange in many places – it was not uncom-
mon to see Germans trailing smoking GIs to pick up the discarded
butts. The Soviets developed tobacco fields in their zone to raise a
crop and their Rasno Company built up a lucrative business with
imported tobacco from the USSR which was made into cigarettes
in Saxony.[5]

The harsh winter of 1946/7 hit the country hard, accentuating the
lack of fuel and shelter. In Cologne, Adenauer slept in his suit and
coat, shaking with cold like most of his compatriots. Then came an
extremely dry summer when crops and people starved in the sun.
In the Western sectors of Berlin, the Russians kidnapped technicians and other experts. Hitler's intention that his nation should
be destroyed along with him and his Reich risked becoming reality
as the stalemate between the Allies prevented coordinated action,
rivalry between the West and the USSR deepened and life was a
constant struggle for the survivors.

## II: Realism takes over

Despite its ruined condition, fear of a militarist revival of the
defeated enemy was extremely strong; Germany 'will recover and
very quickly', Stalin told a Yugoslav delegation in 1945. 'Give them
twelve to fifteen years and they'll be on their feet again.' Bevin
stressed the importance of ensuring that the country evolved in 'such
a form that she could never again menace Europe'. The Treaty of

Dunkirk between Britain and France, which went into operation in the autumn of 1947, was designed to guard against an attack from the immediate east.[6]

The nearest thing to a plan of how to deal with Germany had been the wartime proposal by US Treasury Secretary Henry Morgenthau, that the country should be shorn of its industry and reduced to a pastoral state. FDR bought into the idea and Churchill agreed in the hope that his accord might make Roosevelt more malleable on renewing Lend Lease Aid. But the war secretary, Henry Stimson, who foresaw the need for a strong Germany as a barrier to Soviet expansion, mounted a campaign against it in Washington, and Goebbels seized on it to rally German morale. Roosevelt reversed himself, refusing to see Morgenthau and denying that he had ever signed the document.

However, the US joint chiefs of staff drew up a directive which echoed the Morgenthau Plan in many respects. It instructed the government of the American occupation zone to 'take no steps looking toward the economic rehabilitation of Germany [or] designed to maintain or strengthen the German economy'. The aim was 'to prevent Germany from ever again becoming a threat to the peace of the world' with, as a first step, its 'industrial disarmament and demilitarization'.

The economy was to be decentralised, cartels broken up, war industries dismantled and management shorn of Nazis. Output of factories would be limited to half the 1939 level with car production down by 90 per cent and no locomotives to be built until 1949. The industrial and coal heartlands of the Ruhr and Saar were to be detached – the French were particularly keen on getting control of the second to fuel their steel mills. The banking system was to be dismantled. This harsh line was backed by the USSR and France, which both extracted plant and equipment. Morgenthau told his staff he hoped nobody realised it was really his plan being put into effect.

Lucius Clay, a leading army engineer and an expert in supply and procurement who had never served in combat, had not been told of the directive by the joint chiefs when appointed chief of the Military Government in the US zone, with his headquarters in Frankfurt. When informed, he quickly came to see it as inappropriate at a time

when ensuring minimum food supply was costing American taxpayers $700 million a year.

'It seemed obvious to us even then that Germany would starve
unless it could produce for export and that immediate steps would
have to be taken to revive industrial production,' Clay recalled. His
adviser, Louis Douglas, lambasted the directive as 'assembled by
economic idiots. It makes no sense to forbid the most skilled workers
in Europe from producing as much as they can in a continent that
is desperately short of everything.' From the British side, Hector
McNeil, under secretary at the Foreign Office, noted, 'To keep the
German people permanently in chains means to keep ourselves permanently in rags.' Hugh Dalton groused privately that 'we are getting
nothing out of Germany for feeding the brutes'.[7]

Signalling reconsideration of the punitive policy in his Stuttgart
speech in 1946, Byrnes said the US would 'oppose harsh and venge-
ful measures which invite the breaking of the peace'. The American
people wanted 'to help the German people to win their way back to
an honourable peace among the free and peace-loving nations of the
world,' he added. He also made plain US troops would stay in Europe
for as long as necessary, reversing Roosevelt's wartime remark to
Stalin that they would be back home within a couple of years of the
end of the fighting.[8]

Once the State Department had identified the reconstruction of
West European economies as a key policy objective, it was impossible to prevent Germany from playing a central role. Morgenthau's
departure from the Treasury helped the reorientation of policy. French
governments were hesitant about encouraging German revival and
feared that it would provide fuel for a Communist campaign, but Clay
argued that this risk must be taken. Congress could see no logic in
reducing industrial capacity at a time when the US was pumping in aid
and American firms were anxious to invest in Germany or reclaim
pre-war assets. 'We cannot attain our basic objectives unless we are
ready to move rapidly to reconstruct German life from its present
pitiful and chaotic condition,' Averell Harriman, commerce secretary
at the time, warned Truman. 'We cannot revive a self-supporting
western European economy without a healthy Germany playing its
part as a producing and consuming unit.'[9]

In another message to Washington, Clay made the point that revival of industry should not be seen as a security threat since Germany would have no war plants. In the summer of 1947, the original directive was replaced 'on national security grounds' by one recognising that 'an orderly and prosperous Europe requires the economic contribution of a stable and productive Germany'. An economic council was set up for the US–UK Bizonia.[10]

Recovery in the western zones was still only in its early stage as the foreign ministers met in London. Manpower was still short due to war deaths. Coal supplies were insufficient. But industry was starting to increase output and transport equipment was significantly expanded, especially on the railways. Infrastructure repairs were stepped up. Above all, the revival of Western Germany was essential for the success of the European Recovery Plan. Though the USSR continued to press for a united Germany which it hoped might come under its sway, the separation path was clear by the winter of 1947. As Clay told the Soviets, if they continued the demand for $10 billion in reparations and a share in control of the Ruhr, Washington would inevitably be led to treat the Western zones as a separate economic unit and integrate them closely with the economies about to receive Marshall Plan aid.

Economics was not all that mattered. East and West Germany were both post-fascist, post-war societies facing a huge psychological task in adapting to the legacy of total war and total defeat. Many Germans saw themselves as victims, displaying 'patriotic defiance' to the end. Reporting from Cologne, George Orwell wrote that, in the eyes of some he met there, he detected 'a beaten defiance which ... seemed to me to mean that these people were horribly ashamed of having lost the war'. Other correspondents noted how Germans generally shifted the blame for what had happened onto others, taking the Allies to task for not having stopped Hitler sooner and pointing to how non-Jews had been sent to concentration camps. Collective guilt was rejected and support for the Führer buried in denial. Assize courts cleared evident war criminals on the grounds of drunkenness or not being aware of the illegality of their actions.[11]

Claims spread that the Allies were depriving Germans of food to weaken workers to prevent competition on export markets. There were stories of butter and vegetables being flown out of the country for sale in Britain. In the east, the initial policy of blaming all Germans who had stayed in the Reich for what had happened was modified to put the responsibility on 'the Hitler clique' that 'brought its war to the German people'. Communist leaders drew a parallel between the suffering of millions of Germans who 'had been driven to death ... by the Hitler government' and other, unnamed millions who 'had been murdered and tortured to death by an inhuman terror in the concentration camps'. In the ideological language adopted in the east, it was all the fault of 'fascist dictatorships', a term that could be extended to refer to the Western powers as the Cold War took root.

The sheer size of the denazification campaign overwhelmed the courts. The Americans alone tried nearly a million cases; half were handed fines but only 9,000 went to jail and 22,000 were barred from public office. Most of the proceedings hit the small fry hardest since the better off could buy their way out or move to a part of the country where they were not known. In the east, class warfare coloured denazification with the automatic internment of Junker landowners and owners of big businesses.[12]

A 133-part questionnaire issued to 13 million Germans in the west aroused wide disdain because of its apparently irrelevant probing. An instruction that anybody who had been a member of the Nazi Party could do only 'ordinary labour' proved unworkable given the numbers involved. American schemes to re-educate German children ran into public hostility or indifference from a population that did not feel it needed transatlantic tuition. The plan to break up industrial and financial cartels made only limited progress. A ban on Allied troops fraternising with Germans soon broke down in the Western zones; the number of children fathered by American troops has been estimated at 90,000.[13]

## III: APPARATCHIKS AND DEMOCRATS

In the early morning of 30 April 1945, ten German Communists had been driven by bus from the Lux Hotel in Moscow to the airport to fly to Germany. 'Our task was to establish a broad anti-Nazi coalition that would attract voters across the whole country,' the future spymaster Markus Wolf recalled. They were told that the German road to socialism would be long, but it was tougher than they had expected. Having fled the Nazis in the 1930s, they were out of touch with their homeland. They had expected people to welcome the liberation from Nazi rule, but 'few people felt guilty for what had happened under Hitler and nearly all of them hated the Russians', Wolf remembered.[14]

The instructions from Moscow to the returnees in the tightly organised Communist KPD Party were that they should form an alliance with other left-wing politicians to put together a ruling coalition they could control. That meant unity with the Social Democrats. But the two parties had a long history of bitter rivalry. The SPD Democrat leader, Otto Grotewohl, who had been a Reichstag deputy before the Nazi accession to power and was then imprisoned several times, said he harboured a 'deep distrust' of the KPD. However, he was won round and agreed to a merger after being, as he put it, 'tickled by Russian bayonets' and offered the co-chairmanship of the united movement, the Socialist Unity Party of Germany (SED).

The SED's red flag showed the Communist and Social Democratic movements clasping hands. But Social Democrats in the west opposed the merger, as did 80 per cent of party members in Berlin, setting off a Communist campaign of harassment in the city in which thousands were cajoled, imprisoned or even killed by their would-be allies. The united front attracted a few other adherents, including the venerable Weimar-era interior minister, Wilhelm Külz, chairman of the Liberal Democrats, whose participation in Soviet-backed congresses split his party as colleagues denounced him for accepting 'the Russian conception of German unity'. There was no doubting the SED's orientation: 'To learn from the Soviet Union is to learn how to win,' went one slogan; others exhorted people to 'build Soviet man' on German soil.[15]

Grotewohl's co-chairman was the veteran Communist Wilhelm Pieck, whose political career dated back to the first decade of the century. He had been jailed for opposing the First World War, joined the Communist Party after the defeat of 1918 and played a prominent role in the fight against both the Social Democrats and the Nazis before going into exile after Hitler took power, ending up in Moscow where he worked for the Comintern. Now in his seventies, projecting a plump air of bonhomie, with horn-rimmed glasses perched precariously on his snub nose and his residence in a Palace once occupied by Frederick the Great's queen, he was dismissed by Stalin as 'a senile old man, only up to tapping you on the shoulder'. But his long expertise at bending to the Kremlin's whim had made him a useful puppet.[16]

True power in Berlin lay with the goatee-bearded master bureaucrat Walter Ulbricht, the SED general secretary. Born in the trade union centre of Leipzig, he gravitated through the Social Democrats to Communism after deserting from the army in the First World War. Going into exile in Paris and Prague when the Nazis took power, he helped to supervise German cadres fighting in the civil war in Spain, overseeing the liquidation of comrades whose loyalty to Moscow was in doubt. Like Pieck, he had kept in line with whatever policy Stalin chose to adopt, denouncing critics of the Nazi–Soviet Pact of 1939 for displaying 'primitive anti-Fascism' and running an organisation that sought to convert captured German officers to Communism. Returning with the Red Army in 1945, he criticised the working class for having 'failed before history' in 'having obeyed a band of criminals' during the Nazi era.

He wanted to keep a democratic façade through elections, even though the aim was to monopolise power. The SED, a Berlin city councillor noted, was 'not a one-party system but [left] no room for any other parties'. Grotewohl told a friend Ulbricht was 'dangerous', but, having agreed to work with the Communists, there was nothing he could do to stop the political vice closing.[17]

Twice married, Ulbricht was a far from imposing figure, dumpy in shape with an expressionless face and a thin, rasping voice. But he and his colleagues drew on a desire by many in the east to build a new society to show that Germany could break with its past and become a progressive nation at last. Land reform broke up big Junker estates and redistributed 3 million hectares to 330,000 small farmers and labourers. Ten thousand industrial firms were nationalised along with the banks. For those who resisted or were regarded as unrepentant Nazis and class enemies, the NKVD set up detention camps in which anywhere from 40,000 to 65,000 people died. Some escaped more lightly – Joseph Goebbels's secretary spent five years peeling potatoes and sewing laundry sacks in prison before being released. Others with dubious records made themselves useful to the new authorities and had their pasts swept under the carpet.[18]

The east had suffered most from the later stages of the war and then from Soviet requisitioning. Industrial production was sharply reduced. Steel output was one-eighth of what it had been in 1938. The Soviet forces grabbed assets at will. The Ammendorf railway rolling stock company, with 31,000 workers, sent all its output to the USSR. Mines in Saxony became the largest producer of uranium in Europe, with thousands of people working in often-unsafe conditions. More than 450 plants were removed from Berlin alone. Plant and supplies were taken from the AEF and Siemens electrical and engineering works, the Zeiss optical group in Jena, power stations, railways and breweries. The official figure for the cost of all this was $4.3 billion, but other estimates put it far higher.[19]

An Economic Committee was set up, dominated by Communists who pulled the strings in trade unions, cultural associations and other institutions. The authorities moved into social policy, trying to replace traditional family relationships with a direct, all-embracing link between citizens and the regime. A 'democratic school reform' set out to 'propagate the great world history teachings of Karl Marx and Friedrich Engels'. Four-fifths of the judiciary were replaced by 'people's judges'.[20]

The east sought to build itself up as a haven for progressive culture. Berthold Brecht returned to Europe from America after bamboozling congressional interrogators. Following a stay in Switzerland, he became East Germany's cultural icon, though he held on to his Austrian passport and his foreign bank accounts. The prominent writer Anna Seghers moved from West Berlin to the Soviet zone. The first post-war German film, *The Murderer Among Us*, dealing with war crimes and guilt, was shown in the State Opera in East Berlin.

Wilhelm Pieck assured Stalin that German workers understood that the USSR would ensure their country enjoyed strong growth and so would back parties which stood for friendship with Russia. This would mean certain electoral victory for the SED, he added. But, despite close supervision by the occupation authorities and with dissident members of the independent Social Democrats (SPD) barred from standing, the party could not muster a clear majority in local elections in the east in the autumn of 1946.

Worse, in separate municipal elections in Berlin where they were able to stand, independent Social Democrats obtained a majority in all twenty boroughs, gaining first place even in the Russian sector. Ernst Reuter, the party's leader in the city, was a formidable figure – a one-time Communist who had been held for two years in a Nazi concentration camp before going into exile in Turkey where he worked as a town planner and served on the national language reform committee. The Soviets declined to recognise him as mayor but he enjoyed popular support and cordial relations with the Western powers.

'There are more Communists in the Western part of the country, which has not been in touch with Red Army, than in Berlin,' one Soviet official observed. From the Propaganda Administration of the Soviet Military Administration, General Tulpanov warned of the danger of the SED turning to 'extreme nationalism' and noted that 'deviations from Marxist positions pose a substantial danger to the party'.[21]

While Grotewohl succumbed to pressure and blandishments to take the Social Democrats in the east into the SED, his counterpart in the west was fiercely anti-Communist. Born in the West Prussian territories now under Polish rule, Kurt Schumacher had lost his right arm to machine gun fire in the First World War, when he won an Iron Cross. Becoming a radical Social Democratic activist in the 1920s, he joined street battles against Nazis and Communists. Elected to the Reichstag in 1932, he was arrested after Hitler's accession to power and held in a succession of concentration camps. Within a month of being freed by the Allied advance, he was mobilising the SDP in the British zone, and was elected its 'Western leader'. A party congress in 1947 confirmed him in that post by 340 votes out of 341 – the missing ballot may have been his.

Convinced that the best rampart against Communism lay in democratic socialism, Schumacher was an intractable figure, a cadaverous, chain-smoking bachelor described by Ernst Reuter as 'an anchorite sustained entirely by political passion [who] lacked all contact with real life'. He rejected any attempt to pin collective guilt on the Germans, pointing out that some, like himself, had been fighting the Nazis at the time when Western European powers were signing treaties with Hitler. When he spoke to meetings, he clawed the air with his one hand, his neck muscles quivering and his voice rising to a hoarse shout, his head skull-like. Acheson called him a 'bitter and violent man' and the Soviet newspaper *Pravda* branded him 'an eager warmonger' and 'an unscrupulous demagogue'.[22]

As the Western part of Germany moved towards economic recovery, the Americans preferred that it should be guided politically not by Schumacher but by the avuncular Rhinelander Konrad Adenauer, who topped their 'White List' of acceptable political figures. Born in 1876, the career of 'die Alte' ('the Old Man'), as he would come to be known, dated from before the First World War. From 1917 to 1933, he was mayor of Cologne, turning down the chancellorship of the Weimar Republic in 1926. Dismissed and briefly detained by the Nazis, he spent the Hitler years in seclusion, and was reinstated as mayor of Cologne in 1945. The British military authorities then abruptly sacked him, feeling he was not doing enough to put his city back on its feet. Before long they retreated, but the incident played out to Adenauer's advantage. He appeared as a victim of the Allies and his standing rose further as he pursued his quest to head the nascent Christian Democratic Union (CDU), embracing both Catholics and Protestants, getting himself appointed its 'President by seniority'.[23]

Abandoning his chronically ill wife for long periods, he travelled endlessly in his old chauffeur-driven Horch car to drum up support from party branches and unite regional organisation behind his leadership. The creation by the British of the new state of Nordrhein-Westfalen (North Rhine–Westphalia – NRW) gave him a natural power base, moving the centre of gravity for the west of Germany to his home region and blocking French designs on the Ruhr as the British consolidated their hold on the industrial region. NRW was, he said, 'where Germany's windows are wide open to the west'.[24]

Adenauer was further strengthened by elections held in the spring and autumn of 1946 in the British and American zones, which made the Christian Democrats and their allies the strongest grouping in

Bavaria, Württemberg and North Baden as well as the Rhineland. He burnished his credentials with the Americans by heading off proposals to put industry in the British zone into public ownership and by diluting the party's economic programme, which he regarded as too left wing. Playing the elder statesman role, he sat in the furthest corner of the room at key meetings and sent trusted aides into the firing line.

He sidelined rivals in Western zones, and allowed rumours to spread that the CDU leader in Berlin, Jakob Kaiser, who wanted the party headquarters to be in the former capital, had been talking to Soviet officials and former Wehrmacht generals. The arrest of six hundred CDU members in the Soviet zone further weakened Kaiser's position and, as pressure on him increased, he fled to the West, abandoning what remained of his power base.

By the time of the London conference of foreign ministers, Adenauer had established himself as the only possible leader of the CDU. A leading media figure, Marion von Dönhoff, noted that he was 'totally unpretentious but decidedly authoritarian', a great simplifier, reserved and matter of fact. He had a piercing dry wit but, in comparison to Schumacher's fiery speeches, his were wooden and limited. His opponent quipped that 'Goethe had a vocabulary of 20,000 words; Herr Adenauer has only 200 at his disposal'.

He and Schumacher were as mutually antipathetic, personally and politically, as Nehru and Jinnah or Mao and Chiang. The Social Democrat thought Germany needed a strong central administration and would not give up on the idea of German unity, while his opponent championed a federal state and, though paying lip service to unification, was ready to accept the division of the country as a fact of life. The CDU chief insisted the future must lie with 'Occidental Christianity'; Schumacher was an atheist who decried clerical influence in the CDU.[25]

Adenauer pleaded for Nazi fellow travellers not to be prosecuted. Schumacher was implacable towards anybody who had supped with the devil and blamed the bourgeois parties for having helped Hitler to take power; he depicted the CDU as a haven for anti-democratic reactionaries and remnant Nazis. The Christian Democrat participated in the Zonal Council set up by the British; his opponent boycotted it. Adenauer was the epitome of upper-middle-class *gutbürgerlich* in his comfortable home and well-appointed office; the British commander, Brian Robertson, found him 'eminently reasonable, highly intelligent and flexible in negotiation'. Schumacher worked from a bombed-out building and another German politician recalled that when he grasped your hand, 'One had a sense of a feverish clutch on life itself.'[26]

Believing in confrontation and non-co-operation with opponents, the Social Democrat was obsessive about gaining and retaining power, which enabled him to master his party but limited his appeal outside it. That made it easy for Adenauer to hold him up as the embodiment of the 'old Prussian spirit, that ruthless undemocratic aspiration to exclusive power', as he presented his own more emollient and decentralised vision of Germany. When the British brought the two politicians together on a trip to Berlin, the occasion was not a success; they did not exchange a word during the flight.

The CDU drew on the old Catholic Centre movement, but shifted its centre of gravity westwards as it united regional groupings and absorbed the Social Christian movement. In Bavaria, it forged links with the Christian Social Union led by lawyer Hans Erhard, who was a strong proponent of federalism and European collaboration. A pro-business wing made its influence felt with the economist Ludwig Erhard pushing for the freeing markets in his post at the Bizone Economic Council. In November 1947, he published a trenchant article to point out that the dismantling of factories destroyed capital that was badly needed for reconstruction and to supply the domestic market. He also called for increased output of consumer goods and currency reform to create a stable financial system and spur growth.[27]

Despite its leader's advanced years, Adenauer's party could thus claim to be of its age, while the Social Democrats looked back to the Weimar era, the long years of oppression under the Nazis and a traditional togetherness, with 'comrades' calling one another '*du*'. Apart from the Western sectors of Berlin, they had lost political strength in the east and were suspicious of new economic methods to spur recovery. Hanging over the rivalry between the two main parties was the question of how fast the Western Allies would hand back responsibility to Germans and how this would cement the division between a democratic West and a Communist East. As Clay noted in a telegram to Washington at the end of 1947, 'The resentment of the Germans against colonial administration is increasing daily ... two and a half years without a government is much too long.'[28]

~

## MEANWHILE

- In Kashmir and Jammu, Indian troops lift a 32-day siege of the town of Kotli, but Pakistani forces and tribesmen force them to withdraw. Tribal forces capture another sizeable town, Mirpur, with reports of widespread killings. India's Parliament holds its first meeting as the legislature of an independent nation.
- The Chinese Communists take the city of Shijiazhuang, a key rail junction on the line from Beijing to the Yangtze and establish their capital there. In government-controlled areas, elections are held for the National Assembly; the Kuomintang is assured of overwhelming victory as only small parties are allowed to run against it. In places, police round up people and herd them to polling stations where magistrates tell them how to vote.
- The Viet Minh ambush a French convoy in Tonkin, killing fourteen Europeans.
- Forty-six Indonesian Republican prisoners die in a train under Dutch guard; the authorities blame 'a lack of necessary attention'.
- Thai army officers led by a former collaborator with the Japanese set up a State Supreme Council, which installs on the throne Bhumibol Adulyadej, a prince studying in Switzerland who had become heir after the mysterious death by a gunshot wound of his older brother.
- Hollywood film executives agree not to employ anybody known to be a Communist and to suspend those who decline to answer questioning from the Un-American Activities Committee of House of Representatives. The US Screen Actors Guild implements an anti-Communist loyalty oath and the House Committee finds ten Hollywood figures in contempt after they refuse to say if they are Communists.

- US troops report discovering a mass grave outside Frankfurt estimated to contain 13,000 bodies, most of them Russian prisoners of war.
- Evidence is found in Nebraska of human settlements dating from 20,000 years ago.
- Howard Hughes flies his huge and phenomenally expensive wooden seaplane 'Spruce Goose' for a mile off Long Beach, California – its only flight.
- The art forger Hans van Meegeren is sent to prison for having sold a fake Vermeer; he says he will take the sentence as 'a good sport'.

# PART EIGHT

# DECEMBER 1947

## ACTS

*The conference of foreign ministers grinds to a halt; the French government beats the strikers; Greek Communists stage a Christmas offensive; violence in Palestine rises after UN partition vote; Britain battles with austerity.*

## SCENES

*London, Washington, Moscow; Paris; Konitsa, Athens; Palestine, Aleppo, Aden; the United Kingdom.*

## CAST

*Marshall, Bidault, Molotov, Bevin; Moch, Schuman; Markos, Nikos Zachariadis; Arabs, Jews and British; Attlee, Dalton, Cripps.*

# FINAL MEETING

## I: Obstruction, frustration and carping

The London conference of the four foreign ministers was a much shorter affair than its predecessor in Moscow, its seventeen sessions as compared to forty-three at the previous event reflecting the general acceptance that the process stemming from the wartime alliance had reached its end. George Marshall was on top form as he mingled with high society and was guest of honour at banquets hosted by Churchill and other wartime figures. But Bevin was suffering. 'I can't go on for ever like this,' he told his parliamentary secretary, Christopher Mayhew. 'It's the pain in my chest. It's terrible. I can't sleep at night. You know, it gets you down.' The foreign secretary was baffled as to how to get anywhere with Molotov. 'Ernest keeps saying "Will any one tell me what to do next?"' Mayhew noted in his diary. 'He has no idea of Molotov's mind or intentions. No one in the delegation puts a connected logical case and no one is constructive or sounds confident.'[1]

At a trilateral lunch on 8 December, the three Western ministers agreed they were ready to end the discussions. Bevin reported that members of Parliament had 'indicated their disgust at the spectacle of the futile and somewhat undignified proceedings of the past two weeks'. Marshall's main concern was how to present a breakdown to the public. Bidault, according to the US delegation's report to Washington, 'expressed indifference as how the break occurred'.[2]

That evening, Molotov submitted a paper repeating the demand for $10 billion in reparations from Germany for the USSR and attacking the US–UK Bizone for contravening economic unity. He must have known that discussions were going on about enlarging it into a Trizone to include France. As for the European Recovery Program, he said it was 'fraught with danger for the German people and other nations of Europe'.[3]

'The situation here is exceedingly critical,' Marshall warned in a message to Truman:

> We are involved now in very delicate maneuvers against Molotov's evident purpose to secure agreements of a character which would appear well to the public but would permit most frustration of what must be done in Germany in connection with the ERP. It is plainly evident that Molotov is not only playing for time but is consistently, almost desperately, endeavouring to reach agreements which would really be an embarrassment for us in the next four to six months. We must be exceedingly careful in what we say and what we do and it is going to be exceedingly difficult to have our actions understood by the American public and the British public if Molotov can possibly arrange it so.[4]

As the discussions became, in Clay's words, 'chilly and tense', the next Soviet gambit was to propose putting the Ruhr under four-power control. When the others rejected that, Molotov returned to his call for the Bizone to be dismantled. Marshall said this would be done only when there was a general agreement to Germany. As a final thrust, the Russian charged that the US was seeking to turn Germany into a strategic base from which to attack the 'democratic countries' of Europe. Bevin interjected that 'insults would be resented throughout the British Commonwealth'. Barely glancing at notes from his advisers as to how to respond, Marshall replied with what Clay called 'superb and quiet dignity' that the Russian was evidently aiming at another audience and that his conduct made it difficult to foster respect for the dignity of the Soviet government. At that, Molotov winced perceptibly.[5]

'The present Soviet position obviously renders any possibility of achieving an agreement for the economic unity of Germany impossible,' Marshall reported to the president. 'I have consistently taken the position at the conference that without the necessary fundamental agreement by the occupying powers effectively to remove the barriers that they themselves have created to German economic unity and promptly to put into effect measures essential to attainment of German economic unity, establishment – even discussion of the establishment – of a German Government or other related matters is entirely unreal.'[6]

Molotov's last play was to ask the conference to hear representatives of a German People's Congress which had just met in East Berlin. Most were SED members from Eastern Germany whose meeting had criticised Anglo-American policy and called for an all-German government of 'representatives of all democratic parties'. The US, British and French refused to meet the delegation on the grounds that the Congress was not representative.[7]

They also rejected a fresh Soviet paper on reparations, Marshall continuing to refuse to consider taking them from current production in Germany, which would have harmed economic recovery. The secretary suggested an adjournment, 'since no real progress could be made because of Soviet obstructionism'. Molotov accused him of wanting to suspend the discussions to get a free hand in Germany. 'Any suggestions as to time or place of the next meeting?' Bevin asked. There was dead silence.[8]

'The breakdown of the conference has exposed in all its grimness, the cleavage in Europe,' the London *Times* commented. In Moscow, TASS news agency warned of the 'provocative intention' of the Western powers to saddle the USSR with blame. It attacked Marshall on reparations and said Bidault had displayed duplicity 'characteristic of the conduct of the French delegation throughout the session'. The reality was that Moscow had never been ready to offer concessions; nor was Washington minded to do so in any way that would satisfy Stalin given the binary split between the Marshall Plan countries and those in the Soviet camp. As the ministers left Lancaster House for the last time, the Cold War was a fact of life reversible only by the collapse of one side or the other.[9] It was time for each to make the most of the new reality, each with its own narrative now that the wartime gap in the conflict dating back to 1917 had been relegated to history. Or, as Marshall put it in a message to Washington, events should be 'taken at the flood'.[10]

## II: OUT OF THE ASHES

When the secretary of state called at the Foreign Office later in the week, Bevin was in thoughtful mood. Britain had not cut its bridges with the USSR – a trade agreement just concluded provided for the import of 650,000 tons of Soviet grain and future trade in wool, rubber and aluminium in return for the UK waiving claims for the cost of wartime supplies and services. But the foreign secretary was thinking that what was needed was an association of the US, UK, France, Italy, the Benelux countries and the British Dominions in a 'sort of spiritual federation of the West, backed by power, money and resolute action'. The next day, the two men met with senior aides to discuss German political and currency reform and the situation in Berlin.[11]

The British government created a special unit headed by Mayhew to step up what it called the 'ideological offensive' against the USSR and Stalinism.[12] Bevin told Marshall his government wanted to move ahead rapidly with 'a stable peaceful and democratic Germany'. The secretary replied that Germans should be given 'greater initiative and freedom of action commensurate with the extent of the responsibilities which they are to assume'. Returning from London, Clay ordered a halt to reparations deliveries to the Soviets from the US occupation zone.[13]

The Allied attitude was reinforced by news of fresh repression and political pressure on the other side of the Iron Curtain. The main Romanian opposition, the National Peasants Party, was banned. Four non-Communists resigned from the government, and the hard-line Ana Pauker became foreign minister. In Bulgaria, thirty-nine military officers, including a general known as the Liberator of Sofia, were jailed after being accused of seeking to overthrow the state. The Polish Parliament declared Stanisław Mikołajczyk, who had led the largest party and been the wartime premier-in-exile, a traitor; he had fled the country earlier in the year and was now banished for life.

The Hungarian Communists stepped up the campaign against independent political movements, notably the Smallholders' Party, whose right-wing leaders were accused of subversion. Pressure increased further on Cardinal Mindszenty as a focal point for opposition. The leader of the country's Independence Party fled to Austria. The American correspondent of the Associated Press wire service was expelled and several Hungarian colleagues were held on espionage charges. In Czechoslovakia, thirty-six people were arrested for spying for the West. The Communists put pressure on the Slovaks by resigning en masse from the provincial authority, bringing about its collapse. Members of the Slovak Democratic Party were charged with having worked with pro-Axis agents in 1944, and duly convicted.

Yugoslavia, Bulgaria, Albania, Hungary and Romania signed bilateral treaties of friendship and mutual aid. East and Central European countries were required to join a Council for Economic Mutual Assistance, known as the 'Molotov Plan', in a network of agreements designed to answer the Marshall Plan and adding to the division of the Continent. The trade pacts were skewed in favour of the USSR, and promised deliveries were haphazard – Czechoslovakia waited for months for grain needed after a bad harvest.

In Washington, Truman sent a draft bill for the full ERP to Congress. The first $6.8 billion was set for implementation by 1 April 1948. The programme seemed to involve a huge sum, the president acknowledged, but it amounted to less than 3 per cent of US national income and 5 per cent of the expenditure on the Second World War. Despite the growing gulf with Moscow, he told a press conference, he was not downhearted. 'We should get peace eventually,' he added, remarking that he would be delighted to play host to Stalin.[14]

In a radio broadcast on his return home,[15] Marshall set out to rally public opinion by accusing the USSR of 'obstruction, frustration and carping criticisms'. The London meeting had been 'a dreary repetition of what has been said and re-said at the Moscow conference', he went on. The discussion of Germany had been 'futile'. Still, he assured listeners, 'We are confident in the rehabilitation of Western European civilization with its freedoms.' He then took a two-week break, which included quail shooting at Bernard Baruch's estate in South Carolina, during which *Time* magazine made him Man of the Year.[16]

*

At the start of the London conference, Bidault had remarked to Molotov that the Communists were 'making their great bid for power' in his country. To accompany the strikes hitting public services, coal mines and manufacturing, the party's deputies continued to paralyse the National Assembly with filibusters and volleys of insults at ministers, met with shouts from right-wing deputies for them to 'Go back to Moscow!' and reminders of Thorez's wartime desertion from the army.[17]

With Marshall's approval, John Foster Dulles, the Republican on the US delegation at the London conference, had gone to Paris to assess the situation. He had cold-shouldered Bidault in London and returned with alarming news of conditions across the Channel, hailing de Gaulle as 'the coming man'. He even made an approach to the general to ask him whether, in the event of a Communist coup, he would be ready to mount a counter-action with US help. There is no record of the reply, but it can be imagined.[18]

In this fevered climate, the firmness of Schuman and Moch paid off. Popular discontent with the disruption increased. Dissention grew between the central CGT and its Socialist Force Ouvrière section. Workers demanded that strike ballots be held in secret. Civil servants in Paris reversed a decision to stop work. Postmen resumed deliveries. Police dislodged militants from power stations. Rail links with the capital were opened up. At the massive, tiled Communist headquarters, Thorez grew concerned that violence might spiral out of control, and agreed to open discreet contacts with the government.

Police arrested hundreds of strikers and demonstrators and, in the north, fought off CGT raiding parties trying to stop miners going back to work. Nineteen Russians were expelled for 'unwarranted interference in French affairs'. Communist newspapers were seized. Protestors occupying the Montmartre telephone exchange were driven out. Limoges station was cleared and police used tear gas against mobs attacking food convoys in Marseilles.

In a crucial event, the express train from Paris to Tourcoing in the north crashed in the night of 2/3 December after saboteurs who thought it was carrying troops to battle strikers removed twenty-five metres of track. The Communists accused the government of a put-up job, citing the burning of the Reichstag by the Nazis. But the deaths of sixteen passengers and serious injuries to thirty shocked the public as the news was relayed by bleakly dramatic newsreels as well as the press and radio.[19]

On the day after the crash and following six days of acrimonious debate, the National Assembly voted by more than two to one for a law of 'republican defence' asserting the right to work and extending protection to those wanting to return to their jobs. Ninety deputies who had abstained in the previous month's vote of confidence backed Schuman. On 9 December, the CGT ordered an end to the strike. The following week, a congress of Force Ouvrière decided to split from the CGT. The interior minister warned of more trouble to come in 1948, since economic conditions were not likely to improve before Marshall Plan aid arrived in the summer. But, for the moment, the Schuman–Moch duo had triumphed.

# CHAPTER TWENTY-FOUR

# BLOODY NEW YEAR

Protests spread through the Arab world against the UN vote on Palestine. Demonstrators in Damascus invaded the American Legation, tore down the Stars and Stripes and used it to clean their shoes. Big marches were held in Cairo, Alexandria and Baghdad. In Aleppo, with a Jewish population of some 10,000, mobs burned synagogues, schools, houses and shops; the damage was estimated at $2.5 million. Jews fled the city where their community had lived for 2,000 years. Their property was confiscated.

After Arabs in Aden declared a general strike, a crowd burned and looted more than a hundred shops in the Jewish quarter of the old town. Two Jewish schools were set on fire along with synagogues, houses and cars. The attacks went on for three days before British troops from the Suez Canal Zone restored order. Eighty-two Jews were killed and seventy-six wounded.[1]

In Palestine itself, the strike called by the Arab Higher Committee after the UN decision degenerated into violence when two hundred Arabs, some armed with knives and clubs, looted and burned Jewish stores in a shopping centre in Jerusalem. British police did not stop them and troops held back Haganah forces seeking to intervene. Daily clashes set into a deadly tit-for-tat pattern. Arabs evolved a tactic of throwing grenades over the walls of prisons during exercise time for Jewish prisoners. After a raid on a kibbutz, the Irgun set fire to an Arab cinema. A major battle erupted between Tel Aviv and Jaffa; some reports said seventy Arabs died. The British declared a curfew in Arab areas of Jerusalem. An explosive device thrown beside the city's Damascus Gate killed eleven Arabs and two British constables. An attack on Jews in the Old City led to six hours of fighting with three deaths.

Arab snipers fired at Jewish vehicles and road convoys; fourteen people were killed in one attack and another ambush south of Bethlehem took ten lives. A roadblock stopped a bus carrying thirteen staff of the British BOAC airline from Lydda airport to Jerusalem. Armed Arabs forced the driver to head into a nearby field where the ten Arab and three Jewish passengers were separated. The Arab BOAC manager, who had married a Jew, was ordered to join the three, and all four were shot dead.[2]

A hundred people were reported killed or injured in attacks on Christmas Day, bringing the month's casualties to more than a thousand. The British sent reinforcements to Bethlehem. A bomb planted by Irgun at the Damascus Gate killed fifteen Arabs; in retaliation, gunmen shot dead two Jews and two British policemen. At the end of the month, Irgun members threw grenades at Arab labourers waiting for work outside the refinery in Haifa, where the pipeline from Iraq brought oil to be loaded for transport to Britain. Six people were killed and forty-two wounded; Arabs hit back at Jewish workers with pickaxes, tools and stones slaying forty and injuring fifty. Over the New Year, the Hanagah attacked two Arab villages, with orders to 'kill maximum adult males'; deaths were put at anywhere from twenty-one to seventy.

Ben-Gurion understood that partition had never meant peace. The eventual Zionist goal remained to cover all Palestine. That could mean only a wider conflict as Arabs swore to fight partition to the death. Apart from the competition for land, the Jews could not feel secure in a contested state with 40 per cent of non-Jews who had a higher birth rate than them. 'We danced – but we knew that ahead of us lay the battlefield,' as Moshe Dayan recalled about the celebrations of the UN vote. Or, as Yisrael Galili, head of the Hanagah Command, put it, 'I believe there is a war on.'[3]

Syria began to register volunteers and established a training camp as the Arab League backed a Liberation Army. But, from the start, Arab military moves were bedevilled by long-standing and visceral rivalries. The Grand Mufti, who had his own Holy War Army, was a sworn enemy of both Abdullah and the Liberation Army commander, Fawzi al-Qawuqjie. More of a political and public relations operator than an accomplished military leader, he had also spent the war years in Germany broadcasting propaganda for the Nazis. Egypt favoured its own guerrilla warfare and hoped for an eventual diplomatic outcome after a long war of attrition. Iraq and Syria wanted to send in organised forces. Saudi Arabia reserved its position and Abdullah nurtured his ambitions. Recruitment to the Liberation Army fell well short of expectations.[4]

The Mufti's prime card was his nephew, Abd al-Qadir al-Husseini, a charismatic forty-year-old veteran of the Arab Revolt who had a long-standing rivalry with Fawzi al-Qawuqjie. After his uncle sided with the Nazis, al-Qawuqjie had led an Arab unit against the British in Iraq and then organised a 'Sacred Fighters' force. But the hostility his uncle incurred meant that the Arab League directed its funds and weapons to the rival force, obliging him to depend on a collection of often defective Second World War rifles found in the sands of Libya and sold to him by Bedouins at high prices.[5]

At this stage, the Zionist Haganah had some 35,000 members, though only 7,500 were under arms. A recruitment drive launched in October was steadily increasing numbers. Ben-Gurion, who had immersed himself in military matters, was planning a reorganisation to constitute a true army. An arms drive was in full swing in the United States through front organisations including a group of millionaires who set up dummy companies under such names as the New England Plastic Novelty Company. A plan to buy a decommissioned aircraft carrier fell through and shipments were intercepted after the introduction of an American embargo on weapons shipments to the Middle East. But machine tools to make military equipment were despatched along with communications equipment. A TWA engineer helped to put together a fleet of cargo planes, bombers and a single fighter. Half a million gallons of aviation fuel were amassed. Other agents bought artillery and light tanks in France and reached deals with the Czechoslovaks for guns, ammunition and German planes left over from the war in return for hard cash the government in Prague badly needed.[6]

# CHAPTER TWENTY-FIVE

# CHRISTMAS AT WAR

## I: The Party takes command

On Christmas Eve, the leaders of Greece's KKE Communist Party declared the creation of a government that undertook to mobilise popular forces and institute people's justice, land reform and nationalisation of foreign assets, heavy industry and banks. To go with this, the rebels needed to establish a settled territory of their own with a capital as they sought recognition from states in the Soviet bloc. General Markos, the military chief and former partisan who became prime minister and war minister, argued that it would be safer to set up in Albania or Yugoslavia, but he was overruled.

The choice for a capital fell on the town of Konitsa, in an amphitheatre-shaped strategic mountain location in the far north, looking down on a valley where two rivers met. From there, the insurgents could threaten Joannina, the main town of the Epirus region, and command roads to the south as well as securing supply routes to and from the frontier with Albania only a dozen miles away.

The guerrilla army had steadily built up its operations through the year. Aid from Yugoslavia, Albania and Bulgaria included artillery and anti-aircraft guns, rifles and grenades, and the proceeds of public collections of cash and clothes. Yugoslavia set up training camps and hospitals for the wounded as well as a Radio Free Greece. The aid was not without strings – the three countries helping the KKE decided secretly to form a federation to take over Greek Macedonia while Bulgaria would absorb Greek Thrace, giving it access to the Aegean Sea.

There was also a murky KKE campaign to move children from areas they controlled to friendly countries. Involving some 30,000 infants, this was officially to give them protection but seems to have been designed to produce a corps of indoctrinated young fighters. In reaction, Queen Frederika launched a similar movement from government-held areas; 30,000 were taken to 'children towns' and another 12,000 to island camps.

The political nature of the struggle had changed in the autumn after a crackdown by the government on Communist politicians led them to flee to the northern base area. Among them was Nikos Zachariadis, a former teacher who had been trained in Moscow and installed by the Comintern to lead the Greek Party in 1931. He and his comrades set out to increase the ideological nature of the fight with more political commissars. Markos, who had enjoyed a large measure of independence in the past, was subject to tighter control. As always in the Leninist system, the party had the last word.

Zachariadis had long put his faith in revolution through the urban working class. In the mountains, he decided war was the route to power, favouring conventional tactics over the guerrilla approach of Markos, whose forces had hit eighty-three villages, blown up eleven trains and destroyed tobacco crops worth $9 million during the autumn. A Communist plenum meeting voted 'to transfer the centre of gravity of the party's activities to the military-political sector in order to make the Democratic Army the force which will bring about in the shortest possible time the establishment of a Free Greece in all the areas of Northern Greece'. To achieve this, party forces were to be mobilised 'for the unqualified support, expansion and leadership of the Democratic Army's war effort'. Markos was not present at the meeting; when he later objected to the change, he was overruled. Some reports say he was accused of treason.[1]

It was a highly hazardous course. The strength of the Democratic Army had been boosted to 25,000 members by conscription, including girls, but one eye-witness recounted that they were 'in rags, their beards matted, some barefoot, and others wearing shoes held togther with twine'. The rebels were heavily outnumbered by government forces that were receiving a regular supply of American arms and advisers. This inferiority did not matter so much when the rebels

made hit-and-run raids, but if they sought to take and defend territory, the weight of numbers would tell. Diplomatically, the KKE
remained isolated. None of the three countries giving it help had
extended recognition. Stalin remained hostile, telling a banquet at
his dacha at the end of 1947, 'Greece is on a vital line of communications for the Western powers. The United States is directly involved
there – the strongest country in the world ... No hesitation; the
rebellion in Greece must be laid to rest.'[2]

A new government strategy adopted with American encouragement in the second half of 1947 abandoned static defence and
aimed to sweep up the enemy, using air power. Troop numbers were
increased to 132,000, and were set to reach 200,000. US liaison
officers played a more active role than their British predecessors.
Parallel with the renewed military effort, reconstruction began of
roads, railways, bridges and the Corinth Canal. Plans were drawn up
to boost exports and to cut state spending. Ten thousand prisoners
were released under an amnesty.

After meeting Queen Frederika in London, Marshall decided to
send one of his favourite commanders, James Van Fleet, to Athens
with the title of Senior American Official at the head of 250 US
advisers. Government forces were reorganised and expanded under
a new chief of the general staff. Underground Communist cells were
broken up and their members arrested.[3]

The politics in Athens remained as unsatisfactorily small-circle
as ever, however. The US pressed for a more broadly based and
rejuvenated government after the fall of the ministry of the aged
banker Dimitrios Maximos in the summer, but this led only to a new
coalition of familiar faces under 87-year-old Themistoklis Sofoulis,
whose career dated back to leading the unification of his native
island of Samos with Greece in 1912.

## II: BATTLE FOR THE HEIGHTS

The attack on Konitsa began in driving rain on Christmas Day
morning. As a diversionary measure, Salonika was shelled. The
defenders were taken completely by surprise. Thinking the snow
would impede rebel activities, government commanders had allowed

soldiers to go home for the holiday, leaving only four hundred in the town and another 1,300 scattered through nearby posts.

The rebels quickly took the bridge on the main route to the town, meaning that the only access for government reinforcements was by roundabout mountain roads barely usable by motor vehicles and covered by snow. The attackers captured one of four heights overlooking Konitsa and moved in around two others. They laid down an intensive barrage of shells and mortar bombs. Government Spitfire fighters strafed the insurgents, but were hampered by rain and cloud.

Though his troops had the upper hand, Markos was cautious. Anticipating a counter-attack, he kept some of his forces back from the battle, and withdrew from the two peaks that had been surrounded. A break in the weather enabled Dakota transport planes to fly in supplies, while reinforcements cleared the snow on the roads to break through, urged on by the national chief of staff, who flew to a neighbouring town. On New Year's Eve, the rebels attacked the fourth peak, but retreated as government soldiers occupied hills overlooking the bridge to the town.

King Paul, who was ill with typhoid fever, sent a message to tell the soldiers, 'On your strong shoulders rests not only the future of Greece but also the future of humanity.' Queen Frederika drove into the town in a jeep to meet the inhabitants and defenders, wrapped in a sheepskin coat and wearing boots, her eyes bloodshot from tiredness, her face covered with mud, and her shoes and stockings caked with earth.[4]

The battle ended on 4 January when Markos ordered a retreat and his troops fell back to the Albanian border, burying their dead as they went. The National Army suffered 104 dead and 356 wounded. More than 250 Democratic Army soldiers died with hundreds of wounded. Though small-scale compared with the battles in China or the deaths in India and Pakistan, it was the largest engagement of the Greek civil war to date.

Government morale shot up. Conscription was enforced more effectively. The Communist Party was outlawed. Left-wingers in the civil service were purged. Four hundred people were shipped to detention on the island of Ikaria. Washington authorised the diversion of civilian aid to military purposes, and sent a thousand Marines to the Mediterranean with tanks, field guns and flamethrowers.

At a subsequent meeting of the rebel leadership, Markos urged a return to guerrilla warfare but Zachariadis insisted that victory was possible through conventional means. The Yugoslavs did not abandon hope for the time being and maintained their assistance, but knew success depended on improved military performance and a capping of American support for the government – neither of which were in evidence.[5]

# A HIGHER VIRTUE

## I: WORSE THAN THE WAR

As the foreign ministers met in Lancaster House, the national mood in Britain was as sombre as the proceedings in the conference chamber. Twelve days earlier, Hugh Dalton, the chancellor of the Exchequer, had presented a budget that ratcheted up the austerity gripping the nation. The next day he resigned – not over the state of the economy, but because of his leak of information to a journalist on his way through the Palace of Westminster unveiling proposals in his speech.

Britain had emerged from the world war with a justifiable sense of national pride as the only country that had successfully resisted Hitler in the early years of the conflict, had withstood the battering of the Blitz and emerged eventually among the victors, fighting from East Asia through North Africa to the advance into Germany. Reaching further back through the twentieth century, it was the sole major European nation that had not suffered from defeat, occupation or the collapse of the political system.

But the cost of the war drained the nation. A quarter of its wealth was gone on fighting Germany, Italy and Japan. Foreign obligations weighed heavily on national finances. As well as loans from the US, Britain owed money to an array of nations including Argentina, Brazil, Portugal, Egypt and India. 'This great load of debt is a strange and ironical reward for all we suffered for the common cause,' Dalton reflected, calling it 'an unreal, unjust and unsupportable burden, a fantastic commitment beyond [Britain's] strength and all limits of good sense and fair play'.[1]

Real British per capita GDP was only slightly above the 1938 level (whereas the increase was 56 per cent for the US, 60 per cent for Canada and 26 per cent for Australia). Nearly half the export markets had been lost, mainly to the US. For John Maynard Keynes, the Americans used the war to 'pick out the eyes of the British Empire'. Mining and manufacturing output had risen slowly since the end of the fighting but was still below 1937 levels. Government propaganda, delivered through films, articles, advertisements and street posters, hammered home the need for higher production.

Dollars were in short supply and the UK had gone through a currency crisis when it temporarily lifted the controls on sterling in the summer of 1947. The Attlee government introduced restriction after restriction to try to raise revenue, limit consumption and preserve reserves.[2]

Despite the crushing austerity, there was still a belief among many people that the policies of the Labour government marked the path to a New Jerusalem for the good of the country as a whole. After the wartime suffering, it seemed a time to build a new and more just society. Putting into practice the welfare state proposed in the seminal report of 1942 of civil servant William Beveridge was well received by the public at large. Herbert Morrison, Labour's deputy leader, detected a 'genuine social idealism', reflecting an 'altered moral sense of the community ... moving into an altogether different form of society, working in an altogether different atmosphere of ideas'. Socialism was a way of life, not just an economic theory, demanding 'a higher standard of civic virtue than capitalism', Attlee said.[3]

Following an inter-war period dominated politically by the Conservatives and marked by the Great Depression and high unemployment, the 1945 election saw the arrival of true two-party politics. 'LABOUR COMES OF AGE', ran the headline in the left-wing weekly, the *New Statesman*. Labour had formed two brief governments in the 1920s, but the election of 1931 saw it dropping to fewer than fifty seats in the House of Commons as its leader, Ramsay MacDonald, went into a National Government with the Tories. It regained some ground at the next election in 1935, but was geographically concentrated on industrial areas.

Despite Churchill's aura, Labour's campaign in 1945 was far more in tune with the public mood than that of the Conservatives, who carried with them the baggage of the 1930s and did not help themselves by smearing their opponents as threatening to install rule by a Gestapo of the left. Many middle-class voters felt a sense of community, which led them to vote for Attlee's party and add to its solid base among the working class, where trade union membership was doubling. The sense of it being a time for change was seen in the 12 per cent swing to Labour to give it a 146-seat House of Commons majority.[4]

Building on a tradition of social welfare developed since the start of the century, Attlee's government set out to vanquish what Beveridge had termed 'the five giant evils' of Want, Disease, Ignorance, Squalor and Idleness. The 1946 National Insurance Act, based on his report, promised a comprehensive safety net against sickness, unemployment and old age. Fighting against entrenched opposition from the medical profession to launch the National Health Service, the charismatic left-wing health and housing minister Aneurin Bevan declared that 'no society can legitimately call itself civilized if a sick person is denied medical aid because of lack of means'. Realistically, he reasoned that getting doctors to join the new system would mean 'stuffing their faces with gold'.[5]

The government's activism led to more than two hundred acts of Parliament being passed between 1945 and 1948. These included major pieces of legislation affecting industry, welfare, housing, the family, workers' rights, planning and agriculture. Coal, steel, the railways and other industries, together with the Bank of England, were nationalised in the hope of making the 'commanding heights' of the economy serve the nation better and achieving a coordinated approach to help post-war reconstruction. A Town and Country Planning Act sought to introduce order into the expansion of cities, including the creation of green belts, while a New Towns Act aimed to move people from urban centres in the south-east to other parts of the country. The provisions of an Education Act passed in 1944 were implemented to provide free secondary schooling as a right with the leaving age raised to fifteen. Free milk was made available to all schoolchildren. University state scholarships were provided. Teacher numbers were expanded. A Ministry of Education was established.

These reforms further strained resources. Annual spending on education alone increased by half in the five years after 1945, and the 'gold' Bevan offered the doctors to join the NHS came at a high price, while the huge demand for care, false teeth and spectacles sent costs soaring after the system came into existence in the summer of 1948. Before his forced resignation, Dalton announced tax increases while stressing the need to restrain inflation, increase exports and reduce imports. For the Conservatives, Anthony Eden described the chancellor's medicine as 'a dirge in his diaphragm' and Churchill depicted a government set on imposing misery on the nation.

The overwhelming colour of the time was grey, reflected in the prime minister's cautious manner and pinched speaking style when he warned repeatedly of the hard road ahead. As demand outran supply, consumption was held back in favour of investment and exports. The prevailing mood of 'grin and bear it' was tinged with melancholy that victory should have been followed by continuing material hardship. Restrictions and rationing seemed unending. The pressures of austerity could test the façade of family life. A survey of a thousand women in 1948 reported that most felt their marriages were not successful. The divorce rate spiked. Food was in short supply and diets were monotonous. A cartoon in *Punch* magazine showed a woman telling her husband as he left the house to go shopping, 'If you see anything that looks edible, get it.' Cinema attendances hit a record high as films offered a rare avenue of escapism along with music halls and greyhound racing.[6]

The Mass Observation organisation, which tracked public sentiment, recorded a conversation between two middle-aged men on a London bus about the government.

'Gor Blimey Charlie – wot a bloody outlook,' said the first. 'When are they going to stop cutting things I'd like to know. Still the people wanted 'em in, didn't they? Now they've got 'em they've found out a thing or two.'

'Worse than the war mate, ain't it?' the other replied. 'At least you knew wot was 'appening then but yer don't know wot to expect now, do yer.'[7]

The severe winter of early 1947 made things even worse. Industry was hard hit by power shortages. Offices were lit by candles or hurricane lamps. The state of the roads forced the king and queen to use a limousine rather than the state coach when they went to Waterloo on their way to start a state visit to South Africa. The 1948 Olympic Games in London symbolised the nation's plight; no new venues were built and athletes were subject to food rationing. Attlee's approval rating fell from 66 per cent in 1945 to 51 per cent a year later and 44 per cent at the start of 1948.[8]

The historian Correlli Barnett has made a forceful case that it was folly to give priority to social reform over economic regeneration and that the cost of the welfare state, which rose from 10 per cent GDP in 1945/6 to 14 per cent at the end of the decade, was unsustainable while the country was held back by the amateurism of business and economic policy. But the national mood backed the policies of the Attlee government, for the time being. Short-term survival and the realisation of long-cherished dreams took priority over the future.[9]

The royal wedding on 20 November of Princess Elizabeth and Philip Mountbatten, who took the title of Duke of Edinburgh, provided some reason for public cheer, though a poll showed that 40 per cent of people opposed the heir to the throne marrying a foreigner and many thought she should fit in with the ethos of the time and wed a commoner. Big crowds lined the streets to Westminster Abbey and the proceedings were broadcast to the world. The royal family appeared on the balcony at Buckingham Palace to wave to those below until 11 p.m.[10]

'TUMULTUOUS WELCOME FOR BRIDE AND BRIDEGROOM', read the main headline in *The Times*. The groom's uncle, Mountbatten, flew back from India to attend the wedding he had helped to promote – his daughter recalled that he had hesitated to leave India amid the troubles there but Nehru argued that, if he and his wife did not go, people would think things were even worse than they actually were. Seven thousand congratulatory telegrams flooded in and London was thronged with visitors. Among the wedding gifts was a piece of cloth spun by Gandhi – the Queen Mother called it 'a ghastly piece of fabric' and thought it had come from the mahatma's loin cloth.[11]

The groom was 'devastatingly handsome', Mountbatten's daughter, who acted as a bridesmaid, remembered. 'What a pleasant, innocent event that was!' wrote the *Manchester Guardian*. 'It is many a year since we saw Londoners so simply happy [at] the beginning of a new age of hope in their country.' George Marshall thought Britain might draw 'rejuvenation from the wonderful demonstration of loyalty, respect and devotion'. The couple went to the Mountabattens' home in Hampshire for the honeymoon, the future queen's favourite corgi hidden under a rug in their car. Ten thousand people flocked to the country church where they went to worship the following Sunday, earning a reproof from *The Times* for invading their privacy.[12]

## II: PINK JERUSALEM

The Labour government based itself on moderate Fabian Socialism, Keynes and Beveridge, not Marx. Its leaders were pragmatists rather than ideologues. The Leninist path held no appeal for Attlee, while Bevin had been turned against Communism during his time as a trade union leader in the 1920s. Fair shares was the watchword, not revolution, as the prime minister reflected that 'everything will depend upon the willing co-operation and determined effort of all sections of the population'.[13]

Attlee was a highly practical operator who had been deeply moved by the poverty he saw as a pre-war MP for the East End of London. In a book he wrote in the 1930s, he condemned the 'revolutionary idealist' who would 'criticize and condemn all methods of social advance that do not directly square with his formulae and will repeat his shibboleths without any attempt to work out their practical application. The dreamer must keep his feet on the earth and the thinker must come out of his study.' In one of the rhymes he was fond of composing, he noted that, in Britain, the people's flag for the new Jerusalem would be 'palest pink. It's not blood red, but only ink.' While striking in its breadth, the legislation of his government built on provisions and thinking dating back to the introduction of old-age pensions in 1908. Beveridge belonged to the Liberal Party, not Labour.[14]

Attlee's undemonstrative manner was made for the times. He was driven to Buckingham Palace for his investiture after the 1945 election by his wife in the Standard 10 family car.[15] Churchill had swiped at him as a modest man who had much to be modest about, and others underestimated him, too. Stalin remarked after they met at the Potsdam summit that 'Mr Attlee does not look to me like a man who is hungry for power'. Within the Cabinet, Dalton called him 'a little mouse' and Morrison said he sometimes 'doodled when he ought to have led'. But he saw off recurrent plots by colleagues to replace him with Bevin while remaining on working terms with them, an efficient and resolute manager who knew how to make tough decisions, and had what one contemporary commentator called a 'deceptive capacity for not being noticed'.[16]

Attlee got on well with the most powerful figure in the Cabinet, Bevin, who was key in maintaining support especially among the trade unions. The prime minister maintained a working relationship with the quiff-haired Morrison, despite the deputy's unconcealed belief that he should lead the Labour Party.[17] He also dealt well with the redoubtable Stafford Cripps, who succeeded Dalton as chancellor and was the icon of austerity in both his economic policies and his personal life – a teetotal vegetarian and devoted Christian, he rose at 4 a.m., took a cold bath, worked for three hours before breakfast and followed a raw diet that provided no relief from his chronic bowel inflammation. Relations with Bevan were more turbulent, but the Welsh tribune delighted grassroots Labour supporters as he thundered against the Tories as 'lower than vermin' and stood out from what he called the suburban, middle-class values of his leader.[18]

The importance of the foreign secretary as a political rallying point may have made the prime minister more amenable than he otherwise would have been to high defence and global spending which the country could not afford. Though financial pressure fuelled imperial retreat from India, Palestine and the Eastern Mediterranean, Britain held on to African and Asian colonies and maintained a big navy, as well as military bases and 1.5 million service personnel. As Attlee would reflect, 'We were holding the line in far too many places and the Americans in far too few.' Defence spending took nearly a quarter of every pound raised by taxation (another 15 per cent went on interest on loans). Legislation passed in 1947 provided for eighteen months of military conscription for men aged between seventeen and twenty-one, increasing the burden of defence spending.[19]

This continuing commitment to global presence gave Labour the aura of 'social patriots' who defended national interests abroad while pressing reforms at home and seeking a more progressive form of empire in the Commonwealth. Bevin's world view was founded on a combination of the 'Anglosphere' stretching across the Atlantic, and the belief that the UK could sit at the centre of a web encompassing Western Europe, the Mediterranean, the Middle East and the Commonwealth in association with France's far-flung colonies. He dreamed of a Middle Eastern army under British command, and thought the UK could leverage its international position to make the US 'dependent on us and eating out of our hands in four or five years'.[20]

But, for all the Union Jack flags flying from bases around the world the reality was that his country had been relegated to the second league by the exhaustion of war compounded by the strain of implementing Labour's domestic policies. The nature of what had been the empire was changing as well. Acceptance of European rule was fraying and the Dominions were morphing into different societies. The Second World War had shown how little Britain could, or would, do to defend Australia (and New Zealand) and led governments in Canberra to look to the United States, while immigration of 180,000 displaced people from Europe started a shift in the make-up of its population.[21] Canadian foreign policy was increasingly focused on the United States. The National Party challenging for power in South Africa had opposed backing the Allies in the war and campaigned for Afrikaner culture and values against those of the UK-orientated establishment. The loss of the Raj greatly reduced the red splashes in the atlas. Defeat by Japan in 1941/2 had lowered British prestige in East Asia.

Washington certainly valued British support in the Cold War but, as negotiations over the Marshall Plan were demonstrating, it was not going to let UK interests get in the way of its plans. 'The British have turned out to be our problem children now,' Truman reflected in a letter to his daughter. 'They've decided to go bankrupt and, if they do that, they will end our prosperity and probably all the world's too.'[22]

~

## MEANWHILE

- Communist columns advance in Manchuria, and in Central China, Mao declares that the war has reached a turning point and the PLA has 'turned back the wheel of counter-revolution – of US imperialism and its lackey, Chiang Kai-shek's bandit gang – and sent it down the road to destruction and has pushed the wheel of revolution forward along the road to victory'.

- Dutch soldiers attack the village of Rawagede in West Java, seeking information on the whereabouts of an independence fighter. When the inhabitants insist that they do not know about him, the soldiers kill more than four hundred men. A UN report calls the action 'deliberate and merciless'. No prosecution ensues. After protracted legal proceedings, nine widows and descendants of the dead are awarded (20,000) each in compensation in 2011 and the Dutch state tenders a formal apology.

- Bo Dai meets French High Commissioner Bollaert in Ha Long Bay and signs an agreement and a secret protocol committing him to join a 'solution'. While France would recognise independence and unification, Vietnam would remain in the French Union with the government in Paris retaining control of foreign and military affairs. Most non-Communist Nationalists reject these conditions.

- The Soviet Union announces monetary and price reform.

- King Michael of Romania abdicates after the Communist leader points a revolver at him and threatens to execute students if he does not step down. He goes into exile in Switzerland. The country is declared a republic.

- Scientists at the Bell Laboratories demonstrate the first solid-state electronic transistor.

- Venezuela's Acción Democrática government is re-elected with 70 per cent of the vote.

- Women are admitted to full membership of Cambridge University.

- Joe Louis retains his world heavyweight title against Jersey Joe Walcott, though he is knocked down twice; the split decision is met with booing.

- Marlon Brando has his first starring role on Broadway in *A Streetcar Named Desire* opposite Jessica Tandy.

# PART NINE

# JANUARY 1948

## ACTS

*Truman pursues re-election; Marshall presses his plan;
Britain launches the idea of Western Union against
USSR; Chinese Communists advance in the north-east;
War rages in the Himalayas; India goes to the UN; the
mahatma is assassinated; the Dutch reach an agreement
with Indonesian Republicans while the French seek an
initiative in Vietnam.*

## SCENES

*Washington; London; Manchuria; New Delhi,
Kashmir, the UN; Indonesia; Vietnam.*

## CAST

*Truman, Marshall, Republican presidential hopefuls;
Bevin; Chiang Kai-shek, Mao Zedong, Lin Biao;
Nehru, Patel, Gandhi.*

# HARRY AND ERNIE SET OUT THEIR STALLS

## I: State of the Union

Truman's State of the Union address on 7 January marked the start of his re-election campaign. In private, the president maintained his stream of derogatory comments to his family about 'the impossible administrative burden' on him as well as the 'abuse and lies from liars and demagogues'. From what he called the Great White Jail on Pennsylvania Avenue, he wrote to his sister to say that a president was no more than 'a glorified public relations man who spends his time flattering, kissing and kicking people to get them to do what they are supposed to do anyway'.[1]

However, as he geared up to run for re-election in November, he had positive results to show. The administration won a court battle against the formidable union leader John Lewis, with whom Roosevelt had been careful not to tangle. Fears that the end of the wartime economic stimulus and the return of troops to join the labour force would bring a recession and raise unemployment proved unfounded. Manufacturing and mining output had ended the previous year at double the pre-war level and was still rising. Interest rates were low. Fourteen million more people had jobs than ten years earlier and average earnings were up by 50 per cent. A federal government budget surplus of $7.5 billion was forecast for the year.[2]

There were setbacks. Wholesale prices were 40 per cent above the mid-1946 level and retail prices were up by 23 per cent as consumer demand pent up by wartime restrictions blossomed amid supply bottlenecks. Real purchasing power had fallen by 8 per cent since the beginning of 1946. Savings were down. Congress overrode a presidential veto of the Taft–Hartley Bill placing restrictions on organised labour. Well-financed and well-organised conservative groups financed by business elided their anti-Communist crusade with attacks on the administration. To protect himself from charges of disregarding national security, the president bowed to pressure from Republicans and FBI director J. Edgar Hoover to establish a loyalty programme for federal employees. Over the following four years, 3 million people would be investigated. Only 212 were dismissed and none were charged.

Still, Truman clearly felt he had grown into the job. 'The feelings of inadequacy that had so troubled him after Roosevelt's death were by now past,' as his biographer David McCullough put it. 'He liked being in charge. It showed in his face and the way he carried himself.' More thoughtful than his public persona suggested, he enjoyed taking big decisions and was not intimidated by the exercise of power. His self-confidence had expanded and he was keen to be elected in his own right in a political battle in which he could prove his detractors wrong, once and for all. To do so, he would run a high personal, populist campaign on the key issue of whether to continue the path of the New Deal or to switch to a conservative, fiscally tight course as proposed by the Republicans under the unbending Senator Robert Taft.[3]

A Gallup survey for December/January gave Truman a 46–41 per cent margin of popularity over the most likely Republican candidate, Thomas Dewey, who had lost by 53–46 to FDR in 1944. On the left, Henry Wallace polled 7 per cent after announcing his third-party run. Despite such ratings, few believed Truman would be re-elected in November and other polls showed him losing to Dewey, though beating other potential opponents. People might quite like the president and his ways, but the conventional wisdom was still to see him as a Midwestern bumpkin not cut out for national leadership. There was also a wide assumption that the electoral cycle would put a Republican in the White House after fifteen years of Democratic presidents. Only 'stubborn pride' would make Truman run for a new term, Walter Lippmann wrote.[4]

Taft, the patrician son of a president and his party's leading figure in the Senate, had been a staunch opponent of the New Deal and supported a non-interventionist foreign policy. 'Mr Republican' was a poor public speaker who lacked popular appeal and whose opposition to government spending and pro-business agenda linked him to the Great Depression. There was some support among Republicans for Arthur Vandenberg, a large, somewhat old-fashioned figure given to rhetorical flourishes; but, though he would let his name go forward for nomination, he preferred to keep to the international arena, exercising authority through the bipartisan foreign policy crafted with the administration. The House speaker, Joe Martin, was another marginal runner but he was a short, square, uncharismatic politician whose speciality was back-room management, not winning a presidential election. If there was a surprise, it was more likely to be in the shape of the progressive Harold Stassen, who had become governor of Minnesota in 1939 at the age of thirty-one, served in the forces in the war and was now poised to score upsets in the party primaries.

The joker in the election pack was Dwight Eisenhower. The former Allied supreme commander in Europe was reckoned to be the most popular person in America and was credited with 48 per cent support against Truman's 34 per cent if they faced one another. When the possibility of him running for the White House had come up during the war, the ultimate bureaucrat-at-arms had replied that he could not imagine wanting to be considered for any political job, 'from dogcatcher to Grand High Supreme King of the Universe'. Disregarding this, enthusiasts entered his name for all the Republican state primaries. According to the secretary of the army, Kenneth Royall, Truman even offered to run for the vice-presidency if Ike decided to go for the top job.[5]

With grassroots support swelling ahead of the New Hampshire primary in March, the five-star general issued a statement at the end of January that he was 'not available for and could not accept nomination to high political office'. 'Life-long professional soldiers, in the absence of some obvious and overriding reason, [should] abstain from seeking high political office,' he added. Another war hero, Douglas MacArthur, had no such inhibitions and let it be known that he would not decline the Republican nomination if it was offered to him, but he was far away in Japan and, though popular with the right of the party, lacked a wide following.[6]

That left Dewey, the governor of New York State who had made his name prosecuting the Mafia in the 1930s and headed the moderate, internationalist wing of the Republicans. In his 1944 defeat by Roosevelt, he carried only twelve states. But a report to Truman by aides described him as a 'resourceful . . . highly dangerous' challenger who had a better chance second time around. Dewey controlled the party machine with a staff of highly skilled operatives who steadily built up support among delegates to the party convention in June.[7]

The 32-page report sent to the President by Clifford but largely written by a young attorney, James Rowe, said the key to victory lay in mobilising support in western states and among farmers, industrial workers and black voters. The crucial Jewish electorate in New York was at risk unless the Palestine issue was 'boldly and favourably handled'. As for foreign policy, the report saw the Cold War as a positive for the president. It warned, however, that the Democratic apparatchiks were 'fat, tired and even a bit senile'. This was a campaign Truman would have to wage on his own to appeal to the grassroots and build on what he had done since Roosevelt's death. There was nothing he could have relished more.[8]

The president started the State of the Union by striking a lofty moral tone, saying the basic source of America's strength was spiritual, 'for we are a people with a faith. We believe in the dignity of man. We believe that he was created in the image of the Father of us all.' Then he got down to brass tacks, proposing to raise the minimum wage from 40 to 75 cents an hour and grant every income taxpayer a $40 cost-of-living credit with as much for each dependant, create a national health insurance scheme and increase support for farmers, education, housing and conservation of natural resources. Inflation, he said, was 'the one major problem which affects all our goals' and held 'the threat of another depression'. The way to fund additional spending was to raise taxation of corporate profits, which reached a record post-tax level of $17 billion in 1947. Hitting them would make it possible to 'give relief to those who need it most' without cutting total tax revenue and increasing the federal deficit.[9]

The speech was also notable for its commitment to civil rights, which, as so often with Truman, stemmed from genuine feeling but was also likely to bring electoral benefit. The president had been shocked by lynchings in the South, the shooting of four black people – including a war veteran – in Georgia and extreme violence against other Afro-American war veterans like a young sergeant pulled by police from a bus in South Carolina, beaten and blinded. He now pledged in his address that 'our first goal is to secure fully the essential human rights of our citizens'.

Truman was listened to in grim silence. Republicans were dismissive, calling the speech a blatant attempt to buy votes, which moved him to the left of Wallace. There was little applause from Democrats. While the civil rights passage hit the electoral buttons in the Rowe-Clifford report, it inevitably alienated Southern congressmen, especially when it was followed by a message from the president to the legislature calling for protection of voting rights, outlawing of discrimination in the workplace, transport and the armed forces and a federal law against lynching.

In a letter to a friend who advised him to go easy on the issue, Truman said the South was eighty years behind the times, law enforcement was 'in a pretty bad fix' and 'something is wrong with the system'. Citing violence and discrimination, he added that 'I can't approve of such goings-on and I shall never approve of it, as long as I am here ... I am going to try to remedy it and if that ends up in my failure to be reelected that failure will be in a good cause.' At the end of the month, he signed an Executive Order to end segregation in the armed forces.

Fifty-two Southern Democrat congressmen pledged to fight civil rights legislation. Missouri Democrats said they would withdraw from the party's convention unless 'anti-Southern laws' were abandoned. Governor Strom Thurmond of South Carolina promised to defend white supremacy and warned that the South's vote was no longer in the bag; a senator from his state boycotted a dinner addressed by the president because he and his wife might find themselves sitting 'next to a Nigra'.[10]

## II: A VITAL MEASURE

In his State of the Union speech, the president told Congress that swift action was needed on the European Recovery Program, which he termed 'the vital measure of our foreign policy'. The $540 million interim allocation would run out in April. George Marshall warned the Senate Foreign Relations Committee that the $6.8 billion to follow was the 'absolute minimum' needed to prevent Western Europe collapsing into a 'dictatorship of police states' which would threaten US security.

Republicans questioned the administration of the plan and expressed concern that the recipient countries were not doing enough to bolster their economic co-operation. Though still true to the bipartisan approach, Vandenberg asked for assurances that the aid would be effective in spreading the American Way across the Atlantic. Reflecting US support for West European collaboration, some of his colleagues began referring to a 'united states of Europe', with Dulles suggesting that the best way of speeding things up would be to link assistance to the pace at which recipients met targets of economic progress and co-operation. Summing up the support for the ERP as an arm of wider foreign policy, Republican Senator Henry Cabot Lodge wrote to Vandenberg that 'the aid which we extend now and in the next three or four years will in the long future result in our having strong friends abroad'.[11]

As they waited for the promised assistance, West European countries struggled through the winter with continuing food shortages and high inflation. Floods and snow caused havoc in east France. Official data showed that French prices rose by 59 per cent in 1947. The franc was devalued by 44 per cent. Communist and right-wing deputies again came to blows in the National Assembly, where the lights had to be turned out to get deputies to leave. But the Schuman government survived five confidence votes while three independent trade unions joined the new non-Communist Force Ouvrière grouping.

Protests against food shortages were staged in the Ruhr. Grain and fat levels fell dangerously in Hamburg. As well as the civil war, Greece was in the grip of runaway inflation accompanied by severe lack of food. The number of refugees from the fighting was estimated at half a million. The currency plunged and hoarding of gold increased. Correspondents noted that the number of beggars in the street multiplied.[12]

As the Marshall Plan debate dragged on in Washington, the US and UK military governors plunged ahead with schemes designed to speed up the revival of their occupation zones, including monetary reform to introduce a solid currency. General Clay noted that, after the breakdown of the London conference, 'the wraps were off' and 'heavy going' lay ahead. Fears that the Western Allies might pull out rose in Berlin.

When Clay pressed for strengthening the bi-zonal organisation the French were dismayed. Bidault hurried back from a winter break on the Riviera and implored the American ambassador to 'persuade your people to make it a little easier for us'. The Communists and Gaullists warned of the dangers of a revival of the hereditary foe, and the foreign minister said the Anglo-American moves made his position 'well-nigh impossible'.[13]

Marshall tried to assuage the concerns in Paris but told the ambassadors in Paris and London that 'French preoccupation with Germany as a major threat at this time seems to us both outmoded and unrealistic'. The priority, he went on, was '(a) economic and political reorientation of Germans, fostered by common policies of Western occupation powers; and (b) integration of Western Germany into Western European community'. The government in Paris reacted with a decree extending French economic and financial legislation to the Saarland as a reminder of its claims and got the UK and US to agree to an increase in coal shipments from the territory.[14]

On the other side of the Cold War, the Communist grip continued to tighten with increased pressure on opponents and a web of mutual assistance and trade treaties. Meeting in Italy at the beginning of January, the Cominform concluded that action was needed in Czechoslovakia before the election there in May; the Communists there knew that support was shrinking. Gottwald left Prague for a mountain resort near the border with Poland to plot the next move.

His villa was surrounded by police and visitors arrived secretly. In his absence, Communist ministers sought to boost their popularity with initiatives for land reform and the nationalisation of the textile industry, followed by a proposal from their trade union branches to take all firms with more than fifty employees into public ownership and to establish a state monopoly of foreign trade.[15]

The prime minister's confidence that the Communists could win power by electoral means was being undermined by popular disapproval of its methods, particularly by the heavy-handed, opaque Interior Ministry, which dismissed eight police commanders and replaced them with Communists; their posts gave them power to distribute arms and ammunition. When the justice minister, Prokop Drtina, objected and pointed to Communist dirty tricks in a series of murky events, Gottwald warned him, 'You will meet a bad end. Remember my words.' 'Your Drtina is rushing straight to his doom,' a Communist member of Parliament remarked to one of the justice minister's party.[16]

## III: TIME FOR CONSOLIDATION

Against this background, Bevin addressed Parliament on 22 January to lay the ground for what would become an enlarged treaty structure in Western Europe leading to the NATO Alliance. After the breakdown of the London conference, he had spoken to Marshall about an association of the US, UK, France, Italy, the Benelux countries and the British Dominions in a 'sort of spiritual federation of the West, backed by power, money and resolute action'. Now he fleshed out the idea in a lengthy speech on international affairs delivered at a time when the US embassy in London reported back to Washington that 'virtually the whole British Labour movement has, step by step, abandoned its sentimental attitude towards the Soviet Union and ranged itself behind Bevin'.[17]

It had never been so difficult to make peace, the foreign secretary told the Commons, because 'it is not a question of sitting down together, as it was at Versailles and at the end signing a treaty. This time it is systems, conceptions and ideologies which are in conflict.' The Communist consolidation of power in the east increased the

importance of 'the conception of the unity of Europe and the pres-
ervation of Europe as the heart of Western civilisation,' he added.
'No one disputes the idea of European unity. That is not the issue.
The issue is whether European unity cannot be achieved without
the domination and control of one great Power. That is the issue
which has to be solved. The European Recovery Program brought all
this to a head, and made us all face up to the problem of the future
organisation.'[18]

The collapse of the four-power talks and Communist behaviour
in Central and Eastern Europe, he went on, 'point to the conclusion
that the free nations of Western Europe must now draw closely
together. I believe the time is ripe for a consolidation of Western
Europe.' This should involve 'the closest possible collaboration
with the Commonwealth and with overseas territories, not only
British but French, Dutch, Belgian and Portuguese'. The power and
resources of the US, 'clearly part of our common Western civilisation', would be needed to create a solid, stable and healthy world.

CHAPTER TWENTY-EIGHT

# A SNOWSTORM OF DEFEATS

## I: The more battles the better

On 1 January, Chiang Kai-shek flew to Mukden to inspect the troops and declared that the Communist threat to the Manchurian capital had 'disappeared'. The government commander on the spot, General Chen Cheng, who had persuaded the generalissimo to make the trip, said the Nationalists could 'contemplate the future with serenity'. Though the severe weather held him back for the moment, he planned to advance to split the PLA in Manchuria from northern China, mop them up in the north-east and drive any remnant units into Mongolia and the USSR. He believed his adversaries had overextended their lines and not taken sufficient account of the rigours of the winter, and would be prey to his armies and air force.[1]

Such confidence was ill placed. The government's position had been weakened as, in line with Chiang's distrust of the Manchurians, Chen dissolved local regiments which had collaborated with the Japanese; that cut his forces by more than 50 per cent. Defending the Manchurian capital had meant transferring troops from further north, opening up territory for the Communists to occupy there. The economy was in a mess as inflation soared and the local currency was devalued amid extensive illicit transfers of gold with northern China. The Communists were, meanwhile, consolidating their position by underlining the security offered by the PLA and moderating land reform to win over better-off farmers by denouncing 'leftist deviation' and halting 'killing without discussion'. Some cadres still encouraged extreme measures elsewhere in China – a missionary in Hunan reported landlords being tortured or starved to death as peasant committees sought revenge on their enemies. But, in early 1948, Mao issued general instructions that middle peasants should be encouraged to work in county associations. More radical forms of reform of land ownership, taxes and rents risked causing chaos that would hinder the military effort, and could always be turned on again if needed, he added.[2]

No sooner had Chiang left Mukden than the PLA launched its eighth north-eastern offensive. Lin Biao had initially wanted to delay and prepare a campaign which mirrored Chen's in seeking to cut off government supply lines, especially rail links with the south. (He may well have learned of his opponent's plan from spies at their headquarters.) But Mao had egged him on – getting Lin to mount a big offensive was more difficult than getting a cow to jump a fence, the chairman remarked.

Despite the high icy winds, seven columns of his troops advanced through the forests and frozen countryside north of Mukden. The weather prevented reconnaissance aircraft taking off to spot them. After overcoming one of Chen's armies, Lin proposed widening the attack. Mao was enthusiastic. 'The more battles, the fewer of the enemy troops are left,' he noted. The PLA attacked more towns and cut railway links, forcing the Nationalist to use air transport, which could move fewer men and supplies than trains.[3]

Lin was a man of changeable moods who kept his distance from others and had phobias about moving air and water. Slight and short, with deep black eyes, he had trained at the Whampoa military academy in the south when it was headed by Chiang and, like most of the other PLA leaders, had taken part in the Long March of 1934–5 alongside Mao. He made his name in the early stages of the war with Japan when he led an ambush of an enemy supply chain in a narrow defile in the Pingxingguan region of northern China. It was actually quite a small-scale affair by the standards of the time, with a death toll of around 1,000 and the capture of a hundred trucks, but it was a valuable propaganda tool amid the catalogue of Chinese defeats.

Soon afterwards, Lin was presented with an imperial army

uniform and sword by Japanese soldiers who were serving under him after deserting to the Communists. He put them on and rode away on his horse. A Chinese sniper caught sight of him in the hills and, thinking he was an enemy officer, opened fire, wounding him in the head. Falling from his mount, Lin hurt his back.

The continuing pain from his injuries led to addiction to morphine and opium, and he also contracted tuberculosis. He spent four years in Moscow undergoing military training before returning home to be elected to the Central Committee of the Chinese Communist Party as the hero of 'the Great Victory of Pingxingguan'. Adopted as a protégé by Mao, he moved to Manchuria in 1945 as head of the Northeast Military District, the best-equipped Communist force because of captured Japanese materiel handed over by the Soviets. His uniform was cut so tightly that it seemed like a second skin and he liked to wear a cap to cover his baldness. But, for all his peculiarities, he was a strong leader with an excellent planning staff who evolved effective battlefield tactics.[4]

The Nationalists outnumbered the PLA by 400,000 to 320,000 in Manchuria and included crack troops brought in from the south. But they were tied down by their strategy of defending cities while their highly mobile opponents moved as they wished, concentrating on chosen targets and pummelling urban targets with artillery that included Japanese guns and American equipment captured from government forces. The Communists were also receiving aid from the USSR, mainly in the form of clothing, helmets, boots, ammunition and blankets, while getting other supplies and hard currency for raw materials they sent across the Siberian border. At the same time, they remained experts at living off the land, making their own hand grenades, using captured equipment to set up telephone communications and employing peasants for logistical support. An Australian journalist visiting a war zone saw a convoy of 3,000 wheelbarrows transporting supplies.[5]

Flying back to the north-east, Chiang replaced Chen Cheng, who went 'to rest' in Formosa and soothe his recurrent stomach problems. Chen's replacement, Wei Lihuang, had taken over command of Chinese troops in the successful push into Burma with the Americans in 1944–5, earning the nickname of 'Hundred Victories

Wei'. But his record in the north-east was singularly negative as his troops were besieged in a string of cities and lost a quarter of a million men, most of them captured and taken into the PLA after indoctrination.

The Communists moved on to attack the industrial town and railway junction of Siping,[6] which they had twice failed to capture. With 100,000 men, five times as many as the defenders, Lin's army hit the town with heavy artillery and occupied the surrounding valley in a battle that would end with victory in March. Chiang lamented that 'reports of failure come in like snowflakes' but would not authorise a change of strategy, leading Mao to urge Lin to plan fresh attacks on government troops to 'eliminate them one by one'.[7]

## II: Reticence in Washington

Receiving a letter from the generalissimo's wife, Soong Mei-ling, George Marshall reflected that 'China is probably the most unrestful spot in the world at present'. That made him and Truman ever more reticent about extending aid, especially given the demands of the ERP. The secretary warned Congress that full victory over the Communists could only be achieved by the US funding the Nationalists 'on a wide and probably constantly increasing scale' and being prepared 'virtually to take over the Chinese government and administer its economic, military and governmental affairs'.[8]

As for the president, towards the end of his life he would look back and reflect that there was nothing that could have been done to save Chiang and his regime. 'He was as corrupt as they come,' Truman went on. 'I wasn't going to waste one single American life to save him, and I didn't care what they said. They hooted and hollered and carried on and said I was soft on Communism and I don't know what all. But I never gave in on that, and I never changed my mind about Chiang and his gang. Every damn one of them ought to be in jail ... They're all thieves, every damn one of them.'[9]

Though Chiang could not relinquish the hope of victory, high officials around him seemed to lose faith in defeating the Communists, John Melby judged in Nanking. 'The best they hope for is that events will precipitate another world war which will bail them out,' the

American diplomat went on. 'Failing this, and if they cannot win on their own terms, particularly the right wing groups, they would rather go down to defeat – a primitive blind and collective sense of self-immolation, perhaps even of knowing they are doomed by any terms other than complete victory.'[10]

The regime and its high command were split by factionalism. Co-operation between the army, air force and navy was poor; pilots tended to keep to high altitudes to avoid the risk of being hit by ground fire, resulting in inaccurate bombing. Politically, the government had less and less appeal for the urban middle class, intellectuals, writers, teachers and students as repression increased. Liberals claiming to be the true heirs of 'the Father of the Republic', Sun Yat-sen, set up the Revolutionary Committee of the Kuomintang; among its leading members was the KMT founder's widow, sister of Soong Mei-ling.

The generalissimo looked to the US presidential election in November for the victory of a Republican who would increase help for his regime, but he had to get through a year until a more amenable successor could take Truman's place in the White House. If the Americans did not change their Europe First policy, 'they are sure to regret it in the future', he wrote in his diary. Yet he had nowhere else to turn. Contacts with the Soviets were fruitless. Their military attaché in Nanking told Kuomintang representatives that Moscow could bring influence to bear on the Communists to stop fighting only if the government came up with economic and political concessions, which Chiang would not do. His aides mentioned the contacts to US diplomats in the hope of making Washington more pliable. But that cut no ice.[11]

The Nanking regime thus found itself in an increasingly impossible situation, even if most people still could not envisage a complete Communist conquest of the whole country. The Nationalists were paying for the weakness from which they had suffered since the start in 1927. The military and small cliques of feuding politicians remained dominant, and the regime had lost any popular support it had once enjoyed. The generalissimo's main concern was his own survival, which he achieved for two decades, but at a huge cost to the country. In 1945, he had decided that the future lay in military victory but he had been unable to clinch decisive outcomes. Not only had the PLA evolved into a regular army that could win set-piece battles, but the Communists had also wrecked much of the infrastructure and communications on which the government forces depended, while Nationalist troops had lost an estimated 40 per cent of their American supplies to the enemy – further aid, Truman remarked, would amount to not more than 'pouring sand in a rat hole'.[12]

As the head of the US military mission, David Barr, wrote in an analysis that summed up the military path to defeat:

The Nationalist army is burdened with an unsound strategy which was conceived by a politically influenced and militarily inept high command ... Attempting to do too much with too little, it found its armies scattered along thousands of miles of railroads, the possession of which was vital in view of the fact that these armies were supplied from bases in central China. In order to hold the rail road, it was also necessary to hold to large cities through which they passed. As time went on, the troops degenerated from field armies, capable of offensive combat, to garrison and lines of communication troops with an inevitable loss of offensive spirit. Communist military strength, popular support and tactical skill were seriously underestimated from the start. It became increasingly difficult to maintain effective control over the large sections of predominantly Communist countryside through which the lines of communication passed.

Lack of Nationalist forces qualified to take the field against the Communists enabled the latter to become increasingly strong. The Nationalists, with their limited resources, steadily lost ground against an opponent who not only shaped its strategy around available human and material resources, but also capitalised skilfully on the Government's strategic and tactical blunders and economic vulnerability.[13]

CHAPTER TWENTY-NINE

# WAR AND ASSASSINATION

## I: INDIA GOES TO THE UN

The new year brought fresh outbreaks of murderous violence in India and Pakistan. In West Punjab, 3,000 Pathans armed with guns and hatchets killed 150 non-Muslim refugees on a train. An 8,000-strong Muslim mob burst into a temple in Karachi to slay Sikhs sheltering inside. Violence spread through the city, with a casualty toll estimated at more than 1,000. In Delhi, Gandhi embarked on a new fast, calling on the Hindus and Muslims of Delhi to pledge to live in peace.

In the Himalayas, the new year saw some of the heaviest fighting to date. 'Free Kashmir' forces in steel helmets drove back their adversaries in Jammu in combat over rough terrain, helped by bad weather that grounded Indian planes. In one encounter, two Indian infantry companies and an armoured column were overwhelmed, and, as the London *Times* reported, 'few prisoners were taken'. Tribal fighters were pouring in, the correspondent added, some saying they were shepherds searching for lost sheep. One group found its way to Lahore where it settled in an abandoned hotel, danced in the streets and wandered into the old British club.[1]

At a meeting at the Khyber Pass in mid-January, tribal leaders told the Pakistani prime minister they would not withdraw until the blood that had been shed had been avenged. They reserved particular hatred for the Sikhs – all of whom, they said, should be killed. Hundreds of families trekked across the heights to see Ali Liaquat, greeting him with cries of 'Pakistan zindabad' and offering gifts of goats and sheep. Fighters fired guns in the air and a band played 'God Save the King'. But, after Delhi flew in reinforcements, the front stabilised along what came to be known as the Line of Control, which left two-thirds of Kashmir under Indian control. A series of campaigns followed with the Indians using tanks at high altitudes for the first time and lifting the siege of Poonch.[2]

Faced with the impasse on the ground, the government in New Delhi decided to take the Kashmir question to the United Nations, as suggested by Mountbatten, who argued that the deadlock could only be resolved by 'the introduction of a third party with international authority acting in an agreed capacity'. India charged its neighbour with aggression and warned that if this did not stop it might be compelled 'in self-defence to enter Pakistan territory in order to take military action against the invaders'. Sir Zafrullah Khan, the Pakistani foreign minister, trumped this with a commanding speech, evoking 'an extensive campaign of "genocide"' against Muslims in East Punjab, Delhi and other parts of India'. Much to the discomfort of Nehru and his colleagues, the international body re-classified the issue from 'Jammu and Kashmir Question' to 'India–Pakistan Question'. Britain and the US both backed Pakistan. The Indian prime minister lamented that the world body was dominated by 'power politics and not ethics'. Sheikh Abdullah concluded that partition of Kashmir was the only answer.

India sought another way of putting pressure on Pakistan on one of its most vulnerable fronts – finance – by announcing it would withhold the transfer of the agreed share of the sterling balance debt incurred by Britain during the world war. It was blocking $166 million, it said, 'for fear that the money might be used to finance raiders'. 'Why should we give them the money to buy the arms to shoot our soldiers?' Patel asked. While this played well politically, the legality was highly questionable; the funds were a common asset and not India's to dispose of. Mountbatten considered the move 'both unstatesmanlike and unwise'. Seeing it as unnecessarily confrontational, Gandhi added it to the reasons for his fast. Nehru reversed the policy and agreed to pay the money. Hindu Nationalists were outraged. Patel, who was arguing with the prime minister on a number of issues, submitted his resignation, which was not accepted.[3]

The home affairs minister could, however, take comfort from fresh successes in bringing princely states into the new Indian state. After Delhi sent troops to the border and cut air and postal links as well as fuel supplies, the nawab of Junagadh fled to Pakistan with his pets and his chief minister invited India in, leading to a plebiscite that confirmed accession, though Pakistan refused to recognise it. Such strong-arm tactics were not needed with the champion polo-playing ruler of Jodhpur, who dropped his earlier opposition and agreed to accession, as did Orissa and twenty-seven sub-princedoms.

But Hyderabad held out as tension escalated. The nizam declared the Indian currency illegal while Delhi imposed an economic blockade, stepped up propaganda and worked on an invasion plan. Riots ripped through the state's capital. Along the frontier, Hindu groups attacked customs posts, cut telephone lines, sabotaged railways and attacked Muslim villages. Hundreds of thousands of refugees moved in both directions across the frontier with India.

The militant Muslim movement stepped up its action as did the RSS. The British adviser, Walter Monckton, tried to negotiate an agreement for autonomy even if there was an agreement on accession to India. The ruler played for time, sitting on documents and delaying the despatch of missions to Delhi in a series of manoeuvres that exhausted Indian patience. Patel decried a 'campaign of murder, arson and loot [which] rouses communal passions in India and jeopardises the peace of the Dominion'.[4]

## II: Death of an icon

Encouraged by the government's retreat on the payment to Pakistan and undertakings from a central Peace Committee pledging an end to attacks on Muslims in the capital, Gandhi ended his fast. His health was declining seriously; he suffered headaches and nausea, his kidneys were failing and his weight dropping. Hindu extremists filed past the Birla mansion in Delhi where he was installed, chanting 'Let Gandhi Die'. A Punjabi refugee set off a bomb at a prayer meeting – it did no harm.

During his last fast, Gandhi cited a passage in a letter from a friend criticising factionalism in the Congress leadership and adding, 'the people have begun to say that the British Government were much better'. On 28 January, he reflected, 'If I am to die by the bullet of a mad man, I must do so smiling. There must be no anger within me. God must be in my heart and on my lips.'

Two days later, he received Patel in the late afternoon in his ground-floor room at Birla House where he held nightly prayer meetings in the grounds. As he talked to the minister, he ate his meal of goat's milk, vegetables, oranges and a mixture of sour lemons, ginger, strained butter and aloe juice. He went to the bathroom and, followed by Patel and a group of young women, left the house for the prayer ground, leaning on the shoulders of women he called his 'walking stick'. A 500-strong crowd awaited him at the end of a red sandstone colonnade.[5]

When he arrived, a young man stepped out of the crowd, brushed aside one of the women and fired three shots from a small Beretta automatic pistol at close range. 'Hey Rama' (Oh God), Gandhi murmured as he fell, his steel-rimmed spectacles dropping to the ground, blood stains colouring his white clothes. He was carried into the house where he died.

A gardener overpowered the killer, Nathuram Godse, a militant Hindu Nationalist and member of the Mahasabha movement. He and fellow conspirators were incensed by the seer's last fast, which they called 'pro-Muslim' and an appeasement of Pakistan. Without Gandhi's influence, India would be stronger and better able to retaliate against its neighbour, they believed. The mahatma, Godse would say at his trial, 'always evinced a bias for Muslims, prejudicial and detrimental to the Hindu Community and its interests' and had been 'responsible for a number of calamities which the Hindu Community had to suffer and undergo'.[6]

'The light has gone out of our lives, and there is darkness everywhere,' Nehru declared. Patel appealed to Indians to 'carry the message of love and non-violence', adding, 'We did not follow him when he was alive; let us at least follow his steps now he is dead.' The two politicians buried their differences to confront what the prime minister called 'a different and more difficult world'. Fearing an upsurge in communal violence, they took pains to ensure the media made clear the killer was not Muslim. The RSS movement was banned. Twenty thousand members of the Mahasabha were arrested. Angry crowds turned on high-caste Brahmins, killing some and destroying their property. The RSS headquarters in Nagpur was attacked.[7]

More than 2 million people joined the five-mile-long funeral procession in which the corpse of the apostle of non-violence was placed on a weapons carrier, pulled by fifty people on ropes. After cremation, his ashes were put into urns which were sent across India. Most were immersed in the sacred river waters at Allahabad after a ceremony that bordered on the farcical. An amphibious vehicle carrying the ashes in a temple-like structure got stuck under a bridge and had to have its tyres deflated to get past; then it was swept away by the fast river current while Nehru waved his short stick in frustration. Journalists present chose not to report such mishaps out of respect for the solemnity of the occasion.[8]

After an eight-month hearing and despite appeals for clemency from Gandhi's sons, Godse and another plotter were hanged at the end of 1949 while six others were given life prison sentences.

# CHAPTER THIRTY

# COLONIAL TWILIGHT

## I: INDONESIAN IMBROGLIO

As the year began, the Dutch were jockeying to strengthen their position in Indonesia despite rising opposition to their rule, especially from Washington. They blockaded Nationalist areas and set up a state of East Sumatra, followed on 4 January by a conference of selected representatives from ten regions of Indonesia who agreed to form an interim federal government with the Republicans invited to join as a minority partner.

Under pressure from the United Nations and United States, talks were arranged on an American warship, the *Renville*, anchored off Jakarta. After some haggling, both sides accepted twelve principles put forward by a UN delegation, which included provisions that Dutch sovereignty would continue until transferred to an Indonesian federal state, that referendums should be held in the main areas on joining this state and that a convention would draw up a new constitution. The Republicans gave their agreement after the American member of the UN Group assured them they could rely on his government to ensure that the Dutch kept to their side of the bargain. Given the need of the government in The Hague for Marshall Plan aid, Washington enjoyed powerful leverage.

Sukarno had initially opposed the accord but was persuaded by the situation on the front lines, where a Dutch blockade meant that Republican forces were short of ammunition. He feared a renewed attack by colonial forces which would cause significant casualties.

In mid-January, the accord was signed on the foredeck of the *Renville*, and went into effect immediately. It was unsatisfactory from the start.

The Dutch prime minister said his country would not give up any territory, and that its sovereignty over the whole of Indonesia was to continue. The ceasefire line ran along the most advanced colonial positions, behind which lay many sizeable pockets of Republican strength. The Dutch were not keen on the requirement for referendums in territory they held. The agreement came in for stiff criticism in the Republican camp.

The prime minister, the Socialist Amir Sjarifuddin, was forced to resign at the end of the month and was succeeded by the veteran Nationalist Hatta at the head of an 'emergency presidential Cabinet' responsible directly to Sukarno. Left-wingers split off to form their own group with the Communists, the FDR/PKI which drew support from the military and the main labour organisation.

Conditions in the Republican heartland on Java were chaotic. Virtual civil war broke out in some places. Millions of refugees from Dutch-held areas swelled the population. Food ran short in some areas. The government printed more bank notes and inflation rocketed. A drive to reduce the size and cost of the armed forces alienated the military. The FDR/PKI began organised strikes on plantations pressing for nationalisation of foreign enterprises. Underlying this tenuous situation was an awareness that the colonial army was keen to launch another offensive when its political masters felt able to do so.


## II: Sad reality

In the other big colonial struggle in East Asia, French policy was stuck. After Operation Léa, military strategy boiled down to trying to control urban centres and the main communications routes while ceding the countryside of the north to the Viet Minh. Though Ho Chi Minh rightly observed that 'the key to the problem of Indochina is to be found in the domestic political situation in France', politicians preferred to avoid the subject of what *Le Monde* dubbed 'the dirty war'.

The Indochina policy of coalition governments in Paris was dominated by the Christian Democrats and colonial interests, while the Gaullists would brook no retreat. The right warned that any concessions in Vietnam would encourage Nationalists in North Africa. Socialists went along, embarrassed but with no alternative to offer. Communist support for independence made it difficult for others on the left to rally to the cause for fear of being painted as fellow travellers in the context of the evolving Cold War.

'It's lamentable, absence of statesmen, absence of political conscience, that's the sad reality,' President Auriol wrote in his diary. After talks with Bao Dai in Switzerland, High Commissioner Bollaert announced in late January that they had agreed on 'a concerted line of action'. But it was all words and did nothing to resolve the basic contradiction in the ex-emperor's position as he tried to work with Paris but to avoid appearing as a French puppet, condemning himself to political paralysis.[1]

~

## MEANWHILE

- Burma is declared an independent nation. After the pre-dawn ceremony with beating drums, trumpets and blasts from conch shells, the British presents the new nation with two cars, a Rolls-Royce and an Austin.
- The Japanese Diet passes legislation to break up big economic groups held to have backed the country's military expansion. The firms affected control two-thirds of economic activity.
- Solomon Mikhoels, the artistic director of the Moscow State Jewish Theatre and wartime chairman of the Jewish Anti-Fascist Committee in the USSR, is murdered on Stalin's orders as the dictator prepares an anti-Semitic purge.
- After a debate during which revolvers are flourished and fist fights erupt, the Brazilian Chamber of Deputies votes to deprive fifteen Communist deputies and the party's sixty-one state and municipal representatives of their seats.
- Eleven members of the US Communist Party go on trial in New York.

- The Supreme Court orders Oklahoma to admit a black woman to the State University Law School.
- British railways and ports are nationalised.
- The Co-operative Society opens the first British supermarket in the London suburb of Manor Park.
- A rocket-powered sled is reported to have reached a speed of 1,000 mph in a trial on railway tracks in California.
- Magnetic tape recorders go on sale in the US.

# PART TEN

# FEBRUARY 1948

**ACTS**

*Britain holds secret talks with Transjordan as partition nears while the Mufti's men and Syria attack; Communists take over Czechoslovakia; Model African colony boils over; Japan begins to emerge from defeat.*

**SCENES**

*London, Palestine; Prague; Accra; Tokyo.*

**CAST**

*Bevin, Tawfiq Abu al-Huda; Gottwald, Beneš, Masaryk, Prokop Drtina; Kennan, MacArthur, Hirohito; J. B. Danquah, Kwame Nkrumah.*

CHAPTER THIRTY-ONE

# CLOSER TO WAR

## I: POLITICAL MANOEUVRES

The prime minister of Transjordan, Tawfiq Abu al-Huda, made an unpublicised visit to see Bevin on 7 February. A former army officer who had headed several previous governments, he was on a mission from King Abdullah following a letter the foreign secretary had sent to the monarch the previous month. In line with his ambitions for British influence in the Middle East, this said the UK was determined to stay on in the region after leaving Palestine, that it would not abandon Transjordan and that it would continue to assist the Arab Legion.[1]

The prime minister chose to be lodged away from the accompanying delegation and went to the Foreign Office without any of his colleagues knowing. He told Bevin the Legion should go into Palestine after partition to ensure order and prevent Jews from seizing the whole territory. 'It seems the obvious thing to do,' his host replied. 'But do not go and invade the area allotted to the Jews.' Abdullah saw this as the green light for his expansion plan. After his meeting with Golda Meir, he believed the Jewish Agency was onside – though Ben-Gurion was dubious whether the scheme would work and Meir feared a double-cross.[2]

In another bid to strengthen its position for the future, Britain signed a 'close alliance' treaty with Iraq in pursuit of its policy of buttressing its position in the Middle East. At the ceremony in Portsmouth, Bevin spoke of a 'new series of treaties regularizing and expressing the friendship between the UK and the Arabic world'. But his policy faced at least two obstacles.

As far as Abdullah was concerned, most Arab League states remained hostile to his ambitions, which made it difficult for Britain to back the monarch and continue to fund his army while strengthening relations with other regional states. The agreement signed in Portsmouth, meanwhile, ran into immediate opposition in Iraq with big protest demonstrations in Baghdad in which twenty-nine people were killed. The prime minister who had negotiated the agreement left the country. Bevin's policy was left hanging.

## II: BOMBS AND ARMS

In Palestine, Jews and Arabs moved towards all-out war with reciprocal attacks, bombings and sniping while several hundred Syrians crossed the border to raid a settlement. 'The world will soon see the Arabs rise as one man,' the prime minister in Damascus declared. 'The people's army will be able to teach the treacherous Jews an unforgettable lesson.' British paratroopers, armoured cars and planes intervened to help drive off the Syrians, but cross-border firing at settlements continued.

The Grand Mufti's supporters threw bombs and blockaded the Jewish district of Jerusalem, which depended on food brought into the city and water from surrounding districts controlled by Arabs. At the instructions of the religious leader's nephew, Abd al-Qadir al-Husseini, an Arab drove a canvas-topped lorry into the main Jewish district of the city on the night of 1 February. Two British deserters accompanying him got the truck through the Nablus Gate checkpoint. The vehicle was parked outside the office of the *Palestine Post* newspaper, and the fuse to the explosives lit. The Arab was driven away in a car by the deserters as the blast ripped through the building, killing three people and injuring twenty.

Near to the Jordan River, Arabs from the Liberation Army assaulted the Tirat Zvi religious kibbutz. Despite his pledge the previous month to the British not to attack Jews before the Mandate ended the commander, Fawzi al-Qawuqji felt the need to score a victory to impose himself in the rivalry with el-Husseini. But the settlers beat off his men, leaving forty dead in the mud around the settlement – one Jew was killed. Unable to stomach the outcome, al-Qawuqji reported that his forces had scored a great victory and killed three hundred enemies.[3]

Three weeks after the bombing of the *Palestine Post*, el-Husseini's men, accompanied by four British deserters in an armoured car to get them through police checks, set off an even larger explosion from three lorries in a street market in a Jewish quarter area of Jerusalem. Fifty people died and anywhere from 140 to 200 were hurt. Blaming the British for the attack, Irgun leaders ordered their followers to shoot Mandate troops on sight – nine were killed. At the end of the month, other Irgun militants detonated three mines under a train carrying British soldiers from Cairo to Haifa; twenty-eight died and thirty-five were injured.

The Jewish Agency began to form a government-in-waiting and stepped up the search for arms abroad, able to pay high prices thanks to $50 million brought in for the cause by Meir on a fundraising tour of the US.[4] In the US, crates labelled 'used machinery' being loaded on a ship bound for Tel Aviv in Jersey City were found to contain two hundred tons of explosives.

# CHAPTER THIRTY-TWO

# A CLASSIC COUP

## I: The Leninist moment

A showdown in Czechoslovakia had been brewing ever since the country was put into the Soviet sphere of influence at the wartime summits. Gottwald might follow Lenin's advice that Communists should know when to bide their time and wait for the right moment instead of indulging in the 'infantile disease' of a premature power grab. But circumstances in early 1948 pointed to action. In the deepening context of the Cold War, Stalin needed to crack down on the one country in his zone of influence with a degree of democracy seven months after he had called the country to heel over the Marshall Plan. The creation of the Cominform had increased the stakes; returning from the inaugural meeting, Slánský, the Communist general secretary, complained that the country was 'stuck in the shackles of formal parliamentary democracy'. A directive from Moscow warned against 'right-wing deviation' in waiting to win power through the ballot box.[1]

The party was still strong and confident, tightening its grip on the police, infiltrating the justice system and increasing its influence in the military. It mounted a big campaign for a tax on property worth more than $8,000 to pay for grain subsidies to meet the agricultural crisis, accusing opponents of defending 'millionaires, big landowners, black marketeers' and backing 'foreign reactionaries'. When the Social Democrats replaced fellow traveller Zdeněk Fierlinger as their leader with the less biddable Bohumil Laušman, Gottwald said they must be watched with maximum vigilance. Soviet officials accused 'reactionaries' in the party of 'unbearable provocation'.[2]

The Communists had wide support among workers and a strong network of branches across the country that could be mobilised for action at short notice. They controlled workers' militias and organised international events to boost their appeal. A World Festival of Democratic Youth, arranged by the long-time Communist agent Otto Katz, was attended by 30,000 delegates. The American group marched into the stadium carrying placards showing a Southern lynching. 'Don't play with the Communists,' Fierlinger warned a fellow Social Democrat.[3]

Divisions within the other main parties were encouraged by blackmail of those with dubious wartime records and with offers of preferment. A member of Parliament recalled how Gottwald told him and a non-Communist colleague 'that two of us could be included in the new Cabinet. He said he had seven portfolios to assign and we could choose whichever we liked.' Justice Minister Prokop Drtina denounced 'gangsters and criminal elements who ... wheedled their way into the Communist Party'.[4]

Still, the Communists' own surveys of voting intentions showed them with less than 30 per cent support. Meeting Josef Korbel,[5] the ambassador to Yugoslavia, Beneš forecast that the Social Democrats and National Socialists would win the May poll and the Communist vote would fall by 10 per cent; he discounted the possibility of a coup because he said most of the police and army would remain loyal to him.[6]

In that context, party leaders concluded that it was time to undertake the 'quick liquidation of reactionaries'. They played on divisions in other parties, particularly the Social Democrats, and knew that, after his two strokes, Beneš was much diminished. Their militants were not interested in further compromises within the National Front. As a future party secretary, Zdeněk Mlynář, who had joined up in 1946 at fifteen, recalled, 'it was one side or the other – there was no middle ground ... our experience drummed into us the notion that the victory of the correct conception meant quite simply the liquidation, the destruction of the other'.[7]

## II: No one will help us

### 13 February

At a tense Cabinet meeting, Drtina throws down the gauntlet to the Communists. The dapper justice minister, a leading spokesman on the radio of the government-in-exile in London during the war, says an investigation has established that party members were behind the sending of bombs in perfume boxes to himself, Masaryk and another minister the previous autumn. Communists have also been involved in other murky affairs which the interior minister covered up. Drtina insists on the re-instatement of eight senior non-Communist police officials sacked by the Ministry, and calls an investigation of the security apparatus.

The Communist interior minister, Václav Nosek, is absent on grounds of illness. Standing in for him, Gottwald plays for time. But the Social Democrats side with other non-Communists to give Drtina a majority on the inquiry call.

That afternoon, the Communist Politburo decides 'to mobilize the nation for an effective defence against the reactionaries' attack'. It sends a full report to the Cominform, and resolves to meet twice a day and keep in touch with the Soviet embassy through a dedicated telephone line. The people must be ready 'to frustrate through all necessary force any subversive intentions of the reactionaries', it declares. As Nosek's deputy Jindřich Veselý puts it, 'the million-member colossus of the Communist Party with its transmission belt to mass organizations was set in motion'.[8]

### 14–17 February

Couriers are sent to local Communist branches to get them to mobilise. Workers' militias go on alert. NKVD secret police fly in. Some fan out to work in the regions. Others take rooms at a Prague hotel and work with the Interior Ministry.

### 18 February

Big crowds gather in the snow outside the Communist headquarters and the offices of its newspaper, *Rudé Právo*. Loudspeakers blare out Soviet songs and a manifesto calling for action and denouncing other parties for plotting to break up the National Front. Masaryk hosts a meeting with the Polish and Yugoslav foreign ministers, which insists on the need to continue quadrilateral control of Germany. In the latest sign of the tightening of bonds in the east, the USSR and Hungary sign a treaty of friendship and mutual assistance while the authorities in Albania execute two bishops for treason and jail another for twenty years.[9]

## 19 February

Valerian Zorin, the deputy soviet foreign minister and former ambassador to Czechoslovakia, flies to Prague. He is met at the airport by the Communist deputy foreign minister. The cover story is that he has come to check on Soviet wheat deliveries. He tells Gottwald that Stalin is insistent on a final confrontation and suggests a call for the intervention of the Red Army. Gottwald says military help will not be needed.[10]

Ninety minutes after landing, Zorin drives to the Czernin Palace to see Masaryk who is in bed with bronchitis and fever. The envoy says Stalin still trusts him, but adds, 'Events in your country are intolerable and we shall not tolerate them. The Soviet government cannot follow passively all the extravagances of political parties in Czechoslovakia. Anti-Soviet elements must be eliminated.'[11]

Zorin has protocol meetings with non-Communist politicians, and gets an embassy official to tell the Social Democrats that Moscow will not approve if they line up with the opposition.

## 20 February

Twelve of the twenty-six government ministers send Beneš their resignations in protest against the interior minister's refusal to reverse his decision on the police commanders. They think a show of force will lead to the collapse of the Cabinet and its replacement by one in which the Communists would be weakened. Beneš refuses to accept the resignations, but tells them Gottwald and his colleagues must capitulate. The Communists have miscalculated, he goes on. The election should be speeded up and would bring big losses for Gottwald's party, he adds. 'You can count entirely on me,' he assures the visitors. 'I will not compromise.'[12]

Gottwald cannot believe his luck, saying later that 'I prayed this stupidity over the resignations would go on and that they would not change their minds.' The resigners hold just under half the ministerial seats. To get a majority, they have to win over the Social Democrats and the independent Masaryk. But they make little attempt to recruit either to their cause. Though Fierlinger has been unseated, his faction remains powerful among Social Democrats and the party's ethos is to work with the Communists in a united front of the left. The foreign minister stays in bed, ill and reluctant to join the political fray.

Accusing the resigning ministers of leading 'an anti-State opposition', the Communists appeal to 'good Czechs and Slovaks' to rally round the National Front under Gottwald, who goes to the presidential Hradčany Castle where he charges the twelve ministers with manoeuvring against the higher interest of the nation. Still unable to take a firm stand, the president replies that Gottwald would remain head of any new ministry. The Communist leader says he will not negotiate.

Communists and Social Democrats attend a Cabinet session while ministers from other parties stay in their offices, communicating by messages carried to and fro. Social Democratic newspapers attack a 'police state' and accuse security forces of using methods 'at least as bad as those of Himmler or the Tsarist Okhrana'. The Communists call for the nationalisation of all firms with more than fifty employees; Hubert Ripka, the Social Democratic trade minister, says this would mean the 'ruin of Czechoslovakia's industry and misery for her people'. It is estimated that 3 million working days have been lost due to rallies and strikes.[13]

### 21–2 February

The head of the 7,000-strong Communist-led workers' militia in Prague reports 'a state of battle'. Guns and ammunition are distributed. Local committees are told to be ready to organise defence corps in factories, mobilise workers' militia and purge reactionaries. Party workers drive out of Prague through blizzards to spread the word, which is transmitted by teletype throughout the country. Workers' militia occupy factories. 'Alert squads' take up strategic positions.

Frontiers are sealed as demonstrations surge through urban centres, with armed militia. The Interior Ministry deploys special police forces in sensitive areas. Red Army reinforcements move into border regions. Secret police trail the resigning ministers who are now barred from their offices. Non-Communists are not allowed to broadcast. The Communist youth daily exults that 'newspapers which undermine the confidence of the people in their government cannot be published'.[14]

The Communists appeal to the divided Social Democrats to 'create a revolutionary majority government'. Laušman rejects the proposal, but Fierlinger and his associates preach the necessity of left-wing unity. Several non-Communist deputies telephone Gottwald to say they will work with him. After a late-night meeting, the Social Democrats adopt a motion indicating that the party would not quit the administration. 'If you don't march with us, you will be liquidated with the others,' Gottwald warns them.[15]

In Slovakia, where democratic parties had won 60 per cent of the vote at the last election, the Communists replace their ministers. Thousands of more or less identically worded telegrams arrive at the presidential palace backing the Communists. A stream of delegations of workers calls on the president; Beneš tells one he will not allow street action to determine the outcome, but he also sends a message to ministers of his National Socialist Party asking if it would not be best 'to appease the Communists'; they disagree.[16]

Hundreds of thousands of Communists and sympathisers demonstrate in central Prague. On Sunday the 22nd, 8,000 trade union delegates meet in the capital for a conference, which is meant to be about government proposals on civil service pay but turns into a Communist festival. It threatens strike action and, in his speech, Gottwald blasts 'agents of foreign and domestic reaction'. When a resolution backing the Communist position is put to the vote, only ten delegates oppose it.[17]

Gottwald also speaks at the National Theatre that day. Watched by an impassive Zorin, he vows eternal alliance with the USSR. In Moscow, the Communist daily, *Pravda*, blames the crisis on 'instructions from abroad that placed the State by its agitation in a dangerous situation'. Foreign reactionaries were using Czechoslovak political parties to 'try to divide the ranks of the people's democracy', it adds. 'This attempt will not be successful.'[18]

## 23 February

Beneš meets Drtina and the other ministers from his National Socialist party, colleagues of thirty years' standing and figures of renown. Among them are Education Minister Jaroslav Stránský, a professor, newspaper publisher and outstanding orator, and the party's principal tactician, Foreign Trade Minister Hubert Ripka.

Beneš informs them, 'I told Gottwald flatly "What you are doing is a coup d'état, a putsch, but I will not be pushed around." What you are preparing is a second Munich and I'll have no part of it.' Rather than signing a list of puppet ministers drawn up by the Communists, he vowed to abdicate. 'I will not be their accomplice,' he declares.

What if the Red Army intervened, he asks. 'Obviously, we'd be beaten,' Ripka replies. 'But the whole wide world would know that the Communist regime was imposed on us, that Czechoslovakia was the victim of aggression, defenceless against it . . . This victory would lead us to a new victory.'

'Perhaps,' Beneš responds, 'but no one will help us. The West won't help us. Moscow knows that.' He also warns against the Kremlin: 'You overestimate their intelligence and farsightedness. I overestimated them too. They take themselves for realists; at bottom, they are only fanatics. They are as blind as Hitler.'

'You say that!' Stránský exclaims. 'You who have done more than anyone else in the world to achieve honest co-operation with Soviet Russia.'

Beneš smiles sadly as the meeting ends.[19]

Addressing a huge crowd gathered in Prague's central square under the statue of the mediaeval church reformer Jan Hus, Gottwald attacks his opponents as servants of foreign reactionaries and calls for the creation of 'action committees' to strengthen the struggle. The Politburo sends a letter to Beneš, telling him it 'did not wish to leave him in doubt' about its determination. His request to broadcast to the nation is turned down by the Communist minister of information.[20]

The daily airline flight to London is grounded. Police with rifles patrol outside public buildings. A session of the National Assembly is adjourned. The Interior Ministry orders the National Socialist Party's offices to be searched.

## 24 February

Workers in factories, shops and restaurants stage stoppages to 'enforce the will of the people'. Social Democrats are arrested. Printers refuse to produce the Democratic Party daily in Slovenia. Bohemian railwaymen decline to distribute Catholic and National Socialist papers. Fierlinger and associates hold a meeting with the Communists. Speaking a couple of months later, Gottwald is frank. The tactic consisted of 'finding groups of people with whom we would be able to negotiate and who are at our beck and call ... smashing those parties as we liquidated their leaderships'.

He instructs security forces to move into public buildings. Fifty factories are occupied in Prague. A leading Communist tells Laušman that 'the die is cast. You and Gottwald must lead the working people and create a government of the two Socialist parties.' Ten thousand rifles are brought to the capital from the Brno arms factory.[21]

Ten thousand students march on the castle in support of democracy that evening, eight abreast, waving the Czechoslovak flag and singing the national anthem with its refrain of 'Where is my home?' They are met by platoons of armed men who open fire.

The Communists call a meeting in the Prague City Hall to form a Renewed National Front. The minister of defence assures those present that 'the army goes with the nation. What disturbs the unity of the nation is a menace and must be removed.' More than 2 million workers go on strike; those who do not join in are sacked. The Social Democrats agree a statement accepting the formation of a new government. Fierlinger's supporters occupy the party headquarters, fighting with members of other factions.

Beneš writes to the Communist leadership calling on it to hold talks with other movements to settle the crisis in a peaceful, democratic manner. The Politburo rejects the letter.

## 25 February

In the bitterly cold late morning of 25 February, Gottwald, Nosek and a colleague go to the presidential palace with a list of a new government. 'I do not intend to complicate things for you,' Beneš tells them. 'I will not create unnecessary difficulties. You know that this is not in my character.' Gottwald, wearing a Russian sheepskin cap, leaves with his list signed by the president. He has the names of a majority of members of Parliament ready to vote for the new administration. Later he says Beneš 'knows what strength is, and this led him to evaluate this [situation] realistically'.[22]

Masaryk had been in the adjoining room when Beneš gave Gottwald his agreement. He had gone to the palace to ask the older man about joining the new government. According to the foreign minister's doctor, who was with him, the president said he would not object since he wanted to have at least one reliable member of the new Cabinet. When they went to see him after the Communist leader left, the doctor added, Beneš had his 'face twisted with pain, staring into space, walking slowly towards an easy chair in a curiously stiff manner, as if with the last physical strength left to him'.[23]

The president's 'realism' means that Communists fill half the ministerial seats, with most of the rest taken by Fierlinger's associates and other fellow travellers, though Laušman becomes a deputy premier and Masaryk is retained at the Foreign Ministry. At St Wenceslas Square, under a grey sky amid its sooty nineteenth-century buildings, the Communist leader appears in front of a 200,000-strong crowd. He seems drunk. There is loud applause and thunderous shouts as he announces victory. At the palace, police fire on students trying to stage a pro-democracy demonstration. Armed militia march through the capital.

The civil service is purged. Millions of people gather around radio sets in the evening awaiting a broadcast by Beneš. All they hear is news of the government followed by a recording of a Communist mass meeting. Meeting Marcia Davenport, Masaryk, his face 'like a mask as if he had looked into the pit and was frozen', mutters, 'Lost. Utterly lost.'[24]

## III: The enemies are amongst us

The putsch Beneš had ruled out had been executed with textbook precision matched only by the incapacity of the non-Communists to muster resistance. As Gottwald said of his opponents, 'I knew we'd get them, in the end, but I never thought they'd hand me their arses to kick on a platter.'[25]

## 26 February

The purge extends to the medical profession and education. Action committees are set up to bolster the new regime. One aims to get rid of reactionaries in football and reverse the 'undemocratic' way in which only big teams play abroad.[26]

Meeting in London, the foreign ministers of the US, UK and France condemn the 'establishment of a disguised dictatorship of a single party under the cloak of a Government of National Union'.[27]

Truman, resting in Florida, reflects in a letter to his daughter that 'Things look black. So that now we are faced with exactly the same situation with which Britain and France were faced in 1938/9 with Hitler.' The atmosphere in Washington, write the Alsop brothers in their column, is 'a pre-war'. At the beginning of March, Lucius Clay cables from Berlin to say he and his staff had detected 'a worrisome shift in Soviet attitudes', warning that war could come at any time, 'with dramatic suddenness'.[28]

## 27 February

Beneš says he accepted the change of government after 'long and earnest thought' to avoid 'such a serious rift in the nation that general chaos would have ensued'. The government orders Stalin's portrait to be hung in all schools. The rector of Charles University, the country's oldest institution of higher learning, is sacked. The estate of the Archbishopric of Prague is reduced from 17,800 hectares to 50. Students at the Prague Music Academy are required to sign a resolution that only 'progressive' sounds should be permitted.[29]

## 29 February

As Zorin leaves Prague, police parade in the streets and the Communists organise a rally of farmers. The chairman of the Democratic Party in Slovakia is to be tried for treason. 'Though the crisis is at an end, we must not relax our watchfulness,' the interior minister says. 'The enemies of the state, though defeated, are still among us.'[30]

One of those he has in mind, Drtina, is tailed by police. He has been expelled from the Society of Authors and expects to be arrested at any moment. On the morning of 29 February, he throws himself from the third-floor window of his home. He is found on the pavement with a fractured skull. Much later, he will tell the American journalist, Claire Sterling, the main reason for his suicide bid was Masaryk's decision to join the new government; it removed his last illusion. Taken to hospital, he recovers and is then detained for five years before being given a 25-year jail sentence for 'false accusations of attempted assassination'. After serving half his term, he is released in 1960.[31]

Masaryk tells a French newspaper it was necessary to co-operate with the new National Front. At a lunch with Beneš, he is contemptuous of the way Drtina tried to end his life. Jumping from a window was the way servant girls chose to die, he says. 'It's a stupid way to go about it. Besides, there's no guarantee of success. Suicide doesn't absolve anybody of his responsibilities. It's a very poor escape.'[32]

Events in Czechoslovakia give added impetus to the negotiations for a Western alliance of which Moscow is kept informed through spies at the Foreign Office in London. In Rome, de Gasperi warns that what has happened confirms the danger his country faces. 'Behind the smokescreen of a national front, action committees of various kinds are being formed,' he adds. The Italian election in April would be an 'historic hour – we must win, come what may'.

In Berlin, Ernst Reuter asks who would be next after the Czechoslovaks. His city, is the obvious answer, but, he adds, 'If the world knows this, we will not be abandoned by the world.' The Attlee government announces that Communist Party members and their associates will be banned from state security work; civil servants are investigated while Communists and sympathisers are sacked from the BBC. The British Communist Party produces a leaflet for a by-election in a northern industrial town, declaring, 'Rejoice! Democracy has triumphed in Czechoslovakia.' Workers leaving a cotton mill throw it to the ground and the party candidate gets 1,300 votes.[33]

# MODEL COLONY EXPLODES

As the new regime tightened its hold in Czechoslovakia and Arabs and Jews escalated terrorism in Palestine, a large crowd gathered in the Palladium cinema in the capital of the British West African colony of the Gold Coast. They were ex-servicemen who had fought in the British army in Burma during the world war and were complaining that promised pensions and jobs had not materialised. Life was made especially difficult by the lack of employment and the soaring cost of urban living, which had eaten up their gratuities. A fund for the 65,000 servicemen had only 10 per cent of its capital left.[1]

The British had long seen the Gold Coast as a model colony set on a gradual, reformist path to self-government. The tribal chiefs and the intelligentsia of coastal urban centres both co-existed with the colonial administration. Africans were appointed to the administrative service and then to the governor's executive council in 1942. A new constitution four years later laid down that twenty-two members of the 31-strong legislature were to be Africans, nominated by councils of chiefs, elected by ratepayers in coastal areas or named by the colonial governor.

The economy was buoyed by exports of the key cash crop of cocoa, of which the Gold Coast was the world's biggest producer. Government revenue had doubled since 1930. Roads and railways had expanded. Elementary school numbers had risen markedly. The tribal system was more concentrated than in other African colonies, with half the population sharing a common culture. As a result, the annual British reports on the 92,000-square-mile country of 4.1 million people were able to speak of 'a peace-loving country' which could expect 'orderly and constitutional progress' on a measured path towards self-government.[2]

But the surface calm had been shaken by economic strains as the cost of living soared while real wages fell. Cocoa output was a third below the pre-war level because of the impact of crop disease. Imported goods were in short supply – sugar and flour were three times as expensive as in 1939. This was caused by the manipulations of the European-run Association of West African Merchants, which limited the supply of products its members brought in from abroad to maximise profits, with gross margins averaging at 75 per cent. Goldsmiths complained that they could not get the precious metal. Drivers groused that petrol was only available at high prices on the black market and under the control of 'Syrians' (actually Lebanese).[3]

Nii Kwabena Bonne II, a successful African businessman who was also a tribal chief, organised a month-long boycott of over-priced goods at the beginning of 1948. The big companies agreed to cut their gross profit margins to 50 per cent but discontent continued since most people expected prices to halve, and were angry when they found that the reduction in retail outlets amounted to only one-sixth.

Nationalists among what were known as 'men of property and standing' had set up the United Gold Coast Convention in 1947 to press for 'self-government in the shortest possible time'. J. B. Danquah, a veteran lawyer, became their leading figure. As the group's secretary, the Convention took on Kwame Nkrumah, who had returned home after spending ten years in the US[4] before playing a major role in organising the Pan-African Congress in Manchester which preached a Socialist path to independence for European colonies.

The two men were very different – Danquah urbane and liberal, Nkrumah driven by work and ambition. But they combined to spread the Nationalist message, especially among youth groups, travelling through the country preaching the need for self-government. Nkrumah melded a message of independence, national unity, pan-Africanism and the teachings of Marx, Engels and Lenin. In the north, an Ashanti Youth Association was formed 'to promote the social and political welfare of our dear land of birth'. In the west, a Literary and

A state is created:
Ben-Gurion reads
the Declaration of the
Establishment of the State
of Israel. (Magnum Photos)

Kings at odds: Abdullah of Transjordan and Ibn Saud of Saudi Arabia. (Getty)

The helmsman: Mao Zedong. (Getty)

Economic collapse: crowd besieging Shanghai bank. (Henri Cartier-Bresson/Magnum Photos)

Social Club called for the reduction of the price of imported goods, industrialisation, Africanisation of public services, cheaper education, piped water, telephone and radio facilities and 'self government as early as possible'.[5]

On Saturday 28 February, 2,000 marchers gathered at noon at the city's polo grounds for the ex-servicemen's protest. They walked up a main road to the seat of colonial government at Osu Castle, a white-painted one-time slaving fort on the coast. Urged on by a man with a bugle, they sang and shouted as they marched. Police blocked their progress. Stones and insults were thrown. 'The procession was in a very ugly temper, many taking part being drunk,' a British minister later told the House of Commons.[6]

Seeing his forces heavily outnumbered, the police superintendent shouted 'Stop!' But the crowd continued to advance to the sound of the bugle. 'Fire!' the superintendent ordered his men. None obeyed. So he grabbed a rifle and shot into the crowd. Three demonstrators were killed, among them a wartime sergeant.[7]

When news of the confrontation reached the city centre, rioting broke out. People were killed; shops were looted; the prison was attacked and convicts freed; schoolboys at Adisadel College rampaged over the playing fields. Troops called in to try to restore order opened fire twice. Buildings were set on fire; rioters with cutlasses severed the hoses of the firemen who were then provided with weapons. A curfew was declared and roads closed. Danquah, who had been out of town on a political tour, returned to meet other leaders of the Convention on the veranda of their headquarters to 'plan to take advantage of that day's tragic incidents as a fulcrum or lever for the liberation of Ghana'.[8]

He then filed a thousand-word cable to the government in London and the world press saying that a working committee was ready to take over government and calling for the despatch of a special commissioner 'to hand over Government to interim government of chiefs and people and to witness immediately the calling of a Constituent Assembly'. He also published a manifesto addressed to tribal chiefs declaring, 'The hour of liberation has struck.' Nkrumah sent a message to the United Nations, the *New York Times*, the *Daily Worker* in London, the *New Times* and the

*Pan African* magazine in Manchester demanding the recall of the governor and the establishment of a constituent assembly. The authorities hesitated, unsure of how to respond, and Ghana remained on a knife edge as the death toll in the unrest escalated.[9]

# THREE DS FOR JAPAN

## I: A SENSITIVE MISSION

George Kennan was, meanwhile, on a long and testing flight to Japan. Leaving from Seattle, his plane travelled via Anchorage and then undertook what the head of the State Planning Department described as 'a terrifying refuelling stop in a nocturnal gale at the tabletop landing field of the tiny island of Shemya, fourteen hundred miles from nowhere in the northern Pacific'. He and the general accompanying him reached Tokyo thirty hours after setting out, landing at four in the morning in a snowstorm. The heating had given out on the plane on the last leg so they were frozen as well as exhausted.[1]

Kennan had been analysing the situation in East Asia for some time. While he felt that his containment doctrine should, as a rule, not apply outside Europe, he made an exception for Japan. As Stalin accepted that any hope of playing a significant role in East Asia was dashed by the military realities, Kennan regarded the economic revival of a country 'amenable to American leadership in foreign affairs' and 'reliant upon the U.S. for its security from external attack' as key to the strategic system in the region. In his foreign policy analysis delivered to Marshall before he left, he argued that the US was 'grossly over-expanded' in East Asia and should concentrate on Japan and the Philippines as the cornerstones of a Pacific Security System to protect its interests. 'If we could retain effective control over these two archipelagos in the sense of assuring that they would remain in friendly hands, there could be no serious threat to our security from the East within our time,' he argued,[2] adding that US objective should be to:

> Liquidate unsound commitments in China and try to recover our detachment and freedom of action with relation to that situation;
>
> Devise policies toward Japan which would assure the security of that country from Communist penetration and domination as well as from military attack by the Soviet Union and would permit Japan's economic potential to become once again an important force in the affairs of the area, conducive to peace and stability;
>
> Permit Philippine independence, but in such a way as to assure that the archipelago remained a bulwark of American security in the Pacific region.[3]

On arrival in Tokyo, Kennan was driven to the best lodging place in the city for foreign visitors, the Imperial Hotel was driven with two towers designed by Frank Lloyd Wright, to try to get some rest, but was constantly disturbed by calls from media correspondents. He then went to lunch with the supreme commander for the Allied Powers (SCAP), Douglas MacArthur, at his headquarters in the Dai-Ichi Mutual Life Insurance Building overlooking the imperial palace. The general capped the meal with a two-hour monologue before the diplomat was freed to catch up on some sleep.[4]

Kennan knew how sensitive his mission was. His Long Telegram from Moscow two years earlier had set in motion the administration's policy towards the Soviet Union. Appointed director of policy planning at the State Department in the spring of 1947, he had been at the centre of affairs, through the elaboration of containment and the European Recovery Program. Working closely with George Marshall, he was one of the 'Wise Men' directing US foreign policy. But Japan was different, above all because of the man in charge.

MacArthur was a grandiose figure who compared his role to that of Julius Caesar in Gaul in bringing American-style modernity and Christianity to Japan. A supreme egotist, he bathed in praise and avoided blame, cutting a fine public figure with his corncob pipe and upright bearing. He had been forced to retreat from the Philippines by the Japanese in 1942 but led the fight back as supreme commander of Allied Forces in the Southwest Pacific to vindicate his cry of 'I shall return.'[5] Such was his self-regard that, when it was suggested he should go to the US to brief the administration, he replied 'If I returned for only a few weeks, word would spread through the Pacific that the United States was abandoning the Orient.'[6]

A master of the dramatic gesture from a distinguished military family, he had little time for the joint Allied control committee in Tokyo. Stalin noted that the Soviet representative was 'treated like a piece of extra furniture', but his realism about spheres of influence led him to allow the American to be 'the sole executive authority for the Allied Powers'. US preponderance was backed by troop numbers – there were 400,000 Americans under MacArthur compared to 35,000 Australians, New Zealanders, British and Indians – and no Soviets or Chinese.

The five-star general also took a haughty view of politicians and civil servants back home, ignoring State Department advice and operating through his own organisational framework. 'One has at times the feeling that Washington did not loom very large on the horizon of this highly self-centered occupation command,' Kennan noted. 'Relations between General Marshall and General MacArthur were remote, and, I sense, not cordial . . . MacArthur had a violent prejudice against the State Department . . . Liaisons between the department and SCAP had been distant and full of distrust.'[7]

Acknowledging only George Washington and Abraham Lincoln as influences, the general aimed to carry out 'a spiritual revolution' to bring a new way of life to the 80 million Japanese who he declared to have 'got the spirit of the Sermon on the Mount. Nothing will take that away from them.' They were to enjoy the three Ds of democracy, demilitarisation and decartelisation as feudalism and tradition were swept away in 'an immaculate occupation'. They would be protected as California was protected, he declared. The Ryukyu island chain stretching south from the main area of Japan towards Formosa was, he added, 'our natural frontier'. The island of Okinawa became a vast American base to last for perpetuity, MacArthur arguing that 'the Okinawans are not Japanese', a view not generally shared in Tokyo.[8]

Though some right-wing Republicans hoped the 'Blue Eyed Shogun' would be their party's candidate for the presidency, the programme over which he presided in Japan consisted of radical reform that far outran what was being done in Germany. One of his senior aides, General Courtney Whitney, a conservative Republican, was overheard telling a Japanese politician, 'The only thing that will save your country is a sharp swing to the left.'[10]

For all his projection of grandeur, the commander, now in his mid-sixties, lived and worked quite plainly. He and his wife and son moved into the vacant US embassy residence, where he had the interior painted army green. 'We'll do simply here,' he told his wife. 'This isn't a time for splendor.' At his 54-square metre, sixth-floor office in the Dai-Ichi Building, he attended to business at a lacquer-topped wooden desk with no drawers. The only decoration was two paintings of yachts by the nineteenth-century English artist, Frederick James Aldridge. The general's daily routine was unvaried. Rising at 7 a.m., he said his morning prayers, took breakfast, read cables and went to the office at 10.30. After lunch, he napped and then worked on, sometimes past midnight. He rarely left Tokyo and operated through a clear chain of command whose members lived in awe of him.[9]

## II: Totally levelled

The country over which MacArthur held sway had been traumatised by the outcome of the war it had launched first against the other great Asian power, China, and then across South East Asia and out into the Pacific. This was the first defeat Japan had suffered for more than a thousand years, and the first time foreign troops had invaded its soil. The forces of the Meiji emperor had humiliated China's last dynasty, the Qing, in the war of 1894–5, acquiring the island of Formosa as a colony, positions in Manchuria and a large indemnity. Japan then scored the first military victory of an Asian nation over a European power in the war with Russia in 1905, before allying with the winning side in the First World War, taking over the German concession in north-east China in the process. In 1931, its army seized Manchuria and, six years later, swept across China capturing major cities as it waged a particularly vicious form of warfare, with indiscriminate bombing of undefended cities, massacres of citizens and widespread pillage, driving the Nationalists to seek shelter behind the Yangtze Gorges in their wartime capital of Chongqing as they waited for America to win the war.

At its height in 1942, the 'great empire of Japan', with its 'Great East Asia Co-Prosperity Sphere', extended from the middle of China to the Marshall Islands in the mid Pacific, from the frozen Siberian border with the USSR in Manchuria and the Aleutian Islands to the East Indies, Indochina, Burma and Malaya and the Philippines, taking in Hong Kong and Singapore. Imperial forces humiliated the French, Dutch, British and Americans and laid plans to attack India and Australia.

Now, three years after the peak of military success, Japan was devastated. It had lost all its overseas territories. More than half a million civilians died in all; some 120,000 children were left orphaned and homeless. Five million troops returned home as human symbols of defeat, 'living war dead' who were often treated as pariahs. With them came 3 million Japanese who had followed the army. Cities had been swept by huge fire-bombing raids. Hiroshima and Nagasaki had been hit by atom bombs, their terrifying immediate impact in deaths, destruction and horrifying burns giving way to the longer-term effect of radiation sickness.[11]

For some, it was a time to loot the huge stockpiles that had been built up for the final land battle that never came. One estimate put the value of stolen goods at more than total expenditures in the national budget for 1946. Criminals and prostitutes created their own culture. Messianic cults flourished. A privately funded Recreation and Amusement Association was set up to provide more than a thousand 'comfort women' for the occupiers, serving anywhere up to sixty men a day; their oath said they were 'paying an inescapable courtesy, and serving to fulfil one part of our obligations and to contribute to the security of society'.[12]

Though the destruction was relatively low in heavy industry and chemicals, consumption goods were in short supply because of the conversion of factories to military output. Prices in 1946 reached sixteen times the 1944 level. Fixed capital evaporated. Exports of manufactured goods were 15 per cent below those in 1938 but imports of food soared eightfold. The impact was felt across society. 'The bloodiest years in Japanese history produced a uniquely equalizing force,' as the historian Walter Scheidel put it. 'Total war had levelled totally.'[13]

'In every major city, families were crowded into dugouts and flimsy shacks or, in some cases, were trying to sleep in hallways, on subway platforms, or on sidewalks,' an American general wrote. 'The streets of every major city quickly became peopled with demoralised ex-soldiers, war widows, orphans, the homeless and unemployed – most of them preoccupied with simply staving off hunger.' The descent from military triumphs to utter defeat in three years was vertiginous; 'The hearts of the people have been burned out,' the US expert Edwin Reischauer judged.[14]

The scarcity of food was aggravated by bad harvests and the diversion of supplies onto the black market. The most common diet consisted of barley and potatoes, supplemented by acorns, peanut shells, grain husks and sawdust. Tokyo had a reserve of only three days' consumption of rice, mixed with soybeans to increase the quantity. Newspapers advised that protein deficiencies could be countered by eating silkworm cocoons, worms, grasshoppers, moles, snails and snakes or a powder made from the dried blood of cows, horses and pigs. They also reported that mice and rats tasted like small birds if properly sterilised. Appealing for additional aid at the beginning of 1946, MacArthur told Washington that 30 million people were threatened with starvation and that the resulting unrest and disease would undermine the work of the occupation. Aid to the tune of $100 million was forthcoming in food, fertilisers, petroleum products and medical supplies.[15]

In the absence of a functioning economy, 'blue sky' markets proliferated. By October 1945, there were estimated to be 17,000 across the country; the biggest in Tokyo had a sign made up of 117 hundred-watt bulbs. Many were run by gangs who fought murderous turf wars and were supplemented by Korean and Formosan underworld rings. As well as household effects, cast-off clothes and food brought by farmers and by ex-soldiers who went foraging in the countryside, there were stolen goods, military swords converted into cutlery, American products given to Japanese women by GIs and stews made from the leftovers of US military canteens. In Osaka, the main market, which was controlled by a flamboyant gangster who wore a dagger on his breast and a pistol at his hip, offered garments and blankets taken from the dead in hospitals, sometimes stained with blood.[16]

The Japanese reacted in many different ways to defeat but, as a whole, they wanted to make a new start, forgetting and transcending the era of militaristic aggression. The abrupt ending to the Imperial Way was signified by Hirohito's broadcast in August 1945 – the first time people outside the court, government and military had heard the emperor's voice. With remarkable under-statement, he told listeners that 'despite the best that has been done by everyone ... the war situation has developed not necessarily to Japan's advantage'. So, to avoid more bloodshed, or perhaps even 'the total extinction of human civilisation', Japan would 'endure the unendurable and suffer what is insufferable' and accept the Allied terms which had been decided by the Potsdam summit calling for unconditional surrender, military occupation, demilitarisation and loss of conquered territory.[17]

Six weeks later, Hirohito made the unprecedented gesture of going to visit a foreigner. Formally dressed in frock coat and striped trousers and wearing a top hat, he arrived at 10 a.m. at the US embassy building and was taken by aides to meet MacArthur. 'You are very, very welcome, sir,' the general said as they shook hands. The emperor bowed so low that his hand reached over his head. When they sat down, the emperor said he would entrust himself to the decision of the Allied nations represented by the SCAP.

An army lieutenant entered the room to take what was meant to be a single photograph. But the two men's eyes were shut on the first shot and Hirohito's mouth gaped open on the second. Finally, a satisfactory image was taken, though the emperor looked ill at ease as MacArthur, wearing open-necked uniform and with his thumbs hooked round his belt, towered over him. The photograph was distributed to the press, but editors had a problem. The emperor was still a deity so people were meant to avert their eyes from his image. Newspapers printed the photograph only when the occupation authorities told them to do so.[18]

Because SCAP stood outside Japanese society, with little cultural or linguistic contact, it had to work through the national organs of government and the bureaucracy. Whatever their private reservations about the wholesale changes being made to their country and its society, politicians who escaped the purge of warmongers assured the occupiers that, in the words of Prime Minister Shidehara Kijūrō in 1945, 'We shall construct a new state that is thoroughly democratic, pacifist and rational.'[19]

As in Germany, the US saw itself acting as FDR's 'arsenal of democracy' even as the hardships of life spread a victim mentality among the defeated population. New Deal ideals would be brought to bear by an altruistic occupation force. 'We shall assure ourselves of a "favoured position" in Japan if we succeed in effecting lasting reforms, in giving impetus to a genuine liberal movement, and in starting the process of democratization in Japanese education,' wrote the State Department Japan affairs director, John Emerson. 'Then, perhaps, will Japan become neither a "place d'armes" for the Soviet Union nor a "place d'armes" for the United States.'[20]

In pursuing such an aim, what became known as the State Department's 'Chrysanthemum Club' was at odds with those who saw the former foe as an essential element in the struggle with the USSR, particularly given the way in which China was proving incapable of living up to Roosevelt's vision of it as one of the Four Policemen of the post-war world. 'America must dominate the Pacific,' the navy commander, Ernest King, had declared during the war, a sentiment with which James Forrestal agreed. The problems with this approach were that Europe came first, that the administration's focus on restraining the budget deficit meant it did not want to undertake additional military commitments, and that Asia was far too big and disparate to come under a collective security system.

Proponents of democratic rebirth for Japan took heart when the general election of 1946 attracted a 72 per cent turnout. The Liberals topped the poll with 148 of the 464 seats and formed a coalition with Shidehara's Progressive Party. But the Liberal leader, Ichirō Hatoyama, was unseated and a government formed under Foreign Minister Yoshida Shigeru, the leading political figure of the era. However, fresh elections brought victory for the Socialists who became the largest party in Parliament with 144 seats and took the lead in a reshaped coalition.

The growing Cold War on the other side of the globe and the victories of the PLA in China did not prevent the legalisation of the Japanese Communist Party. Founded in 1922, it had been repressed by the imperial authorities with most of its members being sent to jail, though it never posed any threat to the regime with a membership of below 1,000 and a leadership rent by factional disputes. Now, it formulated a strategy aimed at eliminating the old imperial system, democratisation and land reform, the last two objectives shared with the occupation authorities as it contested elections, attracted some intellectuals and built up a following among workers through its trade union branches.

On May Day 1946, a crowd estimated at half a million gathered in a left-wing demonstration in front of the imperial palace in Tokyo while other cities saw large rallies. Distribution of food fell way behind schedule. 'The political pot is boiling madly,' the journalist Mark Gayn noted. MacArthur issued a warning against 'the growing tendency towards mass violence and physical processes of intimidation under organized leadership [which] present a grave menace to the future development of Japan'. Yoshida wrote that 'Japan had been submerged under a sea of red flags . . . to the accompaniment of revolutionary songs chanted by a mob massed around my headquarters.' But in the elections of 1946–7, the Communists won only 4 per cent of the vote and its trade union activity was limited by rival labour organisations.[21]

## III: CHANGE ALL BUT KEEP THE EMPEROR

The American Initial Post-surrender document for Japan had set as its objectives: (1) to ensure 'that Japan will not again become a menace to the United States or to the peace and security of the world', and (2) to establish eventually 'a peaceful and responsible government', preferably closely conforming to principles of democratic self-government, 'which will respect the rights of other states and will support the objectives of the United States as reflected in the ideals and principles of the Charter of the United Nations'. To accomplish these objectives, SCAP would immediately apply 'the three Ds' – democracy, demilitarisation and decartelization – and impose a sweeping programme of political, economic and social reforms.[22]

In a statement to Japanese newspapers in October 1945, MacArthur stressed the need to rectify 'the traditional social order under which the Japanese people for centuries have been subjugated'. That, he added, would involve a new and more liberal constitution, the 'democratization' of the economy, the emancipation of women, the encouragement of labour unions and an overhaul of the education system.[23]

As politics was democratised, twenty-eight senior high-ranking government and military leaders were put on trial before an international tribunal sitting in a former army building in Tokyo. Seven were sentenced to be hanged including General Tōjō, prime minister from 1941 to 1944; he and others were coached by the Americans so that their evidence would not attribute responsibility to the emperor. Another 5,700 people appeared in court in Japan and formerly occupied territories accused of atrocities; nine hundred were convicted.

The Tokyo trials attracted some criticism as merely seeking 'victors' justice'. A few critics felt that Truman should be tried for deciding to drop atomic bombs on cities. The judge from India argued that, since 'nothing of that magnitude' could be held against the twenty-eight Japanese, they should be acquitted and released. An American general involved in deciding who should be in the dock dismissed the trials as 'mumbo jumbo'. George Kennan called them 'a hocus-pocus of judicial procedure ... political trials, not law'. It would have been better, he thought, if those responsible for the war had been shot out of hand. But the trials were accepted by the public as the least to be expected; they aroused little attention while people, thoroughly tired and relived that the fighting had stopped at last, got on with their lives as best they could.[24]

British and Soviet representatives wanted to charge Hirohito as a war criminal. They were outweighed by the American belief, nurtured by the influential pre-war ambassador in Tokyo, Joseph Grew, and adopted by MacArthur, that, shorn of his powers, the emperor could contribute to stability and help to get the co-operation of the bureaucracy. The general argued that charging the emperor with war crimes would 'undoubtedly cause a tremendous convulsion among the Japanese people, the repercussions of which cannot be over-estimated as he is a symbol that unites all Japanese. Destroy him, and the nation will disintegrate.' It was not a question of guilt, which was hard to deny, but of how Hirohito could be most useful.[25]

MacArthur estimated that a million US troops would be needed to ensure stability and order if Hirohito went to court. At a time when the existing cost of the occupation was a live political issue in the US, this was a telling economic reason to sweep the emperor's complicity in aggression since 1931 under the carpet. It was yet another of the deals done to try to eradicate the awkward past for the better future most people believed in at the time. In January 1946, the former living god formally renounced his divine state; as a historian put it, 'He came down from the clouds, a bookish, uncharismatic figure in ill-fitting clothes.' MacArthur insisted that he was the most democratic person in the country and that the healthy nature of the Japanese was attested to by their love and respect for the occupant of the throne, though Hirohito himself said privately that the people were like children who 'lacked calmness' and were 'blind followers' of imported customs.[26]

But old habits died hard. The change in his status did not mean the emperor and those around him were ready to renounce political influence altogether. Though excluded from formal involvement in government, Hirohito insisted that the new prime minister who took office in June 1947 present a formal report to him at the palace in Kyoto. He also arranged to be briefed on foreign affairs. He issued a statement asserting Japanese sovereignty over Okinawa that was, strictly speaking, unconstitutional and diverged from the line taken by MacArthur. When he convoked the Parliament, some members practised the 'crab walk', bowing deeply in front of him and then left walking sideways or backwards to avoid the disrespect of showing him their backs.

Imperial provincial tours attracted a huge, emotional following. Politicians jostled with one another to be part of the hundred-strong cortège. Roads over which Hirohito travelled were repaired; flowered arches were erected at the entrance to squares; matting was laid on paths where he walked; railings he touched were covered with cloth.

Though officially banned, the rising sun flag, the symbol of militaristic aggression, flew from rooftops and was waved by cheering crowds.[27]

In December 1947, on the sixth anniversary of Pearl Harbor, Hirohito visited Hiroshima. The streets were specially cleaned for the occasion. Thousands of people lined the route of his motorcade. Orphans of the atomic bombing waited for him on their knees. Injured mothers stood with their disfigured children in their arms. As he got back into his car, an Australian diplomat recorded, 'The crowd went berserk. Shouting banzais at the top of their voices, the people rushed forward, their eyes shining and all their mask of unemotionalism wiped off their faces.'[28]

On New Year's Day 1948, the emperor greeted tens of thousands of people at the plaza outside the palace in Tokyo. Twelve days later, the occupation authorities prohibited more imperial tours and cracked down on the flying of the rising sun flag. They had to bring Hirohito down from the clouds. It is unclear how far the emperor set out to provoke the adulation he aroused – he often appeared ill at ease on public appearances and said little. But conservative politicians and court officials wanted to make the most of his remaining special status while the occupation authorities needed to make sure he could not be used to obstruct the changes.

As demonstrated by the Hirohito–MacArthur photograph incident, the occupation authorities ensured that the right messages were transmitted to the public through their control of the media. Though the behaviour of the occupation troops was not always without reproach, Japanese civilians, women in particular, were relieved when fears the victors would conduct themselves as badly as imperial troops proved baseless. American aid, particularly food, was welcomed. If the elite suffered, the people in general benefited from the changes SCAP was introducing.

Japan's military forces were abolished and a purge launched at other wartime institutions. Two hundred thousand 'ultranationalists' were expelled from holding office. But the senior central bureaucracy managed to protect itself, a task made easy since its members staffed the committees that screened the accused – only 145 leading functionaries were obliged to leave office. The education system was reformed with decentralisation, co-education and junior high schools on American lines. Shinto was discontinued as a state religion.

Almost 2 million hectares changed hands in land reform, which brought a major change to agriculture in a country where food production was limited by the mountains and forests that took up to 80 per cent of the land areas on the four main islands. The size of farms was restricted. Farms owned by absentee landlords were bought by the government and re-sold to farmers.

One major target identified in wartime planning was the big business groups that were estimated to control three-quarters of Japan's industrial and commercial activity and were held to have played a key role in backing militarisation and territorial expansion. The leader of a State Department mission to Japan wrote that the 'concentration of economic control enabled the *zaibatsu* to continue a semi-feudal relationship between themselves and their employees, suppress wages, and hinder the development of independent political ideologies. Thus the formation of the middle class, which was useful in opposing the militarist group in other democratic countries, was retarded.'[29]

The conglomerates had their defenders. Yoshida told foreign correspondents that it was a mistake to judge them as having done only bad things. He defended the long-established *zaibatsu* such as Mitsui and Mitsubishi and said it was new groups that had reaped big profits from collaboration with the military. But MacArthur thundered that 'if this concentration of economic power is not torn down and redistributed peacefully, and in due order under the occupation, there is no slightest doubt that its cleansing will eventually occur through a blood bath of revolutionary violence'.[30]

The head offices of big conglomerates were dissolved, followed by the break-up of the giant Mitsui and Mitsubishi Trading Companies and a law for the dissolution of any firm judged monopolistic – eighteen were affected in steel, mining, manufacturing and other sectors. Competition increased and new firms emerged in metals, vehicles and electronics. Six hundred corporate officers found their names added to the purge list; others resigned rather than face investigation. In all, nearly 25 per cent of top-level executives quit their jobs though many soon reappeared at other firms. Under US pressure, Parliament passed an anti-monopoly law and other measures against market domination.[31]

The right of workers to organise and bargain collectively was established, along with the eight-hour working day. In 1946, there were 260 industrial disputes involving 845,000 workers. By the end of 1948, union membership was nearly 7 million, grouped into 17,000 company branches and three national federations. The emancipation and enfranchisement of women was ordered. MacArthur wrote later that 'of all the reforms established by the occupation of Japan, none was more heartwarming than this change in the status of women'. The eighty or so female candidates in early post-war elections included doctors, dentists, teachers and Buddhist nuns – and a prostitute.[32]

There was periodic talk of a peace conference but nothing materialised. What did transpire was a new constitution. This provided a key example of the way MacArthur and his staff used their enormous powers to force through reforms. The government argued that it would be enough to expand the existing constitution with a few new provisions such as granting the vote to women. SCAP disagreed and a committee of scholars and bureaucrats was set up to consider constitutional revision. When MacArthur received its report, he told his aide, General Whitney, to draw up a model constitution to 'guide' the government. A task force of US officials spent a week doing this in the sixth-floor ballroom of the Dai-Ichi Building.

When presented with its recommendations, Japanese representatives 'appeared visibly surprised and disturbed', according to those present. The proposals included limiting the emperor to ceremonial functions, as well as stipulating that he could act only with the advice and approval of the Cabinet. Parliament, the two-house Diet, became the highest organ of state power and sole law-making organ of the state. The Cabinet would be collectively responsible to the legislature, which appointed the prime minister, who must resign with all ministers in the event of a no-confidence vote. Non-parliamentary agencies such as the Privy Council were abolished. Under Article 9, 'The Japanese people forever renounce war as a sovereign right of the nation and the threat or use of force as a means of settling international disputes.' In addition, 'Land, sea, and air forces, as well as other war potential, will never be maintained.'

The American draft provided for free choice of occupation, marriage based on mutual consent, the right of workers to organise and bargain collectively, academic freedom, free universal education, provision of public health and social security, and the right of all 'to maintain the minimum standards of wholesome and cultured living'. Local government functions were devolved. The judiciary was separated from the executive.

MacArthur told the government that if it did not accept the draft, he would put it directly to the Japanese people. On 3 November 1946, the new constitution was promulgated. While it was generally popular, many politicians were unconvinced that such major change was required. But they knew that, as representatives of a defeated nation with a bad war record, they were best advised to accept what was handed down from the Dai-Ichi Building and to wait to see whether events would turn the victors in their direction.

## IV: ECONOMY AND SECURITY

The US Secretary of the Army, Kenneth Royall, had noted in a speech at the beginning of the year that, if Japan was to achieve political stability and free government, it had to have a 'sound and self-supporting economy' so that it could 'serve as a deterrent against any other totalitarian war threats'. The US, he added, could not continue to provide hundreds of millions of dollars in aid indefinitely.

This line was pushed strongly by the Japan lobby in the US, at whose centre stood ex-Ambassador Grew and several former State Department officials who saw a revived Japanese economy with strong companies as a prerequisite for long-term peace in the Pacific. Businessmen added their voices to the call to reverse the reform course. Averell Harriman, Herbert Hoover, Truman's friendly oilman Edwin Pauley and the right-wing senator William Knowland all backed the call to help Japan grow by relaxing the reforms.[33]

MacArthur hit back by charging that ten family groups controlled 'every phase of commerce and industry' with a record of 'economic oppression and exploitation at home, aggression and spoliation abroad'. But the campaign backed by the Japan lobby in the US took on a life of its own. After a trip to Tokyo, the influential right-wing publisher of the *Chicago Tribune*, Colonel Robert McCormick, denounced SCAP's 'socialist economic policies' and switched his support for the 1948 presidential election from MacArthur to Taft. In October 1947, Joseph Keenan, the chief prosecutor at the war crimes trials, said that the business community, like the emperor, did not bear responsibility for the war.[34]

Prominent senators and congressmen complained that the occupation was proving too expensive for the US, and that economic revival was needed to provide relief for the American taxpayer. What SCAP should do, they argued, was to end the *zaibatsu*-busting and restrain labour unions. For their part, Japanese business leaders predicted economic ruin if policy did not change and, in the evolving Cold War context, some of MacArthur's aides proved susceptible to the anti-Communist arguments. 'If the deterioration of the situation in China did not seem to constitute in itself any intolerable threat to our security, what it did do was to heighten greatly the importance of what might now happen in Japan,' as Kennan wrote later. All he had to do was convince MacArthur that it was time for a change of course.

~

## MEANWHILE

- *Falsifiers of History*, personally edited by Stalin and purporting to show that the West colluded with Hitler to launch the Second World War, is published in Moscow.
- Rebels assassinate the king of Yemen and his prime minister.
- Ceylon (now Sri Lanka) gains independence from Britain. D. S. Senanayake of the United National Party becomes prime minister at the head of a coalition.
- After the flight of its ruler to Pakistan, the state of Junagadh votes by 190,000 to 91 to join India. The last British troops in India, from the Somerset Light Infantry, leave Bombay, slow-marching through the Gateway of India to the strains of 'Auld Lang Syne' and applauded by thousands of spectators.

- In Greece, heavy fighting is reported around Mount Olympus, in Western Macedonia, the north and parts of the Peloponnese. Thirteen people convicted of treason are shot in Athens and 350 suspects arrested.
- Aneurin Bevan makes a stinging attack on the doctors who had rejected his National Health Service proposals as 'a small body of raucous-voiced politically poisoned people engaged in a squalid political controversy'.
- Charles de Gaulle's daughter, Anne, who suffered from Down's syndrome and to whom he was hugely attached, dies at the age of twenty. After her funeral in the country church at Colombey-les-Deux-Églises, the general collapses at the tomb side into the arms of the parish priest.

# PART ELEVEN

# MARCH 1948

ACTS

*Masaryk dies; Marshall Plan goes to Congress; Five West European nations sign defence treaty; the Great Reversal sets in for Japan; Britain clamps down in the Gold Coast; Violence rises even further in Palestine as US wavers.*

SCENES

*Prague, Washington, London, Brussels; Tokyo; Accra; Jerusalem.*

CAST

*Masaryk, Gottwald, Beneš; Truman, Marshall; Bevin, Bidault; MacArthur, Kennan, William Draper; Danquah, Nkrumah; the Grand Mufti, Ben-Gurion.*

# DEATH OF A MINISTER

## I: Defenestration in Prague

Jan Masaryk's corpse was found at 6.30 a.m. on Wednesday 10 March in the courtyard below the Czernin Palace, the official residence of the foreign minister in Prague. Two of the staff who had been told to go to the roof to lower a ceremonial flag saw it as they came down. The body lay splayed on the frozen ground. The ankles were broken, the bones protruding. The legs were bent, but not broken, the left arm folded, the right one reaching straight out. The minister's head was bruised. His blue silk pyjamas were soiled. Under his fingernails were traces of paint and plaster. The corpse was carried on a stretcher up the three storeys of the palace to his apartment before being taken to a mortuary for an autopsy.

Senior officials arrived and went to the apartment in the lift. First was the Communist interior minister, Nosek, followed by a police inspector, a doctor and Masaryk's deputy at the Foreign Ministry, Vladimir Clementis. According to the chief criminal investigator of the Prague police force, Gottwald also came. The non-Communists present were told to leave along with the building manager and his wife.[1]

The case was declared closed after six hours. The authorities announced that the foreign minister had killed himself by jumping from the window of his bathroom. Masaryk's doctor went to see Beneš in the countryside. The president said he did not believe it was suicide.

Hundreds of thousands of people watched the state funeral the following Saturday. The cortège to the Pantheon cemetery was headed by boys and girls from the semi-military Union Defence Force, dressed in khaki uniforms. All windows along the route were kept shut on official orders. The coffin was carried on a gun carriage covered by the national flag. A bunch of snowdrops was placed by the body's right ear.

Beneš, old and tired as his arteriosclerosis grew ever more aggravated, attended the ceremony at the Pantheon with all the Cabinet before the body was taken to be buried alongside Masaryk's father and mother in the family tomb, in the village where the family had its country home. A small bronze marker for Jan was added to those of his parents bearing simply their names and the dates of their births and deaths. The Communist Clementis took over as foreign minister.[2]

Beneš thought of resigning. Instead, he decided to 'remain as President but not to function'; he ordered the national flag not to be raised outside his house. Receiving Gottwald, he said he had agreed to appoint the new government to prevent bloodshed and wanted to avoid a complete split in the nation. He disliked what the new regime was doing, but would wait and watch for the time being. During the visit, the prime minister asked him to let the flag be raised. Beneš agreed.[3]

In his speech at the Pantheon, the prime minister repeated the official line that the foreign minister had killed himself because of 'a concerted attack' from the West for having stayed on in his post after the Communist takeover the previous month. The death had come 'like lightning out of a clear sky', he went on. 'We can never forgive the foreign enemies of the Republic for this.' As far as the authorities were concerned, the case was closed. Files on the death were kept sealed in Prague and Moscow.[4]

Masaryk's British friend, Robert Bruce Lockhart, who had speculated several times that he might kill himself, thought he had committed suicide because 'he could no longer bear seeing all that his father created being ruthlessly destroyed'. The dead man's secretary, Antonín Sum, said later that the minister had 'offered his life' in 'a very, very great sacrifice ... to protest against the Communist terror. He had to show so that everybody – especially the Western powers – could see that things were in very bad shape; that the Communist coup was a very bad sign for all of Europe.'

Attlee issued a statement saying Masaryk was 'essentially a lover of freedom and it may well be that he could not endure to live in the suffocating atmosphere of totalitarianism when all that he had striven for was being ruthlessly destroyed'. Marshall stated that Czechoslovakia was under a 'reign of terror' and Truman called the death 'a dramatic symbol of the tragic end of freedom in his nation', which fell into a pattern of tightening Soviet control in the east that looked like the beginning of a Russian 'big push'.[5]

Observers had noted that the foreign minister had appeared older than his sixty-one years ever since the visit to Moscow the previous July. The *Guardian* correspondent who interviewed him a few days before his death wrote that 'weariness characterized his former jovial self', though added that suicide would have been 'a negation of his whole life's work'. The tightening of Communist control gave him every reason for despair. Nationalisation was extended. Refugees flooded over the borders. Independent politicians and senior figures were ruthlessly purged. Non-Communists were expelled from the Journalists' Association. Churchill Square in Prague was renamed Trade Union Square. The ambassador to Washington resigned in protest at the way his country had become 'a fully totalitarian state'.[6]

In his last weeks, Masaryk had been accompanied everywhere by two Interior Ministry guards. He had little privacy; and was not allowed to see official visitors alone. His office and rooms were certainly bugged. 'Every statement he had made in the last two weeks was censored. Masaryk was a prisoner in every sense of the word,' the *Guardian* correspondent reported. The British ambassador, Pierson Dixon, wrote privately that Masaryk had been 'suffering from the torture after joining the new government. 'The lamps of civilization are really extinguished here,' he added in a letter to Bruce Lockhart.[7]

The minister had been shaken by a visit to Beneš at his country home on the first weekend of the month, during which he told the president he planned to leave the country. When he called on Marcia Davenport that evening, he described Beneš as 'totally broken, his tenure of the presidency a phantasm'. His own face, she recalled, was 'absolutely ghastly'. He told her she should leave the country to avoid being arrested as a foreign agent. He had money salted away abroad. They would marry and go to live in Arizona. She was reluctant and he relented.

As he left her home, she helped him put on his loose brown over-coat. 'God bless,' he said, walking down the stairs after donning his flat-crowned, floppy-brimmed hat. In the street, two guards fell into place behind him. Crossing the road in the lamplight, he looked back at the window from which she was looking out. She watched until he disappeared from view, his head bent, the two leather-jacketed men tracking him.[8]

The next day, Davenport changed her mind and left for London with her daughter. When she heard of Jan's death, she broke down. 'He made me come here, and now I know that, if I had stayed, he would still be living,' she told Bruce Lockhart when he visited her in her suite at Claridge's. 'My life is finished. I am forty-five. People talk about hair turning grey in a night – look at mine.' The visitor could see no sign of greying but noted in his diary, 'She seemed suddenly an old woman.' She moved to an old rectory in the Thames Valley where she put two photographs of Jan in the drawing room.[9]

## II: Murder most likely

From the start, the official version of Masaryk's death was open to question. He had reacted to news of the attempted suicide of the former justice minister Prokop Drtina by describing killing oneself as 'a very poor escape' since there was no guarantee of success. Given that, why had Masaryk, a man known to shrink from physical pain, thrown himself to his death rather than taking an overdose of the sleeping pills by his bedside? Why had this physically large man chosen the small window in the bathroom, rather than the larger window in the bedroom? Why had the body been found five feet away from the trajectory from the bathroom? Why had the snowdrops been placed beside his head in the open coffin? To conceal a bullet wound or injury, perhaps? What was the explanation for the paint and plaster under his fingernails or for the scratches on his body?

On the night he died, Masaryk had changed into pyjamas after returning to his official apartment, saying he had a cold, was feeling tired and planned to work in bed on a foreign policy speech. He ate a dinner of cold roast chicken, potatoes and salad on a tray, told his butler how much he enjoyed the food and settled in bed with a big writing pad and glasses of beer and mineral water on the night table, together with his father's bible. After asking to be called at 8.30 a.m., he took two sedatives.[10]

The condition of his apartment, which was not made public, told of a struggle. The bedroom was a shambles – chairs overturned, broken bottles, glasses and a cup on the floor, the bed a mess, sheets torn off. The ashtray was full of stubs of different brands of cigarettes. In the green-tiled bathroom, the floor was scattered with broken glass and razor blades, and the contents of the medicine chest. The towels lay in crumpled heaps. A pillow was in the bathtub. The lavatory bowl was filthy. Excrement was smeared on the windowsill. A cord made of pyjama drawstrings hung from a hook on the door.[11]

When journalist Claire Sterling investigated the case during the relaxation of the Prague Spring of 1968, she found that the wife of the building manager had spoken of a big, blue bruise on the dead man's forehead. As she bent to kiss his head, she saw a little hole behind his ear with dried blood around it. When she cried out, 'What is this?', the police doctor told her and other staff to get lost. Masaryk's doctor was convinced it was murder to stop him leaving the country. A string of witnesses were arrested and several were executed by the new regime. The police doctor expired after administering an injection on himself for his lumbago with a syringe that was unaccountably full of poison.[12]

As proposed by Sterling, Masaryk's death seems to have come about as follows:

Two men climb over the garden wall of the palace in the early hours, slip in through an unguarded door and go up to the apartment – a dozen points of entry by stairways, passages and a lift make access easy. The guard in the courtyard is asleep. The attackers wake the minister and try to persuade him that he should jump out of the window, smoking as they do so and filling the ashtray with cigarette stubs. Masaryk refuses.

The two attackers try to force him through the bedroom window but he resists. The three of them wrestle, overturning furniture and smashing bottles, and fighting on into the bathroom. Masaryk clutches at the wall, getting paint under his nails. Somebody collides with the medicine cabinet, sending its contents tumbling out. The attackers get the minister into the bathtub where they hold a pillow over his face and he weakens. Finally, they manage to haul him to the window and throw him out, after which they leave as silently as they arrived, having hung the pyjama drawstring cord in the bathroom to heighten the belief that the foreign minister was planning to do away with himself.[13]

CHAPTER THIRTY-SIX

# CRITICAL SITUATION

## I: Cornerstone of European unity

On 1 March, Truman sent the European Recovery Program bill to the Senate to start its legislative passage, which ended at the end of the month as the House of Representatives added its assent. The president, who had just declared that he would run for re-election, delivered an address to a joint session of Congress in which he said he was 'sure that the determination of the free countries of Europe to protect themselves will be matched by an equal determination on our part to help them protect themselves'. Events in Czechoslovakia, he added, had 'sent a shock through the civilized world' and highlighted the 'critical situation in Europe today'. 'The free nations are drawing closer together for their economic well-being and for the common defence of their liberties', the president noted.

Soviet pressure on Finland to sign a treaty aroused worries about Scandinavia. In Greece, the Communist rebels were actively supported by Communist neighbours. In Italy, where parliamentary elections were due the following month, Truman wrote that 'a determined and aggressive effort is being made by a Communist minority to take control ... the methods vary but the pattern is all too clear'.[1]

Bidault wrote twice to Marshall 'to point out to him that the Soviet menace now threatened the whole of Western Europe. The Russian armies were only 200 kilometres from the Rhine, so 'it was absolutely necessary for us to have a formal agreement with America to provide a force to help us re-establish our threatened security'.[2] With that in mind, the Frenchman joined Bevin in pressing for an extension of the Dunkirk Treaty between their two countries. Representatives of Britain, France, Belgium, the Netherlands and Luxembourg opened talks in Brussels on 4 March.

Thirteen days later, they signed a treaty which represented a significant evolution from the earlier bilateral agreement. That Franco-British accord had been simply to guard against a revival of the threat from Germany; the signatories to the new five-nation pact also had Germany in mind but their main concern was to provide collective security against the Soviet Union. The five-party accord contained cultural and social clauses, and provided for a Consultative Council which could foster political association.[3]

Bidault hailed the treaty as 'the cornerstone of European unity'. In a speech to Parliament in Paris, he said the time had come 'for us to do all we can as quickly as possible to persuade what remains of Europe to get together'. He tied together the economic and security aspects of the developing Western system which France sought to extend through a bilateral customs union with Italy, though progress on Germany was held back by the opposition of Gaullists, Communists and some other leading politicians to any revival of the enemy of three wars.[4]

The Cold War was rapidly deepening. 'Each side now believed it was time to put its house in order,' as historian Charles Maier put it. Though an exception such as Finland could maintain a democratic regime while keeping up a wary relationship with Moscow, other countries had to choose between east and west – or have the choice made for them. Had Stalin been ready to permit political pluralism, as was the case in Western countries with strong Communist parties, the US might have felt less need to intervene across the Atlantic, but that was not the case, and the reaction of the world's most powerful nation was inevitable once it had turned its back on isolationism.[5]

The USSR's web of 'friendship treaties' with military clauses took in Bulgaria, Romania, Hungary and Finland. Moscow put pressure on Norway to sign a non-aggression pact, though the prime minister, Einar Gerhardsen, pledged to 'fight the Communists by democratic means and spiritual weapons'. The Soviet-sponsored German People's Congress held its second conference in East Berlin to coincide with the hundredth anniversary of the revolution of 1848. Attended by 1,898 delegates, 512 of them from the west, it rejected the Marshall Plan and repeated the call for national reunification while accepting the new frontier with Poland. A People's Council was elected; three-quarters of its four hundred members came from the east. In a clear move towards creating a separate state, a Constitutional Committee, chaired by Grotewohl, was established to draft a constitution for a German Democratic Republic.

In Washington, Robert Lovett was presented with a proposal for the creation of a new currency for the western occupation zones of Germany to replace the old Reichsmark and the barter economy. Seen as essential for economic revival, it would clearly mark a new step in the division of the country and the end of any co-operation there between the West and the Soviets. 'Better act fast,' the Under Secretary scribbled on the proposal.[6]

In London, delegates from the US, UK and France met in snowy weather to discuss the establishment of a devolved political authority in Germany. They did not invite the Soviets. The reaction was swift. Moscow said its absence meant that the meeting was a violation of the Potsdam agreement. Marshal Vasily Sokolovsky, deputy chief of Soviet forces in East Germany, walked out of a session of the Allied Control Council in Berlin, preventing it from operating. Soviet control of transport routes into the former German capital was tightened – no formal provision had been made between the Allies for free access to the city from the west. The path was laid to the biggest Cold War confrontation to date.[7]

## II: Cossacks in Brest

The sombre atmosphere was underlined by the cable from Lucius Clay saying that he and his staff had detected 'a worrisome shift in Soviet attitudes' and warning that war could come at any time and 'with dramatic suddenness'. The general said later that he wrote in response to a request from the army in Washington for helpful information to support a request to Congress to approve selective conscription as military chiefs grew concerned about a cut in spending and the rundown of their forces, despite their growing global mission. But, coming after events in Czechoslovakia, the impact of his warning was significant when the message was leaked to the press, even if Kennan considered that the Russians were already unable to meet their commitments.[8]

The atmosphere in Europe was certainly growing ever more tense. Looking back, Clay recalled that Soviet officers showed 'a new attitude, faintly contemptuous, slightly arrogant and certainly assured'. Returning to the political fray after the death of his beloved daughter, de Gaulle spoke of an invasion from the east with 'Cossacks reaching Brest'. 'I am quite simply frightened,' the English author Nancy Mitford wrote from her home in Paris to her friend, Evelyn Waugh. 'I wake up in the night sometimes in a cold sweat. Thank goodness for having no children, I can take a pill and say goodbye.'[9]

The confrontation between Gaullists and Communists ratcheted up once more with street clashes and rumours of Soviet arms drops in Lyons. The general's followers offered prefects 'shock troops'. Schuman and Moch laid plans to outlaw the Communist Party and arrest its leaders if it launched a new offensive on the state. Duclos thundered against the Gaullist 'illegal and fascist paramilitary organization aimed at the establishment of a dictatorship'. The PCF formed 'action committees' in industry, farming, films and aviation to defend national independence and oppose 'Anglo-American imperialism'.[10]

At the United Nations, the chief soviet delegate, Andrei Gromyko, described criticism of events in Czechoslovakia as 'old rubbish taken from Goebbels' kitchen of propaganda'. In Italy, where the Communists had scored well in municipal elections in February and the left organised demonstrations for an Easter wage bonus, the CIA worked to help the Christian Democrats on the ground and fuelled money to non-Communist parties. In Germany, the devolution of authority to local politicians in the West was pushed ahead when a Christian Democrat, Hermann Pünder, was elected director of the Administrative Council for the US–UK Bizone; he got forty votes from his party members but forty-eight Social Democrats and Communist members abstained.[11]

# KILLINGS AND POLITICS

## I: SEE WEIZMANN!

In Washington, the president was growing increasingly fed up with the contradictory pressures on him over Palestine. Forty governors and more than half the Congress signed petitions calling for the creation of a Jewish state. Thirty-three state legislatures passed resolutions in the same vein. Democratic Party managers warned Truman that if he did not 'give in' on Palestine, he could expect the delegates from New York to oppose his nomination for re-election. Hundreds of thousands of postcards from Jewish groups flooded the White House – Truman said he had them burned without reading them. A stream of letters to the State Department demanded the dismissal of the senior official Henderson Loy for being pro-Arab.[1]

The president refused to see Zionist spokesmen or to have another meeting with Chaim Weizmann. 'Individuals and groups asked me, usually in rather quarrelsome and emotional ways, to stop the Arabs, to keep the British from supporting the Arabs, to furnish American soldiers, to do this, that, and the other,' Truman wrote in his memoirs. Countervailing pressure continued from the State Department. Marshall told the National Security Council the US was 'playing with fire while having nothing with which to put it out'. Forrestal repeated his argument that the Arabs would push out the Jews and that America's interest lay with their oil.[2]

On 13 March, Truman's old Jewish haberdashery partner, Eddie Jacobson from Kansas City, walked into the White House. He had been telephoned in the middle of the night by an American Zionist leader and told to go to New York to meet Weizmann, who was ill in the Waldorf Astoria Hotel after being brought across the Atlantic. 'We took this man [Jacobson] to Weizmann and his head spun with awe and respect,' Abba Eban of the Jewish Agency Delegation to the UN recalled. 'We explained to him "You have to say only one thing to the President; See Weizmann!" We told him "Eddie, don't get involved in arguments! Concentrate on one thing. There is an old man, a great man, who has devoted his entire life to this dream. And fairness demands that you listen to him!"'[3]

At the White House, an aide told Jacobson the president was seeing him on condition he did not mention Palestine. It was Saturday and the building was largely empty. The two men chatted about their families. Truman asked about his friend's business, and then enquired as to what brought him to Washington.

'Harry, you know me,' Jacobson replied. 'I'm no diplomat. I don't know how to beat around the bush. Please. I want you to talk to Dr Weizmann.'

'You what! I can't believe this,' the president exploded. 'Despite my objection, you dare ask that I see Weizmann?'

'Well, Mr President, at least I honored your request. I didn't mention Palestine.'

Truman grew tense and grim faced, speaking in a hard, abrupt way, angry at how Jacobson was being used. He complained how 'disrespectful and mean' some Jews had been towards him and said he would leave Palestine to the United Nations. 'Eddie, I'm fed up,' he added. 'I'm sick and tired of Zionists who think they can tell me what to do. They will eventually prejudice everyone trying to help them.' Then he repeated his sour reflection that 'If Jesus couldn't please them when he was on earth, how can you or anyone else expect me to have any luck?' Jacobson reflected that his 'dear friend ... was at that moment as close to being an anti-Semite as a man could possibly be'.

The visitor tried to argue back but got nowhere. Then he had a brainwave. Pointing to a bronze figure of Truman's hero, Andrew Jackson, he said that he, too, had a hero: Weizmann, 'the greatest Jew who ever lived'. 'He is a very sick man, almost broken in health, but he travelled thousands of miles just to see you and plead the cause of my people,' Jacobson said. 'Now you refuse to see him just because you are insulted by some of our American Jewish leaders, even though you know that Weizmann had absolutely nothing to do with these insults and would be the last man to be party to them. It doesn't sound like you, Harry, because I thought you could take this stuff they have been handing out.'[4]

Wheeling round in his chair, the president stared out into the garden. There was silence for what, to Jacobson, seemed 'like centuries', then, turning back to face the room, Truman said, 'You win, you bald-headed son of a bitch. I will see him.' Jacobson left the White House and walked to the Statler Hotel, where, for the first time in his life, he knocked back a double bourbon.[5]

Weizmann arrived in Washington five days later. He entered the White House by a side door in the late evening. The State Department was not told of the meeting. Even Marshall was kept in the dark. The conversation went on for three-quarters of an hour. The president assured the visitor the US would support partition.

## II: Amazing reversal

Events quickly outran the president and the Zionists. During a break in Key West earlier in the month, Truman had seemed to go along with a reversal of policy to back a trusteeship for Palestine. Not having been informed of the meeting with Weizmann, the State Department announced through Warren Austin, the ambassador at the United Nations, that America was withdrawing its support for partition and advocating a temporary UN trusteeship. Among permanent Security Council members, France and China expressed their agreement.

There was an immediate outcry. The Jewish Agency rejected even temporary trusteeship and announced that the new state would be established on 16 May. 'We are at an utter loss to understand the reason for this amazing reversal,' the head of its team at the UN said. Protest petitions, cables and letters flooded into the White House. Eleanor Roosevelt submitted her resignation from the UN delegation (which was refused). In the Middle East, Arabs were jubilant and

Jews depressed – Irgun denounced American 'treachery'. In Kansas City, though Weizmann urged him by telephone to have confidence in the president, Jacobson called the day 'Black Friday' and took to his bed for the weekend.

Truman learned of Austin's speech when he read the morning newspapers at 6 a.m. 'This morning I find that the State Dept. has reversed my Palestine polity,' he wrote in his diary. 'The first I know about it is what I see in the papers! Isn't that hell? I am now in the position of a liar and a double-crosser . . . There are people on the 3rd and 4th levels of the State Dept. who always wanted to cut my throat. They are succeeding in doing it.' He told Clifford that Weizmann 'must think I'm a shitass'.[6]

Marshall was on the West Coast where he told a press conference he had recommended the change, thinking it the wisest course. By the time he went to the White House on 22 March, the president had calmed down, acknolwedging that he had agreed to back trusteeship while at Key West but adding that it was only a temporary expedient. He could but be unhappy at the way State had ignored his instruction to consult him, but could not disown the new position without disavowing the man he said he most admired, and risking the secretary's resignation. So he prevaricated, continuing support for enlarged Jewish immigration and seeking to keep open the partition option, though he acknowledged at a press conference that it 'cannot be carried out by peaceful means'.[7]

## III: Bombs, assaults and sniping

That was self-evident as fighting escalated around Jerusalem. The Grand Mufti's militia tightened its blockade of the 100,000 Jews in the city who were in a perilous position given their dependence on Arab villages for food and water. Arabs set up a roadblock at the Jaffa Gate – the British agreed to bring supplies through another entrance to the Jewish quarter, checking packages for arms. The Mufti's nephew, Abd al-Qadir al-Husanyi, grasped that the best strategy lay in cutting Jewish communications lines. 'He exploited our weak points to the maximum,' the Haganah chief operations officer, Yigael Yadin, recalled. 'He was everywhere. He was our most dangerous enemy.'

Snipers concealed behind trees ambushed Jewish convoys on the narrow, poorly paved road to Jerusalem as they navigated the ascent from the valley with steep inclines and forests on either side. One attack killed fourteen people in a convoy from Nablus while another trapped nineteen vehicles. 'The convoy was in flames,' one driver recalled. 'Drivers jumped from their burning trucks and were killed in the ditches. The armoured vehicles returned fire. Through this hell, I began to advance and suddenly, right in front of me, a vehicle went over a mine and was blown into the air.'[8]

The Haganah fitted as many vehicles as it could with armoured plating, though the inclusion of steel in a US arms embargo on the region made this difficult. It used a light aircraft for reconnaissance. Ben-Gurion reorganised Haganah forces around the crack Golani and Carmeli brigades, and made military training obligatory for all Jews. Refugee ships continued to arrive and their passengers to be turned away; nearly a thousand were taken off a vessel called *Builders and Fighters* and shipped to Cyprus. In contrast, Jews pointed out the infiltration of Arab volunteers and mercenaries – the Army of Liberation even advertised its presence by inviting foreign correspondents to its bases.

In a secret move, the commander, Fawzi al-Qawuqji, invited a Jewish Agency official, Joshua Palmon, to visit to his headquarters. As they sipped coffee, al-Qawuqji dismissed the Mufti's officers as 'corrupt, bandits, not worthy to be called soldiers' and whispered to his guest, 'If you kill them, I will not intervene.' When Palmon suggested an agreement for their armies to refrain from attacking one another, the Arab general agreed – on condition that his forces were allowed to score a face-saving victory. Palmon objected that, if attacked, the Jews would have to fight back, to which al-Qawuqji smiled and said, 'Don't worry' – it would be just for show.[9]

Azzam Pasha of the Arab League appealed secretly to Britain to extend the deadline for its withdrawal from Palestine, but the Attlee government was determined to quit on schedule in May. Though some troops had already started to leave, the UK still refused to hand over responsibility for running Palestine to anybody else. A UN commission was not allowed to visit the territory. Its request for an international force to implement decisions by the world body met with no response.[10]

Increasingly confident Arab forces staged manoeuvres in the hills around Jerusalem, impressing foreign observers who thought they would win the conflict. To relieve the tightening siege of the city, the Jewish Agency decided to switch to offensive operations to capture the positions from which Arabs were launching attacks. It might seem a mad policy, Yigael Yadin of Haganah said later, 'but many things that appear mad at first glance develop into a situation where there is no other choice'.[11]

CHAPTER THIRTY-EIGHT

# THE GREAT REVERSAL

## I: THE FIVE Rs

The day after he arrived in Tokyo, Kennan attended the first of a series of briefings from MacArthur's staff. They told him nothing new. So, that evening, he sat down in his hotel room and wrote a note to the general thanking him for the briefings but adding that he has 'questions of some moment which I was under instructions to discuss personally with him and about which I would be expected to have enquired his opinion by personal consultations'.

What he got was another day of briefings followed by a conversation with one of MacArthur's aides and an invitation to deliver a lecture to senior staff at SCAP. It was only after this that the general received him for an evening meeting. At this, MacArthur recognised the need to modify some of the occupation policies but said he was worried about encountering opposition from other members of the Far Eastern Commission – Kennan must have known how the pro-consul rode roughshod over them as a matter of course. MacArthur restated his view that Okinawa was a vital element in the US security umbrella. He agreed that economic recovery should be a primary goal but complained that other nations in East Asia were adopting a 'shameless selfish and negative' attitude towards Japan. As for 'academic theorizers of a left-wing variety' on his staff, he thought they were few in number and did not do much harm.[1]

The changes in occupation policies that were now required were related to the objective of the economic rehabilitation of Japan and 'the restoration of her ability to contribute constructively to the stability and prosperity of the Far Eastern region', the visitor recalled. The defeated enemy could become the eastern end of a great crescent arching down to South East Asia and up to India. This geo-strategic view, which included Korea on the edge, did not flow from the surrender as such and so MacArthur and the US government could act independently of the Allied commission. At that, the general slapped his thigh approvingly and the meeting ended.[2]

American policy on Japan had, in fact, begun to shift from the previous summer, when the cotton, rayon and fishing industries were allowed to expand. A steady stream of other measures followed as the course modification urged by the Japan lobby came into effect. A $100 million fund was established by the US to finance cotton credit. Reparations shipments to China ceased after some equipment and warships had been sent and trade between the two countries resumed, provoking street protests in China against imports from the former enemy.

Conversations began between Japanese firms and foreign businesses. To move away from dependence on US food aid, the country began to export to accumulate the foreign exchange needed to buy supplies. The national gold reserves worth $137 million were put at the disposal of the SCAP command in Tokyo to be used to build up industries that would produce goods to be sold abroad. A fund was set up to extend loans for reconstruction. Production of steel and iron was allowed to reach the 1934–5 level.

Kennan might have determined what changes were wanted in policy towards Japan but he recognised that 'in no respect was Japan at that time in a position to shoulder and to bear successfully the responsibilities of independence that could be expected to flow at once from a treaty of peace'. The country was disarmed. Occupation costs were absorbing a third of the budget.

In contrast to the positive spin generated by MacArthur's public relations machine, the visitor feared that the way SCAP had implemented changes were leading to 'a high degree of instability in Japanese life in general'. He found 'great confusion' arising from land reform while the break-up of big industrial groups, which he said had been conducted with 'almost wild enthusiasm', had produced uncertainty that undermined management. Reparations deliveries to other Asian countries were damaging the economy.

The purges in government, education and business meant that 'important elements of Japanese society essential to its constructive development were being driven underground [and had] brought Japanese life to a point of great turmoil and confusion'. The ideological concepts on which these measures rested bore a very close resemblance to Soviet views about the evils of 'capitalist monopolies', he added, and 'their relation to the interests of Japanese recovery was less apparent'.[3]

Viewing his diagnosis through a Cold War lens, Kennan felt Japan would suffer from 'a high degree of vulnerability to Communist pressure' if the occupation ended. The weakness of the police and lack of counter-intelligence meant that 'it was difficult to imagine a setup more favourable and inviting from the standpoint of the prospects for a Communist takeover'. To avoid this, the three Ds of the initial reform programme were to be replaced by the five Rs of reconstructing the economy, restraining labour, rehabilitating people driven from their jobs because of their wartime records, rearming a security force and realigning Japan with the West.

On his return to Washington, Kennan sent Marshall a report which was then accepted by the Far Eastern division of the State Department. Looking back, he wrote that its effect was, apart from the Marshall Plan, the most significant constructive contribution he made to government.

The regime of control by SCAP over the Japanese government should, I recommended, be relaxed. The Japanese should be encouraged to develop independent responsibility. No further reform legislation should be pressed. The emphasis should shift from reform to economic recovery. The purges should be tempered, tapered off, and terminated at an early date.

An effort should be made to reduce occupation costs. Reparations should be generally halted, the opposition of the other Far Eastern Commission powers notwithstanding. The settlement of property claims should be expedited.

Meanwhile, we should not press for a peace treaty. Precedence should be given, for the time being, to the task of bringing the Japanese into a position where they would be better able to shoulder the burdens of independence ... Pending conclusion of a treaty, we should retain tactical forces in Japan; but their numbers, their cost to the Japanese, and their adverse impact on Japanese life and economy should be reduced to a minimum.[4]

As for regional strategy, Okinawa, which was not regarded as being under Japanese sovereignty, should be the centre for US air power. Combined with the fleet, this would serve to 'prevent the assembling and launching of any amphibious force from any mainland port in east-central or northeast Asia'. No bases would be set up in Japan and the Philippines, 'provided that they remain entirely demilitarized and that no other power made any effort to obtain strategic facilities on them'. From this position, the US could seek to influence events on the mainland of Asia but would not regard any area there as vital, Kennan added.[5]

This policy appeared to answer Washington's desire to guarantee its security in the Western Pacific while limiting its commitment. But it assumed that the Japanese would be happy to see Okinawa designated as an American protectorate and overlooked the importance of Korea for Japan. There was also the question of the US military presence – the navy staff estimated that three aircraft carriers would be needed, but budget cuts meant that only one was available while the army's strength was also being reduced. Kennan's approach also underplayed the importance of regional supply links for Japan, with its lack of resources and loss of empire.[6] Still, it won wide acceptance – MacArthur announced it as US policy the following year, not including Korea in the defensive line running between Japan and the Philippines.[7]

During Kennan's visit, the urbane Liberal Party politician, Hitoshi Ashida, became prime minister at the head of a coalition of Democratic and Socialist parties which continued the classic SCAP line by saying it would fight 'the remnants of feudalistic bureaucratism'. But he allied himself with the shift in economic policy which was given added impetus by the presence of a delegation headed by William Draper, the under secretary of the army, a former investment

banker who had served on Clay's staff in Germany. Sitting in on
Kennan's third meeting with MacArthur, Draper mentioned the
possibility that Japan should be allowed a 'small defensive force',
but his main concerns were economic. He was disturbed by the cost
of the occupation, the scale of reparations, the campaign against big
businesses, the impact on productive capacity and high inflation.[8]

The delegation accompanying him urged Washington to make a
strenuous effort to rebuild industrial output and stop demanding reparations from Japan. Privately, Draper made it clear that he thought
some of MacArthur's staff were overzealous and naïve. The administration responded by putting through a $150 million appropriation
for Japanese economic rehabilitation. The bargaining rights of the
2.5 million government employees were restricted.[9]

MacArthur agreed to the creation of a De-concentration Review
Board, which exempted hundreds of companies from the decartelisation measures. The original list of 325 firms to be broken up was
winnowed down to nine, and the number of subsidiaries big groups
had to dispose of was significantly reduced. Nor was any action
taken when enterprises started to 'de-purge' managers. While the
pacifist element of the constitution remained sacrosanct, MacArthur
ordered the formation of a National Police Reserve of 75,000 men
equipped with M-1 rifles, machine guns, mortars, flame-throwers,
artillery and tanks – and with American advisers. Given China's
weakness, the Cold War had produced a reversal of policy as radical
as that in Germany and with equal repercussions for global development felt to our day.

# CHAPTER THIRTY-NINE

# EVERY OPPORTUNITY

After nearly two weeks of rioting in Ghana, the British took action on 11 March, by which time the upheaval had claimed twenty-nine lives with 237 injured. The commercial district of Accra was in ruins. Colonial policy faced a major test.

An order was issued for the arrest of six leading members of the anti-colonial convention and their removal to the north of the country pending the arrival from London of a Commission of Inquiry. J. B. Danquah and Kwame Nkrumah were among the six. Having been taken by surprise by the unrest, the authorities declared that the trouble had been the work of Nationalists who, while ostensibly seeking self-government by constitutional methods, were, in fact, revolutionaries. A document was produced on the existence of a group called The Circle, alleged to have been organised by Nkrumah to conduct civil disobedience, boycotts and strikes while binding members together with secret signs, fast days and threats of reprisal against traitors.[1]

The Commission found that the disturbances were planned but produced no evidence as to by whom. Steered by a progressive civil servant, Andrew Cohen,[2] it saw the violence as evidence of the need for more political enfranchisement. 'The constitution and government must be so reshaped as to give every African of ability an opportunity to help govern the country,' its report said. 'In all appointments or promotions in the public services the first question to be asked is: Is there an African capable of filling the appointment?'[3]

The arrests raised the Convention's profile while the sergeant killed at the start of the violence became an icon for Nationalists. Nkrumah was the hero of the 'veranda boys' – young men who slept outside the homes of the rich because they could not afford accommodation of their own. The divide widened between him and more cautious self-government advocates epitomised by Danquah.

Nkrumah went on to set up his own movement, the Convention People's Party, to press for a more radical course, while Danquah and his colleagues stepped up their co-operation with the tribal chiefs who had reacted to the riots by sending a message of loyalty to the king in London and had turned on the young radicals. The British would offer a new constitution and increased devolution of authority (within strict limits) leading to an election in 1951, after which Nkrumah became prime minister within a day of being released from prison by the British.

The riots and the jailing of the six Nationalists marked a watershed in the history of the colony, which was to become the first British possession in Africa to gain independence in 1957, with Nkrumah as its leader. Danquah was detained subsequently on subversion charges before dying of a heart attack in 1965. Nkrumah was deposed by a coup the following year after which Danquah was given a national funeral and rehabilitated.

~

## MEANWHILE

- Bao Dai accepts the creation of a 'provisional central government' for Vietnam under the control of General Nguyen Van Xuan, whom he neither likes nor trusts.
- Negotiations between the Indian government and Hyderabad break down. The nizam rejects the idea of a Constituent Assembly with a non-Muslim majority and Delhi turns down any compromise for fear of contagion to other states.
- The US Supreme Court rules that religious instruction in public schools violates the constitution.
- Singapore holds its first election.
- Civil war breaks out in Costa Rica.

- Statistics show that the US birth rate rose by 50 per cent between 1940 and 1947; 'obstetricians and maternity wards are over-worked,' the London *Times* reports.
- *Gentleman's Agreement*, depicting anti-Semitism, wins the Oscar for Best Picture, while James Baskett becomes the first Afro-American to win an award for his portrayal of Uncle Remus in the Disney film *Song of the South* – because of his colour, he was barred from the film's premier in Georgia.
- The world's longest locomotive, measuring 154 feet, goes into service on the Chesapeake and Ohio Railway, powered by electric motors on its axles.
- The Hells Angels motorcycle gang is formed in California.

# PART TWELVE

# APRIL 1948

## ACTS

*The Cold War deepens in Europe and Korea;
Yugoslavia and the USSR fall out; Italy chooses between
Christian Democracy and Communism; tension rises
in Berlin; the woes of the Chinese government escalate;
Korea divides; battles, ambushes, massacres and flight
mark Palestine as the British Mandate nears its end.*

## SCENES

*Washington; Belgrade, Moscow; Italy, Berlin; Seoul,
Pyongyang, Jeju Island; Deir Yassin, Jerusalem, Jaffa.*

## CAST

*Truman, Stalin, Tito; De Gasperi, Togliatti; Syngman
Rhee, Kim Il-sung, John Hodge; Begin, Ben-Gurion,
Abd al-Qadir al-Husseini, Fawzi al-Qawuqji,
Amichai Paglin.*

CHAPTER FORTY

# WHERE NEXT?

## I: GUIDEPOSTS TO WAR

The spring of 1948 was a time of high anxiety in Europe and Washington. A sense of perpetual crisis installed itself in the Truman administration as it pushed ahead with the European Recovery Program. Events in Czechoslovakia were 'only one more guidepost on the road to war', Robert Lovett noted. 'WHERE NEXT?' asked the headline to a front-page map of Europe in the *Washington Post* with arrows pointing at France, Italy, Austria and Finland. 'A general stiffening of morale in Free Europe is needed,' wrote the chief of the Office of European Affairs, John Hickerson. Marshall agreed.[1]

The administration proposed a $3 billion increase in the military budget and decided on a rapid build-up of the atomic arsenal. The army secretary asked for a report on how long it would take to transport atom bombs to the Mediterranean. Senior State Department officials and West European diplomats discussed a joint defence structure to build on the five-nation Brussels agreement. (Moscow was kept informed by a participant from the British embassy, the spy Donald Maclean.) Bevin advised firmness but also 'a determination not to be provoked into any ill-considered action'. A Foreign Office memorandum recorded his feeling that the Soviets 'intend to do all they can to wreck the ERP and to cause us the greatest political embarrassment everywhere, but without pushing things to the extreme of war. The danger of course is that they may miscalculate and involve themselves in a situation from which they cannot retreat.'[2]

White House aides reckoned that the increased tension should help the president in his re-election bid. The report on the political outlook by Clark Clifford earlier in the year had noted that 'in times of crises the American citizens tend to back up the President. On the issue of policy toward Russia, President Truman is comparatively invulnerable to attack because of his brilliant appointment of General Marshall, who has convinced the public that as Secretary of State he is nonpartisan and above politics.'[3]

Truman certainly needed all the help he could get. He seemed tired and worn, telling a journalist he felt 'walled in'. His ratings dropped and the Democrats lost a by-election in a normally safe part of New York. Henry Wallace posed an electoral threat from the left. Furious at the president's support for civil rights, Dixiecrats from the South were lining up a challenger for the nominating convention in July. New Dealers compared him unfavourably with Roosevelt. One of their most outspoken members, Harold Ickes, wrote to Truman that he had 'the choice of retiring voluntarily and with dignity, or of being driven out of office by a disillusioned and indignant citizenry'. A movement to get Eisenhower to run as the Democrat candidate drew increasing support, even though nobody knew if the general was any more ready to represent the party than he had been to be drafted by the Republicans.[4]

Alleged scandals swirled around some of the president's cronies; Truman's doctor and his oilman associate, Edwin Pauley, were accused of speculating in commodities, a practice he had condemned. The Republicans pushed a tax-cutting bill through Congress. Arthur Krock, head of the *New York Times* bureau in Washington, opined that 'the President's influence is weaker than any President's has been in modern history'. There was a noisy controversy over his plan to build a balcony on the White House, which had to begin a thorough rebuilding programme after the discovery of structural weaknesses, including weak beams whose collapse could have precipitated the president in his bath into the Blue Room below.[5]

Still, Congress approved the first $6 billion tranche of the ERP. Signing the bill, the president called it a 'momentous occasion in the world's quest for an enduring peace'. In London, Attlee expressed 'deep gratitude at this act of unparalleled generosity and statesmanship'. Bevin and Bidault issued a joint statement calling it 'a signal demonstration of statesmanship'.[6]

A Gallup poll reported that only 17 per cent of Americans opposed the programme. In the UK, one person in five had not heard of it, but among those who had, the approval rating was 80 per cent. The Organization for European Economic Co-operation (OEEC) was established with its headquarters in Paris. Paul Hoffman, the Republican head of the Studebaker automobile company, was appointed as ERP administrator: Washington wanted the programme to be headed by a businessman and chose a marketing expert with a taste for cheeseburgers who held that selling was 'the process of transferring a conviction from the mind of the seller to that of the buyer' and that 'You industrialize by building markets.'[7]

Harriman became ambassador at large for Foreign Economic Co-operation and attended the first session of the OEEC to oversee the collaborative process the Marshall Plan was intended to foster. The parsimonious multimillionaire installed his office in the gilded one-time Parisian residence of Talleyrand on the Place de la Concorde, surrounded by eager young bureaucrats working in parallel with planners under Jean Monnet as they evolved schemes to revive the economy of Western Europe, starting with the creation of a coal and steel community linking France and Germany. The Americans were, literally clean-cut; the personnel officer refused to hire anybody with a beard.

On the other side of the Iron Curtain, the Czechoslovak government signed a friendship and mutual assistance treaty, including military clauses, with Bulgaria. Receiving the new Soviet ambassador, Beneš spoke of their two nations being 'imbued with the desire to strengthen European peace and security'. Gottwald said the purge that had dismissed more than 8,000 officials must continue, because 'reaction has not been destroyed'.

The workers' militia was turned into an auxiliary police force. Eighteen Slovaks were sentenced to jail for separatist activities. The government said 644 people had been arrested trying to leave the country. The Social Democrats agreed to run jointly with the Communists in the May election; the Communist general secretary, Slánský, hailed this as 'a victory for Marxism-Leninism which has proved its supremacy over the harmful theories of the Blums and Bevins'. Amid this tightening of ranks on both sides of the east–west divide, Stalin was about to face the biggest internal challenge to the Soviet bloc since the end of the war, and from a source that surprised many.[8]

## II: THE BALKAN APOSTATE

Yugoslavia had been an enthusiastic promoter of Communism in Eastern Europe, where it was the largest of the states associated with the USSR. Buoyed by his wartime partisan leadership, Tito, who had fought in the Bolshevik ranks in 1917 when embarking on a revolutionary life, had not needed to go through the process of coalition government but had imposed the new order without showing compunction. The Yugoslav constitution was a replica of the Soviet document. Its army, police and economic planning followed the Soviet pattern, with advisers from the USSR. The new regime conducted a purge of richer peasants similar to Stalin's elimination of the kulaks in the 1930s as it sought to extend its reach to the countryside. Disputes with the West flared over Trieste, the shooting down of a US plane and the war in Greece. The Yugoslavs followed Moscow in rejecting the Marshall Plan, took a leading role at the inaugural meeting of the Cominform, which chose Belgrade for its headquarters, with 362 staff – 211 of them Russian – and then embarked on a new round of political repression.

However, relations between the Yugoslav partisans and Moscow had been uneasy as far back as 1941, when, as Tito later recalled, 'the Soviet leaders revealed a tendency to direct our whole uprising neither in the interests of the Yugoslav people nor of the struggle against Hitlerism in general, but mainly in the way that best suited the interests of the Soviet Union and its Greater-Russia policy'. In the later stages of the war, the Yugoslavs sent a message to Moscow about the lack of supplies, which said flatly, 'If you cannot send us assistance, then at least do not hamper us.' In 1944, Tito rejected a suggestion by Stalin that King Peter of Yugoslav be allowed to return home, if only temporarily, and ignored objections by Moscow to some appointments to his new administration in preference to its candidates.[9]

The atmosphere had been 'very cool' at his first meeting with Stalin in Moscow in 1945, Tito remembered. At a dinner, the Soviet leader had compared the Yugoslav army unfavourably with that of Bulgaria, leading his guest to shout out in defence of his country's forces. Though the dictator told a Polish official the Yugoslav leader was 'a tower of strength', there was a deep difference about how to implement Communist policies – Stalin's top-down, bureaucratic state system was the opposite of the bottom-up 'People's Front' which the Yugoslavs favoured (even if it was, in practice, also based on a strong central authority with an active police presence).

Unlike other Communist states, Yugoslavia had not needed the Red Army to liberate it from the Nazis and the ruling party had genuine nationalist roots, its senior ranks reflecting the different regions brought together in the Republic.[10]

The Yugoslavs resented the way post-war economic agreements were tilted to benefit the USSR and attempts by the Soviet agents to recruit associates in the government, the Communist Party and the political police. Tito's efforts to assert regional leadership in the Balkans irked the Kremlin as Belgrade offered financial credits to Albania and planned to integrate the two economies as well as stepping up military coordination.[11]

By 1948, the Yugoslav leader had become unwilling to accept Moscow's dogmatic leadership and saw himself as the natural leader of the Southern Slavs, whatever the Kremlin said. His party's roots in its fight for national liberation gave it a belief in crafting its own course absent in the leadership of other Soviet bloc countries. Stalin was revered as an icon, but he was an abstract figure, far away from the daily reality, which Tito dominated. The partisan chief was now head of the Communist Party, the government and the armed forces, while running the country through a close-knit group of associates and surrounding himself with a personality cult. That was part of the problem; he was too like Stalin in power terms for the Kremlin's comfort and made no secret of his ambitions.

In January 1948, the Soviet ambassador in Belgrade had handed Tito a message from Stalin asking for a member of the Politburo to go to Moscow to discuss unspecified matters. Djilas and a military delegation made a five-day train journey to the Soviet capital where

Stalin opened the first meeting by talking about Albania, saying Yugoslavia was free to 'swallow' it whenever it wished.[13] Pursuing a charm offensive, and perhaps hoping to enlist Djilas as an ally, he then offered military aid. The Yugoslav suspected that Stalin would try to force his nation 'down to the level of the occupied East European countries'.[12]

The following month, Yugoslav ambassadors to Moscow and East European capitals were called home. Belgrade declared closed zones on its frontiers. Military spending was increased. Security was tightened around the homes of leading figures. Stalin criticised Yugoslavia's independent behaviour and repeated his call for an end to the rebellion in Greece.[14]

The atmosphere deteriorated after Dimitrov suggested the creation of a federation of Balkan and Danubian states. The Bulgarian leader appeared anxious to make amends for his country's alliance with Hitler and the horrific behaviour of its troops during their occupation of East Serbia. Stalin was displeased. His concern about the emergence of a power bloc he might not control increased when Albania asked Yugoslavia to send in two army divisions as defence against any attack by Greek government forces. Tito despatched the foreign minister, Edvard Kardelj, to join Djilas in Moscow while Dimitrov made his way north as well to represent Bulgaria.

At a meeting in the Kremlin in mid-February, Molotov opened the proceedings by saying there were serious differences between the USSR and the other two countries that were 'inadmissible both from the Party and from the State point of view'. Stalin, sitting at the head of the table surrounded by senior officials, glowered as he doodled on a pad in front of him before launching into a fierce attack on Dimitrov for a 'childish attempt' to attract attention with 'conceptions different from our own'.

When the Bulgarian apologised, the dictator repeatedly interrupted him, saying he was bandying words 'like a woman of the streets'. Stalin then turned to Kardelj, attacking Yugoslavia for failing to consult Moscow in advance on matters such as its earlier treaty with Bulgaria. When the visitor tried to respond, the dictator browbeat him with interruptions. Then he said that three bilateral federations should be created – between Poland and Czechoslovakia,

Hungary and Romania, and Bulgaria and Yugoslavia. Moscow, as he did not need to say, would control the process and would not be faced by the wider, and potentially challenging, regional grouping.[15]

Late the next night, Kardelj was summoned to Molotov's office where he was ordered to sign a two-page undertaking to consult with Moscow on foreign policy matters. Though 'boiling with rage', the Yugoslav did so. In his anxious state, he put his name in the space reserved for Molotov and a new copy of the document had to be drawn up. As soon as that was done, the Yugoslavs headed home. By now, Stalin had concluded that Tito was 'a nationalist ... infected with the bourgeois spirit ... an opponent of Socialism', Molotov recalled. According to the foreign minister, the dictator considered that 'getting rid of Tito required no more than the lifting of his little finger'.[16]

Back in Belgrade, Djilas told the Central Committee that 'the fundamental question is whether socialism is to develop freely or through the expansion of the Soviet Union'. Moscow suspended negotiations to renew a trade agreement and withdrew military and civilian advisers. 'We are amazed, we cannot understand, and we are deeply hurt,' Tito responded in a message to the Kremlin. He insisted that he and other members of the leadership had always been co-operative and asked Moscow to say 'what the trouble is, that it points out everything which it feels is inconsistent with good relations between our two countries'.[17]

An eight-page reply from Moscow was delivered by the ambassador to the Yugoslav leader at his villa outside Zagreb. Reading its opening lines, Tito felt 'as if a thunderbolt had struck me', he recalled. '[But] I never winced; I contained myself as much as I possibly could.'[18]

'When shall we have an answer?' the ambassador asked.

'We shall consider the letter,' Tito replied. The diplomat left.[19]

'We regard your answer as incorrect and therefore completely unsatisfactory,' the missive from Moscow began. It accused the Yugoslavs of having been 'hoodwinked by the degenerate and opportunist theory of the peaceful absorption of capitalist elements' as associated with Trotsky and other ideological renegades. They lacked democracy, fell short in pursuing the class struggle and failed to check the rise of capitalist elements. Insulting remarks said to have been made about the Red Army by Djilas were dug up – he had once noted that popular feeling was warmer towards British troops than towards Soviet soldiers. Leading figures in Yugoslavia were accused of circulating anti-Soviet rumours. 'The criticism is neither open nor honest,' it added. 'It is both underhand and dishonest and of a hypocritical nature.' The letter concluded by pointing the finger at Assistant Foreign Minister Vladimir Velebit, a former ambassador in London who was branded as an English spy. So long as he remained in his job, the Soviet government would refuse to communicate with Belgrade through official channels.

Tito set out the response in large handwriting on thirty-two sheets of heavy paper. This made clear the Yugoslavs would stand their ground, continuing the combination of nationalism and ideology that characterised the regime. 'No matter how much each of us loves the land of Socialism, the USSR, he can, in no case, love his own country less which also is developing socialism – in this concrete case the Federated People's Republic of Yugoslavia for which so many thousands of its most progressive people fell,' the letter argued. Rebutting the Soviet charges, it listed efforts the authorities had made to increase 'love for the USSR' and added that, while their forms of socialism might differ, Yugoslavia was 'the most faithful ally of the USSR'. As for Velebit, his case was being investigated and he could not be removed from his post while that was being done.[20] Tito suggested that Moscow should send a delegation to Belgrade for talks to iron out the differences.[21]

He then told the Central Committee that their country should show that it was taking 'a big and beautiful step for the progressive movement in the world'. A purge was launched against Soviet sympathisers, starting with the economic planner Andrija Hebrang, who was convicted of having worked with wartime collaborators and having promoted a chauvinist Croatian policy as well as disclosing state secrets to the Soviets. Taken to prison, he was officially reported dead in 1957, though he was also said to have hung himself in his cell five years earlier.[22]

While Tito was in no danger at home, he forfeited backing from fellow leaders in Eastern Europe for whom the unity of the

Communist camp was the prime duty. When Dimitrov stopped in Belgrade on his way to sign the friendship treaty in Prague, he told Djilas, according to the Yugoslav, to 'Stand firm' at a meeting in his railway compartment. On the return journey, he stayed in the train instead of going to see Tito. A delegation that went to Czechoslovakia found that a session with Gottwald was cancelled at the last minute.[23]

## III: GOD SEES YOU – STALIN DOESN'T

Italy's second national election since the end of the war pitted the Christian Democrats' vision of a conservative, capitalist Catholic nation moored in the West against the socialist secular society offered by the Communists and their allies. The previous poll, in 1946, the first in which women had been allowed to vote, had resulted in a coalition government headed by the Christian Democrat Alcide De Gasperi that included Communists. But Togliatti and his comrades were dropped from government in May 1947, and the growing east–west tension made the electoral battle eleven months later key for both sides in the Cold War.

A republican constitution had gone into effect at the beginning of 1948, eighteen months after a referendum abolished the monarchy. It declared that sovereignty belonged to the people and asserted the right of all citizens to a job, a living wage, free health care and education. What one historian has described as 'vain and empty generalizations' included a pledge that workers would share in corporate profits and management. It also provided for the continuation of the Concordat between the Catholic Church and the state, giving priests privileges and banning divorce.[24]

Three years after the death of Mussolini, the country was still saddled with the cost of his rule and the war. Fascist atrocities in Ethiopia were swept under the carpet. The country was reckoned to be capable of supporting 32 million people but the population was 45 million. Poverty was widespread with huge wealth gaps; 1 per cent of Italians owned half the land. Food was a constant concern. The high birth rate increased the population by nearly half a million each year. The prime minister joked to an American visitor that he would give up Marshall aid if 400,000 of his compatriots could be sent to live abroad annually.[25]

Fascist autarky left Italy with an atrophied bureaucracy and a legacy of industries with bloated labour forces and plant as output stagnated far below the pre-war level. Investment capital was scarce. Trade and budget deficits soared. Unemployment was close to 2 million. Inflation was high. Key sectors such as the banks, steel and shipbuilding stayed in state hands if only because there was no private capital to take them over.

Though land reform redistributed 2 million hectares of land to peasants, most used backward cultivation methods. There was a major divide between the poor south, where three-quarters of voters in Naples had backed the retention of the monarchy and the Sicilian Mafia revived, and the more prosperous north with its history of resistance to Fascism and a strong Communist presence. George Kennan forecast that, if the Communists won the election, civil war would break out and suggested Italy should be divided into the north under Soviet control and a Western-orientated south.

The campaign for the election on 18 April was passionate and, at times, dirty. The tight Communist organisation was matched by 'civic committees' set up by their opponents in every parish across the country. Togliatti denounced the Christian Democrats for 'having completely betrayed the cause of Italian democracy' and branded them as 'totalitarian in nature', while declaring that his party was set on 'finding the Italian way to a new kind of democracy'. In the event of victory, he foresaw the possibility of a right-wing coup, which would have to be met by a violent reaction from the left.

De Gasperi cut a modest figure. Born in the Tyrol when it was under Austro-Hungarian rule, he often appeared detached from the hurly-burly of politics around him, an ascetic father of four daughters (one a nun) who lived simply and had had no interests outside his work since age forced him to give up his hobby of mountaineering. Arrested several times by the Fascists, he had spent the war years out of sight in the Vatican library. It was said that he had become head of the post-Mussolini government because there was nobody else around not tainted by association with the dictator.

His party was split between reactionary and more progressive wings, leading Togliatti to compare it to a bat – 'one does not know whether it is a bird or a mouse'. But this did not stop it waging a full-blooded campaign. 'Italians! On April 18, you will be able to save or destroy your freedom,' the Christian Democratic manifesto declared. 'The choice is between an inhuman totalitarianism that concentrates and suffocates everything within the state, and a human conception of political life in which citizens, associations and parties may collaborate in free competition for the achievement of the common good.' The party's emblem for the election was a shield emblazoned with the single word 'Libertas'.[26]

The opposition's economic programme was, in the words of veteran leftist Lucio Magri, 'at the level of generalizations (and) useful only to back up trade unions demands'. Togliatti saw the route to victory as being a long march to combine revolution and reform and there was no practical, coherent programme to address structural weaknesses and galloping inflation. The PCI's leadership also faced the shadow cast by Moscow.[27]

The main wing of the Socialist Party, led by Pietro Nenni, who had fled Mussolini's Italy in 1926 and then returned to become deputy prime minister and foreign minister, formed a united front with the Communists. That provoked another group in the party led by Giuseppe Saragat to split off with fifty-two of the 115 Socialist deputies. A Socialist Congress meeting in London backed them over the Nenni wing.

Both right and left used strong-arm tactics. Togliatti said his party would employ all means offered under the parliamentary system; action should be directed primarily at 'the struggle of the masses for the realisation of their demands'. Communist militants were particularly active in the 'Red Triangle' of the north, while the Mafia used its influence on behalf of the right in the south where big landowners backed action against the left which promised to break up big estates. In Sicily, a trade union leader was murdered and police reported the formation of paramilitary units. Arms caches were found in Lombardy. Neo-Fascists staged a big goose-stepping rally in Naples and held a torch-lit parade at the Spanish Steps in Rome, where there was street fighting with Jews in which iron bars and clubs were wielded. The government stepped up frontier defences near Trieste to stop infiltration from Yugoslavia.[28]

The Church played an important role in combatting the united-front left and its promises of more drastic land reform, which would hit the extensive ecclesiastical holdings. The Catholic Action movement mobilised 1.8 million members. In his Christmas message, the conservative Pope Pius XII had warned that 'he who gives his support, his services and his talents to those parties and forces that deny God is a deserter and a traitor'. 'To be with or against Christ; that is the whole question,' he decreed. The Vatican threatened withdrawal of the sacraments from those who backed the left, saying there was to be 'total opposition to atheistic Communism in every field with no appeasement or compromise'. The Popular Front appealed to the Vatican to be less hostile, but the Christian Democrats warned voters that 'in the secrecy of the polling booth, God sees you – Stalin doesn't'.[29]

While Soviet funds went covertly to the PCI, the American involvement was in plain view. The State Department said a Communist victory would jeopardise Marshall Plan aid. America had been sending in assistance since the Allied landings in 1943 and Washington made sure that the first ERP shipment of wheat and lard went to Italy.[30] It also transferred twenty-nine merchant ships to the De Gasperi government as a 'gesture of friendship and confidence in a democratic Italy', while the House Appropriations Committee approved $18.7 million in additional 'interim aid' funds. Food supplies were stepped up and the return of gold taken away by the Nazis was promised. US coal supplies were laid on. An anti-Communist letter-writing campaign was organised among relatives of voters in America. A 'Friendship Train' toured the US collecting gifts which were distributed in Italy from trains painted red, white and blue. The Voice of America warned of a repetition of events in Czechoslovakia; *Time* magazine wrote that a PCI victory would take the country to 'the brink of catastrophe'. The British joined in the blandishments by talking of returning Trieste to Italian control.[31]

The importance of the election was reflected in the very high turnout of 96 per cent. The smaller parties were largely marginalised except for some traditionalist areas in the south. Boosted by voter loyalty, the Christian Democrats increased their support of 1946 to win 48 per cent of the vote, attracting electors from other parties and improving their performance even in traditionally left-wing regions. The stock market boomed.

The Communists and Socialists took 31 per cent, their combined backing declining slightly on the previous election. The PCI increased its seats from 104 to 133 and the real losers were Nenni's Socialists, whose representation halved. Togliatti reflected that 'these are the best results we could have obtained. This is fine.' The Communist leader in Milan, Luigi Longo, warned of 'dangerous tension' and promised, 'We shall overcome the adverse current ... the election was no Waterloo.' Still, the attempt to build a left-wing coalition that could challenge the centre-right and the Catholic establishment had suffered a significant blow, especially when, instead of forming a purely Christian Democratic government, De Gasperi chose to rule with a coalition containing other parties, including Saragat's Socialists, promising improved welfare services, agrarian reform and an attack on unemployment.[32]

De Gasperi would show himself a master at steering centre-right combination governments over the following six years as he also became a big player in moves towards European co-operation. The coalitions he headed strengthened the power of the Roman and Catholic establishments and of regional barons who were often hostile to much-needed reform. Hobbled by defeat at the polls and Christian Democrat inroads into some of its fiefdoms, the PCI ceased to be an alternative party of government, though it would be capable of attracting 34 per cent of the vote in its reformist phase in the 1970s and ran urban centres, notably the showcase city of Bologna with its innovative health, education and housing programmes. But the centre-right now constituted the hub of Italian national political power, to the relief of Washington as it faced the biggest direct challenge of the early Cold War.

## III: CITY UNDER SIEGE

As April began, the east–west confrontation in Germany escalated after the Soviet walkout from the Allied Control Commission in protest at US–UK–French discussions of setting up a devolved political authority in their occupation zones without consulting Moscow. After the integration of the west of the country into the European and international community became a key economic element under the Marshall Plan with a new currency to replace the devalued Reichsmark, counter measures from the east were inevitable with Berlin as the nodal point of the conflict. The headlines of the London *Times* told of the unfolding crisis day by day.

### 2–3 April:

### Russian ring round Berlin, Russians adamant in Berlin

The Soviet authorities start to check Western personnel moving through their zone and inspect freight shipments. Their troops block the road and rail corridor that carries supplies to Berlin from the Western occupation zones. Four trains are halted at the border. Road vehicles without documents translated into Russian are stopped. Soviet troops set up double barriers across the highway and build sentry boxes at control points while moving Germans out of houses to make room for soldiers. The Western powers step up cargo flights to Tempelhof airfield in the US sector of the city and Gatow in the British sector. Soviet fighters buzz the planes.[33]

### 6 April:

### British aircraft down near Berlin – collision with Russian fighter

A British Viking airliner and a Soviet Yak-3 fighter collide near Gatow. Eyewitnesses report that, as the Viking was coming in to land, the fighter dived under it, climbed steeply and clipped its wing. The ten passengers and four crew in the Viking die, as does the Yak pilot. The airliner crashes inside the Soviet zone and explodes. British fire engines and ambulances, which drive to the scene, are told to leave. The Yak comes down in the British zone; crossing the demarcation line, Soviet soldiers set up a cordon around the wreckage. A British investigation will conclude that the collision had been an accident but that any fault lay with the fighter pilot who had been in disregard of the accepted rules of flying.[34]

**7 April:**

UNITY WEST OF IRON CURTAIN

Bernard Montgomery, chief of the Imperial General Staff, arrives in Berlin for an inspection tour. In a speech in Düsseldorf, General Robertson urges people in the Western zones to stand up against those who 'with democracy on their lips and truncheons behind their backs would filch freedom from Germany'.[35]

**12 April:**

MORE RUSSIAN DEMANDS IN BERLIN

The Soviets ask the British and Americans to close aid stations and withdraw telegraphic maintenance units on roads to and from their zones to Berlin. Clay proposes breaking through any Soviet attempt to cut supply routes by sending an armed convoy, but Washington tells him this was not a favoured option. It would have escalated the confrontation and the convoy might have been cut off in the middle of Soviet-controlled territory.[36]

**19 April:**

DISSENSIONS IN BERLIN

Parcel mail between Berlin and the Western zones is delayed. The Americans reject a request from the People's Council in the east to be allowed to circulate a petition in favour of German unity in the US zone.[37]

**21 April:**

NEW TRAFFIC BAN IN GERMANY

The Russians temporarily halt water traffic to and from Berlin; barges had been bringing 25–30,000 tons of supplies to the city each month, most of it food.[38]

**23 April:**

BERLIN RAIL LINK CUT

The Russians cancel the last civilian passenger train link, the Nord Express between Berlin and Paris.

## 26 April:

### SOVIET CHARGES IN BERLIN; US ADMINISTRATION ATTACKED; 'RACKETS' AND 'GANGS'

General Kotikov of the Soviet command complains of 'gangsterism' in the Western sectors and says 'a reign of terror' existed on zonal frontiers before the transport restrictions. 'No respectable German wife will trust herself to venture near certain buildings occupied by the Americans,' the Russians observe.

The US army chief of staff, Omar Bradley, asks Clay for an estimate of the situation in Berlin and whether the West should hold on there.

'I do not believe that we should plan on leaving Berlin short of a Soviet ultimatum to drive us out by force if we do not leave,' the military governor replies. 'The exception which could force us out would be the Soviet stoppage of all food supplies to German population in western sectors. I doubt that Soviets will make such a move because it would alienate the Germans almost completely, unless they were prepared to supply food for more (than) two million people.'

The planned currency reform would 'develop the real crisis', he adds, linking Berlin with the wider Cold War. 'Why are we in Europe?' he asks.

> We have lost Czechoslovakia. We have lost Finland. Norway is threatened. We retreat from Berlin. We can take it by reducing our personnel with only airlift until we are moved out by force ... After Berlin, will come western Germany and our strength there, relatively, is no greater and our position no more tenable than Berlin.
>
> If we mean that we are to hold Europe against communism, we must not budge. We can take humiliation and pressure short of war in Berlin without losing face. If we move, our position in Europe is threatened. If America does not know this, does not believe the issue is cast now, then it never will and communism will run rampant. I believe the future of democracy requires us to stay here until forced out. God knows this is not [a]heroic pose because there will be nothing heroic in having to take humiliation without retaliation.[39]

In Moscow, Stalin discusses the situation with the SED leader, Wilhelm Pieck. The German says his party faces electoral defeat in Berlin later in the year. Victory would be possible, however, if the Western Allies could be removed.

'Let's make a joint effort,' the dictator replies. 'Perhaps we can kick them out.'[40]

CHAPTER FORTY-ONE

# EAST ASIAN CONFLICTS

## I: THE WORLD'S WORST LEADERSHIP

Despite his formulaic plea that he did not want the job, Chiang Kai-shek was elected president of the Republican China on 20 April. Standing against a token opponent, he got 90 per cent of the vote from the 2,700 National Assembly delegates who gave him 'extraordinary powers' to fight the Communists. Despite those results and an optimistic speech by the generalissimo, the delegates were less supportive than in the past. Fights broke out on the floor of the chamber.

The disquiet showed up in the assembly's creation of seven special inquiry commissions that produced hundreds of resolutions. Chiang's candidate for the vice presidency, Sun Yat-sen's son Sun Fo, was beaten by Li Zongren, a militarist from Guangxi in the south who had fought for the Nationalists since 1927 and scored a notable victory over the Japanese in 1938. Known for his independence of mind, he had avoided being integrated into the Kuomintang and was now associated with other regional warlords, liberals and some minor parties. This made him a threat the generalissimo did not relish, and Chiang did little to share power with his deputy.

The right-wing Kuomintang politician, Chen Lifu, warned of the lack of willpower in the ruling party and army, the effect of corruption and the need for a moral crusade. Though he did not mention this, the regime's increasingly authoritarian nature, which he backed, had alienated intellectuals and students. Political groups banned on the mainland set up in Hong Kong where Communist agents worked on them. Still, Chiang continued to see himself as the national saviour and shuttled around battlefields, reshuffling commanders, issuing orders and preparing for the crucial encounter he sought with the PLA. Yet his preparations of a fall-back base in Formosa denoted less than complete confidence in the outcome of the war.

The PLA took the major centre of Loyang in the middle of China after a month-long battle in which it changed hands four times. This gave the Communists a broad belt of territory reaching into Shanxi province and enabled them to prepare to attack the strategically placed city of Kaifeng. To the east, they captured ports and railway lines in Shandong and blocked off the capital city, Jinan, as well as the major harbour of Qingdao, where 3,000 US marines were stationed.

These victories freed Communist forces to move south and threaten the centre of Nationalist power in the Lower Yangtze Valley around the commercial capital of Shanghai and the government seat of Nanjing. Reckoning the government had lost the initiative almost everywhere north of the river, Mao calculated that final victory would come within three years.[1]

In the US, Republicans used China as a stick with which to beat the administration in the run-up to the presidential election. Calling for increased aid as he sought the Republican nomination, Thomas Dewey said he did not know if it would be 50 per cent or 80 per cent effective but 'of one thing I am sure, it would be immensely more effective than nothing'. The administration pressed for military aid to be channelled to generals it thought competent, but Chiang feared this would strengthen them against his central rule. The principal US military adviser, David Barr, told Washington that, in his experience, no battle had been lost for lack of equipment. 'Military debacles in my opinion can all be attributed to the world's worst leadership and many other morale destroying factors that lead to a complete loss of will to fight.'[2]

## II: SHRIMP BETWEEN THE WHALES

Across the border from Manchuria, Japan's surrender in 1945 ended its 35-year occupation of Korea. The peninsula was divided along the 38th parallel, with the USSR assuming trusteeship to the north and US forces under General John Hodge establishing a military government in the south. Attempts to bring the two together got nowhere. When the issue was taken to the United Nations, the international body passed a resolution calling for a general election under its supervision in May 1948.

Korea had long been a stage for conflict between China, Japan and Russia – a 'shrimp crushed in the battle of whales' as a saying had it. The Japanese had occupied it after routing China in their war of 1894–5 followed by formal annexation in 1910. The next thirty-five years were an extremely bitter time for the Koreans, who were subjected to forced labour with hundreds of thousands killed and women turned into sex slaves as 'comfort women' for the imperial forces. The occupation authorities tried to eradicate the national identity. Despite this, almost a million people emigrated across the Strait to Japan to seek a better living, most ending up in extreme poverty in slums marked by high levels of violence.

After the Soviet Union entered the war in Asia by invading Manchuria in August 1945, the Red Army advanced into the Korean peninsula. On their way, its soldiers, many from Central Asia, practised the looting and rapes that had become familiar in Europe. Some women in their path disguised themselves as men to escape their attentions. In Washington, future secretary of state Dean Rusk and another young official were told to define an American occupation zone in the south in line with a wartime agreement for a temporary division of the country. On a *National Geographic* magazine map, they drew a line along the 38th parallel. That left the capital of Seoul in the US zone, which would contain 16 million people to 9 million in the north. Moscow quickly accepted this as its troops took the major city of Pyongyang. American forces arrived in the south the following month and Washington and Moscow agreed on a joint trusteeship for five years to be followed by a unified government.

As the end of Japanese rule arrived, Koreans organised People's Liberation Committees and a conference in Seoul set up a People's Republic, whose aims included distribution to peasants of land seized from the Japanese, nationalisation of banking, mining, transport and communication, an eight-hour working day, a minimum wage, universal suffrage gender equality, and an end to child labour, It wanted 'close relations with the United States, USSR, England, and China, and positive opposition to any foreign influences interfering with the domestic affairs of the state'.

For the Soviets, the main aim was to ensure that the peninsula provided a buffer zone in Stalin's global security map stretching from Germany to East Asia. So long as that was assured, Moscow had little interest in the country as a whole – its army could have taken the south had it wished to before the Americans arrived. To head the regime in its zone, it chose a man whose subsequent personality cult makes it difficult to disentangle fact from fiction.

Kim Il-sung appears to have become attracted to Communism as a teenager living in Manchuria, where his family had moved to get away from the Japanese. However, the police of the local warlord arrested him for subversion and when he was nineteen the imperial army staged its coup to take over the region in 1931. That year, he was said to have joined the Chinese Communist Party – the small Korean party had been expelled from the Comintern for being too nationalistic. According to the official narrative, Kim spent his twenties and early thirties in guerrilla activity against the Japanese directed by the Chinese Communists, becoming a political commissar and taking the name Kim Il-sung, meaning 'Kim becomes the sun'.

From 1937, the Korean-Japanese press ascribed a number of attacks to 'Kim Il-sung bandits'. In 1940, he crossed to the Soviet Union and was sent to a training camp for Koreans. Becoming an officer in the Red Army, he reportedly had several meetings with Beria, who was in charge of post-war policy towards his homeland. By the time he returned in 1945, he knew that the road ahead lay in allying himself with the Soviets to overcome his significant disadvantages.

He had been away for two decades, knew only rudimentary Korean and was a poor public speaker – his first speech, written for him by the Russians, was described as being delivered in a 'quacking voice'. He faced an array of Nationalist and Communist figures with much more experience and standing than him. Short and plump, he hardly lived up to the description of him in a Pyongyang newspaper as an 'incomparable patriot, national hero, the ever victorious, brilliant field commander with a will of iron ... the greatest leader our people have known for the last several thousand years ... a man equipped with exceptional powers'.[3]

When the Korean Workers Party was set up in August 1946, Kim did not immediately become its leader. As in Eastern Europe, Moscow was happy to work through a left-leaning coalition headed in this case by Cho Man-sik, a veteran Nationalist and scholar who had led a government-in-exile in China. But, as in Europe, the Communist grip tightened steadily. Cho was shunted upstairs while another popular figure who refused to go along with Soviet plans for the country was put under house arrest and then disappeared. A third potential rival to Kim was assassinated while riding in a lorry through Pyongyang. Pak Heon-yeong, a founder of the Korean Communist Party and still regarded as its national leader, remained based in Seoul after the war and was thus somewhat isolated from the evolution of the north.[4]

Backing from the Soviet commander, General Shtykov, ensured that Kim became the power in the land. By 1948, he was in firm control of the Communist Party and able to draw support away from other leftist groups and personalities as his power increased. There were recurrent purges to eliminate real or supposed competitors. The regime absorbed and built on the people's committees set up as Japanese rule collapsed, turning the north into a regimented state with an omnipresent police and a People's Army led by former guerrillas and soldiers who had gained combat experience during the war in Manchuria.

Representing a generational change from older Nationalists, Kim presided over a programme of land reform, nationalisation of industry and the strengthening of the political machine. Education was boosted; the ministry claimed that, by the end of 1948, 2.3 million illiterates had learned to read and write. Living standards remained very low and some 800,000 people moved from north to south in the three years after the defeat of Japan. Twenty-five thousand went the other way. The leader's taste for playing Christian hymn tunes on an organ at his home was kept from the public.[5]

The Soviets maintained a low profile, but controlled the leadership.

The opprobrium directed at the Red Army for the widespread rapes of Korean women by its soldiers lessened when Russian commanders introduced draconian regulations on their behaviour. Several non-Communist parties that were allowed to continue to operate were co-opted into a united front and kept under strict control. Alternative power centres were eliminated. Self-criticism sessions became common to enforce the party line. Individualism was squashed into group life run by the regime in a pattern that persists to our day.

After landing in the south, the US Military Government under General Hodge dissolved the People's Republic administration set up immediately after Japan's defeat because of its left-wing character. From the start, the occupation administration were worried about the volatility of the situation and sought to instil order. 'Southern Korea can best be described as a powder keg ready to explode at the application of a spark,' one report warned. 'Korea is completely ripe for agitators.' There was no basis for a moderate democracy.[6]

That made the Americans all too ready to back the veteran right-wing agitator for independence, Syngman Rhee, despite the objections of the State Department, which regarded him as a dangerous mischief-maker. Rhee, born in 1875 and converted to Christianity as a young man, had a long record as a political activist dating back to assassination plots against the former royal family at the end of the nineteenth century. In 1905, he moved to America and met President Theodore Roosevelt in an unsuccessful attempt to get the US to intervene with Japan to preserve Korean independence. Returning to Korea after studying at Harvard and Princeton, he was arrested for alleged involvement in a plot to kill the Japanese governor-general, but escaped back across the Pacific to run an academy in Honolulu, publish a magazine, set up a church and agitate for Korean independence. As head of foreign affairs for the Korean provisional government based in the Chinese Nationalist capital of Chongqing during the Second World War, he worked with the American Office of Strategic Services (OSS) and headed the Korean delegation to early meetings of the United Nations.

Now seventy, Rhee got back to Korea via Tokyo after the Japanese surrender thanks to an American associate and a meeting with

MacArthur. He established himself at the head of three political bodies, helped by rivalries among his opponents and the way other right-wingers were tainted by collaboration with the Japanese and economic interests. His fluent English and familiarity with the United States also helped and he drew on the rightist sentiment in the bureaucracy. Not that he was easy to get on with.

Hodge, who had fought in the First World War and commanded infantry in the Pacific campaigns under MacArthur, called him an 'old rascal' and described Rhee and his Austrian second wife as the leaders of a 'Capone Gang' of carpetbaggers. To try to bolster support in the US, the politician spent four months in Washington to mobilise supporters there, but a CIA study noted that his 'vanity has made him highly susceptible to the contrived flattery of self-seeking interests in the US and Korea. His intellect is a shallow one, and his behaviour is often irrational and childish.' Yet, it concluded that 'Rhee, in the final analysis, has proved himself to be a remarkably astute politician.'[7]

Hodge recognised from early on that the US-led regime's identification with conservative forces and landlords plus the refusal to grant immediate independence came at a cost. The presence in the police of an overwhelming number of men who had served the colonial Japanese regime added to the discontent. If land reform was being introduced, society remained backward; only a fifth of the population was literate. Inflation was high. There was, the American general reported, 'growing resentment against all Americans in the area including passive resistance ... The word pro-American is being added to pro-Jap, national traitor and collaborator.' But he judged that the country was not ready to run itself and that US withdrawal would open the door to Communism. After a visit in 1946, Truman's friend, oil man Edwin Pauley, advised the president that 'Communism, in Korea, could get off to a better start than practically anywhere else in the world.'[8]

At the beginning of 1947, Hodge warned Washington of the danger of civil war if the US and USSR could not find a joint solution in the peninsula. Moscow rejected a proposal by Truman for a meeting to discuss early elections in the two occupation zones leading to the formation of a provisional national government and legislature. US–Soviet talks which had dragged on since 1946 ran into the sand and an interim government was proclaimed in the south. The Truman administration then put the matter before the UN General Assembly which recognised Korea's independence and set up a temporary commission to prepare for the planned election in May 1948. The Soviet bloc abstained in the voting at the international body and the Red Army commander in the north refused to have anything to do with the commission or allow preparations for the election.

While the Truman administration committed itself to the election and the defence of the south, others in Washington were minimising the importance of the peninsula to US global interests. Kennan ranked it below Japan and China in the list of Asian priorities. He thought it was likely to become a Soviet satellite but this did not worry him. 'Our policy should be to cut our losses and get out as gracefully but as promptly as possible,' he advised. His colleague and Asian expert John Carter Vincent said the aim was to 'neutralise' Korea as an irritant for American foreign policy.[9]

The joint chiefs of staff judged that, from the standpoint of military security, the United States had little strategic interest in maintaining its 45,000 troops and bases in Korea. They could become a liability and were better deployed elsewhere. James Forrestal agreed that any advance by the Red Army in Asia would bypass the peninsula so the US military had no reason to stay there. Still, the defence secretary noted that 'precipitate withdrawal ... would lower the military prestige of the United States' and Acheson pointed to Korea as a place where 'the line is clearly drawn between the Russians and ourselves'.[10]

In their report to the president, the joint chiefs warned that the presence of American troops might be rendered untenable by conditions in the south and the potential for 'violent disorder'. A series of peasant uprisings started in the autumn of 1946, fostered by clan rivalries. As well as reflecting discontent with economic conditions and a range of frustrations among small farmers, these were spurred by the way that right-wingers in Seoul and their associates in the provinces were imposing their rule on regions that had strong left-wing leanings.

Militancy filtered down to local village groups. Though maintaining a fair degree of independence, the South Korean Labor Party
(SKLP) came under the increasing influence of the north, which sent
instructions to infiltrate the government and police and to stock
food for guerrilla warfare. The establishment of anti-leftist groups
at village level and the organisation of right-wing youth gangs added
to the tension. Workers who went on strike were arrested. A leading
left-wing Nationalist figure, Yo Un-hyung, the man most capable
of challenging Syngman Rhee, was assassinated. There were battles
between villagers and police. After visiting Korea in 1947, the head
of the US Civil Liberties Union described the south as 'literally in
the grip of a police regime and a private terror'.[11]

## III: BLOODY ISLAND

The 700-square-mile island of Jeju in the Korea Strait is a place
of considerable natural beauty with wide beaches, caves, orange
groves and the extinct volcanic crater of Hallasan standing 6,000
feet up.[12] Most inhabitants lived along the coast, building black
stone walls to ward off the heavy ocean winds. The relationship
with the mainland had been uneasy since an independence struggle
in the thirteenth century. After that, the 'province across the sea'
was used for breeding horses and as a place of exile, its people
treated as foreigners by other Koreans. In isolation, family and
clan ties grew strong as fresh rebellions broke out against the
mainland and the Japanese. After 1945, in the words of historian
Bruce Cummings, it became 'a magnifying glass, a microscope on
the politics of postwar Korea'.[13]

The Americans reckoned that two-thirds of the island's population were 'moderate leftists' and that Communist influence was
small. But the rightist governor, Yu Hae-jin, classified anybody
who did not support Rhee as a danger, telling visitors that there
was 'no middle line'. Islanders backing a call by the SKLP to
oppose the division of the peninsula and the May election set up
bases on Mount Hallasam. Police were attacked and government
installations damaged. In response, the governor, who blamed
agitators from the north for the trouble, brought in paramilitaries.

A left-wing demonstration was broken up with 2,500 arrests. The body of one of those detained was later found in a river; he had been tortured.[14]

This set off fresh clashes between police and local people, leading to a wholesale revolt on 3 April. There were differing accounts of what happened – either that the trouble began when police fired on a demonstration commemorating the fight against Japanese rule or that the leftists were putting into operation a planned rising. Five hundred SKLP guerrillas flooded down from the volcano's slopes, moving under the cover of high grass, to join 3,000 protestors in attacking a dozen police stations, killing thirty of those inside. The authorities demanded a complete surrender of the rebels but they insisted that the police must be disarmed, officials sacked and the paramilitaries sent away as well as calling for the unification of the peninsula. Guerrillas set fire to government buildings, blocked roads, brought down bridges and cut telephone lines. Administration broke down. Villagers supplied the guerrillas with food. Blood ties made it hard for the authorities to gain information. Police reinforcements were shipped in. The governor's forces had the help of American spotter planes but their pursuit of the rebels was hampered by poor roads, bad weather and the shelter afforded by steep ravines on the sides of the volcano.

Anywhere from 14,000 to 30,000 people died before the rebellion ended after a year, according to a later inquiry. Like an American investigation, this concluded that 86 per cent of the deaths were inflicted by security forces. There were atrocities on both sides. Government forces levelled villages and massacred the inhabitants. In one case, American soldiers caught police forces executing seventy-six villagers, including women and children. In the central mountain area, 95 per cent of dwellings were destroyed.

Forty thousand people fled to Japan. Thousands were imprisoned, some of them subsequently executed during the Korean War. The event was hushed up for decades; it was not until 2006 that the government in Seoul offered an apology to the people of the island, and set up a Truth and Reconciliation Commission. Its report found that the SKLP had staged the rising 'to protest against oppression by the National Police and the North West Youth and against the

South Korean Government' and laid responsibility for the killing on local commanders and, at a higher level, on Rhee and on the US occupation authorities, given that a US officer was in overall control of security forces on Jeju – though only half a dozen Americans were stationed on the island.[15]

# TAPESTRY OF ESCALATING VIOLENCE

## I: Under attack

At the beginning of April, David Ben-Gurion backed a proposal by the Haganah Operations Division to change tactics and aim to capture all territory awarded to their new state with special focus on the link between Jerusalem and Tel Aviv to protect convoys ahead of partition. 'When an officer proposed that this should be done with a unit of four hundred men, the head of the Jewish Agency responded, 'Nonsense! We need 1,500.'[1]

They would have the benefit of arms arriving from Czechoslovakia under contracts that would bring in 50,000 rifles, 6,000 machine guns and 90 million bullets, as well as uniforms and Messerschmitt aircraft captured from the Nazis at the end of the war, plus training for pilots. A batch of guns had already been brought ashore after being transported through Yugoslavia and shipped on an Italian ship, the *Nora*, to Tel Aviv. Zionist agents took the British port inspectors out for drinks while the weapons were transferred to small vessels to be brought ashore clandestinely.[2]

The new Haganah strategy was launched with Operation Nachshon as the month was marked by a rising tide of fighting. It was the largest action to date designed to take and level Arab villages from which the Jerusalem road could be threatened. An initial attack was directed at the hill of Kastel with a Roman fortress. Taken by surprise, the Arab defenders fled. The Mufti's charismatic nephew led a counter-attack on Kastel. Dressed in his trademark fighting outfit of khaki British battledress, steel helmet and crossed bandoliers, he carried a long-barrelled submachine gun. As he and two others moved forward, they were spotted and shot at. Two were wounded but escaped. The third fell to the ground. 'Water, water,' he begged before dying. On the body, the Jews found an ivory-handled pistol, a gold fountain pen, a gold watch and a Lebanese driving licence identifying the man al-Husanyi.[3]

After the attack was beaten off and the position was reinforced by three armoured trucks which arrived with 60,000 rounds of ammunition. But a heavier assault by 2,000 Arabs drove the Jews down the slope. The body of al-Husseini was recovered and taken to Jerusalem where he was buried on the Temple Mount amid tumultuous scenes. Some of the crowd of 30,000 people fired into the air causing several deaths. With most of the Arab fighters away for the funeral, a Jewish attack re-captured the position without resistance.

West of the Jordan, the Arab Liberation Army launched its first heavy artillery bombardment as Fawzi al-Qawuqji sought the victory he had spoken about to his Jewish visitor the previous month. The target was the Mishmar Haemek kibbutz in the Jezreel Valley. Though the kibbutz held out, the Arabs were so anxious to proclaim a success that they announced it had fallen. A second attack also failed. An infantry company commander in the Liberation Army wrote afterwards that there had been no battle plan, no communication, no arrangements to distribute food and water or clothing against the cold. 'The artillery fired without discrimination and the armoured cars wandered as if they were independent agents without any connection with us.'

In the early morning of 9 April, members of Jewish terrorist organisations staged an attack on the village of Deir Yassin which would become a symbol of the struggle between Jews and Palestinians. The Zionists were anxious to build an airstrip on flat land near the village which lay on the route Arab troops took on their way to besiege Jewish Jerusalem. The 120 Irgun and Lehi attackers had been summoned to help in the battle for Kastel but had not been ready to participate. Now they were fired up for action with nowhere to go except Deir Yassin, their action authorised by the Hanagah commander so long as it was 'a seize operation, and not a hit-and-run mission'.[4]

There was no effective communication between the units. A loudspeaker van sent to warn the four hundred villagers to flee turned over into a ditch. The assailants were met with fire from a schoolhouse. Most of the first platoon were hit. The attackers moved from house to house, throwing grenades inside, spraying the interior with small arms fire and blowing up buildings. In alleyways, fleeing villagers were shot down. A group of men was taken to a quarry and executed. Homes were looted. Villagers were stripped of money and jewels. There were unconfirmed allegations of rape. One of those killed, the son of the village chief, had been a Haganah secret agent. 'The conquest of the village was carried out with great cruelty,' a local Jewish commander reported. 'Whole families – women, old people, children – were killed.' 'Some of the prisoners moved to places of detention, including women and children, were murdered viciously by their captors.'[5]

Five of the attackers died and thirty-one were wounded, a casualty rate of almost 33 per cent. The death toll among villagers was a little over a hundred, but Irgun and Lehi inflated it to 250 for propaganda reasons. Begin called the attack 'a great achievement' in spreading panic among Palestinians. Arab authorities joined the exaggeration in the hope that this would stiffen resistance. Instead it swelled the exodus of Arabs and fuelled the 'psychosis of flight' that would lead to the departure of 200–300,000 Arabs between April and June on top of 75,000 who had left earlier in the year.[6]

Saying he was filled with shock and disgust at the episode, Ben-Gurion sent a cable to King Abdullah expressing deep regret and disclaiming responsibility. The monarch replied that the Jewish agency was responsible for Jewish actions. The Arab League discussed sending in regular army troops; it's Iraqi military commander said Palestine was lost unless an invasion was undertaken. Transjordan indicated that its Legion would cross the border once the Mandate ended. Syria and Lebanon were keen for action but Egypt pleaded that it could not participate because of British bases on its supply lines.[7]

Jerusalem was the key sector for both sides. On 13 April, ten vehicles set off at 9.30 a.m. for the Hassadah Hospital and Hebrew University campus on Mount Scopus, which had been cut off by Arab mines and sniping along the narrow access road. The convoy carried 105 passengers in two ambulances and three buses accompanied by three logistical trucks and two armoured cars. The civilian vehicles were marked with a red shield image to denote their medical nature. The British, who had a small detachment from the Highland Light Infantry posted along the road, assured the Jews their path was safe.

At 9.45 a.m., a mine was set off electrically in front of the convoy which was raked by heavy rifle fire. 'Minshan Deir Yassin' ('For Deir Yassin'), the gunmen shouted. Five vehicles backed out, accompanied by an armoured car. The others waited for Haganah troops to come to their aid. But the British command blocked them on the grounds that their arrival could hamper negotiations to stop the fighting while the Highlanders provided what cover they could.

At 11 a.m., a two-hour ceasefire was arranged by the British. As it expired, the British commander in Palestine, General Gordon MacMillan, arrived. He decided to leave the Arabs and Jews to fight it out themselves.

At 2 p.m., Molotov cocktails set two buses on fire; only one of the occupants of each survived. A Haganah attempt to tow out vehicles with an armoured car failed.

At 4 p.m., a British force with three armoured cars reached the scene, laying down heavy rifle and bazooka fire and collecting twenty-eight survivors.

Seventy-eight Jews died in the ambush, among them the hospital's director. Fifteen Arabs died. One British soldier was killed. Most of the bodies were so badly burned as to be unidentifiable. Arab casualties were unknown. A week later, thousands of Arabs swept down to attack another convoy of three hundred vehicles heading for Jerusalem, one carrying Ben-Gurion. All but six got through. The politician was unharmed.[8]

The UN General Assembly convened on 16 April, with a month to go till the end of the Mandate. The US was still backing trusteeship rather than partition. Moshe Sharett, the Jewish Agency's chief foreign affairs official, recalled 'threats' from the State Department if the Zionists did not agree to a ceasefire and an indefinite post-ponement of independence. He warned the UN Security Council that Arab nations 'are now reliably reported to be preparing plans for the occupation of the whole area of Palestine'.[9]

Zionist representatives and Andrei Gromyko formed what future foreign minister Abba Eban would describe as 'an atmosphere of partnership, of a covenant. Together we will foil the American plot.' At late-night meetings in the Soviet delegation on Park Avenue, they planned tactics and enlisted allies. American Jews proclaiming 'Partition – Not Trusteeship' staged a big demonstration in Washington, picketing the White House. Truman's adviser, Samuel Rosenman, called on Weizmann at the Waldorf Astoria to say that the president had told him, 'I have Dr Weizmann on my conscience' and asked for suggestions on how to proceed on Palestine. In a fresh example of the separate tracks being pursued by the president and State, Rosenman informed Weizmann three days later that Truman had said he would recognise the state of Israel as soon as it was proclaimed; he stressed this must be kept secret. That evening, at the home of friends, the Zionist leader recited the first part of the Seder service and ate a hearty Passover dinner.[10]

In Tel Aviv, Ben-Gurion sought to strengthen his grip on the military by abolishing the post of head of the national command held by Yisrael Galili. The shrewd and popular 38-year-old officer objected, and a political-military crisis erupted two weeks before the end of the Mandate and a probable Arab invasion. News of Deir Yassin and of Jewish forces taking Palestinian villages heightened the call for action. Azzam Pasha of the Arab League reflected that Arab leaders 'would probably be assassinated if they did nothing'. In a foretaste of what was to come, an Egyptian group from the Muslim Brotherhood assaulted a kibbutz in the Negev; the attackers wore parchments declaring that, as true Muslims, they would be immune to 'lead and steel'. They were beaten off.[11]

On the west shore of the Sea of Galilee, the Haganah moved against the ancient city of Tiberias, home to 6,000 Jews and 4,000 Arabs. After attacking a hilltop village, it mortared Arab quarters and, moving forward, dynamited houses. Eighty people were killed. Thirty trucks from Transjordan took the Arab population away, most leaving their possessions behind. Their homes were looted. People fled from nearby villages.[12]

On the coast, the British began to evacuate their positions in Haifa. Two Jewish officials suggested responsibility for the city should be handed to them. The British commander on the spot accepted the proposal and wagered a bottle of whisky that the Zionists could not implement control within a week. After chaotic conflict, they did so and claimed their prize. Forty thousand people, 80 per cent of the Arab population, fled. 'We shall return!' they shouted as they boarded ships and sailed away.[13]

Irgun fighters attacked the Arab city of Jaffa in an operation kept secret from the Haganah. The six hundred men were led by the tall, charismatic Commander Amichai Paglin, a sabra born in Palestine who had organised the bombing of the King David Hotel and supervised the hanging of the two British sergeants the previous summer. The assault began at 4.30 a.m. after a speech by Begin. There was heavy house-to-house combat before the Jews broke through and reached the sea, jumping into the waves and firing weapons in the air.[14]

Bevin was not ready to see a major urban centre allocated to the Arabs by partition fall under Jewish control. So British tanks were ordered to riposte, but they were halted by Paglin's men as Spitfire fighters circled overhead. Criticised by the Jewish press, Begin ordered a retreat. Paglin refused, and told his men to dynamite more houses. The fighters dived on the Irgun positions. A destroyer appeared off-shore. But a fresh British advance was beaten back, confirming the Irgun victory. Fewer than 5,000 of the 80,000 Arabs inhabitants were still in the city. When the British demanded to be left in control of the main police station, Paglin had it blown up.[15]

~

## MEANWHILE

- Unable to reach agreement on Kashmir, India and Pakistan ask a UN commission to come up with solutions. The international body proposes a ceasefire with force reductions on both sides, but Delhi reacts badly to its suggestion of a plebiscite while Pakistan has trouble controlling the tribesmen.

- Manuel Roxas, first president of the independent Republic of the Philippines, dies of a heart attack after one year and ten months in office.
- Revolutionaries storm the National Palace in Bogotá following the assassination of the Liberal Party presidential candidate. Police with tanks and armoured cars put down the rising. The death toll reaches 250 with more than a thousand hurt. The violence disrupts a meeting of American states attended by George Marshall, which still ends with the signature of the charter of the Organization of American States (OAS).
- The World Health Organization and the International Court of Justice start work.
- Harold Stassen wins the Wisconsin and Nebraska Republican primaries. MacArthur and Taft do poorly. Dewey stays in the race.
- Elections in Algeria produce a big Gaullist victory. Seven people are killed in clashes during the closing stages of the campaign.
- Twenty SS men are sentenced to hang after being found responsible for the deaths of more than a million people they considered 'racially and politically inferior'.
- The US conducts a nuclear test above Enewetak Atoll in the Marshall Islands with a total yield of 104 kilotons.
- Scientists pick up 'a cacophony of screams, wails, whistles, hoots, a honk honk and a cow-like mooing' from fish 200 feet down in the sea off Bermuda.
- The US Atomic Energy Commission unveils a plan for a cyclotron to be built by the University of California to produce up to 10,000 million electronic volts.
- Don Bradman opens the Australian Ashes cricket tour of England with a century in his first innings.

# PART THIRTEEN

# MAY 1948

## ACTS

*The state of Israel is declared and Arab armies invade as war engulfs Palestine before the UN accepts a British ceasefire plan; Cold War tensions deepen in Europe while the Yugoslavs resist Kremlin pressure; Chinese Communists score fresh victories; Elections are held in South Korea and in South Africa, which returns a pro-apartheid parliamentary majority.*

## SCENES

*Palestine/Israel, Washington, the United Nations; Berlin, London; Luoyang, Shandong, Shanxi; Seoul; South Africa.*

## CAST

*Ben-Gurion, Abdullah, Truman, Marshall, Bevin; Stalin, Tito; Mao, Chiang; Jan Smuts, Daniel Malan.*

CHAPTER FORTY-THREE

# THE BIRTH OF ISRAEL

## I: Violence and fear

### 1 May

Colonel Desmond Goldie, commander of the first brigade of the
Arab Legion, crosses the Majami Bridge and drives in his Ford V8
car through an angry Arab crowd to a kibbutz in the Jordan Valley
for a secret meeting with Haganah officers. Speaking in the name of
his superior, Glubb Pasha, as they sip coffee, Goldie indicates that
Transjordan wants to divide Palestine peacefully with the Zionists
but has to be careful not to be seen to be betraying the Arab cause.[1]

At the United Nations, the British Colonial Secretary, Arthur
Creech-Jones, tells the senior Jewish diplomat, Moshe Sharett, that
the UK is exerting pressure on Arab states not to launch an invasion.
Abdullah, he adds, wants to annex Palestinian territory, but not to
fight the Jews.[2]

### 3 May

Ben-Gurion is convinced the Jewish state will be attacked from all
sides as soon as it is proclaimed. French intelligence reports that
Saudi Arabia, Syria and Egypt have decided Abdullah should invade
first, that he would then be assassinated and a government established under the Mufti.[3]

Ben-Gurion proposes the abolition of the post of head of the
national command held by Yisrael Galili. The security forces would

in future receive instructions exclusively from himself as director of security. Several department heads threaten to resign. A compromise is patched up for the time being but Ben-Gurion comes under severe criticism from the left-wing Mapam Party to which most senior commanders belong. They see the armed forces as the embodiments of progressive Zionist ideals.

## 4 May

The Arab Legion with armoured cars, cannons and Bren guns attacks the main unit in the Kfar Etzion kibbutz in a section of the Judaea hills allocated to the Palestinians by the UN. An Arab attack had been beaten off in January and a supply convoy had subsequently been ambushed. The assault is driven back but the Legion plans a new assault. In the south, Jewish troops surround more villages whose inhabitants either flee or are expelled.[4]

## 5 May

A delegation from the General Staff meets Ben-Gurion to press for Galili's reinstatement. The politician agrees 'on condition that he served as the acting commander in chief, not as head of the national command – not even provisionally'. Ben-Gurion calls in Galili and asks him to continue in his post. He demands to stay as head of national command, which Ben-Gurion refuses. The Haganah chiefs tell Ben-Gurion they consider it essential to restore the general's full responsibilities and warn that 'if this matter is not settled within the next twelve hours, the heads of department would cease to consider themselves responsible for the conduct of affairs'. Refusing to concede, the politician suggests Galili should be restored to the General Staff without specific responsibilities. The stand-off continues.[5]

## 7 May

After its leaders meet the Syrians, Lebanon says it will join an invasion.

## 8 May

Moshe Sharett flies from New York to tell Marshall and Lovett that statehood is a matter of 'now or never.' Lovett argues for a truce. 'There will very likely be an invasion and you will be in trouble,' he warns. 'In that event you shouldn't come to us for help.' 'If it turns out that you are right and you do establish the Jewish state, I'll be happy,' Marshall adds, 'but you are undertaking a very grave responsibility.' Failure could mean annihilation, he warns.[6]

Returning to New York, Sharett takes a colleague waiting for him at the airport aside and says, 'Marshall said that he was talking to me as a general, as a military man. We'll be annihilated!' He tells senior Jewish Agency staff the plan for a truce and postponement of statehood should be considered to avoid antagonising the US. When he sees Weizmann, who is ill in bed at his hotel, the patriarch is adamant there should be no delay.[7]

## 9 May

In East Galilee, Haganah units storm the town of Safed, home to 10,000 Arabs and 1,500 Jews. They take the main strong points as thousands of refugees stream out and Jewish inhabitants dance and sing in the streets. In the south, Zionist forces attack more Arab villages to create panic and flight. The soldiers are told to 'cleanse [them] of inhabitants [and] burn the greatest possible number of houses'. There is also looting.[8]

Subsequent Israeli accounts would pin responsibility for the mass flight of Palestinians on instructions from Arab leaders but most went because of fear or forcible expulsion. Though there is no explicit overall plan to drive them out, Ben-Gurion and his colleagues have no doubt that the new state will be more secure without an Arab population of the size envisaged by the UN partition. For Weizmann, the mass exodus is 'a miraculous clearing of the land; the miraculous simplification of Israel's task'.[9]

As a Haganah intelligence report put it:

The big Jewish offensives ... instilled fear also in the Arab fighters and exaggerated rumors, influenced by the Oriental imagination, spread about Jewish secret weapons and great damage and losses that the Arabs suffered. The fear and depression grew with each new offensive ... After these victories the Arabs reached the conclusion that there is no place in the country where they are safe, and flight began also from purely Arab areas ... A psychosis of flight [took

hold] and massive flight and a complete evacuation of Arab settlements [began], even before any action was taken against them, or
solely on the basis of rumors that they were about to be attacked . . .
The Arab population in large parts of the country was destroyed in
every way, many Arab settlements ceased to exist, economic life was
paralysed and a vast amount of property was lost.[10]

## II: MEETING IN AMMAN

### 10 May

Disguised in Arab dress, Golda Meir arrives in Amman to meet
Abdullah. She is accompanied by Ezra Danin, head of the Haganah
intelligence service's Arab section. Danin, also dressed as an Arab,
had set up the meeting at an Arab friend's home.

The king looks tired and depressed. He proposes that Zionist statehood be cancelled and the Jews settle for autonomy while Transjordan
absorbs the whole of Palestine. There would be a joint Parliament in
which half the members would represent Jews who might make up
half the government. The only alternative is war. Meir points out
that this contradicts his earlier undertaking. The king replies that
conditions have changed. Arab feelings had been heightened by Deir
Yassin and development on the ground. He does not understand why
the Jews are in such a hurry. 'A people that has waited 2,000 years
can hardly be described as being in a hurry,' Meir replies.

'You must know that the Jews are the only friends you
have,' she adds.

'I know that very well,' the king responds. 'I have no illusions. I
know you and I believe in your good intentions.'

He says he thinks divine providence has brought the Jews back to
the region, which needs their knowledge and initiative. 'Only with
your help and your guidance would the Semites be able to revive
their ancient glory. We cannot expect genuine assistance from the
Christian world, which looks down on Semitic peoples. We will
progress only as a result of joint effort. I know all this and I believe
it sincerely, but conditions are difficult. One dare not take rash steps.
Therefore, I beg you once more to be patient.'

Meir replies that his proposal cannot even be considered. 'If Your Majesty had turned his back on our original understanding and wants war instead, there will be war,' she adds. 'Despite our handicap we believe that we will win. Perhaps we should meet again after the war when there will be a Jewish state.'

As the king gets up at the end of the hour-long conversation, he hooks his little finger round Danin's and walks with him to the door. 'You didn't help me this time,' he says with a sad smile as he steps into his car. The two Jews dine with Danin's friend – Meir hardly eats. They pass troop formations as they drive towards the border. The driver loses his nerve and drops them a couple of miles from the frontier. So they have to climb over hills and crawl through barbed wire before reaching Jewish territory at 3 a.m.[11]

The meeting gives rise to various interpretations. One is that Abdullah went back on his word and showed his untrustworthiness. Another was that Meir was simply delivering a warning, not seeking to negotiate. The decision to send a woman was, again, a matter of some controversy, given the king's conservative views. He would later claim that Meir had been the person most responsible for the ensuing war; she was certainly not adept in the arts of diplomacy.[12]

The most reasonable overall verdict comes from Yaacov Shimoni of the Jewish Agency's Political Department, who argued that the king had neither completely betrayed the earlier agreement, nor remained entirely faithful to it but had ended up somewhere in the middle, seeking to expand his realm, but without trying to conquer Jewish territory. By this line of reasoning, Zionist relations with Amman had to be maintained; how feasible that would be in the heat of war was to be tested.[13]

## 11 May

Distrust among other Arab rulers towards Abdullah is at a high level as the Arab League political committee meets in Damascus. The Syrians retail a story of a plot between the monarch and the Jews by which the Zionists would stage an invasion of Syria but give way to a Jordanian advance and thus enable the king to claim the crown of Syria. This plays into Egyptian and Saudi fears of an expanded Hashemite kingdom – there are rumours that Saudi volunteers

ostensibly heading for Palestine would, in fact, be used to attack
Transjordan. One thing unites the delegates – apprehension about
popular anger if they do not go to war. 'We must invade, otherwise
the people will kill us,' the Syrian foreign minister warns.[14]

## III: WE DID IT!

Returning to Tel Aviv from New York, Sharett is driven to Ben-
Gurion's home to report on his conversation with Marshall before
a meeting of their Mapai Party's central committee. As he left New
York, he had been paged at the airport. It was Weizmann on the
telephone who instructed him to tell everybody, 'It's now or never.
Fear not, nor be dismayed.'

Sharett tells Ben-Gurion of Marshall's warnings of potential annihilation and his suggestion of a postponement of the proclamation
of the Zionist state. He then adds, 'I think he's right.' At that, Ben-
Gurion locks the door and says, 'Moshe! I ask you to give a full and
precise report of your conversation with Marshall exactly as you
reported to me. But you're not going out of here before you promise
me one thing. Those last four words you said, you won't say them
at the Central Committee!' Sharett agrees.[15]

### 12 May

At 4 p.m., Marshall and Lovett go to the White House for a meeting with Truman on Palestine. Also present are the pro-Zionist
aide, David Niles, and Clark Clifford, from whom the president
had commissioned a briefing paper on the issue of recognition of
a new Jewish state. Marshall asks Lovett to put the case for trusteeship and says he, himself, had warned Sharett of the dangers
Zionists faced. Truman calls on Clifford who argues that the US
should recognise a new Jewish state before the Soviet Union and
announce this the following day, before the Mandate ends. As
he talks, he recalled, 'I noticed the thunder clouds gathering –
Marshall's face getting redder and redder.'

'This is just straight politics,' the secretary says. 'I don't even
understand why Clifford is here. This is not a political meeting.'

'General, he is here because I asked him to be here,' Truman replies.

As Marshall glares at him, Clifford says recognition would be consistent with Truman's approach. Everybody must feel some responsibility for the survivors of the Holocaust, he goes on, quoting from the book of Deuteronomy to justify the Zionist homeland claim. There is no alternative to partition and a separate Jewish state is inevitable, he adds.

Lovett responds that the whole issue should be left with the UN. He produces intelligence reports that immigrants to Palestine include Communists and Soviet agents. Premature American recognition would hurt US prestige and be seen as a 'very transparent' bid for the pro-Zionist vote in the November election, he argues.

Barely controlling his anger, Marshall insists that 'the great office of the president' is at stake. Domestic political considerations must not be allowed to intrude on foreign policy. Looking straight at Truman, he adds that if the president follows Clifford's advice and if he votes in November, he would cast his ballot against him.

Clifford would recall this as 'the sharpest rebuke' Truman had received. 'The president, I think, was struck dumb by it. There was this awful, *total* silence.' But he remains calm, raising his hand as he says he is well aware of the difficulties and dangers involved. Despite his message to Weizmann through Rosenman about recognition, he adds that he is inclined to agree with Marshall, but thinks it best to sleep on the matter. When he leaves, Marshall refuses to look at Clifford.

'That was rough as a cob,' Truman says to his aide. He tells Clifford not to feel bad about what has happened: 'Let's not agree that it's lost yet.'

That evening Lovett telephones Clifford to say they must meet as soon as possible. Over drinks at the under secretary's home, they agree that everything must be done to prevent a breach between Marshall and Truman. The nightmare is that the secretary might resign, which would hugely damage the president.[16]

Meeting in Damascus, the Arab League's political committee endorses an invasion of Palestine with a campaign in which Lebanese, Syrian and Iraqi armies would carry out a pincer movement and move on Haifa while Transjordanian units press towards the Mediterranean and the Egyptians advance from the south towards Jaffa and Tel Aviv. An Iraqi general is named as commander. The Palestinians are given no role.[17]

The Arab Legion is already engaged in a fresh attack against the Kfar Etzion kibbutz in the Judaea hills defended by five hundred Haganah troops and its residents. The assault begins before dawn with a mortar and artillery barrage after which armoured cars and infantry move in. 'Our situation is very bad,' the defenders radio. 'Every minute counts.' The artillery attack resumes and that night the defenders appeal: 'Extricate us immediately. There is no hope of holding out.'

At the same time, the Jewish administration begins an eleven-hour meeting in Tel Aviv to decide whether to declare a state immediately. The Mandate ends two days later. Three of its thirteen members are absent, two stuck in Jerusalem and one in New York. Sharett reports on the American position without mentioning his own views, while Golda Meir tells of her meeting with Abdullah. Yigael Yadin, the head of military operations, is called in to advise on the outlook. 'To put it cautiously, I would say that at this moment our chances are very balanced,' he says. 'To be more frank, I would say that [the Arabs] have a considerable advantage.' Galili adds that, before weapons arrive from abroad, 'the situation would be very grave'. Summing up as night falls, Ben-Gurion speaks of a perilous short-term situation. But, when arms are received, 'we would be able to land a powerful blow to the Arabs at the opening of their invasion and undermine their morale'. The outcome depended on wiping out most of the Legion, he says.[18]

There is a six to four vote in favour of declaring statehood on the fourteenth. Sharett casts the deciding vote. Ben-Gurion opposes defining the frontiers of the new country since, 'if our strength proves sufficient', the Jews could extend their borders. After intense discussion on what the new state should be called – 'Judaea' and 'Zion' had their advocates – Ben-Gurion backs Israel, which is adopted.[19]

In Cairo, a secret session of the Senate votes overwhelmingly to go to war. Driven by anti-Zionism, a desire to burnish his reputation, the wish to counter the Hashemite ambitions and the pressure of street demonstrations, King Farouk backs action. The army chief looks forward to 'a parade without any risks'. The whole affair would be a military picnic, the prime minister declares. Azzam of the Arab League says the Jews will be swept into the sea. Abdullah still has his doubts. 'The Jews are too strong – it is a mistake to make war,' he says. But popular pressure is building on him and the Legion is already attacking the Judaean kibbutz. 'The politicians, the demagogues, the press and the mob were in charge – not the soldiers,' Glubb would recall. 'Warnings went unheeded. Doubters were denounced as traitors. The Arabs believed themselves to be a great military people and saw the Jews as a nation of shopkeepers.'[20]

## 13 May

In Washington, Lovett telephones Clifford about the storm of the previous day's meeting. The presidential aide tells the under secretary he will have to persuade Marshall he is mistaken. Truman says the secretary needs a little more time.[21]

Glubb dispatches an experienced Arab Legion commander to take over command of the attack on the main section of Kfar Etzion. He finds the troops and militia spread out without any plan. They have had no food or drink for twenty-four hours. Under his orders, the attack resumes, armoured cars and infantry breaching the defences. After being ordered to surrender at noon, a hundred men and women assemble in an open area in the centre of the settlement where a photographer takes pictures of them. Then they become targets for rifle fire while a crowd surges forward shouting 'Dear Yassin'. Almost all the men and women are murdered, though Legion officers save a few, one officer shooting dead two men who try to rape a Jewish woman.[22]

## 14–15 May

As the declaration of statehood is being completed in Tel Aviv, a Red Cross convoy reaches the three other sections of Etzion. The Legion pulls back. But militia men fire at disarmed Jews, killing several. The Red Cross gets a Legion detachment to intervene to restore order. Trucks take 357 residents to Transjordan.[23]

The British high commissioner drives in his armour-plated black Daimler limousine to the airfield outside Jerusalem to fly to Haifa and sail away in a Royal Navy flotilla. The British commander in Jerusalem tells the Hanagah his men will be gone by 4 p.m. On the

coastal plain, Zionist forces clean out villages. As the inhabitants
flee, the Arab Liberation Army makes them pay for safe passage.[24]

In Tel Aviv, Ben-Gurion rises at 7 a.m. and goes through his usual
morning routine, reading documents and sipping black coffee.
After lunch he is driven with his wife to the white-painted Tel Aviv
Museum for the ceremony to declare the new state. They travel in
a black limousine, rented for the occasion. He wears a black suit,
white shirt and, unusually, but to mark the historic nature of the
event, a tie.

The event was supposed to have been kept secret but a flag-waving
crowd and Haganah cadets line the street. The politician walks
briskly up the steps to the hall, returning a salute from a policeman.
The hall is too small to accommodate all who want to attend so the
orchestra is sent to the upper floor. The heat is intense.

Ben-Gurion pauses to be photographed by Robert Capa, who
appeals for a smile, which he gets. Then, at 4 p.m., his face shiny
pink with emotion, Ben-Gurion strikes the table with his gavel. A big
portrait of Herzel hangs behind him. All sing the national anthem,
'Hatikva' ('The Hope'), with its lines

> Our hope is not lost
> The hope of two thousand years;
> To be a free people in our land
> The land of Zion and Jerusalem!

Ben-Gurion, who will become prime minister three days later, reads
out the scroll on the Establishment of the State of Israel before
formally declaring its existence. The crowd applauds. Golda Meir
sheds tears. The proclamation is accepted by acclamation. 'Hatikva'
is sung again and Ben-Gurion declares, 'The State of Israel is established! This meeting is adjourned.' The inauguration of the new state
lasts thirty-seven minutes. While it is going on, the Arab Legion, by
coincidence, halts a bombardment of Jewish Jerusalem to take tea;
by the time the session is finished, they resume the attack. Weizmann
is elected president two days later, but he is abroad and is not sworn
in till the following February. Ben-Gurion will not let him add his

signature to the document establishing Israel, formally because he had not been present on 14 May but as a sign of the power balance between them.[25]

'You see, we did it!' Ben-Gurion remarks to a reporter on his way out as people around him cheer, weep and dance in celebration. In his diary that night, he notes, presumably referring to the impending attack by Arab armies, 'In the country there is celebration and profound joy – and once again I am a mourner among the celebrants.'

In Washington, Truman makes an early call to Clifford to tell him that Marshall has agreed to de facto recognition of Israel. The secretary still does not support the course the president favours, but will not oppose it publicly. 'That is all we need,' Truman tells his aide. Clifford gets the head of the Jewish Agency in Washington to draft a letter requesting recognition. Clifford and Lovett meet for lunch in a club and work on a statement for the president. The under secretary has told his boss that recognition is Truman's choice, and the secretary says a president has the constitutional right to make such a decision. But he never speaks to Clifford again.

Eleven minutes after the declaration of statehood in Tel Aviv, the White House announces de facto recognition.[26] At the United Nations, Ambassador Austin is told by telephone and goes home after a brief session with his delegation, some of whom broke into laughter on hearing the news, thinking it was a joke. State Department officials backing the trusteeship option are furious, both because of the policy switch and because they think their country will be ridiculed for lack of clear purpose.

Meeting Lovett later in the day, Truman refers to his problems with State – to which the under secretary replies softly, 'They almost put it over on you.' Eddie Jacobson flies from Kansas City to New York to see Weizmann. Going on to Washington, he presents himself at the White House as the 'temporary, unofficial ambassador of Israel'. The chief rabbi of Israel telephones Truman to tell him, 'God put you in your mother's womb so you would be the instrument to bring the rebirth of Israel after two thousand years.' When Niles looks at the president during the call, he sees tears running down his cheeks.[27]

At midnight, King Abdullah holds up his revolver, fires a single shot and cries 'Forward' to the Arab Legion troops deployed on the eastern bank of the River Jordan. 'He who will be killed will be a martyr; he who lives will be glad of fighting for Palestine,' he tells them. 'I remind you of the Jihad and the martyrdom of your great-grandfathers.' A long column of jubilant troops in trucks moves across the bridge. Their vehicles are decorated with green branches and pink flowers. 'The procession seemed more like a carnival than troops going to war,' Glubb would recall.[28]

As the Legion advances, Ben-Gurion is awakened in the early morning and taken, over his wife's protests, to broadcast to sixty American radio stations. As he starts to speak, Egyptian planes attack a nearby airfield and power station. The walls of the broadcasting hut shake. The control panel lights blink. 'The explosions you can hear are Arab planes bombing Tel Aviv,' the prime minister says in a low voice as his wife hammers on the door for him to go home. He visits the airfield to see the damage, and is then driven home where he sits at his desk and writes in his diary of the aerial attack, 'Outside stood people in pyjamas. I looked at them and saw that there was no fear in their eyes. I knew then that we would win.'[29]

## IV: OPPOSING FORCES

The Arab forces that moved into Palestine totalled 22–28,000 men from Egypt, Iraq, Syria, Transjordan, Yemen, Saudi Arabia and Lebanon as well as 2,000 members of the Arab Liberation Army already there. They had superior firepower and would be able to concentrate on each of the fronts set down in the attack plans whereas the Jews would be dispersed between the different theatres of war. The Legion was well trained, led and equipped with fast armoured cars and big mortars and cannons. Other Arab forces were less impressive.

Egypt had tanks, armoured cars and heavy field guns but a British assessment at the beginning of the year concluded that its army would 'hardly warrant consideration as a serious invading force'. Gamal Abdel Nasser, who was in the infantry, recalled that 'there was no concentration of forces, no accumulation of ammunition and equipment ... no reconnaissance, no intelligence, no plans'. The army had to rent trucks from Palestinians to carry troops. Though its air force was the largest in the Arab world, it was short of qualified pilots, ground crews and spare parts.

Iraq had two undersized infantry divisions and a poorly equipped artillery brigade, some of whose equipment dated from the First World War. Most of its planes were old and lacked proper maintenance. Only one Syrian brigade of 2,000 men was operational, and its air fleet was unfit for action.[30]

Against this, Israel could field 27–30,000 troops plus 6,000 Home Guard and 2–3,000 Irgun and Stern irregulars. On 14 May, it had only two heavy tanks, a makeshift force of armoured cars, a few mortars and some Piper Cub planes which carried no weapons and could be used only for reconnaissance and to drop bombs by hand. But the new state would shortly receive significant arms supplies, including ten Messerschmitt fighters from Czechoslovakia along with rifles, machine guns and ammunition. Agents had bought tanks, half-track vehicles, mortars and mountain guns elsewhere in Europe and in the US, where a few decommissioned bomber transport planes and half-tracks were listed as 'agricultural equipment'. Haganah had cargo ships waiting to transport the weapons but had not been able to do so until the British arms embargo was lifted with the end of the Mandate.

Despite the argument at the top between Ben-Gurion and Galili, the defenders were highly motivated, had experience from the clashes with Palestinians, were about to receive substantial arms shipments and were fighting on their own territory with short lines of communication.

As the Legion pushed across the Jordan, the Egyptians moved up from the south, the Iraqis advanced in the north and the Syrians into the Golan. Egyptian Spitfire planes kept up the attack on Tel Aviv, killing forty-two people and wounding a hundred, but most of the planes were lost by the end of the month, five of them shot down by the British when they bombed an airfield near Haifa still held by the former mandatory power.

In the Negev, Egyptian troops attacked a series of Jewish settlements. Most held out but they could not halt the advance which the Israelis feared would threaten Tel Aviv. Surrounded by barbed wire and zigzag trenches, one kibbutz resisted a force of tall Sudanese urged on by smartly uniformed officers walking behind them waving revolvers. After five days, however, machine gun and mortar fire forced the Jews to leave.[31]

In the north, the Iraqis crossed the Jordan to attack a strategically located kibbutz but were beaten off and retreated over the river. The Syrians took a Jewish village on the southern edge of the Sea of Galilee which was recovered by IDF reinforcements under Moshe Dayan. In Damascus, the defence minister and chief of staff resigned. To the west, the Lebanese army occupied an abandoned Arab village, lost it at the end of the month but then recaptured it to open up a supply route to the Arab Liberation Army in Galilee.

Even as their troops moved, discord continued among the Arab leaders. The Syrian president telephoned Amman to counsel against an advance by the Legion, saying the Palestinians should be given all possible aid instead. Abdullah wrote later that this 'strange proposal' aroused his apprehension. On the ground, his forces were pursuing their own agenda – instead of heading north as laid down by the Arab battle plan, they concentrated on occupying the West Bank of the Jordan. Cheering crowds greeted them. There was no resistance.

But Jewish operations around and inside Jerusalem provoked a stream of appeals to Abdullah and Glubb to intervene in the city, which they did not wish to do since this would string out their troops along a lengthy front and bring them into conflict with Israeli forces. They also foresaw diplomatic complications and knew that the Legion was not trained for urban fighting.[32]

But it became increasingly difficult for the king to stand aside from the fight for the holy city if he was to aspire to leadership of the Arab side. Azzam Pasha warned he would have to speak out if the Legion did not enter Jerusalem. 'Don't worry,' the king replied. 'I'll send the necessary troops. My ultimate objective is the head of the snake – Tel Aviv. That should make you happy.'

'If you take Tel Aviv, I shall place the crown of Palestine on your head,' the Arab League official responded.

Glubb was handed a message from Amman as he visited the front. 'His Majesty the King orders an advance towards Jerusalem from the direction of Ramallah,' it read. 'He intends this action to threaten the Jews in order that they accept a truce in Jerusalem.'[33]

A hundred legionnaires advanced into the Old City, driving out defenders and manning the wall, their rifles pointing through crossbow apertures. But they were outnumbered, and Glubb summoned help from the Arab Liberation Army, which began shelling. Back in Amman, playing with a string of amber beads, he ordered more men to be transferred to the Jerusalem front.[34]

Outside the city, a fierce battle erupted for the rolling, scrubby Latrun hills overlooking the road link with Tel Aviv. Successive Jewish attempts to dislodge the Legion from its positions on the heights, which had been allocated to the Palestinians, failed. In Jerusalem itself, the Legion advanced through the sixteenth-century Zion Gate and attacked the big, stone-faced monastery Notre Dame de France, where they were embroiled in hand-to-hand fighting before being forced to retreat.

Elsewhere, the new state's Carmeli Brigade established control over the invasion route along the coast from Lebanon; the troops were told 'to kill adult males, to destroy and torch [villages]'. The town of Acre, which was filled with refugees from Haifa and where a typhus epidemic broke out, was the theatre of a fierce 22-hour street battle before a priest carrying a white flag walked from the Old City to signal surrender to the Israelis. But an Egyptian armoured column advanced from the south towards Tel Aviv while the Iraqis were poised to threaten the centre of the country and cut it in two by reaching the sea. 'There was nothing left to fight with,' Ben-Gurion recalled. 'One of the heads of staff said to me, "Another seventy-two hours and it will all be over."'[35]

However, the Egyptian progress halted and the Iraqi threat did not materialise for the time being, while the Haganah held on to its strategic positions in Jerusalem. A ship carrying 5,000 rifles and forty-five cannons was on its way and the first five Messerschmitts arrived with Czechoslovak technicians. Ben-Gurion's confidence rose. The exodus of Palestinians continued; the Israeli command put the total at almost 400,000 at the end of the month. The government adopted a ban on the return of refugees at least for the duration of hostilities. The Mapam Party, whose government ministers opposed expulsion of Palestinians, wanted to allow 'peace-minded' refugees to come back. But Ben-Gurion looked to an agreement with Arab states to absorb them permanently.[36]

The prime minister felt confident enough to send a message to the General Staff saying that, when arms shipments arrived, an attack should be launched on Lebanon to establish a Christian state with which Israel would make an alliance. Transjordan would be bombed and the Legion smashed. After this, Syria would fall. 'If Egypt still dares to fight on, we shall bomb Port Said, Alexandria and Cairo. And in this fashion, we will end the war and settle our forefathers' accounts with Egypt, Assyria and Aram,'[37] he added.[38]

More immediately, Ben-Gurion was fixated on the battle in the Latrun hills outside Jerusalem but a fresh Israeli assault failed. The Legion defenders were well trained and equipped while the attacking infantry was disorganised – some were newly arrived immigrants in shorts and sandals who had never handled a rifle and did not understand the orders in Hebrew. They suffered from a blisteringly hot wind and swarms of noxious flies. Water soon ran short. At one point, Robert Capa arrived with a canteen of arak spirit which soldiers swilled down. The Israeli advance was uncoordinated and they soon fell back in the face of the Legion's professionalism. 'The plan was good,' an American eyewitness recorded. 'The artillery was good. The armour was excellent. The infantry was disgraceful.'[39]

Still, the attacks tied down Legion forces and covered the forging of a rough road to Jerusalem through the hills. Known as the 'Burma Road' after the Second World War route into China and snaking over 400-feet drops into the valley, it enabled lorries to take supplies to the city. A new water pipeline was also laid.

Inside Jerusalem, the Legion blew up the main synagogue and killed thirty-nine defenders. But a ceasefire was signed after two old rabbis carrying a white flag advanced towards the Arab troops. The Legion protected the Jews from the mob. In all, 340 men were taken prisoner. More than a thousand inhabitants were conveyed to the Zion Gate and freed. Arabs then pillaged the quarter and brought down many of its buildings.

## V: Ceasefire

The Attlee government was growing embarrassed both by the war which had followed the ill-prepared ending of the Mandate and by the involvement of British officers in the Legion's battle for Jerusalem. Bevin had a ceasefire proposal drafted to be put to the United Nations and lobbied Abdullah to accept it. British officers with the Arab Legion were told to return to Transjordan if it attacked territory allocated to Israel.

Abdullah knew his Legion needed a pause to re-equip itself with men and munitions, so he urged other Arab leaders to accept the ceasefire. But the League's political committee rejected this as a sign of defeat which would arouse public anger. The people had been fed false news of victories over the Jews; to admit the truth would be highly dangerous. Though explanations might be crafted as a shield for Arab honour, the invaders also knew a truce was likely to benefit Israel as it brought in weapons and men.

On 29 May, Bevin put his proposal to the UN for a four-week suspension of military activity accompanied by an arms embargo. British officers with the Arab Legion were temporarily withdrawn as a symbolic gesture. Accepting the plan, the international body named a Swedish diplomat, Count Folke Bernadotte, as mediator. A member of the royal family who had negotiated with the Nazis for the lives of Jews, he believed privately that partition had been a mistake; the British hoped he might alter some boundaries set down by the UN.

Meeting the experienced UN diplomat Ralph Bunche in Paris, the count asked, 'What do they want me to do there?'

'To go and stop the war,' Bunche replied.

'How?'

'With bare hands.'

'OK, let's go.'[40]

# CHAPTER FORTY-FOUR

# ASIAN ENCOUNTERS

## I: THE QUAGMIRE DEEPENS

While the US set out to make Japan its principal ally in the east, the PLA scored fresh victories across the East China Sea. Liu Bocheng's army, which had crossed the Yellow River the previous summer, consolidated its position in Luoyang on the central plains, establishing a link with Communist units pressing against the veteran warlord Yan Xishan in coal-rich Shanxi province to the north.

In Manchuria, the capture of the strategic railway city of Siping opened the way to Changchun, the one-time capital of the Japanese puppet state of Manchukuo, which the Communists had identified as a prime target. In the last week of May, the PLA started its encirclement of the city on the huge Manchurian plain, cutting it off from KMT forces elsewhere and bombarding the city continuously.

Government planes tried to drop supplies, but the Communists brought their anti-aircraft guns to bear. Inside the city's defences were 100,000 government troops and half a million civilians, including refugees stopped on their flight towards the Great Wall. Trenches were dug and three lines of defensive pillboxes erected. Chiang initially ordered that nobody should be allowed to leave and, to increase pressure on food supplies, the PLA followed suit, turning back those who tried to flee as a big no-man's land opened up around the city.[1]

Though the Nationalists still controlled the air, the PLA was now clearly superior in the north-east in terms of manpower and territory while also advancing across northern China. It also staged raids on the border with Mongolia to seize large stores of grain and munitions before melting into the mountains. The Communists suffered some setbacks – one army suffered heavy losses when trapped in the Wei Valley in the north. But, in his headquarters in a one-storey house in the small Hebei provincial town of Xibaipo, Mao worked on coordinating advances in the north-eastern, northern and central regions. A North China Liberated Area covering five provinces was announced and plans drawn up for a unified North China People's Government. At the end of the month, the chairman told Lin Biao to build up food supplies for a big offensive against more than 400,000 government troops hunkered down in major Manchurian cities.

The generalissimo reshuffled his top command and appointed a new prime minister. But conditions even in the Nationalist heartland grew ever more strained. Chiang faced a growing challenge from a loose coalition of regional barons and liberals headed by vice president Li Zongren. Local warlords were increasingly looking to their own futures and exploring the prospect of understandings with the Communists. The National Assembly was unable to open its scheduled session in Nanking for lack of a quorum because many Nationalists stayed away.

Inflation continued to roar ahead; the army and Kuomintang officials became ever more rapacious. At one point, the price of a sack of flour rose by 40 per cent in thirty-six hours in Shanghai and the value of the currency halved in a month. The government proved itself unable to cope with the mounting problems of social unrest, economic depression and corruption – a wealthy textile merchant from the south complained in a letter to KMT headquarters that the party was made up of 'thieves and highway robbers, (worse than socialists)'.[2]

'Shanghai was the same rat race, only more jittery,' John Melby wrote in his diary. 'I have never seen a place where the rumors are quite so numerous, so fantastic, or so readily accepted by people who should know better. Of course a cost of living index which is now 150,000 times what it was ten years ago is hardly calculated to be reassuring.'[3]

## II: Korea divides

Nearly 8 million people took part in the first elections ever held in Korea on 10 May, supervised by the UN. Following a Coalition Conference in Pyongyang which called for a united country, the end of 'monopoly capitalism' and withdrawal of foreign forces, the North and non-Communist leftists opposed to the division of the peninsula boycotted the poll. So voting was confined to the South, accompanied by rioting that took ninety-three lives in the preceding days. Several prominent Nationalist politicians denounced the event for cementing the division of the peninsula.

Turnout was 95.5 per cent for a Parliament that would pick the president and approve a new constitution. Syngman Rhee's National Association for the Rapid Realisation of Korean Independence emerged as the largest party but with only 26 per cent of the vote and fifty-five of the two hundred legislative seats. Independents took eight-five, so there was plenty of room for horse-trading.

The split over the election among Nationalists led the veteran independence campaigner Kim Koo to break with Rhee and found his own party, but he got the backing of only thirteen legislators for the presidency compared with his opponent's 180. The South declared its statehood and, as a result of the election outcome, was set on a path of autocratic, American-allied rule, while the North established the Democratic People's Republic of Korea in September with Kim Il-sung as prime minister.

# CHAPTER FORTY-FIVE

# CHANGING OF THE GUARD

## I: Ou Baas counts on victory

'I feel the air of victory here,' Jan Smuts, South Africa's prime minister, told the biggest rally he had addressed in the campaign for the country's general election at the end of May. The United Party (UP) headed by the veteran statesman, soldier and philosopher felt it had every reason for confidence. It held eighty-nine seats in Parliament to forty-eight for the National Party (NP). Its period in office had seen significant industrialisation though the economy remained over-dependent on mining and finance was in the hands of banks linked to London. There had been some reforms of race relations and social conditions, but they had been timid enough not to scare the overwhelmingly white electorate.[1]

The Witwatersrand region remained the world's major source of gold. Diamonds were an important source of revenue. Coal production was expanding. Johannesburg was the largest city in southern Africa. Urbanisation rose from 18 to 30 per cent of the population in three decades as black labourers and white rural dwellers moved into cities to work in industry.

Modern sectors began to emerge in farming which became increasingly commercialised. The war brought a boost in demand for food exports, notably in the shape of contracts from Britain, followed by a post-war jump in demand for wool. The number of tractors rose from 6,000 in 1937 to 22,300 in 1947. But there was still a dependence on the large poor black labour force in virtual servitude and a system of land rights which allowed black ownership of less than 10 per cent of the countryside.[2]

The son of prosperous Afrikaner farmers, Smuts was by far the best-known South African. He had long-standing friendships with Churchill and Chaim Weizmann – he was an ardent supporter of Zionism. In the 1920s, he developed the concept of holism, which he summed up as the 'fundamental factor operative towards the creation of wholes in the universe' leading to a great international body uniting all nations.

Now seventy-eight and known as Ou Baas (the Old Man), he had gained a double first-class degree at Cambridge University, and then led a commando raiding party against the British in the Boer War at the turn of the century. He played a major role in negotiating the end of the conflict and then in engineering self-rule for the Transvaal followed by the granting of a constitution to the Union in 1909. After a spell as minister of the interior, defence and mines, he commanded Allied armies against the Germans in Southern Africa in the First World War and then moved to London to join in military planning before participating in the Versailles Peace Conference, from which he retired home to take up the premiership.

After five years in office, his coalition government was unexpectedly defeated in 1924 by the National Party. Ten years on, after the Great Depression hit the economy and the NP suffered by-election losses, Smuts and the National Party leader, J. B. M. Hertzog, formed a coalition known as the Fusion government, with the latter as prime minister. But they then split over their attitude to the Second World War – Smuts favoured backing Britain while, reflecting Afrikaner sentiment, Hertzog held that South Africa had no reason to become involved in a European struggle, and argued for neutrality.

After losing a parliamentary vote on the issue, Hertzog resigned and was replaced by Smuts. Leadership of the Afrikaner cause passed to the harder-line Daniel Malan, a stout Dutch Reformed Church minister who had formed the Purified National Party to advocate stricter racial segregation. Flirting with pro-Nazi groups, it mined the heritage of 'ox cart' fundamentalism from the heritage of the Great Trek of Boers in the 1830s in search of a homeland free from British rule.[3]

## II: 'THE BLACK THREAT'

Smuts sat in at the Second World War Cabinet in London, becoming the only foreigner with the rank of a British field marshal. South Africans fought alongside the British in Africa and Italy as well as flying with the RAF, while the naval base at Simonstown became an important strategic asset for the Allies when Axis control of the Mediterranean forced shipping to take the route around the Cape to and from Asia. This did not endear Smuts and his government to Afrikaner voters, who made up 57 per cent of the electorate. While the prime minister extolled South Africa's links with Britain and the Commonwealth in his speech to the rally in Johannesburg, many of the Boer descendants wanted the country to strike out on its own, reducing the Anglophone influence and tightening racial segregation.

Malan and the NP offered them what they sought as it trumpeted the need to do more for poor whites and strengthen defences against the *swart gevarr* (Black Threat). Afrikaner Nationalists attacked the government over housing and food shortages, inflation and supposed weakness in combatting the *root gevaar* (Red Peril). 'A vote for Jan Smuts is a vote for Joe Stalin', proclaimed a party slogan, with a cartoon of the two men shaking hands. Smuts's wartime remark that he 'doffed his cap' to the Soviet leader was made much of.

The core of the National Party's 1948 election campaign was the interlocking of racial fear and Afrikaner values. Its apartheid policy promised to maximise segregation, protect white workers, abolish the slim African representation in Parliament, outlaw marriage between racial groups, set aside designated reserves as the home of blacks and control their entry into towns while removing the right to vote from non-black coloured people and sending Indians back to their original family home. To put a gloss on the policy, the theory was promulgated that apartheid would help the black population – since they were doomed by divine wisdom to inferiority, the 'Bantus' would be able to develop in special reserves free from competition from superior whites while gaining from wages earned working for the masters.

Malan asked whether the European race would be able to 'retain its rule, its purity, its civilisation, or will it float along until it vanishes without honour in the black sea of South Africa's non-European population'. 'We can act in only one of two directions,' the NP declared. 'Either we must follow the course of equality, which must eventually mean national suicide for the white race, or we must take the course of apartheid through which the character and future of every race will be protected.' The message was, as the historian Deborah Posel put it, one of 'simplicity, and appeal to the voters' desire for security in a world which seemed to be moving too fast in a liberal direction and turning its wrath against South Africa as it did so'.[4]

Religious, social and educational societies proved a powerful network of grassroots support along with bodies ranging from Boy Scouts to automobile clubs and a small business organisation. Secret societies, including the Broederbond, to which Malan and leading colleagues belonged, provided a militant ideological line that the 'Afrikaner nation was put in this land by the hand of God and is destined to continue in existence as a nation with its own nature and calling'.[5] The Ossewabrandwag (OB) organisation, with its seal proclaiming fealty to 'My God My Volk My Land Suid-Afrika', claimed to 'perpetuate the spirit of the ox wagon ... protecting and promoting the religious, cultural and material interests of the Afrikaner, fostering patriotism and national pride'. Storm troopers from its paramilitary wing sabotaged railways and power lines. 'We wanted to be free of the English and we wanted our own Republic,' as one member, future prime minister B. J. Vorster, explained.[6]

Malan ordered the National Party to break with the OB in 1942 and marginalised other far-right groups. But he faced dissidence from the Transvaal, where Afrikaner fundamentalists regarded his grouping of politicians, financial institutions and the influential *Die Burger* newspaper as dangerously capitalistic and insufficiently radical in support of the community's value and the white community. However, the mainstream NP recognised that complete racial separation was impossible since white-owned factories and firms needed the labour of the 80 per cent black population.

Against this message rooted in religious fundamentalism, the UP's message of national unity and realism sounded weak. Smuts's role in drafting the charter of the United Nations, drawing on his holistic thinking, did not impress voters concerned with issues closer to home. A token enfranchisement of Indians won little support. The arrival of 60,000 skilled European workers under an immigration scheme was depicted by the opposition as a bid to 'plough the Afrikaner under'. Retail inflation reached 6.5 per cent and the all-important gold industry was hit by strikes. Government campaigning was lacklustre. The NP made inroads among lower-paid white industrial workers and in rural areas which had a disproportionate share of parliamentary seats.

Strikes for wage increases and better conditions by black workers fuelled white fears, as did a document of 'African Claims' presented to the government by the African National Congress (ANC), including full citizenship and an end to discriminatory laws. As nothing changed, more radical voices increased their influence in the movement, including the young Nelson Mandela. But, at this stage, black militancy had more of an effect in providing the NP with a bogey than in achieving concessions from the white establishment.

## III: A GREAT SHOCK

Despite Smuts's optimism, the government's majority was not as firm or strong as it appeared. At the previous 'khaki election' in 1943, fifteen of its seats were won with majorities of under six hundred votes. The NP had done better and the Afrikaner vote for the government had fallen. The UP then lost a series of by-elections and, while the prime minister was still alert, trim and vigorous, many voters felt it was time for a change. Popular feeling was growing increasingly volatile – hundreds of striking building workers broke up a Smuts election rally as campaign rhetoric grew more heated.

His immensely hard-working deputy and probable successor, J. H. Hofmeyr, who thought discrimination on grounds of race alone was morally wrong, was regarded as a dangerous liberal and traitor to the Afrikaner cause, even if his liberalism was extremely cautious and defined mainly by the National Party's extremism (he acknowledged that he found the idea of racial mixing repugnant). On the other hand, Malan and his colleagues had no doubt that the separation of the races was divinely ordained as part of their special destiny. Whereas the UP had equal numbers from both the two white linguistic groups, the NP did not field a single candidate from the English-speaking community.[7]

When South Africa voted on 26 May, the result was a major shock. The United Party and its allies got 53 per cent of the votes, but the lopsided distribution of constituencies in favour of rural areas gave the National Party a majority of seats. Only 20–25 per cent of Afrikaners backed the government. 'At last, we have got our country back,' the NP jubilantly declared as Malan became prime minister, a post he would hold for six and a half years. Nelson Mandela, who had been elected to the ANC Committee for the Transvaal, was reported to have been stunned and dismayed at the outcome.

With increased backing from farmers in the Transvaal and among the white working class, Malan's party took seventy seats, plus nine for an allied Afrikaner group. This enabled it to finish ahead of the UP's sixty-five seats plus six for its ally, the Labour Party. Smuts was beaten in his constituency by 3,759 votes to 3,535. Despite his iron self-control, the old man could not hide his bitter disappointment. On a drive in the countryside to try to calm himself, he was so self-absorbed that he did not notice when he ran over a cockerel.[8]

# EUROPEAN
# CONFRONTATIONS

The Kremlin took three weeks to come back on Tito's letter rebutting its attacks on the Yugoslav leadership. It had circulated Stalin's original charge sheet around the Cominform to rally support among East European leaders, many of whom resented the way Tito paraded his partisan credentials in contrast to their wartime stays in Moscow. In Budapest, Rákosi annotated his copy with fiercely critical remarks. The Bulgarian Central Committee warned against 'possible harmful influence of the anti-Marxist views of one part of the leading Yugoslav comrades'.[1]

The 10,000-word missive sent to Belgrade in early May dismissed the Yugoslav message as childish, bourgeois, groundless, laughable and lacking honest intent. It demeaned the partisans' wartime struggle against the Germans and accused the authorities of letting the US ambassador in Belgrade act 'as though he owned the place'. The suggestion that Moscow should send a delegation for talks was rejected since the Yugoslav party was 'crudely destroying the principal directive of Lenin' and refused to admit or correct its errors. Rather, the matter would be put before the Cominform.

In further exchanges, the Yugoslavs insisted on their intention to 'resolutely construct socialism and remain loyal to the Soviet Union, loyal to the Doctrines of Marx, Engels, Lenin and Stalin'. But they were told they had 'gone a step further in aggravating their crude mistakes of principle [and] cut themselves off from the united socialist peoples' front'. They had put their own interests and ambitions first and made mistakes which would be fatal for the Yugoslav people. They were too proud of their successes against the Germans and failed to acknowledge that the Red Army had saved their country from destruction. When Tito's birthday came on 27 May, there was no greeting from Stalin.

The following day, a fifteen-hour meeting between Soviet and Western military delegates in Berlin that dragged on till 1 a.m. underlined the depth of east–west differences. The senior British general accused the Russians of 'sheer effrontery' and added that he 'would like to warn the Soviet commander that he is not the dictator of Berlin'. *Pravda* sounded off against 'the aggressive plans of the instigators of a new war'.[2]

The Russians put off one four-power meeting and stormed out of another, their military delegates shouting as they went. In Washington, Chief of Staff Omar Bradley warned of 'an alarming menace to the security of the United States' in the form of 4 million Soviet troops and 14,000 military aircraft which were 'capable of quickly over-running most of Europe, the Near and Middle East, Korea and even China'. Bevin told the House of Commons that Britain was in Berlin as a matter of right and would stay there. A settlement to the east–west differences over the city was unlikely, he added, because of the 'ideological attitude on the part of the Kremlin'.

At the Labour Party's annual conference, the foreign secretary said Britain was 'not prepared to sit idly by and see a ... process of Communization carried on over a weakened, distracted and disunited Europe'. He was frank about the inability of the West to influence the other side of the Iron Curtain. 'We cannot change the Communism of Russia, and I am not going to try,' he said. 'We cannot pursue, and we have no intention of pursuing a policy in Eastern Europe of trying to change by force many of the things done in those states with which we do not agree. Those things will have to be worked out in the process of time.'[3]

So, there was nothing to be done about Czechoslovakia, where the government parties got 89 per cent of the vote in the May election though there were 1.5 million blank papers or abstentions. The new regime installed its nomenklatura of some 15,000 cadres to take charge as the civil service underwent a fresh purge, remaining private firms were nationalised and, at Moscow's urging, an intensive programme of industrialisation was pursued in both the Czech lands and Slovakia.[4]

Meeting Gottwald, Beneš said he had decided to resign as president. 'You are throwing down the gauntlet, and we will be compelled to pick it up,' the prime minister replied. The head of state remained in seclusion in the Bohemian countryside as Parliament adopted the constitution which declared Czechoslovakia a people's democracy. As the dictatorship of the proletariat under the Communist Party was enshrined, eight Czechoslovak airmen defected to the UK after 'borrowing' a passenger plane.[5]

To the south, the Greek justice minister, Christos Ladas, was killed outside a church in Athens by a hand grenade thrown into his car. The assassin, wearing a blue air force tunic, was captured after being seriously wounded. More than 150 Communist prisoners were reported to have been executed in the following days. The body of an American radio correspondent, George Polk, was found floating in Salonika harbour, bound, gagged and shot through the head. His reports for CBS had been outspokenly critical of the government and the Truman administration's support. At the time of his death, he had reportedly been on his way to interview the rebel commander, Markos.[6]

Still, there were expressions of hope at a conference in The Hague of 750 delegates who issued a call for Europe's political, economic and monetary union. 'We must aim at nothing less than the union of Europe as a whole,' Churchill told the meeting, looking forward to 'a happier sunlit age, when all the little children who are now growing up in this tormented world may find themselves ... the heirs of all the treasures of the past and the masters of all the science, the abundance and the glories of the future'.[7]

~

## MEANWHILE

- Truman signs an order for government seizure of US railways amid a crippling strike and broader labour unrest.
- Thomas Dewey wins the Republican primary in Oregon,

blunting the momentum of the outsider Harold Stassen and putting himself on track for the nomination. During the primary battle, he and Stassen held the first radio debate between candidates; it focused on whether the Communist Party should be outlawed in the USA – Stassen favoured this but Dewey argued that 'you can't shoot an idea with a gun'.

- British imports rise to a record level, pushing the trade deficit up to £650 million on an annualised basis. The government lifts rationing for ties, gloves and unfashioned women's cotton stockings.

- British doctors vote 13,891 to 12,799 against the National Health Service proposed by the government but, given the narrowness of the outcome, the Council of the Medical Association advises co-operation with the scheme to come into effect in July.

- General Xuan is elected president of the Provisional Central Government of Vietnam – he and the French announce that they are in agreement.

- The head of the Food and Agriculture Organization of the UN says the 'whole human race is rumbling to destruction' because of shortages of supply and rising populations.

- Screenwriters Dalton Trumbo and John Howard Lawson are sentenced to a year in prison for contempt of Congress after refusing to say if they were members of the Communist Party.

- Princess Elizabeth and the Duke of Edinburgh pay a triumphant visit to Paris, attending a gala ballet evening at the opera and, after official events, having dinner in a restaurant and going to cabarets.

# PART FOURTEEN

# JUNE 1948

ACTS

*UN brokers Israel–Arab ceasefire; Truman gets out of
the Washington bubble while Republicans nominate
Dewey; USSR expels Yugoslavia from Communist fold
as East European grip tightens; Chinese Communists
take first provincial capital amid further government
economic woes; India and Pakistan deadlocked in
Kashmir while Hyderabad and India shape up for a
fight; South African government starts to implement
apartheid; Anti-colonial revolt spreads to Malaya; direct
confrontation unfolds over Berlin and airlift starts.*

SCENES

*Tel Aviv, Amman; Berlin, London; The Ferdinand
Magellan train, Philadelphia; Belgrade, Bucharest;
Kaifeng, Nanking; Hyderabad, Delhi, Jammu and
Kashmir; Pretoria.*

CAST

*Ben-Gurion, Abdullah, Begin; Truman, Bevin, Stalin,
Clay, Vasily Sokolovsky; Cardinal Mindszenty, Beneš;
Tito; Menon, the nizam of Hyderabad; Malan, Smuts;
Malay guerrillas, Malcolm MacDonald.*

# TRUCE

## I: The initiative shifts

This was a month in which many of the themes laid out in this book moved ahead at the same time – from Berlin to China, Palestine to South East Asia, South Africa to the United States and India to the Balkans – underlining how the world was shifting on so many fronts.

On 1 June, Israel and the Arab nations which had invaded Palestine cabled the United Nations to accept the ceasefire put forward by Count Bernadotte who was in Amman that day for talks with King Abdullah. During his visit, Israeli planes dropped fifteen bombs on the city, killing six people. Both sides realised that they needed a respite as the fighting bogged down on all fronts. Arab forces were exhausted and Israeli commanders recognised the benefits of a pause to build up their strength and train tens of thousands of refugee recruits. The commander of the Carmeli Brigade called it like dew from heaven. A four-week ceasefire was agreed to run from 11 June.

Basic political positions did not change. The Arabs refused to recognise Israel and the new state was not going to relinquish advantages gained on the battlefield. Before the ceasefire came into effect, the IDF made a fresh and unsuccessful attempt to take the Latrun heights outside Jerusalem while Arab Legion troops shouting 'Deir Yassin' attacked a kibbutz in central Israel, killing nearly half the sixty-eight defenders. The Carmeli Brigade briefly occupied Jenin on the West Bank of the Jordan, but retreated with heavy casualties.[1] To the south, hundreds of Egyptians backed by planes, tanks, artillery and armoured cars took one Jewish settlement but were driven back from another. Syrian troops backed by fighter bombers overwhelmed a kibbutz west of the Jordan to give them a launching pad for operations in Galilee. As well as bombing Amman, Israeli planes raided Damascus and the Israelis beat off an Egyptian naval attack on Tel Aviv and Jaffa.

Despite some setbacks, Israel not only held on to territory allocated to it but also gained some areas set down for the Arabs by the UN. The war was making its IDF into an army that could defend a nation while weapons were pouring in from Czechoslovakia, Western Europe and the United States. The new government needed time to develop its institutions and sort out its internal politics – the Irgun agreed to meld its fighters into the army, and Begin, no longer having to operate in hiding, busied himself with the creation of a new party, Herut. However, Irgun militants continued to operate as a fighting unit, and planned to use an arms shipment on its way from France aboard a freighter they called the *Altalena* after the pen name of the Revisionist founder, Jabotinsky.[2]

The Arabs made much less use of the ceasefire. Nasser, who led his battalion on the southern front, contrasted the activity he saw on the other side of the lines with the laxity, laughter and lethargy among Egyptian troops. Talks between Abdullah and the kings of Egypt and Saudi Arabia made no progress.[3]

'At the termination of the truce,' the IDF's head of operations, Yigael Yadin, recalled, 'we took the initiative into our own hands; and, after that, we never allowed it to return to the Arab forces'. Still, the Palmach commander Yigal Allon calculated that

> because the enemy was so strong and so close to the most heavily populated Jewish areas, the Israelis dared not adopt a purely defensive strategy. It was clear that if the invading armies were allowed to enjoy the advantage of offensive action, they might break Israel's sparse line, crush its forces and gain possession of all Jewish-held territory, which because it lacked the dimension of depth was all too easy to subdue.[4]

## II: Blessed be the cannon

The *Altalena* freighter chartered by Irgun to carry arms and refugees arrived off Israel on 20 June. It was greeted by Begin, who asked the government to send a fifth of its cargo to fighters in Jerusalem while the rest would go to Irgun members absorbed into the IDF. The government rejected this for fear that it would create an army within the army.

Most of the refugees went ashore and those suitable for military service were taken to an army camp for induction. Irgun supporters thronging the beach unloaded 2,000 rifles and 200 Bren guns, 2 million rounds of ammunition and 3,000 shells. A Cabinet session in Tel Aviv instructed that the arms must be handed to the government forces; otherwise the IDF would fight to get hold of them.

An army brigade with armour and artillery surrounded the beach and its commander issued an ultimatum to Begin to order his followers to hand over the arms. The politician had a meeting with government representatives, returning to confer with Irgun men on the beach. Rifle fire sounded as night fell; who started the shooting was unclear. Boarding a rowing boat, Begin headed to the *Altalena* under fire from naval corvettes moored offshore. Irgun men on the beach were overwhelmed. Six died together with two IDF soldiers. A ceasefire was negotiated by which the IDF took the weapons. Aboard the *Altalena*, Begin gave an order to head for Tel Aviv, where Irgun members assembled on the beach.

The government's credibility was at stake only five weeks after the proclamation of the new state. Ben-Gurion planned to have the freighter bombed but Israeli pilots refused to attack fellow Jews. However, the corvettes directed machine-gun fire at the *Altalena*, which her Bren gunners returned. At midnight, the ship ran aground.

The chief of naval operations was called at dawn to General Command headquarters. He found the senior military commanders sitting silently on chairs along the walls while a furious Ben-Gurion strode about 'like a lion in a cage'. He was intent on destroying the vessel as a symbol of conflict among the Jews. All necessary steps should be taken to force an unconditional surrender, he insisted. When some ministers at a subsequent Cabinet advocated talking to

Irgun, he slapped them down. 'What is happening endangers Israel,' he argued. 'This is an attempt to destroy the army, and this is an attempt to murder the state.' There could be no compromise.[5]

The prime minister ordered the IDF to shell the ship. The first gunner refused to do so but the second carried out the order after some hesitation. A hail of artillery and small arms fire followed. Amichai Paglin, the Irgun operation chief, headed for the government quarter of Tel Aviv where clashes broke out as radicals sought to foment a putsch. IDF soldiers detained Paglin and others. A white flag was hoisted over the *Altalena* as the ship began to burn and those aboard jumped into the sea.

Begin left by boat after the last of the wounded had been taken off. He went to a clandestine radio station from where, in line with his general desire to avoid setting Jews against Jews, he broadcast instructions to Irgun members not to fight back. Instead, he said, they should quit the IDF and go to Jerusalem to join the battle for the Old City. His highly emotional address lasted for two hours. He cursed Ben-Gurion as 'that fool, that idiot' and accused the prime minister of having wanted to kill him.[6]

The government temporarily detained two hundred soldiers who had followed Begin's instructions to desert. Remaining Irgun members of the army were dispersed among different units. In all, sixteen Irgun fighters and three IDF soldiers died in the clashes. The government had established its supremacy. Begin turned to party politics within the system. Paglin, who escaped from guards in Tel Aviv, was rejected when he tried to join the IDF – nominally on health grounds. Ben-Gurion had no regrets. 'Blessed be the cannon that shelled that ship!' he said. The enmity with Irgun supporters would last a generation.[7]

## III: BACK TOWARDS WAR

On 27 June, Count Bernadotte issued a proposal that Palestine and Transjordan should form a single union with the Negev desert going to the Arabs' territory and Israel taking Western Galilee. Jerusalem would be Arab. Haifa would become a free port. The union would coordinate defence and foreign policy while fostering the two economies. The proposal took no account of the entrenched positions that the invasion had strengthened on both sides. The government in Tel Aviv would have nothing to do with any lessening of its territorial hold or sovereignty. It rejected Arab domination of Jerusalem. Ben-Gurion gave voice to the idea that the Swede was acting as a British agent.

The Arabs went back to their basic position that Palestine should be a unitary state. The Syrian prime minister said the plan was worse than partition and would be an even greater threat to the Arab world. The proposal reopened the prospect of Transjordan dominating Palestine, a prospect that did not go down well with Abdullah's fellow rulers.

Both sides looked to fighting on when the truce ended on 9 July. Anxious that his Legion should not be put at risk, Abdullah expressed his concerns to the UN envoy, but he was as isolated as ever. Meeting in Cairo, the Arab League called for fresh action while Ben-Gurion set as prime targets the Old City of Jerusalem and establishing a solid link with the rest of Israel.

# THE PRESIDENT
# TAKES A TRIP

Two days after the Palestine ceasefire agreement, Harry Truman left Washington to travel across the country. Despite the forecasts of electoral doom, he was as chipper as ever: 'If I felt any better, I couldn't stand it,' he said as he boarded the Ferdinand Magellan train, an armour-plated 83-foot-long monster first used for presidential transport by FDR. Its windows were of bullet-proof, three-inch-thick glass and it contained an oak-panelled dining and conference room, four staterooms, five bedrooms with baths, as well as an observation lounge and platform. Air conditioning and telephones could be hooked up at stations. There were loudspeakers on the roof.[1]

Officially, this was a non-partisan journey to receive an honorary degree at the university in Berkeley. But the trip and the train suited Truman's political purpose perfectly. Accompanied by fifty reporters, he went to eighteen states covering 9,500 miles and was seen by perhaps 3 million people. He made seventy-six speeches, most off the cuff or based on scribbled notes in the down-home manner at which he excelled. There were enthusiastic turnouts even in Republican strongholds such as Omaha, where he marched on 5 June with his First World War unit. In Los Angeles, a million people were said to have turned up on the parade route. At one station, the president appeared on the train's back platform to greet the locals in the middle of the night in his pyjamas and bathrobe.

Parts of the trip were mismanaged and the president went

off-script when he riffed about Stalin in Oregon, saying, 'I like Old Joe! He is a decent fellow. But Joe is a prisoner of the Politburo. He can't do what he wants to.' Lovett called presidential aides on the train and they confronted Truman with his gaffe. 'I guess I goofed,' he admitted.[2]

In his speech at Berkeley, he insisted that the administration would pursue 'peace with freedom and justice', but his main theme was to set out an electioneering programme of price controls, expanded social security and health insurance, more housing and support for farmers. He slammed the 'Do-Nothing, Good-for-Nothing' Congress for favouring the 'special privilege boys' and blocking his progressive agenda. His style was uncompromising and provocative. 'If you send another Republican Congress to Washington, you're a bigger bunch of suckers than I think you are,' he told one crowd. 'I wonder how many times you have to be hit on the head before you find out who's hitting you?' he asked another.[3]

'President Truman ... decided that it is time to be aggressive on a grand scale,' the New York Times wrote. 'The trip to the Pacific is the full challenge of battle to all his foes.' At one stop in Washington State, the local newspaper reported that a voice from the hall exhorted him, 'Lay it on, Harry!' The presidential notes rendered that as 'Pour it on, Harry!' Some of those present, and a plaque at the spot, insist that it was the origin of the subsequent campaign catch-phrase 'Give 'em Hell, Harry!' Whatever the truth, the president responded, 'I'm going to! I'm going to!'[4]

The trip was both personally and politically bracing as it took the president out of the bubble of the capital where he felt 'walled in', but he had other reasons for confidence. The economy was doing well, with rising industrial and agricultural output. Median family incomes were double those of 1941 and holdings of liquid assets had trebled in the same period. Though the labour force had expanded by 10 per cent, unemployment was less than a quarter of its 1939 level. Asked at a press conference if he would win the nomination at the Democratic convention in mid-July, the president, his lips cracked and his nose peeling from exposure to the sun, replied simply, 'Sure.'[5]

Truman's confidence was heightened when the Republicans chose the New York governor Thomas Dewey as the party's candidate for

the November election. The convention in Pennsylvania was a trium-
phalist affair. The party's prima donna, Clare Boothe Luce, declared
that the president was 'a gone goose' and the correspondent of the
London *Times* reported that 'It is difficult to see how the Democrats
can have any chance at all.'[6]

The convention was noteworthy as the first to be televised.
Delegates were told to behave themselves for fear of cameras pick-
ing up unseemly conduct. The arch-conservative Taft, the venerable
Senator Vandenberg, the primary shooting star Harold Stassen and
Governor Earl Warren of California had their names put in conten-
tion while MacArthur's dwindling fan club made sure he was not
forgotten. But, having overcome his initial primary bumps, Dewey
got the unanimous vote on the third ballot, with Warren as his running mate. MacArthur received eleven votes on the first round and
seven on the second.

Truman thought that Taft would have been a stronger opponent
than Dewey, who, advised that his 1944 campaign had been too
strident, tried to antagonise nobody and sounded as if he lacked
conviction; his bland, set-piece speeches no match for the president's
fighting spirit. The Republican platform played right into Truman's
negative characterisation with an agenda of lower public debt, tax
cuts, restrictions on trade unions, reduced governmental intervention
and regulation.

He also had a foreign policy bonus thanks to Vandenberg, who
beat off a bid by conservative Republicans to cut Marshall Plan
spending, while Dewey and Taft backed the European Recovery
Plan. Vandenberg also drew up a resolution designed to assure allies
that the US would come to their aid in the case of armed conflict with
the USSR if the president decided to work with 'regional and other
collective arrangements as are based on continuous and effective self-
help and mutual aid, and as affects its national security'. Another
significant step had been taken towards the web of international
alliances that would mark America's global involvement.

# CHAPTER FORTY-NINE

# AT HOME IN OUR LAND

As Harry Truman began his trip west, Daniel Malan formed the Nationalist government in South Africa, saying that, for both whites and non-whites, apartheid would bring 'peaceful relations with each other and co-operation in the common interest'. Non-Europeans would enjoy greater independence, opportunities and self-respect 'in accordance with their nature and abilities'. The election result, he declared, had been a miracle through which 'we have come into our own' – 'where once we were strangers in our own country, today we feel at home in our land'.[1]

A substantial budget surplus meant that the government had room for a bountiful approach of state finances under the veteran finance minister Nicolaas Havenga, leader of the Afrikaner Party, who had rallied to the Nationalists in the election. But, with a majority of only five seats in the lower house of Parliament and opposition control of the Senate, Malan had to balance the Cabinet carefully – his 'miracle' had to be consolidated, in the first place by giving parliamentary seats to six members from the contested territory of South West Africa who could be counted on to line up with him.

Smuts was still a considerable figure and re-entered Parliament after a Unionist MP stepped down to clear the way for a by-election. In his role as a world statesman and thinker, he travelled to England to take on the chancellorship of Cambridge University. In a speech in London, he accused the Nationalists of having loosed 'a cloud of poison gas' on South Africa and added that the Unionist Party must 'scotch once and for all this native bogy'.[2]

But the Nationalists were bent on applying social engineering to reshape the country for the ideological, political, economic and social interests of white inhabitants. An extreme advocate of apartheid and future prime minister, Johannes Strijdom became minister for lands. Apartheid laws were swiftly drawn up including legislation to ban mixed-race marriage. A scheme to train non-white artisans was cancelled. School meals were stopped for black children while recognition was removed from black trade unions. A citizenship bill restricted the influence of recent immigrants from Europe. Five far right-wingers jailed for sabotage and subversion during the war were released. A committee was established to investigate subversion. The civil service was purged.

The inevitable effect was to radicalise those the government regarded as its enemies. The African National Congress (ANC) and the outlawed Communist Party formed an alliance. Meeting in Bloemfontein the following year and electing a new and more militant leadership from its Youth League, the ANC adopted a programme calling for militant action against apartheid and white minority rule.

CHAPTER FIFTY

# LEGACY OF PARTITION

In India, the level of communal violence had lessened, particularly in Punjab, but the new country still faced huge difficulties. The UN agreed that its commission on Kashmir should consider Pakistan's allegations of genocide. On the ground, Indian troops relieved the town of Poonch, 3,000 feet up in Jammu and Kashmir, but tribal forces remained active elsewhere in the region and the involvement of the Pakistan army was no longer concealed.

The refugee problem was enormous: West Bengal counted 1.7 million displaced people. There were half a million refugees in Delhi and the same number in Bombay, where one camp had ten water taps for more than 10,000 inhabitants, no doctors and no electricity. The government's scheme to find and bring home abducted women had recovered only 12,500 by the early summer. For all the suffering, however, the Indian Communist Party had no success in calling for a peasant uprising as it denounced the government in Delhi for siding with the Anglo-Americans in an 'irreconcilable conflict' with the 'democratic camp' headed by the USSR.[1]

Hyderabad continued to resist attempts by India to get it to join the new country. Talks with V. P. Menon, working in consultation with Patel, got nowhere. The Indians demanded full control of defence, external relations and communications as well as the immediate establishment of a Hindu-majority government. Mountbatten met the Hyderabad prime minister, but to no avail; he then handed over the governor-generalship to the Indian politician C. Rajagopalachari and returned home at the end of his sixteen months in the subcontinent.

In the absence of any progress in negotiations with Hyderabad, the prospect of Delhi's forces escalating frontier incidents into an invasion was rising steadily. India blocked off petrol supplies to the state and the nizam's police raided shops selling imported goods. An Australian aviator, Sidney Cotton, organised flights from Karachi to take in weapons and equipment bought by agents in Europe. The first sortie, flying mainly through cloud on 4 June, took place without any interference from Indian planes. Sixteen flights followed before the British government tried to intervene, but Cotton used foreign company registrations to evade regulations and continue the supply.[2]

# CHAPTER FIFTY-ONE

# EMERGENCY

On 14 June, the head of the Security Service in Kuala Lumpur reported to London that there was 'no immediate threat to internal security in Malaya though the position is constantly changing and is potentially dangerous'. The following day, Communist guerrillas killed three Britons at a rubber plantation in the state of Perak; two had their hands bound behind their backs and were shot on the veranda of their office before the attackers fled on bicycles with cash from the safe. Three miles away, the British manager of another rubber estate was shot dead. In the following weeks, police stations were attacked and prominent Kuomintang supporters in the Chinese community assassinated. Planters in Johor organised a defence corps which the authorities supplied with weapons.

Malcolm MacDonald, Britain's commissioner-general in South East Asia, spoke of 'a bestial campaign' by the Malayan Communist Party (MCP) trying to impose 'the rule of the gun and the knife'. If the 'impatient directors' of international Communism were checked in Europe, he warned, they might try an offensive in the east. There was, in fact, no evidence of Soviet involvement as emergency measures were introduced to give police draconian powers and outlaw the MCP and other leftist groups. In the first security forces swoop, six hundred people were arrested.[1]

With its rich reserves of tin and rubber, Malaya was unusual among colonies in that the main movement of the majority population was in no hurry for the European power to go. It had never been a nation and was run by the British as an association of the four

Federated Malay States and five unfederated ones with Singapore in the Crown colony of the Straits Settlements. Of the 6 million population, 40 per cent were Malay, almost as many were Chinese and the remainder Indian, Europeans or others.

The sultans, who were in nominal charge of their states but had to follow the advice of British officials, were coerced immediately after the war into agreeing to a British scheme for a Malayan Union with an equitable distribution of influence under the colonial authority between the three main ethnic groups – Malays, Chinese and Indians. When the proposal was made public, there was an outcry both from Malays and colonial officers. Having apparently not considered the depths of opposition, the British were caught flat-footed by the formation in 1946 of the United Malays National Organisation (UNMO) to object to their scheme. As well as its impact on the various communities, the plan would make Malaya 'a colony with no rights', the party's chief, Dato' Onn Jaafar declared.

The proponents of the scheme began to redraft it while UNMO launched a campaign of civil disobedience, including boycotting meetings of colonial advisory councils and the installation of a new governor. Recognising the impasse, the British dissolved the Union in early 1948 and replaced it with a Federation of Malaya consisting of states ruled by sultans as British protectorates plus Penang and Malacca as colonial territories and Singapore as a separate entity – a degree of political reform was introduced in the port city with the popular election of six of the 22-member legislative council.

This retreat from a proposal to give them a greater say in internal affairs alienated the Chinese community, who made up a third of the population. The predominantly Chinese MCP, which had fought the Japanese alongside the British,[2] defined its three enemies as the colonial power, the sultans and exploitative business tycoons, many of them Chinese. For the moment, the Communists concentrated on industrial action and the British were able to monitor their activities by having enlisted the MCP secretary-general, Lai Teck, as an agent. When he was replaced in early 1947 and fled with the party's ready cash, the party became harder to track as its new leader, Chin Peng, built up a network among labourers in rubber plantations and established bases in the forests and jungles.

In May 1948, a meeting of the MCP leadership in an isolated
jungle clearing set up the Malayan People's Anti-British Army,
organised into eight regiments of three to eight hundred fighters
each, the vast majority Chinese. Ten per cent of the new force were
women. There were also a hundred Japanese left over from the war.
A network of civilian supporters provided food, finance and information, often gleaned from workers in British premises. The MCP
controlled the operation through political commissars and cells.[3]

The initial targets were exposed plantations and police posts,
aiming to drive the British into towns and undermine the economy.
After spreading revolution through the countryside, the People's Army
would attack the colonists in their urban centres, where it hoped to
benefit from discontent at economic and social problems stemming
from a decline in world demand for natural rubber, inflation, low
wages, unemployment and repression of strikes and protests.

At the start, the security forces numbered around 20,000 – police
numbers would eventually swell to 70,000. They faced 8,000 guerrillas. The British had the advantage of aircraft for reconnaissance
and bombing, but the MCP made the most of its hiding places
and guerrilla skills, slipping away from patrols and regrouping. Its
support from Chinese living on the edge of forests and jungles led
the authorities to forcibly relocate half a million people into camps
surrounded by barbed wire, police stations and floodlit areas.
Troop reinforcement had to be sent in as Malaya joined Vietnam
and Indonesia as a theatre for armed struggle against colonialism
in South East Asia. The emergency declared on 16 June would continue until the independence of Malaya in 1957 and the Communists
would continue to fight the new government even after that.

# CHAPTER FIFTY-TWO

# STRATEGIC MORASS

The day after Truman settled back into the White House, the Chinese Communists advanced to take Kaifeng in the centre of the country, the first provincial capital they had captured. Chiang Kai-shek flew to the region to assume command. He called in heavy reinforcements, and ordered the air force into action. The attack was indiscriminate. 'The east–west road was littered with dead animals and human bodies,' a European doctor working with the Communists recalled. 'The stench was indescribable. Pigs and dogs were feeding on those bodies which had not yet putrefied. Flies and maggots covered the swollen bodies of others. Nobody was in the streets, for the planes were in the habit of machine-gunning anything that moved.'[1]

In the face of the big build-up of government forces, the PLA soldiers slipped out on 25 June, reckoning that it was not worth fighting to retain control of the city. They had succeeded in diverting a large body of troops from other theatres of the war and preferred mobile warfare rather than trying to hold urban centres where they were vulnerable to air and artillery attacks. Their brief period in the city had burnished their reputation for good behaviour with no looting or assaults on civilians.[2]

The PLA units moved to a triangular area south of the east–west railway line into which they lured the enemy at the start of a major battle which lasted until early July, costing the Nationalist significant casualties. Government commanders received contradictory and confused orders. One recounted that Chiang ordered him to enter

Kaifeng, but then the Defence Ministry told him to pursue the PLA across the railway. He was instructed to assist a beleaguered infantry division but a message dropped from a plane warned that his unit was about to be attacked. 'I turned round, but there was nothing there,' he recalled. 'This false report must have been put out by the Communists ... and the Ministry, as usual, fell for it.'[3]

The government still held major areas in the north and centre of the country. But the Communists had overwhelmed three Nationalist divisions in one battle in the east and tightened the noose in Shandong where, in what was becoming an increasingly common practice, many defenders laid down their arms or defected. The PLA was also advancing in the Central Plains while it tightened the siege of Changchun.

On 12 June, Chiang lifted the ban on people leaving the Manchurian city, but those who went ran into the tightly held PLA lines with barbed wire, deep trenches and sentries every 50 metres. They knelt in front of the Communist troops begging to be let through. Some hanged themselves in desperation or abandoned babies and children. By the end of June, 30,000 people were caught in the no-man's land, eating grass as they baked in the scorching sun.

Inside the city, starvation spread. Government aircraft could deliver only a quarter of the grain needed for survival and troops grabbed any food. Civilians ate tree bark, leather belts, insects and then human flesh on sale at street markets. Families committed collective suicide or died in their beds. While its artillery maintained constant shelling, the PLA kept up a loudspeaker barrage of appeals to government troops to defect, which they did in growing numbers while their commanders sheltered behind the thick walls of the central bank building.[4]

Once a hit-and-run guerrilla force, the PLA had evolved into six field armies, well equipped, disciplined and ready to fight set-piece battles or enforce sieges such as that of Changchun. At a secret session of the legislature in Nanking on 24 June, the Defence Ministry reported that, in the past three years, the initial preponderance of government forces had fallen sharply. They now numbered a little over 2 million men while the PLA had 1.5 million soldiers plus 700,000 irregulars with slightly more artillery pieces, most captured from enemy forces.[5]

Mao Zedong juggled with strategy to combine operations in the north and east. Preparations were pushed ahead to form a People's Government. On 15 June, the party published the first edition of its flagship newspaper, *People's Daily*. In central China, it pressed ahead with land reform and propaganda that promised to put right local problems, only occasionally attacking the Americans – probably because, as a World Health Organization official reported, 'out in the countryside they have never heard of the United States'.[6]

Refugees streamed into the central provinces under government control. Torrential rains flooded 4 million acres round the Yangtze. Students demonstrated against the war, the regime and American plans to restore the economy of Japan. There were rice riots in Chongqing, Ningbo and other big cities. Strikes stopped construction in Nanjing. The legislature was in fractious rebellion and the government's top military officers split into backstabbing cliques. The generalissimo was finding it increasingly difficult to lay down the law. But he refused to relinquish personal control or to promote able figures who might become rivals.

Inflation was so out of control that the figures made no sense any more. Exports were half the pre-war volume, steel output was less than 10 per cent of the level of the 1930s and production of machinery had, in the words of the United Nations annual report, 'dwindled to insignificant proportions'. It now took 2 million yuan to buy one American dollar. A US diplomat had to hire a rickshaw to carry the notes needed to pay for a new pair of shoes. Commodity prices were estimated at 130,000 times the pre-war level. A director of the Central Bank said it was 'out of foreign exchange'. New calculating machines had seventeen columns to handle all the numbers.[7]

Ministers worked on a plan for economic reform designed to provide monetary stability and reduce inflation. Wage and price increases, strikes and demonstrations would be prohibited. But the size of the government deficit and the tax shortfall, particularly from the richest families including big landowners and insiders headed by the generalissimo's relatives by marriage, undermined reform. As Washington refused a fresh loan, Chiang became ever more estranged from the Americans. His wife found her only welcome in Washington was from Republicans as Truman refused to invite her to the White House. Dewey said that, if he got to the White House, he would send massive financial and military aid. But the State Department China expert John Paton Davies Jr drafted a policy paper for George Kennan to warn that China 'more closely resembles a strategic morass than a strategic springboard'.[8]

CHAPTER FIFTY-THREE

# SHOWDOWN

## I: HOTTER THAN A FIRECRACKER

By the summer of 1948, the Western powers were committed to the revival of their occupation zones in Germany and set on forging ahead politically and economically whatever the Soviets said. Meeting fellow foreign ministers in London, Georges Bidault rallied to the Anglo-American position on the establishment of a constituent assembly for the Western occupation zones – on condition that the Saarland was financially merged with France and that the Ruhr was put under international control. This exposed him to political attacks at home ranging from Communists to Gaullists, whose leader warned that a revival across the border would put France in a state of permanent danger; the foreign minister was heckled as he defended the London agreement in Parliament.[1]

Though generally happy with the political progress offered by the Allies, West German parties took exception to the continuing economic control by the Allies provided for in the London agreements. It was, said the Christian Democrats, 'a form of annexation'. The Soviet reaction was much more strident. Marshal Sokolovsky, the commander in Berlin, denounced 'lies' and 'hypocrisy'. The Soviet delegation to the four-power commission for the city charged the West with creating a 'puppet government'.

The rising tension led Robert Lovett, who kept in touch by following messages flashed up on the screen at the State Department's telex room, to say that the city was becoming 'hotter than a firecracker'.

Freight trains travelling to and from the former capital were subjected to increased Russian inspection. Inter-zonal trains were not allowed to stop in the British sector. Road traffic was delayed by sudden repair work. Newspaper distribution was put under the control of the Soviet authorities.[2]

## II: FOLLOW THE MONEY

Losing patience with the ritualised exchanges at a late-night meeting of the four-power Kommandatura in Berlin on 17 June, the chief American delegate jumped to his feet and said he was going home to bed. That prompted the head of the Russian team to stand up and announce that, in that case, the joint body was at an end. He and his colleagues would leave, too. The French general chairing the meeting pointed out that no date had been agreed for the next session. 'As far as I am concerned, there won't be a next meeting,' the Russian said over his shoulder on his way to the door.[3]

The next day, the Americans, British and French announced the implementation of currency reform for the following weekend in their zones of Western Germany, now known as Trizonia. One new deutschmark would be issued for ten old Reichsmarks. After being flown secretly to Western Germany in boxes labelled 'door-knobs', the notes were in storage in 23,000 boxes weighing 1,035 tons in the old Reichsbank building in Frankfurt. Denouncing the move, the Russians declared the new currency invalid in greater Berlin, implying that the whole city belonged to them. Possession of deutschmarks would be a criminal offence as they clamped on fresh transport restrictions.

Clay was called to Washington to meet Truman, Marshall and the joint chiefs of staff. The general expressed confidence that the Western powers could stay in Berlin indefinitely without war. The meeting agreed to his request for 160 C-54 transport planes, though delivering them would take time. Always worried about his country's military capability, James Forrestal noted in his diary that the US troop reserves for an emergency amounted to only 30,000 men.[4]

Ludwig Erhard, the pudgy director of the Administration for Economics for the Western occupation zones, had been working relentlessly on plans to abolish rationing and free up the economy to go with the introduction of the new currency. In the process, he met Adenauer at the start of a long and sometimes disputatious relationship; the politician's focus on appealing to voters running counter to Erhard's focus on applying economic theory. Not that the economist was an ivory-tower visionary. A British official, Con O'Neill, described him as 'a tough character ... with a strong but remarkably narrow mind ... utterly lacking in any political sense ... like the Fat Boy, whom physically he much resembles, he asks incessantly for more, and, if he gets it, he appears to regard the giver not with gratitude but with contempt'.[5]

With Clay's backing, Erhard set out his argument in a speech on 21 June that 'the decisive break from the state's coercive economy was the precondition for the success of the [currency] reform and our return to economic health'. He laid into companies that benefited from regulations and linked the introduction of the free market to progress towards democracy. Four days later, price liberalisation started in the US and UK zones, followed at the end of the month by a Guiding Principles Law to end most rationing and wage controls, though, for the time being, restrictions remained on food and raw materials while free trade in grain, potatoes, meat, iron and steel was subject to official approval. Monopolies would be controlled. There would not be a free market in housing or transport. The government kept significant powers in the template that would evolve into West Germany's social market model.[6]

Sixty new marks were distributed to each adult in the Western zones to help restore purchasing power. Hoarded goods were brought out to be sold. Farmers stepped up the supply of fruit and vegetables. The American military government judged a month later that 'no event since the capitulation of the German armies has had such an impact upon every sector of life ... Overnight the financial and commercial life of tens of millions of persons was transformed. The foundation upon which normal ways of life could be reestablished, had been erected ... Job efficiency has risen and there are indications of increased output in almost all fields of manufacturing.' By the last quarter of the year, production in the Western zones was 50 per cent up on 1947.[7]

At Clay's suggestion, a four-power meeting was held on 22 June to discuss the situation. The Soviets dismissed a proposal for a special currency for Berlin. They said the integration of the city and the Soviet Zone economy meant that the two had to have the same money, which they would control. The following day, they announced currency reform for the eastern zone and all sectors of Berlin. The Western commanders declared this currency null and void in their sectors and issued their own new marks into Berlin stamped with the letter 'B'.

## III: Squeeze play

There were food stocks for thirty-six days and coal for forty-five for the 2.25 million Germans in the US, British and French zones of the former capital. Though these had been built up in anticipation of a crisis, they would be insufficient if the city was cut off for any considerable period. Clay estimated that a minimum of 4,000 tons of supplies were needed each day. The price of coffee, bread and cigarettes shot up as provisions dwindled and the Russians cut coal supplies.[8]

Visiting Berlin at the time, the American journalist John Gunther found it 'like a horrible dream after the world has stopped'. The city, he wrote, 'looks like death warmed over ... old men in grimy overcoats worn to the stump peering enviously into cheap jewelry shops ... withered and brutalised old women walking the streets and surreptitiously trying to sell chocolate bars which they sometimes get in lieu of wages; bleak auction stalls at street corners ... in a food shop, salted meat from Mexico with no identification except for Carne sold by the gramme out of a dirty open can'.[9]

Behind the immediate challenge posed by the Russians lay the issue raised between Clay and Omar Bradley in April. With 6,500 combat troops in the city compared to 18,000 from the Red Army (and another 300,000 in the east as a whole), were the Western powers ready to make a stand? Or would they cave in when faced with what George Kennan described as 'a species of squeeze play' to test the West and, above all, the man in the White House?[10]

The City Assembly of Berlin made its view clear at a meeting held in a building in the Russian sector. The Social Democrats were the major party represented, but the Soviets refused to recognise their leader in the city, Ernst Reuter as mayor; so his deputy, Louise Schroeder, who had sat in the Weimar Republic Parliament, took the chair. In the streets outside, thugs beat up non-Communists; police stood by without intervening. Despite the intimidation, the assembly voted to accept the deutschmark in the Western sectors and keep the Ostmark for the Soviet sector only.

Sokolovsky rang Molotov to ask if he should take military action. The foreign minister turned that down for fear of provoking an armed Western response. Instead, the decision was to clamp a complete blockade.

At 6 a.m. on 24 June, all rail, road and water links between Berlin and West Germany were cut, together with electricity from power stations in the east of the city. 'Coal shortages' was given as the reason. Eighty thousand people demonstrated in the Western section in support of the vote taken the previous night. Clay telephoned Curtis LeMay, the burly, cigar-chomping commander of the US air force in Europe, an innovative if extreme thinker who had been in charge of the aerial assault on Japan. Clay asked him if he had planes that could carry coal.

'Carry what?' a surprised LeMay asked.

'Coal,' Clay repeated.

'General, the air force can carry anything,' LeMay said when he was assured that he had not misheard. 'How much coal do you want us to haul?'[11]

Clay outlined the need for an air supply bridge to Berlin and LeMay agreed to make all transport aircraft available – the first arrived the following day.[12]

The pilots had conducted an earlier airlift of supplies into Berlin in April. LeMay had also set up a network of air bases in North Germany stocked with bombs, ammunition and fuel. C-54 Skymaster planes arrived from Texas, Alaska, Hawaii and Panama, joined by flying boats that landed by the yacht club on the Havel River.

In a teleconference with Washington, Clay said he did not expect armed conflict. 'Principal danger is from Russian-planned German Communist groups,' he added. 'Conditions are tense ... Our troops and British are in hand and can be trusted. We both realize desire of our governments to avoid armed conflict. Nevertheless, we cannot be run over and a firm position always induces some risk.' He stressed the importance of not undermining the confidence of West Berliners and concluded, 'If the Soviets want war, it will not be because of Berlin currency issue but because they believe this is the right time. I regard the probability as remote, though it cannot be disregarded entirely. Certainly we are not trying to provoke war. We are taking a lot of punches on the chin without striking back.'[13]

A motor torpedo boat was sent to pick up Bevin from a break cruising on a friend's yacht in the Solent off Southampton. Returning to London, he reacted to a pessimistic report about the supply outlook from the deputy UK military governor in Berlin by setting up a small committee under his own leadership to deal with the problem. Since close coordination with the US was essential, it established a direct link with Washington, bypassing the British embassy.

The foreign secretary set great store on getting American strategic bombers capable of carrying atom bombs moved to West Europe as a key stage in the transatlantic military co-operation that was his aim.[14] Abandoning Berlin, he told the American ambassador, would have disastrous consequences in Western Germany. In Washington, Truman directed that the airlift should be put on a full-scale organised basis, seeing the pressure on Berlin as 'international Communism's counter-attack' after setbacks elsewhere in Europe. In the former German capital, Sokolovsky was stopped for speeding, but allowed to continue his journey.

On 28 June, Bevin told the Cabinet that there could be no question of yielding on Berlin. The under secretary of the army, Draper, informed him that the US could initially fly in 1,500 tons a day; not enough, but a start. Looking back, Attlee felt the risk of war over Berlin was one which had to be accepted, though he did not think the USSR was in a position to attack: 'They hadn't really begun to rebuild their economy and I didn't think they were ready for a showdown.' But, he added, 'one couldn't depend on it'. In Washington, Truman was emphatic. 'We are going to stay, period,' he told a White House meeting. 'The Russians have no right to get us out by either direct or indirect pressure.'[15]

## IV: Dealing with a heretic

As the crisis over Berlin built up, the Cominform met in Bucharest to lower the boom on Yugoslavia, which was not represented. Zhdanov and Malenkov headed the Soviet delegation. Many leading figures from other satellite states were present, as well as Duclos from France and Togliatti from Italy. 'We possess information that Tito is an imperialist spy,' Zhdanov announced. From Moscow, Stalin decreed that he had flouted the 'unified Communist front' and taken the road to Nationalism. There was only one possible outcome. The meeting adopted a resolution expelling the Yugoslav party.

To tighten control, Communist parties in Hungary, Czechoslovakia, Poland and Bulgaria absorbed their coalition partners in forced mergers along the lines of the SED in Eastern Germany. The fight against the churches was stepped up not only in Hungary but also in Bulgaria, where the Orthodox primate came under pressure which led him to resign and retreat to a monastery. Returning to Italy, Togliatti condemned Tito and his comrades as militaristic and undemocratic, and their state as a police state marked by Oriental despotism, 'confusion and error'. But then, reflecting the religious need for Communist leaders to toe Moscow's line, he added, 'It's not possible to ask whether Tito is right in some respects; he must be totally wrong.' The Stalinist church had found a new heretic and could now uncover a new set of internal enemies to put on trial in the interest of consolidating power.[16]

Unbowed, the Yugoslav Central Committee decided to publish the Cominform resolution and its own reply rejecting the charges. The popular reaction boosted the popularity of Tito and the regime. The Yugoslav delegation at a youth sports festival in Prague ended their gymnastics display by lining up to spell out the letters TITO, to cheers from spectators. The leadership in Belgrade received overwhelming backing at a Party Congress the following month; old Communists who owed prime allegiance to Moscow were greatly outnumbered by younger activists brought up during the war who sided with Tito. Soviet supporters were swiftly purged as hundreds of thousands of people were arrested, most of them innocent victims of suspicion and denunciation, and about a quarter of them ended up being punished.

In his concluding speech to the Congress, Tito promised to accelerate the implementation of socialism. 'Comrades, I warn you we are in a difficult situation, in a trying time,' he declared. 'Our party is faced with a hard test; if only we maintain profound vigilance, unity and firmness, if only we do not lose our nerve, our victory will be certain.' But then, reflecting the fundamental belief in the Big Brother in the soul of every true Communist of the era, he ended by calling out, 'Long Live the Soviet Union, long live Stalin!'[17]

Only complete subservience could have saved the Yugoslavs from being cast out of the Stalinist fold. Tito's independence of mind had to be sanctioned in the cause of Moscow's leadership of the Communist camp. As the Soviet ambassador in Belgrade remarked during the crisis, the Yugoslavs had 'a lot to learn'. But Tito could not compromise. To have bowed to Stalin would have fatally undermined his position and that of the nation he headed.

As the former Czechoslovak ambassador Josef Korbel put it, the Kremlin 'failed to understand that Marshal Tito, Prime Minister of the People's Federal Republic of Yugoslavia, the Commander-in-Chief of the Yugoslav Army, Partisan leader, national hero and dictator, was a different person from Josip Broz, once underground agent of the Third International'. The half-million-strong army was determined, experienced and well trained. Support for Moscow was weak, whereas the legacy of the wartime resistance had left a high degree of self-confidence in the regime's ability to confront even the Big Brother in the Kremlin. As a result, divorce was inevitable.[18]

The break took the West by surprise and some thought it was all a trick. But the US came round and offered assistance. Tito initially rejected this since he hoped for a reconciliation with Moscow. Instead, Yugoslavia bought expensive grain from Sweden. But as the shutters went down even further in Eastern Europe as a result of Belgrade's apostasy and frontier incidents multiplied, the country opened up and began to pursue its own path between East and West, steered by its unique historical leader.[19]

As the Cold War deepened, the Communists in Czechoslovakia tightened their grip after their election victory the previous month. In retreat in his modest country home in Bohemia since the February putsch, Beneš resigned as head of state. Weak, physically and psychologically, from his two strokes and the second political disaster of his life, the 64-year-old politician was more solitary than ever. Jan Masaryk was dead. His close lieutenant, Prokop Drtina, was in jail accused of subversion. The president's resignation letter stated that his conscience, democratic convictions and attachment to human and civil rights prevented him from agreeing with the new constitution adopted after the election. Since he would not be able to sign the document, he had to step down. He addressed the letter to the chairman of the National Assembly, not the prime minister. It was taken to Gottwald, all the same. He edited it before it was made public to remove Beneš's reasons for stepping down.[20]

In Greece, government troops staged their largest operation of the war against Communist forces in the Konitsa region, preceded by an intensive artillery and air bombardment using US napalm bombs. In hand-to-hand fighting, they took control of the main rebel supply route but ran into heavy resistance on the heights by the Albanian border. Heavy rain and cloud limited aerial operations and a stalemate set in as reinforcements were rushed in on both sides. The government offensive raised fears in Albania of an invasion and, at Hoxha's request, the Yugoslav began to train an intervention force.[21]

In Hungary, the battle intensified between the authorities and the Roman Catholic Church and its primate, Cardinal József Mindszenty, whose strong-minded defence of his religion and its rights had marked him as the regime's leading critic. Seen by the government as the epitome of clerical reaction, the cardinal had denounced the 'revengeful spirit' of land reform which seized the large holdings on which many Catholic institutions depended for their funding. He decried 'the loosening of the indissolubility of marriage' and signed a letter on behalf of the bishops expressing shock at how the new rulers 'seem to delight in throwing men into prison on grounds of mere suspicion, personal spite, individual injury or secret party machinations'. The pope's rejection of compromise with Communism and threat of excommunication to any member of the faith who co-operated with 'irreligious, pagan, anti-Christian forces', bolstered Mindszenty in his unyielding position.[22]

A violent confrontation erupted in a rural area in early June between Catholics and police anxious to put down what the government denounced as 'pulpit agitation'. A policeman was shot dead; a man accused of having fired the gun was hanged. A wider struggle between church and state revolved around a government decision to nationalise religious schools, which were attended by 1.8 million pupils. A church circular instructed priests, monks and nuns to refuse to work in educational establishments under state control, and headmasters who had to hand over school property should declare that they were doing so under duress. In pastoral letters, Mindszenty called for prayers 'that through the Grace of God and through the good offices of our Lady and Our Hungarian Saints, the rights of the parents and of the Church in its schools may soon be triumphant' and that 'Satan prowling amongst us like a roving lion be driven away'. Church bells were to ring to protest while the faithful were told to prevent their families reading pro-government newspapers.[23]

When the new law went into effect in the middle of the month, Protestant churches went along with it but the cardinal kept up his fight with a fruitless exchange of letters with the Education Ministry. The government accused him of neglecting the real interests of Catholics and serving Western interests. Catholic associations were dissolved and the church decided to stop broadcasts of services because of state interference and because they were 'usually preceded and followed by other programmes unsuitable for the dignity of religious broadcasts and for the truths proclaimed in them'.[24]

## V: No surrender

By the end of the month, it was clear that the blockade of Berlin had served only to reinforce the unity and resolve of the Western Allies. 'If the intention is to make trouble for us in Berlin, Her Majesty's Government cannot submit to that,' Bevin told the House of Commons, adding, 'We recognize that as a result of these decision a grave situation might arise ... Her Majesty's Government and our Western allies can see no alternative between that and surrender – and none of us can accept surrender.'[25]

In the former capital, Ernst Reuter became the focus for resistance to Soviet pressure. The refusal of the Russians to recognise him as mayor only served to heighten his standing. Kurt Schumacher was confined to bed with illness at the time, giving his Social Democrat colleague greater freedom of action. As he made the most of this and multiplied his contacts with the Western powers, relations between the two men grew strained, but this did nothing to lessen the determination of Berliners in the west to stand firm as supplies began to arrive overhead in increasing quantities. 'We cannot abandon those stouthearted Berlin democrats who are refusing to bow to Soviet pressure,' Bevin told the Commons.[26]

'The sound of aircraft can be heard day and night and the orderly unending procession of Dakotas and Skymasters is visible and audible proof of the Western Allies' determination to do their best,' a British newspaper correspondent reported. 'Today and yesterday the sight has done more to raise Berliners' morale than the most rousing proclamation could ever done.' In the Eastern sector, Grotewohl called for a clear commitment to 'an Eastern orientation' as the Russians prepared to cut off water to the West. The path towards a Western alliance that would produce NATO the following year was clear and Stalin had suffered a major reversal as the Cold War was set in the shape it would assume for the following four decades.[27]

~

## MEANWHILE

- The former German cruise liner the *Windrush* arrives at Tilbury Docks in London with the first organised group of 492 Caribbean immigrants, among them a tailor, a boxer, a valet and several calypso singers. 'Surely, there is nothing against us coming for we are British subjects,' one tells reporters. 'If there is, is it because we are coloured?'
- The US Congress passed the Displaced Persons Act to admit 200,000 homeless Europeans; one-third had to be farmers and half from the Baltic States absorbed by the USSR.
- The French high commissioner, Bollaert, meets Bao Dai again and reaches another insubstantial agreement on the Franco-Vietnamese relations.
- The Dutch and Indonesian Republicans break off talks because of lack of progress.

- The military strongman of Paraguay, Higinio Morinigo Martinez, is bundled off by former associates to exile in Argentina.
- The House of Representatives Committee on Un-American Activities distributes booklets on 'How to know a Communist' by the way he/she speaks and works.
- William Shockley files a patent for the growth-junction transistor while a machine in Manchester, England, nicknamed 'Baby', becomes the first stored-programme computer to operate successfully.
- Britain pushes ahead with a grand scheme to grow groundnuts in Tanganyika, although the land and weather are totally unsuitable.
- Three armed men carry out the first aircraft hijacking, of a Cathay Pacific airliner, which crashes, killing all but one of the twenty-seven people aboard, after the pilot is shot.
- An earthquake kills 3,769 in Japan.
- Columbia Records markets the first long-playing 33⅓ rpm record.

# FROM THEN TO NOW

As the 1940s moved towards their close, the events of 1947–8 found their logical conclusion. The Berlin airlift continued until 12 May 1949 when the USSR lifted the blockade after 2.3 million tons of supplies had been flown into the city, with a peak of nearly 13,000 tons on one day in April 1949, and planes sometimes landing every three minutes. Unwilling to escalate the confrontation, the Kremlin did not try to bring down any of the aircraft, but twenty-five conflagration crashed and 101 people died in accidents connected with the operation. Having failed to cow the West, Stalin desisted from further probing in Europe until his death in 1953. If Sun Tzu was right in *The Art of War* in believing that every battle is won or lost before it is fought, the Berlin airlift was a good example, given the determination of the Western Allies, the mood of the people of the Western sectors, the transport capability of the US and the Soviet reluctance to risk a hot war.[1]

The division of Germany became the hallmark of European Cold War and reflected the gap between the reality and the aspirations expressed on both sides of the Iron Curtain. While constantly deplored in public, and rarely free from the possibility of escalation, the long stand-off could only be welcomed in private. It removed fears of revanchism from a revived nation and gave each of the superpowers control over their halves of the continent, the presence of their armed forces acting as a further brake on any prospect of a renewal of the threat faced in two world wars. The Federal Republic's neighbours, above all France, were reassured by its focus on its economic role and desire to rehabilitate itself for the sins of the Nazi era while Moscow knew it had a reliable front-line ally in the centre of Europe. When the Soviet Empire collapsed, the dynamics changed but, for the time being, many could subscribe to the French author François Mauriac's remark, 'I love Germany so much I'm glad there are two of them.'

On a broader front, the Cold War acquired a more threatening aspect when the USSR tested nuclear weapons in 1949, while Stalin's ever-growing paranoia combined with Tito's apostasy to provoke a rash of show trials in satellite states, often coloured by anti-Semitism that contributed to his reversal of support for Israel. These purges saw 2,000 executions and 150,000 imprisonments with 'Titoists' joining 'Trotskyists' as designated enemies out to destroy the Soviet system while the heretic in Belgrade built his country into a leader of the non-aligned world.

Among those killed in the Soviet-ordained repression, which targeted everybody from 'right deviationists' and 'Titoists' to 'left deviationists' and 'cosmopolitan Zionists', were Rudolf Slánský in Czechoslovakia. According to some reports, Stalin had Dimitrov slowly poisoned – he died in 1949. Ana Pauker, who had shown signs of defiance towards the Moscow-lining Romanian leadership and facilitated Jewish emigration, was accused by Stalin of pursuing 'peasantist, non-Marxist policies' but was saved from execution by the dictator's death in 1953. Gomułka also avoided death but was expelled from the Polish Communist Party. In February 1949, a Hungarian show trial delivered a life sentence for treason and espionage on Cardinal Mindszenty, who showed signs of having been tortured. He was released during the uprising of 1956 and took refuge in the American embassy for fifteen years after the Soviet invasion – he eventually left for Vienna where he died in 1973 after a row with the pope over his refusal to retire from his archdiocese. In the USSR itself the Leningrad Communist Party was purged and only Stalin's death headed off his last lunge into anti-Semitic paranoia in the alleged 'doctors plot of 1952–3.

In the hot war in southern Europe, Greek government forces succeeded in moving into the rebel area by the Albanian frontier they had attacked in June, claiming to have killed more than 3,000 of the enemy while losing eight hundred men themselves in some of the most savage fighting of the war before the rebels, outnumbered ten-to-one, were trapped at the top of the Grammes mountains. But it was not until 1949 that Athens could clinch final victory after clearing key disputed regions of people and cutting the Democratic Army off from its bases. The defection of Yugoslavia from the Soviet camp and the Greek Communist Party's continuing loyalty to Moscow further weakened the rebels as their ideological commitment ran counter to their main source of aid. The three-and-a-half-year war ended with a death toll of 160,000, leaving a legacy of bitterness still evident in the turmoil around the country's economic woes in the twenty-first century.

The Cold War continued till the collapse of the Soviet Empire at the end of the 1980s followed by the dissolution of the USSR in 1991. Satellite nations of East and Central Europe regained their freedom. Germany was reunited after the four decades of separation that had taken shape in 1947–8. But Yugoslavia unravelled ten years after Tito's death in 1980, the different regions he had held together separating amid vicious wars.

On the other side of the Iron Curtain, the Marshall Plan revived recipient countries, ten of which joined the US and Canada in the NATO alliance that now has twenty-nine members. A good harvest, the first since the end of the war, also helped. Inflation slowed. Increased trade across the Atlantic reduced the dollar gap as the US embraced imports to drive growth and currency convertibility in the non-Communist world. Japan and Germany pursued the material revival that now makes them the third and fourth largest global economies respectively. The movement towards West Europe integration promoted by Robert Schuman, Benelux politicians, Alcide De Gasperi and Konrad Adenauer, and powerfully backed by Washington, led to the Coal and Steel Community of 1950, the Treaty of Rome of 1957 and then the European Union of twenty-eight member states.[3]

In France, the Schuman government fell in July 1948, but the Fourth Republic withstood the attacks of Gaullists and Communists and lasted for another ten years until it was finally brought down by an army revolt in Algeria and a masterful political display by de Gaulle as he went on to found the Fifth Republic. Germany and France drew closer with their friendship treaty of 1963 signed by de Gaulle and Adenauer, which became a central plank in European collaboration.

Across the Channel, Attlee's government was returned for a second term in 1950 but then lost office to the Conservatives as an increasingly infirm Churchill became prime minister again before giving way to his long-time dauphin, Anthony Eden. The main elements of the Labour Party's programme – the Western alliance, a global presence, the National Health Service and nationalisation – remained in place, as did the weakness of the economy. Rationing was not lifted until 1954. The ambivalence towards Europe evident in the early post-war years persisted as the UK sought a role between the Continent, the Anglosphere and the wider world, leading to the 2016 vote to leave the EU.

The war between Arabs and Israelis resumed on 8 July 1948 and continued for ten days before another truce was agreed, during which Lehi terrorists assassinated Count Bernadotte. In a third phase of fighting starting in October, as the IDF expanded to a 96,000-strong force and other Arab states failed to come to Egypt's aid against a southern offensive, the Israelis drove back the Arab armies and reached the southern edge of Palestine on the Red Sea where their soldiers raised a handmade flag on 10 March 1949. An armistice was concluded with Egypt, followed by Lebanon, Transjordan and Syria, while the Iraqis handed their positions to the Arab Legion and went home. The Israeli death toll in the establishment and defence of the new state was almost 6,000, a quarter of them civilians. More than half the military fatalities came in offensive actions and 60 per cent were in areas outside the borders laid down by the UN. Estimates of deaths of Arab troops varied from 3–7,000 and those of Palestinians were put at up to 13,000. Some 700,000 Palestinians were displaced from their homes in a diaspora that continues seven decades later as the Arab–Israeli conflict shows no sign of resolution. The failure to prevent the establishment and expansion of Israel, and the poor performance of their armies, fuelled discontent with Arab leaders, especially among young military officers.

The Kashmir ceasefire proposed by the United Nations in April

1948 went into effect on the following 1 January. But Indian and Pakistani armies remain pitted against one another across the Line of Control. India categorises Pakistan as the aggressor who must pull out while Pakistan objects that there was no guarantee of a subsequent Indian withdrawal. When Pakistan infiltrated forces into the region in 1965, India launched an assault on West Pakistan with massed tank forces that gave it the upper hand before the fighting was stopped by a UN ceasefire after taking some 7,000 casualties. The 50,000 dead in the Vale of Kashmir since the mid-1980s, most of them civilians, has come to symbolise the antagonism between the two neighbours which has remained a constant of regional geo-politics, given a sharper edge by their mutual possession of nuclear weapons.

Jinnah was the first of the major actors in this book to die. His body reduced to 37 kilos by tuberculosis and cancer, he developed pneumonia in September 1948, and expired at the age of seventy-one, thirteen months after Pakistan's creation. A million people gathered for his funeral and he was succeeded by his deputy, Liaquat Ali Khan, who himself died in 1951. Nehru remained prime minister of India until his death in 1964. His daughter Indira held the post from 1980 to 1984 and, after her assassination, was succeeded by her son Rajiv as dynastic politics ruled before the rise of the Hindu-based BJP Party and the decline of Congress in the general election of 2014.

The People's Liberation Army continued its advance across China for the rest of 1948 and 1949, besieging and taking the major cities of the north-east and expanding their control elsewhere. The defenders of Changchun surrendered in October after a siege of 150 days; 160,000 civilians were estimated to have died, the same number as at Hiroshima, most of starvation. At the end of the year, the Communists were victorious in the huge Huaihai battle in eastern China, involving some 1.5 million troops with 300,000 killed. The following October, Chiang Kai-shek fled to Formosa and Mao Zedong declared the People's Republic with himself as the Great Helmsman who would unleash enormous disasters on the Chinese people before his death in 1976. The nation's subsequent emergence onto the world stage as its second largest economy and a major global force could not have been foreseen. But, for all the death and destruction caused by the chairman, the Communist victory presaged by the campaigns and policies described in this book reunited the Middle Kingdom in a way that, after Mao's toll of scores of millions of lives, would enable his successors to change not just China but the world once the one-time political commissar of the Central Plains Army, Deng Xiaoping, had charted a new economic course while retaining the autocratic power of the monopoly party.

The Republic of South Korea came into formal being on 15 August 1948, with Syngman Rhee as president. The constitution provided for the separation of executive and legislative powers and an independent judiciary, but a ban against supporting the North was used to detain some 30,000 people and impose authoritarian rule. The US provided $400 million in aid while, in Pyongyang, the Democratic People's Republic was declared in September 1948 under Kim Il-sung. In Japan, conservative Shigeru Yoshida became prime minister for the second time in October 1948, remaining in office until 1954 and pursuing a policy of economic revival and a close alliance with Washington to frame the country's foreign policy – a peace treaty was signed in 1951 leading to the end of the occupation the following year, though the US retained a powerful military base in Okinawa.

Japan's revival helped the Truman administration to show a large measure of sangfroid at the Communist victory in China in 1949 despite attacks from Republicans and Madame Chiang Kai-shek for having 'lost China'. East Asian policy was designed to create 'a great crescent' of containment on the lines proposed by Kennan; Senator Vandenberg pictured this as enabling America to adopt 'sort of a wait, look, see policy'. But, in June 1950, North Korea upset the strategic calculations with its invasion of the South.

Stalin approved the action, reckoning the Americans would remain out of the conflict, a belief reinforced by a statement by Dean Acheson, which, in line with Kennan's thinking, did not include South Korea in the US security perimeter. After Truman decided, on the contrary, to send in troops under UN auspices along with those of a dozen other nations, fighting lasted until 1953, with more than 700,000 military dead, at least 3 million civilians killed or injured and millions displaced. A peace treaty has still not been signed as North Korea pursues the Kim legacy with the development of missiles and nuclear weapons which makes the peninsula potentially the most dangerous global trouble spot. More generally, the lack of coherent US policy for East Asia, in contrast to the construction of Europe, meant that the region was marked by a series of 'hub and spoke' bilateral relationships and hostilities which persist to the present.[4]

France conquered the last rebel stronghold in Madagascar in November 1948, and quenched the revolt: the island became an independent state ten years later. Successive governments in Paris continued the efforts to hold onto Vietnam until defeat at Dien Bien Phu in the spring of 1954 led to its withdrawal, the division of the country and deepening American involvement.

The Dutch launched a second military offensive in Indonesia at the end of 1948, taking the Republican capital of Yogyakarta and capturing Sukarno. In September of that year, the Republican army put down a revolt by Communist-led troops in the Javanese city of Madiun, killing thousands of the insurgents. After international criticism and the threat of suspension of Marshall aid forced the Netherlands to cede sovereignty, independence was declared in 1950. But Sukarno's rule grew increasingly authoritarian and he dallied with the Communists, leading to the bloody coup of 1965 that ushered in three decades of military rule before democracy returned as part of the international economic aid programme following the Asian economic crisis of 1997–8.

The emergency in Malaya stretched on to 1960, three years after the country gained independence, as the new rulers continued the fight against Communist guerrillas. That same year, 1957, Ghana became a sovereign nation, a decade after the Accra riots. In South Africa, apartheid lasted for almost half a century before the 1994 elections brought the African National Congress to power.

Truman was re-elected in November 1948, with 303 votes in the Electoral College to Dewey's 189 and thirty-nine for the Dixiecrat Strom Thurmond. His popular vote margin over the Republican ran to more than 3 million. He had the side satisfaction of being able to hold up one of the most celebrated instances of fake news, the 'DEWEY BEATS TRUMAN' splash headline in the Republican *Chicago Tribune*. The global policy he oversaw in his first three years in the White House became the model for his successors, though the application of the doctrine that bore his name led to engagements which brought it into question even after its brand of capitalist, democratic internationalism had emerged apparently triumphant at the end of the Cold War.

If the templates set in 1947–8 inevitably evolved over the following decades, what is striking is how many remain as the building blocks for much of the world we know today. The great power contours of Europe set at wartime summits dissolved with the end of the Cold War but most borders drawn then remain in force. The ideological division of the Continent has been replaced by an economic union with its roots in collaborative post-war experimentation which accounts for 23 per cent of the global economy. NATO continues to link the North Atlantic continents. There has been no fresh outbreak of war between major European nations.

For all its economic and social development, China continues to be ruled by the Communist Party, with its current leader vying to match Mao Zedong in authority. The Kim family hold sway in North Korea. The US–Japan strategic link remains in place. Peronist presidents ruled in Argentina between 1989 and 2015. The long war in Colombia which sprang from *La Violencia* following the assassination of the Liberal presidential candidate in 1948 dragged on until a peace accord in 2016.

The democracy established in the period of this book has persisted in Germany, Japan, Israel, India and (albeit with periods of military rule) Pakistan, and has been restored in Indonesia. Following the struggle for freedom that took shape in Asia and Africa in the later 1940s, independent nations have replaced European imperialism. Though now gone, the apartheid era ushered in by the 1948 election has left its legacy on South Africa. The United Nations and other international organisations set up in the wake of the world war continue to function with varied degrees of effect. The GATT trading umbrella has been succeeded by the World Trade Organization. The IMF and World Bank are still central organs of the international economy. The decolonisation process which began in India and Pakistan has boosted the number of nations from the fifty-one that formed the original United Nations to 193 sovereign states.

Despite the criticism it has come to attract, globalisation, whose roots can be traced back to post-war policies, has shaped today's world. Technologies developed in the later 1940s have advanced exponentially, with the West retaining major advantages in modern industry, military strength and soft power built on foundations laid in the second half of the 1940s. Even if questioned, the state has come to be widely accepted as a necessary provider of welfare and education as well as security. The cat's cradle of alliances, economic agreements and international exchanges that emerged from the roots set in 1947–8 provided the framework for the broadly liberal internationalism of recent decades, which even an outlier such as China found it in its interest to join.

But, beside these constants, divisions stretching from 1947–8 remain without resolution. Israel has survived, but is rejected by most of its neighbours and faces rising internal tensions. The Arab world is split. The Palestinians are dispersed and without a settled state of their own. India and Pakistan are as antagonistic as ever, with Islamic military in the latter and Hindu zealotry overturning the Nehru legacy in the former. Though claimed by Beijing and having evolved from Chiang Kai-shek's dictatorship into democracy, Taiwan remains separate from mainland China. Korea is still divided on the 38th parallel. Russia once more tests the West's resolve as Vladimir Putin laments the collapse of the USSR as a great tragedy[5] and a 2017 poll puts Stalin in first place among great historical figures.[6]

Still, the settled state inherited by the West from the crucible of the late 1940s is changing both internally and externally as accepted elements of society, notably the welfare state and entitlements, come under challenge, nationalism, sectarianism and the threat of Islamic terrorism are on the rise, and the global structure unravels or takes new forms. Populism is on the rise almost everywhere. In the West, the centrist consensus is fraying fast as the political establishment is seen by voters as failing to give them what they deserve in an age of radical uncertainty and, in Europe, social democracy has given way to more radical left-wing prescriptions or the loss of traditional supporters to extremist movements of the right. The post-war attempt to contain capitalism within a system that favoured general welfare has been replaced by the primacy of finance as the link between democracy and capitalism has become increasingly strained. Though nations have become more equal with one another economically, domestically many have seen growing wealth disparities internally. Uncertainty about the future is on the increase as living standards stagnate and technology changes the way we live.

Central to this is the country that became the key to the international order under Harry Truman at a time when the White House seems minded to pull back from its global role in the face of what Henry Kissinger has dubbed the 'congenital ambivalence' of reconciling force and diplomacy, realism and idealism, power and legitimacy. Pax Americana rested for seven decades on internationalist alliances and an economic system that offered advantages for all; now the world is moving towards a series of zero-sum games replacing the incrementalism of post-war policy but without a road map such as that provided by the Cold War.[7]

The revival of Europe and Japan and the rise of China have radically altered the balance of economic power away from the US, whose share of world output is likely to fall to 15 per cent by 2020 from 50 per cent in Truman's day. Beijing is setting up financial institutions to challenge those established under US leadership (and with American veto power) after the Second World War. NATO is seeking a fresh role for itself, though unable to discount a possible renewed threat from Moscow. Relations between the superpowers on either side of the Pacific are scratchy, mistrustful and ill defined. American society is increasingly divided as inequalities mushroom and millennials outnumber baby boomers. The unifying domestic American narrative – what the commentator David Brooks calls 'the civic mythology' – is fragmented by demagogic rhetoric with no equivalent of the Wise Men or of the allies they found to chart a united political and economic purpose. Protectionism threatens the free trading system that underpinned turn-of-the century prosperity as President Emmanuel Macron of France warns that, in Europe, 'sovereignty, democracy and trust are in danger'.[8]

The prospect of 'the essential power' turning in on itself with a foreign policy branded by former secretary of state Zbigniew Brzezinski as 'chaotic, unclear, unfocussed' – and the dangers the international community sees in that – demonstrate the importance of the course adopted in 1947–8 in an era in which the globe now faces fragmentation and deep uncertainty. In place of the constructive optimism that reigned after 1945 at home and in dealing with the rest of the world, the challenges of the twenty-first century arouse fear and inward-looking nationalism as President Trump thunders about the world's strongest power being traduced and cheated while its infrastructure slides to twelfth place in world rankings and bipartisanship becomes a forgotten way of getting things done for the general good. 'The fundamental question of our time is whether the West has the will to survive,' the President declared in a speech in the summer of 2017. 'Do we have the confidence in our values to defend them at any cost?' Truman asked a similar question when faced with Soviet power. His response was the Marshall Plan and all that flowed from it, the revival of Japan and Germany, internationalism and partnerships (even if it was always clear who was in the driving seat). Today, the question is asked once more, but there is no coherent proposal in answer from the White House only disjointed tub-thumping.[9]

The United States is not alone in replacing internationalism with an inward-looking mentality, blaming others for domestic problems amid a fraying of social bonds and mounting uncertainties. Many of the structures set in place in the later 1940s are still with us, but are often under threat with no evident replacement in sight, as the secretary-general of the NATO alliance warns that the world is 'more unpredictable and more difficult' than it has been for a generation. Whether the international system can modify itself to bring stability and progress is the prime question for our times. The thirteen months of 1947–8 present trenchant examples of how realpolitik can serve a wider purpose if those in power know how to use it on a planet as fragmented or challenging as it was seven decades ago.[10]

# CAST LIST

**Abdullah bin Al-Hussein,** King of Transjordan (1882–1951). On the throne since 1921, he aimed to expand his realm through secret negotiations with the Zionists and use of his Arab Legion. He was assassinated on the steps of Al-Aqsa mosque in Jerusalem by a member of the Grand Mufti's Husseini Palestinian clan.

**Sheikh Mohammad Abdullah,** the 'Lion of Kashmir' (1905–1982). He was prime minister of Jammu and Kashmir until 1953 when he was arrested and jailed for eleven years, accused of conspiracy against the Indian State. Interned from 1965 to 1968 and exiled in 1971 for eighteen months, he became chief minister again from 1975 until his death.

**Dean Acheson,** American diplomat (1893–1971). Under secretary of state 1945–8, he was central to the evolution of early Cold War policy. Returning to the Truman administration as secretary of state from 1949 to 1953, he played a key role in US involvement in the Korean War and strengthening the Western alliance.

**Konrad Adenauer,** German Christian Democratic politician (1876–1967). Elected as the first chancellor of the Federal Republic of (West) Germany in 1949, he stayed in office until 1963, presiding over its economic growth and political re-integration in Europe as he signed the Friendship Treaty with France in 1963 and pressed for co-operation in the west of the Continent.

**Clement Attlee**, British Labour Party politician (1883–1967). He became prime minister in 1945 after his party's sweeping general election victory, and remained in office till 1951 and leader of the Labour Party until 1955, after which he was ennobled as Earl Attlee.

**Menachem Begin**, Israeli politician (1913–1992). Leader of the Irgun underground movement, he headed the Herut Party after the creation of Israel. As prime minister from 1977 to 1983, he signed the peace treaty with Egypt for which he shared a Nobel Prize. He authorised the bombing of the nuclear plant in Iraq and the invasion of Lebanon in 1982.

**David Ben-Gurion**, Israeli politician (1886–1973). First prime minister of the new state, he remained in office until 1954 and returned from 1955 to 1963. During the second period, Israeli forces invaded Egypt in collusion with the UK and France after Egypt nationalised the Suez Canal.

**Edvard Beneš**, Czechoslovak politician (1884–1948). President at the time of the 1938 Munich Agreement to dismember his country, he headed the government-in-exile in London in the Second World War. He returned as president in 1945, thinking he could contain the Communists but was out-manoeuvred by the putsch in 1948, dying soon afterwards.

**Ernest Bevin**, British Labour Party politician and trade union leader (1881–1951). After serving as labour minister in the wartime coalition, he was foreign secretary from 1945 to 1951, when he reluctantly agreed to be moved to become Lord Privy Seal on account of failing health. He died a month later. 'There's the man I miss,' Attlee said.

**Georges Bidault**, French politician (1899–1983). A resistance leader, he became a leading Christian Democrat after the Liberation and a virtual fixture as foreign minister, also spending eight months as prime minister. After he backed violent opponents of granting independence to Algeria, he went into exile in Brazil in 1962, moving to Belgium in 1967 and returning to France in 1968 following an amnesty.

**Bolesław Bierut,** Polish Communist politician (1892–1956). President and prime minister of post-war Poland, ensuring its loyalty to the Kremlin, he became General Secretary of the Communist Party in August 1948. His mysterious death in Moscow gave rise to speculation of poisoning or suicide, though officially attributed to a heart attack – possibly after reading Khrushchev's denunciation of Stalin.

**Léon Blum,** French politician (1872–1950). Prime minister of the pre-war Popular Front, he was imprisoned in Nazi concentration camps and returned to play a leading role in the early years of the Fourth Republic as prime minister and conscience of the non-Communist left.

**Chiang Kai-shek,** Chinese Nationalist leader (1887–1975). The generalissimo headed the Kuomintang Nationalist Republic from 1927 but never managed to establish a viable state. He was unable to prevent Japan occupying Manchuria in 1931 and suffered a series of defeats when full-scale war broke out between the two countries in 1937. Defeated by the Communists in the ensuing civil war, he fled with his followers to Taiwan where he presided over an authoritarian regime which received US backing as the Korean War made it a strategic asset.

**Lucius Clay,** American soldier (1898–1978). US commander in Germany with a front seat to the evolution of the Cold War, particularly during the Berlin blockade and airlift. He left Germany in 1949 and returned home to take on a wide variety of posts as well as acting as unofficial envoy to Europe of the Eisenhower administration and accompanying President Kennedy on his 1961 visit to Berlin.

**Deng Xiaoping,** Chinese Communist leader (1904–97). PLA political commissary during the civil war who went on to play a leading role in the early People's Republic. After Mao's death, he made himself China's paramount leader, setting the country on a new and more open economic path that changed the world.

**Georgi Dimitrov,** Bulgarian Communist (1882–1949). Veteran apparatchik who headed the Comintern after winning fame when acquitted after being accused of involvement in the Reichstag fire in Berlin in 1933. He led Bulgaria until 1949. There was speculation that his death in a sanatorium near Moscow was the result of Soviet poisoning.

**Milovan Djilas,** Yugoslav politician (1911–1995). Partisan fighter and member of the post-war regime involved in negotiations with Stalin about which he wrote published accounts. Once seen as a potential successor to Tito, his advocacy of greater democracy led to his expulsion from the Communist Party and his imprisonment before he was released and continued to write and speak as a dissident.

**Jacques Duclos,** French Communist politician (1896–1975). A fierce opponent of 'bourgeois' governments of the Fourth Republic known for his fiery rhetoric, he went on to take 21.27 per cent of the first-round vote in the 1969 presidential election.

**Ludwig Erhard,** German economist and politician (1897–1977). The architect of post-war recovery served as economics minister in Bonn from 1949 to 1963, and then became the second chancellor of West Germany from 1963 but was obliged to resign three years after his support dwindled.

**Mohammad Amin al-Husseini,** Grand Mufti of Jerusalem, (1897–1974). Palestinian leader born into a prominent landowning clan, he opposed British rule and collaborated with Nazi Germany, meeting Hitler in Berlin, before seeking a major role in opposing the creation of Israel. After joining in the establishment of an All-Palestine Government in Egyptian-ruled Gaza, he was marginalized by the Palestine Liberation Organization in the last decade of his life.

**Mohandas Karamchand Gandhi,** Indian seer and leader of non-violence independence movement (1869–1948). After initial experience in South Africa he headed the drive for Indian independence from the 1920s using civil disobedience as the tool against the Raj. Increasingly depressed by the violence of partition, he staged a series of fasts before being assassinated in early 1948.

**Alcide De Gasperi,** Italian Christian Democratic politician (1881–1954). He headed eight successive coalition governments until 1953 and was a founding father of the European Union.

**Charles de Gaulle,** French soldier and politician (1890–1970). After challenging the Fourth Republic with his RPF movement from 1947 to 1955, he staged his return to power in 1958, founding the Fifth Republic, ending the war in Algeria and seeking to make his country the leader of Western Europe. After the student revolt and strikes of 1968, he held a referendum he was bound to lose and retired to his country home, where he died while playing patience waiting for the evening television news.

**Władysław Gomułka,** Polish Communist (1905–82). Purged in 1948, he came back in a leadership role from 1956 to 1970 when clashes between security forces and Baltic shipyard workers forced his resignation and retirement.

**Klement Gottwald,** Czechoslovak Communist (1896–1953). He consolidated the regime after the 1948 putsch, presiding over purges in the early 1950s before dying of heart disease.

**Hirohito,** Japanese emperor (1901–89). Though losing his divine status after Japan's defeat in 1945, he remained the potent national figurehead and travelled to meet foreign leaders while continuing his studies of marine biology.

**Ho Chi Minh,** Vietnamese leader (1890–1969). Head of the Viet Minh, he became prime minister and then president of the Democratic Republic in the north of the country as it fought against the south and the French and Americans.

**Eddie Jacobson,** American businessman (1891–1955). Truman's close friend and former business partner who intervened with him to support the creation of Israel, he continued to run his Westport Menswear store in Kansas City, visiting Israel in 1949.

**Muhammad Ali Jinnah,** founder of Pakistan (1876–1948). Initially a proponent of Hindu–Muslim unity, he backed a separate state after being rejected by the Indian Congress Party but described the new nation as 'moth-eaten'. A whisky-drinking secularist, he allied himself increasingly with Islam and became ever more intractable. In bad health for years and shaken by the violence of partition, he died thirteen months after the creation of Pakistan.

**Kim Il-sung,** North Korean leader (1912–94). Consolidating his position with Soviet and Chinese backing, he established an authoritarian state that implemented land reform, nationalisation and repression, preaching patriotism and *Juche* self-reliance. In 1950, he engineered the invasion of South Korea in a still unfinished war.

**George Kennan,** US diplomat and planner (1904–2005). He laid out the containment strategy towards the Soviet Union but subsequently regretted how his analysis had been used as the basis for his country's military build-up.

**Osman Ali Khan, nizam of Hyderabad,** Indian princely ruler (1886–1967). A Muslim ruling a predominantly Hindu state of 83,000 square miles, he was once reputed to be the richest man in the world, but extremely parsimonious. After the Raj ended, he manoeuvred to gain independence but India annexed Hyderabad by force, allowing him to stay on as Rajpramukh (governor) until 1956.

**Lin Biao,** Chinese Communist general (1907–1971). Commanded successful civil war campaigns in Manchuria before becoming a leading figure in the People's Republic. Designated for a time as Mao's successor, he was involved in a murky plot to seize power and died in a plane crash fleeing the country.

**Douglas MacArthur,** American soldier (1880–1964). Supreme commander of the Allied Powers in Japan from 1945, he ruled as pro-consul and then became commander-in-chief in the Korean War before being sacked for insubordination by Truman.

**Daniel Malan**, South African politician (1874–1959). Nationalist leader, he steered his party to electoral victory in 1948 to launch apartheid policies which were tightened during his six years as prime minister.

**Mao Zedong**, China's 'Great Helmsman' (1893–1976). Leader of the Communist Party from the Long March in the mid-1930s, he set military as well as political strategy during the civil war with the Nationalists. Unchallenged chief of the People's Republic, he launched mass repression campaigns and the disastrous Great Leap Forward followed by a famine that took more than 40 million lives and then the vastly destructive Cultural Revolution. Now officially seen as '70 per cent good, 30 per cent bad', he remains the Chinese regime's iconic figure.

**George Marshall**, American soldier and statesman (1880–1959). Army chief of staff in the Second World War, he was appointed secretary of state in 1947 and, at Truman's insistence, gave his name to the post-war American assistance programme for Europe. He resigned on health grounds in 1949 but then became secretary of defence from 1950–51. Awarded the Nobel Peace Prize in 1953 for the Marshall Plan.

**Jan Masaryk**, Czechoslovak diplomat (1886–1948). An iconic figure, the son of the founder of the country, he tried to steer an independent path but was caught by the tightening grip of the Communist Party and the USSR. His death was officially reported as suicide but evidence points to murder.

**Golda Meir**, Israeli politician (1898–1978). A senior figure at the Jewish Agency, she conducted negotiations with King Abdullah of Transjordan and undertook a highly successful fundraising tour of the US. After serving as minister of labour and foreign minister, she became Israel's fourth prime minister in 1969, described as the 'Iron Lady' of the nation's politics.

**Vacheslav Molotov**, Soviet foreign minister (1890–1986). Long-serving deputy to Stalin and prime minister from 1930–41, he signed the 1939 pact with Germany. Falling out of favour in the later 1940s, he lost the foreign affairs post but defended Stalin's policies and legacy until his death. Dismissed from the Presidium of the Central Committee in 1957, he was expelled from the Communist Party in 1961.

**Jawaharlal Nehru,** Indian politician (1889–1964). Congress Party leader, he became India's first prime minister, a post he retained till his death. Under his leadership, Congress won three consecutive elections and he founded a dynasty that continues to dominate the party to this day.

**Vallabhbhai Patel,** Indian politician (1875–1950). Prime manager of the Congress Party. He became first deputy minister of India and minister of home affairs after independence.

**Mátyás Rákosi,** Hungarian Communist (1892–1971). Long-time party activist imprisoned before the Second World War, exiled to Moscow and then returning to power with Red Army. Imposed one-party rule, describing himself as 'Stalin's best pupil'. Forced to relinquish office and move to the USSR in 1956, where he died. His ashes were taken home to Budapest.

**Paul Ramadier,** French politician (1888–1961). Post-war Socialist prime minister who expelled Communists from the coalition government in 1947.

**Syngman Rhee,** South Korean politician (1875–1965). Long-time independence advocate, he became president after elections in 1948. An ardent anti-Communist, he ordered thousands of extra-judicial killings and was forced to resign after protests against a disputed election in 1960. He died in exile in Hawaii.

**Raoul Salan,** French soldier (1899–1984). In Indochina, he organised offensives against the Viet Minh and later became commander of forces in Algeria in 1956, leading the attempted putsch in 1961 and becoming head of the *Organisation armée secrète* (OAS). Charged with treason, he was condemned to death but pardoned in 1968.

**Karl Schumacher**, West German politician (1895–1952). Severely wounded in the First World War, he became a leading Social Democrat and was arrested and held by the Nazis in concentration camps where he was badly beaten. At the head of his party after the end of the war, he was a passionate speaker and firm anti-Communist who could not, however, compete with the appeal of Adenauer's Christian Democrats.

**Moshe Sharett**, Israeli politician and diplomat (1894–1965). Second prime minister of Israel in 1954–5 and then foreign minister until 1956, when he fell out with government policy.

**Yoshida Shigeru**, Japanese politician (1878–1967). After serving as a diplomat before the Second World War, he became prime minister in 1946 and again in 1948, holding the post until 1954 and guiding Japan into a close alliance with the US as its economy grew.

**Robert Shuman**, French politician (1886–1963). Prime minister from 1947–8 and foreign minister 1948–53. His first government mastered a major challenge from Communist-led labour action. As foreign minister, he became one of the founding fathers of West European co-operation.

**Jan Smuts,** South African statesman and soldier (1870–1950). A veteran of the Boer struggle against the British, he held senior military posits with the Allies in both world wars and headed governments at home, but was overwhelmed in 1948 by Afrikaner nationalism.

**Joseph Stalin**, Soviet dictator (1878–1953). He cemented his supremacy after the death of Lenin and embarked on 'Socialism in One Country' with industrialisation accompanied by mass purges, forced labour and deportations. After concluding the pact with the Nazis in 1939, he was caught by surprise by the German invasion two years later but led the USSR to victory in 1945. The post-war regime soon returned to the repression of the 1930s and tightened its grip on the security belt of Communist regime to the west.

**Sukarno**, first president of Indonesia (1901–70). He led the Republican movement to independence in 1950, but then suppressed the parliamentary system in favour of an authoritarian 'Guided Democracy'. Deposed by the army in 1966, he was put under house arrest, denied medical care and died of kidney failure.

**Maurice Thorez**, French Communist (1900–64). A miner as a young man, he proved himself a Moscow loyalist as leader of the Communist Party from 1930, but the party was in perpetual opposition after being expelled from the coalition government in 1947.

**Josip Broz Tito**, Yugoslav leader (1892–1980). His record at the head of the partisans fighting the German occupation forces gave him a dominant post-war power base to install a new regime. After splitting with Moscow in 1948, he became a founding member of the Non-Aligned Movement. In 1980, he had his left leg amputated due to arterial blockages and died of gangrene.

**Palmiro Togliatti**, Italian Communist (1893–1964). As party leader, he tried to forge a left-wing front against the Christian Democrats but lost repeated national elections while establishing party control of several major cities. Severely wounded in an assassination attempt in July 1948.

**Harry Truman**, US president (1884–1972). After winning the 1948 election against expectations, he steered the country through the early stages of the Cold War, enunciating the 'Truman Doctrine' of anti-Soviet intervention, and then took it into the Korean War. He sought to continue New Deal legislation at home but ran into congressional opposition. Though often disparaged during his years in the White House, he is now widely rated as being among the top ten best presidents.

**Walter Ulbricht**, East German Communist (1893–1973). Hard-liner trained in Moscow, he guided East Germany through the Cold War. His rejection of détente led to a loss of Soviet support and he was forced to resign from most of his functions in the early 1970s.

**Markos Vafiadis**, Greek Communist (1906–1992). Commander of rebel army and head of the Provisional Democratic Government 1947–49. After defeat by the US-backed government in Athens, he went into exile for thirty-three years, returning home in 1983 and being elected an honorary member of Parliament.

**Arthur Vandenberg**, American politician (1884–1951). Republican senator from Michigan, foreign affairs spokesman, he participated in the creation of the United Nations and pursued a bipartisan policy to back the Truman Doctrine, the Marshall Plan and NATO.

**Chaim Weizmann**, Zionist patriarch (1874–1952). A leading bio-chemist, he was instrumental in Britain's Balfour Declaration of 1917 promising a national home to the Jews. Amid the debate about partition in 1947–8, he met Truman twice. But his relations with Ben-Gurion soured and he was sidelined in the figurehead presidency after the new state was established.

**Andrei Zhdanov**, Soviet official (1896–1948). Boss of Leningrad before the Second World War and an accomplice in the Great Purges, he became the regime's ideological enforcer and imposed the 'two camps' doctrine on other Communist parties. He was widely seen as Stalin's most likely successor, but died in 1948 of heart failure.

# NOTES

## Preface

1 First use of the term is variously attributed to the British writer George Orwell, the American financier Bernard Baruch and the French politician Jules Moch while US columnist Walter Lippmann took it as a book title in 1947.

2 Though political isolationism did not prevent a significant growth in trade, investment and personal and cultural links between the US and Europe, Latin America and Asia. (See Westad, *Cold War*, pp. 29–30).

3 Mackinder, pp. 421–37.

4 This provided for the USSR to have maximum influence in Romania, Bulgaria and Hungary while Britain dominated in Greece and Yugoslavia was split 50-50. The UK and US had already tacitly accepted the inclusion of Poland and the Baltic states in the Soviet sphere.

5 MacDonald, Lawrence and Logevall, p. 121.

6 He also depicted white settlers as 'reactionary and troublesome in their own way as niggers'.

7 Meredith, pp. 94–6; Morrison, Meredith, pp. 11–12; Dalton, Burleigh, p. 128.

## Chapter One: Legacy of War

1 Capa, p. 232.

2 UN Report, 1948, p. 3.

3 Manila, Doctor, Connaughton et al., *Milwaukee Journal*, 1 November 1945.

4 Russia, Mark Harrison, 'The Soviet Union After 1945: Economic Recovery and Political Repression', http://www2.warwick.ac.uk/fac/soc/economics/staff/mharrison/public/pp2011postprint.pdf; Nove, p. 285; Berlin, MacDonogh, *Berlin*, p. 354.

5 Manchuria, van de Ven, p. 239; Mayor, Gunther, pp. 160–1.

6 Judt, pp. 16–17, 83; Scheidel, p. 147; Fenby, *The General*, p. 263; China, van de Ven, p. 222.

7    Japan, McClain, pp. 532–3.

8    Vienna, MacDonogh, *Reich*, p. 287; Czechoslovakia, Kaplan, *March*,
     p. 79.

9    USSR, Michael Ellman, *Cambridge Journal of Economics*, 24 (2000),
     pp. 603–30; China, van de Ven, pp. 227–8.

10   Sargent, Coal, Bruce Lockhart, *Diaries*, pp. 572, 584.

11   Fish, Kirby, p. 53; UN Economic Report, 1948, pp. 7, 90, 208, 212.

12   It was preceded by a commercial for Jell-O.

13   Truman, London *Times*, 7 October 1947; Heinz, Museum of New York
     exhibition, May 2017; MGM, *New Yorker*, 21 February 1948.

14   Hoover, Yergin, *Peace*, p. 305; Clayton, FRUS 1947, III, Document 136,
     https://history.state.gov/historicaldocuments/frus1947v03/d136.

15   Spaak, Judt, p. 41.

16   Orphans, Mazower, p. 22.

17   Melby, *Mandate*, p. 219.

18   Journalist, Melby, p. 243; Missionary, Westad, *Encounters*, p. 135.

19   Rapes, Beevor, *Berlin*, p. 410; Applebaum, *Curtain*, p. 32; 128 times,
     *Reich*, p. 166; Romania, *Literary Review*, August 2016, p. 31.

20   Djilas, *Wartime*, p. 435; Clay, Smith, p. 244.

21   United Nations, van de Ven, p. 223.

22   Gomułka, MacDonogh, p. 478; Ben-Gurion, Flapan, p. 84; Weizmann,
     Shlaim, *Israel and Palestine*, p. 56.

23   Attlee, Williams, *Prime Minister*, p. 189; McCormick, *New York Times*,
     23 October 1946.

24   Still, several hundred thousand ethnic Germans remained in Silesia, their
     presence not recognised officially until it came to light in the late 1980s
     (Held, p. 257); Beneš, MacDonogh, p. 128; Schechtman, *Population
     Transfers*, part 2, Czechoslovakia, pp. 65–6; 'The Savage Peace', BBC2,
     24 May 2015; Snyder, *Bloodlands*, pp. 314–15, 320, 322; Journalist,
     Connell, pp. 91–2.

25   Camps, Judt, pp. 30–2; Observer, MacDonogh, *Reich*, pp. 182, 191–5.

26   Clay, pp. 313–14.

27   Smolar, Snyder, *Bloodlands*, p. 355.

## Chapter Two: New Departures

1    The work of the technocrats enabled the Fourth Republic established
     in 1946 to maintain a stability that belied the political theatre of its
     revolving-door governments until it was finally brought low by the
     Algerian conflict in 1958.

2    Thorez, Asselain, pp. 108–9.

3    State of Union, https://www.trumanlibrary.org/whistlestop/tap/1748.htm

4    Agreements, UN Economic Report, 1948.

5    King, Ziegler, *George VI*, p. 78.

6    Hirohito, Little man, Gayn, pp. 137–8; Crowds, Role, Bix, pp. 625–7.

7    During the world war, Bush headed the Office of Scientific Research and
     Development, which was responsible for overseeing the development of

the atom bomb. He did early work on analogue computers and envisaged
ways of assembling information similar to those later developed with
hypertext.

8  Bush, *Guardian*, 27 June 2017.
9  On their retreat from Italy in 1943–4, the German army caused a major
    epidemic of the disease, whose name comes from the Italian for 'bad air',
    by flooding the Lazio Plain. More than 50,000 cases were declared in
    the province of Littoria alone. Smith, *Italy*, p. 494.
10 It would go into production three years later.
11 The equivalent of $53,000 today.
12 Dior, Sebba, pp. 325–6.
13 Mini-cameras, George Rodger, http://inmotion.magnumphotos.com/
    about/history.
14 The Act was intended mainly to facilitate white immigrants from
    Australia, New Zealand and South Africa, and only one to two
    thousand people came from the Caribbean in its early years.
15 Qutb, 'Amrika allati Ra'aytu (The America I Have Seen)', *al-Risalah*,
    June 1978. https://archive.org/stream/SayyidQutb/The%20America%20
    I%20have%20seen_djvu.txt
16 Only one prototype was built before lack of interest from airlines led to
    the project being abandoned.
17 One American woman was so taken with the ship that she spent fifteen
    years aboard.
18 Exaggerated modern, Hall, p. 836.

## Chapter Three: The Superpowers

1  De Tocqueville, p. 395; Hitler, *Testament*, 2 April 1945; Rome, Beisner,
    p. 57.
2  First by the French finance minister and future president, Valéry Giscard
    d'Estaing.
3  UN Economic Report for 1947, p. 30.
4  Vectors, Daniel Runde, International *New York Times*, 19 July 2017;
    Clinton, Democratic Party Convention, 31 August 2008 https://www.
    npr.org/templates/story/story.php?storyId=94045962; Thinkers, https://
    www.project-syndicate.org/commentary/trump-china-kindleberger-trap-
    by-joseph-s--nye-2017-01?barrier=accessreg
5  Meijer, Vandenburg, pp. 304, 309; Haas, Lawrence, lays out the
    Truman–Vandenberg relationship.
6  Among those born in 1946–7 were Donald Trump, Bill and Hillary
    Clinton and George W. Bush.
7  Grass, Laundry, *New York Times* International, 24–25 June 2017.
8  As many as Japan, Germany and the UK combined.
9  Construction, James Stewart, *New York Times*, 19–20 November 2016;
    Truman, *Memoirs*, 11, p. 110.
10 Levitt, *New York Times* International, 24–5 June 2017.
11 Madariaga and Nicolson, Mayne, pp. 113, 116.

12   De Beauvoir, Mayne, p. 108.

13   The phrase was coined by the *New Yorker* writer E. B. White, who
     celebrated the 'convergence and concentration and diversity of its
     peoples, talents, ambitions and egos ... leadership, internationalism,
     culture, education, business, finance, medicine, trade, transportation
     [with] the common thread of creativity'.

14   Rothko, Conrad, p. 560.

15   Artists, production, Conrad, p. 555, 582–3; Figure (Harriman), Yergin,
     *Peace*, p. 172; Attlee, Williams, *Prime Minister*, p. 172; Lewis, *New
     York Times* International, 22 August 2017.

16   *New Republic*, June/August 1947.

17   Hopkins, Reynolds, *Origins*, p. 6; Luce, Kennedy, p. 360, Cummings,
     *Origins*, p. 35.

18   Roth, Speech on receiving the National Book Foundation's medal for
     Distinguished Contribution to American Letters, 20 November 2002.

19   Djilas, *Conversations*, p. 153.

20   Recover, Djilas, *Conversations*, p. 106.

21   System, Djilas, *Conversations*, p. 114.

22   George Orwell, 'You and the Atom Bomb', *Tribune*, 19 October 1945. I
     am grateful to D. J. Taylor for drawing my attention to this article.

23   Miłosz, 'Child of Europe', 1946.

24   Bevin, David Reynolds, *Foreign Affairs*, May–June 1997, https://
     www.foreignaffairs.com/articles/europe/1997-05-01/marshall-plan-
     commemorative-section-european-response-primacy-politics.

25   Loyalty, Tracy Strong in Drolet and Dunkerley, p. 129; Spy, Mazower,
     p. 250.

26   Prisoners, Applebaum, *Gulag*, pp. 516–18.

27   Strong blow, Applebaum, *Gulag*, p. 415.

28   Roberts, Hobsbawm, p. 226.

29   Old Bolshevism, see Yuri Slezkine, *The House of Government*
     (Princeton University Press, 2017).

30   The initial stood for nothing but was bestowed on the baby to honour
     his grandfathers who both had the letter in their names.

31   Partners, Miller, p. 109.

32   Kotkin, pp. 5–6.

33   Health, Teeth, Sebag Montefiore, *Court*, pp. 454–6; Flabby, Djilas, *Rise
     and Fall*, pp. 154, 159; Arteriosclerosis, Fine, Conquest, p. 297; Accident
     airbrushed, Soft-spoken, Kotkin, pp. 3–5.

34   Daughter, Margaret Truman, p. 71.

35   Kitchen, Fields, p. 120.

36   Block, McCullough, p. 388, Jackson, Truman, *Memoirs*, 11, p. 161; Ivan,
     Conquest, p. 295.

37   Gestapo, Miller, p. 220.

38   His first wife died of typhus in 1918.

39   Like her husband, she enjoyed her bourbon, preferring it on the rocks in
     a large glass.

40 Crippled, Sebag Montefiore, *Court*, pp. 17, 143–4; Bess, *Time*, 10 November 1947; Anniversary, HST Letter, 28 June, Truman Library; Officer, McCullough, p. 435.

41 Lenin text, https://www.marxists.org/archive/lenin/works/1922/dec/testamnt/congress.htm; Prosecutor, Reynolds, *Origins*, p. 5.

42 Boys, https://www.trumanlibrary.org/lifetimes/whouse.htm

43 Acheson, Miller, p. 376; Wallace, *New York Times*, 19 November 1975, http://www.nytimes.com/1975/11/19/archives/wallace-memoirs-tell-of-ousting-by-truman.html?_r=0

44 Nobody, Miller, p. 215

45 Molotov, Truman, *Memoirs*, pp. 81–2, Leahy, Diary, 23 April 1945, Yergin, *Peace*, pp. 83, 100.

46 Larsh, p. 275; Messer, p. 82; Anna Cienciala, *The Polish Review*, LV/4 (2010), pp. 445–63.

47 Moran, chapter 27.

48 Potsdam, Moran, pp. 282, 285; Kennan, *Memoirs*, pp. 258–9; Truman letter, http://www.shapell.org/manuscript/truman-potsdam-conference-wwii

49 Babying, Poen, p. 124.

50 Iran developments, Arfa, chapters 17–18, Yergin, *Prize*, pp. 451–3; Cooper, p. 62; Beisner, p. 31.

51 Kennan, *Memoirs*, p. 293.

52 Telegram, Kennan, *Memoirs*, annexe C.

53 Kennan, *Memoirs*, p. 294.

54 He had used the term in a message to Truman three days after the end of the world war (Rupnik, p. 71).

55 Speech, Churchill Archive, Cambridge, CHUR 2/226; Reaction, Stalin, McCullough, pp. 488–9.

56 Hog wild, Davis diary, 10 September 1946.

57 Report, Accaia, p. 43, Yergin, *Peace*, pp. 241–5; Harriman, Bruce Lockhart, *Diaries*, p. 567.

58 Novikov, Jensen, p. 3; Tracy Strong in Drolet and Dunkerely, p. 135, note 31.

59 Commie, Ferrell, *Truman*, p. 538; No liberal, Jenkins, *Truman*, p. 128.

60 Stature, McCullough, p. 614.

61 Speech, Pogue, p. 162.

62 *Time*, 25 March 1946; Churchill, Moran, p. 273; Critics, Daniels, p. 317.

63 Trivia, Isaacson and Thomas, p. 405; Smith, *My Three Years in Moscow*, pp. 213–14; Kennan, *Memoirs*, p. 345.

64 Not a diplomat, Pogue, p. 171.

65 Harriman urged him to shave off the moustache, saying, 'You owe it to Truman', but Acheson demurred (McCullough, p. 753).

66 Fish, Isaacson and Thomas, p. 131; White, Beisner, p. 17; Smarty pants, Pogue, p. 146; Low boring, Isaacson and Thomas, p. 465; Moustache, Boring point, Character, Beisner, pp. 27, 79, 88, 100.

67 Beisner, p. 100.

68   War Department, Rajak, p. 13.

69   Acheson, pp. 218–19, Issacson and Thomas, pp. 393–6; Map, Chace, p. 154; No dissent, Truman, *Memoirs*, p. 103.

70   Molotov said he could not understand how a man with so much money could look so unhappy.

71   Crocodile, Tank, Isaacson and Thomas, pp. 20, 443.

72   Harriman, FRUS, 1944, IV, pp. 802–3; FRUS, 1945, IV, pp. 988–90.

73   He would return as secretary of state in 1949.

74   Bohlen, Isaacson and Thomas, p. 225; Kennan on Lovett, Kennan, *Memoirs*, p. 404.

75   Hopkins, Sherwood, p. 34, Harriman, pp. 81, 536.

76   Kennan, *Memoirs*, p. 279; Eden, Thorpe, p. 146; Attlee, Williams, *Prime Minister*, pp. 71, 77.

77   Benelux, No, Djilas, *Rise and Fall*, p. 169, Dedijer, p. 330.

78   Gluttony, Record, Djilas, *Rise and Fall*, pp. 154, 159.

79   Divorce, Watson, p. 238.

80   Leading groups, Watson, pp. 235–6; Djilas, *Conversations*, p. 100.

81   Finished, Fitzpatrick, p. 188.

## Chapter Four: Allies and Adversaries

1    Wife, Ferrell, *Bess*, p. 522; SOB, Knebel and Bailey, pp. 1–2; Liked a lot, hat, *Truman Speaks*, pp. 67–8.

2    Exiled by a coup in 1952, he collapsed and died thirteen years later after a heavy meal in a Rome restaurant.

3    His left leg was amputated in September 1948.

4    Milk, Coffee, MacDonogh, p. 265; Colleagues, Chancellor, Bew, p. 453.

5    Doctor, Bullock, pp. 82, 288.

6    Marshall, Lovett, Isaacson and Thomas, pp. 417, 449; Kennan, *Memoirs*, p. 404; Tito, Ridley, p. 291.

7    Nehru, Khan, *Partition*, p. 85; Run down, Fatima Jinnah manuscript.

8    Spender, Mayne, p. 57.

9    Good fellow, Bevin, *Molotov Remembers*, pp. 50, 83; Bidault, Demory, pp. 156, 247, 261.

10   Markos, Brewer, p. 230.

11   Jinnah, Hajari, p. 93, Heren, *Growing Up*, pp. 54–6.

12   Opiate, Australian ambassador Walter Crocker quoted in Perry Anderson, 'After Nehru', *London Review of Books* (2 August 2012); Leather, Guha, *India*, p. 138.

13   Pharmacist, Fauvet, p. 131.

14   Antipathy, Berman, Mark Kramer in Snyder and Brandon, pp. 274–5.

15   Umbrella, Gunther, pp. 119–20.

16   Vandenberg, Dumaine, p. 60; Stalin, Djilas, *Rise and Fall*, p. 105.

17   Blum, Mazower, pp. 188–9.

## Chapter Five: Power Polarisation

1 Beisner, p. 72; Clayton, McCullough, p. 561, FRUS, 1947, III, 27 May 1947, https://history.state.gov/historicaldocuments/frus1947v03/d136.

2 FRUS, 1947, III, p. 335.

3 See Benn Steil, 'The Marshall Plan and "America First"', *Project Syndicate*, 4 August 2017, ahead of his book, *The Marshall Plan: Dawn of the Cold War* (Simon & Schuster, 2018).

4 Speech, Marshall Foundation, http://marshallfoundation.org/marshall/the-marshall-plan/marshall-plan-speech/.

5 Hogan, *Plan*, pp. 21–2. This book places the plan in a US foreign policy process stretching from the First World War.

6 Conversation, Miller, p. 245.

7 https://history.state.gov/historicaldocuments/frus1947v02/d85; Put in, Marshall report on Moscow conference, http://avalon.law.yale.edu/20th_century/decade23.asp.

8 https://history.state.gov/historicaldocuments/frus1947v02/d107.

9 Truman speech, *Memoirs*, II, pp. 105 et seq., http://avalon.law.yale.edu/20th_century/trudoc.asp.

10 Acheson, Beisner, p. 62; Aide, Pogue, p. 175; Speech, Bruce Lockhart, Diaries, p. 588.

11 Letter, Williams, *Prime Minister*, pp. 154–9; Western ministers, Gaddis, *Know*, p. 117.

12 FRUS, II, pp. 139 et seq.

13 Meeting, Memorandum by Charles Bohlen, Bland and Stoler, pp. 97–104; http://marshallfoundation.org/library/digital-archive/6-053-memorandum-conversation-stalin-april-15-1947/.

14 Reparations, Reynolds, *Origins*, p. 18.

15 Bohlen, p. 263; Marshall, Pogue, p. 196.

16 Marshall, http://avalon.law.yale.edu/20th_century/decade23.asp.

17 Kennan, FRUS, 1947, III, 23 May 1947, pp. 224–5, https://history.state.gov/historicaldocuments/frus1947v03/d135.

18 Clayton, FRUS, 1947, III, 27 May 1947, https://history.state.gov/historicaldocuments/frus1947v03/d136; Acheson, Yergin, *Shattered Peace*, pp. 308, 310; Speech, Programme, Acheson, pp. 227–9, 231.

19 Grain, 82 million tons, $9 billion, *Times*, 2 July 1947, p. 4.

20 Stalin, Yergin, *Peace*, p. 298.

21 Margin, FRUS, 1947, III, pp. 344–6; Bevin, FO371/62420/UE678.

22 Stalin, Developments, Borhi, p. 68.

23 Hoover, Hogan, *Plan*, pp. 33–4.

24 Truman, *Memoirs*, p. 113; Kennan, Hogan, *Plan*, p. 41; Clayton, FRUS, 1947, III, pp. 230–2; Appeal, *New York Times*, 18 April 1947; Lippmann, *Washington Post*, 5 April, 1 May 1947.

25 Truman, Press conference, 22 June 1947.

26 Rayburn, Miller, p. 246

27 $130 billion at current value.

28 Lovett, Krock, p. 238.

## Chapter Six: Volcano of Hidden Fires

1 Upright, Campbell-Johnson, p. 165; Keel, http://news.bbc.co.uk/1/hi/world/south_asia/6926464.stm.

2 Wavell, Das, Manmath, pp. 17, 44; Mansergh, pp. 119, 197; French, pp. 253–4.

3 Calendars, Campbell-Johnson, photograph opposite p. 224.

4 Wavell, *Viceroy's Journal*, 8 April 1946, p. 239; Mosley, pp. 26–70.

5 Khan, *Partition*, pp. 63–4; Pistol, Das, p. 38; Suhrawardy, *Statesman*, 8 May 1946.

6 Killings, Lorries, Khan, *Partition*, pp. 65–6; Burrows, Mansergh, XI, p. 244.

7 Patel, Chatterji, p. 233; *Statesman*, 20 August 1946.

8 Wavell, Journal entry for 27 August 1947; Gandhi, Seervai, p. 78.

9 Gandhi, Adams, p. 254.

10 Bihar, Max Harcourt in Low, p. 315 et seq.; Nehru, *Works*, II, 1. pp. 47, 83.

11 Long, pp. 397–9; League membership, Islam, Guha, *India*, p. 43.

12 Jinnah, Hajari, p. 107.

13 The title referred to his time as a school teacher.

14 *Express Tribune*, 19 October 2013.

15 *Times*, 25, 27 August 1947.

16 Singh, Das, pp. 175–6; Nehru, *Works*, IV, pp. 14, 23.

17 Jenkins, Jinnah, http://apnaorg.com/articles/bbc-1/, Das, p. 158.

18 Jinnah, Nehru, Ghose, p. 118, Hajari, pp. 43–4; Gandhi, French, p. 27, Singh, p. 469.

19 Bogey, Fischer, *Gandhi*, p. 427.

20 Gandhi, Singh, p. 469; Window, Bolitho, p. 8.

21 Congress, Ghose, p. 191.

22 Inspidity, Early life, Moraes, pp. 22–50, French, *Liberty*, pp. 55–7, Misra, *Temple*, pp. 175–7, Nehru, *Autobiography*, p. 520.

23 Nehru, *Works*, 1/XIV, p. 503.

24 Bose would end up seeking the assistance of the Axis powers for independence and leading an Indian army allied with the Japanese. He died in a plane crash in 1945.

25 Birla, Patel, Misra, *Temple*, p. 198; Nehru, Bowles, Report, p. 59.

26 Resolution, Pirzada, p. 341.

27 Jinnah, Long, pp. 391–4, Singh, pp. 481–3.

28 Jamaat-e-Islami, Lieven, Antol, pp. 150–1.

29 India's role in the war and its impact is covered in Raghavan.

30 Mission, Mansergh, I, pp. 539–40.

31 Mutinies, Strikes, Food, Cholera, Misra, *Temple*, pp. 230–1, Hansard, 22 February 1947.

32 Jinnah, Hajari, p. 214, quoting BBC correspondent Robert Stimson.

33 Simla, Nehru, Mansergh, X, p. 756.

34 Staff Officer, Collins and Lapierre, II, p. 310.

35 Menon, Menon, *Transfer*, p. 365.

36    Moth-eaten, http://www.nationalarchives.gov.uk/wp-content/
      uploads/2014/03/fo371-635331.jpg.
37    Camps, Hajari, p. 158; Militias, Khan, *Partition*, p. 117; Patel, Das,
      p. 20.

## Chapter Seven: Battle for Palestine

1     Transformation, *New York Times*, 8 October 2017.
2     Demonstrations, Libya, Alexandria, Morris, *1948*, p. 176; Ben-Gurion,
      Shindler, pp. 43–4, Shlaim, *Israel and Palestine*, p. 58.
3     https://unispal.un.org/DPA/DPR/unispal.nsf/0/7651F1007D32B88
      E852575AD0068CE3C.
4     Abdullah, Shlaim, *Collusion*, p. 92.
5     Hitch, Shlaim, *Israel and Palestine*, p. 140.
6     Survey of Palestine, United Nations, 1946, p. 185; Society, Shindler,
      p. 30.
7     Soars, Thomas, *Fight or Flight*, p. 37; Khalidi, pp. 107–8.
8     Wingate went on to lead the Chindit guerrillas in Burma before dying in
      a plane crash in India in 1944.
9     Policy, Shlaim, *Collusion*, p. 19; Official, Sanger, p. 160.
10    Falapan, p. 240, Bar-Zohar, p. 107.
11    Bar-Zohar, pp. 108–9.
12    At Wise's request, this charge was deleted from the minutes.
13    Bar-Zohar, pp. 109–12.
14    Attacks, Barr, pp. 316–17; Meir, Rees, p. 124.
15    Named after its founder who had been killed by the British in 1942.
16    Attacks, Barr, pp. 337–44.
17    Cunningham, Barker, Sebag Montefiore, *Jerusalem*, p. 467.
18    National executive, Bevan, Shindler, pp. 57, 59.
19    Bevin, Gilbert, *Israel*, pp. 141–2; Odessa, Shindler, p. 59.
20    Crossman, pp. 69–70; Mayhew, pp. 118–19.
21    Tether, Hennessy, *Never Again*, p. 239; Paper, Wilson, pp. 181–2;
      Dalton, Barr, p. 353; Gurney, Shlaim, *Collusion*, pp. 218–19.
22    Israe*lites*, Kurzman, p. 7.
23    Gilbert, *Israel*, p. 144.
24    Mayhew, Lapping, p. 135.
25    Truman, *Memoirs*, II, p. 162.
26    Niles, Kurzman, pp. 7–8; UN, *Leader*, 4 October 1947.
27    Gentlemen, Lapping, p. 123, Barr, p. 313.
28    Bevin, Truman, Lapping, p. 125; Hecht, *A Flag is Born*, Internet
      Broadway Database.
29    Depreux, Blum, Sartre, Bidault, Barr, pp. 339–4.

## Chapter Eight: Anihilate the Enemy

1     Mao, Westad, *Encounters*, note 51, p. 360.
2     Losing one eye in battle to give him his nickname.
3     Westad, *Encounters*, pp. 169–70.

4   Westad, *Encounters*, p. 170.

5   O'Balance, *Red Army*, pp. 220–1.

6   Source note. The historian Frederic Wakeman came up with the term
    Confucian Fascism. See Wakeman, Frederic, and Edmonds, Richard
    Louis, *Reappraising Nationalist China* (Oxford University Press, 2000).

7   Stilwell, Fenby, *Generalissimo*, p. 425; Meat, Fenby, *Generalissimo*, p. 390.

8   Marshall, Fenby, *Modern China*, pp. 332–3, 336; Truman, Fenby,
    *Generalissimo*, p. 463.

9   Recognised, Melby, p. 167; Chiang, Marshall, Fenby, *Generalissimo*,
    pp. 467–71; Bad, McCullough, p. 508.

10  Domination, State, Pogue, pp. 265–6.

11  French way, van de Ven, p. 232.

12  Molotov, 14 April 1945, http://www.chinaforeignrelations.net/node/242.

13  Mao, Reynolds, *Origins*, p. 61.

14  The trip would have to wait for another two years and, even then, the
    visitor was treated coolly, leading him to complain at one point that all
    he had to do was to 'eat, sleep and shit'. Message, Westad, *Encounters*,
    p. 167, Fenby, *Modern China*, p. 364.

15  Now Shenyang.

16  Levine, pp. 237, 244–6, Westad, *Encounters*, pp. 124–8; Observer,
    Levine, pp. 108, 130.

17  These groups were not finally eliminated until 1950.

18  In due course, Gao would be purged; Mao was said to have marvelled at
    his sexual appetite.

19  Pepper, Eastman et al., *Nationalist*, pp. 321–2.

20  Westad, *Encounters*, p. 124.

21  O'Ballance, *Red Army*, p. 157.

22  Westad, *Encounters*, pp. 1567, van de Ven, pp. 246–7.

23  Mao, Pepper, Eastman et al., p. 338

24  Hankow, Melby, p. 218; Cost of living, Fairbank and Feuerwerker,
    *Cambridge History*, p. 744.

25  Production, Revenue, Expenditure, Fiscal, Shun-hsin Chou, *The Chinese
    Inflation 1937–49* (Columbia University Press, 1963), pp. 58, 70, 106.

26  Pepper, *Civil War*, pp. 58, 107, 109, 110, 111, 161.

27  Commentator, Discontent, Pepper in Fairbank and Feuerwerker, p. 739.

28  Consul General, Chassin, p. 120; Rea and Brewer, pp. 125–6.

29  As the chronicler of Mao's Thought, Stuart Schram, noted, this was
    remarkably similar to Lenin's belief that class consciousness had to
    be imposed on the proletariat. (Schram in Fairbank and Feuerwerker,
    p. 822.)

30  Resolution, Melby, p. 221.

## Chapter Nine: A Matter of Friendship

1   Bear, Kindleberger, p. 100; Contacts, FRUS, 1947, III, pp. 228, 235,
    Beisner, p. 73; Caffery, FRUS, 1947, III, p. 260; Bevin, Cromwell, p. 242.

2   Varga, Parrish and Narinsky, pp. 17, 19–20, 29–31.

3 FRUS, 1947, III, p. 301.

4 Djilas, *Rise and Fall*, p. 127.

5 Bidault, Mayne, p. 102; Cable, Parrish and Narinsky, p. 45.

6 FRUS, 1947, III, 296–9, 299–301, 303–6, Molotov, p. 61, Mayne, p. 103.

7 CVCE records, http://www.cvce.eu/content/publication/1999/1/1/ f692bc11-0049-4b78-ba99-bc0ac81aedeb/publishable_en.pdf, *New York Times*, 3 July 1947.

8 Molotov, p. 61; Marshall, FRUS, 1947, III, p. 308; Truman, Ferrell, Bess, p. 545.

9 Molotov to ambassador in Belgrade, 5 July 1947, Parrish and Narinsky, p. 48; FRUS, 1947, III, 297–3, 306–7.

10 Gottwald, Korbel, *Subversion*, p. 29; Parliamentary speech, Prague, 21 December 1929, quoted in Molloy, p. 63

11 Attlee, Williams, *Prime Minister*, p. 55, 76; Beneš, Sterling, p. 115.

12 Beneš, Kaplan, *March*, p. 11, MacDonogh, p. 127, Lukes, p. 138; Swallow, Rupnik, p. 91; Masaryk, Albright, p. 13.

13 Kennan, *Memoirs*, p. 253.

14 Masaryk, Bruce Lockhart, *Friends*, p. 135; Davenport, *Fantasy*, p. 317.

15 Villa, Drinking, Lukes, pp. 163, 167; Djilas, *Rise and Fall*, p. 123.

16 Taylor, Manchester *Guardian*, 24 July 1946; General, Rupnik, pp. 93–4, 99.

17 Party, Kaplan, *March*, p. 46.

18 Kaplan, *March*, p. 49.

19 Beneš, Zeman and Klimek, p. 247.

20 Including the 'show' concentration camp of Theresienstadt.

21 Woman, McDonough, pp. 136–7; Guillotine, Davenport, *Fantasy*, p. 309. For details of treatment of Germans, see MacDonogh, chapter 4; Joseph Chechtman, *Postwar Population Transfers in Europe 1945–1955* (University of Philadelphia Press, 1963), http://archive.org/stream/ Schechtman-Postwar-Population-Transfers-in-Europe-1945-1955/ Schechtman--PostwarPopulationTransfersInEurope1945-1955_djvu.txt; 'The Savage Peace', BBC2, 24 May 2015; Czechoslovak government decrees, 5/1945 3 June 1945, 33/1945 2 August 1945, 108/1945 25 October 1945; Massacres, Steffen Prauser and Arfon Rees (eds), 'The Expulsion of "German" Communities from Eastern Europe at the end of the Second World War' (European University Institute, Florence, 2004), http://cadmus.eui.eu/bitstream/handle/1814/2599/HEC04-01.pdf;jsessionid=1FA53D45E1EB08851160F016A0327B13?sequence=1.

22 Survey, Lukes, pp. 139–40, 141.

23 Ambassador, Bruce Lockhart, *Diaries*, p. 608.

24 *Times*, 2 January 1947; Byrnes, Lukes, p. 141.

25 Plot, Hydra, Kaplan, *March*, p. 94.

26 Kopecký, Kaplan, *March*, p. 57; Masaryk, Davenport, *Fantasy*, p. 337.

27 Russians will do, Zeman and Klimek, p. 261; President, Bruce Lockhart, *Diaries*, pp. 599–600.

28  Parades, Lusman, Poll, Lukes, p. 171; Beneš, Bruce Lockhart, *Diaries*, p. 599.

29  Letter, Gunther, pp. 215–16.

30  Bruce Lockhart, *Diaries,* pp. 579, 609–10; Sling, Albright, p. 17.

31  Davenport, *Fantasy*, pp. 277–8, 320, 327, 353–4.

32  Holtsmark et al., p. 16.

33  Embassy, FRUS, 1947, III, pp. 313–14; Masaryk, Ambassador, Holtsmark et al., pp. 13–14, 35.

34  Rejoicing, Davenport, *Fantasy*, p. 348; Masaryk, Holtsmark et al., p. 15; Cable, Parrish and Narinsky, p. 28, Lukes, pp. 171–2.

35  Cow, Mayne, p. 104.

36  Davenport, *Fantasy*, pp. 351–2.

37  Gracious, Davenport, *Fantasy*, p. 354; Stalin, Parrish and Narinsky, p. 31.

38  Beneš, Government, Holtsmark et al., p. 20; Parrish and Narinsky, pp. 32, 45, 50–1; Korbel, *Subversion*, pp. 181–3.

39  Gottwald, Lukes, p. 173; Molotov, p. 61; Masaryk, Bruce Lockhart, *Masaryk*, p. 66.

40  Official, Kennan, Bullock, pp. 540, 571.

41  *Foreign Affairs* (July 1947), https://www.foreignaffairs.com/articles/russian-federation/1947-07-01/sources-soviet-conduct.

42  Lovett, Yergin, *Shattered Peace*, p. 327.

### Chapter Ten: Hanging On

1   Poll, Lawrence and Logevall, p. 16.

2   'La guerre d'Algérie a commencé à Sétif', *Le Monde Diplomatique* (May 2005), http://www.monde-diplomatique.fr/2005/05/HARBI/12191; Fenby, *The General*, pp. 289–90, Burleigh, pp. 92–4; Eyewitness accounts, http://www.algerie-dz.com/article611.html.

3   A member of the royal family, Andriamanantena Paul Razafinkarefo, made a signal contribution to Afro American culture. His father, a nephew of Queen Ranavalona, was killed in the French invasion of the island. His mother, the daughter of the American consul to the court, escaped, pregnant at fifteen. Born in Washington in 1895 and taking the name of Andy Razaf, he became a poet and wrote the lyrics for more than two hundred songs including 'Ain't Misbehavin'', 'Black and Blue', 'Honeysuckle Rose', 'Stomping at the Savoy' and 'In the Mood'.

4   In 1937, Poland explored a proposal to deport the country's Jews to the island which got nowhere. The Nazis picked up the idea after the defeat of France in 1940, with Adolf Eichmann recommending that Madagascar should become a police state run by the SS and that a million Jews should be sent there each year. A British naval blockade prevented this and the scheme was shelved after the Final Solution was adopted in 1942.

5   Thomas, *Fight or Flight*, pp. 193, 200–1.

6   Junction, *Times*, 19 June 1947; Revolt, Tronchon, Rioux, p. 165,

Thomas, chapter 7, *Le Monde*, 27 March 2007, http://www.
lemonde.fr/afrique/article/2007/03/27/en-1947-l-armee-francaise-
reprimait-violemment-l-insurrection-malgache_888584_3212.
html#hUyko4FgLXi4ZlJa.99, *Le Monde Diplomatique*, March 1997,
https://mondediplo.com/1997/03/02madagascar.

7   Jean Fremigacci, *Le Monde*, 27 March 2007, Thomas, p. 203.
8   A small stone column in the 16th arrondissement of Paris pays tribute to
    Malagasays who 'defended the freedom of their country and France' in
    two world wars but makes no mention of the events of 1947–8. 300,000,
    Thomas, *Fight or Flight*, p. 195; Commissioner, *Times*, 19 June 1947.
9   Goshca, pp. 178–9.
10  Goscha, pp. 187–90.
11  He was said to have lived in Ealing and Crouch End, in London, and to
    have trained as a pastry chef under the famed chef Escoffier at the Carlton
    Hotel. A plaque records the latter event but proof is lacking. He was also
    said to have made a brief visit to the United States working on a ship.
12  Only, Westad, *Cold War*, p. 32; Beguiling, Vu, pp. 91–4; Protocol,
    Quinn-Judge in Guha, *Makers*, p. 74.
13  Army, David Marr in Lawrence and Logevall, p. 76.
14  Banners, Goscha, p. 193.
15  Assembly, Goscha, p. 252.
16  Advances, Pacification, David Marr in Lawrence and Logevall, pp. 77,
    81; Sects, Goscha, pp. 182–6.
17  Embrace, Folin, p. 166.
18  Dissuade, Salan, 1, pp. 389, 402–3.
19  Thinh, Goscha, pp. 235–6.
20  Ho, Salan, 1, p. 402, 11, p. 77, *Time*, 13 April 1998; Journalist,
    Schoenbrun, p. 234.
21  Ho, David Marr in Lawrence and Logevall, pp. 99, 102.
22  David Marr in Lawrence and Logevall, pp. 102–3.
23  Mark Philip Bradley in Lawrence and Logevall, p. 28, David Marr, ibid.,
    pp. 75–6.
24  D'Argelieu, Folin, p. 190; Ambush, *Times*, 12 April 1948; Lerclerc,
    Folin, p. 189, Irving, p. 20.
25  Folin, p. 189.
26  Bollaert, Government, Parliament, Goscha, pp. 258–9.
27  He had only one name.
28  Intoxicate, Electricity, Observer, Sukarno, p. 86; Kahin, p. 43.
29  Sukarno, Vickers, p. 97.
30  Historian, Ricklefs, p. 249.
31  Bogarde, *Backcloth*, p. 140.
32  Van Mook, Keay, *Last Post*, pp. 260, 262.
33  Economy, Zanden, p. 123.
34  Van Mook, article in *International Affairs*, Royal Institute of
    International Affairs, London, July 1949; Keay, *Last Post*, p. 262

## Chapter Eleven: Next Year in Jerusalem

1  Weizmann, Ben-Gurion, Gilbert, *Israel,* pp. 146–8, Lossin, p. 471, *Times,* 17 June 1947.
2  Lossin, p. 469.
3  Study, UNSCOP report, chapter 2, point 19.
4  Organisation, Routes, *Leader,* 17 May 1947.
5  Ship, Halamish, pp. 68–77.
6  Bevin, *Jewish Chronicle,* 8 May 2008; Eban, Gilbert, *Israel,* p. 145.
7  *Humanité,* Lapping, p. 133; Moch, Thomas, p. 117.
8  Bevin, Julius, p. 331.
9  Eyewitness, Commander, *Jewish Chronicle,* 8 May 2008.

## Chapter Twelve: The Birth of Two Nations

1  He was ignoring substantial parts of the world which were not slumbering – in Washington it was mid-afternoon and evening in London, and one doubts that Truman or Attlee were slumbering – but the rhetoric went with the occasion.
2  Ceremonies, Singh, pp. 401–2, Campell-Johnson, p. 154; Envelope, Campbell-Johnson, p. 157.
3  Sen, p. 193; Du Bois quoted by Pankaj Mishra, *New York Times International,* 12–13 August 2017.
4  Speech, Jalal, p. 530 et seq., Singh, pp. 481–3.
5  *Times,* 12 August 1947; Mudie, Guha, *India,* p. 27.
6  Baxter, pp. 24, 37, 40.
7  Patel, Seervai, p. 135; Jinnah, Hajari, p. 9, 12; Moon, Guha, *India,* p. 44.
8  Tharoor, *Inglorious Empire,* pp. 216–17.
9  Fear, *Times,* 13 August 1947.
10 Das, p. 148; Poison, Guha, *India,* p. 26.
11 Das, p. 148.
12 Marcuse, Gopal, *Nehru,* 11, p. 14.
13 Jinnah, Radio broadcast, 2 September 1947; Radcliffe, Bruce Lockhart, *Diary,* 27 August 1947.
14 Nehru, *Works,* IV, p. 107; Aide, Campbell-Johnson, p. 180.
15 Officials, Mountbatten, Wolpert, pp. 321–2; Corpse, Von Tunzelmann, p. 238; Handkerchief, Fatima Jinnah manuscript; Bourke-White, p. 290.
16 Minister, *Times,* 18 August 1947.
17 Jinnah, Singh, pp. 481–3, http://www.nationalarchives.gov.uk/wp-content/uploads/2014/03/fo371-635331.jpg; Campbell, Doon, p. 165.
18 *Civil and Military Gazette,* 6 May 1947; Lahore, Talbot and Kamran, pp. 171–2.
19 Jinnah, National Archive, PREM 8/568.
20 Packing cases, Thorns, Improvised, Khan, *Partition,* pp. 120–1, 150; Hamid, Singh, p. 400.
21 Minister, Von Tunzelmann, p. 279; Train, *Times,* 11 August 1947.

22  Regiments, Ordinance, *London Review of Books*, 19 July 2012.

23  US credit, see Brown, *United States*; Cadillac, Wolpert, p. 346.

24  Bridge, Heren, *Growing Up*, p. 41; *Times*, 22–3 August 1947.

25  *Gazette*, 16 August 1947.

26  Moon, *Divide*, p. 115; Sikhs, *Times*, 22, 27 August 1947.

27  Lahore station, Grand Trunk Road, Talbot and Kamran, p. 171.

28  Survivor, SikhNet, 12 November 2009; *Times*, Manchester *Guardian*, 28–9 August, 1947; Nehru, Von Tunzelmann, p. 261, *Times of India*, 2 September 1947.

29  Surgeon, Khan, *Partition*, p. 139.

30  RSS, Baxter, pp. 31, 41, Hajari, p. 113, Misra, *Temple*, p. 198; Gandhi, Guha, *Leaders*, p. 33; Moon, *Divide*, p. 115.

31  Pamphlet, Chatterji, p. 243.

32  Secretary, Zakaria, pp. 177–80; *Times*, 29 August 1947.

33  Von Tunzelmann, p. 281.

34  Mountbatten, Ziegler, *Mountbatten*, p, 436.

35  Corfield, Misra, *Temple*, p. 242.

36  Arrogant, Low, p. 462.

37  He used a 280-carat diamond as a paperweight.

38  Father, Cameras, Graveyards, Hospitals, Copland, p. 11.

39  Champagne, Chenevix-Trench, p. 199; Office, Montgomery-Hyde, p. 138.

40  Belly, Guha, *India*, p. 67.

41  Jinnah, Teleagana, Guha, *India*, pp. 66–7

42  Monckton, Ziegler, *Mountbatten*, p. 413; 90,000 guineas, Replica, Guha, *India*, pp. 66–7.

43  Travancore, Low, pp. 444, 461.

44  Bose, pp. 47–50, Guha, *India*, pp. 49, 57.

45  Land, Guha, *India*, p. 59.

## Chapter Thirteen: Land and Lives

1   Official Records of the Second Session of the General Assembly, Supplement 11, September 1947, https://unispal.un.org/DPA/DPR/unispal.nsf/0/07175DE9FA2DE563852568D3006E10F3.

2   Meeting, Kurzman, pp. 8–9, Lossin, p. 482, Shlaim, *Collusion*, p. 96.

3   Arab warnings, Morris, *War*, p. 410.

4   Ben-Gurion, Gilbert, *Israel*, pp. 149, 151.

5   Abdullah, Shlaim, *Collusion*, pp. 78, 82–3, 85.

6   Arabs, Shlaim, *Collusion*, pp. 87–90.

7   Rabbi, *Times*, 8–9 September 1947; *Punch*, 24 September 1947.

8   *Punch*, 24 September 1947.

9   Rusk, Lossin, p. 487.

10  Morgenthau, Margaret Truman, *Truman*, p. 385; Jesus, McCullough, p. 598.

## Chapter Fourteen: Separate Camps

1 Timing, Dedijer, p. 301, Mark Kramer in Snyder and Brandon, p. 284.
2 Djilas, *Conversations*, p. 135.
3 Statement, Parrish and Narinsky, pp. 37–8.
4 Djilas, Clissold, p. 174.
5 http://genius.com/Andrei-zhdanov-speech-at-the-founding-of-the-cominform-annotated.
6 Parrish and Narinsky, pp. 38–9, Yergin, *Peace*, p. 326.
7 Duclos, p. 220; Translator, Djilas, *Rise and Fall*, pp. 134–5.
8 Robrieux, pp. 355–6, Djilas, *Rise and Fall*, p. 135.
9 Gomułka, Prazmowska, pp. 147–52.
10 Slánský, Lukes, p. 163; Plot, *Times*, 9 September 1947.
11 Broadcast, Truman, *Memoirs*, II, p. 17.
12 Wife, Ferrell, *Bess*, pp. 550–1, https://www.trumanlibrary.org/whistlestop/study_collections/trumanpapers/fbpa/index.php?documentVersion=both&documentid=HST-FBP_16-024_01&pagenumber=5; Daughter, Margaret Truman, *Letters*, p. 352.
13 Kennan, Pogue, p. 231.
14 Italy, *Times*, 17 September 1947; Delegation, Dirksen, http://marshallfoundation.org/library/wp-content/uploads/sites/16/2014/04/Studies_Prior_to_the_Marshall_Plan.pdf.

## Chapter Fifteen: The General Reports

1 Committee, USSR, Melby, pp. 233–4; Delegation, China White Paper, pp. 265–8.
2 Wedemeyer, pp. 396–8, http://www.general-wedemeyer.com/1947-2.html; Manchuria, Pogue, p. 274.
3 Kennan, *Memoirs*, pp. 373–4, War College speech, 6 May 1947.
4 Trade, Offensives, Westad, *Encounters*, pp. 175–6; Technicians, Japanese, Van de Ven p. 244.
5 When they did so late in the civil war, he flew off to Formosa with the provincial treasury. Yan, Gillin, p. 286–7, Fenby, *Generalissimo*, p. 489.
6 Shandong, Fenby, *Modern China*, p. 338.
7 Melby, p. 237.

## Chapter Sixteen: My Head Hangs in Shame

1 Diplomat, Hajari, p. 159.
2 Gopal, *Nehru*, II, p. 16.
3 Campbell-Johnson, pp. 200–1.
4 Resident, Ahmed, p. xxxiii; Low and Howards, p. 61.
5 Low and Howards, p. 58.
6 *Times*, 19, 30 September 1947.
7 Correspondent, *Times*, 5 September 1947.
8 Jinnah, Speech, 14 September 1947.
9 Gandhi, French, p. 358.

## Chapter Seventeen: A Republic Under Siege

1   Fenby, *General*, p. 332.
2   De Gaulle, Rioux, I, p. 153.
3   Fenby, *General*, p. 326.
4   Fenby, *General*, pp. 327–8.
5   Malraux, De Gaulle, Fenby, *General*, p. 328.
6   $120 million, *Le Monde*, 4 October, 1947.
7   Thorez, Robrieux, p. 357.
8   Frogs, De Gaulle, *Lettres* (1947), p. 231.
9   Stalin, Kaplan, *Ghosts*, p. 102.
10  Greece, *Times*, 6, 10, 15 October 1947; Czechslovakia, Kaplan, *March*, pp. 136–7, 141, *Times*, 14 October 1947.
11  Congress, Fulbrook and Port, pp. 60–1.
12  *Daily Express*, *Economist*, 4 November 2017. Thomas Zeiler's book gives details of the GATT negotiations.
13  Salan, *Mémoires*, II, p. 119.
14  Operation, Salan, pp. 119–21.
15  Valluy, Letter, Salan, p. 117.
16  Perelman, p. 60.
17  Hoped, Reuters, 13 October 1947; Peace, Ministère de la France d'Outre Mer, 15 October 1947.
18  Bollaert, Devillers, p. 408.
19  Bao, Xuan, Devillers, pp. 410–12, 416–18, Hammer, pp. 214–17.
20  Xuan, Bollaert, Devillers, pp. 418–19.

## Chapter Eighteen: The Great Game

1   Whoever, Hajari, p. 188.
2   Switzerland, Queen, Guha, *India*, pp. 73, 79.
3   Sting, Chenevix-Trench, pp. 175–6.
4   Visit, Eyes, Heren, *Growing Up*, pp. 52, 56.
5   Jinnah, Hajari, pp. 184, 187.
6   Appeals, Hajari, p. 184.
7   A post he relinquished only in 2001. Grady, Guha, *India*, p. 96.
8   Road, Perry Anderson, *London Review of Books*, 19 July 2012; Nehru, Brown, *Nehru*, p. 177.
9   Sheikh, Guha, *India*, pp. 91–2.
10  *Times*, 10 November 1947, Guha, *India*, p. 82.
11  Hajari, pp. 191–2, Guha, *India*, pp. 82–3, Campbell-Johnson, p. 224.
12  Very large number, Low and Brasted, p. 61.
13  Abdullah, Nehru, *Times*, 30 October, 1, 12 November 1947, Guha, *India*, p. 85; Amity, Guha, *India*, p. 84.
14  Gilgit, *Times*, 2 January 1948; Schofield; *Journal of Imperial and Commonwealth History*, 38 (1), pp. 117 et seq.
15  Jinnah, p. 359; Depression, Campbell-Johnson, p. 229.
16  Conversations, Wolpert, pp. 351–3; Obtuseness, Call off, Campbell-Johnson, pp. 225, 229.

17   RSS, Baxter, p. 39, Misra, Maria, p. 245; Ambush, Testimony
     of Mazhar Malik, *Guardian*, 3 August 2017; Journalist, *Times*,
     24 November 1947.

### Chapter Nineteen: The Republic Shows Its Guts

 1   Purchasing power, Asselain, p. 116; Strikes, *Le Monde*, 10–20
     November 1947, Rioux, p. 183, Lacouture, *Blum*, pp. 543–5, Moch,
     p. 318.
 2   Italy, Togliatti, *Times*, 13, 16, 17, 21, 29 November 1947;
     Pandemonium, *Times*, 13 November 1947.
 3   Blum speech, *Le Monde*, 21 November 1947.
 4   Riposte, *Le Monde*, 22 November 1947; Communists, Thorez, pp. 227,
     231.
 5   De Gaulle, Mauriac, p. 299.
 6   My government, *Times*, 24 November 1947.
 7   Schuman, *Le Monde*, *Figaro*, 29–30 November 1947.
 8   Telegrams, Beevor and Cooper, p. 301; CIA, Jeffreys, p. 155, Marchetti
     and Marks, pp. 25, 165.
 9   Executioner, *Times*, 27 November 1947.
10   De Gaulle, *Le Monde*, *Times*, 11–12 November 1947.
11   Passy, Beevor and Cooper, p. 298.
12   Schuman, Vote, *Le Monde*, 29–30 November 1947.
13   Robrieux, p. 359.
14   Calas, *Le Monde*, 3–4 December 2016, *Times*, 3 December 1947.

### Chapter Twenty: Mission Accomplished

 1   Lossin, p. 489.
 2   Filibuster, Lobbying, Lossin, p. 489.
 3   Devices, Kurzman, pp. 17–19.
 4   Baruch, Barr, p. 355; Silver, Cohen, pp. 163–4.
 5   Saudi, Lossin, p. 487.
 6   Forrestal, Lossin, p. 515.
 7   Aides, Look here, McCullough, pp. 601–2.
 8   Pile, https://www.trumanlibrary.org/israel/palestin.htm; Truman,
     McCullough, pp. 595–9.
 9   Truman, McCullough, p. 599; Acheson, Benson, p. 121
10   Truman, Weizmann, McCullough, p. 605, Benson, p. 121, Kurzman,
     pp. 12–13, Lossin, p. 486, Truman, *Memoirs*, II, p. 158.
11   Abdullah, Shlaim, *Collusion*, chapter 20.
12   Shlaim, *Collusion*, pp. 110–16.
13   Gromyko, http://www.jewishvirtuallibrary.org/
     united-nations-debate-on-partition-november-1947.
14   Indian, Morris, *War*, p. 56.
15   Jacobson, McCullough, p. 602.
16   Begin, p. 433.
17   Celebrations, Gilbert, *Israel*, p. 154, *New York Times*, *Times*,

30 November 1947; Meir, Lossin, p. 495; Ben-Gurion, Morris, *War*, p. 65.
18 *Times*, 1–2 December 1947; Mufti, Kurzman, pp. 34–5.
19 Warnings, Morris, *War*, p. 187.
20 Abdullah, Shlaim, *Collusion*, p. 121.

## Chapter Twenty-One: The Great Divide

1 Marshall, Murphy, Yergin, *Peace*, p. 350.
2 Unhappy, Benelux, Adenauer, pp. 102–4; Bevin, *Times*, 18, 29 November 1947; Smith, Galambos et al., p. 213.
3 Molotov, Vyshinsky, *Times*, *New York Times*, 7, 12 November 1947; Tulpanov, Tessier and Davidson, p. 181.
4 http://www.history.com/this-day-in-history/london-council-of-foreign-ministers-meeting-begins.
5 Conference reports in FRUS, 1947, 11, https://history.state.gov/historicaldocuments/frus1947v02, http://avalon.law.yale.edu/20th_century/decade24.asp.
6 *Times*, 28 November 1947; Bevin, Smile, Molotov, Tolerance, *Times*, 27 November 1947.
7 Nicolson, p. 393.
8 When I say, *Times*, 28 November 1947.

## Chapter Twenty-Two: Reviving Germany

1 McCloy, Judt, p. 39.
2 Rapes, Beevor, *Berlin*, p. 410; Takings, Cairncross, p. 209; Take everything, MacDonogh, *Reich*, p. 478.
3 Döblin, MacDonogh, *Reich*, p. 277.
4 Truman, Ferrell, *Bess*, p. 520; Wilder, Communist, Taschen, p. 278; Galbraith, Holt, p. 58.
5 Markets, McDonogh, *Reich*, p. 377; Berlin, One-third, Diamonds, Opium, Cigarettes, Rasno, Zierenberg, pp. 128–9, 154–7, 167, 174, 199.
6 Stalin, Djilas, *Rise and Fall*, p. 155; Bevin, *Times*, 26 April 1947.
7 Clay, Barnet, p. 40; Douglas, Murphy, p. 251; McNeil, Barnet, p. 34; Dalton, Ian Locke, *History Today*, 8 August 1997.
8 Byrnes, pp. 190–1, Gatzke, p. 173.
9 Clay, Smith, *Clay*, pp. 390–1; Congress, Cairncross, p. 180; Companies, Barnet, p. 35; Harriman, Truman, *Memoirs*, 11, p. 121.
10 Clay, Smith, *Clay*, p. 447.
11 Nicholas Stargardt's book deals in depth with the German psychology of the time; Orwell, *Observer*, 1 April 1945; Correspondents, Connell, pp. 24–5; Courts, Food, Connell, pp. 23, 108–9.
12 Cases, Sentences, Gatzke, p. 166.
13 Ban, Gatzke, pp. 163, 170.
14 Barrass, p. 50.
15 Applebaum, *Curtain*, pp. 227–9, Spilker, pp. 45–50; Learn, Soviet Man, German Historical Museum, Berlin.

16 Stalin on Pieck, Djilas, *Rise and Fall*, p. 105.

17 Ulbricht, Applebaum, *Curtain*, pp. 46–52, Judt, p. 59; Dangerous, Stern, p. 116.

18 Secretary, *Economist*, 18 February 2017.

19 Childs, pp. 137–8; Ammendorf, Uranium, German Historical Museum, Berlin.

20 Gatzke, pp. 171–2; Relationship, Biess, p. 151.

21 Tulpanov, Westad and Hanhimäki, pp. 87–9.

22 Reuter, Edinger, p. 134; Meetings, *Leader* magazine, 10 May 1947; Acheson, *Pravda*, Barnet, p. 49.

23 Sacking, Adenauer, pp. 31–5, Prittie, pp. 105–10, Williams, *Prime Minister*, pp. 298–306, *Daily Express*, 15 October 1963.

24 Windows, *Die Welt*, 30 November 1946.

25 Dönhoff, pp. 27–9; Christianity, Williams, *Prime Minister*, p. 306; Schumacher and CDU, Edinger, p. 197.

26 Robertson, Prittie, p. 122; Politician, Theodor Heuss, Prittie, p. 129, footnote 10.

27 Erhard, *Der Wirtschaftsspiegel*, 15 November and 1 December 1947 in Mierzejewski, pp. 56–7.

28 Social Democrats, Edinger, pp. 108–110; Clay, Parrish, p. 127.

## Chapter Twenty-Three: Final Meeting

1 Mayhew, pp. 107–8.

2 Council of Foreign Ministers; Germany and Austria, FRUS, 1947, http://digicoll.library.wisc.edu/cgi-bin/FRUS/FRUS-idx?type=turn&entity=FRUS.FRUS1947v02.p0710&id=FRUS. FRUS1947v02&isize=M.

3 Molotov, FRUS, 8 December 1947.

4 FRUS, 8 December 1947.

5 Exchanges, FRUS, 12 December 1947; Chilly, Dignity, Wince, Clay, p. 348.

6 FRUS, pp. 769–70, http://digicoll.library.wisc.edu/cgi-bin/FRUS/FRUS-idx?type=goto&id=FRUS. FRUS1947v02&isize=M&submit=Go+to+page&page=769.

7 FRUS, pp. 770–2, http://digicoll.library.wisc.edu/cgi-bin/FRUS/FRUS-idx?type=turn&entity=FRUS.FRUS1947v02.p0804&id=FRUS. FRUS1947v02&isize=M.

8 FRUS, 1947, II, pp. 770–2.

9 Though talks on Austria would continue.

10 Marshall, FRUS, 1947, II, pp. 764–5.

11 FRUS, 1947, II, pp. 769–72, 812, 826.

12 One recruit was a young man called Guy Burgess who had attended the conference of foreign ministers as private secretary to Hector McNeil, minister of state at the Foreign Office. He showed 'a dazzling insight into Communist methods of subversion and propaganda' at his interview, Mayhew recalled. Naturally, nobody knew that he was part of a Soviet

spy ring, but he did not last long, sacked after a few months for being 'dirty, drunken and idle'. Burgess, Mayhew, pp. 109–10, Lownie, p. 165.

13  Bevin, Marshall, Pogue, p. 287.

14  Truman, *Memoirs*, II, p. 118.

15  The networks wanted to limit him to fifteen minutes but the secretary insisted on having half an hour of air time.

16  Marshall, Bland and Stoler, pp. 296 et seq.

17  Bidault, FRUS, 28 November 1947, II.

18  Dulles, Beevor and Cooper, p. 308.

19  *Le Monde, Figaro*, 1–4 December 1947.

### Chapter Twenty-Four: Bloody New Year

1  Marches, Attacks, *Times*, 3 December 1947, Lossin, p. 496–7.

2  Attacks, *New York Times, Times*, 1, 15 December 1947, Gilbert, p. 155; BOAC, Kurzman, pp. 38–9.

3  Dayan, Gilbert, p. 154; Galili, Lossin, p. 495.

4  Shlaim, *Collusion*, pp. 123–4, Kurzman, pp. 58–9.

5  El-Husseini, Rifles, Kurzman, pp. 70–1.

6  Morris, *1948*, pp. 201–2.

### Chapter Twenty-Five: Christmas at War

1  The discord was similar to one between Mao and the Chinese Communist leadership in the early 1930s. Plenum, Woodhouse, p. 217; Treason, Gage, p. 238.

2  Rebels, Gage, p. 243; Stalin, Djilas, *Rise and Fall*, p. 169.

3  Queen, Mosley, pp. 411–14; Forces, O'Ballance, Greek, pp. 165–7.

4  Paul, *Times*, 31 December 1947.

5  Woodhouse, pp. 222–3, *Times*, 31 December–2 January 1947.

### Chapter Twenty-Six: A Higher Virtue

1  Marcelo de Paiva Abreu, 'Britain as a debtor', *Economic History Review*, 70/2, May 2017.

2  Cigarettes were not rationed for fear of the reaction among voters – 80 per cent of adult males and half as many women consumed tobacco products; but taxation sent the price up by 50 per cent. (Keynes, *Documents on British Policy Overseas*, 1, III, p. 29; Output, *UN World Economic Conditions Report*, 1949; C. C. S. Newton, 'The Sterling Crisis of 1947 and the British Response to the Marshall Plan', *The Economic History Review*, 37/3 (August 1984), pp. 391–408, Hogan, *Plan*; GDP, Bashford and Macintyre, p. 312; Tobacco, Cancer Research Organisation statistics.)

3  Equality, Socialism, Bew, pp. 347, 401, 464; Well received, Morrison, Kynaston, pp. 37, 181.

4  Middle class, Unions, Kynaston, pp. 37, 181, 452.

5  Bevan, p. 100; Brivati and Heffernan, pp. 69, 76; For creation of welfare state, see Timmins, parts I and II.

 6   Survey, *Leader*, 10 July 1948; *Punch*, 15, 22 October 1947;
     Cinema, http://www.launchingfilms.com/research-databank/
     uk-cinema-admissions.
 7   Kynaston, p. 41.
 8   Gallup, Bew, p. 459.
 9   Correlli Barnett, *The Lost Victory: British Dreams, British Realities,
     1945–1950* (Pan, 1996).
10   Poll, Kynaston, p. 243.
11   Daughter, Loin cloth, *Sunday Telegraph*, 19 November, 2017.
12   *Times*, 29 November 1947; Manchester *Guardian*, 31 December 1947;
     Marshall, Bland and Stoler, p. 276.
13   Depend, Tomlinson, p. 22.
14   http://blogs.lse.ac.uk/lsehistory/2017/03/29/a-man-for-all-seasons-the-
     life-and-times-of-clement-attlee/; Welfare state, see Chris Renwick's
     authoritative account; Rhyme, John Bew, *New Statesman*, 31 July 2015.
15   Churchill had gone to the palace to tender his resignation in a chauffeur-
     driven Rolls-Royce. Mrs Attlee drove her husband on his election tours
     but was known as a bad driver who made passengers shield their eyes.
16   Morrison, Bew, p. 394; Stalin, Dilkes, p. 772; Deceptive, Kingsley
     Martin quoted, Bew and Cox.
17   On the other hand, when somebody remarked that Morrison was his
     own worst enemy, Bevin was said to have muttered, 'Not as long as I'm
     alive.'
18   Spivvery, Vermin, Bevan speech, *Times*, 5 July 1948.
19   Attlee, Williams, *Prime Minister*, p. 172; Tax, Government
     advertisement, 16 April 1948.
20   Bevin, Weiler, pp. 150, 168, 175, 177.
21   The questioning of the British link dated back to the late nineteenth-
     century Prime Minister, Alfred Deakin, but it was the Second World
     War that led Prime Minister John Curtin to conclude, 'I make it quite
     clear that Australia looks to America, free of any pangs as to our
     traditional links or kinship with the United Kingdom.' (Judith Brett,
     *Lowy Interpreter*, September 2017, https://www.lowyinstitute.org/
     the-interpreter/alfred-deakin-s-strategic-thought, Curtin, http://www.
     pacificwar.org.au/battaust/Britain_betrays_Australia.html)
22   Truman, Margaret Truman, p. 352.

**Chapter Twenty-Seven: Harry and Ernie Set Out Their Stalls**

 1   Letter, 14 November 1947, HST Library.
 2   President's Economic Report to Congress, 14 January 1947.
 3   McCullough, p. 585.
 4   Polls, *Gallup Presidential Election Trial-Heat Trends, 1936–2008*,
     http://www.gallup.com/poll/110548/gallup-presidential-election-
     trialheat-trends-19362004.aspx#4, *Times*, 12 January 1947.
 5   Royall, McCullough, p. 585, *New York Times*, 11 July 2003;
     Dogcatcher, Pusey, p. 1.

6   Eisenhower, Pusey, p. 6.
7   Report, McCullough, pp. 589–91.
8   Report, McCullough, pp. 586, 590–1.
9   Speech, HST Library, Annual Message to the Congress on the State of the Union, 7 January 1948, www.trumanlibrary.org/whistlestop/tap/1748.htm.
10  Letter, Connolly, McCullough, pp. 588–9, 593.
11  President, HST Library, Annual Message to the Congress on the State of the Union, 7 January 1948, www.trumanlibrary.org/whistlestop/tap/1748.htm; Marshall, Committee, *New York Times*, *Times*, 9–10 January 1947; Dulles, Pruessen, p. 356; Lodge, Steil, Project Syndicate article, August 2017.
12  Germany, Greece, *Times*, 19, 21 January 1947.
13  Frankfurt, Bidault, Pogue, pp. 287–8, FRUS, 1948, II, pp. 20–1.
14  Marshall, FRUS, 1948, II, pp. 70–3.
15  Korbel, pp. 206–7.
16  Bad end, Korbel, p. 93; Doom, Sterling, p. 95.
17  Embassy, FRUS, 1948, III, p. 1069.
18  Text, Hansard, 22 January 1947.

### Chapter Twenty-Eight: A Snowstorm of Defeats

1   Chiang, Chen, Chassin, p. 136, Westad, *Encounters*, p. 176.
2   Pepper, pp. 179–80, 316–18, Chassin, pp. 250–1. Missionary, Land reform Westad, *Encounters*, pp. 135–7, 138–9.
3   Spies, Mao, Westad, *Encounters*, pp. 173, 177.
4   Lin, Fenby, *Modern China*, p. 429, Snow, p. 135; Tactics, van de Ven, p. 246.
5   Journalist, Chassin, p. 162.
6   Transcribed then as Ssupingkai.
7   Chiang, Mao, Westad, *Encounters*, pp. 172, 176–7.
8   China White Paper, Stanford, August 1949, pp. 382–3.
9   Truman, Miller, pp. 283, 288.
10  Melby, p. 247.
11  Westad, *Encounters*, pp. 163–40, FRUS, 1947, VIII, pp. 404–10.
12  Wrecked, Truman, van de Ven, pp. 236, 238.
13  Department of State, p. 336.

### Chapter Twenty-Nine: War and Assassination

1   Tribesmen, *Times*, 3 January 1948.
2   *Times*, 15 January 1948.
3   Raiders, *Statesman*, 1 January 1948; Patel, Mountbatten, Campbell-Johnson, pp. 252, 265.
4   Patel, Sunil Purushotham, 'The "Police Action" in Hyderabad', *Comparative Studies*, Cambridge, 57/2 (2015), pp. 435 et seq.
5   If I am, Fischer, p. 15.
6   Excerpts From Nathuram Godse's Deposition Before Justice Atma

Charan of the Special Court, *Jana Sangh Today*, January 2006;
Nathuram Godse's deposition in the Red Fort court case (8 November
1948), Indian Court Records.
7   Guha, *India*, pp. 38–9, Baxter, pp. 41–2.
8   Allahabad, Heren, *Growing Up*, pp. 58–9.

## Chapter Thirty: Colonial Twilight

1   Auriol, *Le Monde*, Folin, pp. 195, 201; Bollaert, *Times*, 29 January
1948.

## Chapter Thirty-One: Closer to War

1   Shlaim, *Collusion*, p. 131.
2   Shlaim, *Collusion*, p. 136.
3   Kurzman, pp. 63–5.
4   Earning her the accolade from Ben-Gurion of being 'the Jewish woman
who got the money which made the state possible' (*Haaretz*, 7 July
2008).

## Chapter Thirty-Two: A Classic Coup

1   Slánský, Kaplan, *March*, p. 76; Cominform, Korbel, *Subversion*, p. 190.
The February events are described in detail in Lukes, chapters 10–11.
2   Gottwald, Soviets, Kaplan, *March*, pp. 130–1, 140–1.
3   Festival, Miles, p. 268; Feirlinger, Korbel, pp. 199, 201.
4   Preferment, Rupnik, p. 98; Drtina, Kaplan, *March*, p. 165.
5   Korbel, father of future secretary of state Madeleine Albright,
subsequently defected.
6   Survey, Sterling, p. 100.
7   Mlynář, Judt, p. 201.
8   Politburo, Korbel, *Subversion*, pp. 208–9; Veselý, Sterling, p. 96.
9   Albania, *Times*, 19 February 1948.
10  Gottwald, Kaplan, *March*, p. 175.
11  Korbel, p. 222, Sterling, pp. 78–9.
12  Faith, Kaplan, *March*, p. 194; Beneš, Korbel, pp. 214–15, Sterling,
p. 106.
13  Cabinet, Social Democrats, 3 million, Ripka, *Times*, 21 February 1947.
14  Newspapers, Sterling, p. 102.
15  Gottwald, Sterling, p. 99.
16  Appease, Sterling, p. 107.
17  Conference, Rupnik, p. 101; Gottwald, Resolution, Korbel, p. 210.
18  Gottwald, Korbel, p. 221; *Pravda*, 23 February 1948.
19  Korbel, Subversion, pp. 228–9; Sterling, pp. 108–9.
20  Letter, Broadcast, Korbel, p. 220.
21  Gottwald, Laušman, Kaplan, *March*, pp. 180, 187; Pavel, Rupnik,
p. 102.
22  Beneš, Gottwald, Rupnik, p. 103.
23  Doctor, Sterling, p. 164.

24 Davenport, Maria, pp. 360–1.
25 Gottwald, Sterling, p. 88.
26 Football, *Times*, 27 February 1948.
27 Statement, *Times*, 27 February 1948.
28 Truman, Clay, Alsops, McCullough, p. 603.
29 *Times*, 28 February 1948.
30 Nosek, *Times*, 1 March 1948.
31 Sterling, p. 9; http://www.radio.cz/en/section/czech-history/post-wwii-political-leader-prokop-drtina-subject-of-new-biography.
32 Masaryk, Sterling, p. 164.
33 De Gasperi, *Times*, 1 March 1948; Reuter, MacDonogh, p. 524; By-election, Kynaston, pp. 223–4.

## Chapter Thirty-Three: Model Colony Explodes

1 Fund, Austin, p. 68.
2 Revenue, Trade, Roads, Railways, Schools, Reports, Austin, pp. 3, 5–6, 130.
3 Prices, Syrians, Austin, pp. 67–8.
4 At one point, he sold fish on a street corner in Harlem.
5 Ashanti, Club, Austin, pp. 56, 67–8.
6 Minister, Hansard, http://hansard.millbanksystems.com/people/mr-james-hudson/.
7 Riots, Apter, pp. 169–70, Meredith, pp. 19–20, BBC Witness, 7 March 2014, http://www.bbc.co.uk/programmes/p01t10s9, *Times*, 6 April 1948.
8 Hoses, Lapping, p. 367; Danquah, Austin, p. 75.
9 Austin, p. 75.

## Chapter Thirty-Four: Three Ds for Japan

1 Kennan, *Memoirs*, p. 383.
2 Exception, Amenable, Reliant, Cummings, *Origins*, pp. 52, 57; Kennan, *Memoirs,* p. 381.
3 Kennan, *Memoirs*, p. 381.
4 Kennan, *Memoirs*, p. 384.
5 Characteristically, he rejected a suggestion from Washington that he should use the first-person plural.
6 If I, Manchester, p. 483.
7 Kennan, *Memoirs*, p. 382.
8 Protect, Ryukus, Okinawa, Bix, pp. 625–6.
9 *Japan Times*, 28 April 2002, http://www.japantimes.co.jp/community/2002/04/28/general/where-history-was-made/#.WM5j5YXXLno; Dai-Ichi statement, http://www.dai-ichi-life.co.jp/english/news_release/2012/pdf/index_004.pdf.
10 MacArthur, Whitney, Manchester, pp. 469, 479, 483, 494.
11 Children, Dower, *Defeat*, p. 63.
12 The scheme was ended in 1946, officially because it was undemocratic

and violated women's rights, but also because it spread venereal disease – by the end almost 90 per cent of RAA women tested positive for the disease (Dower, *Defeat*, p. 130). Estimate, Comfort women, Dower, *Defeat*, pp. 26, 117, 126–32.

13   Exports, Imports, Fleet, *UN Economic Report*, 1948, pp. 126, 130; Scheidel, p. 129.

14   General Walter Krueger, quoted in Dower, *Defeat*, p. 48; Descent, Reischauer, Barnet, pp. 60, 64.

15   Tokyo, Food, Dower, *Defeat*, pp. 91–3.

16   Black markets, Dower, *Defeat*, 139–48.

17   Broadcast, Beasley, p. 279.

18   Meeting, *Japan Times*, 9 September 2014.

19   Shidehara, Bix, p. 563.

20   Emerson, Green, p. 264.

21   Though it increased its score to nearly 10 per cent in 1949 elections, the party would soon afterwards fall foul of the impact of the Korean War. Yoshida, Dower, *Empire*, p. 293.

22   MSCAP Political reorientation of Japan, Washington, 1945, pp. 423–6.

23   McClain, p. 534.

24   Judge, Storry, p. 249; Mumbo jumbo, Dower, *Defeat*, p. 451; Kennan, FRUS, 1948, VI, pp. 717–19, 794.

25   MacArthur, FRUS, 1948, VIII, pp. 395–7.

26   Historian, Clouds, Storry, pp. 247-8; MacArthur, Hirohito, Bix, p. 623.

27   Tours, Bix, pp. 625, 630.

28   Diplomat, Bix, p. 629.

29   Dower, *Empire*, pp. 297–8.

30   MacArthur, Finn, p. 161.

31   McClain, pp. 497–8.

32   Candidates, Imamura, p. 273; MacArthur, pp. 304–5.

33   Finn, p. 161.

34   McCormick, Manchester, p. 495; Keenan, Bix, p. 627.

### Chapter Thirty-Five: Death of a Minister

1   Chief, Sterling, pp. 47–8.

2   Funeral, Tomb, *History Today*, 3 March 1998.

3   Beneš, Korbel, p. 6.

4   Gottwald, *Guardian*, 11 March 1948.

5   Attlee, *Times*, 11 March 1947; Marshall; http://www.history.com/this-day-in-history/strange-death-of-jan-masaryk; Truman, *Memoirs*, 11, p. 241.

6   *Guardian*, 11 March 1948.

7   *Guardian*, 11 March 1947; Ambassador, Bruce Lockhart, *Diaries*, p. 653.

8   Davenport, *Fantasy*, pp. 365, 368, 378.

9   Bruce Lockhart, *Diaries*, p. 652.

10   Davenport, *Fantasy*, p. 379.

11  Davenport, *Fantasy*, pp. 381–2; Sterling, pp. 33–4, 56–7, 63, 66–8.
12  Wife, Doctor, Sterling, p. 168.
13  Sterling, pp. 347–8.

### Chapter Thirty-Six: Critical Situation

1  Truman, *Memoirs*, XI, pp. 241–2; Norway, Westad and Hanhimäki, pp. 57–8.
2  Bidault, pp. 115–16.
3  'The First Five Years', *RUSI Journal*, 1993.
4  Bidault, pp. 156–8.
5  Charles Maier, 'The Marshall Plan and the Division of Europe', *Journal of Cold War Studies*, 7/1 (Winter 2005), https://muse.jhu.edu/article/179567; Michael Cox and Caroline Kennedy-Pipe, 'The Tragedy of American Diplomacy: Rethinking the Marshall Plan', same volume.
6  Isaacson and Thomas, p. 455.
7  Council, Gatzke, p. 177; Sokolovsky, http://www.cvce.eu/en/education/unit-content/-/unit/55c09dcc-a9f2-45e9-b240-eaef64452cae/43750634-b7c4-47a8-ba6c-f46e632f3d5d/Resources#db4f4c77-6b80-4bda-bf28-12db50702b0a_en&overlay; *Times*, 2 April 1948.
8  Message, Smith, *Clay Papers*, pp. 568–9; Said later, Clay, p. 354; Kennan, *Memoirs*, p. 401.
9  Clay, p. 354; De Gaulle, Fenby, *General*, pp. 339–41; Mitford, Beevor and Cooper, p. 321.
10  Prefects, Schuman, Duclos, Beevor and Cooper, pp. 322–3.
11  Gromyko, *Times*, 24 March 1948.

### Chapter Thirty-Seven: Killings and Politics

1  McCullough, pp. 603–4.
2  Truman, *Memoirs*, II, p. 160; Communism, Kennan, *Memoirs*, p. 380; Marshall, McCullough, p. 604; Forrestal, Isaacson and Thomas, p. 452.
3  Complaining, Took this man, Lossin, p. 515.
4  Meeting, American Jewish Archives, April 1958, Samuel Montague, 'The Reform Jew Who Changed Truman's Mind', *Reform Judaism*, http://www.reformjudaismmag.net/rjmag-90s/998sam.html, McCullough, p. 606.
5  American Jewish Archives, April 1958.
6  Truman diary, 20 March 1948, *Off the Record*, p. 127, McCullough, pp. 610–11.
7  Marshall, *Times*, 21 March 1948; *Times*, 27 March 1948.
8  Driver, Lossin, p. 519.
9  Meeting, Kurzman, pp. 67–9.
10  Azam, Kurzman, p. 206, footnote.
11  Yadin, Yossin, p. 519.

## Chapter Thirty-Eight: The Great Reversal

1  MacArthur–Kennan, FRUS, 1948, VI, pp. 700–12.
2  Kennan, *Memoirs*, pp. 385–6.
3  Kennan, *Memoirs*, pp. 387–9.
4  Kennan, *Memoirs*, pp. 391–2.
5  FRUS, 1948, I, II, pp. 531 et seq.
6  Apart from squeezing South East Asia, the war effort had been fed, in part, by grain imports from North China and minerals and food from Manchuria.
7  That omission would be repeated by Acheson as secretary of state in 1950 and encourage Kim Il-sung to conclude that the US would not resist an invasion of South Korea. Green, pp. 273–4.
8  Bureaucratism, Dower, *Empire*, p. 314; Draper, Finn, p. 196.
9  Draper, Delegation, Aduard, pp. 84–5.

## Chapter Thirty-Nine: Every Opportunity

1  Circle, Austin, p. 76, footnote 52.
2  He liked to say that 'Self-government is better than good colonial government' (Lapping, p. 370).
3  Report, Lapping, p. 371.

## Chapter Forty: Where Next?

1  Lovett, Post, Hickerson, Isaacson and Thomas, pp. 446–7, 450, 457.
2  Bevin, Bullock, pp. 556–7.
3  McCullough, p. 59.
4  Ickes, McCullough, p. 632.
5  McCullough, pp. 612–13; Rebuilding, Bath, Klara, prologue.
6  Truman, Attlee, Bevin–Bidault, *Times*, 4, 6 April 1948.
7  Gallup, McDonald, p. 40; UK poll, *Times*, 12 April 1948; Hoffman, Obituary, *New York Times*, 9 October 1974, http://www.nytimes.com/1974/10/09/archives/paul-g-hoffman-is-dead-at-83-led-marshallplan-and-un-aid-paul-g.html?_r=0.
8  Beneš, Slánský, *Times*, 2, 12 April 1948.
9  King, Appointments, Unkovski-Korica, p. 28.
10  Dinner, Djilas, *Conversations*, p. 103
11  Stalin-Tito, Dedijer, chapter 16; Tower, Differences, Swain, pp. 76, 85; System, Unkovski-Korica, pp. 33–4.
12  Source note: I am indebted to Dr Svetozan Rajak for his insights into Tito and the split with Moscow.
13  Swallow, Djilas, *Conversations*, p. 130. Arriving at the delegation's hotel, Djilas had changed rooms. After he had settled into his new suite, workmen came in to carry out 'electrical repairs' (Dedijer, p. 320).
14  Lees, pp. 47, 53.
15  Dedijer, pp. 325–7.
16  Kardelj, Dedijer, p. 333; Molotov, p. 84.
17  Exchanges in RIIS, Bass and Marbury.

18  Tito, Dedijer: chapter 16 gives chapter and verse.

19  Dedijer, p. 341.

20  He was later moved from the Foreign Ministry, but given another government job in trade.

21  Accusation, Reply, Pavlowitch, p. 210; Breach covered in books cited above and Clissold, pp. 172 et seq, Kardelj, pp. 217 et seq, Rusinow, pp. 28 et seq.

22  Central Committee, Unkovski-Korica, p. 60; Hebrang, http://www.andrija-hebrang.com/eng/chronology.htm

23  Dimitrov, Gottwald, Korbel, *Tito's Communism*, p. 288.

24  Historian, Smith, *Italy*, p. 495.

25  Land, Joked, Gunther, pp. 4–5.

26  Togliatti, Agosti, pp. 191, 195; Manifesto, Clough and Saladino, pp. 542, 565.

27  Magri, pp. 54–6.

28  Togliatti, Agosti, p. 191; Fascists, *Times*, 7, 9 April, 1948.

29  Pope, Falconi, p. 266, Cheetham, p. 290; Catholic Action, Clark, pp. 324–5.

30  A later shipment to Italy would contain 177 million tons of bad-quality spaghetti which the manufacturers wanted to offload.

31  US involvement, Mario Einaudi, 'The Italian Elections of 1948', *Review of Politics*, July 1948 (Cambridge University Press), http://www.jstor.org/stable/1404569; https://williamblum.org/chapters/killing-hope/italy.

32  Togliatti, Longo, *Times*, 22 April 1948.

33  *Times, Guardian*, 2 April 1948.

34  *Times, New York Times*, 6 April 1948; Foreign Office, 'Report of the Court of Enquiry into the circumstances of the collision between a Viking Airliner and a Soviet Service Aircraft on 5th April 1948'.

35  *Times*, 7 April 1948.

36  *Times*, 12 April 1948.

37  *Times*, 19 April 1948.

38  *Times*, 21 April 1948.

39  Clay, https://www.trumanlibrary.org/whistlestop/BERLIN_A/PAGE_2.HTM.

40  Parrish, p. 143.

## Chapter Forty-One: East Asian Conflicts

1  Mao, Fairbank and Feuerwerker, pp. 775–6.

2  Republicans, Dewey, Westad, *Encounters*, pp. 186–7; Barr, China White Paper, p. 358.

3  Newspaper, French, p. 53.

4  When he transferred to Pyongyang in the summer of 1948, he became deputy premier and foreign minister but was executed as an American spy in the mid-1950s.

5  Education, Movement, Scalapino and Lee, pp. 380, 384; I am indebted to John Everard for information about Kim's hymn playing.

6   Report, Cummings, *Sun*, pp. 192–3.
7   Hodge, Cummings, *Origins*, p. 250; Support, Cummings, *Origins*, II, p. 64; CIA, Cummings, *Sun*, pp. 213, 214–15.
8   Hodge, Pauley, Cummings, *Sun*, pp. 198, 199; Inflation, UN Report, 1948, p. 127.
9   Kennan, FRUS, 1947, VI, p. 814; Vincent, Green, p. 266.
10  Chiefs, Truman, *Memoirs*, II, p. 325; Forrestal, Acheson, Green, p. 267.
11  Labor Party, Yo, Union, Cummings, *Origins*, I, pp. 209, 218–19.
12  It is now the most popular honeymoon destination in South Korea.
13  Cummings, *Origins*, II, p. 251.
14  Americans, Governor, Police, Cummings, *Origins*, II, pp. 252–3, 256.
15  See John Merrill, 'The Cheju-do Rebellion', *Journal of Korean Studies*, 2 (1980), pp. 139–97; Official report, http://www.jeju43peace.or.kr/report_eng.pdf, *Newsweek*, 19 June 2000; Cummings, *Origins*, II, pp. 250–59; Kim, pp. 13 et seq.

## Chapter Forty-Two: Tapestry of Escalating Violence

1   Lossin, p. 525, Kurzman, p. 103.
2   Arms, Shindler, p. 47; http://www.palyam.org/English/ArmsShips/Nora; Lossin, p. 521.
3   Lossin, p. 527, Morris, *1948*, pp. 123–4.
4   Perlmutter, p. 214.
5   Morris, *1948*, pp. 126–7.
6   200–300,000, Shindler, pp. 44–5; Begin, p. 164; Perlmutter, p. 215; Benny Morris, 'The Historiography of Deir Yassin', *Journal of Israeli History*, 14 (1 March 2005).
7   Kurzman, pp. 139–49, 206, 220, Morris, *1948*, p. 182.
8   Kurzman, pp. 188–99.
9   Sharett, Lossin, p. 535, Morris, *1948*, p. 202.
10  Kurzman, pp. 211–12.
11  Morris, *1948*, pp. 181–2, 183; Azzam, Morris, *1948*, p. 187.
12  Morris, *1948*, pp. 138–9.
13  Kurzman, pp. 153–8, Lossin, p. 532.
14  Kurzman, pp. 175–9.
15  Kurzman, pp. 180–5.

## Chapter Forty-Three: The Birth of Israel

1   Shlaim, *Collusion*, p. 181, Kurzman, pp. 207–8, Morris, *1948*, p. 94.
2   Creech-Jones, MacMillan, Shlaim, *Collusion*, p. 186.
3   French, Bar-Zohar, p. 157.
4   Morris, *1948*, p. 162.
5   Bar-Zohar, p. 156.
6   Kurzman, pp. 213–14.
7   Bar-Zohar, p. 158, Kurzman, p. 214.
8   Morris, *1948*, pp. 157–62.
9   Flapan, Part Three, Shlaim, *Israel and Palestine*, pp. 54–61; Weizmann,

Shlaim, *Israel and Palestine*, p. 59; Morris (*Birth*), Pappé (*Making*) and Masalha deal at length with the issue.

10 Morris, *1948*, pp. 171–2.

11 Meeting, Shlaim, *Collusion*, pp. 205–10, Meir, pp. 176–81, Kirkbride, pp. 21 et seq., Kurzman, p. 209.

12 The historian Avi Shlaim calls the decision to send Meir 'one of the worst blunders in the annals of Zionist diplomacy' (Shlaim, *Collusion*, p. 213).

13 Shlaim, *Collusion*, pp. 211–12.

14 Plot, Saudi, Foreign minister, Shlaim, *Collusion*, p. 193.

15 Bar-Zohar, p. 159; Kurzman, p. 214.

16 Meeting, McCullough, pp. 614–17, FRUS, 1948, v, p. 972.

17 Morris, *1948*, pp. 187–8; Glubb, p. 85.

18 Yadin, Galili, Ben-Gurion, Bar-Zohar, p. 160, Kurzman, pp. 246–7.

19 Name, Kurzman, p. 248.

20 Egypt, Morris, p. 185; Abdullah, Shlaim, *Collusion*, pp. 227–8, Glubb, pp. 93, 152; Shlaim, 'Israel and the Arab Coalition in 1948', Rogan and Shlaim, p. 82.

21 McCullough, p. 617.

22 Morris, pp. 169–70, Kurzman, pp. 226–33.

23 Morris, pp. 170–1.

24 Morris, pp. 163–4.

25 Bar-Zohar, pp. 162–3, Morris, *1948*, p. 177, Kurzman, pp. 250–1, Lossin, p. 545.

26 The USSR announces recognition on 17 May.

27 McCullough, pp. 617–18, 620, Kurzman, pp. 251–6.

28 Glubb, p. 99.

29 Ben-Gurion, Kurzman, pp. 257–8.

30 Forces, Morris, *1948*, pp. 233, 251, Kurzman, p. 244, Nasser, *Memoirs*, p. 10.

31 Egyptian advance, Kurzman, pp. 270–87.

32 Ben-Gurion, Glubb, Shlaim, *Collusion*, pp. 236, 239.

33 Abdullah–Azzam, Message, Kurzman, p. 354.

34 Kurzman, pp. 357–62.

35 Told, Morris, *1948*, p. 166; Acre, Kurzman, p. 329.

36 Return, Refugees, Shindler, pp. 45, 48; Mapam, Flapan, p. 110.

37 The ancient state located primarily in Assyria.

38 Bar-Zohar, p. 166.

39 Capa, Arak, Eyewitness, Kurzman, pp. 414, 424.

40 Morris, *1948*, p. 265.

## Chapter Forty-Four: Asian Encounters

1 Dikötter, pp. 4–5.

2 Flour, Currency, *Times*, 14 May 1948; Merchant, Westad, *Encounters*, p. 183.

3 Melby, p. 253.

### Chapter Forty-Five: Changing of the Guard

1 Economy reforms, Ross, pp. 216–17, 221–3, 246–7.
2 Exports, Tractors, Horwitz, pp. 276–7; Ross, pp. 216–17, 235, 241.
3 Smuts, *Times*, 18 May 1948.
4 NP, Barber, pp. 135-9; Deborah Posel, Ross et al., p. 322.
5 The Smuts government banned Broederbond adherents from working as civil servants. But, since membership was secret, this was impossible to implement.
6 Broederbond, Horwitz, p. 269; OB, Vorster, Barber, p. 119.
7 Hofmeyr, Repugnant, Welsh, p. 413; Destiny, Ross, p. 325.
8 Election, Horowitz, p. 267; Smuts, *Smuts*, p. 511.

### Chapter Forty-Six: European Confrontations

1 Rákosi, Bulgarians, Dedijer, pp. 358–60.
2 Meeting, *Pravda*, *Times*, 29 May 1948.
3 *Pravda*, Bevin, *Times*, 5, 10, 15, 20 May 1948; Bradley, *Times*, 1 June 1948.
4 Cadres, Purge, Nationalisation, Industrialisation, Krejci and Machonin, pp. 159, 161–3.
5 Gottwald–Beneš, Korbel, Subversion. pp. 8–9.
6 Prisoners, *Times*, 3 May 1948.
7 Churchill, *Times*, 9 May 1948, http://www.churchill-society-london.org.uk/WSCHague.html.

### Chapter Forty-Seven: Truce

1 Abdullah Yusuf Azzam, the future 'Father of Global Jihad', was a boy living in a village near Jenin at the time.
2 Weapons, Morris, p. 268.
3 Nasser, pp. 17–19.
4 Yadin, Bar-Zohar, p. 179; Allon, Shindler, p. 46.
5 Kurzman, pp. 464–83.
6 Broadcast, Kurzman, p. 484.
7 Blessed, Kurzman, p. 484.

### Chapter Forty-Eight: The President Takes a Trip

1 Any better, http://www.thedailybeast.com/how-truman-reinvented-campaigning.
2 Stalin, Hamby, p. 443.
3 http://www.thedailybeast.com/how-truman-reinvented-campaigning.
4 Lay it on, http://www.historylink.org/File/5466.
5 Trip, McCullough, pp. 628–30; HST diary, 28 June 1948; Production, Employment, UN, *1948*, pp. 9, 227; Incomes, Assets, *Federal Reserve Bulletin Survey of Consumer Finance*, 1949, p. 1324.
6 Luce, *Chicago Tribune*, 22 June 1948; *Times*, 21 June 1948.

## Chapter Forty-Nine: At Home in Our Land

1 Malan, Reuters, 4 June 1948.
2 Smuts, *Times*, 1 July 1948.

## Chapter Fifty: Legacy of Partition

1 Refugees, Women, Communists, Guha, *India*, pp. 102–3, 108, 109–10.
2 See Cotton's autobiography.

## Chapter Fifty-One: Emergency

1 Attacks, MacDonald, *Times*, 8, 17, 22, 29 June 1948.
2 Party representatives who had fought the Japanese had been invited to victory celebrations in London where they were given medals and a gratuity of £45 each.
3 Burleigh, pp. 165–71.

## Chapter Fifty-Two: Strategic Morass

1 Doctor, Lippa, p. 53.
2 Reputation, Chassin, pp. 175–6.
3 Confusion, Chassin, pp. 176–7.
4 Dikötter, pp. 6–7.
5 Battlefield situation, Minister, Chassin, pp. 177–82.
6 Land reform, Official, Melby, pp. 262–3.
7 Inflation, Exports, UN Report, 1948, pp. 124, 127, 129; Refuges, Floods, Shoes, House, Director, Melby, pp. 262, 268, 275; Dollar, *Times*, 25 June 1948; Machines, *Leader*, 10 July 1948.
8 Davies, *China*, p. 303.

## Chapter Fifty-Three: Showdown

1 De Gaulle, *Times*, 8, 10 June 1948.
2 Lovett, Isaacson and Thomas, p. 457; Soviet measures, *Times*, 12 June 1948.
3 Rodrigo, p. 17.
4 Clay, p. 368; Forrestal, pp. 410, 431.
5 O'Neill, Edinger, pp. 77–8.
6 Erhard would criticize the execution of the Marshall Plan for favouring state planning over free markets. Speech, Edinger, p. 70.
7 Last quarter, UN Economic Report, 1948, p. 137; Judged, https://www.trumanlibrary.org/whistlestop/BERLIN_A/PAGE_3.HTM.
8 Stocks, Needs, Clay, p. 365.
9 Gunther, pp. 292–4.
10 Kennan, *Memoirs*, p. 420.
11 Parrish, p. 194.
12 An earlier flight had taken place on 23 June, when a Skymaster plane chartered by the military from American Overseas Airways in Frankfurt took in a cargo of potatoes (Parrish, p. 198).
13 Clay, p. 366.

14  Though the first planes sent to Europe were not equipped to carry atom bombs.

15  Bevin, FO 800/468/GER/48/31, Bullock, pp. 575–6; Bombers, Bullock, pp. 576–7, FO 800/467/GER/48/34; Vandenberg, Meijer, p. 329, Atlee, Williams, *Prime Minister*, p. 172, Truman, American Presidency Project, 14, May 1998..

16  Togliatti, Agosti, p. 197.

17  Prague, Ridley, p. 290; Tito, Dedijer, p. 381.

18  Ambassador, Failed, Korbel, *Tito's Communism*, pp. 289, 300.

19  I am grateful to Dr Svetozar Rajak for information on this and other aspects of the Soviet–Yugoslav split.

20  Beneš died three months later. He was buried in the garden of his country house. Letter, *Times*, 8 June 1948, Korbel, p. 4.

21  Lovett, Isaacson and Thomas, p. 457.

22  Mindszenty, Boer, pp. 36–7; Pope, Cheetham, p. 290, Falconi, p. 266.

23  Schools, Letter, Bells, Boer, pp. 200, 220; Satan, *Times*, 9 June 1948.

24  Broadcasts, Boer, pp. 226–7, 235; Education Ministry, Mindszenty, pp. 311–12, 316–17.

25  Hansard, 30 June 1948.

26  Schumacher, Edinger, pp. 133–4; Bevin, Hansard, 30 June 1948.

27  Sound, *Guardian*, 30 June 1948.

## Afterword: From Then to Now

1  Tonnage, Jackson, p. 142.

2  Equivalent to $800 billion today.

3  Gap, Imports, Steil, Project Syndicate article, August 2017.

4  Hub and spoke, Dr Hahm Chaibong at Korean Global Forum, October 2017.

5  One assumes that he was referring to the Soviet Union as the embodiment of traditional Russian power rather than as the home of Communist ideology.

6  Stalin, Levada Centre poll, June 2017.

7  Kissinger, *Order*, p. 279.

8  Macron, Athens speech, 6 September 2017; Brooks, *New York Times*, 27 May 2017.

9  Brzezinski, *Economist*, 3 June 2017; Infrastructure, *FT*, 15 September 2017; Trump, Warsaw speech, 6 July 2017.

10  NATO, *Guardian*, 9 September 2017.

# BIBLIOGRAPHY

Acacia, John, *Clark Clifford* (Kentucky, 2009)

Acheson, Dean, *Present at the Creation* (Hamish Hamilton, 1970)

Adams, Jad, *Gandhi* (Quercus, 2010)

Agosti, Aldo, *Palmiro Togliatti* (I. B. Tauris, 2008)

Ahmed, Ishtiaq, *The Punjab Bloodied, Partitioned and Cleansed* (Oxford University Press, 2012)

Akbar, M. J., *Nehru* (Viking Penguin, 1988)

Albright, Madeleine, *Madam Secretary* (Macmillan, 2003)

Alexievich, Svetlana, *Second-Hand Time* (Fitzcarraldo, 2016)

Andrew, Christopher, *The Defence of the Realm* (Allen Lane, 2009)

Annan, Noel, *Changing Enemies* (HarperCollins, 1995)

Applebaum, Anne, *Iron Curtain* (Allen Lane, 2012)

——, *Gulag* (Penguin, 2003)

Apter, David, *The Gold Coast in Transition* (Princeton University Press, 1955)

Åsbrink, Elisabeth, *1947: When Now Begins* (Scribe, 2017)

Arfa, Hassan, *Under Five Shahs* (John Murray, 1964)

Asselain, Jean-Charles, *Histoire économique de la France*, Vol. II (Seuil, 1984)

Attlee, Clement, *As It Happened* (Heinemann, 1954)

Augstein, Rudolf, *Konrad Adenauer* (Secker & Warburg, 1964)

Austin, Dennis, *Politics in Ghana, 1946–1960* (Oxford University Press, 1964)

Axworth, Michael, *Iran: Empire of the Mind* (Penguin, 2008)

Barber, James, *South Africa in the Twentieth Century* (Blackwell, 1999)

Barnet, Richard J., *Allies* (Jonathan Cape, 1984)

Barr, James, *A Line in the Sand* (Simon & Schuster, 2011)

Barrass, Gordon S., *The Great Cold War* (Stanford University Press, 2009)

Bar-Zohar, Michael, *Ben-Gurion* (Weidenfeld & Nicolson, 1978)

Bashford, Alison, and Macintyre, Stuart (eds), *The Cambridge History of Australia*, Vol. II (Cambridge University Press, 2013)

Bass, Robert, and Marbury, Elizabeth (eds), *The Soviet–Yugoslav Controversy, 1948–58* at https://babel.hathitrust.org/cgi/pt?id=mdp.39015003763102;view=1up;seq=9)

Baxter, Craig, *The Jana Sangh* (University of Pennsylvania Press, 1969)

Bayeh, Joseph, *A History of Stability and Change in Lebanon* (I. B. Tauris, 2017)

Beasley, W. G., *The Modern History of Japan* (Weidenfeld & Nicolson, 1973)

Beckman, George, and Genji, Okubo, *The Japanese Communist Party, 1922–1945* (Stanford University Press, 1965)

Beevor, Antony, *The Fall of Berlin 1945* (Penguin, 2003)

——, and Cooper, Artemis, *Paris: After the Liberation 1944–1949* (Penguin, 2007)

Begin, Menachem, *The Revolt* (Nash, 1951)

Beisner, Robert, *Dean Acheson* (Oxford University Press, 2006)

Belden, Jack, *China Shakes the World* (New York Modern Readers Press, 1949)

Ben-Gurion, David, *Memoirs*, Vol. IV, (World Publishing, 1970)

——, *Israel: A Personal History* (New English Library, 1972)

——, *Israel: Years of Challenge* (Massadah-PEC Press, 1963)

Benson, Michael T., *Harry S. Truman and the Founding of Israel* (Praeger, 1997)

Berstein, Serge, *Léon Blum* (Fayard, 2006)

——, *Histoire du Gaullisme* (Perrin, 2001–2)

Beschloss, Michael, *Our Documents* (Oxford University Press, 2006)

Bessel, Richard, *Germany 1945* (Simon & Schuster, 2009)

Bevan, Aneurin, *In Place of Fear* (Heinemann, 1952)

Bew, John, *Citizen Clem* (Quercus, 2016)

—— and Cox, Michael, *A Man for All Seasons* (London School of
    Economics, 2017; http://blogs.lse.ac.uk/lsehistory/2017/03/29/a-
    man-for-all-seasons-the-life-and-times-of-clement-attlee/)

Bidault, Georges, *D'une Résistance à l'autre* (Les Presses du siècle,
    1965)

Billotte, Pierre, *Le passé au futur* (Stock, 1979)

Birkenhead, Lord, *Walter Monckton* (Weidenfeld & Nicolson, 1965)

Bix, Herbert P., *Hirohito and the Making of Modern Japan*
    (Duckworth, 2001)

Bland, Larry, and Stoler, Mark, *The Papers of George Catlett
    Marshall*, Vol. VI (Johns Hopkins University Press, 2013)

Boer, Nicholas, *Cardinal Mindszenty* (BUE, 1949)

Bogarde, Dirk, *Backcloth* (Penguin, 1987)

Bohlen, Charles, *Witness to History, 1929–1969* (W. W. Norton &
    Company, 1973)

Bolitho, Hector, Sharif al Mujahid, *In Quest of Jinnah* (Oxford,
    2009)

Borhi, Laszlo, *Dealing with Dictators* (Indiana University Press,
    2016)

Bose, Mihir, *From Midnight to Glorious Morning?* (Haus, 2017)

Bourke-White, Margaret, *Portrait of Myself* (Simon & Schuster,
    1963)

Bowles, Chester, *Promises to Keep* (Harper & Row, 1971)

——, *Ambassador's Report* (Collins, 1954)

Boyd, Douglas, *De Gaulle: The Man Who Defied Six US Presidents*
    (History Press, 2013)

Bren, Paulina, and Neuberger, Mary (eds), *Communism Unwrapped*
    (Oxford University Press, 2012)

Brendon, Piers, *The Decline and Fall of the British Empire* (Cape,
    2007)

Brewer, David, *Greece, the Decade of War* (I. B. Taurus, 2016)

Brivati, Brian, and Heffernan, Richard (eds), *The Labour Party*
    (Macmillan, 2000)

Brown, Judith M., *Nehru* (Longman, 1999)

——, *Gandhi: Prisoner of Hope* (Yale University Press, 1989)

——, *Ghandi and Civil Disobedience* (Cambridge University Press,
    1977)

Brown, W. Norman, *The United States, India, Pakistan and Bangladesh* (Harvard University Press, 1972)

Bruce Lockhart, Sir Robert, *Diaries: Vol. II, 1939–1965* (Macmillan London Ltd, 1980)

——, *Jan Masaryk* (Dropmore Press, 1951)

Bryant, Chris, *Stafford Cripps* (Hodder & Stoughton, 1997)

Bullock, Alan, *Ernest Bevin* (Heinemann, 1983)

Burks, Ardath W., *Japan* (Westview Press, 1981)

Burleigh, Michael, *Small Wars, Far Away Places* (Macmillan, 2013)

Buruma, Ian, *Year Zero* (Penguin, 2013)

Byrnes, James F., *Speaking Frankly* (Harper, 1947)

Cairncross, Alec, *The Price of War* (Basil Blackwell, 1986)

Campbell, Doon, *Magic Mistress* (No publisher given, 1998)

Campbell-Johnson, Alan, *Mission with Mountbatten* (Robert Hale, 1981)

Capa, Robert, *Slightly Out of Focus* (Modern Library, 2001)

Casey, S., and Wright, J. (eds), *Mental Maps in the Early Cold War Era, 1945–68* (Palgrave, 2011)

Cesarani, David, *Final Solution* (Pan Macmillan, 2016)

——, *Major Farran's Hat* (Heinemann, 2009)

Chace, James, *Acheson* (Simon & Schuster, 1998)

Chassin, Lionel Max, *The Communist Conquest of China* (Weidenfeld & Nicolson, 1966)

Chatterji, Joya, *Spoils of Partition* (Cambridge, 2011)

Chaudhuri, Sukanta, *Calcutta* (Oxford University Press, 1990)

Cheetham, Nicholas, *Keepers of the Keys* (Scribner, 1983)

Chenevix-Trench, Charles, *Viceroy's Agent* (Jonathan Cape, 1987)

Childs, David, *East Germany* (Benn, 1969)

Clark, Martin, *Modern Italy, 1871–1982* (Longman, 1984)

Clarke, Peter, *The Cripps Version* (Allen Lane, 2002)

Clay, Lucius D., *Decision in Germany* (Heinemann, 1950)

Clissold, Stephen, *Djilas* (Maurice Temple Smith, 1983)

—— (ed), *Yugoslavia and the Soviet Union, 1939–1973* (Royal Institute of International Affairs, London, 1975)

Clough, Shepard B., and Saladino, Salvatore M., *A History of Modern Italy* (Columbia University Press, 1968)

Cohen, Michael Joseph, *Truman and Israel* (University of California Press, 1990)

Cohen-Solal, Annie, Goldberger, Paul, and Gottlieb, Robert, *New York Mid-Century* (Thames & Hudson, 2014)

Collins, Larry, and Lapierre, Dominique, *Mountbatten and the Partition of India* (Vikas Publishing House, 1982)

——, *Freedom at Midnight* (Vikas, 1975)

Connaughton, R., Pimlott, J., and Anderson, D., *The Battle for Manila* (Bloomsbury, 1995)

Connell, Brian, *A Watcher on the Rhine* (Weidenfeld & Nicolson, 1967)

Conquest, Robert, *Stalin: Breaker of Nations* (Weidenfeld & Nicolson, 1991)

Cooper, Andrew Scott, *The Fall of Heaven* (Henry Holt, 2016)

Conrad, Peter, *Modern Times, Modern Places* (Thames & Hudson, 1998)

Corsellis, John, and Ferrar, Marcus, *Slovenia 1945* (I. B. Tauris, 2005)

Cotton, Sidney, with Barker, Ralph, *Aviator Extraordinary* (Chatto & Windus, 1969)

Cromwell, William C., *The Marshall Plan, Britain and the Cold War* (Cambridge University Press, 1982)

Crossman, Richard, *A Nation Reborn* (Hamish Hamilton, 1960)

Crowder, Richard, *Aftermath* (I. B. Tauris, 2015)

Cummings, Bruce, *Korea's Place in the Sun* (W. W. Norton & Company, 1997)

——, *The Origins of the Korean War* (Princeton University Press, Vol. I, 1981; Vol. II, 1990)

Dahm, Bernhard, *History of Indonesia in the Twentieth Century* (Pall Mall Press, 1971)

Dalton, Hugh, *The Second War Diary of Hugh Dalton 1940–45* (Cape with LSE, 1986)

Daniels, Jonathan, *The Man of Independence* (Victor Gollancz, 1951)

Daniels, Robert, *A Documentary History of Communism* (Hanover, University Press of New England, 1984)

Das, Durga (ed.), *Sardar Patel's Correspondence 1945–50* (Navajivan Publishing House, 1971)

Das, Manmath Nath, *Partition and Independence of India* (Vision Books, 1982)

Davenport, Marcia, *Too Strong for Fantasy* (Collins, 1968)

Davenport, T. R. H., *South Africa: A Modern History* (Macmillan, 1987)

Davidson, Eugene, *The Death and Life of Germany* (Jonathan Cape, 1959)

Davies Jr, John Paton, *China Hand* (University of Pennsylvania Press, 2012)

——, *Dragon by the Tail* (W. W. Norton & Company, 1972)

Davies, Joseph, *Diary* (Library of Congress, Washington)

Dayan, Moshe, *Story of My Life* (Morrow, 1976)

Dedijer, Vladimir, *Tito Speaks* (Weidenfeld & Nicolson, 1953)

Demory, Jean-Claude, *Georges Bidault 1899–1983* (Julliard, 1995)

Department of State, *United States Relations with China with Special Reference to the Period 1944–1949* (Washington US Government Printing Office, 1949)

Desai, Meghnad, *The Rediscovery of India* (Penguin, 2009)

Devillers, Philippe, *Histoire du Vietnam* (Seuil, 1952)

Dijk, Ruud van, *Encyclopedia of the Cold War*, Vol. 1 (Taylor and Francis, 2008)

Dilks, David (ed.), *The Diaries of Sir Alexander Cadogan, 1938–1945* (Faber, 2010)

Dikötter, Frank, *The Tragedy of Liberation* (Bloomsbury, 2013)

Dixon, Piers, *Double Diploma* (Hutchinson, 1968)

Djilas, Milovan, *Rise and Fall* (Macmillan, 1985)

——, *Wartime* (Secker & Warburg, 1977)

——, *Conversations with Stalin* (Harcourt Brace, 1963)

Dobbs, Michael, *Madeleine Albright* (Holt, 1999)

Dönhoff, Marion, *Foe into Friend* (Palgrave Macmillan, 1982)

Dower, John W., *Embracing Defeat* (Allen Lane, 1999)

——, *Japan in War and Peace* (New Press, 1993)

——, *Empire and Aftermath* (Harvard University Press, 1979)

Dreyer, Edward, *China at War, 1901–1949* (Longman, 1995)

Drolet, Jean-François, and Dunkerley, James, *American Foreign Policy* (Manchester University Press, 2017)

Duchêne, François, *Jean Monnet* (W.W. Norton & Company, 1994)

Duclos, Jacques, *Mémoires*, Vol. IV (Fayard, 1971)

Dumaine, Jacques, *Quai d'Orsay* (Chapman & Hall, 1958)

Duus, Peter (ed.), *The Cambridge History of Japan*, Vol. VI
    (Cambridge University Press, 1988)

Easterbrook, W. T., and Aitken, Hugh G. J., *Canadian Economic
    History* (Macmillan Toronto, 1956)

Eastman, Lloyd, Ch'en, Jerome, Pepper, Suzanne, and Van Slyke,
    Lyman, *The Nationalist Era in China* (Cambridge University
    Press, 1991)

Eban, Abba, *Personal Witness: Israel through My Eyes* (Jonathan
    Cape, 1993)

Eden, Anthony, *Memoirs – Full Circle* (Cassell, 1960)

Edinger, Lewis J., *Kurt Schumacher* (Stanford University Press, 1965)

Eisenberg, Caroline, *Drawing the Line* (Cambridge University Press,
    1996)

Engelstein, Laura, *Russia in Flames* (Oxford, 2017)

Fairbank, John, and Feuerwerker, Albert (eds), *The Cambridge
    History of China*, Vol. XIII, Part 2 (Cambridge University Press,
    1986)

Falconi, Carlo, *The Popes in the Twentieth Century* (Weidenfeld &
    Nicolson, 1967)

Fauvet, Jacques, *La IVe République* (Fayard, 1959)

Feigel, Lara, *The Bitter Taste of Victory* (Bloomsbury, 2016)

Fenby, Jonathan, *The General* (Simon & Schuster, 2010)

——, *The Penguin History of Modern China*
    (Penguin, 2008)

——, *Alliance* (Simon & Schuster, 2006)

——, *Generalissimo*, (Simon & Schuster, 2003)

Ferrell, Robert (ed.), *Truman: A Centenary Remembrance* (Thames
    & Hudson, 1984)

——, *Dear Bess* (W. W. Norton & Company, 1983)

Fevziu, Blendi, *Enver Hoxha* (I.B. Tauris, 2016)

Fields, Alonzo, *My 21 Years in the White House* (Coward-McCann,
    1961)

Finn, Richard B., *Winners in Peace* (University of California Press,
    1992)

Fischer, Louis, *The Life of Mahatma Gandhi* (Cape, 1951)

Fitzgerald, C. P., *The Birth of Communist China* (Penguin Books, 1976)

Fitzpatrick, Sheila, *On Stalin's Team* (Princeton University Press, 2015)

Flapan, Simha, *The Birth of Israel* (Pantheon, 1987)

Folin, Jacques de, *Indochine, 1940–55* (Seuil, 1987)

*Foreign Relations of the United States* (FRUS), 1947, 1948 (US Government Printing Office)

Forrestal, James, *The Forrestal Diaries* (Viking, 1951)

French, Patrick, *Liberty or Death* (Flamingo, 1998)

Fulbrook, Mary, and Port, Andrew, *Becoming East German* (Berghahn, 2013)

Gaddis, John Lewis, *George F. Kennan* (Penguin, 2011)

——, *We Now Know* (Clarendon Press, 1997)

——, *The Cold War* (Allen Lane, 2005)

Gage, Nicholas, *Eleni* (Vintage, 2006)

Galambos, Louis et al. (eds), *Papers of Dwight David Eisenhower*, Vol. ix (Johns Hopkins University Press, 1978)

Gatzke, Hans H. W., *Germany and the United States* (Harvard University Press, 1980)

Gayn, Mark, *Japan Diary* (Sloane Associate, 1948)

Gellhorn, Martha, 'Journey Through a Peaceful Land', *New Republic* (June/August 1947)

Gerwarth, Robert, *The Vanquished* (Allen Lane, 2016)

Ghose, Sankar, *Jawaharlal Nehru* (Allied Publishers, Bombay, 1993)

Giangreco, D. M., and Moore, Kathryn (eds) *Dear Harry: Truman's Mailroom, 1945–1953* (Stackpole, 1999)

Gilbert, Martin, *Israel: A History* (Doubleday, 1998)

——, *Never Despair* (Heinemann, 1988)

Gildea, Robert, *France Since 1945* (Oxford University Press, 1997)

Gillin, Donald, *Warlord: Yen Hsi-shan* (Princeton University Press, 1962)

Girling, J. L. S., *People's War* (Allen and Unwin, 1969)

Glubb, John, *A Soldier with the Arabs* (Hodder & Stoughton, 1957)

Gopal, Sarvepalli, *Jawaharlal Nehru* (Oxford University Press, 2004)

Gordon, Andrew, *Postwar Japan as History* (University of California Press, 1993)

Gori, Francesca, and Pons, Silvio (eds), *The Soviet Union and Europe in the Cold War, 1943–53* (Palgrave Macmillan, 1996)

Goscha, Christopher, *The Penguin History of Modern Vietnam* (Allen Lane, 2016)

Gray, Jack, *Rebellions and Revolutions* (Oxford University Press, 2002)

Green, Michael, *By More Than Providence* (Columbia University Press, 2017)

Greilsammer, Ilan, *Blum* (Flammarion, 1996)

Grieder, Peter, *The East German Leadership, 1946–73: Conflict and Crisis* (Manchester University Press, 2000)

Grosser, Alfred, *Affaires Extérieures* (Flammarion, 1984)

Guha, Ramachandra, *Makers of Modern Asia* (Harvard University Press, 2014)

——, *India After Gandhi* (HarperCollins, 2007)

Gunther, John, *Behind Europe's Curtain* (Hamish Hamilton, 1949)

Haas, Lawrence J., *Harry and Arthur: Truman, Vandenberg, and the Partnership that Created the Free World* (Potomac Books, 2016)

Haas, Richard, *A World in Disarray* (Penguin, 2017)

Hajari, Nisid, *Midnight's Furies* (Amberley, 2015)

Halamish, Aviva, *The Exodus Affair* (Syracuse, 1998)

Hall, Peter, *Cities in Civilization* (Phoenix, 1999)

Halle, Louis J., *The Cold War as History* (Chatto & Windus, 1967)

Hamby, Alonzo, *Man of the People* (Oxford University Press, 1950)

Hammer, Ellen Joy, *The Struggle for Indochina, 1940–1955* (Stanford University Press, 1966)

Harriman, Averell, *Special Envoy to Churchill and Stalin, 1941–1946* (Random House, 1975)

Hathaway, Oona, and Shapiro, Scott, *The Internationalists* (Simon & Schuster, 2017)

Harper, Townsend, *The Devil and John Foster Dulles* (André Deutsch, 1974)

Held, Joseph (ed.), *The Columbia History of Eastern Europe in the Twentieth Century* (Columbia University Press, 1992)

Hennessy, Peter, *The Secret State* (Allen Lane, 2003)

——, *Never Again: Britain, 1945–51* (Vintage, 1993)

Heren, Louis, *Memories of Times Past* (Hamish Hamilton, 1988)

——, *Growing up on* The Times (Hamish Hamilton, 1978)

Herman, Arthur, *Gandhi and Churchill: The Rivalry That Destroyed an Empire and Forged Our Age* (Arrow, 2009)

Hermann, A., *A History of the Czechs* (Allen Lane, 1975)

Hibbert, Reginald, *Albania's National Liberation Struggle* (Pinte Publishers, 1991)

Hicks, Pamela, *Daughter of Empire: Life as a Mountbatten* (Weidenfeld & Nicolson, 2012)

Hobsbawm, Eric, *The Age of Extremes* (Michael Joseph, 1994)

Hodson, H. V., *The Great Divide* (Oxford University Press, 1986)

Hogan, Michael J., *A Cross of Iron* (Cambridge University Press, 1998)

——, *The Marshall Plan* (Cambridge University Press, 1987)

Holt, Richard (ed.), *Selected Letters of John Kenneth Galbraith* (Cambridge University Press, 2017)

Holtsmark, Sven, Neumann, Ivar, and Westad, Odd Arne (eds), *The Soviet Union in Eastern Europe, 1945–89* (Springer, 2016)

Hopkins, Michael, *The Cold War 1945–1991* (Palgrave Macmillan, 2006)

Horwitz, Ralph, *The Political Economy of South Africa* (Weidenfeld & Nicolson, 1967)

Huneidi, Sahar, *A Broken Trust* (I. B. Tauris, 2001)

Hyde, H. Montgomery, *Walter Monckton* (Sinclair-Stevenson, 1991)

Imamura, Anne (ed.), *Re-imaging Japanese Women* (University of California Press, 1996)

Innis, Mary (ed.), *Essays in Canadian Economic History* (University of Toronto Press, 2017)

Iokobe, Makoto, *The Diplomatic History of Postwar Japan* (Routledge, 2011)

Isaacson, Walter, and Thomas, Evan, *The Wise Men* (Faber & Faber, 1986)

Iyengar, Uma (ed.), *The Oxford India* (Oxford, 2007)

Jackson, Robert, *The Berlin Airlift* (Endeavour Press Ltd, 2016)

Jacobs, Jack (ed.), *Jews and Leftist Politics* (Cambridge University Press, 2017)

Jalal, Ayesha, *The Struggle for Pakistan* (Belknap Press of Harvard University Press, 2014)

Jarausch, Konrad, *Out of the Ashes* (Princeton University Press, 2015)

Jeffreys-Jones, Rhodri, *Cloak and Dollar* (Yale University Press, 2002)

Jenkins, Roy, *Churchill* (Pan, 2002)

——, *Harry Truman* (Collins, 1980)

Jenkins, Simon, *A Short History of England* (Profile, 2012)

Jenner, W. J. F., *The Tyranny of History* (The Penguin Press, 1992)

Jensen, Kenneth (ed.), *Origins of the Cold War* (United States Institute of Peace, 1993)

Jinnah, Fatima, *My Brother* (Unpublished memoirs in National Archive of Pakistan, Islamabad)

Jinnah, Muhammad Ali, *Speeches* (Lahore, 1989)

Jones, Joseph, *The Fifteen Weeks: February 21 – June 5, 1947* (Houghton Mifflin Harcourt, 1965)

Judd, Denis, *Empire* (I. B. Tauris, 2011)

Judt, Tony, *Postwar* (Vintage, 2011)

Julius, Anthony, *Trials of the Diaspora* (Oxford University Press, 2012)

Kahin, George, *Southeast Asia: A Testament* (Routledge, 2003)

Kaplan, Karel, *The Communist Party in Power* (Westview Press, 1987)

——, *The Short March* (C. Hurst & Company, 1987)

Kaplan, Robert, *Balkan Ghosts* (Vintage, 1994)

Kardelj, Edvard, *Reminiscences* (Blond & Briggs, 1982)

Keay, John, *Midnight's Descendants* (Collins, 2015)

——, *Last Post* (John Murray, 1997)

Kedward, Rod, *La Vie en bleu* (Allen Lane, 2005)

Kendall, Bridget, *Cold War* (BBC Books, 2017)

Kennan, George F., *Memoirs* (Hutchinson, 1968)

——, *Russia and the West under Lenin and Stalin* (Little, Brown, 1961)

——, *American Diplomacy, 1900–1950* (University of Chicago Press, 1951)

Kennedy, Paul, *The Rise and Fall of the Great Powers* (Unwin Hyman, 1988)

Kershaw, Ian, *To Hell and Back* (Allen Lane, 2016)

Khalidi, Rashid, *Iron Cage* (Beacon, 2007)

Khan, Yasmin, *The Raj at War* (Bodley Head, 2015)

——, *The Great Partition* (Yale University Press, 2007)

Khrushchev, Nikita, *Khrushchev Remembers*, Introduction, Commentary and Notes by Edward Crankshaw (André Deutsch, 1971)

Kiernan, Ben, *Viet Nam* (Oxford University Press, 2017)

Kim Hun Joon, *The Massacres at Mt Halla* (Cornell, 2004)

Kindleberger, Charles, *Marshall Plan Days* (Allen & Unwin, 1987)

Kirby, E. Stuart, *Economic Development in East Asia* (Allen & Unwin, 1967)

Kirkbride, Alec, *From the Wings* (Cass, 1976)

Kissinger, Henry, *World Order* (Allen Lane, 2014)

——, *Diplomacy* (Simon & Schuster, 1994)

Klara, Robert, *The Hidden White House* (Thomas Dunne, 2013)

Knebel, Fletcher, and Bailey, Charles, *No High Ground* (Weidenfeld & Nicolson, 1960)

Korbel, Josef, *Twentieth-Century Czechoslovakia, 1938–1948* (Columbia University Press, 1977)

——, *The Communist Subversion of Czechoslovakia* (Princeton University Press, 1959)

——, *Tito's Communism* (University of Denver, 1951)

Kotkin, Stephen, *Waiting for Hitler* (Allen Lane, 2017)

Kralevska-Owens, Nassya, *Communism versus Democracy: Bulgaria 1944 to 1997* (American Research Center, Sofia, 2010)

Krejčí, Jarolsav, and Machonin, Pavel, *Czechoslovakia, 1918–92* (Macmillan, 1996)

Krock, Arthur, *Memoirs* (Cassell, 1970)

Kurzman, Dan, *Genesis 1948: The First Arab-Israeli War* (Da Capo Press, 1992)

Kynaston, David, *Austerity Britain, 1945–1951* (Bloomsbury, 2008)

Lacouture, Jean, *De Gaulle* (Seuil, 1994–6)

——, *Léon Blum* (Seuil, 1977)

Landes, David, *The Wealth and Poverty of Nations* (Little, Brown, 1998)

Lane, David, *Into the Heart of the Mafia* (Profile Books, 2009)

Lapping, Brian, *End of Empire* (St Martin's Press, 1985)

Larkin, Maurice, *France since the Popular Front* (Clarendon Press, 1988)

Larsh, William, 'Yalta and the American Approach to Free Elections in Poland', *Polish Review*, Polish Institute of Arts and Sciences of America, XL/3 (1995)

Lawrence, Mark Attwood, and Logevall, Fredrik (eds), *The First Vietnam War* (Harvard University Press, 2007)

Leahy, William, *I Was There* (Whittlesey House, 1950)

Lees, Lorraine M., *Keeping Tito Afloat* (The Pennsylvania State University Press, 1997)

Leffler, Melvyn P., *A Preponderance of Power* (Stanford University Press, 1993)

——, and Westad, Odd Arne, *The Cambridge History of the Cold War*, Vol. 1 (Cambridge University Press, 2010)

Legum Colin, *Pan-Africanism* (Pall Mall Press, 1962)

LeMay, Curtis, *Mission with LeMay* (Doubleday, 1965)

Levine, Steven, *Anvil of Victory* (Columbia University Press, 1987)

Lieven, Anatol, *Pakistan* (Allen Lane, 2011)

Lippa, Ernest, *I Was a Surgeon for the Chinese Reds* (Harrap, 1953)

Long, Roger D., *A History of Pakistan* (Oxford University Press, 2015)

Lossin, Yigal, *Pillar of Fire* (Shikmona, 1983)

Louis, Roger, and Stookey, Robert Wilson (eds), *The End of the Palestine Mandate* (I. B. Tauris, 1985)

Low, Donald (ed.), *Congress and the Raj* (Heinemann, 1977)

——, and Brasted Howards (eds), *Freedom, Trauma, Continuities: Northern India and Independence* (Sage, 1998)

Lowe, Keith, *The Fear and the Freedom* (Penguin, 2017)

Lownie, Andrew, *Stalin's Englishman* (Hodder, 2015)

Lukes, Igor, *On the Edge of the Cold War* (Oxford University Press, 2012)

MacArthur, Douglas, *Reminiscences* (Heinemann, 1965)

McClain, James L., *Japan: A Modern History* (W. W. Norton & Company, 2002)

McCullough, David, *Truman* (Simon & Schuster, 1992)

McDonald, Bryan, *Food Power* (Oxford University Press, 2017)

MacDonogh, Giles, *After the Reich* (John Murray, 2008)

———, *Berlin* (St Martin's Press, 1998)

Mackinder, Halford, *The Geographical Pivot of History* (Geographical Journal, London, Vol. 23, No. 4, 1904)

McMahon, Robert J., *The Cold War in the Third World* (Oxford University Press, 2013)

Magri, Lucio, *The Tailor of Ulm* (Verso, 2011)

Maier, Charles, and Bischof, Günter, *The Marshall Plan and Germany* (Berg Press, 1991)

Manchester, William, *American Caesar* (Hutchinson, 1979)

Mauriac, Claude, *Un Autre de Gaulle* (Hachette, 1971)

Mansergh, Nicholas (ed.), *Constitutional Relations between Britain and India: The Transfer of Power* (TOP) (HMSO, 1970–83)

Mao Zedong, *Selected Works* (University Press of the Pacific, 2011)

Marchetti, Victor, and Marks, John, *The CIA and the Cult of Intelligence* (Cape, 1974)

Marseille, Jacques, *Nouvelle Histoire de France* (Perrin, 1999)

Marshall, George, *Papers* (Johns Hopkins University Press, 2013)

Masalha, Nur, *Expulsion of the Palestinians* (I. B. Tauris, 1994)

Matthews, Kenneth, *Memories of a Mountain War: Greece, 1944–1949* (Longman, 1972)

Mayhew, Christopher, *Time to Explain* (Hutchinson, 1987)

Mayne, Richard, *Postwar* (Thames & Hudson, 1983)

Mazower, Mark, *Dark Continent* (Allen Lane, 1998)

Meijer, Henrik, *Arthur Vandenberg* (Chicago, 2017)

Meir, Golda, *My Life* (Weidenfeld & Nicolson, 1975)

Melby, John F., *The Mandate of Heaven* (Chatto & Windus, 1969)

Menon, V. P., *The Transfer of Power in India* (Orient Blackswan, 1957)

Meredith, Martin, *The State of Africa* (Simon & Schuster, 2011)

Messer, Robert, *The End of an Alliance: James F. Byrnes, Roosevelt, Truman and the Origins of the Cold War* (University of North Carolina Press, 1982)

Metz, William, *The Political Career of Mohammad Ali Jinnah* (Oxford University Press, 2010)

Mierzejewski, Alfred C., *Ludwig Erhard* (University of North Carolina Press, 2004)

Miles, Jonathan, *The Nine Lives of Otto Katz* (Bantam, 2010)

Miller, Merle, *Plain Speaking* (Gollancz, 1974)

Milward, Alan, *The Reconstruction of Western Europe, 1945–51* (Routledge, 1987)

Mindszenty, Jozsef, *Memoirs* (Weidenfeld & Nicolson, 1974)

Misra, Maria, *Vishnu's Crowded Temple* (Allen Lane, 2007)

Misra, Udayon, *India's North-East* (Oxford University Press, 2014)

Mistry, Kaeten, *The United States, Italy and the Origins of Cold War* (Cambridge, 2014)

Mitchell, Maria, *The Origins of Christian Democracy: Politics and Confession in Modern Germany* (University of Michigan Press, 2012)

Moch, Jules, *Rencontres avec Léon Blum* (Plon, 1970)

Molloy, Peter, *The Lost World of Communism* (BBC Books, 2009)

Molotov, Vyacheslav, *Molotov Remembers* (Ivan Dee, 1993)

Monnet, Jean, *Mémoires* (Fayard, 1976)

Montagnon, Pierre, *La France coloniale* (Pygmalion/Gérard Watelet, 1988)

Montefiore, Simon Sebag, *Young Stalin* (Weidenfeld & Nicolson, 2007)

——, *Jerusalem* (Phoenix, 2011)

——, *Stalin, The Court of the Red Star* (Weidenfeld & Nicolson, 2003)

Moon, Penderel (ed.), *Wavell: The Viceroy's Journal*, 2 vols (Oxford University Press, 1973)

——, *Divide and Quit* (University of California Press, 1962)

Moraes, Frank, *Jawaharlal Nehru* (Jaico Publishing House, 2008)

Moran, Lord, *Winston Churchill: The Struggle for Survival* (Sphere, 1968)

Morris, Benny, *1948: A History of the First Arab-Israeli War* (Yale University Press, 2008)

——, *Righteous Victims* (John Murray, 2000)

——, *The Birth of the Palestinian Refugee Problem, 1947–1949* (Cambridge University Press, 1989)

Morwood, William, *Duel for the Middle Kingdom* (Everest House, 1980)

Mosley, Leonard, *Marshall* (Methuen, 1982)

Mouzelis, Nicos, *Modern Greece* (Macmillan, 1978)

Murphy, Robert, *Diplomat Among Warriors* (Collins, 1964)

Naimark, Norman, *The Russians in Germany* (Harvard University Press, 1995)

Nanda, B. R., *Mahatma Gandhi* (Oxford University Press, 1989)

Nasser, Gamal, *Memoirs of the First Palestine War* (Akher Sa'a (Cairo), 1955 – Translation at https://www.scribd.com/document/155304102/Nasser-Gamal-Abdel-Nasser-s-Memoirs-of-the-First-Palestine-War)

Nehru, Jawaharlal, *Autobiography, Toward Freedom* (John Day Co Inc., 2012)

—— (ed. Gopal and Uma Iyengar), *The Essential Writings of Jawaharlal Nehru* (Oxford University Press, 2003)

—— (ed. Sarvepalli Gopal), *Selected Works* (Jawaharlal Nehru Memorial Fund New Delhi, 1972–82, 1984 )

Neiberg, Michael, *Potsdam* (Basic Books, 2015)

Nicolson, Nigel (ed.), *Harold Nicolson: Diaries and Letters, 1945–62* (Phoenix, 2004)

Nove, Alec, *Economic History of the USSR* (Penguin, 1990)

O'Balance, Edgar, *The Greek Civil War 1944–49* (Faber, 1966)

——, *The Red Army of China* (Praeger, 1962)

Ostrovski, Max, *The Hyperbole of the World Order* (Rowman & Littlefield, 2006)

Paddock, Paul, *China Diary* (Iowa State University Press, 1977)

Pappé, Ilan, *The Rise and Fall of a Palestinian Dynasty* (University of California Press, 2011)

——, *The Making of the Arab–Israeli Conflict, 1947–51* (I. B. Tauris, 1994)

——, *Britain and the Arab–Israeli Conflict, 1948–51* (Palgrave, 1988)

Parrish, Scott, and Narinsky, Mikhail, *New Evidence On the Soviet Rejection of the Marshall Plan, 1947* (Woodrow Wilson International Center, March 1999)

Parrish, Thomas, *Berlin in the Balance, 1945–1949* (Addison-Wesley, 1998)

Pavlowitch, Stevan, *Yugoslavia* (Ernest Benn, 1971)

Pelling, Henry, and Cox, Michael, *Britain and the Marshall Plan* (Palgrave Macmillan, 1988)

Pepper, Suzanne, *Civil War in China* (Rowman & Littlefield Publishers, 1999)

Perelman, S. J. *Westward Ha!* (Simon & Schuster, 1948)

Perlmutter, Amos, *The Life and Times of Menachem Begin* (Doubleday, 1987)

Pimlott, Ben (ed.), *The Political Diary of Hugh Dalton* (Cape, 1986)

———, *Hugh Dalton* (Cape, 1985)

Pirzada, S.S. (ed.), *Foundations of Pakistan* (All-India Muslim League Documents, 1906–1947, National Publishing House, Karachi, 1970)

Plokhy, Serhii, *The Gates of Europe* (Allen Lane, 2015)

Poen, Monte (ed.), *Strictly Personal and Confidential, Letters Truman Never Mailed* (Little, Brown, 1982)

Pogue, Forrest, *George C. Marshall, Vol. IV: Statesman, 1945–1959* (Viking, 1987)

Poidevin, Raymond, *Robert Schuman* (Imprimerie Nationale, 1986)

Prittie, Terence, *Konrad Adenauer, 1876–1967* (Tom Stacey, 1972)

Prüssen, Ronald, *John Foster Dulles* (Free Press, 1982)

Pusey, Merlo, *Eisenhower the President* (Macmillan, 1956)

Pye, Lucian, *Guerrilla Communism in Malaya* (Princeton University Press, 1956)

Quinn-Judge, Sophie, *Ho Chi Minh: The Missing Years ,1919–1941* (Hurst & Company, 2003)

Raghavan, Srinath, *India's War: The Making of Modern South Asia, 1939–1945* (Allen Lane, 2016)

Rajak, Svetozar et al. (eds), *The Balkans in the Cold War* (Palgrave, 2017)

Ray, J. K., *Transfer of Power in Indonesia, 1942–1949* (Manaktalas, 1967)

Rea, Kenneth, and Brewer, John, *The Forgotten Ambassador* (Boulder, 1981)

Rees, Phil, *Dining with Terrorists* (Pan, 2006)

Renwick, Chris, *Bread for All* (Allen Lane, 2017)

Resis, Albert (ed.), *Molotov Remembers* (Ivan Dee, 1993)

Reynolds, David (ed.), *The Origins of the Cold War in Europe: International Perspectives* (Yale University Press, 1994)

Ricklefs, M. C., *A History of Modern Indonesia since c. 1200* (Palgrave, 2001)

Ridley, Jasper, *Tito* (Constable, 1994)

Roberts, Andrew, *Eminent Churchillians* (Weidenfeld & Nicolson, 1995)

Robrieux, Philippe, *Maurice Thorez* (Fayard, 1975)

Rodrigo, Robert, *Berlin Airlift* (Cassell, 1960)

Rogan, Eugene, *The Arabs* (Penguin, 2012)

——, and Shlaim, Ari (eds), *The War for Palestine* (Cambridge, 2001)

Romanus, Charles, and Sunderland, Riley, *Time Runs Out* in CBI (Department of the Army, Washington, 1959)

Ross, Robert, Kelk Mager, Anne, and Nasson, Bill, *The Cambridge History of South Africa*, Vol. II (Cambridge University Press, 2011)

Royal Institute of International Affairs, *The Soviet–Yugoslav Dispute* (RIIS, London, 1948)

Rowan, Roy, *Chasing the Dragon* (Lyons Press, 2004)

Ruoff, Kenneth, *The People's Emperor* (Harvard University Press, 2003)

Rupnik, Jacques, *The Other Europe* (Schocken, 1989)

Rusinow, Dennison, *The Yugoslav Experiment, 1948–1974* (California, 1982)

Salan, Raoul, *Mémoires*, Vols I and II (Presses de la Cité, 1971)

Salisbury, Harrison, *The Long March* (Macmillan, 1973)

Sanger, Clyde, *Malcolm MacDonald* (McGill-Queen's University Press, 1995)

Sarkar, Sumit, *Modern India: 1885–1947* (Macmillan, 1985)

Scaff, Alvin, *The Philippine Answer to Communism* (Stanford University Press, 1955)

Scalapino, Robert A., and Chong-Sik Lee, *Communism in Korea* (University of California Press, 1992)

Schechtman, Joseph, *Postwar Population Transfers in Europe 1945–1955* (University of Pennsylvania Press, 1963)

Scheidel, Walter, *The Great Leveller* (Princeton University Press, 2017)

Schoenbrun, David, *As France Goes* (Gollancz, 1957)

Schofield, Victoria, *Kashmir in Conflict* (I. B. Tauris, 2000)

Schurmann, Franz, and Schell, Orville, *Republican China* (Penguin, 1968)

Sebba, Anne, *Les Parisiennes* (Weidenfeld & Nicolson, 2016)

Sebestyn, Victor, *1946* (Pan, 2015)

Seervai, H. M., *Partition of India: Legend and Reality* (Oxford University Press, 2005)

Segev, Tom, *One Palestine Complete* (Little, Brown, 2000)

Sen, Amartya, *The Argumentative Indian* (Allen Lane, 2005)

Shavit, Ari, *My Promised Land* (Spiegel & Grau, 2013)

Sherwood, Robert, *Roosevelt and Hopkins* (Harpers, 1948)

Shilon, Avi, *Menachem Begin* (Yale University Press, 2012)

Shindler, Colin, *A History of Modern Israel* (Cambridge University Press, 2008)

Shlaim, Avi, *The Iron Wall* (Penguin, 2014)

——, *Israel and Palestine* (Verso, 2009)

——, *Collusion Across the Jordan* (Clarendon Press, 1988)

Short, Philip, *Mao: A Life* (Hodder & Stoughton, 1999)

Singh, Jaswant, *Jinnah* (Oxford University Press, 2010)

Sisson, Richard, and Rose, Leo, *War and Secession* (University of California Press, 1990)

Sklar, Martin, *Creating the American Century* (Cambridge, 2017)

Smith, Denis Mack, *Italy: A Modern History* (University of Michigan Press, 1969)

Smith, Jean Edward, *Lucius D. Clay* (Henry Holt and Co., 1990)

—— (ed.), *The Papers of General Lucius D. Clay* (Bloomington, 1974)

Smith, Walter Bedell, *My Three Years in Moscow* (Lippincott, 1950)

Smuts, J. C., *Jan Christian Smuts* (Cassell, 1952)

Snow, Edgar, *Red Star Over China* (Penguin, 1973)

Snowden, Frank, *The Conquest of Malaria* (Yale University Press, 2006)

Snyder, Timothy, *Bloodlands* (Vintage, 2011)

——, *The Reconstruction of Nations* (Yale University Press, 2003)

——, and Brandon, Ray (eds), *Stalin and Europe* (Oxford University Press, 2014)

Spilker, Dirk, *The East German Leadership and the Division of Germany* (Clarendon Press, 2006)

Srodes, James, *Allen Dulles* (Regnery, 1999)

Stargardt, Nicholas, *The German War* (Bodley Head, 2015)

Sterling, Claire, *The Masaryk Case* (Godine, 1969)

Stern, Carola, *Ulbricht: A Political Biography* (Pall Mall Press, 1965)

Storry, Richard, *A History of Modern Japan* (Penguin, 1961)

Sukarno, *Sukarno: An Autobiography as Told to Cindy Adams* (Bobbs Merrill, 1965)

Swain, Geoffrey, *Tito: A Biography* (I. B. Tauris, 2011)

Taft, Robert, and Wunderlin, Clarence, *The Papers of Robert A. Taft* (The Kent State University Press, 2001)

Talbot, Ian, and Kamran, Tahir, *Colonial Lahore* (Hurst, 2016)

Taschen, Benedikt, *Berlin Porträt einer Stadt* (Taschen, no date)

Taubman, William, *Khrushchev* (Free Press, 2003)

Taylor, Frederick, *Exorcising Hitler* (Bloomsbury, 2011)

Tharoor, Shashi, *Nehru: The Invention of India* (Arcade, 2003)

——, *Inglorious Empire* (Hurst, 2017)

Thomas, Hugh, *Armed Truce* (Hamish Hamilton, 1986)

Thomas, Martin, *Fight or Flight* (Oxford University Press, 2014)

Thorez, Maurice, *Fils du Peuple* (Editions Sociales, 1949)

Thorpe, D. R, *Eden* (Chatto & Windus, 2003)

Timmins, Nicholas, *The Five Giants* (Fontana, 1996)

Tocqueville, Alexis de, *Democracy in America* (Doubleday, 1969)

Tomlinson, Jim, *Managing the Economy, Managing the People* (Oxford University Press, 2017)

Topping, Seymour, *Journey Between Two Chinas* (Harper & Row, 1972)

Townshend, Charles, *Terrorism* (Oxford University Press, 2011)

Tronchon, Jacques, *L'Insurrection malgache de 1947* (Karthala, 1986)

Troup, Freda, *South Africa* (Eyre Methuen, 1972)

Truman, Harry S., *Mr Citizen* (Hutchinson, 1961)

——, *Truman Speaks* (Columbia University Press, 1960)

——, *Memoirs: Vol. II, Years of Trial and Hope* (Doubleday, 1956)

Truman, Margaret, *Letters from Father* (Pinnacle, 1982)

——, *Harry S. Truman* (Hamish Hamilton, 1973)

Tudor, Daniel, *Korea: The Impossible Country* (Tuttle, 2012)

Tunzelmann, Alex von, *Indian Summer* (Simon & Schuster, 2007)

United Nations, *World Economic Reports, 1947 and 1948* (United Nations Department of Economic Affairs, Lake Success, New York, 1948, 1949)

——, *Economic Report, Salient Features of the World Economic Situation, 1945–47* (Lake Success, New York, 1948)

Unkovski-Korica, Vladimir, *The Economic Struggle for Power in Tito's Yugoslavia* (I. B. Tauris, 2016

Vatikiotis, Michael, *Blood and Silk* (Weidenfeld & Nicolson, 2017)

Ven, Hans van de, *China at War* (Profile, 2017)

Vickers, Adrian, *A History of Modern Indonesia* (Cambridge, 2011)

Vinen, Richard, *A History in Fragments* (Little, Brown, 2000)

Vinogradova, Lyuba, *Avenging Angels* (MacLehose Press, 2017)

Vu, Tuong, *Vietnam's Communist Revolution* (Cambridge University Press, 2017)

Walker, Martin, *The Cold War* (Bloomsbury, 1993)

Watson, Derek, *Molotov* (Palgrave Macmillan, 2005)

Wedemeyer, Albert, *Wedemeyer Reports!* (Holt, 1958)

Weiler, Peter, *Ernest Bevin* (Manchester, 1993)

Weir, Alison, *Against Our Better Judgment* (CreateSpace Publishing Platform, 2014)

Weizmann, Chaim, *Trial and Error* (Harper, 1949)

Welsh, Frank, *A History of South Africa* (HarperCollins, 1998)

Westad, Odd Arne, *The Cold War* (Allen Lane, 2017)

——, *Restless Empire* (Bodley Head, 2012)

——, *Decisive Encounters: The Chinese Civil War, 1946–1950* (Stanford University Press, 2003)

——, and Hanhimäki, Jussi, *The Cold War* (Oxford University Press, 2003)

——, *The Soviet Union in Eastern Europe, 1945–89* (Palgrave, 1994)

Whitson, William, *The Chinese High Command* (Praeger, 1973)

Wilkinson, Steven, *Army and Nation* (Harvard University Press, 2015)

Williams, Charles, *Adenauer: The Father of the New Germany* (Little, Brown, 2000)

Williams, Francis, *A Prime Minister Remembers* (Heinemann, 1961)

——, *Ernest Bevin* (Hutchinson, 1952)

Wilson, Harold, *The Chariot of Israel* (Weidenfeld & Nicolson, 1981)

Wilson, Jon, *India Conquered* (Simon & Schuster, 2016)

Winock, Michel, *François Mitterrand* (Gallimard, 2015)

Wolferen, Karel van, *The Enigma of Japanese Power* (Vintage, 1990)

Wolpert, Stanley, *Jinnah of Pakistan* (Oxford University Press, 2005)

Woodhouse, C. M., *The Struggle for Greece, 1941–1949* (Hart-Davis, 1976)

Yergin, Daniel, *The Prize* (Simon & Schuster, 1991)

——, *Shattered Peace* (André Deutsch, 1978)

Zakaria, Rafiq (ed.), *A Study of Nehru* (Times of India, 1960)

Zanden, Jan van, *The Economic History of The Netherlands, 1914–1995* (Routledge, 2005)

Zeiler, Thomas, *Free Trade, Free World* (North Carolina, 1999)

Zeman, Zbyněk, *The Masaryks* (Weidenfeld & Nicolson, 1976)

——, and Klimek, Antonín, *The Life of Edvard Beneš* (Oxford University Press, 1999)

Ziegler, Philip, *Mountbatten* (HarperCollins, 1985)

——, *George VI* (Penguin, 2014)

Zierenberg, Malte, *Berlin's Black Market, 1939–1950* (Palgrave Macmillan, 2015)

# INDEX

Jacobson, Eddie, 247, 249,
375–8, 439
Jai Singh of Alwar, ruler of
Rajasthan, 182
Jammu and Kashmir: unresolved
dispute over allegiance, 184,
227–33, 424; violence and
conflicts in, 227, 230, 270, 316–
17; India invades, 231; Muslims
call for jihad, 232; Indian
army presence in, 317; UN
commission on, 471; ceasefire,
495–6; casualties, 496
Japan: occupation and development
of Manchuria, 3–4, 111,
115–16; wartime casualties,
4; economic effect of war,
5; plundering in China, 6;
post-war lawlessness, 8; well-
behaved occupation forces, 10;
emancipation of women, 18,
358; invades Indochina, 149;
occupies Indonesia, 157–8;
demilitarisation, 167; recovery,
221; breaks up major economic
groups, 323; Kennan visits,
345; MacArthur dominates,
346–8; US occupation and
administration, 346–52, 356–7;
condition after defeat, 348–51;
general election (1946), 352;
Communist Party, 353; left-
wing demonstrations, 353;
post-surrender document, 353;
war-crime trials, 354; reforms,
356–8; constitutional revision,
358–9; change in US occupation
policy, 381–5; vulnerability to
Communism, 383; coalition
of Democratic and Socialist
parties, 384; National Police
Reserve with arms, 385; in
occupation of Korea, 410;
earthquake (June 1948), 491;
peace treaty with USA (1951),
497; democracy in, 499; and
balance of power, 501
Jaurès, Jean, 238
Java, 156, 158, 160, 322
Jeju (Korean island), 8, 416–18

Jenkins, Evan, 83, 85
Jerusalem: King David Hotel
bombed (1946), 101, 107;
Jews and Palestinians in,
191; Arab strike in, 233;
Special International Regime
established for, 249; curfew
imposed, 282; in Jewish-
Arab fighting, 422; Arab
forces attack, 442–4; see also
Israel; Palestine
Jewish Agency, 96, 100–1, 192,
244, 247, 327, 329, 377,
380
Jewish Anti-Fascist Committee
(USSR), 52
Jewish State (ship), 233
Jews: killed in Holocaust, 4;
migrate to Palestine/Israel,
11, 97, 163–4; and partition
of Palestine, 95, 191; claim
homeland in Palestine, 162–4;
mobilise for conflict with Arabs,
192; welcome establishment
of homeland state in Palestine,
250; attacked in Arab
states, 282–3; see also anti-
Semitism; Zionism
Jinnah, Muhammad Ali (the
Qaid-e-Azam): demands
separate Pakistan, 55, 57,
59, 80–3, 85–6, 89–93, 173;
as first governor-general of
Pakistan, 172–4; appearance
and behaviour, 177; criticises
Radcliffe's adjudication, 177;
complains to Attlee of Indian
obstructionism, 178; on divided
Pakistan, 178; orders new
Cadillac, 179; on future of
Hyderabad, 185; makes offers
to Junagadh, 186; on communal
violence, 211; hopes to take
over Jammu and Kashmir, 228,
232; and Indian invasion of
Kashmir, 231; health decline,
232; death, 496
Jodhpur, maharajah of, 184, 186
Jordan, Louis, 29
Jovanović, Dragoljub, 220

and Communist rebellion in
Greece, 286–7; presidential
election campaign, 301–5,
466–8; economic difficulties,
302; loyalty programme and
investigations, 302; civil rights,
305, 323; debates Marshall Plan,
307; Bevin emphasises need for
support from, 309; Communist
Party members tried, 323;
occupation and administration
of Japan, 346–52; uncertainty
over Palestine, 375–7; modifies
policy on Japan, 382–4; Supreme
Court rules against religious
instruction in public schools,
387; intervention in 1948 Italian
election, 402; presence in South
Korea, 415; recognises state
of Israel, 434, 439; economic
buoyancy under Truman, 467;
admits homeless Europeans
under Displaced Persons Act,
490; and international order,
501; current uncertainty,
502

Vafiadis, General Markos, 59,
285–6, 288–9, 457
Valluy, General Jean Étienne, 224
Vandenberg, Arthur Hendrick, 26,
49, 62, 303, 306, 468, 497
Varga, Evgenii, 34, 128
Velebit, Vladimir, 398
Venezuela, 298
Veselý, Jindřich, 332
Viet Minh, 9, 122, 148, 149–51,
153–5, 222–5, 322
Vietnam: Ho Chi Minh heads
government, 122, 150–2;
independence movement, 148,
298, 323, 490; violence and
resistance struggle in, 151–2,
154–6, 270; French operations
in, 222–5; provisional central
government formed, 387; Xuan
elected president, 458; French
withdraw from, 498
Vincent, John Carter, 415
Volkswagen company, 23

Vorster, B. J., 452
Vyshinsky, Andrey, 253

Walcott, Jersey Joe, 298
Waldron, Francis Xavier ('Eugene
Dennis'), 122
Wallace, Henry, 40–1, 45–6,
122, 302, 392
Wallenberg, Raoul, 167
Warren, Earl, 468
Warsaw: wartime damage, 4
Washington, George, xiii
Wavell, Archibald, Earl, 79–81
Wedemeyer, General Albert,
167, 202–4
Wei Lihuang, General, 312
Weizmann, Chaim: Zionism, 12,
56, 97, 162, 247, 250, 375–8,
423, 431; differences with
Ben-Gurion, 99–100; elected
president of Israel, 438–9
Welles, Orson, 47
West Bengal, 471
West Germany: new currency
proposed, 373
White, Harry Dexter, 48
White House, Washington:
deterioration, 392
White, Theodore, 50
Whitney, General Courtney, 358
Wilder, Billy, 257
Wilhelmina, Queen of the
Netherlands, 160
Willkie, Wendell, 112
Wingate, Orde, 98
winter (1946–7), 6, 73, 293
Wise, Rabbi Stephen, 99–100
Wolf, Markus, 263
women: violated post-war, 9–10,
410, 413; increasing role in
society, 17–18; emancipation
in Japan, 18, 358; admitted to
full membership of Cambridge
University, 198; violated in
India, 209–10; enfranchised
and emancipated, 211; in
Germany, 256–7
World Bank, 17, 26, 499
World Festival of Democratic
Youth, 331